J. P. Gordy, Noah Porter

Descartes and his school

J. P. Gordy, Noah Porter

Descartes and his school

ISBN/EAN: 9783743336698

Manufactured in Europe, USA, Canada, Australia, Japa

Cover: Foto ©Thomas Meinert / pixelio.de

Manufactured and distributed by brebook publishing software
(www.brebook.com)

J. P. Gordy, Noah Porter

Descartes and his school

HISTORY OF MODERN PHILOSOPHY

BY KUNO FISCHER

DESCARTES AND HIS SCHOOL

Translated from the Third and Revised German Edition

BY

J. P. GORDY, Ph.D.

PROFESSOR OF PEDAGOGICS IN OHIO UNIVERSITY

EDITED BY

NOAH PORTER, D.D., LL.D.

LONDON

T. FISHER UNWIN

26, PATERNOSTER SQUARE

1890

Presswork by Berwick & Smith, Boston, U.S.A.

INTRODUCTION.

A MONG the many histories of philosophy for which we are indebted to modern research, the history of Modern Philosophy by Professor Kuno Fischer of Heidelberg is conspicuous for the courage with which the author grapples with the difficulties of his task and the success with which he overcomes them. Though he is by no means removed from criticism or controversy in respect to the interpretation which he gives of the writers and schools which he encounters, and in the positive and pronounced estimates and criticisms which he does not hesitate to give of their leading positions, he is uniformly clear, spirited, and exhaustive. He is also popular in the best sense of the term, being neither technical nor abstract beyond the necessities imposed by his theme, and connecting with the thorough and masterly discussion of schools and opinions as much of personal and general historic interest as could be expected or desired. For these reasons his history is, perhaps, more readable than any other, and is uniformly confessed by competent critics, whether friendly or otherwise, to be eminently attractive and exciting to the general student.

Hitherto only a small portion of this history has been translated into English, — for one reason among others, that the history itself is not yet complete, having as yet been finished to the end of Schelling's system and life, where it rests for obvious reasons with the author's unsatisfied desire satisfactorily to expound the development of the Hegelian theory of Being and of Knowledge. Meanwhile the result of his attempt to do this is awaited with more than ordinary interest by both the disciples and antagonists of Hegel and his critics. During this interval, there seems to be no reason why the earlier portion of this history should not be given to the English public, especially when we consider that the history of the school of Descartes, in many senses, and especially as treated by our author, stands by itself, and holds closer relations to all the forms of modern speculation than is commonly supposed.

It should be remembered also, that this portion of the history has meanwhile passed to a third edition, and been carefully elaborated by the author. The general Introduction will be found to possess an independent interest.

For these reasons the publishers have decided to publish in two separate volumes a translation of that portion of this history which treats of Descartes and his school (including Spinoza), leaving the question at present undecided whether they shall publish the remainder of the history, being satisfied that the volumes which they offer to the public will in any event constitute a valuable addition to the library of the student of modern philosophy, which will, in an important sense, be complete by itself.

They are assured that the translation has been made by a competent German scholar, who, in addition to his knowledge of the German language and his familiarity with German philosophy, has had the very great advantage of giving the study of several months to the critical study of the school of Descartes previously to undertaking this translation.

NOAH PORTER.

YALE COLLEGE, Dec. 14, 1886.

AUTHOR'S PREFACE.

THE first volume of this work has been out of print for some time. I have been unable to complete a thorough revision of it until during the present year, and I here present it in a *third* edition. When I published the second edition, I had written my history of modern philosophy as far as Kant. Since then, I have added Fichte and his Predecessors, and Schelling and his Period. Hegel, his School, and his Opponents, and the course of development of philosophy since Hegel, are still lacking. On account of the great difficulty of the subject, I have been obliged, for the sake of clearness, to treat it in such detail that the size and expensiveness of the work have increased beyond what I intended. For it is impossible to estimate the difficulties of one's own work, until one has realized them, and sought to overcome them. And if he should be so fortunate as to travel the toilsome road a second time, he will have acquired the strength to advance more easily and rapidly, as is often the case with long and fatiguing journeys. Brevity without injury to clearness is possible only after the most detailed exposition.

The size of the work in this new edition will be diminished by the more compact form in which the matter is printed. I seek to comply with this just desire of my publisher, while I oppose every kind of abridgment that is unfavorable to clearness. With my method of exposition, I cannot attain brevity by omissions, but only by a corresponding treatment of all the various parts of the whole. This was one reason for this new revision, and is an essential part of it. It also seemed desirable to enlarge the introduction, especially the sections treating of the Renaissance and the Reformation : besides, it appeared necessary to add the results of recent investigations concerning Descartes. The stand-point and arrangement of the work are unchanged. It is unnecessary to repeat in the preface what is shown in the work itself. When a third edition of a work so extensive and expensive as the present is called for, I can venture, with some satisfaction, to regard it as a proof that it has been of some service in the instruction of my contemporaries.

KUNO FISCHER.

Heidelberg, Oct. 23, 1878.

CONTENTS.

CHAPTER V.

CHAPTER VI.

CHAPTER VII.

BOOK I.

DESCARTES' LIFE AND WRITINGS.

CHAPTER I.

CHAPTER II.

CHAPTER III.

CHAPTER IV.

CHAPTER V.

CHAPTER VI.

CHAPTER VII.

CHAPTER VIII.

BOOK II.

DESCARTES' DOCTRINE.

CHAPTER I.

CHAPTER II.

CHAPTER III.

CHAPTER IV.

CHAPTER V.

CHAPTER VI.

CHAPTER VII.

CHAPTER VIII.

CHAPTER IX.

CHAPTER X.

CHAPTER XI.

BOOK III.

DEVELOPMENT AND MODIFICATION OF THE DOCTRINE OF DESCARTES.

CHAPTER I.

CHAPTER II.

CHAPTER III.

INTRODUCTION

TO

THE HISTORY OF MODERN PHILOSOPHY.

HISTORY OF MODERN PHILOSOPHY.

CHAPTER I.

THE HISTORY OF PHILOSOPHY AS SCIENCE.

THE subject of this work is modern philosophy. However peculiar the conditions of life which this philosophy
implies, however natural and plain its problems, proposed
through its own insight, it is still conditioned in its origin
by the history of the philosophy which precedes it. To be
sure, it arises in a thoroughly conscious break with the
past. It has the distinct and outspoken certainty that an
entirely new beginning must be made, and declares at the
start that it intends to be free from all presuppositions, perfectly independent of all traditional doctrines, of all the
authorities of the past. And it actually realizes this ideal
as it conceives it. But this freedom of mind is itself an
historical event: this freedom from presuppositions has historical conditions. The path that leads to it is gradually
broken, and preparations are made for it by a further and
further departure from the principles of the earlier philosophy. There are definite crises in which the human mind,
weary of that which is, falls back upon its original powers,
and, from its inexhaustible sources, renews its culture. The
foundations of such crises are laid deep in the progress of
humanity: they are dependent upon a long series of historical conditions, and, therefore, they are rare. They never
appear except in the fulness of time. Such a fulness of

1

time, modern philosophy required for its origin. Hence, this philosophy, with all its independence of thought, with all the originality of its foundations, remains in constant intercourse with its historical presuppositions. It contradicts them in its first period, and sharpens this contradiction to a complete contrast; as it progresses, it inclines to them, and feels a kinship with them; and, in its most recent period, it renews this antagonism and this relationship. Thus, modern philosophy always sustains a definite relation to the philosophy of ancient times, and never permits it to vanish from its horizon. We must, therefore, in the introduction to this work, become clear as to the historical conditions from which modern philosophy proceeds, and as to the connection of its first period with the great march of human development.

In the very concept of the history of philosophy, certain difficulties are contained which might make the possibility of such a history doubtful. For a concept is difficult when its characteristics cannot be at once combined, and impossible when they cannot be combined at all. Now, between the concept of history and that of philosophy, such an opposition seems indeed to exist. History is inconceivable without a succession of events in time; philosophy, without the knowledge of truth. Now, only that concept is true which completely corresponds to its object. There are, therefore, but two possibilities, — either this correspondence between a concept and its object exists, or it does not: in the first case, the concept is true; in the second, it is false. Truth is a *unit:* it has no series or succession of cases, and, therefore, as it seems, no history. And so a history of philosophy, a succession of different systems, often in the most direct contradiction, and never in perfect harmony with each other, appears as the manifest contradiction of philosophy itself, and the plainest testimony to its impossibility. Therefore the contradictions of philosophers, the multiplicity and diversity of their systems, have always been urged by those who have doubted the possibility of true knowledge. Among the objections which the sceptics of ancient times brought against philosophy, the conflict of systems was one of the first and most important. It is evident, that, from this point of view, the history of philosophy, in the strict sense of the term, is impossible. Either the many so-called systems are accepted as mere historical facts, and the history of philosophy is resolved into a history of philosophers, — of their lives, opinions, and schools, — which the historian sets forth as well as the sources of information concerning permit, and as he understands those sources, or these systems are regarded merely as having failed to reach the unity of true knowledge, and criticised without reference to their historical character. In such a consideration of the history of philosophy, history is entirely separated from philosophy. In the first case, the history of philosophy is a subject merely of a narration: in the second, it is a subject merely of critical examination. The narration of the first is as uncritical as the criticism of the second is unhistorical. From the one-sided historical point of view, there is indeed a history, but no philosophy: from the one-sided critical point of view, there is indeed a philosophy, but no history. This philosophy, without historical interest and without historical insight, either regards the problem of true knowledge as insoluble, and the given systems as nothing but errors, or it maintains, on practical grounds, a certain knowledge of the truth, valid in all cases, but which those systems only imperfectly attain, and mingle with false opinions. Thus, it deals with historical systems either absolutely *sceptically*, rejecting them all, or *eclectically*, separating and culling out the true according to a completely subjective principle. Now, these critics are not what they aim to be, by far. They suppose that they judge these systems with entire freedom from prejudice, and in absolute independence, as though they stood *above* the history of philosophy. They do not know that they have received their stand-points from this very history; that these stand-points are historical events with historical conditions; that they are necessary products of an entirely definite historical position of philosophy, and that this very fact gives them their authority for the time.

These two points of view — the historical and critical — are naturally the first from which the history of philosophy is considered. It is written at first either by historians or by sceptics and eclectic philosophers. Three important sources of the knowledge of ancient philosophy are so many examples of these historical, sceptical, and eclectic stand-points, — Diogenes Laertius, Sextus Empiricus, Johannes Stobäus. And among the first writers who, in modern times, have expounded and criticised the systems of philosophy, there are three with corresponding points of view, — Thomas Stanley, Pierre Bayle, and Jacob Brucker.

But this separation of the historical and critical points of view does not solve the problem of the history of philosophy, but merely evades the difficulty. From the one, we have history without philosophy; from the other, philosophy without history. It is impossible to comprehend how the history of philosophy is possible from either of these stand-points. And so the question returns, *How is the history of philosophy as science possible?*

Let us inquire somewhat more rigorously whether philosophy, as love of wisdom, as striving for truth, is really incapable of a history. Let us admit for the present the usual explanation, according to which truth consists in adequate conceptions; i.e., in perfect agreement between our concept and its object. If we assume that the object is a given, in itself completed, thing, which remains unchangeably like itself, certainly only two cases are possible: our concept either does, or does not, correspond to this so constituted object. And if we assume that there is just as certainly a completed concept, only two cases are possible: either we have, or do not have, this true concept; either we are in conplete possession of the truth, or we are completely deprived of it. In either case, every kind of history is excluded from the territory of truth.

But this is *never* the case. However definite and un-changeable may be the object of our knowledge, the concept corresponding to it is never so perfect that with *one* grasp, as it were, we lay hold of the object, or miss it altogether. Even if true concepts were innate, we should have to become gradually conscious of them : we should pass from the twilight to the noonday of knowledge, in a succession of experiences which would be equivalent to a *history* of our conscious-ness. And, if true conceptions are not innate, they must be produced by the mind, — i.e., be formed, — and, there-fore, pass through a process of development which can be nothing else than a gradual correction of our concepts, which, in their first state, are not conformable to objects. Every true concept in the human consciousness *has become* so : there every truth has a history upon which its existence depends, and this history forms an essential part of the progress in the culture and development of the individual. The greater the difficulties to be overcome, the more numerous the problems to be solved in order to bring the truth into the light, the longer, of course, continues its development. Whole periods remain involved in errors, and it requires the strength of a new age to detect and correct and overcome them. Cen-turies work on such a process of development. Such a truth has a history on a large scale. Every science is an historical growth, and could only become what it is by a gradual de-velopment. The fabric of the world, in its constitution, its laws, its mechanical order, remains unchangeably the same as an object of human contemplation ; but astronomy had to develop and fix a series of conceptions, then dissolve and abandon them, before it could reach true knowledge after so many centuries. However erroneous the old system, it formed the necessary vestibule to the new and correct one.

The second of the above suppositions is, therefore, *never*

true. True concepts are never once for all stamped upon
the mind, and perfect. On the contrary, they are always
problems to be solved. But even the first of them is not
always true. The object of our knowledge does not always
remain unchangeably the same. What if this object itself
forms a process, is undergoing a change which is constantly
renewed, not in such a change as is continually repeated
according to the same laws, like motion in nature, and
the circulation of life, but in a creative activity, in a really
progressive development? What if this object not merely
has, but unfolds and represents its entire nature in, a history,
without being exhausted in any period of it whatever? If,
in brief, this object is of a living, spiritual nature? It is
evident that the knowledge of such an object not merely
requires development, in common with all human knowledge,
but, in order to correspond to its object, must itself be in a
state of historical progress. A process of progressing development can only be conceived by a process of progressing
knowledge.

This process of progressing development is the *human
mind:* this progressing process of knowledge is *philosophy*
as the self-knowledge of the human mind. Since it is clear
that the human mind, as self-conscious, must be an object to
itself, it must be a problem to itself. It must seek to solve
this problem: it cannot exist without this effort. This effort
is philosophy. Without it the mind could not be a problem
to itself, could not be its own object, could not, therefore, be
self-conscious. Human self-consciousness is a problem which
philosophy solves. The human mind is like an historical
development which ramifies into a variety of modes and into
a series of systems of culture which the mind produces from
itself, consummates, and outgrows, and out of which, as its
material, produces new forms of civilization. What can the
knowledge, which seeks to correspond to this object, be,
except a variety and series of systems of knowledge, which,
like their object, lead an historical life? What, therefore,

can philosophy be in this relation, except the history of philosophy? It is like a quantity whose value is made up of a series of quantities. At the first glance, it seemed as if the concept of philosophy excluded from itself the possibility of a history, as something incompatible with it: we now see, that, on the contrary, philosophy not merely admits historical development as a possibility, but demands it as a necessity; that to every philosophical system with its historical worth, belongs also its historical truth; that each of these systems demands as rigidly to be understood in its historical characteristics as in its truth; that, therefore, the history of philosophy as science unites in the closest manner the historical point of view with the critical, the historical interest with the philosophical. If its object were the philosopher's stone, its truth would be something found, a prize, which is either won or lost. If its object is the human mind, its truth itself is a living history, and it must develop and advance within the great march of the civilization of humanity.

This must be true if indeed the human mind is the real object of philosophy; if in its fundamental characteristics, in its distinctive problems, philosophy is nothing else than the self-knowledge of the mind, the self-knowledge of humanity universally. But is this true? Is not this explanation too narrow and limited? Does not the problem of philosophy embrace more than the human mind? We call it *self-knowledge:* it calls itself *knowledge of the universe (weltweisheit).* And the only relation which the knowledge of self can sustain to the knowledge of the universe, is that of the human mind to the universe; i.e., that of a part to the whole. Have we not, therefore, drawn a fallacious inference, and extended to philosophy in general what is true of it only in a limited sense, asserted of it universally what is only true partially?

It is certainly true that all historical systems have by no means put the problem of human self-knowledge in the front, and made all others depend upon it. Rather only in rare moments in the course of time, has the Delphic inscription been written on the portals of philosophy, with the full and distinct consciousness of being the first of all philosophical problems. But, as often as it has, a definite crisis has at the same time appeared in philosophy, as in antiquity in the Socratic epoch, and in modern times in the Kantian. It is easy to show that the meaning of these crises extends to the whole of preceding and the whole of succeeding philosophy; that it is the fruit of the one and the seed of the other; that it absolutely brings to an end the philosophy of the past, as it absolutely dominates that of the future. And thus it becomes clear, and is proved by the experience of the history of philosophy itself, that human self-knowledge constitutes the fundamental theme of all systems, — *of all*, if they are not isolated, but considered in their inner relations with each other. It is indeed the universal problem, for the clear perception of which the systems of the one series prepare, and the distinctly conscious starting-point of the systems of the other series. The epochs in which the consciousness of this problem breaks through would not illuminate the path of philosophy on both sides so brilliantly, they would not enable us to see so easily and simply the significance of all the schools of philosophy, if they did not reveal the nature of the subject in its entirety.

And what the experience of history thus shows, is taught also by the concept of philosophy when rightly considered. For human self-knowledge is not merely the profoundest, but also the *most comprehensive*, of all scientific problems. Philosophy as knowledge of self, plainly includes philosophy as knowledge of the universe. A thoughtless conception of the matter certainly represents the knowledge of self as related to the knowledge of the universe — the self to the universe — as a part to the whole. It sees in self a single thing; in the universe, the conceived totality (*inbegriff*) of things: how, therefore, can it be that that is not less than this? And yet it is not difficult to see that the world as the conceived totality of things presupposes a being that conceives this totality, therefore a conceiving being, since conceived totality is nothing in itself. It is not difficult to see that the world as the object of our contemplation, as the problem of our knowledge, is only possible under the condition of a being that makes it an object, therefore, of a perceiving, conceiving, in a word, self-conscious, being ; that this itself as a single thing, as a part of the universe, belongs among the objects which require to be reflected upon, conceived, made into objects, and presupposes, therefore, an original self, which forms the inmost core of our being. Here is the great problem of things that presses for solution, the problem of all problems. The universe and self are related as subject and object, as the conditioned to the condition, not as the whole to a part, also not as the two sides of a contrast which exclude each other, as the real to the ideal, to use the favorite formula for expressing the relation between object and subject, the world and self. The world is our object, our presentation : it is nothing independent of our presentation of our self. *We ourselves* are the world. Every false view of the world is always likewise a self-delusion : every true view of the world is always likewise a self-knowledge. As there is no world independent of our self to whom it appears, by whom it is conceived, so there is no knowledge of the world capable of being independent of, or disjoined from, human self-knowledge. Only two cases are here thinkable : either our self-knowledge is made dependent upon our view of the world, or our view of the world is made dependent upon our self-knowledge. From the nature of the case, the second must be true ; but the perception of this necessity had to be gained by toil, and philosophy made and abandoned a series of presuppositions before it could acquire it. And thus its fundamental tendencies are distinguished. At first, the world appeared first, and self as second, until the self-delusion which lies at the foundation of this point of view became evident, and now their relation in the consciousness of philosophy is reversed.

Thereby we hope to have established that philosophy by means of its concept can be nothing else than human self-knowledge, and, as soon as it has gotten rid of the first self-delusion, that it also consciously seeks to be nothing else. The course of its historical development confirms this truth.

We can draw a number of self-evident inferences from this conception, which throw much light upon the history of philosophy, and clear away a multitude of prejudices that hinder a right view of it.

The first is, that philosophy, like the human mind itself, is capable of, and requires, an historical development; that it participates in the life of systems of culture which ages and nations consummate, and, therefore, shares in their progress, and is subject to their destinies. It is the self-knowledge of humanity, of humanity in the highest form of one of its stages of development, controlled by one of its definite and distinct modes of culture. It is the problem of philosophy to comprehend the inmost motives of this form of culture, and explain its nature and its ideal. This inmost motive must appear, the mind must be conscious of it if it is conscious of *itself*, for *it* is *itself* this inmost motive. And there is no other means of solving this problem than philosophy.

The richer and more multiform the world of culture which philosophy must comprehend and explain, the more difficult its problem. A multitude of different and opposing movements and interests are clashing with each other on the animated theatre of the world; so different and conflicting must be the motives at work in the human mind; and so different and conflicting must be the philosophical systems of such an age. It is self-evident that the contradictions of the time must appear in conflicting systems, each of them representing one phase of the spirit of the age, and supplementing the rest in order to solve the philosophical problem of the time.

Every period has its *predominant* tendencies, either manifesting themselves alone or with unmistakable ascendency, and employing the active forces of history: they are based either upon the great problem of the age, upon the highest interests of the human mind, which obscure all others for a time, and drive them into the background, or upon the interests of mere bulk, which, with the value of its aims in life, presses to the front, and temporarily chokes all other forms of culture. Hence also in philosophy there are predominant systems contrasted in character; profound systems probing the depths of the human mind, and popular philosophies comprehending no more than the masses desire.

But whatever may be the spirit of a time which is portrayed in philosophy, this portrait is always more than a mere likeness. Philosophy is related to the historical spirit of man as is self-knowledge to our own life, and this enables us to bring this great question into a smaller compass. Now, what is involved in an act of self-knowledge? We withdraw our attention from the outer world, and reflect upon ourselves. It is our own life which we make the object of our thoughts; and while we, in contemplation of it, stand opposite to it, as it were, we ourselves become a phenomenon. We cease to be what we have been: we rise above our past self, like an artist above his work. The artist absorbed in labor sees with different eyes from the artist who has put down his tools, and stepped back from his work, and, from a well-chosen point of view, critically surveys the whole. He discovers faults undetected before; here he sees an incongruity in the parts, there a lack of symmetry. He sees how one part harmonizes with another, and what disturbs this harmony. What will he do? Abandon the work because it is not yet perfected, because it seems to him very defective? Will he not rather

seize his tools again, and strive to realize that true conception which entered his mind in the moment of that critical survey? Let us leave the figure. We are the artist;
the work of art is our life; the critical survey is the
knowledge of self which interrupts our life. We withdraw
from the life we have been living, like the artist from his
work, to a point of view from which we make it our object,
and get a distinct perception of ourselves. Thereby we
leave our old life, and we shall *never* return to it again.
Thus, the knowledge of self determines the moment in
our existence which concludes one period in our life, and
begins another; it forms a crisis in our development; it
makes a turning-point in our lives. It is not merely a
copy, it is a transformation of our lives. We free ourselves from our passions as soon as we think them; they
cease to be our state as soon as they become our object;
we cease to feel them as soon as we begin to reflect upon
them. Therein lies the whole significance of the knowledge of self; the crisis which it effects in our lives. It
transforms our *state* into our *object:* it places the power
under which we have lived over against us as an object.
What is the necessary result? We are no longer involved in that state; we are no longer controlled by that
power; we are, therefore, no longer what we were. Thus,
earnest self-knowledge is always a fundamental freeing
and renewing of our lives: it is really the crisis in which
the present separates itself from the past, and prepares for
the future. The acts of self-knowledge in our lives are
like the monologue of a drama: the action withdraws from
the animated theatre of the outer world into one's inmost
mind, and there, in the quietness of self-reflection, it solves
old problems, and proposes new ones.

Such crises are wanting in no actively intellectual life, and
every one has experienced them. It is impossible for us
continually to pour out our being without remainder, as it
were, into the particular states of life and culture by which

we are controlled. Insensibly begins, and gradually grows, the rebellious consciousness. In the same proportion, our interest in the old forms of culture dies; in the same proportion they cease to satisfy us; we are weary of them. A feeling of satiety and dissatisfaction becomes more and more definite, more and more painful, until, at last, we remain alone with ourselves. One thing is certain: we are estranged from the life we have been living; we are inwardly free from it. For the first time we become conscious of our independence; and we indemnify ourselves in our thoughts for every thing that we no longer desire or believe with the great consciousness that we no longer desire it. Now begins reflection upon ourselves, upon the problem of our existence, upon the problem of the world. We begin to philosophize so far as our faculties and culture permit us. This philosophy is a fruit of our culture, however mature or immature it may be. Its foundations are laid in the state of culture from which it proceeds, and from which it frees us. It will, therefore, necessarily give expression to this state of culture also. Thus, from the experience and development of a single life, I have described the state of mind in which the will inclines to reflection and self-knowledge, and the first motives to philosophize are conceived. Those are the moments when intense natures become conscious of a passionate desire to become acquainted with philosophy, and receive from it the satisfaction that life no longer gives.

What those significant meditations upon self are in the life of the individual, the prominent systems of philosophy are in the life of humanity. They not merely accompany the advancing spirit of man, but they exert a quiet though powerful influence upon its progress. They make that an object of thought which was before a mastering state: they free the world from this dominion, and so tend to complete existing states, and prepare and lay the foundations of a new human culture. They act as inner factors in originating, developing, and bringing to an end, the great systems of culture in the history of the world, and in determining the great crises of culture. Humanity is a problem that becomes more and more developed in history, is ever more and more profoundly conceived. That, in brief, is the entire content of the history of philosophy, a content indeed of great historical significance. We first see the history of philosophy in its true light, when we see in it the course of development in which the necessary problems of humanity are defined with all distinctness, and so solved that from every solution ever new and profounder problems arise. We must trace out the fundamental lines in this course of development, in order to fix the point where we ourselves take up its exposition.

CHAPTER II.

THE COURSE OF DEVELOPMENT OF GREEK PHILOSOPHY.

THE entrance of Christianity into the history of the world forms the boundary between the two great periods of the history of the world, — the pre-Christian and the Christian. By this boundary we mean the whole time which Christianity required to overcome the old religion and to become itself a great power in the history of the world.

In the pre-Christian world, there was *one* nation which beyond all others was philosophical. It exercised almost undivided mental sway for more than a thousand years, and its systems still remain a school of culture and education for the nations of Christianity. The predominant philosophy of antiquity was the *Grecian*. It began in the sixth century before Christ, and ended in the sixth of the Christian era. Its beginnings coincided with the foundation of the great Persian empire, and its last school died about a half-century after the downfall of the Western Roman Empire. A peculiar fate willed that Grecian philosophers of the first period should flee from the Persians, whose victorious arms already threatened the Grecian world, and that, more than a thousand years later, the last philosophers of Greece, driven from Athens, should seek refuge with a Persian king, protected by the edict of a Christian emperor.

A comparison has often been made between the philosophy of Greece and that of modern times. In this relation, Socrates has often been compared with Kant, and the pre-Socratic, with the pre-Kantian, philosophies; and, even in the

post-Kantian philosophers, some have sought to find many
noteworthy points of resemblance to the Post-Socratic Attic
philosophers. Still, on the whole, the fundamental principles
of the two periods are essentially different. Nevertheless, I
will make the comparison in one respect, if only to make the
survey more rapidly. If one can distinguish the periods of
the development of antiquity according to the universal
scheme of historical division, into the earlier, middle, and
later times, Grecian philosophy, in the last of these divisions, begins in an unmistakably reformatory epoch. The
founders of ancient philosophy were impelled by the desire
for a universal religious-moral reformation of the Grecian
world, and philosophy itself appeared in the service of this
reformatory effort. I need only mention Pythagoras to denote a type and example of a tendency which stamped itself
on Grecian philosophy even in its origin, and which was continually re-appearing during its progress. Ancient philosophy
began in the reformatory age of the Grecian world; modern
philosophy in that of the Christian world. Between the end
of the former and the beginning of the latter, lie a thousand years of that specifically Christian culture in which
the new principle of faith developed its order of the
world in the supremacy of the Church, and based its view
of the world on theological foundations. Thus, it is the
philosophical problems of antiquity, and the theological
problems of Christendom, which, generally speaking, constitute the course of development which precedes our subject
as its historical condition.

In the development and succession of its problems, Grecian
philosophy is a wonderful and an incomparable example of a
profound and, at the same time, entirely natural and simple
growth. Nothing is forced, nothing is artificial. Nowhere
is there a break in the progressing course of thought. Everywhere the uniting terms are thoroughly thought out and distinct. A connection of the most vital character binds the
members of this long series into a whole, in whose magnifi-

cent forms we recognize the plastic influence of classic art. No other philosophy makes this impression. The thought-world of Greece was born of *one* people, of *one* language, and has nothing, therefore, of the fragmentary character of those philosophies in whose elaboration different peoples co-operate. And how full of meaning, and rich, is the development of Grecian philosophy! In its origin, it was in contact with the cosmogonal fictions of the religion of nature: at its close, it stood in the presence of Christianity; and it was not only an essential factor in its production, but is still an indispensable means in its education.

I. THE PROBLEM OF THE WORLD.

Its first problem was the explanation of the world, as it appeared as nature to the perceiving mind. Its first thoughts were the simplest, which naturally first occurred for the solution of that problem. Of what does the world consist? What is the *basal material* of which it is formed and constituted? But the world is not merely substance and material: it is likewise form and order, system, cosmos. In what consists its *fundamental form*, its principle of order? These two problems were the first and simplest. The Ionic school undertook to solve the first, — the determination of the basal material; the Pythagorean philosophy the second and higher, — the determination of the principle of world-order, or the fundamental form of the world.

If we combine these two questions in one, we have the fundamental problem of Grecian philosophy, the problem which was first solved in the zenith of its classical development, — How are stuff and form united? How does stuff acquire form? How is the world formed? How do things arise? This formation or origin, taken in its simplest sense, is a becoming, a process, a change. And so the third natural and great problem that here arises relates to the *world-process*, the origin of the world. When the principle, the real ground of things, is determined, whether it be stuff or form, plainly

the next question must be, How do things result from their
real ground?

The solution of this question results in new contradictions.
The concept of becoming, of genesis and decay, in a word,
of the world-process, is a great problem. We must comprehend how something arises, — i.e., passes from non-existence
into existence; how something changes, — i.e., how this thing
becomes another thing, passes from this condition into
another. Such a transition seems incomprehensible, inexplicable, underivable. And so there are for this problem of the
world but two solutions at first. We cannot deduce, cannot
explain, cannot think the genesis of things; it appears, therefore, unthinkable and impossible; it cannot be. That is one
solution. Or we cannot, to be sure, deduce becoming, but
we can just as little deny it: it must, therefore, be declared
original and eternal. It does not follow from the principle
of the world, it is itself the principle of the world. That
is the second solution. The two solutions form the most
decided contradiction. The first solution declares that *nothing* is in a process or becoming: the second declares that
every thing is in a process, in a constant and continuous
change which never begins, never ceases, never pauses.
Both recognize in the concept of becoming, the contradiction that something is, and, at the same time, is not. This
contradiction is impossible, declare the Eleatics: this contradiction is necessary, declares Heraclitus, "the incomprehensible sage of Ephesus." The problems on both sides are
clear. How must the world be conceived, since it does not
endure that contradiction, since being necessarily excludes
from itself not-being in every respect, therefore, all becoming
and all multiplicity, since, in a word, becoming and multiplicity are concepts, which are full of contradictions, unthinkable, impossible? This is the exact problem of the Eleatics.
They first made the great discovery, that contradictions are
contained in, and impossibilities asserted by, our natural
thinking; that, therefore, the natural concept of the world,

based on the reports of the senses, cannot be true. This trend of thought is, therefore, rich in results for all time. The world-process cannot be derived: how the primary being passes over from a permanent state into changing states cannot be conceived. Such a transition is unthinkable, therefore impossible. There is no becoming; the primary being remains always like itself; there is in it no difference, no multiplicity: it is the *all-one*. The fundamental concept of the Eleatics is, the necessarily to be thought, as the contradictory of the impossibly to be thought (Xenophanes, Parmenides, Zeno, Melissus).

How must the world be conceived, since it excludes from itself motionless, unchangeable being, as entirely contrary to nature? That is the question of Heraclitus. The world-process cannot be denied: *it is*. It cannot be deduced, since it is incomprehensible how an unchangeable being should at any time begin to change. The world-process is, therefore, original; the primary being itself is in eternal, uninterrupted change; it is itself the world-process, the eternally arising and vanishing world; it is the one divine entity, the principle of world-order, the logos, the primitive fire. That is the solution of Heraclitus.

As the Ionic and Pythagorean problems together constitute the fundamental question of Greek philosophy, so the Eleatic and Heraclitic philosophies constitute its deepest and most fundamental contradictions. To answer the first question, to comprehend the true relation of stuff and form, or their union, the metaphysics of Aristotle was necessary. To answer the second question, to comprehend the true relation of the one and the many, the existing and its changeable phenomena being in becoming, — this union of the fundamental thoughts of the Eleatics and Heraclitus, — the Platonic dialectics was required.

But the problem of philosophy is still occupied with the world-process as nature. This problem must be solved: the world-process, the origin and formation of things, must be

made comprehensible or explained. Now, to explain is to
deduce. Such an explanation of natural becoming, is impossible both to the Eleatics and Heraclitus: they declare
the world-process impossible; he, original. From neither
of these points of view can there be any question of a
derivation.

If the world-process is to be deduced, something must lie
at the foundation of it which has itself not become, and which
itself does not enter into change; something, therefore, original and unchangeable, something in which no genesis or
destruction takes place; a something existing in the sense
of the Eleatics. The world-process is: it cannot take place
in the existing. What remains? How alone can it be conceived, since it plainly must be so conceived that that which
is does not itself change? That is the precise form in which
the problem of Grecian philosophy now stands. The solution is evident, the only one possible. That which exists
cannot be conceived as one, but as many, a *multiplicity*
of primary beings. The world-process — i.e., all natural
changes, all genesis and destruction — can only be conceived
as a union and separation of primary beings; i.e., as a
mechanical process.

Since these primary beings must be united and separated,
they can, of course, be nothing else than materials, fundamental materials. But what are these fundamental materials? The first answer is that of Empedocles: they are the
four *elements*. But the elements are changeable and divisible,
and the fundamental materials must be unchangeable. This
is required by the principle of the Eleatics, to which this
trend of thought remains loyal, in this respect, and certainly
on logical grounds. But if they must be unchangeable, they
cannot have this or that property, cannot, therefore, be different kinds of elements; hence, not the four elements at all,
but an indefinite multitude of fundamental materials, destitute of quality and divisibility; i.e., numberless *atoms*, only
quantitatively different, whose manifold unions or aggrega-

tions constitute things (Leucippus, Democritus). But if only blind, mechanical motion results from the weight of the combined atoms, what is the explanation of the form and order of things? Evidently without such a law-giving motion the problem of the world cannot be solved; evidently such a law-giving motion cannot result from the fundamental materials; evidently there must be an intelligent principle by means of which this motion, and thereby all motion whatever, is produced, since mechanical motion is, at the same time, conformable to purpose. That primordial mind must, therefore, be separated from that fundamental material, and the *dualism* of mind and matter must be explained. In itself, therefore, the matter of the world is a motionless, unseparated mass, a chaos in which there is no separation of materials, but a universal mingling of each with every other. The fundamental materials, therefore, can no longer be conceived as atoms, but qualitative materials, each of which is mingled in every part with the parts of the other, therefore materials divided in an equal number of parts, or homœomeria as Aristotle called them (Anaxagoras).

Here the first period of Greek philosophy naturally closes. This period, usually called the period of natural philosophy, has so far thought through the problem of the world, that from its solutions *mind* necessarily resulted. There are three great problems which occupied this first period, — the problem of the world-material, that of the world-order, and that of the world-process (genesis of things). These investigations lead to *one* result, and this to a new and higher problem.

II. THE PROBLEM OF KNOWLEDGE.

If the nature of things is in truth as these first natural philosophical systems have defined it, it appears, at first sight, inconceivable, and therefore impossible, for the mind of man to know things. Knowing is a mental process. Now, if there is no process whatever, as the Eleatics maintained, there is no mental process. If there is nothing but process, and nothing whatever that is permanent, as Heraclitus maintained, neither subject nor object continues; there is neither a knowing nor a thing to be known, therefore no knowledge. If there is nothing but mechanical process, nothing but the unions and separations of basal elements, as Empedocles and the atomists maintained, there is no mental process, therefore no knowledge. And if the mental process depends upon a being outside the world, as Anaxagoras maintained, there is no natural process of knowledge, therefore no human knowledge. The total result is, — *human knowledge is impossible.* It is impossible from all the points of view of the philosophy which has been heretofore taught: it cannot exist in nature as that philosophy conceived it. At first sight, therefore, nothing seems to remain but to deny it. There is no knowledge, therefore no truth, therefore nothing whatever in itself, or universally valid, neither in science nor in ethics. Nothing remains but subjective opinion, and the art of making it accepted; nothing but the individual man, who declared himself the measure of all things, — the theme of the *Sophists* (Gorgias and Protagoras). The theory of the sophists forms the transition from the knowledge of the world to the knowledge of self, — the crisis of Greek philosophy: it decided the new problem which occupied the following period, the classical time of Attic thought. It turned a blaze of light upon the then existing state of thought, by showing with entire clearness, that, under this state, knowledge and, along with it, philosophy itself, was an absolute impossibility. The sophists themselves were really convinced of this impossibility, at least the ablest of them, since they saw no means of escaping this conclusion. In this conviction they were by no means without philosophical principles; and if we correctly and completely understand them, we shall have to say that they not merely made the culture of their time fruitful, but that they threw such light upon the condition of philosophy that the new problem was self-evident to the progressing mind. They completely illuminated the state of thought of the Greek mind; and the confusion of concepts which they are charged with having produced, was the necessary result of the existing condition of thought,—a condition which they apprehended with perfect clearness, and made clear to the consciousness of others.

The first who saw the new problem, and was himself possessed by it against his will, as it were, who brought on the crisis of self-knowledge, and made it a matter of distinct consciousness in the philosophy of Greece, was *Socrates*. The doctrine of the Sophists forms the transition from the pre-Socratic philosophy to the Socratic. The central point of the pre-Socratic problems related to the genesis of things. The problem of Socrates was to explain the genesis of the *process of knowing*. This was the problem of Attic philosophy. Attic philosophy conceived and solved the problem of the world under the presupposition of the problem of knowledge. Its question was, How must the world be thought, if it is to be thought as a knowable world, as an object of knowledge?

The question which occupied Socrates was nothing else than the genesis of knowledge, the passage of the mind from the state of not-knowing into that of knowing, the seeking of truth, the production and uniting of true concepts, the factual refutation of the sophists who declared that knowledge is impossible, because there is no concept, no judgment, the contradictory of which cannot just as well be affirmed. The continual contradiction of human opinions was regarded by the sophists as a proof of the impossibility of knowledge. Socrates regarded the harmony produced out of the contradiction of opinions as the proof of the contrary. He could only find truth, therefore, in intercourse with men, in animated conversation, in ordinary, conversational thought.

Universal concepts — those in which all men agree — are true concepts, the objects of true knowledge, therefore true objects in general. Are we not obliged to conclude that those species or ideas which express the nature of things, are also really the nature of things? that the objects of true knowledge constitute the truly real and primordial being, are, therefore, the true world, the intelligible or archetypal world, which appears in the sensible world as in its copy, like an idea in a work of art? If there is true knowledge, its object must be the truly real. That is the step from Socrates to *Plato.* From this point of view, philosophy becomes a doctrine of ideas, and the world appears as a copy of ideas, as an eternally living work of art; the cosmos as a natural, the state as a moral, work of art. An ideal world arises in the philosophical consciousness, accessible to man only through elevation to his thinking and ideal nature; and this elevation is only possible through purification from his sensuous nature, from that which constitutes its roots, — namely, the desires which obscure the bright world within us, and draw us down into material things. This philosophy requires the turning from desire and to ideas: it makes the elevation of man to the world of ideas dependent upon his inner purification, upon his moral transformation. Now the conception of an eternal purpose in the world is gained, a living and moulding power which unfolds itself in the order of things, and appears to man as an example for his moral life. In this tendency towards the transformation of the moral life of man, the Platonic philosophy is reformatory and religious. In this phase of his doctrine, Plato feels a kinship with Pythagoras, and future centuries will feel their relationship with Plato. The time will come when men with ardent longing will look towards that intelligible world which Plato, like a master of the plastic arts, conceives, and holds before his world as the only deliverance from the ruin that had already begun.

The opposition of idea and matter, of the intelligible and material worlds, of the natures of thought and sense, is peculiar to the Platonic philosophy, and is grounded in its entire nature. Simply expressed, it is the dualism between form and stuff. The philosophical consciousness, in its demand for unity and coherence, struggles against this dualism. And so the next question — which results from the Platonic philosophy, and which we have called the fundamental problem of Greek thought — is, How does stuff acquire form? How is their union explained? If they were separate from each other, their union would only be comprehensible through the action of a third principle, of external machinery ; and this itself would remain incomprehensible. Form, therefore, must be conceived as dwelling in stuff, as a formative force, i.e., as energy ; and stuff must be conceived as containing form potentially in itself, as the foundation for, and tendency to, this particular formation, i.e., as energy ; and every actual thing must be conceived as self-forming stuff, which achieves its form, realizes its inner purpose, i.e., as entelechy. And things altogether must appear to us as a series of such forms, the lower of which always contains the foundation for, and tendency to, the next higher, i.e., as a gradation of entelechies. And the world-process itself can only be conceived as a motion, in which stuff forms itself, form completes itself, potentiality actualizes itself, and that which has already become a thing, is constantly becoming stuff and material for higher formations ; i.e., it must be conceived as development. By this concept, *Aristotle* got rid of the Platonic dualism. Even knowledge, according to Aristotle, is a process of development. Thus, through the concept of development, both the problem of the world and the problem of knowledge were solved. This concept is established as soon as form is conceived as the energic, and matter as the dynamic, principle, or, what is the same thing, as soon as ideas are regarded as the purpose dwelling in things. Matter, then, must be explained by the concept of potentiality, or capacity for assuming form. Plato regarded stuff as μὴ ὄν, Aristotle as δυνάμει ὄν. The difference between these two philosophers cannot be stated more briefly and forcibly.

Here ends the classic period of Greek philosophy. The succeeding period takes another direction, pointed out by the Socratic schools and the Platonic-Aristotelian doctrine. It ceased to be what it had been, — cosmology, — since before and after its transition in Socrates it was constantly trying to solve the problem of the world. The problems of the world-stuff, world-order, world-process, occupied the attention of the pre-Socratic philosophers: How can the world be known? was the question of Socrates. Anaxagoras gave the last solution of these first problems, Aristotle of the last. Anaxagoras founded the dualism between mind and matter which Aristotle sought to overcome by the doctrines of entelechy and development, but he was by no means entirely successful : since, at the conclusion of his system, this dualism appears again and again. If we attend merely to this separation of mind from matter, Aristotle's system seems to conclude in a dualism similar to that from which Anaxagoras started.

III. THE PROBLEM OF FREEDOM.

This dualistic mode of thought, though certainly inconsistent with the principle of Aristotle, was nevertheless a natural result of his philosophy. This philosophy sees in the world a series of gradations of entelechies: it conceives this series as a completed whole, and, therefore, requires a last member, a highest entelechy, i.e., such a one as can proceed from no higher, which, therefore, in no wise contains a potentiality for new formations, is, therefore, not at all of a material nature, but is completely immaterial, hence one which must be thought as pure form, as mere energy which is an end only to itself, i.e., as thought which thinks itself, as mind, as God. Moving every thing, he is himself unmoved. Unaffected by the world-process, he is exalted above the world, and in this exaltation is absolutely perfect. He is sufficient to himself. This self-sufficiency appears as the most perfect state, attainable only by mind which reposes in its self-consciousness, and holds itself aloof from the motions of the world. Man also is a self-conscious personal being: if he were free from the world, he would be

perfect. This perfection becomes his ideal, his highest problem. What he seeks is the most perfect state of life, his
personal ideal. Philosophy which takes this direction is
practical rather than theoretical. The object of this philosophy is not so much idea as *ideal*, not so much truth as
the wise man whose archetype it only seeks to know in order
to realize it in life. Its fundamental direction is practical:
its problem is the restoration of divine perfection in man, an
inner perfection, which approximates divinity. Its goal is
this divine-human state, or, if I dare so speak, this God-be-
coming of man. The solution of this problem is only possible through becoming free from the world; and in this sense
I call the new problem, *the freeing of man from the world*.
Here we see already how Grecian philosophy, filled by the
ideal of man, renounces the world, and seeks a goal that,
without its knowledge, guided it into the path that terminated in Christianity.

But how is the freeing from the world possible, through
which personal self-sufficiency is obtained? So long as the
world lays hold of us, and insnares us, we remain dependent.
This dependence is profound so long as we permit the world
to excite our desires, our passions, and our efforts; so long
as we allow ourselves to be influenced by its goods, its evils,
its problems. To free ourselves thoroughly from the world,
we must cease to desire, to suffer, to struggle; i.e., to strive
for the solution of the problems of the world. We must put
ourselves in a condition in which the world offers us no more
goods, in which there is nothing worthy of desire, in which
our desires and passions become dead, in which the will is
affected and influenced by nothing. This state is the virtue
of the *stoics*. We must lead a life — in order to protect ourselves against the world — which is free from suffering. or,
not to ask too much of nature, in which we suffer as little,
and enjoy as much, as possible. This state is the happiness
of the *Epicureans*. Finally, in order to get rid of unrest of
mind, we must cease to strive, and must give up the solution

of the problems of the world, being convinced that they are insoluble. This doubt is the indifference of the *Sceptics.* What, after Socrates, was begun in the cynic, Cyrenaic, and Megaric schools, again appears after Aristotle, in the related trends of thought, in the Stoics, Epicureans, and Sceptics, raised to a higher power, as it were, and so conceived that these different tendencies there spring from *one* motive, and go hand in hand to *one* goal. This common motive is the ideal of freedom from the world, a self-consciousness resting in itself, entire self-sufficiency. In this common ideal, Stoics, Epicureans, and Sceptics unite.

If we compare the means which they employ for the attainment of their ideal, with the power from which they wish to become free, the impossibility of their undertaking is manifest. They wish to become free from the world; but the world is more powerful than they are, and the ideal of the wise man is wrecked on the abiding power of things. The virtue of the Stoics stands opposed to the ever-renewing power of natural impulses; the happiness of the Epicureans, to the course of nature with its army of evils, and unless the Epicureans fly to their gods in the interspaces of the universe, they cannot escape the evils of the world; finally, the course of nature, with the power of its predominant conceptions and purposes, which the Sceptic cannot expel, of which he cannot get rid, makes the indifference which he seeks impossible. It is impossible to wring the ideal of self-sufficiency from the world, to bear it triumphantly away, unspotted by the powers of the world. This ideal is the weaker party in the conflict, and must at last succumb.

The means which are here opposed to nature, are, in the last analysis, taken from nature herself. The Stoic seeks to become free from nature through the independence of the will, and this he calls virtue; but this virtue is the proud consciousness of one's own worth, and this egoistic feeling is of the character of human vanity which is a part of nature. The Epicurean seeks to become free from nature through enjoyment, which he would change into a permanent state : this enjoyment is the agreeable consciousness of one's own well-being, and this consciousness is a part of nature.   The Sceptic seeks to become free from nature through doubt : he wishes to destroy our natural beliefs, and to regard the problems that naturally arise as insoluble.   But this doubt itself is supported by natural grounds, by the perceptions of the natural understanding ; and this itself is a part of nature.   The ideal which seeks to overcome nature is constituted by the powers of nature.

And so each of these trends of thought falls into a peculiar contradiction with itself.   The Stoic is happy in the consciousness of his virtue ; he feels exalted in it, and has in this exaltation that agreeable consciousness which the Epicurean finds only in the enjoyments of the senses ; he contents himself with the consciousness that he does not need and desire the goods of the world ; in this consciousness he can enjoy them, first really enjoy them.   In brief, the Stoic makes an enjoyment of virtue.   The Epicurean seeks enjoyment as the most perfect state of life ; he avoids all suffering as far as possible : but the greatest enemy of pleasure are pleasures ; and the Epicurean, therefore, carefully avoids pleasures, and, for the sake of pleasure, practises a renunciation and temperance which would do credit to many a Stoic.   In brief, the Epicurean makes a virtue of enjoyment.   And thus the two opposing trends of thought and systems of life, in their actual manifestations, may become like, even to the degree of being confounded with each other.   Finally, the Sceptic makes a certainty of doubt, and falls into a contradiction no matter whither he turns.   For if his doubt is certain, he is no longer a Sceptic ; and if his doubt is doubtful, it destroys itself, and with it scepticism is at an end.   Enough, these trends of thought are on the road to the human ideal ; but all their attempts fail, and at last resolve themselves into nothing but problems which require a new and deeper solution.

IV. THE PROBLEM OF RELIGION.

We ourselves are the world. Our natural love of self and our natural understanding are also world: they are fundamentally powers of the world, since without them there is no world which we conceive or desire. And just this world which is identical with ourselves, which we ourselves are in a certain sense, is, in the ideal of the Stoics, Epicureans, Sceptics, so little overcome that it is rather deified in it. To get rid of this world, of this our own nature which is of the world, which is indeed experienced as evil, to free ourselves thoroughly from it, to fling away and break through this self that takes us prisoner, and holds us down, — this is now the problem of philosophy and, at the same time, the longing of all who are sensible of the calamities of the time, and the deep inner ruin of man. This ardent desire for freedom from our own worldly and selfish nature is the *desire for salvation;* and so it is an absolutely religious motive which now animates philosophy, and urges it directly towards human redemption. It seeks the way to this goal: it aims itself to be the means of salvation, it announces itself as a doctrine of salvation. In this spirit, and in this motive, must we judge its conceptions and its effects. Its problem is the last of antiquity, — the salvation of the world. What it would call into life, is a world religion: and it seeks to attain it, first, through a purification of the old faith in the gods; and second, through a restoration of it. With this thought, it prepares for, and goes to meet, Christianity, contends and struggles with it for the victory, which it finally loses. But the idea of a world-saving religion was received in, and nourished by, the consciousness of the Grecian world; and when aspiring Christianity broke through the limits of Judaism to work for the salvation of the world, it found here the most fruitful soil.

That desire for salvation which animated the last philosophy of antiquity, and determined its mode of thought, consists in the effort of man to get rid of the world, to escape from the world, or, what is the same thing, to unite himself with a being who is <u>entirely aloof</u> from the world of the senses, free from its limits and evils. The stand-point of this philosophy, therefore, requires, in the strictest sense of the word, the oppositeness of God to the world. To satisfy this desire of human salvation, God cannot be transcendent enough, or enough opposed to the world. Exactly because of his aloofness from the world, exactly because he is free from every thing from which man desires to be free, does he become an object of religious aspiration. And exactly for this reason is there in the conception of a great chasm between God and the world a religious satisfaction. God must be so conceived that man can say to himself, "If I were with him, I should be happy. In his presence there is nothing of that which disturbs and oppresses me." The dualistic mode of conception is, therefore, a characteristic of this philosophy, and the fundamental cause of it is absolutely religious. God here stands opposite the world, not as the principle of order in the presence of chaos, not as the moving purpose in the presence of the moved cosmos, but as the principle of blessedness in opposition to the principle of evil. He is not a principle for the explanation of things, but the ideal of man striving for salvation. Religious aspiration widens to the uttermost the chasm between God and the world: at the same time it desires their union. But how is this union possible? Certainly not by natural, therefore only by supernatural, means: on the part of God by supernatural revelation; on the part of man by supernatural intuition, by inner, mysterious, illumination. The highest state possible to man is now regarded not as self-sufficiency or independence, but enthusiasm, a being filled by God. This state has nothing in common with the natural reason, and is not attainable by it. It is mysterious, and the philosophy which seeks this state is *mystical*. It is a wonderful exaltation in which philosophy now participates, and which tears it away from its natural consciousness;

a state of ecstasy which cannot arise by natural means, but rather suddenly comes and vanishes like a moment of divine illumination. Of himself, man cannot produce this state: he can only experience it, and, so far as in him lies, make himself ready to receive it by a constant purification of his life, a continued renunciation of the world, and control of the natural desires, even to the extremest abstinence. Hence the strictly *ascetic* form of life which this pious philosophy adopts. But the infinite chasm between the divine and the human nature remains. Only in the moment of ecstasy is man lifted above it; but the moment of illumination passes, and man sinks back again into the obscure and unholy world of his natural consciousness. Religious aspiration must throw a bridge across this chasm. Natural beings cannot, therefore higher, supernatural beings must, be mediators between God and man. From the world, no gradation of beings ascends to God; therefore, a gradation of beings must descend from God to the needy world of man. These mediators are, therefore, demons, — beings above man, and below God. Faith in demons takes possession of this religious philosophy; and the same motive, which, in its mode of conception, separates God and the world to the uttermost, and relates the two dualistically, putting the being of God entirely beyond and outside of the world, which makes man's consciousness of God mystical, and his life ascetic, — this motive makes philosophy demonological in relation to the mediation between God and man.

Of course, from such conditions a new scientific system cannot arise, nor does it lie in the need and tendency of the time. It goes back to the past, and what it finds in those systems akin to it, is taken by it, and transformed and renovated in the religious spirit which now animates philosophy. And it finds there two trends of thought pre-eminently which meet its great want, and, therefore, even appear as prefigurations, because they are the fruits of the same kind of reformatory and religious motives; viz., the doctrines of Pythagoras and Plato, who are now surrounded with the

halo of a divine authority.   Both these philosophies are
theologically transformed in the religious spirit of the time,
and in this character they appear as Neo-Pythagoreanism and
Neo-Platonism. To transform and renew the Pythagorean
doctrine in this spirit, its doctrine of the orders of the world
must be conceived as thoughts of God; the numbers, which
express this order in the old Pythagorean system, must be
taken symbolically, — as signs or symbols of concepts, —
themselves, therefore, thought as ideas, the doctrine of numbers as a doctrine of ideas; i.e., the old Pythagorean philosophy must be conceived as the Platonic. And so it is
principally the Platonic philosophy which offers material for
the development of that religious view of the world which the
last period of antiquity required. We may, therefore, call
this entire trend of thought *religious Platonism*, which begins
with the Neo-Pythagoreans, and systematically culminates
and dies in the Neo-Platonic schools (Plotinus and Porphyry, Jamblichus, Proclus). In fact, the aspiration for a
supersensible, purely intelligible world, the ardent desire for
freedom from the world of the senses, for salvation from evil,
the desire for inward purification, — these fundamental impulses which imbue philosophy with the religious spirit, find
no greater or more luminous example than Plato's doctrine of
ideas.   And the Platonic ideas themselves, descending from
the highest unity step by step to an ever-increasing multiplicity, down to the extremest limit where forms enter into
matter, appear here as intermediate beings, as uniting terms,
as ladders, descending from God to the world. This world
of ideas offers itself as a welcome design into which philosophy, with its faith in demons, works its conception of
mediators.

From this point of view, it is easy to determine the systematic form in which the last school of antiquity conceived
and solved its problem. It required a system which fulfils
these two conditions: first, the chasm between God and the
world must be made as wide as possible; and second, this

chasm must be bridged over by a series of intermediate beings infinite in number. These intermediate beings must be conceived as a gradation, a descending gradation, and, therefore, of decreasing perfection, which proceeds from the most perfect being, and ends in the most imperfect; i.e., in the world of the senses, with the effort to return to its original source. The divine primordial being must be thought as not merely beyond the world, but also all activity of mind, as beyond even thought and will, since as such it is inaccessible to man. Those intermediate beings, therefore, cannot proceed from their divine Cause by means of will and thought, but only as a necessary result, flowing from the fulness of his Being without diminishing this fulness, as an effect from which again new, less perfect effects emanate; i.e., that gradation of intermediate beings must be conceived as a gradation of divine *emanations*. What, in the old Platonic system, are ideas, are emanations in the Neo-Platonism, in which the salvation of the world or the soul returning from the greatest distance from God to union with him, is thought in the form of an eternal process of the world and nature. Here we see plainly how the religious motive is conceived in its typical pagan form. These emanations are the most plastic material for all forms of mythology. What in Plotinus are still emanations, are in Jamblichus races of gods and demons, which Proclus methodically orders and arranges.

From the central point of religious Platonism, in which it is grounded, this mode of thought describes a wide horizon, extending beyond Pythagoras and the bounds of the Grecian world. Religious feelings, as such, are indeed kindred. Every phenomenon of a distinctly religious character is important to the interests of this period. As it is itself of a mystical nature, it is particularly attracted by such forms of religious culture as are of a mysterious character, by such religious knowledge as has the character of a divine revelation. Hence the powerful and fanciful attraction which the mysteries of Greece, the Orphic rites, and the Oriental religions, exercise on this temper of mind. The more mysterious the phenomenon, so much the more powerful and magical its impression ; and the obscurer it appears, i.e., the further removed from the present, so much the more mysterious can it assume to be. Hence the effort of this Platonic trend of thought to push the sources of its religious knowledge out beyond the bounds of authentic history, and to sink them in the darkness of the past. There it would find the origin of its wisdom, and would see it borne on in religion and philosophy by a succession of world-illuminating minds from then until the present in which the old and mysterious revelations are renewed. It is characteristic of the faith of this time, of the dogmas of this philosophy, that it feels itself in harmony with all the religious minds of the past, and brings them in a connection which corresponds to its own religious presuppositions. It looks everywhere as in a mirror, and finds everywhere the reflection of its own mode of thought: it perceives its conceptions in the philosophy of Plato, in the wisdom of Pythagoras, in the mysteries of the Egyptians, in the wisdom of the magicians and Brahmins, in the illuminations of the Jewish prophets. It feels itself a link in the great chain of minds through which divine revelations are communicated to humanity. Its reflection, which it throws back into the past, appears again as the prefiguration of that from which it claims to have received its own light. As these religious Platonizing philosophers think, so must Plato and Pythagoras themselves, the old Platonists and old Pythagoreans, have thought. And at the same time this perfect harmony is justified and proved. A multitude of writings appear written in the spirit of the new mode of thought, under the names of an Orpheus, Pythagoras, and old Pythagoreans. The connection believed in is substituted for the actual one, and this is completely obscured by dogmatic conceptions ; in like manner, under the dominion of these conceptions, historical sense and historical criticism are obscured until they are completely lost.

Among the religions of the East, there is particularly one which spontaneously feels and acknowledges a spiritual kinship with religious Platonism, — *the Jewish.* The decline and ill fortune of the Jews under the oppression of foreign rule; the consciousness of this calamity, and the longing to be delivered from it; the hope of a future restoration; faith in a transcendent God; the religious animation, extension, and purification of the idea of God through the prophetic consciousness; the prophets themselves, with their religious and reformatory efforts, and their illuminations enhanced even to ecstasy; faith in miracles; the conception of angels as intermediate beings between God and man, already old and familiar in the faith of the people, — all these characteristics gave to Judaism a kinship with the Grecian philosophy, which we have just expounded, and made the Mosaic religion hospitable to the Platonic. Even the external conditions for mental intercourse existed in Alexandria, that centre of the Hellenic Orient. Judaism recognizes this kinship: it can only comprehend the harmony between itself and Platonism by conceiving the latter as based on the Old Testament, the holy records of its own faith; and now it can only so interpret the records of its own faith as to vindicate their harmony with Platonism. In this way the allegorical mode of interpreting the Old-Testament Scriptures originated, and on its basis the Jewish-Alexandrian religious philosophy. This philosophy culminated in Philo, as religious Grecian Platonism did in the later Neo-Platonists.

This Jewish philosophy is also religious Platonism, under which name we accordingly include all the factors in the spirit of the time immediately preceding the Christian era. Not to lose ourselves in details, since we are here concerned only with the motive that impels philosophy onward, we seek the central point of this entire trend of thought. Its chief problem is the salvation of the world: the fundamental thought in which its solution is sought is that of a world-saving principle. Now, this principle can only be conceived as the divine purpose in the world, as the motive of creation, as the world-arranging idea — present in the formation of things — which enters into the universe, while God himself remains entirely aloof from the world in his transcendent existence. The principle, therefore, which creates and saves the world must be different from God ; it is not God himself, but it goes out from God as the word from the mind ; it is, to express it allegorically and typically, the word of God, the divine *logos*. All the intermediate beings between God and man, however they are named, whether demons according to the Greeks, or angels according to the Jews, meet in this conception as in their unity. The *logos* is regarded as the *mediator* between God and man.

The idea of the logos was developed in the Grecian philosophy. In order to enter into human consciousness, this idea required a trend of thought which, from the beginning, made the principle of the world its problem. Grecian philosophy from its very origin reflected upon the principle of the world : it developed these reflections in its pre-Socratic period, and applied them to the explanation of things ; in its classic period, to the explanation of the knowledge of things ; in its first post-Aristotelian period, to the realization of the human ideal ; in its last period, to comprehend from thence the salvation of man from the world. If we denote that principle of the world by the term logos, since even under the logos a principle of the world must be thought, although this name was by no means the one always used, we can say that Greek philosophy was almost always occupied with this theme, with this question, What is the logos ? In the series of solutions with which we have become acquainted, I will call attention to three principal forms in which we meet the Grecian concept of the logos most distinctly. The principle of the world must be conceived as the order of the world, which is equivalent to the eternal world-process ; but this order of the world cannot be conceived without an eternal purpose in the world, which expresses itself in the world-process, and appears as changeless being in ceaseless becoming. But this eternal purpose in the world cannot be conceived, without at the same time conceiving in it the forming world-energy, or the powers that form the world, and are the germ, as it were, from which the world is developed. In the first form, we recognize the Heraclitian explanation of the world; in the second, the Platonic; in the third, after the appearance of the Aristotelian philosophy, the Stoic. In the first explanation, the logos appears as the order of the world or world-process, as nature or cosmos; in the second, as the archetypal or ideal world, as the world of ideas; in the third, as the fulness of forming forces the λόγοι σπερματικοί. And in the Heraclitian-stoic form, we even meet the word logos.

But the *Platonic* mode of thought forms the real central point of the Grecian logos-idea. The Heraclitian mode of thought involves it as a conclusion: the Stoic involves it as a premise. For one cannot conceive the world-process without the world-idea, and just as little can be conceived the forming powers of the world without the same idea. The Platonic conception of the archetypal world includes the human archetype as the intelligible ground of our existence and the goal of our becoming. In the presence of this archetype, we can only understand our earthy existence, our embodiment in the material world, as a fall of the soul, which is guilty of desire, and our return to that archetype is only possible by means of a purification, which entirely overcomes desire in our minds. But if this is the goal of man, should it not also be the goal of the world — this salvation of man from the world? Here the Platonic philosophy appears in its religious significance; and, from this point, it gives rise to, and explains, the religious state of mind and mode of thought which characterized Greek philosophy in the last centuries of its existence. The logos now appears as the world-saving principle, as the divine thought of the salvation of the world, in which the secret, i.e., the inmost purpose of creation is contained, as the real motive of creation, as the creative word of God.

The word is realized in man who overcomes the world, or restores in himself the pure archetype of man.

Now the Grecian and Jewish problems of salvation come in contact, and show in very many kindred conceptions their religious affinity. That rests in the thought of the *logos*, this in the conception of the Messiah. The logos is a universally conceived principle of the world, and seeks personification: the Messiah is an ideal of a people conceived as a person, and seeks universalization. Both trends of thought need to supplement and penetrate each other: this supplement is sought on the Jewish side. To introduce Platonism into Judaism is to think the logos idea into the conception of the Messiah. This problem, already adumbrated in the Jewish-Alexandrian book of wisdom, is solved by Philo, who makes the logos-Messiah the central point of his philosophy, the Mediator and Saviour of the world.

The problem of salvation demands a *personal solution*. It is solved if a man appears who actually overcomes the world in himself, who, in the deeper meaning of the word, is truly free from the world, in whom humanity recognizes its archetype, and in whom it, therefore, believes as the Saviour of the world. This is the only possible form in which the solution of the religious problem of the world can be effected. A person must appear, who saves himself from the world, and, through faith in him, the world itself; a person of whom one can say that in him salvation has taken place, the idea has appeared, the logos has become flesh, God has become man. Only through faith in such a person can the desire of men for salvation be satisfied.

From the point of view of the logos idea, as this was developed in the consciousness of Greek philosophy, this man was *not* to be found, for this idea had no reference whatever to a particular individual, to an actual man: it gave to the faith which it animated no direction whatever towards a person. From the logos to man, there was an impassable chasm, a chasm that could not be bridged by any conceivable num-

ber of orders of divine beings. The logos idea sought personification, but it was utterly incompatible with the natural
life of man. The thought of salvation was inconsistent with
human nature; it remained on the other side of reality, something universal and inanimate; and so under this conception
the desire of salvation was without expectation and without
hope.

The Jewish desire for salvation, on the other hand, was
filled with a definite expectation and hope. An ideal of their
people was given to it in the person of the Messiah. It waited
patiently for this Saviour who was to come to be the deliverer
of a people, a people whom God had chosen and preserved
to rule the world. This world-ruling Messiah, whom the
prophets beheld in the future of Israel, was the object of the
highest hopes of the faith of the Jews. Now, when a Messiah
appeared who became a saviour, not in the Jewish sense, but
the Grecian, a saviour from the world, the conditions were
fulfilled under which the religious problem of the world received its solution. Its starting-point lay in the centre of the
Jewish people. Their Messianic ideal gave the personal direction which the idea of the logos lacked. The desire for
salvation had, therefore, to accept this ideal in order to reach
its goal, in which, as a phenomenon of history, the logos was
believed to have become flesh, God to have become man.
Faith had at first no path from the logos to man; but there
was a path from man to the Messiah, and from *this* Messiah,
who was not a deliverer in the Jewish-worldly sense, to the
logos. Historical development took this path, a roundabout
one indeed, but the shortest one because it led to the goal;
and, as Lessing has said in the "Education of the Human
Race," "It is not true that a straight line is always the
shortest way."

CHAPTER III.

CHRISTIANITY AND THE CHURCH.

I. PRIMITIVE CHRISTIANITY.

THE person Jesus realized that desire for salvation which humanity felt most deeply, most purely, and most simply; and simplicity always triumphs. Through him the Jewish Messianic ideal was spiritualized and transformed: through him it was animated from the beginning of its history with a new spirit, whose aim was not the exaltation of a people, the subjugation of the world, but the transformation and regeneration of man. In him was solved the deepest and most difficult of the problems of the world, — the salvation of man from the world; he himself was the personal solution of this problem; he forms, therefore, the decisive crisis in the development of humanity, as Socrates was in the development of Greek consciousness. This comparison shows likewise the difference between the two.

At this point in the history of humanity, a fundamental spiritual renewing began. Before this was possible, it was necessary for the divine idea to be embodied in a person who restored and revealed the human archetype in himself; then it was necessary for humanity to recognize this archetype as its own, and believe in the person Jesus as the Saviour of the world. This faith in Jesus Christ forms the foundation and the principle of Christianity: it contains the problem which from that time occupied humanity, and out of which new problems are progressively developed. We follow here these problems in their philosophical relations, so

far as they give rise to, and promote, a new view of the
world corresponding to the Christian faith. The principle
of this faith is absolutely religious: it is concerned only
with the eternal welfare of man, with the salvation of the
world, with the relation of man to God. The view of the
world corresponding to it is, therefore, absolutely theological. The theological mode of thought forms the fundamental characteristic of Christian philosophy, by which we mean
that system of conceptions which is grounded on faith in
Christ as its principle.

Christian philosophy, therefore, as a system, could not be
developed until the religious principle of Christianity was
thoroughly established, — the principle that fitted it to be
the religion of the world. In its primitive form, Christianity
was not a system of thought, but the proclamation of a fact;
not a series of dogmas, but a gospel. As it developed, it
passed through a series of different stages, and got rid of the
contradictions which were discovered in its first records.
Christian faith regarded Jesus from higher and higher points
of view. First he was the *Messiah* of the chosen people;
then he was the *Saviour of the world*, who came not to glorify the Jews, but to save the world; and finally he was the
saving principle of the world, the eternal logos, God become
man, and in this light his person and life were represented.

To follow and point out those developments in the New-
Testament records, those contradictions, forms of transition,
and interminglings of Jewish and Hellenic conceptions,
those great conflicts which deeply and passionately agitated
primitive Christianity, and were necessary to free it from its
first limits, and fit it for a great career in the history of the
world, was the special task of a searching examination of the
Bible. It was necessary to decide between the Jewish faith
in the Messiah, and the faith in the Saviour of the world;
between Christianity as the religion of the Jews and the religion of the world; between the Jewish and Gentile, the
Petrine and Pauline, conceptions. These controversies were

carried on and settled by *primitive Christianity,* which, in its Pauline form, broke through the barriers of Judaism, and severed the bond that still fastened it to a single nation. Thus only did Christianity attain that universal value which made possible a great career in the history of the world.

II. THE CHURCH.

The decisive step towards the realization of this career was the fixed and permanent organization of the Church, an empire of faith which rose in the midst of the ruins of the old world, and laid the foundation for a new one. But such an organization was impossible until Christianity laid aside its apocalyptic conceptions of the imminent end of the world. If Christ was about to come from the clouds of heaven, and establish a millennial kingdom, there was no need of a permanent ecclesiastical institution. But as faith in Christ abandoned its Messianic form, and became spiritualized ; as the idea of its universal value was emphasized, and, consequently, as the need for a new fellowship and regulation in the life of humanity was felt, — the organization of the Church seemed a necessity. The Church was the earthly kingdom of the invisible Christ instead of the millennial kingdom expected by those who believed in his immediate second coming. That kingdom of the invisible Christ promotes the unity of believers, and this unity must be the central fact and governing principle in the new regulation of life. Now, Christ himself must be the bond of union between Christian believers. But for its value on earth, this union requires a visible form. The community of believers need to know that they are united under one head, a head which represents Christ in their midst, steps into his place, as it were. The idea of a representative office, i.e., the idea of an *episcopacy,* alone solves the problem of the unity of faith, which is identical with the problem of the Church. Now, only in one way can bishops be regarded as the representatives of Christ on earth. The apostles were the immediate successors of Christ: bishops must be the successors of the apostles, and, through them, of Christ. Thus, the value of the episcopacy depends upon the idea of apostolic succession. But there are many bishops; and the idea of unity, which, it must be borne in mind, is identical with that of the Church, requires their union under a supreme bishop; and, from the idea of apostolic succession, it follows that he must be regarded as the successor of the chief apostle, i.e., of *Peter*. Now, the Church was organized in the Roman empire: the political institutions of Rome were, therefore, the external conditions under which it began to exist. Hence her political centres seemed the natural centres for the ecclesiastical organization; the capitals of provinces became the natural seats of bishops; those of states, of archbishops and patriarchs; and the metropolis of the world, the seat of the supreme bishop. Thus, Rome was the seat of the ecclesiastical unit, the episcopal primate; while it followed, from ecclesiastical grounds, that this primate was regarded as the successor or representative of *Peter*. From the co-operation of the two causes, therefore, it followed that the Roman bishop was regarded as the successor of Peter, and the apostle Peter as the founder of the Christian community in Rome. Thus the idea of the papacy arose and was realized in the Western Church. The idea of Peter's residence in Rome and his labors there first grew out of anti-Pauline tendencies, then adapted itself to the reconciled form of the Petro-Pauline legends, and grew into an established tradition, on the basis of which the Roman bishops claimed ecclesiastical primacy. (This conclusion is clearly made out by a highly instructive investigation, which has thrown much light upon the nature and development of the Jewish-Christian modes of thought.)

In the various departments of human life, and the various forms of human culture, perhaps no greater example can be found of an historical development, springing merely from an idea, and perpetuated and controlled by it, than the Christian Church. It sprang from the idea of the unity of Christian faith; and this idea determined its form, and developed it into a power that ruled the world. Its fundamental form was very simple. It was so constituted that believers felt themselves united with Christ by a living, historical bond: that the person of Christ seemed united with believers by an unbroken series of connecting links. Those links were the bishops and the apostles and the apostolic fathers. Hence the historical reality of Jesus was accepted as an axiom of incontestable truth.

In a short time, the Church became a living and indestructible power. Its influence increased in spite of the persecutions of Rome, and because of them. In the midst of the disintegrating empire of pagan Rome, the Christian Church, after a few centuries, was the only strong unit with inward life. The unity of the state consisted in imperialism; the unity of faith, in the Church; and already it stood in the presence of that empire as an imposing, and, even in its outward form, invincible, power. In *one* respect, imperialism and the Church resembled each other, — in their striving for centralization; and this was why the Church exercised an attraction on the imperial power. Each of these powers could strengthen itself by forming an alliance with, and using, the other. Constantine the Great appreciated this fact, and it might very well have appeared to him in a religious light.[1] It was not so much the cross in the clouds, as the cross in the world, before which he bowed. Imperialism professed Christianity, and thereby advanced to the power of the world. What Constantine established in the beginning of the fourth century, and Julian, fifty years after the first edict of toleration, vainly sought to overthrow, was confirmed by Theodosius the Great, at the end of that century, even before the division of the empire.

The first inner problem of the new religion consisted in the

---

[1] F. Chr. Baur: Christianity, and the Christian Church of the First Three Centuries (1853), pp. 443-7.

development and adjustment of the apostolic oppositions, —
the grounding of *Catholic* Christianity. Externally, its work
was to conquer the Roman empire. It gained the victory
after enduring all sorts of political persecutions, in the course
of the three first centuries, from Nero to Diocletian, and
experiencing every attack of philosophy from Celsus to
Porphyry.

III. THE DOCTRINE OF THE CHURCH.

1. *The Problem.* — Unity of faith demands perfect harmony
in the conceptions of faith. The Church must make these
conceptions universally valid or symbolical. Only the
Church can do it, since, by virtue of its bishops and synods,
it alone has the power to decide what is true. Christian
faith must be definitely determined, freed from all arbitrary
conceptions, from all opposing points of view. This was required by the Church, since unity of faith demands also unity
in the consciousness of faith: only thereby is the Church
inwardly and thoroughly established. The men who laid
the foundations of the ecclesiastical edifice, who put the doctrines of the Church in a definite form, are justly called the
fathers of the Church, *patres ecclesiæ*. They changed faith
into *dogmas;* they grounded the doctrines of the Church, and
therewith the inner unity of the faith of the Church; they
solved the fundamental problems of theology (called patristic
. in this part of its development).

These problems were solved from a regulative point of
view. The criterion of the unity of faith was determined by
the teachings of Christ and the apostles. That is true which
they taught, which has been handed down as their doctrine
in unbroken succession by the successors of the apostles,
with whom the Church believes itself, and only itself, in
living historical connection. As apostolic succession forms
the unity of faith, so apostolic tradition forms the criterion
of the doctrines of faith.

From the point of view, and the fundamental idea, of
Christianity, we can see the principle that determined the

conception and solution of the patristic problem. What must be believed, is Christ as the Saviour of humanity. He must be accepted as the person in whom the salvation of the world is accomplished. Faith in this fact forms the fixed presupposition on which the Church rests; the sure guiding principle which regulates and arranges its conceptions. What contradicts this principle is false, that which agrees with it is true. Thus orthodoxy and heterodoxy were distinguished in the concepts of the Christian faith. And the problem of the Church was to develop and establish the doctrines of orthodoxy in accordance with this principle.

In that fact of faith itself lies the fundamental question of Christian theology. The fact of the salvation of the world is accomplished in the person of Christ. Christ, therefore, must be accepted as the Saviour of the world; as the world-saving principle, which is eternal; like the divine purpose in the world, like the divine motive in creation; eternal, therefore, like God himself. This world-saving principle must be identified with the person Jesus, with this definite, historical person. The two moments of faith must have equal authority, and must be united in the doctrine of the Church. If a certain mode of thought requires the saving world-principle in Christ to be so acknowledged and emphasized that the historical, human Jesus is thereby made unreal, the fact of salvation ceases to be an historical, actual fact, and this mode of thought is, therefore, false. If another mode of thought requires the finite and creatural character of the Saviour to be so emphasized that his divine nature is thereby degraded and invalidated, this mode of thought is likewise, therefore, in contradiction with that which must be believed. Thus, the doctrine of the Church must develop its own principles in conflict with opposing views of faith. It is threatened on two sides, each a contradiction of the other. On the one, the divine manifestation of Christ is maintained at the expense of his historical and human reality: on the other, reversely, his creatural nature is maintained at the expense

of his divine.   There, the Gnostic-Docetic mode of thought
must be contested; here, the rationalistic-Arian.

If we presuppose salvation in Christ as the primarily
given fact, the problem of patristic theology is, to bring the
conceptions of faith into harmony with it, to make them
conformable to it, to so determine them that they do *not* invalidate that primary fact.   Humanity must be saved; i.e.,
reconciled with God through Christ.   This fact, therefore,
appears as a product of three factors, — God, Christ, humanity.   In reference to all three, a multitude of conceptions are
possible which are *not* consistent with the fact of salvation:
all those conceptions are, and must be, false in the opinion
of the Church.   In respect, therefore, to all three, only certain conceptions are true; and this brings us to the problem,
What are those *true* conceptions?   If God is not so conceived that from him goes out a world-saving principle, which
appears in the person of Christ, and makes real the fellowship of believers, the fact of salvation is null.   If the person
of Christ is not so conceived that salvation takes place in
him, there has been no salvation.   If man is not conceived as
needing, and, therefore, capable of receiving, salvation, the
fact of salvation is without purpose and meaning.

These are thus three problems, in respect to that primary
fact of faith, which affect the doctrine of the Church: how
must the natures of God, Christ, and man, be conceived, that,
in all three points, our conceptions may be conformable to
the fact of salvation?   The first question is the *problem of
theology;* the second, of *Christology;* the third, of *anthropology.*   Athanasius, the bishop of Alexandria, determined the
ecclesiastical solution of the first question in a controversy
with the presbyter Arius: he is related to dogma, as Baur
aptly says, as Gregory VII. to the Church.   Cyril, the patriarch of Alexandria, determined the solution of the second,
in controversy with Nestor, the patriarch of Constantinople;
and the solution of the third was determined by Augustinus,
the bishop of Hippo, in controversy with the monk Pelagius.

The solution of the first question requires the distinction of the divine persons and their consubstantiality, the determination of the divine economy, the concept of the *trinity;* that of the second, the distinction and union of both natures in Christ, the concept of *theanthropism;* that of the third, the doctrine of divine *grace* and of the *sinful nature* of man, by which the concept of human freedom is determined. Here the ecclesiastical system of faith culminates in decided and absolute opposition to paganism. Augustine defined this opposition, conceiving them as fundamentally opposed systems, — paganism as the kingdom of this world, "*civitas terrena;*" Christianity as the kingdom of God, "*civitas dei.*" Filled and illuminated with the faith in a new world, in the midst of the on-rushing destruction and devastation of the old, he laid the foundation of the specifically Christian and ecclesiastical view of the world.

2. *Augustinianism.* — Augustine was the ablest of ecclesiastical thinkers; and if "ecclesiastical" includes "theological," he was the greatest of Christian theologians. He made the Church clear concerning herself: he kindled the light in which she saw her own nature; and in this sense we can say with truth of this father of the Church, that he was her greatest light. He not merely completed the faith of the Church, but at the same time grounded faith in the Church, drawing from the fact of salvation all the inferences that relate to human nature.

Human nature must be conceived as adapted to the fact of salvation from sin. It must, therefore, be regarded as needing salvation, or *sinful.* It can be saved only through Christ: it appears, therefore, as incapable of salvation of itself, or as *destitute of freedom* in its sinfulness. Sin, accordingly, is the power which controls the will; it is a property of the will from which the will cannot free itself, it is the nature of the human will. But sin is guilt, and guilt presupposes freedom, since a being without freedom cannot incur guilt: a sin which excludes freedom is a contradiction.

Thus, sin appears as the fact of freedom, and likewise as its loss. Man originally had power not to sin: he sinned, and thus lost his freedom, and certainly forever. Since then he can do nothing but sin. In the first sin, the human race fell: in Adam, all have sinned. Sin is free in its origin; in its consequences, slavery, causing the permanent corruption of human nature, *original sin*. That is the fundamental thought of Augustine, — a thought which he first made valid in this sense, raised into full consciousness, and made the central point of the doctrine of salvation. In this state of original sin, man cannot acquire salvation; he can neither give it to himself, nor can he of himself merit it; it can only fall to his share contrary to his deserts, i.e., through *grace*. There is nothing in man to deserve this favor: it is, therefore, unconditional, groundless, an act of the divine Arbitrary Will. God bestows his grace on man without his co-operation; i.e., he elects him to salvation. Salvation, therefore, is the *election of grace*, — an election completely independent of human actions and works: it was made before man existed, and must accordingly be conceived as divine predetermination or *predestination*. To elect is to prefer.' Some are elected by God to salvation, others to damnation. Now, according to the divine decree, revealed in the fact of salvation, man can receive divine grace only through Christ, and communion with Christ is possible only through the Church. The Church, therefore, is the kingdom of grace, the divine institution of grace on earth, the condition and means of human salvation. There is no salvation except through redemption, none, therefore, outside of the Church: this is the doctrine that the Church alone saves.

The fact of salvation presupposed by faith demands that human nature be conceived as under the dominion of original sin. The concept of God and that of the Church lead to the same requirement.

God must be conceived as unconditional, i.e., all-powerful, will. He is not merely power, but will: this concept nega-

tives all emanation. He is *unconditional* will, — will limited
by nothing without him; without him, therefore, there is
nothing that can limit him: this concept negatives all dualism. The mode of thought of religious Platonism, the Neo-
Platonists, and the Christian Gnostics, was dualistic and
emanational. The theology of Augustine is completely
opposed to these modes of thought. If God is will, the
world is the work of his will, — i.e., creation, — and the divine
activity is creative. If God is unconditional will, the world,
since it does not emanate from the divine nature, can only
be created out of nothing by the divine will: it is "*per deum
de nihilo.*" So the conservation of the world, since the world
is nothing in itself, is a continual creation of God, "*creatio
continua;*" so every thing which happens in the world is
determined, predetermined, by the divine will; so men also
are predestined, some to salvation, the rest to damnation: so
from the side of men salvation can be conditioned by nothing,
i.e., men appear as of themselves incapable of salvation, as
so under the rule of sin that this constitutes the condition
of their will, — a condition which is transmitted by inheritance
from generation to generation. In this point, the theology
of Augustine results in the doctrine of original sin.

Two principal concepts of the Augustinian system appear
to contradict each other. The concept of God requires the
unconditionalness of the will, and this, the concept of predestination, which destroys human freedom. But if there is
no freedom, there is no sin; and if there is no sin, there is no
need of salvation; and if no need of salvation, no salvation.
What the concept of God denies, the concept of salvation
affirms. Augustine seeks so to remove this contradiction as
not to deny human freedom as such. God gave it to man,
but man has lost it through sin, and corrupted his nature;
and this is why sin has become original sin.

The concept of the Church requires that of original sin.
The perception of this connection turns a blaze of light upon
the system of Augustine. If the Church is the kingdom

within which alone we can commune with Christ, and thereby partake of the divine grace, it possesses the power to forgive sins. Only through and in it can sins be forgiven. Salvation comes to man because the Church takes him into her bosom through the means of grace of baptism. Now, if the Church, as the kingdom of divine grace, is, like this, unconditional, and independent of the co-operation of men, it exists before individuals: it appears, like the state of the ancients, as the whole which is earlier than the parts. It, therefore, receives man in the beginning of his earthly existence, at his entrance in the world: it must incorporate into itself children when it baptizes them. Through baptism, children become partakers of forgiveness of sins, must, therefore, also need forgiveness of sins, i.e., be sinful; and this is only possible because of original sin. It is very significant that a controversy arose between Pelagius and Augustine concerning the damnation of unbaptized children. If there is no salvation outside the Church, and if it can only be reached through the Church, man outside the Church is in a state of sin ; outside of baptism is corruption ; in the kingdom of nature, sin rules, and this leads to damnation. Without original sin, there is no sinfulness of children, no necessity in their case for forgiveness of sin, no necessity for their baptism, no validity to the doctrine that the church exists before individuals, no unconditional existence of the Church, i.e., no Church as the kingdom of grace. Thus, the doctrine of original sin is the central point of the doctrine of the Church. Faith in the Church demands the natural corruption of individuals, and conversely. As to what concerns the eternal welfare of man, every thing depends upon the Church, nothing upon the natural man. That is the central point of Augustinianism, which, regardless of consequences, forcibly and keenly drew all the inferences which that presupposed principle of faith enjoins, even in their unavoidable contradictions.

This system is the basis of the Church of the Middle Ages.

This is the source of its consciousness of unconditional supremacy. But, in the course of the development of the Church, conclusions were necessarily drawn which obscured the principle of Augustinianism. Faith in the Church is unconditional obedience, and this does what the Church requires. Obedience can show itself in but one way, — by obedient conduct, by external works, in this case by ecclesiastical works. Inwardly these works may be merely mechanical: outwardly they may far exceed the measure of what is required, and be meritorious and holy; and, from the nature of works, they must be judged from without. Hence the possibility arises of earning merit, and justifying one's self, by works. But, if works avail as a means of justification, human co-operation is no longer excluded from the conditions of salvation; and in the same proportion as this co-operation is meritorious, validity must be conceded to human freedom also. And thus there proceeded from the faith in the Church, which Augustine grounded, the doctrine of the merit of good works, which, in contradiction with Augustinianism, rests on the Pelagian doctrine of freedom. After this doctrine had reached its extremest limit, Augustine's fundamental thought of the sinful nature of man was emphasized anew as a reforming power. Within the Christianity of the West it broke through the authority of the Roman-Catholic system in Luther, Zwingle, and Calvin; and within Catholicism, as Jansenism, it attacked the system of the Jesuits.

IV. THE DEIFICATION OF THE CHURCH.

If the Church is the kingdom of divine grace, the vessel of the Holy Spirit, and the sphere of its activity, it itself appears as a member in the divine economy, as an eternal ordinance, which, in its hierarchical forms, constitutes the ladder which leads from heaven down to earth. In this conception, the historical origin and development of the Church is obscured: it seems as if it had descended from heaven, become visible in the earthly hierarchy, which rises from the Jewish to the Christian, from the legal to the ecclesiastical, from deacons and presbyters to bishops, and continues beyond the world in the heavenly hierarchy in the orders of angels, whose highest ranks surround the throne of God.

The gradation of Platonic ideas had transformed itself in the last systems of Greek philosophy, in religious Platonism, into the gradation of heathen gods. This conception, which the Neo-Platonic school of Athens, the system of Proclus, developed, was the last of exhausted paganism. The Christian Church has now established its divine authority. It also is a kingdom of orders mediating between God and man, and the type and the form of that Neo-Platonic mode of conception corresponds to its hierarchical constitution. Thus it was that the two entered a union; that that type became Christianized, and in it the Church was deified.

This blending of Neo-Platonic forms with faith in the Church, this deification of the Church, constitutes the character and the theme of those writings which, in the sixth century of the Christian era, were known under the name of "Dionysius the Areopagite," who was one of the first Christians whom Paul converted in Athens, and whom the sage made the first bishop of that city. This conception of the theology of the Areopagite, which sees and worships in the Church the kingdom of heaven on earth, stamped itself deeply on the religious imagination and the mysticism of the Middle Ages. It was the Gnosticism of the Church.

CHAPTER IV.

THE COURSE OF DEVELOPMENT OF THE PHILOSOPHY OF THE MIDDLE AGES.

I. PROBLEM.

CHRISTIANITY has developed into the Church, and Christian faith into a series of dogmas. The fixed presupposition upon which the further development of Christian ideas now rests, is the fact of salvation, represented in the form of the symbols and dogmas which resulted from the labors of the fathers of the Church, and of the great councils of the fourth and fifth centuries. The fact of salvation needed to be proclaimed, devoutly received, freed from every limitation. The dogmas of faith, on the other hand, require to be taught, proved, combined with each other. As the Church forms a hierarchical system of absolute unity, so its doctrine must become a system in complete harmony with the spirit of the Church, and governed by it. The systematization of faith requires their collection and organization in a demonstrative form, by means of which they can be taught and learned. Such a form is impossible unless they are grounded on a comprehensive basis, and logically deduced therefrom. This systematization was the work of scholasticism. The teachers of the Church in the narrower sense of the term, the *doctores ecclesiæ*, take the place of the *patres ecclesiæ*, the fathers of the Church. Dogmas in their hands were materials for instruction : theology was taught. It became scholasticism, and in this form constitutes the philosophy of that ecclesiastical age of the world that we are accustomed to call the Middle Ages.

The character and problem of scholasticism were thereby
determined. It was closely and vitally connected with the
hierarchical system, and was a servant of the Church. Its
labor was essentially *formal:* out of given material, according
to a prescribed plan and an established guiding principle, it
had to erect a system of doctrine in perfect harmony with
the ecclesiastical conception of the world. As theology, it
was a servant of the Church : as philosophy, it was " the hand-
maid of theology."

But though scholastic philosophy was in bondage to theology and the Church, this bondage involved a new and
peculiar relation into which scholasticism entered with faith.
The Church determined what was believed : scholasticism
was to explain why it was true. Dogma says, " *Deus homo :* "
scholasticism asks, " *Cur deus homo ?* " Dogmas must be
evident to the natural understanding : the faculties of human
knowledge must be brought into harmony with faith. This
harmony was the avowed problem, the programme, as it
were, of scholasticism. And this differentiates scholasticism
from the theological development which preceded it, and the
philosophical one that followed it. The doctrine of faith
had to be developed in opposition to Gnosticism, which was
its immediate antagonist, and in opposition to the philosophy
in general which came from paganism, and seemed to it the
mother of all heresies. It regarded philosophy, and, with
it, all the natural knowledge of reason, as inimical to faith ;
and Tertullian regarded its assertions as the criterion of
infidelity, and with his " *credo, quia absurdum,*" struck it to
the ground. In the time succeeding scholasticism, philosophy
threw off its dependence upon faith, and took its own course,
even in opposition to faith. Before and after scholasticism,
faith and philosophy were separated : in it they were united
so long as its power was unimpaired. While this alliance
lasted, scholasticism flourished, and lived in its true element.
When this alliance was dissolved, it fell into decline. When
faith tore itself loose from philosophy, and quit the service of

the latter, the signs of the decay of scholasticism were at hand. And this decay came from within: it was the self-dissolution of scholasticism, since it necessarily advanced to the point in its own development where it demanded the separation of knowledge and faith, and thereby destroyed its own work.

The motive of scholasticism was "*credo ut intelligam;*" its fundamental principle the ecclesiastical "*fides;*" its goal the "*ratio fidei.*" The systematization of faith was likewise its rationalization. Scholasticism is *rational theology* under the control of the Church: therein lay its character and its problem. In scholasticism the Church authorized philosophy, gave it a field of labor, demanded the development of a Christian philosophy, and incorporated rational activity into its own development, as a completely servile, dependent factor, to be sure, to which the faith of the Church prescribed what it had to do. But to serve is to become free. Obedience is the discipline that prepares for freedom. In the service of theology, philosophy laboriously attained its majority, and won the independence with which it finally tore itself loose from the dominion of the Church, and undertook its own development.

II. THE ECCLESIASTICAL AGE OF THE WORLD.

In determining the problem and activity of scholasticism, we have presupposed an ecclesiastical age of the world, that had to be founded historically before this ecclesiastical philosophy began its work of instruction. New states of the world and of nations required to be developed, — nations which received Christianity in the form of the faith of the Church, the education and culture of whom proceeded from the Church. The downfall of the old world; the hostile migrations of nations; the destruction of the Western Roman empire, which, of the powers contemporary with it, the Church alone outlived; the formation of the feudal system; the Christianization of new peoples distinguished into Romanic,

Germanic, and Slavic; finally, the founding of a new, Franko-Carlovingian empire, extending over a large part of the world, — these were the conditions which prepared the way for the ecclesiastical age of the world, and preceded the appearance of scholasticism. Its theatre was the Western world, the Romanic-Germanic, — Spain, France, Italy, Britain, Germany.

Rome was the spiritual centre of this new world, — not the Rome of the Cæsars, but ecclesiastical Rome, in whose rule of the world the age consists that we have called ecclesiastical. The supremacy of the Church was based on its unity and centralization. Rome was the centre of the empire of the world: Rome, therefore, was, also, the Church of the world. The elevation of Roman bishops to authority over the Church was the condition which constituted and realized the character of the ecclesiastical age. This sovereign authority of the Roman bishops is the *papacy*, which gradually, in the course of centuries, step by step, scaled the height from which it saw the Church and the world at its feet.

The first round of the ladder was the ecclesiastical primacy to which the bishop of Rome, as the successor of Peter, laid claim, and which particularly Leo I., a generation before the downfall of the Western Roman empire, succeeded in establishing, on the ground of the *ecclesiastical* dignity and importance of Rome. During the headlong political changes in Italy, — in the course of the immediately subsequent time, the Goths were forced to give way to the Greeks, and these to the Longobardi, — the successors of Peter grew more and more independent. The second great step was taken in the eighth century through the alliance with the Frankish rulers, which even Gregory I. had in mind: this made the bishop of Rome the largest possessor of provinces, and, after the downfall of the rule of the Longobardi, brought about that significant and momentous event very near the beginning of the ninth century, which denoted a new state of the world, — the coronation of Charles the Great by the first bishop of the

West, the ecclesiastical inauguration of the empire of the Cæsars during the Middle Ages, the subjection of the world to two highest, as yet harmonious and co-ordinate, powers, the joint rule of emperor and pope. A dualism was founded, which, in the progress of things, necessarily called forth a conflict between those two powers for the empire of the world. But before this, the final step was taken, which forged for the Roman-ecclesiastical primacy, in the form in which it then existed, the appearance of a legal foundation, through that collection of spurious decretals named after Isidorus. The form into which it had developed was the original one according to the decretals, — the Roman bishop the from-the-first acknowledged bishop of the Church of the world, to whom even Constantine conceded the government of Rome and Italy. Not till then was the hierarchical system finished, the ecclesiastical pyramid: the Roman bishop passed not merely for the first, but the *supreme*, bishop of the Christian world, the head and ruler of the Church. The papacy consists in this central power. The pseudo-Isidoric decretals appeared about the middle of the ninth century : they originated in the Frankish episcopacy, and in its interests, since its immediate subjection to the Roman ruler freed the bishops of the Frankish empire from the secular and ecclesiastical powers (archbishops), who were near at hand to limit the scope of their authority. Independently of the forged decretals, *Nicholas I.* (858–867) defended his ecclesiastical central power, as it had been conceded, with a clear consciousness of its importance, and with great energy.

The papacy, and with it the ecclesiastical age of the world, reaches its highest point in the conflict for the supremacy of the world, and in its victory there. We can trace its course in this period of its greatest ascendency through three points, — its rising, its culmination, and the beginning of its decline as the sovereign power of the world. At its rising stood *Gregory VII.* (1073–1085) ; at its culmination, *Innocence III.* (1198–1216) ; at the beginning of its decline, *Boniface VIII.*

(1294–1303).   It was no longer enough that the bishops of
Rome were regarded as the successors of Peter, they became
his deputies: with this conception of his office, Gregory VII.
ruled.   The feeling of power increased: it was not enough
that they were deputies of Peter; they became the vicars
of Christ, the vicegerents of God on earth, an infallible
authority in human form.   The bishops themselves were
regarded only as their vicars; the pope was not merely the
supreme, but, by reason of his absolute power, the *only*, bishop.
This is the claim of the papacy since Innocence III., supported by a new collection of ecclesiastical decrees from the
hand of Gratian, the so-called " *decretum Gratiani*," which
appeared in the course of the twelfth century.   This highest
elevation of power is the *papal system*.

In these great conflicts for universal power, three great
phases can be distinguished.   In the first, it was a conflict
of principles between the Church and the world, or the State:
it was the controversy between Gregory VII. and Henry IV.
In the second, it was a conflict for secular power, especially
for the possession of Italy: then were kindled those fatal conflicts between the popes and the Hohenstaufen.   In the last,
the controversy was renewed between the Church and the
State, with the peculiar turn that then the *national* consciousness was arrayed on the side of political power, to
oppose to the central power of Rome the independence of
the nation: it was the conflict which the king and the orders
of France waged against Boniface VIII.

At first, the two powerful, pyramid-shaped bodies of the
Middle Ages appeared on the field of battle, — the hierarchical
Church and the feudal State, — the first dovetailed into the
second, exposed to secularization, and in danger of becoming
ungovernable.   The freeing of the Church from the powers
of the world that fetter it; the dissolution of all the bonds
that ensnared the clergy in the world and in the State; the
separation of the Church from the world without abandoning
its power, i.e., the exaltation of it above the State, — Gregory

VII. regarded as his reformatory work. He forbade the marriage of priests, the sale of spiritual offices (simony), the investiture of laymen, the vassalage of bishops. The controversy concerning investiture continued long, and terminated with a compromise between the parties. In the conflict with the Hohenstaufen, the popes won the victory, but the means to which they resorted sowed the seeds of injury to the papacy. Never in the history of the world did Nemesis show her power more sublimely. To destroy the German imperial family, the papal policy founded a French throne in Italy, the necessary result of which was the increase of French influence upon the apostolic see. In the conflict with France, the powerful Boniface VIII. was overthrown; and he, the most positive in his consciousness of power of all the popes, was taken prisoner by the king of France: and the second of his successors, a French pope, went to Avignon (1305) two years after his death. Thus, the destruction of the Hohenstaufen, through the French policy of the popes, resulted in their captivity to the French, that so-called Babylonish exile (1305–1377) by which the papacy was hurled down the abyss at the brink of which Boniface VIII. stood. For the immediate consequence of this exile was the beginning of the great schism (1378), the destruction of the unity of the Church, which the reformatory councils of the fifteenth century restored, and the plans of which were frustrated by their own work. For the reformation of the Church was incompatible with the restoration of the papacy. What remained but the reformation of the Church, — which was necessary, and had been proved impossible through councils, — a reformation beginning at the very foundation? And then appeared Luther, as the time of the upheaval had come.

Thus, the ecclesiastical age of the world, before the reformation of the sixteenth century made the irreparable breech, includes the time from Gregory VII. to the beginning of the German reformation. This is the period of real scholasticism, — scholasticism bound, in its activity of thought, to the service

of the Church; and it extends from the end of the eleventh
to the end of the fifteenth century. Its course of development corresponded to that of the Church. Two periods can
be clearly distinguished in the development of the Church, —
that of the papal rule of the world, or ecclesiastical centralization; and that of its nascent dissolution, or decentralization.
The former includes the twelfth and thirteenth centuries;
the latter, the fourteenth and fifteenth. The first two were
the time of the Crusades (1095–1291), in which the papacy
appeared at the head of the nations, and which (immediately
before Boniface VIII.) ended with the loss of all their con-
quests. Of course, the distinction between those two periods
stamps itself upon the course of the development of scholasticism, which is controlled by the position of the Church in
the world. So, in its first period, the fundamental trend of
ecclesiastical centralization, the idea of the all-powerful,
universal Church, binding together all individual powers,
predominates; and, in the second, the fundamental trend of
ecclesiastical decentralization, the idea of the Church, independent of, and separated from, the world and the State.
The Church and the world are related as the faith of the
Church and natural (human) knowledge. The bond, therefore, between faith and knowledge was strong in the first
period, and weak in the second. Scholasticism changed with
the times. And precisely therein consists its philosophical
significance, that, within its department, it formulated, and
gave expression to, the consciousness of the time. That in
an ecclesiastical age of the world, the consciousness of the
time was of an ecclesiastical character, with ecclesiastical
limitations, was clearly the natural result of the predominant state of the world. It is absurd to make a noise about
empty and unproductive scholasticism, and blame the forest
because it is not an orchard.

III. THE FOUNDING OF SCHOLASTICISM.

1. *Erigena*. — Scholasticism had two beginnings, separated from each other by more than two centuries, — the first, which remained isolated, in the Carlovingian period, in the time of the pseudo-Isidoric decretals and Nicholas I.; the second, with which its real course of development began, in the period that commenced with Gregory VII.

The first founder, a Briton, whom Charles the Bold called to his court in Paris, was *John Scotus Erigena*. He regarded the unity and universality of the divine being as the truly real, and the knowledge of it as the illumination of faith. God is the beginning, middle, and end of all that is, which, in all its distinctions of kind, is determined by the concept of creation and created being. There is one being who creates all things, himself uncreated. He is the creative ground of all things. There is a second, which, though created, works creatively, — the logos. The third nature consists in creatures, without creative power of their own, in the world of time and sense. Finally, there is an ultimate state, in which all creation and creating reach their goal, the end of all things, in their re-union with God. Accordingly, that which is, or nature in its entire extent, is divided into the following distinctions of being: God, the world in God (logos), the world outside of God, the return of the world to God. That is Erigena's "*divisio naturæ*." We perceive at once the Platonic thinker in the form of this classification. In his manner of conceiving the primary being as without distinctions, and distinguishing all other beings as degrees of the *one* life, emanating from God, separated from him, to him returning, in the mode of the pantheistic doctrine of emanation, we see unmistakably the traces of his mental affinity with the fundamental doctrine of Neo-Platonism and the theology of the Areopagite. (It was not an accident that he became the translator of the Areopagite.)

In the system of Erigena, the divine life in the world has
but one origin, — its issue from the father of all things;
and humanity but one final goal, — union with God. With
him, therefore, there is no second divinity equal to the
primary being, no divine twofold nature, no twofold issue
of the Holy Spirit, no twofold choice of grace. If the final
goal of humanity consists in its spiritualization, glorification,
and re-union with God (*adunatio*), its communion with God
in the visible Church, and the presence of Christ in the sacrament, have only a figurative and symbolical meaning.

Thus, this system conflicts with the dogma of the Trinity,
of theanthropism, of the divine election of grace, and with
the nascent doctrine of transubstantiation. After the symbolical sacrifice had gradually transformed itself, in the
imagination of believers, into the real, through the culture
of the century, the doctrine of transubstantiation, formulated
by Paschasius Radbertus, had resulted from that culture
in the time of Erigena; and those controversies concerning
the Lord's supper began, which were renewed under Gregory
VII., between Lanfranc and Berengar of Tours, the result
of which was, that the doctrine of transformation became a
dogma of the Church (1215) under Innocence III., a result
which grew out of the interests and the condition of the
Church. There is no greater example of the development
of a dogma from worship; none in which the obedience of
faith had to stand a more powerful test in opposition to the
certainty of the senses; none that could make more evident
the truth of that sentence of the German poet, " Miracle is
the favorite child of faith," than the faith in this transformation.

Erigena's system stands in opposition to the Romish
Church. It appeared in an age in which the controversy
concerning predestination was renewed, and that concerning
transubstantiation arose. It is, therefore, comprehensible
enough, that such a thinker experienced persecutions from
the Church through synods, bishops, and popes (Nicholas I.).

In his system, Gnosticism and Scholasticism are mingled. He attempted to unify faith and knowledge, but in such a system that the Church rejected it, and even centuries after his death condemned it as a type of heretical ideas. Erigena has been called the "Origen of the West." But scholasticism required for the solution of its problem a "second Augustine."

2. *Anselm.* — This "second Augustine" was found in a contemporary and mental kinsman of Gregory VII. In the year that Hildebrand ascended the papal see (1073), *Anselm* of Aosta became prior of the cloister Bec in France (successor of that Lanfranc who had defended the doctrine of transubstantiation against Berengar): twenty years later he was made archbishop of Canterbury, the first ecclesiastical prince of England. In the controversy with England concerning investiture, he supported the pope against the king; in the political questions of the Church, he was an hierarch; in theology, the orthodox founder of scholasticism. He harmonized the interests of theology and hierarchy as the spirit of scholasticism required.

The faith of the Church was then accepted as the motive and aim of all knowledge, and knowledge itself was only regarded as a means of strengthening the hold of the doctrines of the Church. Where comprehension ceased, faith called a halt, and reason submitted. "Caput submittam." The reality of God and theanthropism were not subjects of inquiry or of doubt, as if they were first to be established: they were incontestable certainties. The question was only as to the arguments for demonstrating them. And the arguments which Anselm of Canterbury made for the existence and incarnation of God in his "*proslogium*" and his "*Cur Deus homo?*" give a good illustration of the character of scholasticism.

He proves the being of God *ontologically*. The reality of the most perfect being is evident from our concept of him. For, if he lacked existence, he would be defective, and, therefore, not perfect, and our conception would not then be what it is, — that of the most perfect being. He proves the incarnation of man, from the conditions through which alone sinful humanity can be saved. For the fall of man is, as disobedience to God, a crime of infinite guilt, and, as such, can neither be forgiven, without some interposition, nor punished according to its deserts; for forgiveness without punishment would be unjust, and deserved punishment would be the destruction of man. The former is incompatible with divine justice: the latter would frustrate the purpose of creation. There is but one way out of the difficulty, — guilt must be atoned for; satisfaction must be made to God. Salvation is only possible through *satisfaction*. But this atoning action, paying our infinite debt, must itself be an infinite merit, of which sinful humanity is incapable. In place of humanity, a sinless being must suffer and outweigh the guilt of sin. Satisfaction is possible only through a *substitutional suffering*. Here God himself alone can take the place of humanity, for he alone is sinless; and, therefore, substitutional suffering requires the *incarnation of God*. This incarnation must not be subject to the conditions through which original sin is transmitted; it can take place, therefore, only through supernatural birth; is possible only in the son of the Virgin Mary, in the person Jesus, who sacrificed himself for humanity, and through this sacrificial death earned infinite merit, — a merit which God cannot put to the account of Jesus himself, but only to that of those for whom the God-man made himself an offering. This merit which God puts to the account of the race is the *forgiveness of sins*, or the salvation of humanity. Now the debt is all paid. Salvation is accomplished through the incarnation of God. The incarnation results from the necessity of substitution, and this from the satisfaction which humanity owes in consequence of original sin. Heirship now steps in the place of original sin; original sin works on in nature; heirship in the Church as the kingdom of grace. Thus, the proofs of Anselm lead us to the central point of the doctrine of Augustine. Justly can we call this first orthodox scholastic the second Augustine.

IV. THE COURSE OF DEVELOPMENT OF SCHOLASTICISM.

1. *Realism and Nominalism.* — Anselm's arguments rest upon a presupposition which, indeed, lies at the bottom of the whole doctrine of the Church, but was first consciously accepted here, where the attempt was made to give a logical and demonstrative proof of dogmas. The two turning-points of the Augustinian doctrine of faith and the theology of Anselm are original sin and salvation: in Adam man fell, in Christ he is saved. If these facts have no *universal* truth, or, what is the same, if these universal determinations have no *actual* (real) being, faith is without foundation. Faith rests, therefore, on the logical presupposition that humanity as species or idea in truth exists, and constitutes the nature of man. What is true of this species must be true of all species (ideas), of all universals. If they are not realities, it is to be feared that the facts of faith are either manifestly unreal or incapable of proof. The Church itself exists by virtue of its idea: its reality rests on its universality. Even Augustine based its authority on its catholicity, its necessary, on its universal, validity. As the Platonic state exists in the idea of justice, independently of particulars, so the Christian Church exists in the idea of the unity of faith. And that is why the comparison of the two is so just and appropriate, as Bauer and Zeller have very significantly shown.

From this fundamental, and, to the Church, natural, view, the proposition now follows in which scholasticism recognizes its principle, *universalia sunt realia.* Species are the truly real. It is characteristic enough that the first scholastic proof of the existence of God was the *ontological* argument of Anselm.

The *realism* of the Middle Ages was based on the reality of universals, — the first fundamental trend of scholasti-

cism; and it evoked its opposite. The problem of scholasticism authorized also the claims of the natural understanding,
but to this, single things appear as the real objects; species,
on the other hand, as mere concepts and abstractions, which
we make and denote by words. The natural understanding,
accordingly, regards *universalia* not as *realia*, but "*vocalia*"
or "*nomina*." On the unreality of universals rests the
nominalism of the Middle Ages, the second fundamental
trend of scholasticism, the first expression of which followed
close upon the heels of realism. These opposing views were
formulated in a controversy between Roscelin and William
of Champeaux, near the end of the eleventh century.

The range of the nominalistic mode of thought can be
easily determined. We know by means of presentations and
concepts, judgments and propositions. If concepts neither
have, nor apprehend, reality, there is no knowledge of the real,
and, since the objects of faith are the truly real, no knowledge
of faith. When, therefore, nominalism, in the spirit of scholasticism, affirmed the reality of the objects of faith, it was at the
same time compelled, contrary to the fundamental principle of
scholasticism, to deny the knowledge of them. As soon as this
mode of thought prevailed, the bond between knowledge and
faith, which constituted the certainty of the theology of the
Middle Ages, was severed: the union of faith and knowledge.
From this vantage-ground we can survey the course of the
development of scholasticism. In the twelfth and thirteenth
centuries, realism prevailed; in the fourteenth, the nominalistic mode of thought became more and more general; and
this led to the downfall of scholasticism, and formed the
transition to a new philosophy, independent of faith. Thus,
the two fundamental tendencies of scholasticism, each in its
greatest predominance, coincide with the two periods which
we have distinguished in the ecclesiastical age of the world.
Realism corresponds to the period of the ecclesiastical rule
of the world and centralization; nominalism to that of its
nascent destruction and decentralization.

Such a course of development has lately been denied ; and, on the other hand, an attempt has been made to limit the point of dispute between realism and nominalism to their first encounter, when Roscelin explained universals as "*flatus vocis.*" If any one wishes to restrict the term nominalism to Roscelin's unsuccessful contradiction of realism, he may choose another name for the later and victorious line of thought, in like manner opposed to it. The matter itself, the well-known contrast between the two scholastic periods, which we have just explained, remains unchanged. And just as little is accomplished by the objection that the progress of scholasticism consisted only in growth in breadth, only in the increased importation of its materials for doctrine, — in other words, in the increasing knowledge of the doctrine of Aristotle. The materials of culture which the Middle Ages received from the ancient world were the scantiest. Of the philosophy of Aristotle, which ruled scholasticism in its zenith, — so some have claimed, — only an unimportant fragment of the logic was at first known, the doctrine of the proposition and the categories, and this only in a translation of Boethius, with an introduction by Porphyry. Not till the twelfth century was the whole organon of Aristotle known, and his real philosophy, his metaphysics, physics, psychology, etc., not till the following, and these through Latin translations, made first from the Hebrew and Arabic, later from the Greek, until at last the study of the ancients in their own language was again renewed. This creeping away into the leading-strings of Aristotle signifies nothing more than the increasing secularization of scholastic theology, from which the separation between faith and knowledge, and the victory of the nominalistic doctrine of knowledge, at last necessarily resulted.

2. *The Platonic and Aristotelian Realism.* — During the period when the ecclesiastical rule of the world was unbroken, the accepted fundamental principle of scholastic theology was, that species or ideas have reality ; that this reality is

either completely independent of individual things, or their active, indwelling principle, either "*ante rem*" or "*in re*." This is not the place to enter into all the possible modifications and intermediate distinctions of those two conceptions. The scholasticism of the twelfth century was untiring in such distinctions. The two norm-giving conceptions were prefigured in Greek philosophy, — the first in Plato, the second in Aristotle. Both affirmed the reality of ideas, but Plato regarded them as that which truly exists independently of phenomena, while with Aristotle they were the truly efficient force in things. With Plato, their reality was the world of ideas; with Aristotle, nature. We have already shown how the second conception necessarily results from the first. *Platonic* realism prevailed in the scholastic theology of the twelfth century, the Aristotelian during the thirteenth. Thus, in the ecclesiastical philosophy of the Middle Ages, three trends of thought can be distinguished, which, generally speaking, coincide with the centuries, — the realistic-Platonic in the twelfth, the realistic-Aristotelian in the thirteenth, and the nominalistic in the two following. *Abelard* (+ 1142) formed the transition between the Platonic and Aristotelian scholasticism; *John Duns Scotus* (+ 1308) between the realistic and nominalistic.

We have already referred to that significant affinity, which, in spite of the fundamentally different ages in which they were developed, and of their fundamentally different conceptions of the world, exists between the Platonic mode of thought of antiquity and the ecclesiastical conceptions of the Middle Ages, between the Platonic state and the Romish Church. In both, the universal prevails unconditionally over the particular; the whole is before the parts, and the idea is the only real power, completely independent of individuals. It is not, therefore, surprising that, under the absolute rule of the Church of the Middle Ages, a Platonic scholasticism was developed, and that the period during which this scholasticism prevailed coincided with the period of the Crusades;

that the Church resisted the increasing departure from this mode of realistic thought, the increasing approximations to the Aristotelian realism, and finally yielded to the necessity which it could not prevent. The physical and metaphysical writings of Aristotle were still condemned in the beginning of the thirteenth century, then hesitatingly permitted, first to artists, then to theologians; and finally the study of the Aristotelian philosophy was even required, and the pagan philosopher was held in the highest regard by the Church itself, in respect to all natural knowledge.

What is the explanation of this remarkable phenomenon, — this union between the Church of the Middle Ages and Aristotle? It is not hard to find. When once natural knowledge was authorized in scholasticism, even if only as an instrument of faith, in the course of its development the point necessarily came where nature also became its object, and where it inserted into, and subordinated to, its system this concept, even as the Church had subjected the State to its authority. The Church itself in the course of time was obliged to recognize this work as necessary and beneficial to its system. Scholasticism required a *theological conception of nature*. In obtaining it, the Church conquered a great territory, that appeared hostile as long as it was foreign to theology. By the theological conception of nature, a mode of thought is to be understood which regards God as the ultimate ground and purpose of nature, and nature herself as a gradation of material and living forms, depending upon the divine purpose, — forms which are animated by God, and have their consummation in him. This conception of nature is found in the Aristotelian philosophy, hence its significance to scholasticism and the Church. Because of its pagan spirit, it at first seemed to be of a questionable character; but its theological aspect recommended it to the Church, and finally it was regarded as a most welcome means for solving a problem, through the solution of which the Church triumphs. Now, the philosophy of Aristotle was almost unknown to the

West.   His logical writings have no bearing upon the solution of this problem.   The culture of the West was remote
from that of Greece, and made still more so by the chasm
between the two churches.   And so, by the most circuitous
path, the Aristotelian philosophy was introduced into the
schools of Western Christendom, through the Arabian philosophers of the eleventh, twelfth, and thirteenth centuries.
Of those, Avicenna (+ 1036) was the greatest of those of
the East ; Averroës (+ 1198) of those of Spain.   The latter
came nearest to the true understanding of Aristotle, through
the extent of his commentaries and the mode of his insight.

During the thirteenth century, scholasticism was in its
zenith.   The problem was, to gain a concept of nature for
the system of theology, and thereby first to complete its
systematization.   The kingdom of grace did not seem to
natural knowledge thoroughly established, until the kingdom of nature was subordinated to it, and could be conceived
as forming *one* coherent whole with it.   In this union of the
two kingdoms lay the problem.   The kingdom of nature
must be regarded as the vestibule to the kingdom of grace ;
so that even in nature the kingdom of grace is outlined, prefigurated, designed, that the ordinances of the Church appear
as the filling out of the outline contained in nature.   That is
the fundamental thought of the thirteenth century ; the real
motive in the systems of the great theologians of this period,
— Alexander of Hales, Albertus Magnus, Thomas Aquinas.
He who solves this problem most perfectly, in the conception
of the Church, sustains the same relation to scholasticism
that Augustine had done to the doctrine of faith.   This
greatest of the scholastics was *Thomas*.   In his system, nature
appears as a kingdom of gradations, planned with reference to,
and leading up to, the Church.   In the natural life of man,
the stages of the body are completed : in the ordinances of
grace, i.e., in the sacraments, the natural life of man is completed.   Thomas's doctrine of the sacraments turns a blaze
of light upon the spirit of this entire theology.   It is the

Aristotelian conception of development which is the foundation of its systems. As the foundation is related to the completed structure, the means to the end, so, in Thomas's view
of the world, is the natural world to the ecclesiastical, the
life of man to the sacraments. His system, in its ecclesiastical spirit, is throughout theological and supernatural; but it
incorporated into itself the conception of nature, and thereby completed the theological-scholastic mode of thought.
Thomas rounded off the faith of the Church into an incomparable system of doctrine, and earned for himself the fame
of being *the* ecclesiastical philosopher.

3. *Sums and Systems.* — The problem of scholasticism was,
to form a theological system out of the material furnished
by dogmatic doctrines and controversies. The first solution
of this problem consisted in the collection, abridgment, and
arrangement of all the materials appertaining to it, — those
so-called "*Sums*" of the twelfth century, the model of which
was the work of *Peter Lombard* (+ 1164). He sustained
the same relation to the doctrines of the Church that his
contemporary, Gratian, did to its laws. He surveyed the
whole field of dogmas or "sentences" in a comprehensive
work, which earned for him the title of "*magister sententi-
orum*," and became the first commonly accepted text-book of
theology, the foundation of theological lectures. The sums
of sentences produced in the twelfth century were still no
systems. The text-book of Lombard furnished the material
out of which, blended with the philosophy of Aristotle, the
theological sums of the thirteenth century were produced, the
works of the great doctors of the Church. To the grounds
of the doctrine of the Church were now added the rational
grounds of the philosopher; to the "*autoritates*," the "*rationes*."
In the exposition, comparison, and contrast of the two, the
new problem was introduced by the English Franciscan, Alexander of Hales (+ 1245). The real representative of the
rationes was the Aristotelian philosophy. So far as this lay
in the horizon and power of comprehension of the time, it

must be set forth along with theology, and the problem thereby explained and illustrated in its entirety. This was done by the "*doctor universalis,*" the German Dominican, *Albert the Great* (+ 1280). His greater disciple, the Italian Dominican, *Thomas Aquinas* (+ 1274), completed the solution of the scholastic problem: he was the author of the ecclesiastical philosophical system in which Augustine, the Lombard, and Aristotle were harmonized with each other. He Christianized the Aristotelian doctrine of development in the spirit of the Church's rule of the world, as the Areopagite had done the Neo-Platonic doctrine of emanation in the spirit of its hierarchy.

4. *Thomas and Scotus.* — In the progress of the Aristotelian Realism, the opposition between Thomas and Scotus arose, which set their schools at variance with each other, and permanently affected the stability of the scholastic theology. If the two kingdoms of nature and of grace are so united that the former is consummated, and realizes its purpose, in the latter, the kingdom of things in general must appear as the best-ordered world, — a world which God chose, by reason of his wisdom, out of all possible worlds, and created by his omnipotence: and the divine will in the creation of the world is thus determined by knowledge; and the divine creation, since it is under the control of an idea, — that of the good, — is necessary and determined. Thus, the system of Thomas, in spite of its supernatural character, is absolutely *deterministic;* and therein is the genuine expression of the ecclesiastical conception of the world, which regards its ordinances as rigidly determined, decided for all cases, and so arranged as to completely exclude individual wills and choice. This "*theodicee*" of Thomas, in which every thing is determined according to divine knowledge, and arranged "*ad deum,*" found an antagonist in the English Franciscan, *John Duns Scotus.* It was no less a controversy than that between determinism and indeterminism, between necessity and freedom, which here broke out in scholasticism. It was the question

of the *freedom of the will*. If the divine causality is necessary, God is bound to his works, and cannot exist without them; then the independence of God must be denied, and, consequently, his existence. If every thing is determined by divine necessity, and this itself by the idea of the good, nothing is either accidental or evil: God is not merely the first, but, in the last analysis, the *only*, cause; he is identical with the nature of things, and pantheism is the manifest and inevitable result. These were the weighty objections which Scotus urged in reply to Thomas. Determinism, according to which the divine will is determined by the idea of the good, is disproved by the fact of accident and evil in the world. The divine will is determined by nothing; it acts without grounds, absolutely arbitrarily; it can just as well create as not create, just as well this world as another, or even none at all. The will is not determined by knowledge, but conversely, — *voluntas superior intellectu*. The good is good, not of itself, but through the determination of the divine will, not "*per se*," but "*ex instituto;*" it is not rational, but positive: God has not willed because something is good, but something is good because God has willed it. With the power of choice, will is destroyed, and the distinction between natural causes and will-causes obliterated; there is then no will at all, either divine or human. Scotus affirms human freedom and its co-operation in the reception of divine grace; the meritoriousness of works which, not by reason of. their own character, also not because of the disposition of mind in which they are done, but merely through this justify, — that God by the exercise of his arbitrary will has united this effect to this work. Spiritual works avail, independently of any state of mind, as external acts in accordance with command as "*opus operatum*." This is the theory of scholastic indeterminism seeking to support the power, and to promote the interests, of the Church. Human freedom includes self-determination, personal will, individual existence, by reason of which every man is not merely a thing among things, but *this* particular, individual being existing for itself. Thus arises in the consciousness of scholasticism the conception of *individuality*, the character not merely of specific but individual distinction of things which are differentiated not merely by their kinds and properties (quiddities), but each from all the rest by reason of its singleness (thisness). Individuality is undefinable, incomprehensible, " *ratio singularitatis frustra quæritur.*" If reality reaches its highest point and consummation in individuality, there is no knowledge of the real. The same is true of arbitrary will: it is groundless in its actions, therefore unknowable. The same is true of divine revelation, of the work of salvation, of the objects of the faith of the Church in general: they exist by reason of the groundless and inscrutable will of God. There is, therefore, no knowledge of the objects of faith, no rational theology, no philosophical system of faith. Theology is practical; faith a direction and consent of the will independent of knowledge, not based on rational grounds, incapable of being overthrown by rational considerations. Thus, indeterminism dissolves the alliance between faith and knowledge.

5. *Occam. The Dissolution of Scholasticism.* — The way was thus paved for that new and last fundamental phase of scholasticism, — the phase which was systematically grounded by the English Franciscan, *William Occam* (+ 1347?), a disciple of Scotus. His was no longer the age of Roscelin, which began with Gregory VII., and terminated with Innocence III. When Scotus stood at the height of his fame, and died, the papal see had been for three years in Avignon. The age of Occam began with Boniface VIII., and the great schism was not far distant.

Occam's work was the destruction of scholastic realism; of the dominion of the ideal world in the faith of the Church. If universals (ideas) are real, they must precede creation in God, and determine his will, and there is no divine freedom, and no creation *ex nihilo.* It was the conflict between faith and scholastic realism.

If universals (genera), though common to things, are themselves things, a thing must be in several things at the same time, which is impossible. Ideas are not things, they are not realities: they are only conceptions which denote things, and are themselves denoted by words, as words are by letters. They are, therefore, signs or "*signa*," the fundamental determinations of which are constituted by the "*termini*." These last are single and universal conceptions, spoken and written symbols, therefore intuitions, conceptions, words. Intuitions represent single actual things; concepts, many single perceptions; words, conceptions. All human knowledge takes place through terms (*termini*): it is therefore terministic, and, so far as the signs which communicate it are "*vocalia*" or names, nominalistic. Knowledge through perceptions is intuitive or real, since they represent things: knowledge through universal conceptions and judgments, through words and sentences, is rational or logical (*sermocinal*). There is, therefore, no knowledge of actual things. Reality consists in single things, individuals, simple substances: our conception is neither thing nor substance nor simple, and its indistinctness is in proportion to its universality. There is, therefore, no agreement whatever between conception and thing; hence, no knowledge of the truth.

Between conception and reality, there lies an impassable chasm; and hence the impossibility of the ontological proof of the existence of God is evident, since its presupposition of the reality of the conception of God is fundamentally false. Also the cosmological proofs are invalid, since they presuppose that there must be a first or ultimate cause, that an infinite regress is impossible. But just this presupposition is fundamentally false; rather, this regress is necessarily to be demanded. There are, therefore, no proofs whatever of the existence of God: there is no kind of rational theology. From the impossibility of this knowledge follows the necessity of faith, guaranteed only by the authority of the Church.

The relation between the Church and the world corresponds to that between faith and knowledge. The question is as to separation in both cases, — as to the separation of faith from knowledge, and the Church from the world. The time has come when the powers of which the Church is the centre begin to become centrifugal, and desire to throw off her control; viz., states and nations, sciences and arts. With the spiritualization of the Church, the independence of the State from the Church is at the same time required. "Defend me with your sword, and I will defend you with my pen," Occam is reported to have said to Louis the Bavarian, in the controversy between the emperor and the pope.

We must carefully observe how this nominalistic doctrine of knowledge, which caused the dissension between faith and knowledge, theology and philosophy, and stamped itself upon the consciousness of the time, is related to both. It desired separation for the sake of faith, for the sake of the Church. It sought to purify and strengthen faith by separating it from knowledge, and the Church by separating it from the world. It is not an accident that these nominalists belonged for the most part to the strictest party of the Franciscans. Faith would no longer keep a common account with fallible knowledge, supported by human authority: it would have nothing more to do with this foreign and dangerous ally. In the same proportion as it renounced all natural and rational knowledge, it strengthened its supernatural character, increased its positive value, its ecclesiastical authority. To strengthen the latter, and make it irresistible and unquestionable, was the ultimate purpose of this nominalistic theology. It was, therefore, in its nature *scholastic*. But it broke with the secular power of the Church, and aimed at her purification, and thus opened the way to reformatory efforts within scholasticism. It also freed philosophy, by separating it from faith, and directing the former to things of the world. Within scholasticism it paved the way for a *new* philosophy. It denied the possibility of a true knowledge of things by human means, and thus led to that *scepticism* with which modern philosophy began, and out of which it proceeded. It conceded to human knowledge, only the intuitive and sensitive, and appeared in this point as the scholastic forerunner of that *empiricism* and *sensualism* with which modern philosophy began its course in the native country of Occam.

CHAPTER V.

THE PERIOD OF THE RENAISSANCE.

I. HUMANISM.

PAGAN philosophy served the ecclesiastical philosophy of
the Middle Ages in a form foreign to its origin and its
nature. Scholastic theology confined human knowledge in
a twofold prison. It was under the control of the Church,
which determined its doctrines; and under the control of a
school which borrowed its mode of teaching, and the form
of its culture, from the authorities of ancient philosophy.
When, now, the chains began to be loosed, and human knowledge began to strive for a fundamental renewing, the first
step was to throw off the bondage of the schools, and seek
out, and search into, the great philosophers of antiquity in
their original form. The philosophy of modern times came
directly from the emancipated schools of antiquity. It
matured in it gradually. Not till it felt itself outgrowing
the leading-strings of that philosophy, did the epoch of its
own independent existence come, and the moment when it
entered upon its majority. The revival of the Grecian-
Roman philosophy was, therefore, the necessary and immediate problem of knowledge, the condition of, and the
transition to, modern philosophy.

This problem forms a part of philological archæology,
and this itself required to be cultivated and understood as
a particular branch of revived antiquity in general. To
guide philosophy from the Middle Ages into our times, that
mental new birth of antiquity which we call the "Renais-

sance," must find and illumine the path. The significance
of the Renaissance is in no way limited to linguistic studies;
since it is not merely a matter of schools and of scholarship,
but an *age* which progressing humanity has lived, and which
has penetrated every department of human culture, — an
inexhaustible age, which lives on in our day, and never will
die. The Renaissance is, in its work and its intellectual
tendencies, as little to be limited as the Reformation; and
if both are limited to particular periods, — that in its bloom
to the second half of the fifteenth century, this to the first
of the sixteenth, — such a chronological limitation applies
only to the outbreak and founding of the two.

The Renaissance radically changed men's conceptions of
life and nature, freed them from the powers which controlled
them in the Middle Ages, and stamped upon them an opposition to those powers which the Church itself, borne along
by the current of the time, did not observe, which it half
promoted, and which it did not recognize till much later,
when the first bloom of the Renaissance had faded, and the
Reformation had become powerful. The fundamental theme
of the Middle Ages was, the restoration and glorification of
the "*civitas dei*," that kingdom of God on earth which,
through its divine ordinances, rules the world and binds individuals. The fundamental theme of the Renaissance starts
from the completely opposite key: it consists in the glorification of man, his greatness and his fame; in the worship
of the individual, his genius, his power, his immeasurable
natural freedom. If there ever was an age that believed in
the universal genius of man, in his omnipotence and magical
power, — an age that produced individuals of powerful minds,
and felt their charm, that deified the world of man in nature,
the state and art, — it was this. Its entire interest went out
to natural man, infinitely enlarged by his energy and his
endowments. In such a sense, far more comprehensively
and universally than we usually understand the term, can
we say of the Renaissance that it made the "Humanities"

its subject. In the Middle Ages, the power to loose and bind, concerning forgiveness of sin and eternal welfare, was with the Church. In the Renaissance, it was the poets, the orators, the historians, who had power to elevate and over-throw, to glorify, and refuse to acknowledge, the merit and the fame of man. Even *Dante*, with whom the first glimmer of the dawning Renaissance began to shine, invented a hell, and peopled it, by means of his absolute power as poetic judge of the world. The Middle Ages reverenced saints: the Renaissance reverenced great men, eminent for their mental achievements; their relics and their graves were honored, and the memorable scenes of their lives. " The ground upon which a good man treads is consecrated : after a hundred years his words and deeds re-echo to his descend-ants." This was spoken in the spirit of the Renaissance (a language foreign to the Middle Ages, but still the native tongue of our thoughts and feelings). We must know how the Renaissance fundamentally changed man's conception of himself, before we speak of the altered course of the sciences and education. It called " modern man " into life, as one of its ablest students has said in a comprehensive and luminous work, setting forth the characteristics of this powerful age.[1]

II. THE ITALIAN RENAISSANCE.

The faith of the Middle Ages was led, by its worship of relics, to Palestine, that it might actually see the Holy Land and the holiest of graves. The Renaissance needed no Crusades by means of which to find relics to worship. *Italy* was its natural birthplace and home, — the classic land, the grave of the most glorious past of the world. In the revival of antiquity, Italy worshipped her own past world. Thus, even in its origin, the Renaissance was not the artificial product of the schools, but the natural course of the soar-ing national self-consciousness, the subject and the theme

[1] Jacob Burckhardt: The Culture of the Italian Renaissance (sec. ed., 1869).

of national joy and self-glorification. Augustine, the last of
the great Fathers of the Church, saw in the old Roman
Empire and its people the consummation of the "*civitas
terrena*," the world devoted to destruction, fallen through the
sin of paganism, the world which in its greatness and earthly
fame had reaped the reward of its deeds, and perished forever. Dante, the first national poet of Italy, extolled anew
the Roman nation as the noblest and first of the world, to
whom the dominion of the world belonged by the favor of
God, independently of Church and pope. He celebrated
Rome as the august widow, waiting in impatient longing for
her Cæsar. The Eternal City, commanding reverence in her
ruins, filled him with enthusiasm. Some decades after Dante,
that adventurous tribune, Cola de Rienza, appeared, and in
the midst of destitute and down-fallen Rome attempted, in
disunited Italy, to improvise the restoration of the Roman
Empire. Augustine, who lived before the beginning of the
Middle Ages, saw the new ecclesiastical kingdom of the
world in its rising; that of the Cæsar's in its setting: Dante,
even at the threshold of the Renaissance, saw the earthly
salvation of the world in a new Augustus.

For the mental regeneration of antiquity, it was well that
such a Roman central power did not exist, that it was nowhere less possible than in Italy. Political unity and centralization would have fettered the powers which, for the
unfolding of the new mental life, required to be in perfect
freedom and activity. That complexity of individuality, that
richness of nature, and enlargement of feeling, that rivalry of
states and cities which called out, and cultivated, talent in
every direction, would, in that case, never have been developed. Decentralized Italy was as favorable to the rise of
the Renaissance as was decentralized Germany to that of the
Reformation. The disintegration of Italy in consequence of
the conflict between the pope and the Hohenstaufen, the
multitude and diversity of little states, the continual and
headlong changes in their fortunes, internal party conflicts

and external wars, the usurpers and despots, the invention
and employment of every means of power to promote political interests, to exalt the fame of princes, to attract and win
the masses, — among others, splendid and imposing works of
art, — all these conditions of Italy during the fourteenth and
fifteenth centuries involuntarily remind us of similar circumstances in Greece in the seventh and sixth centuries before
the Christian era.   Then arose from the most active life that
richness of knowledge of the world and of men, that wealth
of culture, from which Greek philosophy proceeded.   This
analogy is significant.   There are in the history of the world
scarcely two periods which present so many points of resemblance, grounded in the state of the nations between which
comparison is made.   No wonder, therefore, that from such
conditions, from such a like condition of affairs in Italy, a
view of life and a culture were developed that felt their relationship to antiquity, and again seized its neglected treasures; that the Italians — the first of European nations that
became free from the Middle Ages — then recognized themselves as the descendants of the Greeks and Romans, and,
with this conception of themselves, entered upon the inheritance of their past.   We must, indeed, include all these factors, in order to understand the *natural* origin and character
of the Italian Renaissance, which opened the school of a new
universal culture to the rest of Europe.   To the discovery
of ancient ruins, and works of art, was added the recovery of
authors, whose works were copied, multiplied, collected and
arranged in libraries.   In the growing knowledge of these
works consists the literary Renaissance and the widening of
its scientific horizon.

In its greatest extension, this period reaches from the beginning of the fourteenth to the end of the sixteenth century,
from Dante to Tasso.   Its highest development, to fix the
period by means of the popes, extended from Nicholas V.
(1447–1455), the founder of the Vatican library, to Leo X.
(1513–1521), who, among the Muses of the Vatican, would

gladly have failed to hear the outbreak of the German Reformation. The two periods before and after this period of
greatest vigor may be called "early" and "late" Renaissance.

Some events which happened about the middle of the
fifteenth century were of the greatest importance in broad-
ening and deepening this new spiritual current; viz., the
invention of the art of printing, and the renewal of the union
between the Latin and Greek worlds, — between the bloom-
ing Italian Renaissance and Greek scholars. The councils
of union called by Pope Eugene IV. were the occasion of a
meeting, which, although of no value to the Church, exercised a great influence upon the Renaissance. Greek
theologians were invited by a Roman ambassador, *Nicholas
Cusanus,* — a German by birth, who was himself animated
by the deepest ideas of Greek philosophy, — to the council
which was opened in Ferrara, and removed the next year
to Florence. A few years later, the Eastern Empire fell.
The capture of Constantinople by the Turks (1453) increased the number of Greek scholars who fled to Italy,
and found a most welcome refuge there. The continued
settlement in Italy, strengthened by the last victory of the
barbarians, acquired the character of an intellectual colony.
For the second time Italy deserved the name of Magna
Græcia.

III. THE COURSE OF DEVELOPMENT OF THE RENAISSANCE.

We have now to notice more particularly the growth and
development of the *philosophical* Renaissance, which mediated
the transition from the Middle Ages to modern philosophy.
It consisted in a growing separation from scholasticism, in a
growing development of its own enfranchised impulse to
knowledge ; and this determined the law of its development.
It was not enough to reknow the culture and systems of antiquity in their true forms, to excavate them, as it were, and
strip them from the overgrowths and disguises of scholasticism. It was not enough to imitate their philosophy : it was

necessary to imitate their philosophical spirit and originality. The age must exert its own powers in seeking for a knowledge of the world to satisfy its own need. Thus, the Renaissance was *reproductive* in relation to antiquity in the first half of its work, and *productive* in the second, impelled by the spirit of a new time.

1. *The Neo-Latin Renaissance.* — Ancient classic Rome, her orators and poets, her models and instructors of rhetoric, the systems and conceptions of life, of the Post-Aristotelian philosophy, — epicureanism, stoicism, scepticism, — which had become naturalized in her culture, lay nearer to the budding Italian Renaissance than ancient Greece and her culture. The reproduction of this Roman culture is the Neo-Latin Renaissance. The Neo-Latin Renaissance recognized its models in Cicero and Quintilian, and found its ablest representative in the Roman *Lorenzo Valla* (1406-1457). In him the opposition to the Middle Ages and scholasticism was already under full headway. Pure Latin, modelled after Cicero, was opposed to the barbarous Latin of the Church ; philological criticism, to the authenticity of ecclesiastical documents. Valla examined the Vulgate, and pointed out its errors, doubted the genuineness of the Apostles' Creed, refuted the Constantinian origin of the territories of the pope in his famous work " On the Erroneously Believed and Fabricated Donation of Constantine." The Pseudo-Isidoric decretals had, as it were, codified this fiction. The later papal system did not rest satisfied with the donation. Constantine, it held, had only given back to the pope what had always belonged to him as the vicegerent of God. Even Dante rejected the legality of the donation of Constantine, though he did not dispute it as a fact. Valla proved that it was *never* made, that the popes are robbers and usurpers, and that they deserve to be deprived of their power. It is not to be wondered at that this man was persecuted, and found protection among the Aragonese in Naples. Far more remarkable is it that Nicholas V. took him into his service.

Valla intended to write a work, "For the Sake of Truth, Religion, and Honor;" but when he wished to return to Rome, he declared himself ready to abandon it. His boldness was due as much to ambition as to love of truth: he desired it to bring him fame, but not misfortune. The value of martyrdom fell when the new interests of the Renaissance were felt, and we cannot test the strength of his character by a capacity for sacrifice which presupposes the power of unshaken faith.

In a time when scholasticism still appeared the firm ally of Aristotle, particularly in the department of logic, the rejection of the former necessarily affected the latter. The Neo-Latin Renaissance in its anti-scholastic and its anti-hierarchical tendency became likewise the opponent of Aristotle and his logic. That is especially true of Valla and all who followed him. In the text-books and practice of the scholastics, the logic of Aristotle had acquired a ridiculous and barbarous appearance. This was attacked by Valla and his followers. Animated discourse, they urged, must be accepted as a model in place of abstract and artificial forms of thought; instead of logic, rhetoric, instead of the dry and unprofitable school-discipline of a barren manipulation of words, unfettered and beautiful eloquence must serve that form of culture which employs at the same time strength of thought, and vigor of expression.

2. *The Aristotelian Renaissance.* — But the onward marching Renaissance could not leave the great master of Greek philosophy in the hands of scholasticism. One of its tasks was to restore the knowledge of Aristotle by means of his own works, to tear his system from the control of the Church, and to point out the opposition between him and her doctrines. This form of the development of the Italian Renaissance may be termed the *Aristotelian.* Its controversies were continued during the sixteenth century, particularly in the universities of Padua and Bologna. Its most prominent representative, who was most in harmony with the spirit

of the Renaissance, was the Mantuan, *Pietro Pomponatius*
(1462–1525). Since the object of this movement was to
learn the true interpretation of Aristotle, the investigation
necessarily began with his commentators, and, because of the
disagreement between them, took the form of a controversy.
Averroës was the greatest of the Arabian, and *Alexander of
Aphrodisias,* "the commentator" (in the beginning of the
third century of the Christian era), of the Grecian, expounders. Averroists and Alexandrists disputed in Padua
and Bologna. The Italian Renaissance, in the reproduction
of Greek philosophy, naturally preferred Greek expounders,
and followed their guidance. Pomponatius defended their
interpretations against Achillini and Nifo. The doctrine of
Aristotle was a system of development, which, founded on
the immanence of final cause, the unity of form and matter,
natural entelechy and its series of gradations, had led in its
last results again to a dualism of form and matter, God and
the world, mind and body. Thus, in the very nature of his
doctrine the monistic and dualistic tendencies were separated,
and therein lay the possibility of opposing interpretations of
it, according as the immanence of final cause or the transcendence of God was the prevailing point of view from
which it was considered and estimated. The first point of
view determines the *naturalistic,* the second the *theological,*
conception of the philosophy of Aristotle. The former was
first expounded among the Greek expositors by Strato, then
by Alexander, — the latter by the Neo-Platonists, from whom
it passed over to the Arabian philosophers, who made Aristotle accessible in the theosophic form to the scholasticism
of the West. If the Aristotelian system of development is
considered from its theological point of view, it appears as a
gradation of intelligences starting from the supra-mundane
Deity, each of which, embraced in, and ruled by, the higher,
governs a definite sphere in the cosmos of gradations, and
the lowest of which in the sublunary world constitutes the
mind of humanity. This was the fundamental form of the

doctrine of Averroës, which repelled scholasticism through its pantheistic character, though its theological conception of nature and the world attracted it. The aim now was to purify the doctrine of Aristotle from the additions of its Neo-Platonic, Arabian, and scholastic interpreters, to know the true Aristotle, to ascertain the difference between him and Plato, between him and the doctrine of the Christian faith. The Italian Aristotelians, who agreed with Alexander, were on their way back to the true Aristotle. There was no point in which all these oppositions could so distinctly and actively appear, and at the same time so eagerly arouse and hold the attention of the age, as in the question concerning the *immortality of the soul.* Aristotle had taught that the soul is the individual organic purpose of a living body ; that the mind, or reason, is imperishable and immortal. He had made a distinction between passive and active reason, and affirmed immortality of the latter. Now the question here arose, whether this immortal mind of man is also personal and individual, whether there is a personal immortality, the only immortality which has any value to the Church. If it must be denied, according to Aristotle, there is, according to him, no retribution for man in a world to come: there is no world beyond the bounds of this life for the Church to reach, and the power upon which all the authority of the Church depends is gone. There is, in that case, an opposition between the doctrine of the Church and that of Aristotle as great as it is possible to conceive, and the whole structure of scholasticism lies in ruins. If the mind, or active reason (active in true knowledge), is explained both as immaterial and individual, the personal immortality of men, as Thomas intended, is proved by the help of the Aristotelian doctrine of the soul *in majorem Dei gloriam.* But if active reason is identical with the universal mind of man, immortality must be affirmed with Averroës, but personal immortality denied. If, on the other hand, active reason, according to the naturalistic conception, is regarded as a

product of development, and always subject to individual and
organic conditions, there can be no kind of human immortality, neither impersonal nor individual. Pomponatius so
argued in his famous work, "*De Immortalitate Animæ*" (1516).
Immortality is merely a matter of faith ; and, as such, Pomponatius allowed it to pass unchallenged, and even affirmed
it. The already current opposition between faith and knowledge, theology and philosophy, was thus developed in the
sharpest form, concentrated in the weightiest and most practically important of cases. It was an opposition between
Thomas and Aristotle : it related to the whole question of a
world beyond, — a world by means of which the Church
rules the world we live in. What could be more welcome
to the secular and worldly spirit of the Renaissance than
such an indirect reference to the interests of the present
life? A series of great problems, which are immediately
connected with the destiny of man, were proposed anew, —
problems concerning the order of the world and the nature
of its necessity, concerning predestination and fate, concerning the possibility of human freedom, — all of them themes
which Pomponatius discussed also. It was then established
that all phenomena, even pretended supra-natural phenomena,
like presentiments, magic, demons, etc., must be explained
by natural laws. In relation to the art of magic, Pomponatius likewise attempted such an explanation.[1]

Now, if this explanation of things by natural causes could
in no way be obtained through a revival of the philosophy
of Aristotle, since the latter is in conflict not merely with
the doctrine of the Church, but also with *that of nature*, no
resource was left but for the Renaissance itself to attempt
the development of a new, natural philosophy, since that
kind of explanation was demanded. When Pomponatius led

---

[1] For the most detailed account of Pomponatius, we are indebted to the
Italian scholar, *Francesco Fiorentini*, who, in his two works *P. Pomponatius*
(1868) and *B. Telesio* (1872-74), earned for himself great merit for his investigation of the philosophical Renaissance of the sixteenth century.

into the field the Aristotelian doctrine of the soul against the Christian heaven, the time was no longer far distant when the Aristotelian doctrine of the system of the universe was to be overthrown by the discovery of the real heavens.

3. *The Political Renaissance.* — The immediate objects of the modern consciousness of the world, — a consciousness which awoke with the Renaissance, — are nature and the State, the totality of the human cosmos. The time had come when interest in the State also was revived, and when it rejected the guardianship of theology, of the whole scholastic doctrine of the State, determined as it was by the authority of the Church. In a contemporary of Pomponatius, one of the most remarkable minds of the Italy of that time, this Renaissance of the political consciousness reached its highest and most concentrated expression, — in the Florentine, *Niccolo Macchiavelli* (1469–1527). The desire to revive political thought, to devote all his energies to the State, impelled him, with native and irresistible power, to an extent possible only in the perfect freshness of a new time. " Destiny willed that I should be able to speak neither of silk nor weaving of wool, neither of profit nor loss: *I must speak of the State*, or be completely silent," wrote he to a friend when the Medici had banished him. He would pay any price for the privilege of returning to political activity, "even if I should have to roll stones."

From the pattern of the old Roman State, from the study of history, from patriotic interest in the affairs of Italy, he derived his instructions and his tasks. The physical life of man can be known and judged only through nature ; the life of the State only through history. Thus the political horizon is widened to the *historical.* An interest in politics awakens an interest in history ; and from the natural union of the two, political history arises. In this spirit, Macchiavelli studied Livy, and wrote the history of Florence. Man is at all times the same : always like causes have like effects ; effects change and deteriorate in relation to causes. These

are some of the very evident and universal truths which
Macchiavelli repeated, again and again, and applied to his
own time and country. The greatness of ancient Rome,
and the wretchedness of modern Italy: there the increasing
dominion of a growing and powerful people; here the increasing servitude of their descendants who are subject to
barbarians, and are a toy of foreign thirst for conquest: there
Rome rising to the dominion of the world; here Italy disintegrated under foreign rule, invaded. Whence came that
greatness? whence this ruin? Why have the descendants of
the Romans degenerated? Whence the chasm between the
Romans before Cæsar, and the Italians of the present? These
are the great historical questions which unceasingly occupy
the mind of Macchiavelli, which, prompted by Livy, he seeks
to answer in his "Discorsi," according to the laws of historical causality. The Italians of the Renaissance must be told
that they are, indeed, the most direct, but, also, the most
degraded, heirs of ancient Rome; that regeneration requires
new exaltation. "Earn what thou hast inherited from thy
fathers if thou wouldst possess it." This sentence, applied
to the heirs of the Romans, denotes that phase of the Italian
Renaissance which occupied the mind of Macchiavelli as
statesman and author.

He sought through his historical studies the means for the
political regeneration of Italy. This was his aim, his real
patriotic task. The instructive model is the State, of which
Macchiavelli treats in his "Discorsi" on the first decade
of Livy, his comparing glance being constantly directed to
the present. The task of the present is the freeing of Italy
from barbarians, the restoration of its unity. The political
reformation of Italy can only proceed from an Italian city
which through its commonwealth, its republican constitution,
and its political development, is the richest and most experienced. It can only be reached through a despotism which
knows and employs all the means whereby *power* is established, preserved, and extended. This city is *Florence*. The

great-grandson of that great Florentine citizen who had been called the father of his country, is the man who should be the despot of Italy. The political vocation and importance of Florence are evident from its history; and it was to show this that Macchiavelli had written it as far as the death of the man in whose son (Lorenzo II.) he would gladly have seen the ruler of Italy. In his book "On the Prince," he aimed to describe to Italy the ruler which it needed, in order to fulfil the first condition of its political regeneration; namely, to become a power. Thus, his books on the history of Florence are connected with those on the State and the prince. If we clearly realize the distinction between the progressive development of power in an able and vigorous people, a people which endures no despot, and the weakness of a degraded and corrupt nation, that requires a tyrant in order to be brought and kept into unity, we shall see no inconsistency between the author of the "Discorsi," who looks with aversion upon the great Cæsar, and that of the "Principe," who desires for Italy a man like Cæsar Borgia. And since we know that questions of political power, least of all in a corrupt people, can never be solved by moral means, it is foolish to decry the book "On the Prince." Macchiavelli had to describe a ruler, not a lay-brother, — one of those Italian rulers in whom the age of the Renaissance had long been accustomed to admire only their strength and success; and these have nothing in common with moral excellence.

Among the causes which made the Romans great and the Italians contemptible, Macchiavelli lays special emphasis on *religion.* And here the whole opposition between the political Renaissance, and that of the Church, is evident. The religion of the ancient Romans was the religion of the State, and its preservation a patriotic and political duty. Christianity, on the contrary, has been, from the beginning, concerned with a world beyond this: its back is turned upon the present world and the State. In its origin, it was unpolitical; and it has alienated man from the State, and weak-

ened his political power. With this first evil, a second has
associated itself. The Christian religion has not remained
true to its original tendency: it has degenerated. On the
faith in heaven an ecclesiastical power on earth has been
grounded, and this has made itself master of the State. This
second and greater evil is the hierarchy and the papacy,
which has its throne in Rome, and possesses a part of Italy.
There is no greater evil than the ecclesiastical State, the
greatest of all the obstacles to Italian unity. Here Macchiavelli attacks the worst antagonist of his reformatory plans.
Three cases are conceivable in the position of the papacy in
Italy: either the pope rules the whole of Italy, or only the
ecclesiastical State, or he is without all secular power —
merely the supreme head of the Church. In the first case,
Italy is not a State, but only a province of the Church; in
the second, it is disunited — its unity impossible; in the
third, which Dante had desired, the pope requires the protection of a foreign power, which continually endangers the
independence of Italy. There is, therefore, *no* case in which
the papacy is compatible with the political reformation of
Italy. There is thus an absolute opposition between the
two, and Macchiavelli desires the destruction of the papacy.
In it he sees the root of evil. The papacy has corrupted
both religion and the State: it has made religion hypocriti-
cal, and deprived the State of power. It has been a centre
of corruption, and has poisoned the morals of nations. The
nearer they are to the head of the Church, the less religious
they are. Of Christian nations, therefore, the Romanic are
the most corrupt; and of these, the Italians are the worst.
The aim of Macchiavelli cannot be mistaken: it was the
destruction of the Romish Church, — *the secularization of
religion.* His greatest preference was to substitute the religion of ancient, for that of modern, Rome; the State for
the Church; patriotism for religion. He *deifies the State.*
Such a conception necessarily appeared in the course of
the Renaissance. Macchiavelli was filled by it, and he

stamped it upon this period with the incomparable force of genius. •

Pomponatius saw the contradiction between the doctrine of immortality and philosophy: immortality is a matter of faith, not knowledge. Macchiavelli saw the contradiction between Christian faith in immortality and the true policy of the State: man should concentrate his attention upon the State. According to Pomponatius, the ecclesiastical kingdom of heaven is without foundation: according to Macchiavelli, the ecclesiastical kingdom on earth should be overthrown.

4. *Italian Neo-Platonism and Theosophy.* — The spirit of the Renaissance was entirely engrossed with the present world; and in its boldest and most decided characters, this interest amounts to the deification of the State and of nature. We have seen in Macchiavelli one-half, as it were, of this affirmation of the world, — the political, — and now we look for the other. We find it at the end of the sixteenth century as nature-philosophy and pantheism. This pantheistic view of the world, deifying nature and the universe, was in conflict, not merely with the doctrine of the Church, but with that of Aristotle, which separates God and the world, and since it was also the product of the Renaissance of the revival of ancient philosophy, the starting-point of this tendency must be sought in *Neo-Platonism*. Here we find the philosophical Renaissance advancing in a direction exactly the reverse of that taken by ancient philosophy itself. Ancient philosophy proceeded from the problems of cosmology through those of anthropology (Socratic) to those of theology, and resulted at last in that great religious question which lay at the foundation of Neo-Platonism in its most comprehensive sense. The Renaissance, on the other hand, starting from the Middle Ages, sought the path to the problems of cosmology through the theological view of the world which it borrowed from the Middle Ages and still retained. The philosophy of the ancients was naturally at first most evident to the philosophy arising out of Christianity

on the side most in harmony with its theological and religious spirit. This form of the philosophy of Greece, in which the last period of antiquity and the first of modern times touch each other, is religious Platonism. They reach their hands across the Middle Ages; and it might seem as if, after a long pause in which the philosophy of antiquity had been silent, it wished to continue exactly where it had left off in the last Neo-Platonists. We see before us the Renaissance in that trend of thought which advanced from the religious-philosophical view of the world to that of the natural-philosophical. Its starting-point was the *Italian Neo-Platonism;* its conclusion the *Italian* nature-philosophy. There we meet with modes of thought which remind us of Proclus and the last Neo-Platonics; here, on the other hand, with such as are akin to the first conceptions of the Ionic nature-philosophy.

Among those Greek theologians who appeared in Florence, where the union between the Greek and Roman Church was planned according to the view of the latter, were *Giorgios Gemistos Plethon* and his pupil *Bessarion* of Trebizond (1395–1472), the former an opponent, the latter a friend, of the union, soon after cardinal (1439) of the Romish Church, the defender and leader of the Platonic Renaissance in Italy. Plethon promulgated a kind of new world-religion which was to eclipse Christianity, and be not unlike paganism. He was a devout disciple of Proclus rather than of the Christian Church, and won through his animated expositions the first Medici to the Platonic philosophy, and occasioned the founding of the Platonic Academy in Florence, in which that school of Athens seemed to revive which Justinian had suppressed more than nine centuries before. The contest between Platonists and Aristotelians was then renewed. Bessarion defended Plato against those who misrepresented him. He regarded Plato and Aristotle as the heroes of philosophy, in comparison with whom the philosophers of his own time were mere apes. He proposed to divide the territory of knowledge between them, so that

Plato should be the authority in theology, and Aristotle, in the philosophy of nature.

The first problem of the Academy of Florence was the revival of the philosophy of Plato, the knowledge of it from the original sources, the diffusion of this knowledge in the West. The Florentine _Marsilio Ficino_ (1433–1499) solved this problem by translating into Latin the works of Plato and Plotinus. Ficino was educated by Cosimo to be an instructor of philosophy in his family and in the Academy of Florence. His mode of thought was the Neo-Platonic. He found in the philosophy of Plato the essence of all wisdom, the key to Christianity, and likewise the means of spiritualizing and renovating it. The philosophy of Plato, according to Ficino, is the great mystery in which all the wisdom of the past has been deposited, by which all true wisdom of after-times is permeated. Plato is the real heir of Pythagoras and Zoroaster. Philo, Numenius, Plotinus, Jamblicus, and Proclus are the real heirs of Plato, and also the revealers of the mystery of his doctrine. This light has shone upon those teachers of the Christian wisdom, — John, Paul, and the Areopagites.

Now, what is the principle of this mode of thought, the fundamental characteristics of which are not new? It is this: Christianity and Neo-Platonism are to be harmonized, the theological spirit of the one with the cosmological spirit of the other. Neo-Platonism is akin to Christianity in its religious motive, its striving for union with God: it is opposed to Christianity in its pagan deification of the world. The world in Neo-Platonism appears in a natural and necessary connection of divine and eternal orders, as a natural result of the primordial being, as an unfolding of divine powers in a definite order of gradations: the cosmos appears as a divine emanation, which naturally gushes forth from its primitive source, and enters into an order of degrees of decreasing perfection in the forms of the world of sense, that from this point, where the divine life is farthest from its original source, it may struggle back again. In this system of thought, union with God forms a moment in the eternal circulation of the universe, which, at its greatest distance from its eternal and primitive cause, seeks to return. The principle of Christianity is the salvation of the world through Christ: that of Neo-Platonism is the (mediate) emanation of the world from the divine primordial being.[1] Now, if Christianity is brought into harmony with Neo-Platonism, the theological spirit of the first must enter into the emanistic mode of thought of the second; assume, therefore, cosmological forms, and the divine mystery of the salvation of the world must be conceived as revealing itself, not merely in the Church, but also in the life of the world and of nature, and, indeed, as flowing in a pure stream from the very depths of the divine being. Nature is now regarded as a genuine revelation of God, as a guide to union with God. It appears in a religious significance which threatens the authority of the Church. In the depths of nature the mystery of divinity is concealed. He who penetrates nature, looks into the divine being. Nature thus appears as the great mystery which is to be revealed.

If this problem is solved, the veil is removed from divinity, and the word of reconciliation spoken for all the contradictions of the world. If we suppose the knowledge of God dependent upon the fact of the salvation of the world in Christ, we have the principle and form of (Christian) theology. If we suppose the knowledge of God dependent upon the mystery of nature, we have the principle and form of *theosophy;* and this theosophical character is the next form which philosophy, re-animated by Neo-Platonism, takes. It is the first step on the road to the nature-philosophy. But from this point of view, nature does not appear as a subject to be methodically investigated, but as a mystery for which the word of solution is sought; as a sealed book incapable

---

[1] Cf. above, p. 31, and following.

of being opened by earthly powers, — a book for the understanding of which a key, as mysterious as the book itself, is
required. What, therefore, this theosophical spirit sought
was an esoteric doctrine to unfold the hidden meaning of
nature, and to solve its mystery. And as the Grecian logos-
idea went to meet the Jewish ideal of the Messiah, so this
theosophical spirit which Neo-Platonism aroused in the Christian world was attracted by the Jewish Cabala, which claimed
to have received from divine revelation in primitive times
the solution of the enigma of creation. In this union with
the *Cabala*, that Jewish Gnosticism, which in its fundamental
conceptions is akin to Neo-Platonism, we find the Platonic
theosophy distinctly expressed in the writings of *Giovanni
Pico della Mirandola*, the most talented representative of the
Italian Neo-Platonism.

The interest in Cabalistic doctrines and writings was an
active factor in the culture of the time, since attention was
thereby directed to Jewish literature, and the study of
Hebrew promoted. The circle of humanistic studies was
thus enlarged, and made to include Hebrew literature as
well as that of Greece. By the side of Erasmus, *Reuchlin*
arose, who made Hebrew the subject of scientific investigation, with a view of explaining the Holy Scriptures, and
understanding the Cabala. He made the acquaintance of
Pico, and through him became interested in the Cabala, and
eventually the first Hebrew scholar of the West. When the
theologians of Cologne, incited by a converted Jew, demanded the destruction of Hebrew literature, with the
exception of the Holy Scriptures, and, therefore, the ecclesiastical condemnation of the Cabalistic books, Reuchlin
publicly defended this literature, and achieved a victory. It
was the first victorious conflict of Humanism with scholasticism in Germany. The entire cultivated world followed the
controversy with their sympathy: the great parties of the
humanists and scholastics were arrayed against each other.
On one side were the famous men of the time, names

noted in literature and science; on the other, men of little ability and as little reputation. The letters of the famous men who congratulated the victor were followed by "Letters of Obscure Men " (1515–7), that inimitable satire which shows most plainly how far the humanistic mind had gone beyond the scholastic, whose style entertained it only as a subject of the keenest wit and satire.[1]

5. *Magic and Mysticism.* — We follow the further course of this theosophical mode of thought. If in nature divine forces are active in a descending gradation, in which the lower forces proceed from the higher, one divine life must stream creatively through the whole universe: the lowest must stand in an unbroken connection with the highest, the earthly world with the heavenly; and this unbroken connection must transmit the invisible influences from above, and the higher forces penetrate and govern all the lower. Nothing more, accordingly, seems necessary than to appropriate those higher powers, in order to rule nature in the completest sense. Theosophy is now attracted more and more by the image of nature, is more and more absorbed in contemplating it, eagerly listening, as it were, to overhear the secrets of nature, constantly striving to acquire her concealed powers. In this direction it becomes *magic*, the great art which rests on the deepest and most mysterious of sciences. This phase of theosophy, the mago-Cabalistic trend of thought, was developed by *Agrippa von Nettesheim* (1487–1535). It was faith in nature as the problem in which divinity is concealed: it was also faith in the solution of this problem. If there are divine forces in nature, why cannot man acquire them? If he acquires them, and learns how to use them, he becomes a *magician*. This possibility was a belief of the age. In a series of strange characters, this temper of mind was distinctly expressed, which, in the legend

[1] Cf. D. Fr. Strauss, Ulrich von Hutten (sec. ed., 1871), Book I. chap. viii. pp. 176–211.

of Faust, finally found its typical, and, in the poem of Goethe, its Promethean, expression.[1]

> " The spirit-world no closures fasten,
>   Thy sense is shut, thy heart is dead;
> Disciple, up! untiring hasten
>   To bathe thy breast in morning red." [2]

This passage which Goethe puts in the mouth of Faust, was, in the sixteenth century, a really active factor in the beliefs of men. Nor can we better express the conception of the world which lies at the foundation of this belief, than with the words of Faust, as he considers the sign of the macrocosm : —

> " How each the Whole its substance gives,
>   Each in the other works and lives
> Like heavenly forces rising and descending,
> Their golden urns reciprocally lending,
>   With wings that winnow blessing.
> From heaven to earth I see them pressing,
> Filling the earth with harmony unceasing." [2]

But how is it possible to appropriate these higher divine forces in order that we may use them? The first condition is to apprehend them. They are concealed in nature and the lower forms of it: they appear veiled, and, under the hostile influences of external things, are hindered in a variety of ways. These hinderances must be removed: this veil must be torn away. It is, therefore, necessary even to penetrate the material world, not to content one's self merely with the consideration of the great spectacle of the world's forces, but to disclose each in its properties, separating from it every thing which obstructs its action, and so learning the arts of nature. Magic demands chemistry,

---

[1] Cf. my work on Goethe's Faust, chap. i. pp. 21-35 (Stuttgart, Cotta, 1878).
[2] Bayard Taylor's translation.

chemical experiments. If we can remove all obstructions, we can heal all diseases. The idea of a panacea lies in this mode of thought, which, through chemistry, aims likewise to promote medical science. But the important thing is, that this phase of magic begins to have intercourse with nature herself, makes trials of things, handles them, as it were, and thus introduces experiment as the investigation of nature requires. This practical, and therefore important, development of magic was made by *Paracelsus* (1493–1541), a thaumaturge, — still entirely in connection with its theosophical principles.

Now, if the divine life is present and active in the inmost nature of things, will it not likewise be active in the inmost nature of man, in the very core of human nature? Nowhere can the divine mystery shine upon us more directly and brightly and plainly than from the hidden depths of our own being. All we must do is to force our way through the barrier of our outer nature, and penetrate into the depths where the spark of divine light shines. Here, also, a chemistry is necessary to separate every thing of a foreign or hostile nature that penetrates from the outer world into our inmost being, and disturbs our mind. The desires and passions, which draw us into the things of the world, are the dross which is mingled with the gold in the deep mines of our souls. This mixture must be broken in pieces: the gold must be separated from the dross, that the light may shine out of the darkness, and fill all the powers of our soul. There is a path which leads directly to God; it goes through the very centre of our being; it demands absorption into ourselves, the quiet turning into our own inmost being, and away from all worldly selfish pleasure, in a word, perfectly sincere, profound, contemplative piety, by means of which we become what we are in the primary principle of our being. That is not the path of magic, but of *mysticism*. Both are forms of theosophy which seek the path to God through the mystery of things. Magic takes its course through external nature; mysticism, through internal; that through the mystery of nature; this, through that of man. Mysticism is the deeper and more abiding form, since it seeks by a sure way which always leads to new discoveries. They agree in that they seek the same goal, and strive to reach it immediately, through the presageful absorption into life itself. They, therefore, agree in their aversion to tradition, to the instructions of the school, to all learned and bookish knowledge. They reject books with the feeling that something new gushes forth from themselves with original and irresistible power. The passionate revolt against received conceptions is only the expression of their revolt against the past, the sign of the crisis in which the times divide. A mystic like Valentin Weigel is not less satiated with the learning of the schools than Agrippa and Paracelsus!

Mysticism had passed through a series of stages of development in the Christian world before it was borne along, in the sixteenth century, by that theosophical current of thought which started from the Platonic Renaissance, and united it closely with magic. In its simple form, it is the expression of the inner religious life, which, in the quiet depths of the soul, seeks the way to God, the life within God through the change in the human heart, without which Christian piety cannot be conceived. This fundamental characteristic is natural to Christianity, and, in the manifold forms which are subject to the different spirit of different times, forms the continual theme of all Christian mysticism, the inexhaustible source from which a stream of living religion ever anew gushes forth, whenever Christianity, through its ecclesiastical development, is in danger of becoming fossilized in dogmas, and losing itself in a labyrinth of worldly desires and theological systems. Thus, the scholasticism of the Middle Ages was mystical in its tendencies whenever it opposed or supplemented the theology of dialectics and formalism, — periods related to theology as feeling to a mere tenet, and life to a doctrine. In the twelfth century the monks in the cloister of St. Victor in Paris (the *Victorines;* Hugo, Richard, Walter) introduced mysticism into ecclesiastical scholasticism, and with increasing dislike opposed the doctrines of the schools that religion might not be eaten up by theology. In the following century, when the ecclesiastico-scholastic view of the world had reached the final point in its development, mysticism formed its salutary supplement, and found its most powerful expression in *Bonaventura* and *Dante,* who portrayed the life of the soul in the course of its development, as if it were on its way to God. When the nominalistic doctrine of knowledge began to be diffused, and the separation between knowledge and faith, philosophy and theology, began, theology was obliged to confine itself to practical and religious life, and even assume a mystical tendency. But with the first movement towards ecclesiastical decentralization, religious life also strove to throw off the bondage of the Church, and to assert itself more independently than ever before, and demand its own inner transformation as the essential condition of holiness. We find, therefore, in the last centuries of scholasticism, an ecclesiastical and an independent mysticism, the latter independent of the Church. The former was in alliance with the reformatory councils, and found expression in the French theologians *Pierre d'Ailly* (1350–1425) and *Johann Gerson* (1363–1429); the latter was the forerunner of the German Reformation : and its greatest expounder was the Saxon Dominican, Meister Eckardt, whom the German and Netherlandish mystics followed ; viz., *Suso (Heinrich Berg,* 1300–1365), *Johannes Tauler* (1290–1391), *Johann Ruysbroek* (1293–1381), and that unknown citizen of Frankfort, the author of " The German Theology," which Luther published a year after he posted his theses against indulgences. The Reformation of the sixteenth century developed a Protestant mysticism in Germany, which, in opposition to the nascent scholasticism of Lutheranism, to a slavishly literal faith, to a merely outward service of God, to the bodily presence of Christ in the sacrament, renewed the

old and eternal theme of spiritual regeneration, of the hell
of selfishness, of the heaven of self-denial, of the Christ
whom we must experience *in ourselves* in order to be saved
by him. It was this religious, Protestant self-knowledge,
which in *Casper Schwenckfeld* (1490–1561), *Sebastian Franck*
(1500–1545), *Valentin Weigel* (1533–1588), and *Jacob Böhme*
(1575–1624), opposed mechanical Lutheranism, and grew
stronger and stronger until, towards the end of the century,
it was compressed into the *form of concord*, and lost its power.

Jacob Böhme was the profoundest and ablest of those mystics, and in him both these factors were combined ; viz., the
mago-Cabalistic view of the world, united with the Renaissance, — a view of the world which animated Paracelsus, —
and the mysticism which Protestantism called into life. The
divine mystery in man is identical with that in nature : if
the divine mystery in man is disclosed, the enigma and mystery of creation are explained. Religious self-knowledge penetrates the depths, the inmost, most concealed abysses of our
being. In regeneration, Böhme saw the manifestation of the
"inward," and the death of the "monstrous," man, who is
governed by selfishness ; in the birth of the natural (selfish)
will, the birth of things in general, which, by their own will,
tear themselves loose from God. There is, therefore, a primary state of things, or a Nature in God, which is related to
the life and revelation of God, as the natural will in man to
that which is born again. For the revelation of God is the
new birth and illumination of the world (humanity), which
reflects divine, as a mirror does natural, light. Böhme's
mago-mystical conception of the world was a theosophical
view of things, in which pious emotion co-exists with lively
imagination, filled with the images of nature. It was based
on the connection of, and the conflict between, the divine
and natural forces in life, whose goal can be none other than
"a being free from strife."

Religious self-knowledge is the ground of philosophical.
Eckardt's mysticism, which culminated in German theology,

was the forerunner of the Reformation. Protestant mysticism, which culminated in Jacob Böhme, was a forerunner of modern philosophy, and stands close to its threshold.

6. *The Italian Nature - Philosophy.* — We return to the Renaissance to complete the course of its philosophical development in the element peculiar to it. The revival of Neo-Platonism resulted in a theosophical view of nature, which at every step departed farther from the theological conception of nature, of scholasticism, and of Aristotle, expressed its pantheistic character more distinctly, and which finally terminated in a naturalistic view of the world completely opposed to scholasticism. According to this view of the world, nature has a value of her own, manifests law, has in and of herself the power and purpose of her activity, and must, therefore, be explained by means of herself alone, not by theological grounds, but "*juxta propria principia.*" This is the trend of the *Italian nature-philosophy*, the last form of that philosophical development of the Renaissance which began in the Platonic school of Florence.

The very problem which the Italian nature-philosophy proposed, is completely opposed to the fundamental conception of Aristotle. It is impossible to explain nature by means of itself, so long as the supra-mundane God is regarded as its moving ground and cause. This conception of God is closely connected with the doctrine that the universe is limited, with the doctrine of the geo-centric system of the world, of the opposition between the heavens and the earth, of the formation of the elements by means of differences of motion (change of place), through which the opposition between the upper or heavenly element (ether), and the four lower (fire, air, water, earth), is held to be evident. Fire, accordingly, is regarded as matter: warmth and cold, lightness and heaviness, are opposite properties or states of matter. In the foundations of the Aristotelian doctrine itself, there is a conflict between the theological and naturalistic conceptions ; between metaphysics and physics ; between the transcendence and immanence of purpose; between purpose (form) and matter.

This modern naturalism, which opposes that of Aristotle, was founded by *Bernardino Telesio* of Cosenza, in Calabria (1509–1588). He was the leader of the natural philosophical school, the central point of which was the Academy of Cosenza. Avoiding the Church, he took nature alone as his guide. His forerunner was the adventurous *Gierolamo Cardano* of Milan (1500–1577). He based philosophy on the knowledge of nature, the inner connection of all phenomena, the absolute unity of the living universe, and revived the conception of the world-soul, which he conceived as light and warmth. The Telesian doctrine, the real foundation of the Italian nature-philosophy, simplifies principles, and insists on their derivation from the observation of things themselves. Every thing in nature must be explained by means of matter and force, matter and the conflict between its indwelling forces, the activity of which consists in their expansion and contraction, which are identical with light and darkness, warmth and cold, and are concentrated in the sun and the earth. Though the conception of Telesio was undeveloped, the doctrine of *natural forces* and the idea of their unity were already pressing to the centre of natural philosophy. Warmth was no longer regarded as matter, but as motion, and the cause of motion; and fire, air, and water, as its effects. Therewith, the Aristotelian physics was abandoned in one of its principal points, — its doctrine of the elements; and, since every thing is to be explained by natural forces, knowledge must be derived from sensation, reason from sensibility, our moral nature from our desires, virtue from the impulse to self-preservation. Theological and religious questions aside, the system of Telesio is absolutely monistic and naturalistic. His principal work, "On the Investigation of Natural Causes," appeared in its first form in 1565, though the completed work was not published until 1587.

This doctrine, through its opposition to Aristotle, exercised an involuntary attraction upon the Platonic mode of thought, in the form in which it was revived by the Renaissance. *Francesco Patrizzi* of Clissa, in Dalmatia (1529–1593), combined the Neo-Platonism of Italy with the modern Italian nature-philosophy founded by Telesio. The point where the two come in contact is the doctrine of warmth and light, which Telesio regarded as the moving and animating force in nature, and with which the Neo-Platonists have always compared the Divine being and his emanations. Patrizzi distinguished and combined both significations, and regarded the material and the spiritual light as proceeding from the unity of the divine primitive light, the primary source of all things, from which the series of emanations proceeds. That is the fundamental thought which he sought to develop in his "Nova de Universis Philosophia" (1591). In this system the concept of the world-soul also has a place, so that Patrizzi combined the doctrines of Telesio and Cardano within the Italian nature-philosophy. Nevertheless, his doctrine, in its Platonism, which was indeed hostile to Aristotle, but friendly to the Church, appears as a step backward in the course of this modern naturalistic philosophy.

Telesio and his followers were not concerned with the revival of Aristotle or Plato, or with the controversies between their revived schools. The path upon which they entered led to the Renaissance of nature herself in the mind of man, to a naturalism so complete and unreserved that it regarded transcendent conceptions as elements foreign to its nature, as dead scholasticism, as the enslaving of nature by theology, and rejected them accordingly. What Aristotle had said of Plato, "*Amicus Plato, magis amica Veritas!*" was then felt concerning nature itself. It became the subject of intense enthusiasm and affection. As Macchiavelli had deified the State, and had hated the secular power of the pope, and the papacy itself, and had declared that it was the root of political evil, so nature was then deified, and the doctrine of the Church was attacked, — even the foundations of the Christian faith. This bold step, required by the spirit of the Italian Renaissance and its nature-philosophy, was taken by the Dominican monk, *Giordano Bruno*, of Nola in Naples (1548–1600), who rejected the habit of his order, and fled adventurously over the world, as three centuries before him his countryman, Thomas Aquinas, had risked every thing in order to flee out of the world into a cell of the Dominicans. Thus the times change! Bruno represented the naturalistic, as Macchiavelli had done the political, Renaissance. His theme was the deification of nature and the universe, the divine, all-embracing unity, pantheism in opposition to all ecclesiastical conceptions. This doctrine animated his thoughts and poems, and seemed to him an entirely new theory of the world, the new bond of religion and knowledge, which he, as philosopher and poet, proclaimed. He had exchanged the cowl of the monk for the thyrsus! He felt himself related to the philosophers of antiquity, who affirmed and taught the divine cosmos, — Pythagoras and Plato, the Stoics and Epicureans. And they stood the nearer to him, the less dualistic their systems and the more conformable to the natural order of things. This is why he rates Plato higher than Aristotle, Pythagoras than Plato, Epicurus and Lucretius than the Stoics. On the other hand, he rejected scholasticism, particularly that of Aristotle; and the doctrine of Duns Scotus was an object of intense aversion, since the latter made nature subject to the divine arbitrary will. As the system of things can only be one, our concepts must be capable of being arranged systematically; and hence he was interested in, and gave some attention to, the so-called "art of Lully." In opposition to the dualism of God and the world, form and matter, he taught the absolute unity of contradictions, — which the profound Nicholas Cusanus, on the threshold of the Renaissance, had first stated, — and made it the principle of his doctrine. The universe appeared to him as the true and only revelation of God.

Therefore, he opposed the faith in the personal God-man on which Christianity rests, and the sinful nature of man on which Catholicism bases its justification by the Church alone, and Protestantism its justification by faith alone. The axiom of Luther, "*sola fide*," is as little in harmony with his view as the Romish "*nulla solus extra ecclesiam*." Nature alone is the kingdom of God; and it is to be found only in the living and true perception of things, not in books, nor can it be reached through the manipulation of words. Entirely filled by an intense desire for the knowledge of nature, Bruno felt an aversion to the philological spirit of the Renaissance, to formalism, to logic and rhetoric. Here, indeed, naturalism came in conflict with humanism in the narrower acceptation of the term.

From Bruno's fundamental pantheistic conception, which denies the existence of God external to and beyond the world, and regards the universe as his complete presence, the identity of God and the world, the unconditional immanence of God immediately follows. "It pleases him to move the world within himself, nature in himself, himself in nature to enclose." The universe, therefore, is, like God, unlimited, immeasurable, embracing countless worlds; the starry heavens are no longer the boundary of the universe; the earth is no longer its motionless centre; there is no such absolute centre at all; even the sun is only central in relation to the system of the planets. Bruno therefore accepted the *Copernican* theory of the universe (which had already been expounded), and defended it against the Aristotelian and Ptolemaic system, to which the ecclesiastical view of the world had adjusted itself. He went beyond Copernicus in his inferences, and was indeed a forerunner of Galileo. Whether between the pantheistic and Copernican doctrines a necessary connection exists, is not here the question. So much is evident: from the denial of the geocentric system, the denial of the limited and the affirmation of the unlimited universe necessarily follow, whereby the usual conceptions of transcendence fall to the ground, and the equality of God and the world results. One can base the pantheistic conception of the world on the Copernican theory, and, conversely, the Copernican theory can be deduced from pantheism. Bruno chose this method. Through his agreement with Copernicus, he is the most advanced of the Italian natural philosophers, as in his character he is the boldest and fullest of genius.

Now, the divine, all-embracing unity must be conceived as embracing all that is and happens in the nature of things. This is the unity that embraces all in itself, produces and moves all, permeates and knows all, — matter, force, and mind in one. The relation between God and the universe is accordingly identical with the necessary order of things or of *nature*. Bruno's doctrine of the all-embracing unity is naturalistic. God is related to the universe as producing, to produced, nature. He is " *natura naturans:* " the world of phenomena is " *natura naturata.*" God, as causative nature, or all-producing force, is both matter and mind, matter and intelligence, extension and thought. In this point we see in Bruno the forerunner of *Spinoza*. But nature is likewise a living and divine work of art, in which the artist, working within it, reflects and reveals himself, advancing from unconscious to conscious nature, from the material expression of his thoughts to the mental, from the " *vestigia* " to the " *umbræ,*" which are the images of the divine ideas in us. This natural and progressive revelation of God is a *process of development*, in which the divine purposes or world-thoughts dwell as impelling forces, and out of which they proceed as objects of knowledge, like fruit from seed. The universe, considered as a living work of art, is the self-development of God. God is related, accordingly, to the world as the ground of a development to all its forms and stages, like a germ to its unfolding, like a point to space, like an atom to a body, like a unit to a number. God is, therefore, the smallest and greatest, and forms in truth the unity of all contradictions.

The world is contained in him potentially, — as Cujanus had already said, — in undeveloped capacity, in a state of "*implicatio:*" in the world, God is in a state of "*explicatio*," of infinite fulness, and unfolding, of his powers. Thus, the universe appears as a system of development, the germs of which are uninfolded powers, or monads of things. In this point we see in Bruno the forerunner of our *Leibnitz*. The Italian works which he published in London in 1584, lie in the trend of thought which culminated in Spinoza; while the Latin didactic poems published in Frankfort-on-the-Main (1591) shortly before his death, already prefigurated the doctrine of monads. After he had fallen, through treachery, into the hands of the Inquisition, filled by the "*eroici furoris*" of his faith, he would not mitigate his sufferings by any kind of recantation, and endured death by fire without any sign of fear, in Rome, Feb. 17, 1600. "Ye tremble more than I," said he to his judges, in the presence of the stake. He was no atheist, but a "lover of God." His doctrine of the divine and immeasurable universe, which he felt and proclaimed as a new religion, formed the principal count in his indictment. He died for pantheism, on the ground of which he maintained and defended the new theory of Copernicus. Two thousand years after the death of Socrates!

But however characteristic of modern times was Bruno's passionate attack on the Church of the Middle Ages, he, nevertheless, belonged to the philosophical Renaissance, not to modern philosophy. He was not so independent as he seemed to be. He was an innovator in intention rather than in fact; and, though original in his character and individuality, his thoughts belonged, in good part, to the mental atmosphere of revived antiquity, and he appropriated them through sympathy. The needle of the Italian nature-philosophy unmistakably points to modern times; but it was powerfully deflected by the strong currents of the past, and, therefore, still wavered in uncertainty. It was not the beginning and the founding of modern philosophy, but the transition to it from the Middle Ages through the Renaissance. The mental tendencies of the past and future are, therefore, mingled in it; and it felt the threefold attraction of antiquity, the ecclesiastical age of the world, and the spirit of modern times. In none of its advocates does this mingling — which is too peculiar to be regarded as the usual eclecticism — appear more comprehensive, and on a larger scale, than in the last of this series, *Tommaso Campanella* of Stylo, in Calabria (1568–1639), the countryman and younger contemporary of Bruno. Like Bruno, he was a Dominican of a fiery and poetic imagination, who was possessed and overpowered, as it were, by the Telesian nature-philosophy; and, like him, he was persecuted, not so much on ecclesiastical as on political grounds, having been suspected of a conspiracy against the Spanish Government, for which he did penance by suffering seven times at the rack, and imprisonment for twenty-seven years in fifty different prisons (1599–1626). With Telesio, who gave him his starting-point, and Patrizzi and Bruno, he strengthened the anti-Aristotelian character of the new nature-philosophy. Like Patrizzi, he advocated the Telesian-Platonic doctrines, which were friendly to the Church; but, in complete opposition to Bruno, he maintained the ecclesiastical rule of the world, and established, in his doctrine, an alliance between the Italian nature-philosophy and the scholastic doctrine of the State, between Telesio, the founder of naturalism, and Thomas, the theological authority of the Dominicans. From the height of the late Renaissance, Campanella descended, in his political opinions, to a stand-point before Dante, and bitterly opposed Macchiavelli, that genuine representation of the political Renaissance, whom he regarded as diabolical. At the same time, this remarkable mingling of Telesianic-Platonic and Thomistic conceptions, this synthesis of the Italian nature-philosophy, Neo-Platonic (Areopagitic) and scholastic theology, rests on principles which cause Campanella to appear as the progenitor of the founder of modern philosophy. He sustains the same relation to Bacon and Descartes, especially the latter, that Bruno does to Spinoza and Leibnitz.

The natural knowledge of things rests on our experience of external and internal facts: the former consists in sense-perceptions, and is sensualistic; the latter is reflective, and consists in the consideration of self, in the immediate certainty of our own being, in the indubitable "I am." This is the point where Campanella borders on Descartes, and seems to anticipate the beginning of modern philosophy. We know immediately not merely our own existence and its limits, but also *what* we are, and in what the nature of our being consists; namely, in the power of knowing and willing. I am a being with faculties, a conceiving, willing being. These are my immediately evident fundamental properties or "primalities." My faculty is consummated in power; conceiving in knowledge or wisdom; willing in love. But, since my being is of a limited nature, I am subject to the opposites of these perfections, — to weakness, ignorance, and hate. Now, knowledge requires the unity and connection of all beings; and their fundamental properties must, therefore, be analogous to each other. Thus, the certainty of my own existence immediately reveals to me the ultimate principles or primary grounds of things. By means of those "*primalitates*" of his own being, Campanella apprehends the "*proprincipia*," which constitute the subject of his new metaphysic. The unconscious beings beneath me are in a lower potence what I am in a higher. God is in the highest and absolute potence what all finite beings are in a lower. He is omnipotence, wisdom, and love. There is, therefore, no actual thing that does not feel and desire its being, that does not feel and will by reason of its nature, even if in an unconscious, obscure manner. Every actual being has at the same time feeling of itself, will to being, impulse to self-preservation. The living can never result from that which is lifeless, nor conscious feeling and perception from that which is destitute of feeling. The powers of conceiving and willing are, therefore, the primitive forces which ground all existence, the powers which animate and bring forth the gradation of things. In this profound conception we find Campanella on the road to Leibnitz, and opposed to Spinoza, to the same extent as Bruno was related to him. He stands between Telesio and Descartes, with Bruno between Telesio and Leibnitz, but not, like Bruno, also between Leibnitz and Spinoza. The Telesianic doctrine of the opposition of, and conflict between, the forces in the nature of things, Campanella grounds by maintaining that sense and sensation exist in all things; that from their impulse to self-preservation, the will to existence, which already dwells in the resistance of an inert mass, sympathy and antipathy, attraction and repulsion, follow: he bases it on the " *sensus rerum*," the entirely original theme of his first philosophical work, which already contained the fundamental thoughts of his metaphysics, and appeared the same year (1591) in Naples, as Patrizzi's new philosophy in Ferrara, and Bruno's Latin didactic poem in Frankfort.

If the world is viewed from the stand-point of natural things, it appears as a development, as a gradation of increasing perfection and illumination, which terminates in God. If God is taken as the stand-point from which it is considered, it appears as a creation of omnipotent wisdom and love, which, in distinction from God, must be finite and incomplete, and the farther it is from God, therefore, the less perfect and the more obscure the members of the kingdom of gradations which it forms, in which the intermediate kingdoms of ideas, minds, and souls cannot be wanting. The spirit-world also includes the orders of angels, the heavenly hierarchy, which the Areopagite had taught. Campanella's doctrine of creation had its nearest type in Thomas, and his conception of the descending gradation of the universe closely resembles the Neo-Platonic doctrine of emanation. But in man, the world of spirits again ascends, springing out of the dark bosom of nature. It must form a new kingdom of light, a "system of suns," a copy of the divine kingdom. There must be *one* flock and *one* shepherd. Campanella, therefore, requires the unity and centralization of religion, of the Church and the State ; a kingdom of the world, which unites in itself humanity arranged in the form of a gradation, under a universal ruler over whom the vicegerent of God on earth is enthroned, the supreme head of the Church of the world, as a copy of the divine omnipotence, the Romish pope. A poetic, retrospective, earnest reconstruction of the ecclesiastical age of the world of the times of Innocence III., a philosophical dream, after Dante had imprecated the secular power of the papacy, and Macchiavelli, his ecclesiastical power also, and the Reformation had made the incurable schism! But why should not the fancy of the Renaissance, which possessed the magical power of necromancy, again dream this ideal of the Middle Ages in the person of one of its youngest sons? There was still between the Platonic State and the Romish Church an old kinship, which could overcome and inspire the lonely Campanella in his dungeon !

7. *Scepticism as the Result of the Renaissance.* — Even in the last period of scholasticism, faith had no longer felt knowledge as a support, but as an oppressive burden, and had freed itself from it by the nominalistic theory of cognition. Human knowledge was directed to the world of nature and sense, with the consciousness that its powers were insufficient to grasp the nature of things. There was thus a sceptical tendency in that scholastic doctrine which had separated faith and knowledge. The Renaissance unsettled faith in the Church, and in the transcendent and supernatural world : it revived the philosophical systems of antiquity, none of which were able to yield the scientific satisfaction which the spirit of the new time sought and required. It authorized an unfettered variety of individual opinions, and was itself in no way inclined to submit to the trammels of a system. An authority which usurps the empire of knowl-

edge was in irreconcilable and fundamental conflict with the primary origin and nature of the Renaissance. It was, therefore, an entirely natural result, when the culture of the Renaissance, unable of itself to produce a really new system, finally terminated in a scepticism which openly confessed this inability, and reckoned belief in the knowledge of truth among human delusions.

To such a sceptical consciousness the culture of the period naturally suggested a trend of thought which reminds us of the *Sophism* of the ancients, in which doubt was a source of personal enjoyment, and so strongly increased the feeling of intellectual power in the individual, that he seemed to himself to be standing on a height with the kingdoms of belief and knowledge at his feet. Man again imagines himself " the measure of all things." It rests with him whether he will defend belief to-day, or deride it to-morrow. The Italian Renaissance must still develop this idle and boastful sophism ; and it found the corresponding character in a younger contemporary of Bruno and Campanella, a man whose opinion of himself passed over into the extremest presumption. His name was *Lucilio Vanini*, and he called himself *Giulio Cesare Vanini* (1585–1619). In one of his dialogues he makes one of the speakers cry out in the greatest wonder at the power of his reasoning, " Either thou art a God or Vanini !" He modestly answered, "I am Vanini !" In his " Amphitheatre," he appeared as the antagonist of the philosophy of antiquity, and as the advocate of Christianity, the Church, the Council of Trent, and the Jesuits. In the very next year, he wrote the " Dialogues on Nature," " The Queen and Goddess of Mortals," in which he plainly derided the dogmas of religion and Christianity, though his irony was disguised by being expressed in the form of a dialogue. A century had passed since Pomponatius led naturalism into the field against the Church, and cautiously grounded and disguised doubt of the doctrines of faith. Vanini was a disciple of Pomponatius, though he lacked his earnestness and originality of inquiry.

Almost at the same time, he played the roll of the sophistical apologist, and shameless derider, of the Church. But the age that followed the founding of the order of Jesuits, the Council of Trent, the night of Bartholomew, no longer appreciated such jests, and burned Vanini at the stake in Toulouse because of his dialogues (1619). Not because of his character and his works, but only because of this tragic fate, which is greater than the man, does Vanini appear alongside of Giordano Bruno.[1]

There is a sceptical view of the world, which resulted from the Renaissance as the ripe fruit of collective experience and worldly wisdom, and formed the final stage of its philosophical development. In this confused variety of philosophical hypotheses and systems, there was none which had the power to produce a conviction of its truth. Their conflicts with each other were rather a proof of their weakness, which, in such a wealth of culture and intellectual power as the Renaissance possesses, must have its foundations in human nature itself. Therefore, true *self-knowledge*, tested by experience, out of sympathy with intellectual arrogance and the desires natural to it, is the problem to which the whole intellectual condition of the world points. The more correct and clear one's self-observation, the better he knows others, and the more successfully he gains the stand-point from which he can calmly observe things. " *C'est moi, que je peins!* " This is the stand-point of *Michel de Montaigne* (1533–1592) in the last stage of the philosophical Renaissance: this sentence was the acknowledged and universal theme of his self-delineations or essays (1580–1588). He was educated entirely in the spirit of the Renaissance, and his mode of thought was the result of his education. Montaigne knew himself; and no one knew better how to estimate the power of the educating influences which depend upon an age, and which even determine the opinions of men. In the

---

[1] Fr. Fiorentino: Bernardino Telesio, vol. ii. pp. 211-222.

world of men, individuals change ; in these, dispositions and circumstances in life ; with these, opinions. He who knows how opinions arise, will concede to none an objective value, and regard each of them as the result of individual development. A good-natured *tolerance*, therefore, based on a wide knowledge of men, accompanied Montaigne's scepticism, even in relation to the differences of religious beliefs which had given rise to the civil wars in France. He despised the conceit of truth of philosophical systems, and the puffed-up learning which commentators heap on commentators. He respected everywhere the *individual* right of opinions ; and precisely in this respect Montaigne appears as the child of the Renaissance, and his scepticism as the result of his culture. The more changeable and uncertain the world of human conceptions and views, laws and customs, appears, the stronger the contrast between that world and the law-obeying and invariable course of nature, the living book of creation, which *Raymond von Sabunde*, in his "Natural Theology" (1436), had already called the pure revelation of God. Montaigne translated Raymond's work in his youth, and defended it in the most comprehensive of his essays. To faith in human knowledge and its bungling systems, he opposes faith in nature, in its simplicity, and in its harmony with the positive revelation of God. He knew no wiser course than to yield himself to nature, and follow her guidance. In this faith in nature, Montaigne appears as a forerunner of Rousseau, also in that he rests this faith on self-observation, and gives expression to it in the form of self-delineation. " *C'est moi, que je peins!* " "I seek to know myself: this is my metaphysics and physics." This sentence of our sceptic, Rousseau also might have made his motto.

Montaigne stood on the threshold of modern philosophy, but he did *not* cross it. It began where he stopped, with doubt based on self-observation and self-examination, and including belief in the existence and *cognizability* of nature. It was doubt seeking and producing knowledge, which animated Bacon and Descartes, the founders of modern philosophy. Montaigne's father was a countryman of Bacon, who took the form of the "Essays" as the model of his first important work. Montaigne himself was a countryman of Descartes. He was the type and leader of a sceptical mode of thought which formed in Southern France, the last station, as it were, between the Renaissance and Descartes. In the preacher, *Pierre Charron* (1541–1603), this scepticism became an exhortation to religious faith: in the professor of medicine, *Franz Sanchez* (1562–1632), it applied itself to a natural observation of things. Its fundamental thought is expressed in that sentence of Charron's, "The proper study of mankind is man."

CHAPTER VI.

THE PERIOD OF THE REFORMATION.

THE origin of modern philosophy was dependent upon an epoch-making fact which shook the foundations of the culture of the Middle Ages, destroyed its limits, and, by the union of all the forces necessary to the crisis, so transformed the whole human conception of the world, that the foundations for a new period of culture were firmly laid. This comprehensive and fundamental transformation, which is in no way limited to ecclesiastical changes, is the *Reformation*, the boundary between the Middle and Modern Ages of the world. Never in the world has a greater change taken place in a shorter time. In the short space of a half-century, human consciousness in all its principal forms was transformed: a multitude of reforming forces crowded together to bring the Middle Ages to an end. They worked in the most different departments, destroying old conceptions of the world and of life, and acting independently of each other, and yet in wonderful harmony. We have become acquainted with the stages of transition in which the Renaissance was tending towards modern times. We must now show in what respects it was a factor in the Reformation itself.

There are two objects which man immediately presents to himself, — the world and himself. His theory of the world consists in the connection and development of these two conceptions, and in his theory of the world the highest form of his culture. Both are subject to self-delusion, and are true only to the extent to which they have seen through, and freed themselves from, the deceptive appearances of things. The first conception, whose object is the existing world, may be called the view of the external world, the second, whose object is human nature itself, the view of the inner world of man. The latter culminates in the certainty of a highest purpose which we serve, a highest power upon whom we depend: in this form it is *religious*. The view of the outer world, on the other hand, finds its definite objects and problems in the present world. The given world is humanity, in the development of which we are included; the material world, in which humanity lives, the all or the cosmos, in which this material world is comprehended. Humanity, the earth, the universe, are accordingly the objects comprehended in our view of the external world. We, therefore, distinguish in it three great departments of human culture, *the Historical, the Geographical,* and *the Cosmographical.* The object of the first is humanity in its development; that of the second, the earth as the dwelling-place of man; that of the third, the universe as the totality of material bodies. From these forms of our view of the outer world, we distinguish our inner religious consciousness as deeper than any of them. If we compare the modes of thought which prevailed in all these departments before the Reformation, with those which were accepted after it, the greatest changes are evident at the first glance. The human view of the world in all its departments, in all its essential conditions, appears fundamentally and completely transformed. This transformation is the Reformation.

1. THE NEW VIEW OF THE WORLD.

1. *The Historical View* — First of these, the historical view was greatly enlarged, and so transformed that the conception of humanity was freed from the limits by which its horizon was bounded in the Middle Ages. From the point of the Middle Ages, an impassable chasm lies between the pagan and the Christian world. There is an absolute opposition between

them, — an opposite which excludes all connection, and which the doctrine of Augustine had stamped deeply upon the consciousness of the Church. And just as profound were the darkness and ignorance of the Middle Ages with reference to antiquity and classic culture. The Church itself was interested in concealing the historical and human conditions of its development, that it might thereby promote faith in its divine origin. The Middle Ages had only as much knowledge of the human world and its history as the Church permitted, and with such knowledge a scientific historical view was impossible. The revival of classic learning broke through the barriers set by the Church; antiquity was discovered anew; the feeling of kinship with the spirit of its art and philosophy permeated and renovated the Western world, and in the admiration and imitation of these works of classic paganism, men felt their relationship, not merely with Christians, but with the whole human race. Their mode of thought became humanistic at the same time with their studies: art and philosophy followed in the same direction. A new, rich, and comprehensive idea of humanity unfolded itself: an abundance of problems to which no limit was set, and which could only be solved by historical investigation, forced their way into the field of scientific vision. We have already described the period and culture of the Renaissance in their fundamental characteristics, and mention them here, not merely as a transition to the Reformation, but as a constituent of the latter, taking the word in its widest sense. The Renaissance contained, the reformation of the historical view of the world.

2. *The Geographical View.* — The discovery of the *new* world in geography followed the discovery of the *old* in history. In consequence of the former, humanity learned more and more of its development; in consequence of the latter, of the heavenly body which it inhabits. There the knowledge of history, here that of the earth, was immeasurably extended. Even the Crusades, planned and carried on by

the ecclesiastical spirit of conquest, awakened the spirit of travel, which resulted in those first discoveries in the wonderful countries of the Orient. Then came the world-thirsty spirit of the Renaissance, — filled with the spirit of business, — which the Italian seaport cities particularly cultivated. It was no accident that the great Oriental travels were made by Venetians, and the epoch-making discovery itself by a son of Genoa.

In the second half of the thirteenth century, the elder Poli of Venice wandered over Eastern Asia. *Marco Polo*, their younger companion, who accompanied them on their second journey, made his home in China and India (1271–1295), and by the histories which he wrote earned for himself the title of "the Herodotus of the Middle Ages," at the time when the Crusades unsuccessfully ended, and Dante was beginning his career. The sea-route to India was then the great problem of commerce in the West, the solution of which was sought by the circumnavigation of Africa, or by a *transatlantic* voyage. This second thought, tearing itself away from the shores of the old world, was the boldest. If it succeeds, the epoch-making work is done.

If the greatest extent of Asia is from East to West, and if the earth is round, Eastern Asia must approach our portion of the earth from the West, and the smaller the surface of the earth, the closer Eastern Asia must be. Under these presuppositions, both of which are false, *Christopher Columbus* conceived and solved his problem. He had a firm belief in the Western world, and based it besides on some actual indications which were more certain than those assumptions. He discovered land in the West, supposing that he had reached India. Five years later, the Portuguese, *Vasco da Gama*, sailed around the southern cape of Africa, and completed the sea-route to India.

It must now be discovered that the world in the West is not Asia, but forms a continent by itself, separated from the eastern coast of Asia by an ocean. The next problems were the discovery of this ocean, the circumnavigation of America, the circumnavigation of the earth, the discovery, conquest, and colonization of the new continent. All this was done within a single generation. The Spaniard, *Balboa*, crossed the Isthmus of Darien, and discovered the Pacific Ocean (1513) · the Portuguese, *Fernando Magellan* (Magalhaens), sailed around the southern point of America, and discovered the southern ocean. To him belongs the fame of having begun, and made possible, the first circumnavigation of the earth, if he did not himself complete it. The Portuguese, *Cabral*, discovered Brazil (1500) ; *Fernando Cortez*, the greatest of the Spanish conquistadors, conquered Mexico (1519–21); Pizarro discovered and conquered Peru (1527–31). With the victorious wars of the English against Spain, in the time of Elizabeth, a new epoch in transatlantic life began. It consisted in the union between North America and England, in the beginnings of a colonial foundation of a state supported by German culture. *Francis Drake* was the first successful circumnavigator of the globe (1577–80) : some years later *Walter Raleigh* discovered the coasts of Virginia, and planted the first germs of the English North-American colonies.

All these achievements, each of which comprehended new problems, were conditional upon the discovery of Columbus: in it lay the reformation of the geographical view of the world.

3. *The Cosmographical View.* — After the historical view had become so enlarged as to include the whole human race and its history, and the geographical view had made room for the various continents and seas of the earth, but one further step remained, — the discovery of the earth itself in the universe, its place and position in the cosmos, the discovery of the earth among the stars! To the point of view of sense, which is the first, and for the consideration of the heavenly bodies, as it appears is the only possible one, the universe seems to be a sphere, whose arch is the firmament,

and whose fixed centre is the earth itself, about which the moon, the sun, and the planets revolve; between the moon and the sun, the two inferior planets, Mercury and Venus; beyond the sun, the three superior ones, Mars, Jupiter, and Saturn. Each of these heavenly bodies shares the daily revolution of the heavens, and has at the same time a sphere peculiar to itself (transparent to us, and therefore invisible), to which it is attached, and by whose motion the different revolutions of the planets are explained. This geocentric view of the world was the cosmography of the ancients, excepting the Pythagoreans, who, on dogmatic grounds, imagined a central fire in the middle of the universe, and, because of supposed properties of the number ten, maintained the existence of a counter-earth. On false presuppositions, they taught a system of the universe that was *not* geocentric, — a system containing data upon which, unsystematized and disconnected in antiquity, the heliocentric hypothesis was based. The Aristotelian doctrine of the world was based on the geocentric conception and the theory of the spheres. But the motions of the planets contradicted the doctrine of their circular, sphere-determined revolution; and since this was a fundamental part of the theory, the problem remained to account for their irregularities on the theory of the sphere. Finally the Alexandrine astronomer, Ptolemy, gave an ingenious and final solution, in the second century of the Christian era, in his work on the arrangement of the planetary system (Μεγάλη Σύνταξις, called "Almagest" in the Arabian translation). The planets move, as he taught, around the earth in circles, whose centres move on the periphery of another (deferent) circle. These circles are called epicycles, and the curve which the planet so describes, epicycloids. But 'the real path of the planets by no means coincides with the hypothetical. In very many cases, the observed place of the planet does not correspond with the calculated: the planet is not precisely where it ought to be, according to the geometrical construction. New contradic-

tions are constantly appearing between the actual course of
the planets and the theoretical, and new epicycles must constantly be added to set aside these contradictions. A distrust of the Ptolemaic doctrine arises in view of these facts
and the belief in the simplicity and regular course of nature.
It cannot be that nature acts so irregularly and intricately.
The doctrine cannot be true : it must make some false
fundamental presupposition. What is this? is now the
question.

Now, this entire conception is based on the presupposition
that the planets move about the earth, and that the earth is
in the centre of the universe. To get rid of epicycles, the
first of these two suppositions was abandoned : the planets
do not move about the earth. Their orbits are now related
to the sun, and the conception of these orbits is cleared up.
By the true distance of the planets, which the Danish
astronomer, Tycho de Brahe (1546–1601), calculated, it was
proved that the planets actually revolved around the sun.
The Ptolemaic system calculated the relation of the radii of
the epicycles to the radii of their deferents. Tycho calculates
the relation of the first to the radii of the orbits of the planets
about the sun, and found that the radii of the epicycles sustain exactly the same relation to the radii of the deferents
as to the radii of their orbits about the sun. In every
point of its epicycle, Mercury appears at an equal distance
from the sun ; Venus likewise. What is true of the inferior planets, is proved of the superior ones also. Of *all*
the planets, therefore, the sun forms the centre of its epicycles, or, what is the same thing, the deferent is the path
of the sun. In the Ptolemaic system, the centres of the
epicycles are empty : the sun now appears as this middle
point of the orbits of all the planets. In reference to the
sun, therefore, the orbits of the planets no longer appear
epicycloidal, but circular. The epicycles are analyzed : the
planets describe their orbit about the sun in the periphery
of their deferent. Under this presupposition, which annuls

the theory of epicycles, and thereby essentially changes the
Ptolemaic system, the centre of the cosmos is yet an open
question.   It is possible that the sun is the centre of the
orbits of the planets, and yet moves about the earth as
the cosmical centre.   If so, the second fundamental presupposition of the Ptolemaic system is true, and also the
ordinary and ecclesiastical conception.   Both these cases are
conceivable: the planets move about the sun, which itself
moves about the earth as the cosmical centre; or, the planets
move about the sun, which forms also the cosmical centre,
and what appears as motion of the sun is in truth the motion
of the earth, which is, therefore, no longer the motionless
centre of the universe, but a planet among planets.   The
sun and the earth change their places and their *rôles* in the
universe.   According to the one conception, the earth,
according to the other, the sun, is the cosmical centre.
That is the geocentric, this the heliocentric, hypothesis.
Tycho de Brahe defends the first; the German astronomer
and canon, *Nicholas Copernicus* (1473–1543), the second.
Both are distinguished from the Ptolemaic system, in that
they put the sun in the centre of the orbits of the planets;
but the system of Tycho shares with the Ptolemaic the
geocentric supposition; while the Copernican annuls this
also, and, therefore, subverts the old system in its principle.
The Copernican theory precedes that of Tycho, which, therefore, appears not as the preliminary stage of the Copernican,
but rather as an attempt to mediate between that theory and
the Ptolemaic hypothesis.   Copernicus's epoch-making work,
"On the Motions of the Heavenly Bodies," was published
shortly before his death (1543).

From the point of view of Copernicus, the cosmographical
view of the world is very simple and clear.   The conception
of sense is fundamentally denied, while it is explained in an
extremely evident manner.   The actual revolution of the
earth about its axis explains the apparent (daily) revolution
of the heavens: the actual motion of the earth about the

sun explains the apparent (yearly) motion of the sun about the earth, and likewise the apparent epicycloidal orbits of·the planets. This supposition immeasurably enlarges the conception of the universe. If the earth changes its place in space, why does not this change appear in relation to the fixed stars? In the two points of the earth's orbit which are most distant from each other, the axis of the earth points to the same stars. A change of place, therefore, equal to the diameter of the earth's orbit, i.e., to forty millions of miles, appears as nothing in relation to the fixed stars. The fixed stars must, therefore, appear infinitely distant; or, to speak according to the conception of the celestial globe, the diameter of the sphere of the fixed stars must appear infinitely great. This refutation of the Ptolemaic theory is likewise the completest refutation of the conception of sense (common sense), and is, therefore, an exceedingly instructive example for every department of human thought, — an example of which succeeding philosophy often avails itself. Kant gladly compared his work with that of Copernicus. For the fundamental error of all earlier astronomy lay exactly in this, that it was involved in a delusion concerning its own point of view, which it represented to itself, on the authority of the senses, as the motionless centre of the universe: now, the apparent motions of the heavenly bodies must be acknowledged as the actual, the appearances as real facts. The failure to reflect on one's own point of view and one's own procedure produces delusion. There is in this respect no grander and more instructive example than the history of astronomy.

The work of Copernicus was dedicated to Pope Paul III., and in the preface, written by Osiander, was represented as a mere hypothesis, though Copernicus himself was completely convinced of its truth. Tycho, with his re-affirmation of the geocentric doctrine, opposed this system; and so the new theory appeared uncertain, and in a position exposed to scientific attack. The next work, therefore, was so to ground the Copernican theory by a series of new proofs, that its truth should be put beyond scientific question, and Tycho's counter-assumption be deprived of all force. This was done by *Galileo Galilei* of Pisa (1564–1642), one of the greatest natural philosophers of all times, in whom the Italian Renaissance rendered its highest service, and produced a reformer of science. While he was professor in Pisa (1587–92), he reformed the doctrine of motion by discovering the laws of projectiles and falling bodies. The same force of gravity (centripetal force) which attracts bodies on the surface of the earth towards its middle point, attracts the earth towards the sun, and causes its revolution in connection with the force of impetus or projection (centrifugal force) exerted at the same time. The knowledge of this truth must have convinced Galileo of the truth of the heliocentric doctrine, even before he made in Padua (1592–1610) his great astronomical discoveries. In the year 1597, he declared, in a letter to Kepler, that he had been for many years a disciple of Copernicus. The Aristotelian doctrine of the unchangeableness of the heavens (the firmament) was overthrown when Galileo observed the appearance and the vanishing of a star in Ophiuchus (1604). With the aid of the telescope, which he improved after it had been invented, and first applied to the examination of the heavenly bodies, he made in the year 1610 those wonderful discoveries which completely established the truth of the heliocentric system. He discovered the resemblance of the moon to the earth, the satellites of Jupiter, the rings of Saturn, the changing phases of light of Venus and Mercury, similar to those of the moon, and, finally, the spots on the sun and their motion, from which he inferred the revolution of the sun about its axis. The sun is the centre of the planetary system, not the motionless and absolute centre of the universe. The universe is immeasurable in extent. The imagined vault of the heavens falls down as the spirits of knowledge cry out, " Vanish, ye dark vaults of heaven ! "

Galileo's telescopic discoveries are pure triumphs of the

Copernican system. If Copernicus was right, his opponents had replied, the inferior planets must exhibit phases of light similar to those of the moon. Since the effect does not exist, neither can the cause. Galileo discovered the phases of Venus, and silenced his opponents.

There are still in the Copernican doctrine, problems to be solved, and conceptions to be corrected. It represents the planets as revolving in circular orbits about the sun, and with this view still maintains the theory of the spheres of the ancients. But the actual, correctly observed motion of the planets is not uniform: they move, now more rapidly, now more slowly; and this changing velocity depends upon their distance from the sun. The sun, therefore, is not in the centre of their orbits, and their orbits are not perfect circles. The next problem, accordingly, is to find the form and the law of these orbits. The motion of the planets must in like manner be in harmony with law: there must be a definite relation between the time of their motion, and the space through which it extends. To find this relation, is the second problem. The times of the revolution of the planets are different: the farther they are from the sun, the longer the time of revolution. The length of the period of revolution depends upon the greatness of their distance, and between them a definite relation must exist: to find this, is the third problem. When these laws are discovered, the harmony of the world which the Pythagoreans once sought is actually discovered in its true figures and numbers. These problems were solved by *John Kepler*, the German astronomer and mathematician of Weil in Würtemberg (1571–1630), Galileo's contemporary, admirer, and friend. His first discovered law explains the form of the orbits of the planets as an ellipse, in one of the foci of which lies the centre of the sun. His second law defines the relation between the spaces and times of the motion of the planets: a straight line from the centre of the planets to the centre of the sun (*radius victor*) describes equal areas in equal times. The third law defines the relation of the time of revolution of the planet to its distance from the sun: the squares of the times of revolution around the sun are as the cubes of their mean distances from it. Kepler's laws rest on his observation of the planet Mars, which he published in his important work, "Nova astronomia" (1609). But one problem remained to be solved, in order to complete the first epoch of modern astronomy. The laws which Kepler discovered by observation and induction must be derived or deduced from *one* principle, which Galileo had already apprehended. *Isaac Newton* (1642–1727), the greatest mathematician of England, solved this problem by discovering the law of universal gravitation.

As the transatlantic discoveries were conditional upon the achievement of Columbus, so Copernicus furnished the point of departure for those astronomic discoveries which ground the new view of the universe.

4. *Inventions.* — The spirit of invention goes hand in hand with the spirit of discovery. New inventions of the greatest importance were made, in part accompanying and supporting the great discoveries, in part following and promoted by them. The literary discoveries which diffused the light of antiquity over the world were accompanied by the art of printing; the transatlantic discoveries would have been impossible without the compass; new instruments, both of observation and calculation, were required for further progress in astronomical discoveries. There are no inventions of more importance in scientific investigations than the telescope and microscope, neither of which was invented by Galileo himself, though he reconstructed and improved both. For the calculations used by science, there are three mathematical discoveries of the greatest importance: viz., logarithms, by means of which great calculations are simplified and facilitated; analytical geometry, — discovered by Descartes contemporaneously with modern philosophy, — by which geometrical problems are solved by calculations;

the higher analysis, or infinitesimal calculus, — discovered by Newton and Leibnitz, — by which the variations of quantities are subjected to the calculus.

II. THE CONFLICT BETWEEN THE CHURCH AND SCIENCE.

1. *Trial of Galileo.* — Wherever the Reformation overthrew the barriers of ecclesiastical conceptions, the opposition between the old and new theory of the world was manifest; but nowhere else was it so strong as in the transformation of all the old conceptions of heaven and earth, for which a modern Archimides had actually found a fulcrum. And nowhere else had the Church so many and so powerful allies as in the maintenance of the limited and geocentric universe, for which both the senses and the authorities of antiquity bear testimony. The interest of the faith of the Church is here united in the closest manner with the Aristotelian and Ptolemaic system. The two fit each other as scene and action: the earth, the centre of the world; the appearance of God upon the earth; the Church, the *civitas dei* on earth, the centre of humanity; hell under the earth, heaven above it; the damned in hell, the saved in heaven beyond the stars, where the orders of the heavenly hierarchy ascend to the throne of God! This whole structure of limited and local conceptions totters and tumbles as soon as the earth ceases to be the centre of the universe, and heaven its dome. There are indeed far deeper conceptions of heaven and hell, grounded in the Christian religion, and guaranteed by mysticism, than those; but the latter were the home, if I may so speak, of the ecclesiastical consciousness of the Middle Ages — with its conviction of the supremacy of the Church — and of the faith of ecclesiastical people; and that consciousness and faith could not be separated from them. There is in this point, therefore, a comprehensive, fundamental opposition between the ecclesiastical and Copernican systems, — an opposition which could not be concealed, which could not but be evident to the world, and which appeared the more serious

in view of the characters of the founders of the modern view.
They were not freethinkers, like Bruno and Vanini, chal-
lenging the Church; they were her obedient sons, and
desired nothing less than to injure her, though they were
at the same time entirely devoted to science; they merely
sought to explain, and actually did explain, universally
known, enigmatical facts, which were incomprehensible from
the old stand-point.   The suit which the Roman Inquisition
brought against the Copernican system, in the person of
Galileo, is a lasting and memorable monument of this collision between ecclesiastical policy and scientific inquiry.
It occurred in the beginnings of modern philosophy, and, as
we shall see, exercised a momentous influence upon it.

In his controversy with the Jesuits concerning the discovery and explanation of the spots on the sun (1613),
Galileo had for the first time *publicly* declared his belief in
the Copernican doctrine, and thereby so excited the anger
of the monastic orders, that he became an object of suspicion
to the Inquisition, whose attention had already been directed
to him.   The Copernican system, which had been propagated for seventy years, and permitted as an hypothesis, was,
at the command of Paul V., examined and rejected by the
theologians of the holy office, who were acquainted with
the subject.   The heliocentric doctrine must be regarded
as contrary to reason and heretical; the non-geocentric as
contrary to reason and erroneous.   This decree was published Feb. 24, 1616.   On the following day, Cardinal Bellarmin received papal instructions to admonish Galileo, who
was then in Rome, to abandon the Copernican doctrine.   If
he refused, the Inquisition must proceed against him.   Galileo at once submitted (Feb. 26).   No further inquisitorial
action was therefore necessary, no formal, specific prohibition.   That this was the disposition of the matter and the
nature of Galileo's acquittal, is proved beyond doubt by
the papal instructions to Bellarmin, Feb. 25; the report of
the latter in the session of the Holy Office, March 3; the testi-

monial given to Galileo by Bellarmin, May 26; and, finally, by expressions of Galileo himself in letters written at this time. March 5, 1616, by a decree relating to the Copernican theory, issued by the Congregation of the Index, the writings which maintained the truth of that doctrine were entirely forbidden; others provisionally, until they were corrected. The latter denoted those which, after the correction of certain passages, represented the Copernican view, not as truth, but as an hypothesis. Among these was the work of Copernicus himself. It cannot be doubted, therefore, that, after those proceedings relating to Galileo in the spring of 1616, the Copernican theory was still tolerated as a mathematical hypothesis. To gain a wider privilege, — the privilege of proving and defending the heliocentric system as such, — Galileo labored in vain during another stay in Rome (1624), notwithstanding the fact that Urban VIII. was favorably disposed towards him. In the mean time, by a second irritating polemic against one of the Jesuit fathers (1618), he had increased the number of his enemies who wished to destroy him. The wished-for opportunity came. In the year 1632, there appeared with the papal license, "Galileo's Dialogue Concerning the Two Most Important Systems of the World, the Ptolemaic and Copernican." Its form as a dialogue held the matter within the tolerated limits of hypothetical treatment. The title expressly declared that no decision was intended to be given, that only the grounds for each of the theories were to be set forth. But certainly no capable man could doubt on which side the weight of argument lay, according to this dialogue. But a condemnation of Galileo by the Inquisition was only possible if *every* kind of exposition of the Copernican had been formally forbidden to him personally. Such a special prohibition did not exist, and in the position of affairs was impossible. But a means was found of avoiding this difficulty. The prohibition by means of which alone the wished-for condemnation could take place, was forged by his enemies; and the official report of facts of Feb. 26, 1616, was falsified, to bring it in harmony with this forgery. On this forgery, undiscovered until the most recent times, though now proved, rested the unprecedented suit which ended with Galileo's condemnation.[1] June 22, 1633, almost seventy years old, he was obliged to renounce and forswear the Copernican system, in the Church of the Dominicans, Maria sopra Minerva, in Rome. He remained a prisoner until his death, if not in the dungeons of the Inquisition, at least in their power and under their eyes. He was neither imprisoned, nor tortured on the rack; and he was far from retracting his retraction. "But it moves, for all that!" Galileo may have thought; but he certainly did not say it. He suffered every thing patiently, that he might be able to return to the freedom of his thoughts and investigations, which he rightly valued more highly than such a martyrdom. The Romish Church could not forbid the motion of the earth: instead of that, it has put the works of Copernicus and Galileo on its Index, and let them stand there more than two hundred years.

III. THE RELIGIOUS REFORMATION.

1. *Protestantism.* — But however complete the transformation of men's conceptions in the departments of history, geography, and astronomy, — transformations which freed the horizon of man from its limits, and extended it immeasurably, — they would have been insufficient of themselves to introduce a new principle of life into the development of humanity, and make a world-epoch in the comprehensive sense of the term. These reformatory achievements bore their fruits in art and science; i.e., on heights of human culture which in the most cultured ages are accessible only to a few. They can prosper without making a fundamental change in the feelings and education of humanity. The

---

[1] Galileo Galilei and the Romish Curia. According to the authentic sources by Karl von Gebler (Stuttg. Cotta, 1876). Concerning the forgery and the history of its discovery, cf. pp. 95–112.

Church promoted the Renaissance. Generally speaking, the Renaissance was indeed within the pale of the Church, and would have composed its differences, come to terms, with it. It was not the infidelity of the clearing-up period, contented with its enjoyment of culture, which the Church had to fear. It was weak in comparison with the Church because of its numbers, its need of undisturbed leisure, and its indifference to matters of faith. Even the heroes of the reformation of science, the great discoverers, like Columbus, Copernicus, and Galileo, were loyal sons of the Church, who never entertained the idea of breaking with it. The united culture of the Renaissance was incapable of shaking the foundations of the ecclesiastical rule of the world so powerfully as to destroy it.

The Church rests on religious foundations, and rules people through its hierarchical constitution. Only, therefore, by means of *religious* motives which relate to those principles, and force their way into the hearts of people, can the decisive attack be made against the Church. To move the world, the fulcrum must be sought without it. It is otherwise with the Church: he who would overthrow the authority of the Church, and transform the foundations of its faith, must take his stand within it, and, indeed, in the very depths of its faith. This transformation and renovation of the religious consciousness is the *Reformation* in the ecclesiastical sense, without which, the Middle Ages, in spite of all discoveries, would have lived on.

As little as the Church accidentally and suddenly assumed the form of the hierarchy and the Roman papacy, as little did the Reformation accidentally and suddenly appear in opposition to it. It came from the Church itself, in which it gradually matured. There never was an ecclesiastical age without reformatory emotions and desires. Always in the midst of the secularization occasioned by the progress of human affairs, the Church has felt the desire, natural to it because of its Christian spirit, for spiritualization and purification. But the direction in which the reform was sought, varied with the period. To free Christian life from the entanglements of the world, and to alienate it therefrom, the monastic orders of the first centuries arose. To free the ecclesiastical hierarchical state from the bonds of feudalism, Gregory VII. appeared as a reformer of the hierarchy. When the Roman ecclesiastical rule of the world had reached its height, Innocent III. saw the unity of faith threatened by an invasion of heretics, who even then opposed the Gospel to the Church; and he declared the urgent necessity for a reformation of the laity, in reference to ecclesiastical faith. When, finally, the unity of ecclesiastical rule in the papacy itself was destroyed by the schism, the councils of the fifteenth century came with the problem to reform the Church in its head and members. The problem remained unsolved and insoluble. It was impossible to restore the Church by the reformation of the papacy, and the repression of that anti-hierarchical tendency. This impossibility could not have been more glaringly shown than by the flames of the stake, at which the reformatory council of Constance burnt *Huss*. The flames in which he perished, illuminated for the Reformation the road from Constance to Wittenberg. Since it could not come from above, it must come from below, reaching its crisis in *Luther*, when the times were ripe, a hundred years after the death of Huss.

The Reformation of the sixteenth century based the opposition of religion to the Church on the foundation of Christianity. This opposition, which, on religious grounds, attacked the system of the Church all along the lines, we call Protestantism — using the term in a wider sense than its historical origin suggests. Negatively, it consists in the denial of Roman Catholicism; positively, in the ground of faith on which it rests, without which it never would have become a religious power. The principle of Protestantism, what it affirms, is evident from what it denies. The religion of the Middle Ages consists in faith in the Church as a divine and infallible authority, in the *obedience of faith*, which believes what the Church teaches, and does what it commands, which, like all other obedience, has to prove itself by external works. The ideal of this faith is ecclesiastical activity, the performance of the duties of worship, and of actions agreeable and serviceable to the Church. He who does more in the service of the Church than she requires, acts meritoriously. Believers are justified in the eyes of the Church, and therefore before God, by meritorious works. — works done in obedience to the Church. This obedience of faith consists, therefore, in faith in justification by cultus and by works. That is faith in the doctrine of salvation by works which regards human actions as meritorious, and, therefore, concedes and affirms human freedom. The external work is independent of the temper of mind in which it is done ; it is " *opus operatum ;* " and from the point of view of the Church, we can understand why it makes its supremacy independent of the dispositions of individuals, and, therefore, regards obedience to the Church as the characteristic and essence of piety. Now the guilt of sin stands between man and God ; and this can be blotted out only by complying with the ordinances of the Church, by confession and penance ; it can be atoned for only by ecclesiastical penalties, the duration of which is proportioned to . the sin, and may even extend into the world beyond. There are many kinds of ecclesiastical and pious works ; and since the Church determines their worth with a view to her own interests, it is in her power to set one off against the other, for one external work to substitute another of a different character, to accept an equivalent for penance that may shorten its duration, or even atone for the sin altogether. A fine that enriches the Church may even be such an equivalent. Now, if penance, the condition of forgiveness of sin, is sold for gold, forgiveness of sin itself is also sold. But, if penance is once made a matter of ecclesiastical exchange,

there is nothing to hinder the acceptance of a fine as an
equivalent for the sake of the need of the Church. Thus the
system of *indulgences* arose, for which the additional justification by dogma was not wanting as a necessary consequence
of faith in justification by works. Since there are in the
Church so many whose penances more than counterbalance
their sin, so there may also be those who sin more than they
do penance, and make good the deficit by money. If the
surplus of the penance of saints is for this cause transferred
to the account of sinners, the deficit in their penance is
made good.

The system of indulgences makes perfectly evident the
absolute opposition between the Church and religion. Religion requires deep repentance — a repentance that wrings
and transforms the heart — as the condition of forgiveness of
sins: the Church accepts money as an equivalent for repentance! It was here that a religious re-action set in against
the system of the Church. The Reformation began with the
thesis which Luther posted on the door of the church in
Wittenberg (Oct. 31, 1517), since it was the cause of religion against the Church. If it was at first only the misuse
of indulgence which Luther attacked in his theses, — he condemned it as a means of eternal salvation, not as a substitute
for ecclesiastical punishment, — the earnestness of his religious nature compelled him to go on unceasingly. For the
system of indulgences is no accidental abuse: it follows
naturally from the doctrine of the holiness of works, as the
latter does from the obedience of faith required by the absolute authority of the Church, which is independent of
motives and dispositions. And Luther's motive was his
anxiety for the salvation of the human soul, to which the
Romish Church had been unfaithful. This motive urged
him on. He soon rejected the dogmatic ground of indulgence, the doctrine of works of supererogation, faith in saints,
the confession of individual sins as though they were numer-
able. He denied the doctrine of salvation by works in prin-

ciple, and, therefore, attacked its foundation; viz., the hierarchical system of the Church, the primacy of the pope, the infallibility of councils. The final and necessary result was, that he disputed the authority of the Church in matters of faith, therefore the duty of the obedience of faith, and declared, for the sake of religion, the freedom of faith. Then the Reformation was in its element; it appeared, in comparison with the Catholic Church, as the religious work of revived Christianity; in comparison with *Roman* Catholicism, as the national work of the German people. This position, which Luther's epoch-making writings on the Lord's Supper, the captivity of the Church, and the improvement of the Christian state, set forth, was won by the strong man through severe struggles, since the yoke that he shook off was his own, and it pressed heavily upon his conscience.

What Protestantism denies, accordingly, is *justification by works*. No work has a power to atone for sin: every work, however holy it may seem, may be a mere "*opus operatum*," done in a merely outward mechanical way without any feeling whatever, and, as such, is of no avail for salvation — is rather injurious to it because of the trust falsely reposed in it. All ecclesiastical works — even the most thorough renunciation of the world — may be strictly performed without effecting any change in the inner man. Such works, therefore, have no religious value. Religion consists in moral regeneration, in that transformation of the heart which consists in faith, — in faith in justification, not by the Church, but by Christ. The affirmation of Protestantism is, "*Salvation is by faith alone*." This faith is not a work which human free-will can do or deserve, but an act of divine grace which takes hold of man without regard to the dogmas of the Church, which are the works of man. Thus, the Reformation returned to the sources of Christian faith and Christian doctrine, that it might restore Christianity itself from its primary conditions. In opposition to the dogmas of the Church, it rests on the *Holy Scriptures* as the records of the revelation of God; on the doctrines of the apostles, particularly of *Paul*, who first threw off the yoke of the law, and rejected the works of the law, and proclaimed justification by faith; on the doctrines of the Fathers of the Church, particularly of *Augustine*, who first turned a blaze of light upon human guilt in all its extent as the work, and, at the same time, the loss of freedom, and put it in the very centre of the doctrine of the Church — that inalienable guilt, clinging to the very core of human nature, which the Church had made salable! Not the offering of gold, but the sacrifice of the human heart and its selfishness, leads to salvation. That was the theme of that "German Theology," which Luther, for this very reason, prized next to the Bible and Augustine. Every one must make an offering of himself, of his own sinful heart: therein consists the universal priesthood of Christians in opposition to the consecratory priesthood of the Church and the sacrificial priesthood of the sacrament. From this point of view, we see why the reformers opposed the hierarchy and its exaltation in the cultus of the Church, particularly the Lord's Supper; why they transformed the doctrine of the sacraments, especially of the Lord's Supper. This explains why the purification and simplification of cultus was a principal object of the Reformation, one of its essential problems, its starting-point, indeed, where it felt most simply and strongly. The real home of the religion of a people is cultus, and this culminates in the Lord's Supper.

The transformation, therefore, of the doctrine of the Lord's Supper is the most immediate and effective transformation of the religious life of a people.

We have the fundamental facts before us which Protestantism affirmed, — the facts in which the great reformers, *Luther, Zwingle, Calvin,* were agreed; viz., faith in the Scriptures, belief in the teachings of Paul and Augustine, the purification of the cultus of the Church, the transformation of the doctrine of the sacrament. Differences arose within the doctrine of Augustine concerning *predestination*, within that of the sacrament of the Lord's Supper concerning *the real presence of Christ*. Calvin maintained the doctrine of predestination and election, in all its hardness and logical rigor, which even Augustine had not ventured to do. Zwingle denied every kind of mystical or magical transubstantiation, maintaining that the sacrament is purely symbolic. In spite of the conflict which urgently enjoined union against the common enemy, these differences were not composed, and Protestantism was divided in the period of the Reformation into the *Lutheran* and *Reformed* creeds.

The Renaissance began before the Reformation, and also was contemporary with it. The revival of learning, of studies in Greek and Hebrew, necessarily led to new and clearer views concerning the origin of Christianity, to a new and better understanding of the Bible, and therewith to conclusions which the Reformation required for the investigation of history and the Scriptures. It owed its scientific equipment to the Renaissance. When the rising German Reformation, and the German Renaissance, which came from Italy, were at the same time in full bloom, there was a moment when each availed itself of the other, in the clear consciousness of their common origin, and their common national exaltation. The spirit of the new period affected men's minds very powerfully. The regeneration of Christianity wished to go hand in hand with that of antiquity, and that of the German people and empire with both. The scientific and religious Reformation sought to be national and political also. This idea found an expounder in *Ulrich von Hutten*, and was powerfully stated in his last writings (1519–23). But the political Reformation necessarily failed, since the religious Reformation made a deeper chasm in the German Empire than ever before. Moreover, the Reformation and the Renaissance came in conflict. That intellectual aristocracy which wished to live and shine in the quiet enjoyment of the high culture of antiquity, was incompatible with

the revolutionary tumults of people whom the Reformation
had unshackled.   The doctrines of ancient philosophy, —
affirming the freedom of the will, — which the Renaissance
had revived, were inconsistent with the Augustinianism of
Luther's doctrine, that man is completely destitute of freedom.   This opposition between the Renaissance and the
Reformation was embodied with typical completeness in the
controversy between Erasmus and Luther.   But the ideas
of religion were very powerful in that period, and even led
the spirits of the Renaissance into their service.   From this
side came Zwingle, with his simple and natural conception
of the Lord's Supper, which Luther rejected with the characteristic expression, " We have a different spirit from yours!"
But even among the German reformers, there was one who
combined both tendencies, Melanchthon, — who received his
training from the Renaissance, and entered into the service
of the German Reformation, — a kinsman and disciple of
Reuchlin, Luther's associate, nearest friend, and helper.   He
combined the religious and liberal spirit of the Renaissance,
and was able to endure contrasts offensive to Luther, being
inclined to certain compromises between Catholicism and
Protestantism, between the Lutheran and the Reformed tendencies.   Lutheranism would not tolerate these compromises.
After it became dogmatically fixed in the Augsburg confession (1530) ; after it was more narrowly and inflexibly
developed through the settlement of religious differences at
Augsburg (1555) ; finally, after the adoption of the forms
of concord made impossible any compromise with the reformed branch of Protestantism, and destroyed the work of
Melanchthon, — German Protestantism also split into the
Lutheran and Dutch-reformed Churches ; and that ecclesias-
tical-political division of Germany, which paved the way for
the Thirty Years' War, was completed.

The Reformation was not responsible for the political disintegration of Germany, though it did indeed promote it
and increase it.   This consequence was so necessary and

unavoidable, that it affords no ground for reproach. Without
the disintegrated and decentralized Romish Empire of the
German nation, the Reformation would never have been possible, as the Romish Church would not have been possible
without the centralized power of the ancient Roman Empire,
nor the Renaissance without the division and decentralization of Italy. It was not an accident, but an historical necessity in the condition of affairs that then existed, that the
Reformation arose in Germany and Switzerland. Its central
points were Wittenberg, Zurich, and Geneva. Luther was
the leader of the German Reformation in Wittenberg (1517–
1546), Zwingle of the Swiss in Zurich (1519–1531), and
Calvin in Geneva (1541–1564). In the course of the sixteenth century, the Reformation spread from these points
over Europe, and became a great historical power. The
Scandinavian State Church was modelled after the Lutheran
(1527–37), those of Scotland (under Knox, 1556–73) and the
Netherlands after the Reformed (Calvinistic). The Netherlands won their political and religious freedom by a war with
Spain (1566–1609). In England, the Reformed Episcopal
State Church took the place of the Romish (1534–71); in
Italy, the Reformation fermented in isolated phenomena; in
Spain, the fermentation was checked; in France, it produced
the religious civil wars.

2. *The Counter-Reformation and Jesuitism.* — Through the
Reformation the opposition between Protestantism and Catholicism in Western Christianity arose, based on principles
which make compromise impossible. Protestantism denies
the authority of the Church. Its basis is the opinions and
convictions of individuals, who, by their agreement, form
congregations, but do not grant that unconditional authority
which alone constitutes the power of the Church. Hence
the unity of Protestantism in its opposition to Catholicism,
and its divisions as regards itself, which latter appear as
weaknesses in comparison with the Catholic Church. It was,
therefore, the interest and the policy of the Romish Church

to strengthen its unity and authority anew against Protestantism, and, by setting aside certain abuses, to forever exclude from itself, by solemn anathemas, all the motives, which, in its eyes, had made faith weak, and given it a disposition to revolt. This formal denial and condemnation of Protestantism became the theme of the counter-Reformation which the *Council of Trent* accomplished (1545–1563), — the last ecumenical council but one.

But the principle of Catholicism was not satisfied by the simple condemnation of Protestantism : it required the destruction of the enemy, the reconquest of apostate nations, the restoration of the Church of the Middle Ages. A new equipment and organization of ecclesiastical powers were required for the solution of this problem, the first step in which was a conflict with the Reformation. A new order of the Church, devoted to this special purpose, was necessary ; and this was founded (1534) by *Ignatius von Loyola* (1491–1556) in the " Society," or, to use the characteristic and martial title, " Company," of Jesus, which first received the papal sanction in 1540. If the religious objects of the Romish Church are identical with their political ends, that is, the preservation and increase of their power in the world, Jesuitism is identical with Roman Catholicism, and is, as it were, the principle of which the ultramontane system is the result. Two tendencies, so fundamentally different in principle that one would never combine them in thought, were united in the spirit of the order of the Jesuits; viz., the most enthusiastic readiness to sacrifice themselves for an ideal of the past, the restoration of the Church of the Middle Ages, — and that, too, *after* the Renaissance and the Reformation, — and the most far-seeing policy, thoroughly acquainted with all the questions of the present, with every change in the condition of affairs, with every means that promotes power, and at the same time skilled and resolute in their application, and systematic in their combination ! Who would have thought that the dreamy enthusiasm of a

Don Quixote, and the policy of a *Macchiavelli*, could be
united in a common cause?   They were united in the order
of the Jesuits.   Never in the history of the world has the
spirit of Macchiavelli, although hostile to the Church, manifested itself more powerfully, more effectively, more fearfully,
than in the order of the Jesuits, whose sole purpose was to
advance the cause, and increase the power, of the Church.
Jesuitism is *ecclesiastical Macchiavellism.*   And perhaps no
man ever lived who was so much like Don Quixote as his
countryman, Ignatius von Loyola, the founder of the Jesuits,
who first turned from the romances of chivalry to the legends
of saints, from Amadis to Franciscus, and then, before the
picture of Mary on Montserrat, held his nightly watch, as
the knight of La Mancha had done in that village tap-house,
which was to him a knightly castle.   Without that enthusiasm
for the past, ravished by the pictures of the saints of the
Middle Ages, the idea of the order of the Jesuits would
never have suggested itself.   Before Ignatius von Loyola
became a soldier of Jesus, he had vowed to become a knight
of Mary.   It was in the same year that Luther appeared
before the Diet of Worms.   The new order sprang into existence at the same time with Protestantism, and, as the
Company of Jesus, was firmly organized in opposition to its
enemy.

The Church was in danger: it could be rescued, and restored to its old power, only by the unconditional acceptance
of its central authority, by the permanent dictatorship of
the Pope.   Hence unconditional and blind submission to the
will of the Pope, that obedience which is equivalent to military subordination, was the peculiar vow of the Jesuits,
which, in connection with the three customary vows of
chastity, poverty, and obedience, constituted the specific
character of these new monks.   The world which they intended to fight and conquer could not be overcome by re-
treating into a cloister, but only by the most influential life
in the very midst of the world, interested in all that interests

men. In the order of the Jesuits, two characters were united
which elsewhere have always been separate ; viz., the *monk*
and the *man of the world*, the former, in the most inflexible,
the latter, in the most pliant, form. This union, which
marks an entirely new stage in the history of monks, existed
for the exclusive service of the Romish-monarchical Church,
which sent out the disciples of Loyola against unbelievers,
particularly against Protestants, with the injunction, " Go
ye into all the world." As once the Jewish-Christian legends
represented Peter as following the hated apostle, who bore
Christianity to the heathens, step by step, that he might
destroy his work, so these new followers of Peter were appointed to pursue the hated Reformation — this new Paulin-
ism — everywhere, and to undermine it. Their activity in
their character of men of the world was much more powerful in attaining the ends of the Church than the exercises of
ordinary monks, which robbed them of time and strength.
Hence the Jesuits were not required to perform those ascetic
and ceremonial duties which regulate the unoccupied life of
monks.

We have seen that unconditional, instant obedience constitutes the particular purpose of the order and the vow
of the real professed (*professi quatuor votorum*). Corresponding to this was the strictest subordination and gradation in the constitution of the order. It rose from novices
to scholastics, to their worldly and spiritual coadjutors, to
the professors of the three vows, to those of the fourth who
are their real missionaries, and reached its head in the general who ruled the great order divided into colleges, provinces,
and countries. *One* purpose animated every member, producing that uniform and trained type which showed cool,
measured reserve and a winning self-possession in the play
of the features and the expression of the countenance. The
duties of the order enjoined the wisdom of the serpent, which,
in this case, was incompatible with the harmlessness of a
dove. The conversion of heathen nations, which even the

first Jesuits undertook in India, China, and Brazil, formed the foreign part of their mission. At home their effort was to rule over Christian nations. They sought to accomplish this end by the employment of three means, — cultus, education, and the governing of States, — and they were successful. Since the most imposing, splendid, pictorial cultus is the most national, they did all in their power to enlarge and enrich cultus in this direction. Even their art was characterized by rich, overladen gorgeousness, lacking in taste, though it pleased the people. It lay entirely in their interest to favor dogmas relating to cultus, to enlarge the cultus of Mary, and, in the doctrine of immaculate conception, to make common cause with the Franciscans. To be a knight of Mary was the first ideal of their founder! That the doctrine of the infallibility of the pope became a formal dogma of the order, was the immediate result of their principles. To promote the interests of the Church, they adapted their pedagogical system to the cultivation of common people, of people of the world, of scholars, of theologians and preachers, and so fitted it to the needs of the time that even their enemies acknowledged their schools as typical institutions of learning. Through their power over the people, they gained power over the State. For the power of the State rests on the people, as the power of the Church rests on God. The monarchy of the Church (papacy) is an emanation from the divine absolute power, and is, therefore, absolute and unchangeable. Secular empires, on the contrary, rest on the *sovereignty of the people*, and, therefore, are just only so long as they promote the well-being of the people, which is inseparable from the welfare of the Church. Since the Church could not then control the State directly, it had to do it *indirectly* by means of the people, who were absolutely dependent in spiritual matters, and sovereign in political affairs. Hence the Jesuits were the first to proclaim the sovereignty of the people, by means of which princes could be dethroned ; and they had to be dethroned, if, by apostasy from, or disobedience to, the Church, they were unfaithful to the cause of the people. Such an apostasy or disobedience converted princes into tyrants. The same Jesuits, who, in Catholic and orthodox courts, were the aristocratic educators and father-confessors of princes, were revolutionists in the country of apostate or suspected princes, who taught the duty of killing tyrants, and not only caused it to be done, but glorified it. Thus, the Jesuit Mariana praised the murderer of Henry III. in his work on royalty (1598). They taught, that when a prince becomes an apostate, i.e., a tyrant, his people have not merely the right, but the duty, to revolt from him.

The Jesuits were not content with weakening Protestantism through their influence upon cultus, education, and the State: they placed their lever still deeper, and sought to overturn and destroy the very foundations of Protestantism. The doctrine of justification by faith and grace rests on the terribleness of human guilt, on that Augustinian doctrine of original sin, which deprived man of freedom, and made him the slave of his selfishness. To get this cardinal point of the Protestant creed out of the way, and to completely obscure it in the thoughts of men, was the real object of the *Jesuit Morals*, which we only rightly understand when we so conceive its origin and purpose. The more earnestly Protestantism conceived the guilt of sin, and felt it as the ground of anguish of conscience, — this was the source of the Reformation, — so much the less stress did the Jesuits lay upon it. The Protestant doctrine of faith and grace is, in their opinion, a great noise about nothing! Protestants have conceived sin much too mystically and tragically. When it is simply and intelligently considered, it is not such a terrible matter: it does not consist in a mystical guilt of the race, which corrupted every one at once and forever, but in single actions, each of which requires to be considered and judged in its circumstances and intentions. Thus, sin is casuistically conceived, and its importance very greatly diminished. The compact mass of guilt which presses man to the earth, is pulverized, as it were. In their doctrine of Morals, the Jesuits were the most pronounced individualists. The entire object of their system was to make sin a trifling matter, by analyzing the fall of sin into individual falls. Hence their *casuistry*, which finds contradictions everywhere, and transforms scruples into problems of conscience, the solution of which first decides whether man has sinned, or not. When conscience begins to refine, it ceases to judge. To weaken its office as judge, the keenness of casuistry interposes, of which the Jesuits make a great display. In every single action, the purpose must first of all be examined. Who will condemn a purpose, the motive of which is, or may be, the attainment of a worthy end, or the opinion of an approved authority? When the motives of an action are in this way made probable, and transformed into grounds of excuse or approbation, it is in good part justified. Hence the importance of *probability* in the Jesuit Morals. Probability is the art of making conscience a calculation of probabilities, and such a one, indeed, as diminishes the probability of sinful motives. Now, every purpose is, according to its nature, internal: we must, therefore, distinguish between the professed and real purpose, upon which last alone the sinfulness of an action depends. In consequence of secret reserve (the so-called reservation, or restriction), an action may indeed be inconsistent with the professed, but conformable to the true, purpose, and thereby justified. Reservation is the art of excluding wicked motives from actions, or, more correctly, from the judgment concerning them. The greater the sin, the more improbable the assumption that it was committed with perfect clearness of knowledge, and with the purpose of sinning. Hence the greater the sin, the less becomes its probability, so that mortal sins finally become so highly improbable as to be practically impossible. In this way, one brings his purposes entirely under his will: he can bend them, or let them be bent, by reasons of probability and reservations, entirely according to his convenience. It is as easy, with the help of such a system of morals, to get rid of sin, as it appears difficult, according to it, even to sin at all. The freedom not to sin, which, according to Augustine and the reformers, man completely lost, the Jesuits restored to him in full measure; and they laid great emphasis upon Pelagianism in the doctrine of the natural freedom of man.

The moral worth of actions is not, accordingly, determined by the actual disposition and intention, as they seem to be, but by *judgment* concerning such disposition and intention. But the Church is the judge; and the whole Morals of the Jesuits was used, and was intended to be used, as an anti-reformatory instrument and means of power in their hands. The reformers made the Church dismal and unendurable to the sinner with their doctrine of the value of works: the Jesuits made it more comfortable and easy than it had ever been before. After sins have been transformed into pardonable weaknesses, forgiveness itself remains; but it can be bestowed by the Church only after the performance of sacramental duties, otherwise the sin remains unforgiven and condemned. The more frequently one sins, the oftener he must confess; and it is scarcely necessary to say, that, with the Jesuitical confessors, absolution from sin was as simple and light a matter as sin itself. Forgiveness depends merely upon obedience to the Church, upon the strict performance of ecclesiastical duties, upon ecclesiastical correctness, in which alone piety consists. God is the Father of him only whose Mother is the Church. It gives to the dear God very great and particular joy to pardon good children who live to please their Mother, and who earn the approbation of their teachers, the Jesuit fathers. So simple and natural is the grace of God, of which the reformers made so nebulous a doctrine! Not till the probability Morals of the Jesuits had infinitely diminished the guilt of sin, and had made the forgiveness of sins a natural result, was it possible to understand, as the Jesuit Escobar said, the meaning of those words of Jesus, "My yoke is easy, and my burden is light"!

It is the natural inclination of men to regard their sins as a light matter, and to excuse themselves: hence the Morals of the Jesuits accords with the feelings of the world; it is the justification of man in his ordinary life, the self-palliation of the natural man transformed into an art and a system; a theory of Morals arranged to suit the palate of worldly pleasure, plainly more akin to the spirit of the Renaissance and the illumination (*Aufklärung*) than the mystical doctrine of Luther and the gloomy Calvin. The Jesuit Morals sustains the same relation to men's usual modes of action that Macchiavelli's doctrine of the State sustains to the practice of politics. Instead of feeling a virtuous horror at both, people of the world should rather wonder that they have spoken this prose all their lives. "To appear good is better than to be good," said Macchiavelli, because he knew how little genuine goodness of heart accomplishes in political affairs. In like manner the Jesuit Morals necessarily regards the appearance of holiness as better than holiness itself, for holiness can only come from a transformation of the will and a discord in our own nature, which always disturbs faith in authority, and endangers obedience to the Church. With Macchiavelli, the power of the State; with the Jesuits, the power of the Church, — was the one end to which the doctrine of Morals had to be adapted and accommodated. That the Jesuits so successfully showed men how they could remain sinful, and be loyal to the Church, is the explanation, in great part, of the powerful influence which they exercised on the society of an immoral period, particularly on such courts as that of Louis XIV., who had the highest appreciation of the privilege of being able to sin, without detriment to his piety.

3. *Jansenism.* — In opposing the Reformation, the Jesuits also opposed Augustinianism, and in it a principle of the Catholic Church. The question arose whether the Church should of itself subvert this principle, or not rather preserve

and restore it, and upon it as a foundation reform itself?
The Church was exposed to two dangers, — to apostasy from
herself through Protestantism, to apostasy from Augustinianism through Jesuitism.   The two evils must be avoided by a
revival of Augustinianism within the Church, acting there
in opposition to the Jesuits.   This movement originated in
Catholic Netherlands, and fought its fiercest battles in
France.   It might be termed Catholic Protestantism, because,
without apostasy from the Church, it shared with the Reformation its Augustinian-moral principle.   Its founder was
Cornelius Jansen (1585–1638), professor of theology in Lyons,
whose great work on Augustine appeared the same year
that the Jesuits celebrated the first centennial of their
order (1640).

The feeling that the Catholic Church required a religious
and moral purification, existed before the Reformation ; and
it was by no means completely stifled by the Council of Trent
and Jesuitism.   It worked on here and there, and, particularly in France, it awoke anew the spirit of contemplative,
world-renouncing piety, and earnestness of repentance : it
stimulated men to the religious and strictly conscientious
performance of the duties imposed by the Church as the
condition of salvation, and the duties of worship, and hence
prevented Catholicism from being completely absorbed by
Jesuitism.   Augustine's doctrine of the sinful nature of man,
and Jansen's revival of Augustinianism, corresponded to this
feeling.   Under the reforming guidance of a strict and pious
abbess, Angelica Arnauld (made abbess in 1607), a lonely
nunnery in the country, *Port Royal des Champs*, was ready
to receive this doctrine ; and it was propagated in the subordinate cloister, Port Royal de Paris, founded in Paris in 1625 ;
and under the influence of a man, who was Jansen's most
intimate and most congenial friend, Du Verger, abbey of
St. Cyron, it became imbued with the principles of Jansenism.   In the asylum of the country cloister, there were a
number of able men, among them, men eminent in science

and theology, with the same religious aims in life, and living
in the same anchoretic manner, who undertook the defence
of Jansenism, and appeared before the public as an ecclesias-
tical-religious party of great intellectual power. They were
the men of Port Royal, at whose head were the theologian
Antoine Arnauld — " the great Arnauld" (1612-1694) — and
the mathematician *Blaise Pascal* (1623-67), "the genius of
Port Royal."   The Church was already feared within the
Church. The contest with the Jesuits arose of itself: the
contest against the authority of the pope was provoked by
the latter. In 1653 Innocence X. condemned some positions
of Jansen as heretical, which the Jansenists denied to have
been taught by Jansen at all. After a second bull (1654)
had fixed this point also, Arnauld disputed, not, to be sure,
the right of the pope to decide concerning dogmas, but his
power to decide concerning matters of fact (1655). Whether
certain propositions are heretical, the Pope can decide; but
whether they actually occur in the works of Jansen, is a
question as to a matter of fact (*question du fait*), and can be
decided only historically, and not by an authoritative declaration. Such a limitation of the papal authority is the denial of
its infallibility, the characteristic dogma of the Jesuits. The
doctors of Sorbonne condemned Arnauld by a majority of
votes, a third of which were cast by monks. "Our antagonists," said Pascal, "have more monks than reasons!"

As early as ten years before, before the first bull condemned
the assertions of Jansen, Arnauld had taken up the fight
against Jesuitism, supported though it was by the king and
the bishops of the court. We have seen the connection
between the casuistical Morals of the Jesuits, and their
stress on ecclesiastical observances, on frequent confes-
sions and communions, in all of which inward repentance
and earnestness of penance were completely disregarded. In
his work "On Frequent Communion," Arnauld shows the
sterility of the Jesuit Morals; and in another, he attacks the
" Theological Ethics of the Jesuits " itself (1643). To favor

Jesuitism, and condemn Jansenism, papal infallibility was arrayed against historical truth; and the papal authority, whether through its own error or deceit, was misused and degraded to sanction falsehood. It was time to turn a full blaze of light on Jesuitism, upon all its machinery, even to the mainspring of its action, to strip it of disguises, and lay it bare before all the world as a system of falsehood, which converts error into truth, and sin into righteousness. This was done in a series of letters which followed Arnauld's attacks on papal infallibility, and, under the name of "Louis Montalte," were directed to a friend in the province. They were "Pascal's Provincial Letters" ("Lettres provinciales," 1656–57), — one of the greatest and most successful of the few masterpieces of polemical literature because of the importance of its subject, the power of its arguments, and the perfectness of its exposition, which employed all the resources of language, even the burning energy of wit. Of the men of Port Royal, Pascal was the most intellectual, and the most courageous in his convictions. He stripped the disguise from Jesuitism as no one else has done, either before or after him, and denied papal infallibility without the reservations, which he found ambiguous, and even Jesuitical, in the Jansenists. It is impossible to change the nature of things by an authoritative decision of the Church. The decision against Galileo as little proves that the earth rests, as the decision against the antipodes proves that there are none. If popes ever err, they are not infallible, even in matters of faith. In this avowed opinion, Pascal was on the road from Catholicism to Protestantism. He had seen the indecision of Jansenism, since it was unable longer to acknowledge the authority of the Romish Church, and still did not dare to reject it. This indecision was its ruin. The old Port Royal was destroyed: at the instigation of the Jesuits, the Pope issued the bull Unigenitus (1713), condemning Quesnel's New Testament, not caring whether Augustinian and biblical doctrines also fell under the anathema ; in union with the State, he destroyed French Jansenism in 1730.

Catholicism and Protestantism are world-historical *oppositions*, which embrace and exhaust the principles of religious life within Christianity. Hence, no mingling of the one with the other is possible; no compromise between them, no existence of the one in the other, no intermediate forms. Whatever occupies an intermediate position is always a variety of one of the two, and, taken by itself, an impotent mongrel. Faith, submitting to authority, and religious liberty (I mean by the latter, not an empty phrase, but that which Luther demanded), are utterly antagonistic religious principles, the conflict between which led the Reformation to apostasy, and the Church to the decrees of the Council of Trent. That Protestantism cannot prosper in Catholicism, that no temper of mind akin to it can live in the Church, and under the principle that faith must submit to authority, Jansenism experienced in its own case, and proved to the world a second time. French Jansenism of the seventeenth century serves as a proof, as it were, that the German Reformation of the sixteenth century calculated rightly when it declared its revolt against Catholicism.

Catholicism and Protestantism are also *stages* in the religious *development* and *education* of the Christian world. The former is still far from being outgrown: the latter is far from being perfectly developed.

CHAPTER VII.

THE COURSE OF DEVELOPMENT OF MODERN PHILOSOPHY.

THE Reformation was a freeing and renovation of the spiritual life of unlimited range. By putting an end to the Church's control over the conscience, and rejecting the obedience of faith and the doctrine of the holiness of works, it threw off the chains which, for the sake of human salvation, had shackled and bound human *labor*. If the performance of ecclesiastical works does not contribute to salvation, their neglect cannot prevent it: if asceticism, celibacy, voluntary poverty, unconditional obedience, aloofness from civil and political life, do not make religious perfection, as this indeed cannot be made at all, the natural and harmless pleasures of life, marriage and a family, the performance of civil duties and labors, participation in the affairs of State and in the business of the world, do not injure or endanger the well-being of the soul. The victory over the world by the solution of its problems, by self-sacrificing labor, must rather contribute to human purification, and thereby to salvation. The labor of man in the service of civilization is not incompatible with his labor for himself, for his own purification and moral development; and since Protestantism must require these, it cannot hinder that; it must permit it, and, from the stand-point of its own historical problem of education, it must even require it. Thus, religion no longer restrains man from labor and a career in the world: it makes him free, and authorizes him even to seek out and solve the problems of the world. In this point,

the religious spirit of the Reformation again met the humanism of the Renaissance, not to antagonize it, but to increase
its pleasure in secular labor, and to free it more perfectly
than it had itself been able to do. It is a one-sided and
miserable conception, both of the Reformation and the Renaissance, which regards the former as the opposition to, or even
protest against, the latter.

Among the new problems of human labor, the first was
that of science and knowledge. Philosophy had to enter the
road which the Reformation made and opened. It followed
the example of the latter. As the Reformation sought to
restore Christianity out of its original sources, God, man,
and the Bible, so philosophy desired to renew human knowledge out of its inexhaustible sources likewise, independently
of all traditions of the past, of all conditions which do not
lie in itself, i.e., in its own faculty of knowledge. The
Reformation in philosophy consisted in such a renewal. As
soon as this problem was fully and clearly conceived, this
independence declared, new knowledge sought in this spirit,
the epoch of modern philosophy began. Modern philosophy
was founded in the first third of the seventeenth century,
and stretches on to our day. From the time it was founded,
to the development of its last historically notable systems,
about two hundred years have passed by. The countries in
which it has been chiefly developed are England, France, the
Netherlands, and Germany ; and these are the countries which
were most powerfully affected by the Reformation. It suffered its severest contests in France, stood them successfully
in Germany, and victoriously terminated them in England
and the Netherlands. These countries, in part attacked, in
part overcome, by the Reformation, have been the leaders
of modern philosophy ; since the end of the last century, it
has been chiefly in the hands of the Germans, out of whom
the Reformation proceeded.

It is easy to survey the course of its inner development.
It seeks to know things by means of human reason, and

therefore begins in entire confidence in the possibility of such knowledge, in complete trust in the power of human reason. It rests on this assumption, and is *dogmatic*, accordingly, in its first form. Since it presupposes knowledge, it must make the nature of things its object, independently of the conditions of knowableness; and the explanation of all phenomena, even the phenomena of mind, its problem, to be solved by means of the essential principles of nature. In its fundamental tendency, accordingly, it is *naturalistic*. Now, the true faculty of knowledge must be but *one*, like the true knowledge of things. But there are two faculties of the human mind through which things become objects of consciousness; viz., the sensibility and the understanding. In the very beginnings of modern philosophy, therefore, there arises a conflict between opposing theories of knowledge, — a conflict which the common problem and presupposition does not prevent, but rather excites. One party declares that the only true knowledge of things takes place through sense-perception; the other, through the understanding, or clear and distinct thought. The former regards experience (empiricism) as the only means of solving the problem of philosophy; the other, the understanding (rationalism). This solution, therefore, must first be sought in the opposite trends of *empiricism* and *rationalism*. The nominalistic doctrine of knowledge prepared the way for empiricism. As soon as this appears in complete independence, the epoch of modern philosophy begins, and the former causes the development and opposition of rationalism. With what right is obvious. Things must be known as they are, independently of the manner in which we perceive them, in which they appear to our senses. We cannot, therefore, perceive the true nature of things: it can be learned only by thought. This is the point out of which that great controversy proceeds, in which modern philosophy was engaged in the first part of its development, and which marks each of its stages by an antithesis.

The empirical philosophy was founded by the English-man *Francis Bacon* (1561–1626) in the years 1605–1623. It was developed in England by *Hobbes* and *Locke*, the founder of Sensualism (1690). From this point, it separates into two branches, — in the English-French illumination (*Aufklärung*), which terminates in Materialism, and in the logical development and culmination of the sensualistic doctrine in the English philosophers, *Berkeley* and *Hume* (1710–1740). I have expounded this branch of modern philosophy, which recognizes Bacon as its founder, in a particular work, to which I here refer my reader because it is only separated from the present work on account of reasons [1] not connected with its subject-matter.

The Frenchman, *René Descartes*, founded Rationalism. He laid the foundation of a new doctrine of rational princi-ples, the principal stages of which appeared in France, the Netherlands, and Germany. These principal stages are denoted by *Descartes*, *Spinoza*, and *Leibnitz*, as those of Empiricism are by *Bacon*, *Hobbes*, and *Locke*. Parallels are naturally suggested which are likewise antitheses, — Bacon and Descartes, Hobbes and Spinoza, Locke and Leibnitz. Locke forms the starting-point of Voltaire and the French illumination; Leibnitz, of Wolf and the German. The fundamental development of modern metaphysics from Des-cartes to Leibnitz, to indicate the literary limiting points, falls between the years 1636 and 1715.

Now, the fact of knowledge under the dogmatic presup-position, both of Empiricism and Rationalism, is neither explained nor explicable. The necessary consequence, there fore, was a denial of its possibility. This was made by *Hume* in whose Scepticism the opposing trends of thought converge, and complete their course. Philosophy stands at a new and decisive turning-point: it can no longer presuppose the

---

[1] Francis Bacon and his Followers. The History of the Development of the Empirical Philosophy. Second and revised edition. Leipzig: F. A. Brockhaus, 1875.

possibility of knowledge, but must inquire into and establish
it *in the first place*.   The nature of things is conditioned by
their knowableness.   The problem of knowledge is the first
of all problems.   Hume disturbed the dogmatic slumber
of philosophy.   The first whom he awoke was *Kant*, the
founder of the *critical* epoch (1781), which divides modern
philosophy into the dogmatic and critical periods, and controls the philosophy of our century.

BOOK I.

DESCARTES' LIFE AND WRITINGS.

CHAPTER I.

I. TYPE OF LIFE.

WITH the founders of the modern period of philosophy, it was not the business of professorships and schools, but of an inmost call, and a free, independent leisure. It was no longer the aim to transmit a traditional doctrine, but to originate the elements and principles of a new one. The "*munus professorium*" of scholastic times did not, therefore, lie within the scope of these first philosophers: they had enough to do, to come to terms with their own thoughts and desire for truth. Apart from the leisure which they devoted to philosophy, they either lived on the theatre of the great world, in pursuit of objects more satisfying than a professorship to their ambition and their thirst for experience, or they devoted their lives entirely to the quiet service of knowledge. They were either men of the world, like Bacon and Descartes, or recluses, like Descartes and Spinoza. The characteristics of both types were, however, to a certain extent, united in Descartes. Compared with Bacon and Leibnitz, he appears as a philosophical recluse, who, out of inmost inclination, despised both the splendor and obligations of a worldly position, and felt so powerfully the desire for knowledge, that every opposing ambition was silenced, even the desire for scientific fame. "I have no desire at all" said he, at the close of his description of himself, "to be regarded as a man of importance in the world; and I

165

shall always count the enjoyment of undisturbed leisure a greater favor than the highest earthly preferments." In this respect, he strongly resembles Spinoza. Yet, in comparison with the latter, Descartes appears as a distinguished and wealthy man of the world, whose place was in the society of the great, who entered for a short time into their enjoyments, and always remained at home in their customs, carefully preserving, also, an outward harmony with the world in which he lived, and avoiding, even anxiously fleeing from, all conflicts with its regulations, — conflicts which Spinoza certainly did not seek, but which he courageously endured, — finally, who was rich enough to satisfy his burning thirst for the world and experience in a life of varied activity, and in long and numerous journeys. In Spinoza's life, the *Wanderjahre* were wanting, which were to Descartes a school with a long course of study which he thoroughly completed. As his doctrine contained the germs from which Spinoza and Leibnitz develop their systems, so his character and type of life unite the characteristics of both, but so unite them that the man of the world is ruled by the recluse, and the desire for knowledge decides the fundamental direction and form of his entire life.

It was the desire for truth that caused Descartes to enter into the activities of the world, and to lead an almost adventurous life. It was not the great world, as such, that attracted him, but reflection upon it; and when his thirst for experience was satisfied, he found, in the perfect and free leisure of solitude, his true and contented form of life. He lived ever only for himself and his intellectual culture. Both from natural inclination and on principle he sought to avoid all external conflicts. He was not able to do so altogether, but he never sought them. He knew why he sustained a friendly relation towards the world. His conservative attitude was as much the result of deep reflection as it was natural. It was determined not merely by his method and principles, but was a necessary consequence of the nature of his mind: the unrest of his mind was so great that he needed outward quiet, and nothing could induce him to sacrifice it.

But he avoided no *inner* struggle, however great and powerful. When one makes of truth a duty, he owes it first of all to himself. To be true to one's self is the fundamental condition of all truthfulness. Most men boast of their candor towards others, and live in the greatest blindness concerning themselves; and, of all deceptions, *self-deception* is the worst and most frequent. From this most destructive enemy of truth, Descartes wished to protect himself by the most searching self-examination and the boldest doubt. All apparent truth and pretended knowledge consist in an intellectual self-deception which is, at bottom, a moral one. This was the enemy with whom Descartes fought, and he did not let him go until he was certain he had conquered him. In this struggle for truth, in this fight against intellectual self-deception in every form, Descartes was one of the greatest and most fearless of thinkers. A look into these inner conflicts which some of his writings portray exactly as he experienced them, suffices to give us a knowledge of the man, whom a mere surface view so little penetrates, and often so falsely and ignorantly estimates. In the whole range of philosophical literature, there is no work in which the struggle for truth is portrayed in a more animated, personal, captivating manner, and, at the same time, more simply and clearly, than in Descartes' essay on method and his first "Meditation." That irresistible desire for knowledge, that disgust with book-learning, that distrust of all scholars, that aversion to all instruction and improvement by others, that thirst for the world and life, that longing for a fundamental and complete mental renovation, are in those writings conspicuous characteristics; and they are expressed so powerfully nowhere else but in a German poem. If we bring before our minds the profound critic and thinker in the "Faust" of Goethe, who, struggling after truth, falls into a maelstrom of doubts, and resolves to seek it henceforth only in himself and the great book of the world, flees out of his study into the wide world, which he hurriedly and adventurously roams over without being captivated by it; if we seek in actual life for a man corresponding to this picture, who has lived all these characteristics, and experienced all these conflicts and changes, — we shall find no one who exemplifies this exalted type so perfectly as Descartes, who lived not far from the period which began to develop the Faust legend. There was even in his life a moment of search, when he allowed himself to be seized by the hope of help from magic.

The life of the philosopher naturally divides itself into three parts, which cause the course of its development to stand out so distinctly within the above sketched outlines, that their limits and names are self-evident. The first sixteen years is the period of instruction; the next sixteen, the period of travel; the last twenty-two, the time of his mastership and works.

II. THE FIRST PERIOD OF HIS LIFE (1596-1612).[1]

Our philosopher comes from a distinguished and wealthy old French family of Touraine. The name was Des Quartes in the old mode of writing it: in the fourteenth century it appears in the Latin form De Quartis. Distinguished birth was at that time a passport into the highest public offices, in which, especially those of the Church and the army, some members of his family had distinguished themselves. Besides the army and the Church, the parliaments, the highest

---

[1] The most important of Descartes' writings for the knowledge of his life and development is his Discours de la Méthode. In my translation, Rene Descartes' Principal Works for the Grounding of his Philosophy (Mannh., 1863). As biographical expositions are to be mentioned, A. Baillet: La Vie de M. Descartes (2 vols., Paris, 1691. Abridged, Paris, 1692). Thomas : Éloge de René Descartes (1767). Besides, Notes sur l'Éloge de Descartes (Œuvres de Descartes, publ. par V. Cousin, t. i, pp. 1-117). The Notes are given in extracts. Fr. Bouillier: Histoire de la Philosophie Cartésienne (2 vols , Paris, 1854). J. Millet: Histoire de Descartes avant 1637 (Paris, 1867), depuis 1637 (Paris, 1870).

courts of France, offered a field of public activity suited to one of distinguished birth; and the counsellors of parliament formed a particular class of French nobles, an official nobility the most independent of all by reason of its position. One of his family was Archbishop of Tours. His grandfather fought against the Huguenots. His father, Joachim Descartes, took the robe, and became counsellor of parliament in Rennes. The traditions of his family were not adapted to educate a philosopher, to say nothing of a reformer of philosophy and a renovator of knowledge. They were rather fitted to restrict the career of Descartes within the usual and pleasant course of the loyal nobility, and to make him averse to the innovations of the time. But this family spirit was not without influence in the life of our philosopher. It was partly due to it, that Descartes, notwithstanding that freedom of mind which he insisted upon in science as in life, notwithstanding that most fundamental reform in thought which proceeded from him, was deeply averse, not merely on principle, but radically, to every violent and arbitrary reform in public life, to every kind of subversion in Church and State, and, in this respect, never ceased to be an old French nobleman of conservative stamp. But this family spirit, on the other hand, could not prevent him from becoming more and more estranged from his family, since his life was devoted to science, far from the walks of public activity: particularly, it could not prevent the elder brother of Descartes from looking down contemptuously upon him, even when he had made the name of Descartes famous throughout the world. With his father, who marked his scientific tastes even when a child, and wished to indulge them, his relations always remained the most tender.

The estates of the family, upon which the father of Descartes resided by turns during the parliamentary vacation, lay in South Touraine and Poitou. I mention particularly La Haye, which belonged in part to Descartes, and Perron. René Descartes was born in La Haye the last of March, 1596,

— the third child of the first marriage. His mother (Jeanne Brochard) died a few days after his birth, of consumption, a disease which her son inherited. The pale face of the child, his weak body, and a dry cough, permitted, in the opinion of the physician, no hope that he would live. That, nevertheless, the child was kept alive, was due to the care of his nurse, to whom Descartes always showed a grateful memory. To distinguish him from his brother, he was called " René Descartes Signeur du Perron," after the little estate Perron, situated in Poitou, which he was to possess. In the family he was called simply " Perron." He himself attached no importance to his title as a nobleman, called himself in the world simply " René Descartes," in his Latin writings " Renatus Descartes." The Latinized and abridged " Cartesien " was disagreeable to him. Small, and of delicate health, his body required in childhood the greatest indulgence : it was necessary for him to avoid all mental exertion, and he could only prosecute his studies as play. Nevertheless, his extraordinarily strong desire for knowledge showed itself so actively, and at such an early age, that his father was accustomed to call him in jest his little philosopher. When he finished his eighth year, he seemed strong enough to take up a regular course of study. At the beginning of the year 1604, in the royal palace at La Flèche, in Anjou, a new school was started, founded by Henry IV., and intended to be the first and most distinguished school for the French nobility. After the king had sacrificed his faith to his crown, and, through the Edict of Nantes, had assured toleration to those of his old faith, he wished to show favor also to his enemies the Jesuits. By an act of indiscreet magnanimity, he recalled them into the country from which they had been driven ten years before (1594), after the first murderous attack which one of them had ventured upon his life. The father of the "great Arnauld" had already written his philippics against them. The king now gave to the order the palace of La Flèche, and committed to their management the school in which a hundred French nobles were to be educated. It was endowed with royal magnificence and generosity. As a mark of his favor, he had ordered that his heart should be buried in the Church of La Flèche.

Descartes was among the first pupils, and remained there until he finished the course. He had not merely gone through the studies taught in the school, but he had completely outgrown them, when, in his seventeenth year, he left the institution. The rector of the school, Father Charlet, was related to him, and interested himself particularly in the pupil recommended to his protection, who, — which is rarely the case with boys of genius, — through obedience, fidelity to duty, and desire for learning, very soon became a really exemplary scholar. Charlet committed the boy to the special tutorage and care of Father Dinet, who afterwards became provincial of the order, and confessor of the kings Louis XIII. and XIV. To the authority of this man, who was kindly disposed towards him, Descartes appealed when, in the times of his scientific controversies, Bourdin invidiously attacked him. There Descartes first became acquainted with Marin Mersenne, who later entered the order of Minims (hermit brothers of the holy Francesco de Paolo), and whom, when their school-days were over, Descartes again met in a fortunate hour in Paris. I mention his name at once, because he had the first place among Descartes' friends. When the new doctrine began to spread abroad in the scientific world, and to be an object of attack in many points, and when many explanations were necessary, Mersenne, who was in the capital of France, while Descartes was living in the most concealed retirement, was, as it were, the scientific and business agent of his friend. He was called the resident of Descartes in Paris and the dean of the Cartesians. When they met in La Flèche, Mersenne, who was eight years older, was already in the last part of the course of study, while Descartes was commencing it: the former was already studying philosophy when the latter began grammar. The greatest event during the school-life of Descartes which came within the range of his experience, was the murder of Henry IV. He was among the chosen pupils who, on the 10th of June, 1610, solemnly received the heart of the king.

The studies of the school began with the ancient languages, which Descartes learned with ease: he not merely read the ancient poets, but even enjoyed and imitated them. Then followed a two years' course in philosophy, — in the first year, logic and ethics; in the second, physics and metaphysics. It was when the boy was ripening into the young man, and his spiritual consciousness began to be very active, that Descartes became acquainted with the studies of the philosophical course (1610–1611). These branches had the greatest influence upon Descartes, in that they utterly failed to satisfy his thirst for knowledge, challenged his judgment, provoked his criticism, and gave the first occasion to the doubt by means of which he finally cut himself loose from the schools and from science in the scholastic form. ·Finally came mathematics, which completely took possession of his hungry mind, and, among all the sciences taught in the school, was the *only* one which satisfied him, and incited him to further study of it. This fact illuminates for us the nature of his mind. He cared not for polymathy, but only for the certainty, clearness, and distinctness of knowledge; i.e., for actual knowledge, not for the confused knowledge of a multitude of objects, but for the kind of knowledge. His thirst for knowledge was not at all for polymathy, but was absolutely philosophical. What he sought was not the cognition of this or that object, but *truth*, clearness and distinctness of concepts, evident sequence and order in his thoughts. This is why mathematics fascinated him, and satisfied him beyond all other sciences. It gave him an illustration of what *knowing* really is, and wherein true knowledge is distinguished from false. It pointed out the direction which thought must follow in order to find truth. Even then, therefore, mathematics was important to the young scholar, not merely because of its problems, which so eagerly occupied him, but pre-eminently because of its *method*. This method was the criterion by which he judged science in general. And to the same extent to which his mind was accustomed to clearness and distinctness of conceptions in mathematics, to a course of thought by which new truths are reached, he was astonished to find the opposite in the remaining sciences: in the syllogism, the absence of a method of thought by which discoveries are made; in ethics, unfruitful theories; in physics and metaphysics, obscure, dark, and uncertain conceptions, of which, indeed, their systems consist, resting on the most uncertain foundations. Already it is evident that he will not continue to apply himself to mathematics as the particular science which best suits his endowments, but that he will find his attitude with reference to science in general by reflecting upon it; that he will use it as a means of cultivating his mind, and gaining a point of view from which to make an independent and wide survey over the territory of human knowledge as such. Mathematics becomes the criterion by means of which he tests every cognition. It awakens in him the philosophical spirit, which, conformably to the nature of his desire for knowledge, finds its first satisfaction in mathematics, and bears its first fruits there. The preference for this science was in Descartes the first characteristic of the methodical thinker, as his aversion towards the philosophy of the schools was the first manifestation of the sceptical. And so ripens already in the scholar the problem to which he gave his entire life, — *the fundamental reformation of the sciences by means of a new method based on the analogy of mathematics.* At first the goal lay in the dark distance, but already it is clear to him that the right method of thought is the only way to truth; that this method must be discovered, or, what amounts to the same thing, that the spirit of mathematics must be made fruitful in philosophy.

The method which Descartes sought to discover, and which
he wished to introduce into philosophy, was not an art of
orderly exposition: such an art already existed in the syllogism. Its purpose was not to expound the known, but to
discover the unknown, to deduce and develop it methodically from the known. He was less interested, therefore,
in the proof of mathematical propositions than in the solution of mathematical problems, in analysis and algebra.
When he was listening while at school to an exposition of
the ordinary analysis, it is said to have occurred to him that
this analysis is nothing but algebra; that the latter contains
the key to the solution of geometrical problems; that the
magnitudes of geometry can be expressed by means of equations, and its problems, therefore, arithmetically solved.
Therewith the first thought of a new science was conceived, —
a thought in the highest degree fruitful to it, — the science of
analytical geometry, of which Descartes was to be the founder.
This great discovery was the first result of his methodical
thought. He mastered mathematics from the side of method;
regarded it as an instrument for the solution of problems,
and knew how to use it for the most difficult solutions in
a new and skilful manner. In this way mathematics is
studied by its masters, and Descartes intended to become
such a master while he was still a pupil. He continued to
occupy himself quietly with mathematical problems which
he proposed to himself, and solved by means of his method.
Nothing was more agreeable to him than these lonely meditations, which were favored by the indulgence granted to
him on account of his state of health. He was allowed to
rise later in the morning than the rest of the pupils. In these
early hours spent in bed, he communed with his thoughts
in the most undisturbed and active manner. They were
the hours of his most unoccupied and fruitful leisure. He
so accustomed himself to this mode of work, that he continued it in after-life, and gathered in full measure the gold
of the morning hours.

Let us hear how Descartes himself describes the state of mind in which he found himself at the end of his course at school. "From childhood on," says he, glancing back to that time, "I have been educated for the sciences; and as I was made to believe, that by their help I might acquire a clear and certain knowledge of all that is useful in life, I was ardently desirous of being instructed in them. But when I had finished the entire course of study, at the close of which one is usually admitted into the order of the learned, I completely changed my opinion; for I found myself involved in so many doubts and errors, that I was convinced that I had derived no other result from my desire for learning *than that I had more and more discovered my own ignorance.* And yet I was studying in one of the most famous schools of Europe, in which I thought there must be learned men if such were anywhere to be found. I had then learned all that my fellow-students had learned; and, since my desire for knowledge was not satisfied with the sciences actually taught us, I had read all the books that had fallen into my hands, treating of the subjects acknowledged to be the most curious and rare. I knew the judgment others formed of me. I saw that I was considered not less capable than my fellow-students, although among them were some who were already fixed upon to fill the places of our instructors. And finally our age appeared to me as rich and fertile in powerful minds as any earlier one. I was, therefore, led to take the liberty of judging all men by myself, and of concluding that there were no sciences of such a nature as I had previously been given to believe." In this survey of his life, he reviews the sciences taught at the school, — the ancient languages, rhetoric, poetry, mathematics, ethics, philosophy. He states that in each he found something useful, but that none of them, mathematics excepted, had a right to be called science, in the strict sense of the term. Even the existing mathematics seemed to him limited and unphilosophical, and the school-philosophy everywhere uncertain and doubtful. "Therefore," he continues, "I completely abandoned the study of books as soon as my age permitted me to leave the subordinate position of a scholar, and *I resolved no longer to study any other science than that which I could find in myself or in the great book of the world.* I therefore spent the rest of my youth in travelling, in visiting courts and armies, in holding intercourse with men of different tempers and positions in life, in collecting varied experience in the situations into which fortune threw me, in proving myself, and so reflecting upon my experiences that I might derive some benefit from them. And in this way I gradually extricated myself from many errors which darken our natural understanding, and make us less capable of listening to reason. But after I had spent several years in thus studying the book of the world, and in making every possible effort to gather experience, I at length resolved to study *myself* in the same manner, and to employ all the powers of my mind in choosing the paths I ought to follow. And I succeeded, as I think, much better than if I had never left my country and my books."

CHAPTER II.

THE SECOND PERIOD OF HIS LIFE (1612-1628): THE WANDER-JAHRE. (a) LIFE IN THE WORLD AND AS A SOLDIER.

I. ENTRANCE INTO THE WORLD.

IN August, of the year 1612, Descartes left the school of La Flèche. The first sixteen years of his life lay behind him. The wanderings upon which he entered continued as long, — the study of the world, from which, in a riper epoch of his life, he was to return into his inmost self. Upon the period of school-culture followed the period of self-culture, — self-formation in the literal sense of the word. He would accept nothing from without and on good authority, but would deduce every thing from himself; would penetrate, prove, discover every thing by means of his own thought. The school-culture was the result of an aggregate accumulated by many minds, composed of all sorts of confused opinions, without method, internal order or harmony. As soon as he perceived this, his faith in the teachings of the school was gone forever. With all the gratitude and regard which Descartes always felt for his instructors (with a certain preference, indeed, for the Jesuits), he thought himself indebted to his training at school for only the smallest part of his performances. He often remarked to his friends, that, without the education which his father gave him, he would have written the same works, only he would have written them all in French, none in Latin.

It was a long journey from the first doubt of the existing state of science to the discovery of new and sure principles,

and its termination still lay in the dark distance. It was
with Descartes a moment of complete uncertainty as to his
life. The learned professions had no attractions for him,
and he was not sure of his calling to philosophy; he believed that he had talent for the mechanical arts; but his
father intended him for a military career, according to the
custom of the family, after his elder brother entered the
profession of law. But he was not then strong enough for
military service; and in order to strengthen himself, and
prepare for his future calling, he practised riding and fencing
at Rennes, where he staid for a time after he left school.
The path of a French cavalier leads through the distinguished society of Paris. At the commencement of the
following year, Descartes went to Paris, attended by some
servants, in order to become acquainted with the fashions
and customs of the great world through intercourse with
companions of his rank. For some time the excitement of
the new life, with its numerous diversions and enjoyments,
pleased him; and he floated with the stream. But the great
needs of his thinking nature soon awakened when he met
men whose mental natures were akin to his. He became
acquainted with the mathematician Mydorge, and met again,
in the cloister of the Minims, his school-friend, Mersenne,
the philosopher among the monks, with whom he entered
into an intimate and active intellectual intercourse, which
continued, unfortunately, only for a short time, since Mersenne was sent to Revers as instructor of philosophy by the
provincial of his order (1614). Scientific conversation was
dearer to Descartes than play, which was his most agreeable
amusement among the cavaliers. Suddenly he vanished
from the distinguished society. No one knew where he
was. He lived in Paris, in an out-of-the-way house in the
suburb St. Germain, entirely secluded, concealed from his
friends, even from his family. He occupied himself entirely
with mathematics, associated only with some scientific men,
and avoided going out where his acquaintances might see

him. He lived thus two years in the metropolis of the world, sought in vain. Finally, towards the end of the year 1616, one of his friends, whom he had been avoiding, happened to see him on the street. That put an end to his freedom and retirement. He had to consent to go back into the society which had lost all charms for him. It was no longer play, but music, which most delighted him, and at the same time excited his thoughts. He could live a dissipated life, but never a thoughtless one. What occupied him immediately became an object of reflection. He practised knightly exercises, and at the same time wrote an essay on the art of fencing. He played; but what attracted him was, not the winnings, but the calculations by which he endeavored to avoid the chances of play. In music it was chiefly the mathematical relations of vibrations which gave him material for thought. His next work, the first of those which have been preserved, was an essay on music.

II. MILITARY SERVICE IN HOLLAND (1617-19).

The political condition of France had as little power to engage the interest of Descartes as intercourse with the nobility. The greatest event of that time was the summoning of the States-General of the kingdom, the last in France before 1789. While the whole of Paris flocked to see the solemn procession of deputies to the Church of Notre Dame, Descartes, who had already fled to his retirement in St. Germain, was absorbed in mathematical studies. The affairs of the court were at that time in the most wretched confusion. The queen-mother, Maria of Medici, ruled under the influence of an unworthy favorite, Marshall d'Ancre, whom she had elevated to power. The princes forcibly opposed this disgraceful rule; but its overthrow resulted only in the transfer of power from the favorite of an ambitious and corrupt queen, to a weak king who was under a guardian. One favorite put the other out of his way by causing him to be murdered. He was murdered in Paris in 1617, during Descartes' residence there; and under such circumstances, it was natural for him to avoid service in the French army, and to prefer to serve in a neighboring country friendly to his own land.

With the armistice of 1609 the United Netherlands, after a long and persistent struggle, had won the first acknowledgment of their independence.   France favored this rising Protestant power because of her old hatred of the Spanish-Austrian monarchy, and permitted her warlike sons to bear arms there under the leadership of those who fought a common enemy.   Many French nobles had already taken service under Maurice of Nassau.   Descartes followed them. In May, 1617, he went to Breda, and entered as cadet into the service of the Stadtholder.   That the pupil of the Jesuits should be a soldier of the son of the great Prince of Orange will not surprise us when we consider the circumstances of the time.   We shall soon see that the same man, now a volunteer under Maurice, continued his military career under the flag of Tilly.   We have in general no right to make so much noise about his military career as foolish panegyrists have attempted, a thing to which he himself gave no occasion.   He lacked both the military ambition and the bodily strength which make soldiers by profession.   He wished to become acquainted with the great and strange world as a drama in which he could be a spectator, not an actor.   His military services were his first mode of *travelling*, and of finding an opportunity of acquiring a knowledge of the world.   Implements of war interested him from the side of their mechanical inventions, and the methods employed in fortifications and sieges were subjects of his reflections. Every kind of crudeness in camp and field was repulsive to him.   His tabard was a passport, as it were, by means of which he had an opportunity of seeing in the easiest manner all those things which attracted his curiosity.   He was less a soldier than a tourist, and chose a military life, not as a career, but as a costume.   For this reason he remained volunteer, rejected promotion and pay, took the latter but once, for the sake of the name, "as certain pilgrims do alms," and preserved it as a memento of his military life.

In Breda he found an armed peace, which had still to continue four years, and which left him complete leisure. Undisturbed, he devoted himself to his scientific pursuits, and through a happy accident made the acquaintance of a man with whom he could share them. The Stadtholder knew how to value mathematics, and preferred them to all other sciences on account of their importance to the art of war. They were, therefore, prosecuted by the men of ability about him; and it befell that mathematical problems were posted for solution on the walls. One day Descartes saw such a problem, written in the language of the Netherlands, and requested a by-stander to translate it into French or Latin. As chance would have it, this by-stander was the scholarly and highly respected mathematician, Isaac Beeckmann of Middleburg, who, surprised at the request of the French cadet, explained the problem, stipulating, in jest, that Descartes should solve it. The second day after, Descartes brought him the solution; and, in spite of the great difference in their ages, this accidental acquaintance soon developed into a friendly and scientific intercourse. At Beeckmann's urgent suggestion, Descartes wrote in Breda (1618) his "Compendium Musicæ," which he dedicated to his friend, with the earnest request that he keep it secret. This was first printed after his death (1650). Probably he had at that time also written an essay on algebra, and put it in Beeckmann's hands; since it appears from one of his later letters (October, 1630), that the latter had such a work. The friendship of the two was disturbed by the boasting and indiscreet vanity of the latter, who regarded the disparity of their ages as a disparity of knowledge, and pretended that Descartes was his pupil; while the latter was conscious that his old friend had learned much from him, and that Beeckmann had taught him nothing more than he was accustomed to learn from all things, even ants and worms, as he openly told him in the letter above mentioned.

As in Paris, Descartes devoted himself to his thoughts, and gave little heed to the stormy events which were happening around him. While external conflicts in the Netherlands ceased for a time in consequence of the truce, momentous conflicts broke out between political and ecclesiastical parties. The ecclesiastical controversies which disunited Protestantism in the Netherlands, had begun between Jacob Arminius and Franz Gomarus, two professors of theology in the University of Leyden. The controversy related to the question of unconditional predestination and election, which Gomarus maintained in rigid Calvinistic fashion, and Arminius denied, defending the freedom of the human will. It was the opposition between orthodox Calvinism and rationalism which these two men embodied. The controversy passed from lecturers' chairs to pulpits, and soon became so general, and gained such strength, that it divided the ecclesiastical life of the Netherlands into the parties of the Arminians and the Gomarists. Since the year 1610, when the Arminians appeared as a congregation, and brought their confession of faith ("remonstrance") before the States of Holland and West Friesland, with a claim for toleration, these two parties had stood opposed to each other as Remonstrants and Counter-remonstrants. With these parties in the Church, political parties were united, — the monarchical party, headed by Maurice of Nassau (Prince of Orange since February, 1618), and the Republican party, under the leadership of John van Oldenbarneveld, grand pensionary of Holland, and Hugo Grotius, recorder of Rotterdam. The party of Orange sided with the Calvinists, and summoned a universal synod for the condemnation of their opponents: the Republican party sided with the Arminians, and insisted on the right of individual States to self-government in ecclesiastical matters, a right which they guarded with their own militia against the attacks of their fanatical opponents. The Stadtholder then caused the leaders of the opposite party to be taken prisoners, and accused of high treason against the United Netherlands. Oldenbarneveld was beheaded (May 13, 1619); the victory was given to orthodox Calvinism by the decrees of the synod of Dort (1618); the Arminians were condemned, and excluded from the community of churches. *Gisbertus Voëtius* was one of their most violent and intolerant opponents at that synod: we shall meet him hereafter as professor in Utrecht, in the life of our philosopher. When Descartes left Breda, he did not dream how disagreeable the victors of Dort would make his later residence in the Netherlands.

III. MILITARY SERVICE IN GERMANY (1619-21).

1. *Campaigns.* — The first two years of Descartes' life as a soldier were of the most peaceful character. In Breda, he had become acquainted, not with war, but with an armistice; and his most interesting experience there was his intercourse with a mathematician. He could not permit his military career to end in such an unwarlike way, and just then a war broke out in Germany. The news of the disturbances in Bohemia which resulted in the Thirty Years' War had already spread in the Netherlands. The Protestants of the land were in the armed defence of their rights, in open resistance to the authority of the emperor, particularly to prevent the succession of Ferdinand, who was to inherit the crown of Bohemia from his cousin Matthias, and had set himself the task of uprooting Protestantism, first in the kingdom of his inheritance, and then, where it was possible, in the empire also. The counts Thurn and Mansfeld led the insurgents in Bohemia: the forces of the emperor were commanded by Bucquoi. The Emperor Matthias died on the 20th of March, 1619. In spite of the protests of the Bohemians, Ferdinand went to Frankfort as elector of Bohemia, was chosen king of Bohemia, Aug. 28, 1619, and crowned as Emperor Ferdinand II., Sept. 9. Even before his coronation,

the Bohemians had proclaimed a Protestant prince, Frederick V. of the Palatinate, as their king. War for the Bohemian crown was thus inevitable between the new emperor and this counter-king chosen by the Bohemians. This, however, was only the starting-point of a struggle which, from the position of affairs, necessarily and immediately spread. The question was not merely as to the possession of Bohemia, but in a wider sense as to the existence of Protestantism. It was a struggle between the Catholic and Protestant interests in the empire, which stood in opposition to each other in the alliances of the Union and Liga. Thus, the material lay ready for the breaking out of a great European war which was to lay waste the lands of Germany for thirty years.

Descartes exchanged the Netherlands for this scene of action. In July, 1619, he went to Frankfort-on-the-Main, saw there the preparations for the election of an emperor, and was present at the coronation, the most magnificent spectacle which the world of that time could show. Then he took service in the Bavarian army, and so we find him at the commencement of the Thirty Years' War a volunteer esquire of the leader of Liga. The first movement of the Bavarian army was against Würtemberg, the duke of which stood on the side of the union. The army marched against Donawert, but the campaign was interrupted by diplomatic negotiations: they entered winter quarters, and Descartes spent the winter of 1619–20 at Neuburg-on-the-Danube in the most perfect solitude, — a solitude that proved fruitful for his thoughts.

The diplomatic interruption had come from France. The emperor had sought an alliance with the French : the most influential man at the court of Louis XIII., the favorite of the king, the Duke of Luynes, had been won over to the Austrian party ; and under the Duke of Angoulême, a brilliant embassy went to Germany, to arrange the differences of the hostile parties in the interests of the emperor. The embassy at first stopped at Ulm, the imperial city of Swabia ; summoned thither the hostile parties of the empire, and effected an agreement, according to which the war, at first confined to Bohemia, was made the exclusive matter of Ferdinand, and Frederick of the Palatinate; and the Protestant princes of Germany were excluded from participation in it. From Ulm, the embassy went to Vienna. The Duke of Bavaria, as an ally of the emperor, led his troops to upper Austria, conquered there the rebellious Protestants, united, in Bohemia, with the imperial army under Bucquoi, and their combined forces defeated, in the battle of Prague, the Bohemian rebels and their king, Frederick of the Palatinate, who fled to Schlesia the same day that the victorious army entered Prague.

During this time, Descartes was not always with the army in which he served. After the winter in Neuburg, he went in June, 1620, to Ulm, where he met his countrymen, and remained some months on account of his interest in science. In September he went to Vienna, where the French embassy was, and returned to the Bavarian army in Bohemia probably a little before the battle of Prague. He remained in Prague until towards the end of the year, then spent some months in solitude on the southern boundary of Bohemia, engaged in meditation. Since the Bavarian army had ended its campaign, he joined the imperial army under Bucquoi in Moravia in the beginning of the spring of 1621, as he wished to continue for a while his life as a soldier, which just then offered to him an experience of war. The revolt in Hungary, which had been allied with that in Bohemia, still continued under Bethlem Gabor. The campaign of the imperial army, in which Descartes served, was directed against this enemy. His panegyrists pretend that he distinguished himself in this campaign: he himself tells us nothing of it. Bucquoi took Presburg, Tirnau, and other fortified cities, and fell in the heroic battle of Neuhausel, July 10, 1621. The siege of this city was raised July 27; and soon after, Descartes quitted the service of the emperor, and ended his life as a soldier. During these three years (1619–21) he served in the Netherlands

during the truce, was in winter quarters in Neuburg, and
served in the Bohemian and Hungarian campaign. It appears that in Neuburg, where the war called him to Bohemia,
he had already intended to abandon his life as a soldier, and
travelled from Vienna to Venice in order to make a pilgrimage
on foot from that place to Loretto.

2. *His Solitude in Neuburg. An Inner Crisis.* — We must
look deep into the life of Descartes to find the man himself.
We must seek for the events of most importance to him, not
in campaigns and battles, but in the winter quarters on the
Danube and in Bohemia, where he resigned himself entirely
to his meditations. His scientific interests followed him
everywhere. In Ulm he became acquainted with the mathematician Faulhaber, and remained there some months: in
Prague nothing interested him more deeply than reminis-
cences of Tycho Brahe. But of most importance to his
development was that residence in Neuburg, where, in the
deepest solitudes, he found the clew which gradually led to
the founding of the new philosophy. It was the time of a
crisis. Since he left La Flèche, the doubts which there
took possession of him had not let him rest: they had followed him into the society of Paris, had driven him into the
solitude of the suburb of St. Germain, and been his companions in the garrison of Breda. Mathematics alone seemed
to him to give certain knowledge. It satisfied him entirely,
and even became the bond of his friendships. Yet it did
not free him from the doubts that disquieted him. Its clearness did not make the other sciences clearer: the certainty
of its truths did not protect him against the uncertainty of
philosophy. If we could only make philosophy as certain
as mathematics, if we could penetrate the nature of things
with mathematical distinctness, and form a philosophy according to the method of geometry, we could build a system of
true philosophy, very slowly, to be sure, but with perfect
certainty. That was the problem which had gradually taken
shape in his mind, — as sceptical as it was mathematical, —

and the solution of which became united with the inmost aim of his life.   Philosophy lay before him like a dark chaos: mathematics shone upon him from a perfectly clear sky.   If we could only let this light into that chaos!   But how is it possible?   On *this* question the mind of Descartes was concentrated.   He felt that he was standing at the door of truth, and could not enter it.   In every moment of solitude, this importunate problem thrusts itself upon him, though he cannot solve it.   With a feeling of his own impotency, he prays for light from heaven, and vows a pilgrimage to Loretto.   Since he can find no help in himself, he seeks it without.   It seems to him as if some one could explain the riddle, as if the key were somewhere preserved as a secret treasure, like the stone of the Wise, which only adepts possess.   In the midst of his doubts, he feels an impulse towards mystics and magicians.   In this mood he hears of the "*brotherhood of the Rosicrucians*," which arose in a mystical manner, and, consecrated to the service of truth, intends to enlighten the world, and free the sciences from their errors.   It is impossible for any one *outside of the society* to learn who its members are, and they dare not betray themselves in any way.   The imagination of people is so much the more active about them; the most fabulous reports go from mouth to mouth; works are published in defence of them and in opposition to them.   The interest of our philosopher is deeply aroused.   He earnestly seeks to meet one of them, perhaps through a work, the title of which has been preserved, and which was to have been dedicated to the Rosicrucians: but all his efforts were in vain; he never was able to discover a Rosicrucian, for the simple reason that there were *none*.   At the time when Descartes was seeking them, the rumor of such a society had just arisen; and the published writings, which spread abroad their fame, their plans for reformation, the wonderful history of their founder and their order, had just begun to be circulated (since 1614).   The whole matter had no foundation in fact.   It was an invention of the Suabian theologian, Valentin Andreæ (1586–1654), circulated by him for the purpose of disgusting the world with magic and its pretended reformations, by the most extravagant satire, and directing it to a genuine reformation by means of practical Christianity. He wished to scourge a folly of the time, and was compelled to discover that he had promoted it in a high degree, by providing for it new nourishment, which all the world greedily swallowed. The Rosicrucians were sought everywhere: they existed nowhere. Never has a satire so completely failed of its intended effect, and accomplished the exact opposite. It became a universal mystification, gave birth to the fables concerning the Rosicrucians, even duped a Descartes, and made a Leibnitz curious fifty years after its origin.[1] But what shall we say when even in our day the latest French biographer of Descartes accepts the Rosicrucians as an historical fact, and even conjectures that Descartes was a member of that brotherhood, whose founder or head at that time was Andreæ! To be sure, Descartes always denied that he was a Rosicrucian, or that he knew any of them; but that proves nothing, since he dared not acknowledge it.[2]

These moods of despondency in which Descartes felt helpless, and vowed pilgrimages, and longed for the Rosicrucians, passed by. Truth cannot be received from without, but must be sought in a path that one discovers and makes for himself. This right and sure road is *Method*, already typified in mathematics and logic. The point now is, to make it universal, i.e., philosophical; to simplify it, and free it from all defects. Even then Descartes knew certain rules which point out the path the mind must follow in seeking truth: knowledge extends no farther than clear and distinct thought; dark conceptions must be analyzed into their elements, and illuminated step by step; clear ones must be so arranged and united that their connection may be as

---

[1] Vol. iii. of this work (sec. ed.), pp. 72 and following.

[2] Millet: Histoire de Descartes, vol. i. p. 93.

evident as they are themselves. At first all is dark. What is required, therefore, is a universal and fundamental *analysis* of our conceptions, — an analysis of them into their simplest elements, the simplicity of which is equivalent to their absolute clearness and certainty. These rules must not only be given, but followed. They require a knowledge of self illuminating the very core of our being, demanding all the powers of our mind, and, therefore, our entire life, and aiming at the *instruction of self* as the single purpose of life. Every dependence upon the opinions of others is a deviation from this goal, a false step in the direction of the life which must preserve the greatest independence in thought and judgment. But this independence reaches only so far as thought: farther it ought not to reach, and cannot. Here is the limit, and the failure to observe it would be likewise a false step. Self-instruction, therefore, requires the greatest *self-limitation*. Thought takes its own way; and to find this way, and systematize it, one mind is sufficient, and better than many. In the world, on the other hand, complicated human interests prevail, difficult to systematize, laboriously adjusted to each other in the great organizations of society, which have gradually arisen, and oppose every theory arbitrarily obtruded upon them, every methodical regulation which thought would introduce in accordance with its guiding principle. There is in this point a sharp distinction between the theoretical and practical life : the former requires a systematic arrangement governed by *one* fundamental thought; the latter will not tolerate it. The reform of thought, therefore, is entirely different from that of society; and the instruction of self, in its search for the truth, has neither the time nor the ability to improve the world. A direct application of theory to public and practical affairs is, in Descartes' eyes, a most erroneous use of method, and, therefore, an unmethodical procedure of the most vicious character, which he avoided on principle. The instruction of self was for him the task of the whole of life, a purely personal

and private one, which he never sought to have accepted
as an example by others. That saying of Faust, "Do not
imagine that I could teach any thing to improve and amend
men," was with Descartes, not the bitter, but the good-
natured and modest, expression of the aim of his life. This
inability is likewise a nolition on principle. What has
happened in the arrangement of public affairs can be changed
and reformed only gradually. It is better for them to
remain as they are than to be suddenly overturned by an
abstract theory, and what is bad in them become worse than
before. By such considerations Descartes justified his con-
servatism. In his thoughts he intended to be free; and he
avoided, therefore, every public position in life, related himself to the activities of the world, less as an actor than as
a spectator. He made no change in the outward form of
his life. From a feeling of piety and on principle, he remained loyal to the laws of his land, to the religion of his
father, to the customs of his rank; and he resolved beforehand rather not to publish any thoughts that might conflict
with public authorities, than to disquiet men, and disturb
ideas long established in Church and State. This mode of
thought, to which we cannot allow the courage of the
reformer, aiming at the welfare of others, but to which we
must concede a wise caution, a ripe judgment, based on a
wide experience of the world, and a profound knowledge
of men, was already methodically confirmed, when, at the
age of five and twenty, Descartes left the army. His statements concerning this matter are so simple and artless that
no one can read them and regard the cautious, at times
timid, conduct of Descartes as an affectation. "I was then
in Germany," he says, in his essay on method, "attracted
thither by the wars which are still going on in that country;
and, as I was returning from the coronation of the emperor,
I spent the beginning of the winter in a locality, where,
without distracting conversation, and fortunately, also, without any cares or passions, I remained the whole day alone

in my room, with full opportunity to occupy myself with my thoughts. One of the first of these that occurred to me was, that works composed of many parts are often less perfect than those which are the work of a single hand. Thus, one sees that the buildings which a single architect has planned and executed, are generally more beautiful and commodious than those which several have attempted to improve, by making old walls serve purposes for which they were not originally intended." "It is true that it is not customary to pull down all the houses of a city, for the simple purpose of rebuilding them in another form, and of making more beautiful streets; but we certainly do see that many people have their houses pulled down in order to rebuild them, and that they are often even constrained to this when their houses are in danger of falling down, and their foundations are insecure. I was accordingly convinced that it would indeed be absurd for a private individual to think of reforming the State by fundamentally changing it throughout, and overturning it with a view of restoring it amended; and I had the same opinion of any similar plan for reforming the body of the sciences and their systems, as they are established in schools. But I thought that I could do nothing better with my opinions than to cast them off at once and completely, that I might be able, by reflection, to put others in their places, or even to restore the very same ones after they had been vindicated by reason. And I was certain, that, in this way, I should succeed in ordering my life far better than if I built upon old foundations, and held fast to principles which I had taken on trust in my youth, and the truth of which I had not at any time tested. For, although I was conscious of various difficulties in this undertaking, they were not insurmountable, and not to be compared with those which are involved in the slightest reformation in public affairs. Only with great labor can the huge bodies of society be set up again when they are once overthrown, or even held upright when they totter;

and their fall is always very disastrous.   Then their imperfections are always somewhat modified by time; and many
of them, which no sagacity could have reached with equal
success, have thus been insensibly removed or corrected;
and, finally, these defects are in almost all cases more toler-
able than their arbitrary change.   It is in this case as with
the roads that wind between mountains, and which daily use
has made so smooth and easy, that it is far better to follow
them than to seek a straight path by clambering over rocks,
and descending to the bottom of precipices.   I shall never,
therefore, be able to approve of those restless meddlers, who,
called neither by birth nor fortune to the management of
public affairs, are continually projecting theoretical reforms
in public matters.   And if I thought that this essay contained any thing which could make me suspected of such
folly, I should be very sorry that I have consented to its
publication.   I have never intended any thing more than
to reform my own thoughts, and base them on a foundation
entirely my own.   And, although my satisfaction with my
work causes me here to give an account of it, I do not
counsel any one to make a similar attempt.   Others, whom
God has more highly endowed, may, perhaps, entertain
more exalted purposes; but I am afraid that even mine is
too bold for many.   The resolve to strip one's self of all
past beliefs is not an example for every man."   After Descartes had developed his method in its theoretical and practical relations, and stated the maxims by which his life was
governed, he continues, " Having thus provided myself with
these maxims, and put them aside with those principles of
faith which I have ever held in the highest regard, I thought
I could take the liberty to renounce and examine the remainder of my opinions.   And, inasmuch as I hoped to be
better able to accomplish this work by intercourse with men,
than by remaining longer in solitude, where these thoughts
had occurred to me, I began travelling before the end of the
winter.   And during the nine subsequent years, I did noth-

ing but wander, now here, now there, since I wished to be a spectator, rather than an actor, in the dramas of the world; and since in every matter I carefully considered what might be doubted, and prove a source of deception, I gradually succeeded in rooting out all the errors that had crept into my mind. Not that in this I imitated the sceptics, who doubt for the sake of doubt, and seek to be always undecided. My design, on the contrary, was to obtain certainty, and to throw aside the loose earth and sand, in order to find rocks or clay." "Thus, living apparently as those who have nothing to do but to lead a pleasant and innocent life, and who strive to enjoy their pleasures without vices, and engage in all honorable diversions, that they may enjoy their leisure without *ennui*, I was constantly progressing in the execution of my plans, and perhaps making greater gains in the knowledge of truth than if I had done nothing but read books, and converse with scholars." [1]

3. *The Epoch of the Crisis.* — We have allowed Descartes to speak at such length on account of the *biographical* importance of his statements. Although they were not published until eighteen years had passed by after the events of which they give so luminous an account, their historical truth cannot be doubted when we consider that Descartes' love of truth and his accurate self-knowledge would certainly exclude any deception of memory concerning the progress of his own development. This account is the single, perfectly trustworthy and authentic source of our knowledge of the crisis of his life. It is accordingly certain that Descartes left school a sceptic, trying to find truth, but ignorant of the road to it; that the guiding light began to shine into his mind during his retirement in Neuburg in the winter of 1619; that he there first saw the possibility and necessity of applying the *analytical* method to the human mind and its cognitions with the same certainty and success as he had so

---

[1] Discours de la Méthode. Parts II. et III. Cf. my translation, pp. 12-16, 27, 28.

fortunately found in geometry. He had discovered the fundamental principle of analytical geometry when he formed the important resolution to deal with *himself* instead of quantities; to analyze his own mind and its cognitions in order to banish darkness, and come into light; to so order his entire life accordingly that it might be the constant subject of this experiment of which he had no example, and might reward him for his labor. In this resolution, all the rules were contained which he then adopted for his guidance. He still felt far from the goal that he hoped slowly and surely to reach, but he felt that he was on the right road. At the age of three and twenty, one has not yet that knowledge of men or that experience of himself which ought to precede a fundamental and methodical examination of himself. Accordingly, Descartes postponed it until he had completed his "Wanderjahre," which he henceforth arranged with a view to this problem of his life and method. The goal, sought on *this* road, could be none other than the principles of modern philosophy of which Descartes was the founder. Its germ was planted in that solitude in Neuburg, but it required nine years to come to perfect maturity. The certainty of the crisis filled Descartes with enthusiastic joy: the view opened, and in the distance the Olympic peaks of knowledge were ablaze with light; we use his own figure. It seems that we can determine the day of this remarkable epoch in his life: *it was the 10th of November, 1619.* In the diary of the philosopher relating to that time, which, so far, is unfortunately lost, — our knowledge of it is derived from Baillet's accounts, and from incomplete transcripts made by Leibnitz, and published by Foucher de Careil, — there was a note with the heading "Olympica," and in the margin, "On the tenth of November I began to make a wonderful discovery (*intelligere cœpi fundamentum inventi mirabilis*)." In Leibnitz' transcript, the year is 1620: according to Baillet's account, the words of Descartes were, "On the tenth of November, 1619, filled with enthusiasm I discovered the foundations of a wonderful science (cum plenus forem enthusiasms et mirabilis scientiæ fundamenta reperirem)." The published statements of the philosopher without further detaii mark the beginning of the winter of 1619 as the epoch of the crisis. In a longer note in his diary, he says, " I shall be in Loretto before the end of November, shall finish and publish my essay before Easter, as I have promised myself this day, September 23, 1620." The subject of that essay could be none other than that discovery in return for which he had vowed the pilgrimage to Loretto. He made the pilgrimage five years later: seventeen years rolled by before he published the work, — twenty, indeed, if the principles of the system was the work alluded to.

The accounts of the first discovery vary. His most recent biographer supposes that the " *scientiæ mirabilis* " and the " inventum mirabile " refer to different discoveries, the first of which was made Nov. 10, 1619; the second, Nov. 11, 1620. The subject of the first, he thinks, was analytical geometry and also the new method of philosophy ; that of the second is unknown, probably of a particular mathematical character, and relating to equations. Now, this combination is purely arbitrary : in the diary of Descartes, so far as Leibnitz has copied it, and Foucher de Careil has published it, there is not one word under the date of Nov. 11, 1620. In the text of the diary, Descartes says, " In the year 1620 I first began to perceive a wonderful discovery ; " on the margin, Nov. 10 is written as the date of it ; and we are further told, that Descartes intended to make a pilgrimage from Venice to Loretto in November, 1620.

In the light of Descartes' statements, the most certain opinion appears to be, that the 10th of November was the epoch-making day when he conceived the first, fruitful thought of his philosophy. (The year 1620 in connection with this date is probably a mistake made by Leibnitz in copying.)

Baillet informs us, on the authority of the diary, that, immediately after the enthusiastic excitement of the eventful day, Descartes had three remarkable dreams, which he described in detail, and interpreted as allegories of his past and future. In the first, he seemed to be lame, driven by a storm to seek protection in a church; in the second, he thought he heard a sound like thunder, and saw sparks of fire around him; in the third, he suddenly opened the poem of Ausonius and read the words, " *Quod vitæ sectabor iter ?* " After long impotency and many inward struggles, Descartes had on the day before heard the voice of truth, had suddenly seen light, and found the path of his life.[1]

---

[1] In the Olympica (according to Leibnitz' copy) the following sentence comes immediately after the date of his "wonderful discovery:" "In November, 1619, I dreamed of a poem that began with the words, ' *Quod vitæ sectabor iter ?* ' " It is to be inferred from this, that immediately before, not the year 1620, but 1619, was mentioned, with the marginal note, "On the tenth of November," etc.

Compare Foucher de Careil: Œuvres inédites de Descartes, I. (Paris, 1859), Préf. ix.-xiii.; Introd. xi.-xv. Millet: Hist. de Descartes, I. pp. 74-82, 96-98.

CHAPTER III.

CONTINUATION. (*b*) TRAVELS, AND SECOND RESIDENCE IN PARIS.

EIGHT months passed by before Descartes returned to France from Hungary, where he ended his military career. He wished to travel for some time, since his travels were his studies in the great book of the world; and his country at this time had little attraction for him. The renewal of the war with the Huguenots, and the pestilence which had raged for a year in Paris, made a longer absence in foreign lands agreeable. He travelled through Moravia and Silesia, to Mark-Brandenburg and Pomerania, where we find him in the beginning of the autumn of 1621, thence to Mecklenburg and Holstein, thence from Emden by way of the sea to West Friesland; and experienced during the voyage an adventure which he narrated in a note of that time (under the heading " Experimenta "), and in which his presence of mind, and moral force, stood a successful test. The mariners with whom he sailed intended to rob and kill him. Believing that he did not understand their language, they talked about it quite openly; but Descartes perceived their intention, and with quickly drawn sword and determined air so frightened the robbers that he rescued himself and his servant. From West Friesland he went to Holland, where he remained a part of the winter. In The Hague, he visited the court of the Prince of Orange; and, directly after, that of the Infantin Isabella in Brussels. In March, 1622, he returned to France, came into possession of his inheritance from

his mother, and went to Paris in February, 1623. Among
the items of news which then attracted the attention of the
social circles of the metropolis, the events of the war in
Germany, and the brotherhood of the Rosicrucians, were the
most interesting. No one could speak more intelligently
concerning the most recent and important events of the
German war than Descartes, and his accounts were listened
to with the greatest attention. A report was also abroad,
that there were members of the Rosicrucians, that order of
"invisibles," in Paris, that Descartes was very closely connected with them, that he was even a member of that mysterious brotherhood. The Rosicrucians even became a subject
of literary controversies at this time. Mersenne was engaged
in a controversy with the English scientist, Robert Fludd,
who defended them ; while Gassendi, who was afterward to
rival Descartes for the honor of being the first philosopher
of France, opposed them. After nine years Descartes again
met his old friend Mersenne, who had returned to Paris in
the mean time, and then lived near the Palace Royal, and
was working on the edition of his commentary on Genesis.
As to the Rosicrucians, Descartes could only reply in jest, to
the curious questions, that his presence proved that he was
not an "invisible."

He resided in Paris but a few months. After he had
again visited his family in Brittany, and sold his property in
Poitou, he started again upon his travels (September, 1623),
directing his course towards the south. He wished to become acquainted with Italy, and live in Rome during a part
of the year of the jubilee that began Christmas, 1624. The
papal city was then, as it were, an abstract of the whole of
Europe. He went through Switzerland to Tyrol, and visited
in Innspruck the court of the Archduke Leopold; went
thence to Venice, and saw on Ascension Day the imposing
ceremony of the marriage of the doge with the sea; from
thence made a pilgrimage to Loretto, to fulfil the vow he had
made in Neuburg five years before. At the beginning of

the jubilee he was in Rome, and remained there until the following spring. On his return he stopped at Florence, and visited the court of the great duke, Ferdinand II.; but he did not see Galileo, the greatest man of the time, who was afterward to exert a momentous influence upon his life. The statement that he made the acquaintance of Galileo is contradicted by his own declaration in a letter to Mersenne. Before the middle of the year 1625, he returned to France by Piedmont and over the Alps.

Near the beginning of the summer, Descartes went to Paris, where he remained, with some interruptions, during the three following years. Shortly before this, an office suitable to his rank was offered to him in Chattellerault, and he seems to have thought of buying it; but he gave up the idea when he thought of it seriously, and, true to his first resolve, preserved his independence and leisure. The circle of his scientific acquaintances and friends increased; he was sought on all sides, and was even then considered as one of the first mathematicians and philosophers of his time. In this circle were to be found the ablest mathematicians, physicists, and theologians of the metropolis. I mention the names of Hardy, de Beaune, Morin, Desargues, Balzac, the physician Villebressieux, the theologians Gibieuf, de la Barde, de Sancy, and particularly his first patron, the Cardinal Bérulle. In the following years we find the physician Villebressieux and the abbé Picot in intimate relation with Descartes. His most intimate friends were still those of his first residence in Paris, Mersenne and Mydorge, who was then engaged in optical experiments and studies, and stimulated Descartes to the investigations which afterwards bore fruit in his "Dioptrics." Both of them were supported in these studies by Ferrier, one of the first optical artisans of Paris, who was skilled alike in the theory and technics of his art, and who made the instruments sketched by Mydorge, and with whom Descartes practised the art of polishing glasses. Descartes esteemed him so highly, that there was no one with whom he, in after years, would have more willingly shared that so carefully sought and so anxiously guarded solitude in Holland.

From the house of his friend Le Vasseur d'Etioles, where he had at first resided, he again withdrew into the suburb of St. Germain, to spend some time in a more retired way. When he returned into the house of Le Vasseur, and into the larger circle of his friends, the social and scientific intercourse began again; and there was thus formed there a little academy, of which Descartes was the centre. There, in social conversations, he gave the first expression to the philosophical thoughts which had ripened in solitude, and which, through their originality and depth, so surprised his friends, and were at the same time so obviously true, that scholars and booksellers immediately urged him to publish them. But Descartes was resolved to be on his guard against all precipitance and prejudice in the execution of his work, to cultivate the growing crop a while longer, and to wait for the harvest until the time of perfect maturity had come in his own life also. Soon society and visits again wearied him; the irresistible longing for solitude again returned: and he fled from the house of his friend, and concealed himself on the outskirts of Paris, in a dwelling known only to his most intimate friends (summer of 1628). Le Vasseur sought him in vain. Finally he met his servant on the street, and compelled him to point out the dwelling; and there Le Vasseur found Descartes at eleven o'clock in bed, according to his custom, and watched him for a long time unobserved, as he lay, writing from time to time, absorbed in meditation.

When Descartes first left France, Louis XIII. had shaken off the influence of his mother, and abandoned himself to the control of his favorite: when he returned to Paris, this rule was over, and at the side of the weak king an able statesman was rising into power, really called to govern. The year before, Richelieu was made cardinal; two years

later, under the again powerful influence of the queen-
mother, he became a member of the council of state; soon
he was the first minister, in truth the only ruler, in France.
The policy of this man tolerated no power in France that
opposed or threatened the royal rule; and demanded, therefore, the subjection and disarmament of the Protestants and
their fortified cities, of which latter La Rochelle was the
most important. He determined to starve out this city, and
therefore so to invest it as to make relief and the supply of
provisions impossible. The besiegers had the greatest difficulties to encounter from the position of the city; and that
they were able to overcome them, made the siege of La
Rochelle memorable in the history of military science. A
crowd of curious people flocked there to see the military
works, Descartes among them; and he was compensated
before Rochelle for the solitude given up in Paris. His
friend Desargues had, as engineer, assisted in making the
machinery; and he introduced Descartes to Richelieu. The
king himself was present, and it did not suit him for the
nobles whom curiosity had drawn there to be mere specta-
tors. Descartes was among the attendants of the king when
he reconnoitred the English fleet which tried in vain to
relieve the city, and afterwards when he entered it after it
had voluntarily surrendered. At the beginning of November, 1628, Descartes returned to Paris from this his last campaign (if we can give it such a name). Exactly nine years
had passed since in Neuburg on the Danube he first saw the
road whose terminus now lay close at hand.

Some days after his return, Descartes celebrated a victory
which was more memorable to him than his campaigns, — a
triumph of his method; a test which it had stood successfully before a chosen circle of able and influential men.
When new ideas are in the air, many imagine that they have
already grasped them; and along with the true and rare discoverer we always find a crowd of supposed innovators who
deceive themselves and others. Such people usually have all

sorts of knowledge, know precisely as much as they make a
display of, and have an impudent assurance in appearing
before the public, an amazing readiness and social cleverness
in speaking,—all of them qualities calculated to deceive particularly the world of rank and fashion, which often has
difficulty in distinguishing gold from fools' gold. A certain
Chandoux was an example of this class, a doctor and chemist
by profession, who had already attracted attention in Paris.
Aristotle and the scholastics were, in his mouth, abandoned
and obsolete points of view; he could declaim against them
in as modern a way as Bacon, Hobbes, and Gassendi: his
every other word was "the new philosophy," the new and
absolutely certain principles which he boasted that he himself had discovered. This boasting had really deceived the
papal ambassador, Marquis de Bagne; he wished this luminary
to let his light shine in his circle, and invited a company of
celebrated people to hear him. Besides Cardinal Bérulle,
Descartes, Mersenne, Villebressieux, and others were invited.
Chandoux was prepared, and his fluent and plausible exposition won the sincere approval of this select audience. Descartes said nothing. Cardinal Bérulle, observing his silence,
asked his opinion. He answered evasively, as if after the approval of such men nothing further were to be said. Finally,
pressed on all sides, he took up the discourse, praised its flu-
ency, and the freedom with which Chandoux had declared
against scholasticism, in behalf of a completely independent
philosophy; but as to the supposed new principles, he was
obliged to doubt whether they could stand the test of truth.
Descartes saw before him an example of that self-deception
which he had himself experienced, and which he had seen a
thousand times in others, and the nature of which he thoroughly understood. An opportunity of setting an example
offered itself. We must have a test to distinguish truth from
error. He who does not possess it gropes in darkness. He
pledged himself so to refute the most evident truth that might

be proposed to him, and so to prove the most evident error, that his hearers would be forced to admit the validity of his reasonings. The double experiment was immediately made, and Descartes kept his pledge by producing twelve arguments of increasing probability. His object was to show that nothing can be proved or disproved by unproved principles, and that merely apparent principles prove nothing; that all previous philosophizing, no matter how many modern terms it employed, was based on unreal foundations; and that the new philosophy of Chandoux was in this respect not one whit better than the old and traditional one which he despised. Without the touchstone of truth, there is in human knowledge no protection against false coins. Chandoux seems to have understood this art better in other matters than in philosophy: he practised it on money, and was hanged on the Gréveplatz as a counterfeiter.

Descartes made no secret of his criterion; and he declared to his hearers whom his experiment had convinced, and who were, therefore, desirous to know more about it, that all truth can be discovered only by *methodical* thought, and must be tested by it. Cardinal Bérulle was profoundly impressed. He recognized in Descartes the epoch-making mind called to the reformation of philosophy, capable of becoming for France such a renovator of science as Bacon had been for England. In a confidential conversation, he formally pledged Descartes to write and publish a work on method. The exhortations of such a man must have strengthened his already mature resolution to devote himself henceforth to the execution of his work. For the complete collection of his thoughts he needed leisure, and freedom from disturbance, which Paris did not afford him. It appears that he lived for some time in the country in the neighborhood of Paris, and wrote there, perhaps, the first sketch of his doctrine of method "The Rules for the Direction of the Mind" (*Regulæ ad Direc-*

tionem Ingenii), of which only a fragment has been preserved. After carefully considering where it would be best for him to live, with a view to his health and the undisturbed prosecution of his work, he went to Holland, and remained there for the next twenty years.

CHAPTER IV.

THIRD PERIOD (1629-1650). THE PERIOD OF THE WORKS.
(a) RESIDENCE IN THE NETHERLANDS.

I. "THE HERMITAGE IN HOLLAND."

THE *Wanderjahre* were over. Descartes had seen much of the world; had become acquainted with human life in its most different forms, and observed its unconscious deceptions. He had become a great critic of opinions, a master in the detection of error. His mind had been so critically trained, so methodically exercised in distinguishing truth from error, so sharpened by a comprehensive knowledge of men, so undeceived by the false values of the world, that he was then mature enough to undertake the difficult task of self-examination, and to discover the truth in himself. We expect from him no descriptions of his travels, no account of the courts and armies, the countries and cities, which he has seen; but a profound analysis of human knowledge, unrestrained by fear of doubt. He proposed to take himself as a representative of human consciousness, as an example of a mind filled with experiences of the world and of life, even as Montaigne's had been. On this plane must he stand, if he would overcome the doubts which had remained the last and most mature fruits of Montaigne's experiences. Descartes had not travelled in order to recount the adventures of a French cavalier. And we do not understand him if (with a French contemporary writer) we regard the philosopher and the man of the world in him as two different persons. The man of the world was the instructor of the philosopher. This was their relation in the plan of his life, according to his own statements. His studies in the world are completed now, and he has come to the point where he must begin his study of himself. Now he seeks, as Montaigne had done, "a quiet little place."

The world attributed to Descartes more than he had actually accomplished. Up to the time when he left Paris, he had been occupied with the sceptical and negative side of his philosophy, not with the positive. That the world expected such a work from him, and even believed that he had already completed it, incited him to take up the matter in earnest, and without delay. He would not permit the men of whose judgment he thought most highly to be mistaken in their opinion of him. At any rate, seven years later, looking back upon his *Wanderjahre*, Descartes stated this as the motive which had finally caused him to retire into the workshop of the philosopher. "These nine years passed away before I had come to any conclusion concerning the difficulties which occasion the controversies of scholars, or had begun to lay the foundations of a more certain philosophy than the traditional one. The example of so many eminent men who had formed the same purpose before me, and who, as it seemed to me, had failed, made me realize so many difficulties in the work, that I would not have ventured on it so soon, had not the report gone out that I had already completed it. I do not know what were the grounds of this opinion; and if any expressions of mine gave rise to it, this must have happened rather from my having confessed my ignorance more frankly than scholars are in the habit of doing, and expounded the reasons for doubting many things that seemed certain to many, than from having boasted of a system of philosophy. But, too honorable to be willing to be more highly esteemed than I deserved, I thought I ought to bend all my energies to the task of making myself worthy of my reputation. I therefore resolved, exactly eight years ago, to avoid every place where it was possible for me to meet acquaintances, and to retire to a land where the long duration of war has resulted in such discipline that the armies maintained only enable the inhabitants to enjoy more securely the fruits of peace, and where in the midst of a great and very busy people, more careful of their own affairs than curious about others', I have been able to live, without dispensing with the advantages of the most populous cities, as solitary and retired as in the midst of the most distant desert."[1]

Two conditions were necessary to enable Descartes to devote himself to his work with complete freedom, — a favorable climate, and undisturbed solitude. France and Paris offered neither: he found both in Holland, whither he went in the beginning of the spring of 1629, exactly ten years after he left Breda. He took the utmost precautions against every interruption. He bade farewell to his family by letter, and took leave in Paris of only his most intimate friends. The Abbé Picot had charge of his business matters, Mersenne of his literary affairs: in particular, the greater part of the letters that Descartes wrote to France, and received from thence, passed through Mersenne's hands. Importunate curiosity should not discover where he lived. He concealed his place of residence even by false dates, frequently changed it, and preferred those that were most out of the way, — suburbs, villages, remote country-houses. For his correspondence in Holland, also, he had friendly agents in different places, — Beeckman in Dort, Bloemaert in Haarlem, Reynier in Amsterdam, Hooghland in Leyden. He lived in his retirement like a nomad, "like the Jews in the deserts of Arabia." During his twenty years in Holland (1629–49), he changed his residence twenty-four times, and lived in thirteen different places. I mention Amsterdam, Franeker, Deventer, Utrecht, Amersfort, Leeuwarden, the abbey of Egmond in Alkmaar, Egmond van Hoef, Harderwijk on the Zuyder Zee, Leyden, and the palace of Endegeest near Leyden. He was there entirely master of his time, and his mode of life: he could

[1] Œuvres, t. 1., Discours de la Méthode, part iii. pp. 155, 156.

live in populous cities, finding abundant diversion in society, and in intercourse with his friends, and as soon as he desired to return to his work, he could retire to the most out-of-the-way places, where no bore troubled him. There he was safer than in the suburb of St. Germain. In such solitude originated and matured the works which made him the founder of modern philosophy, and an object of admiration to the world. *Franeker* and *Leeuwarden* in Friesland, *Harde-wijk* in Guelders, *Endegeest* near Leyden, and *Eymond* in North Holland, were the places where his most important works originated. The palace of Endegeest is still conse-crated by the memory of Descartes. In Franeker, whither he had gone from Amsterdam, soon after he left France (he wrote his name, "*Renatus Descartes Gallus philosophus*," in the register of the University of Amsterdam), he dwelt in a lonely palace which was separated from the city by a moat, and wrote there the first sketch of his " Meditations," which were finished ten years later in Harderwijk (1639–40). In Leeuwarden his "Essays" originated, during the winter of 1635–36, which were introduced by the "Discours de la Méthode," his first published work. In Endegeest he planned the "Principles," his most important philosophical work (1641–43), and finished it in Egmond. This was one of the most beautiful villages in North Holland, and Descartes liked best to stay there, and, indeed, did stay there longer than anywhere else. His first stay there was during the winter of 1637–38, immediately after the publication of his "Essays:" his last was during the years 1643–49, — the last period of his solitude in Holland, which was interrupted by three journeys to France, made in 1644, 1647, and 1648.

Descartes' life in Holland can accordingly be divided into three periods, the first of which precedes the publication of his important works (1629–36); the second includes it (1637–44); the third succeeds it (1644–49). During the first, Descartes lived for the most part in Amsterdam, Deventer, Utrecht, and Leeuwarden, after he left Franeker;

he lived during the second, first in Egmond, then in Harder-wijk, Amersfort, Amsterdam, Leyden, and the castle of Endegeest; he spent the third in Egmond. Directly after the sketch of the "Meditations," which were finished in their first form in December, 1629, Descartes began a com-prehensive and important work, in which he intended to explain the world according to his new principles: it was to be called "Cosmos," and was to be his first published work. It was about finished, when, for reasons hereafter to be stated, he determined not to publish it at all. He was engaged in this work during the years 1630–33. After he had thus abandoned the idea of appearing before the public as instructor of the world in this first essay, he hesitated whether he should not give it up forever.

Directly after this, occurred an episode not provided for in the method of his life; but inclination is often more powerful than principle. In the winter of 1634–35, he became acquainted with a lady in Amsterdam, with whom he fell in love, and whom he made his wife without observ-ing the forms of marriage. She bore him a daughter (in Deventer, July 19, 1635), who was named "Francine Des-cartes," and whom he cared for with tender love. But he was not long to experience the happiness of a father: the child died in Amersford, Sept. 7, 1640.[1]

Descartes thoroughly enjoyed the independence and leisure which he had always desired, and which he found for the first time in the Netherlands in undivided measure. Some of his letters, particularly those of the first year, reveal a most cheerful and contented state of mind, which communi-cates itself to the reader. He described his idyllic life in Holland, in the happiest mood, to Balzac, the well-known *protégé* of Richelieu, by whom he was esteemed as a his-toriographer and stylist. Descartes wrote to Balzac from

---

[1] All further details are unknown. In the records of baptism of the Reformed Church in Deventer, the mother is called "*Hélène, fille de Jean.*" Cf. Millet: Histoire de Descartes, i. pp. 339, 340.

Amsterdam in the spring of 1631, when the latter had returned to Paris from his family estate: " I really had some scruples about disturbing your quiet, and therefore preferred not to write until you were no longer enjoying the solitude of the country. Though I intended to write the first week, I have left you undisturbed for eighteen months, during the whole of your absence from home, and you have not once thanked me. But now that you are again in Paris, I must beg for my part of the time that is wasted by so many importunate visitors, and say to you, that, in the two years I have spent in foreign land, I have not once been tempted to return to Paris; and only since I have known that you were there has it been possible for me to be happier elsewhere than here. And were it not that my work restrains me, — the most important, in my poor judgment, in which I can engage, — the wish to enjoy your conversation and to see the birth of all those powerful thoughts which we admire in your writings, would alone be strong enough to drive me from this place. Do not ask me, I beg you, what the work is which seems so important to me; for I should be ashamed to tell you. I have become so much of a philosopher, that I set but little value on much that the world esteems, while I put a high estimate on other things that are usually considered worthless. Yet I know that you do not think with the vulgar: you judge me more favorably than I deserve, and at some convenient time I will talk with you frankly about my labors. To-day, only this: I am not in the humor to write books. I do not despise renown when one is really able, as you are, to earn a great and solid reputation. But to the middling and uncertain fame that I perhaps might hope for, I prefer the peace and quiet of mind which I have here. I sleep here every night ten hours, without being awakened by a single care. I dream only of beautiful things, of woods and gardens and the enchanted palaces of legends; and when I awake I find myself with still greater delight in the actual world which surrounds me.

Nothing but your presence is wanting." When Balzac answered that he was inclined to go to Holland, and live also among the hermits, Descartes replied, "I thought that I was dreaming, and rubbed my eyes, when I read that you thought of coming here. And yet it is not at all strange that a noble spirit like yours should no longer endure the restraints of a court; and if God has prompted you, as you write, to leave the life of the world, I should sin against the Holy Spirit if I should seek to dissuade you from such a resolve. Rather, I invite you to choose Holland, and to prefer it, not merely to the cloisters of all Capuchins and Carthusians, to which so many honorable people retire, but also to the most beautiful residences of France and Italy, — even to that renowned hermitage where you sojourned last year. A country-house, however well furnished, always lacks many conveniences which one finds in a city, and even the solitude which one hopes for in the country is never perfect there. I admit that you may find there a brook so magical in its beauty that it turns the greatest talkers into dreamers; a lovely vale, that rejoices and delights you: but there are likewise a multitude of neighbors, who make visits far more inconvenient than those which one receives in Paris. But in this great city I am the only man who is not engaged in business; and every one else is so entirely occupied with his own interests, that I could spend my entire life here without being noticed by any one. I take a daily walk in the midst of a multitude of people, as freely and quietly as you do in your gardens. And I note the men about me as I would the trees in your gardens, or the animals in your meadows. Even the noise of traffic disturbs my reveries as little as would the murmur of a brook. With the same pleasure with which you regard the peasants as they cultivate your fields, I observe that the labor of all these people contributes to make the place where I live more beautiful and comfortable. And as the sight of rich, ripening fruits is a pleasure to you, so I see with delight ships sailing into our

harbor, laden with the productions of both Indias and the
rarities of Europe.　Nowhere in the world can all the pleasures of life be had as easily as here.　There is no country
in which civil freedom is more complete, security greater,
crime rarer, the simplicity of ancient manners more perfect,
than here.　I do not understand why you prefer Italy, where
the heat of the day is unendurable, the coolness of the even-
ing unhealthy, the darkness of the night dangerous since it
conceals robbers and murderers.　You fear the winter of the
North; but what shade, what fans, what springs, can so well
protect you from the heat of Rome as you can here be kept
from the cold by a stove and a good fire?　Come therefore
to Holland: I await you with a little collection of my fancies that may not, perhaps, displease you." [1]

After the publication of his first work, it was reported
that Richelieu intended to make the philosopher offers to
induce him to return to Paris.　"I do not believe," writes
Descartes to Mersenne, "that the cardinal will condescend
to think of a man like me.　Moreover, between ourselves,
there is nothing less suited to my plans than the air of Paris,
on account of the numerous distractions which are there
unavoidable.　And as long as I can live as I choose, I will
rather stay in a village in any country you can mention,
where the visits of the neighbors are as little troublesome as
here in a corner of North Holland.　This is my only reason
for preferring this country to my own, and I am now so accustomed to it that I have no wish to change my residence." [2]

We add to these passages from his letters a sentence from
the beginning of the "Meditations," one of the first which
Descartes wrote in that retired castle in the city of Franeker:
"The present is favorable; I am free from care, and enjoy
undisturbed leisure; I am living in solitude, and will now

---

[1] The first letter was written, in Cousin's opinion, March 29, 1631; the
second, May 15 of the same year. Balzac's answer was written between
them, April 25, 1631. (Œuvres, t. vi. pp. 197-203.)

[2] This letter was evidently written in Egmond, May 27, 1638. (Œuvres,
t. vii. p. 155.)

apply myself earnestly and freely to my task, which at first requires the complete overthrow of all my opinions."

II. INTELLECTUAL LIFE IN THE NETHERLANDS.

1. *The State of Culture.* — Holland, however, would scarcely have been his "beloved hermitage," as he called it, if it had not likewise afforded opportunities for the most active intellectual intercourse. The Netherlands were then one of the first centres of every kind of culture. Art and science, the humanitarian and exact sciences, were in full bloom. Protestantism had given new life to, and excited new controversies in, the Church and theology; which had quickened its neighbor Catholicism also. In Leyden, the controversy already mentioned between the Arminians and the Gomarists had been kindled; in Lyons, Jansenism arose, which in France came in contact with the doctrine of Descartes, and was in part friendly to it. The universities of the Netherlands stood in the van of intellectual culture: new ones were being founded. Particular mention must be made of the University of Utrecht (established in 1636), where the first school of the new philosophy was formed, and where it found its most violent opponents. Science, learning, universal culture, were the order of the day, and spread in the circles of society like a fashion, even among women. Out of the wealth of the interests of culture, there was developed in receptive and gifted women a scientific, scholarly, and artistic culture, which, even in its most masculine forms, was compatible with womanliness; and, in spite of the astonishment which they excited, they did not make the impression of artificially educated "blue-stockings."

2. *Anna Maria von Schurmann.* — Anna Maria Schurmann (1607–78) was then the most remarkable example of this class, "the star of Utrecht, the tenth Muse, the Minerva of Holland," as her admirers called her, a real prodigy of learning and varied culture. She learned the ancient languages even in her childhood; read Seneca, Virgil, and Homer. To

these she added the modern languages, Italian, Spanish, French, and English. She wrote Latin with the accuracy of a philologist, French with the elegance of a Balzac. To read the Bible in the original texts, she studied the Shemitic languages and dialects; and not merely understood but wrote Hebrew. She wrote letters, and composed essays and poems, in Latin, Greek, Hebrew, and French. She edited Spanheim in 1648, and seven years before published a Latin work in defence of the scientific and scholarly cultivation of women. She was versed in poetry, rhetoric, dialectics, mathematics, and philosophy, even in the problems of metaphysics. She was likewise acquainted with the fine arts: she painted with publicly acknowledged talent, and was expert in sculpture and copper-engraving, even in the plastic arts. She set little value on all this culture in comparison with the study of the Bible, the Church Fathers, and scholasticism. She knew Aristotle, Augustine, and Thomas, but did not care to know any thing of the new philosophy. Her deepest interests were religious, which, at last, were not satisfied in the orthodox Church of the Netherlands. She desired a Church of Christ, which, like the primitive communities of the elect, should live in perfect renunciation of the world and in brotherly intercourse, filled by no other love than the "*amor crucifixus*." Her instructor and guide in Utrecht had been Voëtius, the most bitter opponent of Descartes. She finally followed the French preacher *Labadie*, who had gone over to Calvinism from the Jesuits, and was then preaching in favor of the community of the elect. He was the Roumanian forerunner, and in certain respects the type, of Spener, who founded German pietism. She was already an old woman when she called this man to the Netherlands (1667), and wandered with the exile into foreign lands. [1]

---

[1] Gottfr. Arnold's Impartial History of the Church and Heretics, bd. ii. (Schaffhausen, 1741), chap. xxi. pp. 307–319. Dr. P. Tschackert: A. M. von Schurmann, the Star of Utrecht, the disciple of Labadie (Gotha, 1876).

Many years before, more, indeed, than a generation, Descartes visited the famous woman in Utrecht, and found her engaged in studying the Mosaic account of creation. An impassable chasm lay between the biblical Genesis, and the clear and distinct knowledge of the origin of the world which Descartes required, and sought to give in his "Cosmos." The philosopher remarked that for the explanation of things one could learn nothing from Moses; and was afterwards regarded by the zealous pupil of Voëtius as a "profane man," against whom one must be on his guard. A passage relating to that conversation is cited from her writings, in which she thanks God that the "profane man" found no hearing with her. She saw in Descartes an ungodly philosopher; he in her, great talent for art, which Voëtius had spoiled with his theology, — so he said in one of his letters.[1]

III. THE COUNTESS-PALATINE ELIZABETH.

It appeared that this "Minerva of Holland" sought to rival Descartes in her influence upon one of the ablest and most interesting women of the time, whom a tragic fate had led into the asylum of the Netherlands. The family of Frederick V. of the Palatinate, who had lost the crown of Bohemia in the battle of Prague, and had been deprived of his hereditary states in Germany, lived in The Hague, fugitives and exiles. With the death of Gustavus Adolphus, his last hope departed. He survived him only a few days (November, 1632), leaving eleven of the thirteen children whom his wife, Elizabeth Stuart, had borne him; among them four daughters, the oldest of whom was the Princess Elizabeth (1618–80). There has been, in modern times, no royal family which has suffered so many strange and tragical experiences of an extraordinary character as this, and which, on the other hand, has received greater and more extraordinary gifts from fortune, and is more interesting in its

[1] Foucher de Careil: Descartes et la Princesse-Palatine (Par. 1862), pp. 61–63.

descendants. Frederick V. was deprived of two crowns, and ended his life in misfortune and exile. His widow, in the midst of her numerous family, led, as ex-queen of Bohemia, a kind of court life in exile. The eldest son was drowned in the Zuyder Zee (1629). Rupert, the third son, gained and lost a reputation as a commander of cavalry in the English civil war. His brother Maurice went to America, and no one knew what became of him. Edward, the next brother, went to France secretly, and joined the Catholic Church (1645). The second daughter, Louise Hollandine (1622–1709), followed his example: she became the famous and notorious abbess of Maubuisson. Philip, next to the youngest of the sons, killed, on a public street, a French nobleman, Marquis d'Épinay, who had insidiously attacked him the day before (June, 1646); he was banished by his mother forever, — out of revenge, it seems, since she was said to be more devoted to that nobleman than befitted the dignity of the queen, the mother, and the matron. The Countess-palatine Elizabeth, her elder brother Charles Louis (1617–80), and her youngest sister Sophia (1630–1714), through their personal importance, and the importance of their destinies, were undoubtedly the first of the children of the unfortunate elector. The hereditary rights of Charles Louis were restored by the peace of Westphalia, and through the ability of his administration he became the restorer of the Palatinate after the devastations of the Thirty Years' War. His daughter was the excellent Charlotte Elizabeth, the Duchess of Orleans, who knew how to preserve her loyalty to Germany, and maintain the rank of the Palatinate, at the court of Louis XIV. Her son, Philip of Orleans, was regent; her uncle was the Emperor Francis I., the husband of Maria Theresa. Sophia, the youngest daughter of Frederick, was the pride of the family of the Palatinate. She was the first electress of Hanover, "the great electress;" her son George was the first king of Great Britain of the house of Hanover; her daughter, Sophia Charlotte, was the first queen of Prussia. That these three showed favor to the greatest philosophers of the century, increased their posthumous fame. Charles Louis, a man of the most tolerant spirit, invited Spinoza to take the chair of philosophy in Heidelberg; Sophia and her daughter chose Leibnitz for their intimate friend and counsellor; and the Princess Elizabeth was the most enthusiastic pupil of Descartes.

She had spent her childhood, the first years of "the Thirty Years' War," with her grandmother Juliana, the daughter of the great Prince of Orange, at Krosse in Mark-Brandenburg, far from her parents. Under the care of this highly cultivated woman, the powers of Elizabeth were awakened at an early age, and her taste for the sciences and the languages was cultivated when she was very young. When she went, in the first bloom of her youth, to the court of her mother in The Hague, her charms and talents soon made her celebrated. One of the first objects of her admiration was the "star of Utrecht," in whom the intelligent and aspiring Elizabeth saw a brilliant exemplar. She became acquainted with Schurmann, and carried on a friendly correspondence with her. Summoned by extraordinary events from the usual career of princesses, Elizabeth was firmly resolved to devote herself entirely to intellectual pursuits. When (1638) she rejected the suit of the Polish king, she had just begun to study the doctrine of Descartes. She was nineteen years old when the philosopher published his first work. She read the "Discourse," the "Essays," and the "Meditations," and then wished to see and become acquainted with their author. She felt in sympathy with his view of life; and his doctrine, and mode of instruction, so fascinated her by their depth and clearness, that all that she had learned before seemed worthless in comparison. She belonged to the rare class who could understand and judge the mathematician and the metaphysician with equal success. Then the "star of Utrecht" paled before the constellation of Descartes. She made the acquaintance of the philosopher, which she had wished for so ardently.

He responded to the veneration of the young princess with a
full heart, and became her teacher and friend as long as he
lived, — the most faithful, perhaps, that she ever had.   In
order to be near her, Descartes took up his residence in the
palace of Endegeest, in the spring of 1641.   He dedicated to
her his most important work, the " Principles of Philosophy "
(1644); for her recreation in the days of her bodily and mental affliction, he wrote, in the spring of 1645, the letters on
human happiness (a subject discussed by Seneca in his books
" De Vita Beata "), which formed a part of his theory of
ethics, and resulted in "The Passions of the Soul," the last
work which he himself published, and which he composed in
the winter of 1646, and immediately sent to his friend the
princess.   There is no more beautiful memorial of the Princess Elizabeth than the letter with which Descartes dedicated
his most important work to her: " The greatest advantage I
have derived from my writings is the honor of becoming
acquainted with your highness, and of being permitted at
times to converse with you, and thus becoming a witness of
your rare and estimable qualities; and I am sure I shall do a
service to posterity by proposing them as an example.   It
would be folly for me to flatter, or write what I am not
convinced of, on the first page of a book in which I aim to
expound the fundamental principles of knowledge.   I know
your noble modesty, and am sure that the simple and frank
opinion of a man who only writes what he believes, will be
more agreeable to you than the ornate praises of those who
have studied the art of compliment.   I shall say nothing in
this letter that I do not know by experience; and shall write
here, as in the rest of the work, with the accuracy that befits
a philosopher."   With a few strokes Descartes sketches the
true dignity of human nature, and draws the distinction between apparent virtues, which are like will-of-the-wisps, and
real virtues.   Temerity is more conspicuous than true courage,
and prodigality than true generosity.   Genuine goodness of
heart is considered less pious than superstition and hypocrisy.

Simplicity is often the source of goodness, and despair of courage, and that which includes all virtues is wisdom. Wisdom apprehends the good distinctly, and firmly and constantly performs it. It does not shine like the apparent virtues, and is therefore less observed and so less praised; but its demand is for understanding and character. We cannot all have the same faculties of knowledge, but we can have the same strength of will. But where we find a union of a clear understanding, and an earnest effort for culture, with strength of will, there we find the flower of virtue. "These three conditions are found in your highness in great perfection. The amusements of a court, and the usual method of educating princesses, are unfavorable to study; and that these obstacles have been unable to prevent you from appropriating the ripest fruits of the sciences, proves how earnestly you desire knowledge, while the shortness of the time in which you have made such attainments witnesses to the greatness of your ability. But I have yet another proof, that relates to me personally: I have met no one who has such a thorough and comprehensive understanding of my writings as yourself. Even among the best and most highly cultivated minds, there are many that find them very obscure; and it is almost always the case, that those who are familiar with mathematics cannot comprehend metaphysics, while those conversant with metaphysics cannot understand mathematics. The only mind, as far as my experience goes, to whom both alike are easy, is yours; and I am therefore compelled to regard it as incomparable. And what increases my admiration is, that it is not an aged man, who has given many years to study, in whom we find such comprehensive and scientific scholarship, but a young princess whose charms rather resemble the Graces, as the poets describe them, than the Muses or the wise Minerva. I see in your highness all those excellences that are requisite to pure and sublime wisdom on the part not merely of the mind, but of the will and character; magnanimity and gentleness are united with a disposition which an unjust fortune with persistent persecutions has not been able to imbitter or discourage. It is this high-minded wisdom which I reverence in you; and I dedicate to it, not merely this work, because it treats of philosophy, which is the study of wisdom, but myself and my services."

In the same year that Elizabeth received this dedication, Schurmann wrote her a letter which unmistakably cast a wicked side-glance at Descartes. She acknowledged her reverence for the doctors of the Church, who, with no wish to be innovators, modestly trod the path "which Augustine and Aristotle had pointed out, — those two great luminaries of the science of human and divine things, whose light could not be dimmed by any troubled clouds of error with which one sought to obscure them." [1]

The personal intercourse between Descartes and the princess was very active during his residence in Endegeest. He had previously lived a year in Leyden (April, 1640–April, 1641), and then two years in a palace in the country, only a half-mile away (April, 1641, to end of March, 1643), and went from there through Amsterdam to Egmond, that he might be completely undisturbed while he attended to the publication of his "Principles." I do not know whether he saw the princess after he went to Egmond, since it does not appear from his letters, some of which are unfortunately lost. Their correspondence began directly after their separation, and continued from the commencement of his residence in Egmond (May, 1643), until after his arrival in Stockholm (October, 1649). She requested him to solve various problems in philosophy, geometry, and natural philosophy. The first and most important which she proposed to him related to the union of the soul and body, the most important problem of Descartes' system. In a series of letters, he discussed the

---

[1] Foucher de Careil: Descartes et la Princesse-Palatine, pp 11, 12. No one has yet undertaken the instructive and valuable labor of writing a monograph of Elizabeth. The above-mentioned work, with its ignorance of German life and history, can scarcely be considered a contribution to it.

great question of the value and significance of human life (May and June, 1645). Elizabeth sent him Machiavelli's work on "Princes," with her comments, and requested his (autumn of 1646); and it is worthy of remark, that Descartes, already past fifty, first became acquainted with this book through his pupil. Everywhere on the journey of life, Descartes accompanied her with the most sympathetic and friendly counsel. Dark days came to Elizabeth,—sickness and misfortunes of every kind, the apostasy of a brother and a sister from the faith of her father, dissensions in the family of her mother, the overthrow of the Stuarts in England. After the conversion of her brother Edward, and the execution of her uncle Charles I., Descartes wrote to console and cheer her. He thought of Elizabeth and her unfortunate family when he commenced corresponding with the Queen of Sweden ; and he accepted the invitation to Stockholm, in the hope of making the two princesses friends, and of causing the powerful influence of Sweden to be exerted in behalf of Elizabeth and her house. Already he rejoiced in the prospect of living with her, in the near future, in the court of Heidelberg.

After the murder of the Marquis d'Épinay, Elizabeth was obliged to leave The Hague, because she was suspected (probably without reason) of being an accessory to the crime. She spent the next years in Berlin, at the court of her cousin the great elector. When her brother's hereditary rights were restored, she returned to her paternal city, and lived at the court of Heidelberg until the quarrels of Charles Louis and his spouse, Charlotte of Hesse, set the brother and sister at variance, and drove Elizabeth from Heidelberg. She became imperial abbess of the Lutheran abbey of Herforden in Westphalia, and died there on the anniversary of Descartes' death, a generation after him (Feb. 11, 1680). She remained what she had always been, — a gifted and profound student, able to reconcile the interests of philosophy with those of religion. She granted to her old friend Schurmann the asylum which

she asked for in Herforden (1670), when with Labadie and
the Church of Christ she was no longer tolerated in Amsterdam; and resolutely protected the congregation, which had
entered the country, from the hostilities of the State Church.
The same year she was visited by the English Quaker William Penn, who seemed to make a powerful impression upon
her.   The storms of the world had beaten thickly upon the
aged princess, and she needed the peace which comes from
the renunciation of the world.   But through all the changes
of her life, through changing events and moods and circumstances, she thanked Descartes for her highest intellectual
satisfaction ; and this is the recollection of the abbess also
which has been preserved.

CHAPTER V.

(b) THE DEVELOPMENT AND PUBLICATION OF THE WORKS.

I. THE "COSMOS."

1. *Arrangement and Plan.*

NOW that we have followed the important events in the life of Descartes during his residence in Holland, we must direct our attention more particularly to his studies, and the origin of the works to which his residence there was devoted. In the foregoing chapter, we have touched upon them in connection with the account of his life in Holland, and shall give in the next book a systematic exposition of his doctrine: we have here, therefore, merely to give *the history of their development and publication*, and shall mention their contents only when it is necessary to the understanding of their history.

The "Meditations" were completed, in their first form, in Franeker, Dec. 28, 1629; and the foundation was thus laid for a new explanation of things by the simplest and surest principles discovered by methodical thought. Descartes' first discovery was method; and this led him to the principles which required a new knowledge of the world, and at the same time furnished the foundation for it. If he proposed to write and publish his works in the order of the development of his thoughts, the theory of method would come first; the principles of metaphysics, second; and, last, cosmology, the doctrine of nature and of man. From the scanty remains of some writings composed in the years 1619–29, and from

the accounts given by Baillet, it is probable that in a fragment "Studium Bonæ Mentis," and in the "Rules for the
Direction of the Mind," already mentioned, there were outlines of his theory of method.

But Descartes thought that it was safer, and for the instruction of the world better, to take the directly opposite
course, and assume his method and principles provisionally,
and let them stand their first examination by the world in
their application, that is, in the explanation of things. Such
a course seemed to him the best introduction to his philosophy, and would require the world to judge it according to
the declaration, "By their fruits ye shall know them." To
understand the reasons for Descartes' plan, we must glance
at the fundamental thoughts of his system; though I shall
rather state what they were, than enter into their proof.

For years he had been entirely occupied with this question:
What criterion infallibly distinguishes truth from error, true
conceptions from false ones, reality from imagination? That
he had such a criterion, even in the last days of his residence
in Paris, was evident from his remarkable criticism of Chandoux. He had discovered that there is no such criterion in
our presentations; that the so-called actual phenomena may
just as well be mere phantoms, and can in no way be distinguished from them. There remained, therefore, but one
certainty: not that our presentations denote actual things, or
that the objects which appear to us really exist, but that *we*
have such presentations, that such objects appear to *us*.
Certain only is it, that our act of presentation, that our
thought, is; and, since each is certain only of his own thought,
the first incontestable fact is: I am thinking. *I think: therefore I am.* This perception is entirely clear and distinct:
what we know with the same clearness and distinctness has,
therefore, the same certainty. And now we find the criterion
we have been searching for: clear and distinct perception
decides concerning being and not-being; the clearness and
distinctness of a conception proves the reality of its object.

From the conception of a perfect Being, his existence is clearly and distinctly evident; from the nature of this Being, follows his veracity; and from this, the existence of the material world.   For, if there were no material world, its apparent reality would be a deception, which would be inconsistent with the truthfulness, and, therefore, with the perfection and existence, of God.   But if there really is a material world, it must be capable of being clearly and distinctly known; i.e., it must be a world arranged in harmony with laws, a scientific object, a *cosmos* which we can comprehend.   The clear and distinct law of all happening is causality, the connection of cause and effect, the necessity on account of which nothing happens without a cause, and every thing always comes from some other.   If, therefore, the world, the totality of material things or nature, is explained by the law of causality, it is clearly and distinctly known; and its reality is thus proved, and the doubt that it may be a mere phantom world is forever laid.   These considerations open two paths to the philosopher: he can go from universal doubt to the single certainty of his own thinking being, and, from the vantage-ground here won of the criterion of truth, discover the existence of God in the conception of him, and, by means of this, his veracity, and hence the reality of the material world, and its knowableness; and thus vindicate the problem of the natural sciences.   Or, he can begin with the solution of this problem, prove the existence of the world by our clear and distinct conception of it, and thus reach the goal already arrived at in his metaphysical investigations.   The first path is *metaphysical*, the second *physical:* that is deductive, this inductive, in relation to the entire system and its grounding.   In the second, what metaphysics requires is proved by things, as it were, *ad oculos*.   Physics forms the basis on which rests the validity of our philosophical principles: it tests their correctness.   If there is a possible science of the world, there is a world in harmony with law, its existence is beyond doubt, and the existence of bodies is as

certain as the existence of God and the soul. If nature
obeys law, it can be known distinctly, and is therefore not
merely imagined but real.

Descartes takes this path. He intends to give a clear and
distinct picture of the world, if only in a comprehensive outline, that he may thus assure the victory in advance to his
most fundamental thoughts. He could not have proceeded
more pedagogically. He, therefore, discontinues his metaphysical inquiries, and enters upon a series of physical re-
searches, which he intends to compress in a single work,
explaining the world in its broad outlines from the heavenly
bodies down to those of human beings. He calls it " Le
Monde," according to his subject. This cosmology was the
first of his works intended for the world. He sought to
derive the world from the laws of matter, to cause it to arise,
as it were, before our eyes, and leave the reader to discover
that this world, so explained, and presented to him merely
as an hypothesis, is identical with the world we live in.

First the origin of light out of chaos, then the formation
of the heavens and the heavenly bodies, luminous stars, fixed
stars and suns, of the opaque heavenly bodies, planets, comets,
and the earth, are pointed out ; then the history of the earth,
the formation of its atmosphere, surface, and productions, are
stated ; the origin of the elements, of the ebb and flow of
tides, of the currents of water and air (winds), of seas and
mountains, of springs and streams, of metals and plants, of
the bodies of animals and men, down to the union of body
and soul, which constitutes the entire man, and forms the
point of departure of mental and moral life. Here arise
the questions concerning the essential difference between soul
and body, the union of the two in man, the freeing of the
mental and spiritual life from the fetters of the body. The
first is metaphysical ; the second, psychological ; the third,
ethical. The doctrine of principles forms the foundation of
cosmology, and the doctrine of the soul its boundary. The
doctrine of morals is the most important, as well as the final,

chapter of his practical philosophy, which has first to explain
the motion of physical bodies by means of machinery, and
then the proper method of treating, nursing, and healing the
human body. The theory of motion in its relations to practice is *mechanics ;* anthropology, from the same point of view,
is *the science of medicine ;* and the theory of the spiritual nature of man, considered in the same relation, is *ethics.* These
are the fruit-bearing branches of the tree of knowledge,
whose root is metaphysics, and whose trunk is the philosophy
of nature. This trunk Descartes wished to expound in his
" Cosmos." " I wished to embrace in it all that I had learned
of the nature of material things before I took it up. But as
a painter on a plane surface cannot represent all the different
sides of a real object, and, therefore, selects one of the most
important, puts that in the light, but leaves the rest in
shadow, and represents them perspectively, so I feared that
it would be impossible for me to comprise all my thoughts in
my work : I therefore decided to give a minute exposition of
my theory of light, and, along with this, to treat of the sun
and the fixed stars, because these objects are almost the only
sources of light; also, of the medium between the heavenly
bodies, because light passes through it ; of planets, comets,
and the earth, because they reflect it ; and, particularly, of all
terrestrial objects, because they are either colored, transparent, or luminous ; and, finally, of man, because he considers
all these objects. But that I might discuss all these things
with greater security, and express my opinions with more
freedom, without being obliged to accept or refute the theories heretofore accepted, I resolved to leave this entire
world here below to the disputes of lecturers, and to inquire
what would happen in a *new* one if God should cause the
material for it to arise somewhere in imaginary space, to
move in the condition of chaos, and to act according to fixed
and unchangeable laws. Every thing in this world of mine
was to happen in the most natural and intelligible manner.
I showed how the greatest part of matter would have to

order itself in obedience to those laws, and assume a form
similar to that of our heavens, how some parts would become
an earth, others planets and comets, others suns and fixed
stars.   Then I gave a detailed account of the origin, progress, and reflection of light; and left it to the reader to
observe, that, in the heavenly bodies of the actual world, nothing is to be found that must not or can not resemble the
world which I described.   At this point I began to speak
more particularly of the earth, and I showed how without
the assumption of gravity all its parts continually gravitate
towards the centre; how, under the influence of the heavenly
bodies, particularly the moon, an ebb and flow arises on its
surface (which is covered with air and water) first of our
seas, and then a motion of the water and air from east
to west like that noticed in our tropics; how mountains and
seas, springs and streams, are naturally formed, metals come
in mines, plants grow in fields, and how in general compound
bodies are produced.   And since fire is the only cause of light
in the world, excepting the heavenly bodies, I endeavored to
give an exact explanation of its origin, preservation, and
mode of action." [1]

Descartes had already engaged in studies in optics, with a
view to his investigation of light; and he continued them
uninterruptedly.   For the explanation of the complex bodies
on the surface of the earth, particularly of animal and human
bodies, he needed a knowledge of chemistry, anatomy, and
medicine; and he sought to gain it in a practical way.   In
Amsterdam, where he resided after he left Franeker, he was
engaged during the winter of 1630, especially, with studies in
anatomy, which he pursued with the greatest zeal.   He himself bought from a butcher parts of the bodies of animals,
and dissected them: he wished to be able to explain the
minutest part of the body of an animal as precisely as the
formation of a crystal of salt or a flake of snow.   While he

---

[1] Œuvres, i., Dis. de la Méth., part. v. pp. 163-172 (I have given the most
important passage, with some abbreviations).

was engaged in these studies, he was meditating on the plan of the "Cosmos," but he wrote almost nothing.

2. *Composition, and Prevention of Publication.* — At last he began to write, and told his friend Mersenne in April, 1630, that he had made a beginning, and hoped to be able to send him the completed work not far from the beginning of 1633. Soon he was under full headway. "I am just now busy bringing order out of chaos, and deducing light from it, — one of the greatest and most difficult labors in which I can ever engage, since it contains almost the whole of cosmology.[1] Two years after the first report (April, 1632), he thought he could find the key to the deepest human knowledge of material things, the explanation of the order that prevails in the world of the fixed stars, and determines their position. For some months he did nothing to the work, but he still hoped to reach the conclusion before the time indicated: later the date of the conclusion was fixed at Easter. Shortly before this time (March, 1633), he proceeded from his account of the heavenly bodies and the earth, to the explanation of terrestrial bodies and their different properties, and considered whether he should also investigate the origin of animals in this work. He decided to exclude this matter, to avoid increasing the size of his book. It had already grown under his hands, and could no longer serve, as he originally intended, for a convenient "afternoon's reading."[2] Only something concerning human nature still remained to be added. So far he had gone, at the beginning of June, 1633, during his residence in Deventer. "I shall treat of man to a greater extent than I proposed: I intend to explain the principal functions of his body, and have already given an account of some of them, as digestion, beating of the pulse, distribution of nutritious matter, the action of the five senses, etc. I have dissected the heads of various animals, in order

---

[1] Œuvres, t. vi. p. 181. (It is uncertain whether this letter was written June, 1630, or Jan. 10, 1631.)

[2] Œuvres, t. vi. p. 101.

to ascertain in what memory, imagination, etc., consist." In the midst of his labor he received and read Harvey's famous work "On the Motion of the Heart" ("De Motu Cordis"), which had been published five years before. Mersenne had repeatedly called his attention to it. "I find my opinions but little different from his, although I had written my own explanation of the matter before I read his book." [1]

Suddenly the work stopped, and its conclusion seemed to be indefinitely postponed. "My essay," he wrote July 22, 1633, "is almost finished; I have only to make some corrections, and copy it: but I have such an aversion towards it, that, if I had not promised three years ago to send it to you before the end of this year, it might be a long time before I should be able to finish it. Nevertheless, I will try to keep my promise." [2]

What had happened? In this work, which lacked only a final revision, he had explained the universe on mathematical-mechanical principles, in accordance with the law of causality, setting forth the motion of the earth as a necessary link in the mechanical order of the heavenly bodies. Now, the Copernican system had been defended by Galileo, and just then in a new work under the form of an hypothesis. His famous dialogue on the two most important astronomical systems appeared in 1632, and was condemned exactly four weeks before Descartes wrote the above letter. [3] Descartes had not then heard of the sentence, though he had been informed of the trial. But that was enough to make his work disagreeable to him. The decision against Galileo was published in Liège, Sept. 20, 1633; and Descartes then learned that the doctrine of the motion of the earth was not tolerated, even as an *hypothesis*, since the sentence of condemnation contains these words: "*quamvis hypothetice a se illam proponi simularet.*" Almost a year passed by before he read the work itself (August, 1634); and then hastily, since it was lent to him secretly, only for a number of hours. He

---

[1] Œuvres, t. vi. p. 235.   [2] Ib., pp. 237, 238.   [3] See Introduction, pp. 135, 136.

suddenly saw himself threatened by one of those conflicts which he wished to avoid on principle. He saw, that, if he published his work as it was, he would provoke a contest with the Church, and that he would be regarded as one of those dangerous innovators whom he himself disliked. Unless he were willing to mutilate his work, and so make it absurd, there was nothing left for him but to keep it secret, and decline every proposal to publish his thoughts. " I am like wicked debtors," he wrote to Mersenne, Nov. 28, 1633, " who are always asking their creditors for more time, as soon as they see the day for payment drawing near. I had really intended to send you my ' Cosmos ' as a New-Year's present ; and about two weeks ago I was entirely resolved to send at least a part of it to you, if the whole should not be then copied. But I have just been inquiring in Leyden and Amsterdam whether Galileo's system of the universe can there be found, since I thought I had heard that it had been published in Italy the previous year. I am now informed that it was certainly printed, but that every copy of it was immediately burnt in Rome, and that Galileo himself was sentenced to do penance. This has so strongly affected me, that I have almost resolved to burn all my manuscript, or at least to show it to no one. And I am the more inclined to this resolution, because it at once occurs to me, that Galileo, who is an Italian, and, as I am informed, has been in favor with the Pope, is charged with no other crime than his doctrine of the motion of the earth, which, as I know, some cardinals had before pronounced heretical. But in spite of it, if my information is correct, it has continued to be propagated even in Rome ; and I confess, that, *if it is false, all the principles of my philosophy are erroneous, since they mutually support each other ;* and it is so closely connected with all the parts of my work, that I cannot leave it out without fatally injuring the rest. But on no account will I publish any thing that contains a single word that might displease the Church, and I will rather suppress it altogether than allow it to appear in a mutilated condition. I never was inclined to book-making; and if I had not promised the work to you and some other friends, that the desire to keep my promise might stimulate me to more vigorous application, I should never have gone so far. But, after all, I am sure that you will not send an officer to force me to pay my debts, and perhaps you will be glad to be spared the pains of reading worthless stuff. However, I cannot in a sudden humor break so many promises repeated so often during so many years. I will therefore lay my work before you as soon as possible, and beg only for a year's delay that I may have an opportunity to revise it. You yourself quoted to me that sentence from Horace, *Nonumque prematur in annum;* and but three years have passed since I began the work I intend to send you. Write me, I beg you, what you hear of Galileo's matter." In the next letter, which was lost on the way, he recalled this tardy promise. "You will find my reasons excellent," he wrote Jan. 10, 1634, "and you will not have the least disposition to blame me for withholding my work: rather, you would be the first to suggest it. I am sure you know that Galileo was condemned by the Inquisition a short time ago, and his doctrine of the motion of the earth pronounced heretical. Now, the various conclusions of my essay form a chain, and this view of the motion of the earth is one of its links; and, if any one of my positions is false, all my arguments are invalid. And, however certain and evident they might seem to me, I would on no account maintain them in opposition to the authority of the Church. I am well aware that the decision of a Roman inquisition is not a dogma, that the vote of a council is necessary to that; but I am by no means so enamoured of my thoughts as to wish to invoke such extraordinary means for their protection. I desire quiet; I have guided my life so far according to the motto, *Bene vixit bene qui latuit,* and I intend to continue to do so. I am now rid of the fear of having sinned against a desirable moderation of judgment in my work, and this pleasant consciousness more than counterbalances the vexation at the time and labor lost." In a subsequent letter, Mersenne, who ardently desired to become acquainted with the work, jokingly said that somebody would murder Descartes yet in order to be able to read it sooner. "I had to laugh," answered Descartes, "when I read that passage. My writings are so thoroughly concealed that a murderer would hunt for them in vain, and I shall have been dead a hundred years before the world comes in possession of them."[1] Nevertheless, at another time he did not positively declare that the work would not appear, either in his lifetime or after his death. He wrote to one of his best friends, de Beaune (June, 1639), who earnestly requested him not to keep his work secret longer, since it might easily be lost: "We let fruit hang on the tree as long as it improves, although we know very well that storms, hail, and other disasters may destroy it at any moment. Now, my work is such a fruit, and we can never pluck it late enough."[2] It happened as de Beaune feared. Only a short sketch, reduced to the limits originally intended, which was afterwards written or revised by Descartes, was found in his unpublished writings after his death, under the title "The World, or an Essay on Light" (1664).

An unforeseen catastrophe had caused the philosopher to retrace the first step he had taken towards a literary career; and it was necessary to become accurately acquainted with his feelings and reasons, as stated in his own letters, in order to understand it. It is true that he feared the fate of Galileo: he saw here a collision between a doctrine which he believed, and an authority which, in accordance with the practical principles of his life, he held worthy of honor. The case had arisen in which, according to his principles, theory should retire in favor of the absolute value of political and ecclesiastical interests. He felt this conflict in all

---

[1] Œuvres, pp. 242, 243, 137, 138. The letter was written in the summer of 1637, after the publication of the Discours de la Méthode.

[2] Œuvres, t. viii p. 127.

its seriousness, and yet without a trace of the courage of
the reformer which dares, and even desires, opposition.
And he made no secret, either to himself or to others, of his
timidity. Nevertheless, we should not correctly understand,
and could not therefore correctly judge, Descartes' conduct
if we regarded this motive as the only one. He might
have avoided the conflict, left his work unpublished, and
yet have felt the necessity for such a course as painful in
the extreme. But this was by no means the case. On the
contrary, the fate of Galileo was to him a most welcome
reason for freeing himself from an oppressive obligation.
His promises to write and publish the work imposed upon
him a necessity more painful than the alternative demanded
by the Inquisition. Now he could say, "I need not keep
my promise: I can keep my thoughts to myself; I am no
longer in debt to the public, for it will not have my work."
Evidently relieved and in excellent humor, he wrote, in this
mood, to his friends. And he afterwards declared himself
to the world in the same strain, in his first published work.
After he had stated his reasons for entering upon a literary
career, he spoke quite openly of the hinderance which had
occurred, and he declared frankly: "Although my resolution had been fixed, nevertheless my deep aversion to book-
making permitted me to find other reasons sufficient to
excuse me."[1] The condemnation of Galileo served as a
convenient and welcome reason for declining to publish his
works.

It would have been right if Descartes had adhered to the
resolution, formed for such reasons, to withhold his doctrine
of the motion of the earth. That he disguised it in a certain manner, that it might be accepted without hesitation,
is a graver fault. Here his truthfulness came in conflict
with his policy, and the truth had to suffer. He offered to
help secretly an ecclesiastic in Paris who wished to defend
the doctrine of Galileo, but withdrew his offer when he

---

[1] Discours de la Méthode, Part VI. Œuvres, t. i. p. 191.

learned that the theory was not tolerated, even as an hypothesis.   He read the condemned work, and thought he could
find an expedient for rescuing the doctrine of the immobility
of the earth, in appearance, in view of the difference between his theory of motion and Galileo's.   " You see," he
says in one of his letters, " that in words I deny the motion of the earth, while in reality I defend the system of
Copernicus."   Can it serve to justify Descartes, that we are
obliged to admit that Galileo in like manner retracted his
doctrine ?

Towards the end of the year 1633, Descartes had firmly
resolved to keep his works secret.   How did it happen,
nevertheless, that he afterwards published his doctrine ?
To this question his last biographer has found an answer
more touching than true, and he has also neglected to
make his idyllic explanation intelligible.   The anticipation
of the joys of a father is claimed to have brought the philosopher to the resolution to publish books.   " New feelings
awakened in his mind ; and what Mersenne, de Beaune, and
his best friends could not accomplish, the smile of a child
beaming into his face in the bright future was already able
to do."   After the birth of his child, he remained for some
months in Deventer, and then went with the mother and
daughter to Leeuworden to write the " Discours de la
Méthode."[1]   The reader can now guess what connection
there is between the birth of his child, and the publication
of his works, the most important of which were written
after her death !

II. THE PHILOSOPHICAL WORKS.

1. *The Motive for their Publication.* — The reasons that led
Descartes to avoid and then to undertake a literary career,
then abandon it, and finally enter upon it, and publish a
series of works, must be learned from himself and from the
problem of his life; and so much the more, as Descartes

---

[1] J. Millet : Histoire de Descartes avant 1637, p. 340.

declared them in detail, in concluding his first important
work.   His opponents are very ready with the decision that
fear was the motive of secrecy, while ambition incited him to
literary activity.   The first opinion is very superficial, and
the second fundamentally false.   Whatever external influences might have contributed to hinder or promote his
literary activity, the *inner* reason, in harmony with his
character, which first restrained him from publication, and
then led him to it step by step, was the desire for self-
instruction, the guiding principle of his life.   This is the
key to all those contradictions and vacillations.   When he
entered upon his course of self-instruction, he avoided publishing his thoughts, as a loss of time and a disturbance;
when he had made some progress in it, the publication of
his thoughts and the interchange of ideas became a part
of it.   At first Descartes was engaged exclusively in self-
instruction on principle, and was absorbed in his thoughts,
which he did not write, or, if he did, only briefly and hastily.
Then came a time when the maturity and clearness of his
developed thoughts could not be better tested than by
stating them in detail in writing.   He who is his own
teacher must also be his own examiner.   The record of his
own thoughts was such an examination, and Descartes was
much too methodical and thorough to be willing to dispense
with it.   Carefully written works, ready for the press, thus
arose, intended to serve for the examination of his own
thoughts and the instruction of the world; but the world
which they were to instruct was posterity, — not for the
sake of posthumous fame, but because of the great service
they could render.   The more uninterruptedly and constantly he could pursue his discoveries, the richer the results,
and the greater the benefits accruing to the world from his
labors.   He was therefore resolved not to publish his works
during his own lifetime.   He dreaded *the loss of time* which
the publication of his works would certainly involve.   It
would oblige him to parry attacks, correct misunderstand-

ings, engage in controversies with opponents and discussions with disciples. Even the reputation they might bring him would be unfavorable to his leisure. Sharing the territory he had won, would make it impossible for him to acquire more. "I am willing to have it known, that the little knowledge I have gained is almost nothing in comparison with that of which I am ignorant, and to the knowledge of which I hope to be able to attain. For it is with students of science as with those who are growing rich, who make great gains with less difficulty than they experienced when poor in making much smaller ones. Or, they may be compared with generals whose forces usually increase with victories, and who must use greater skill in keeping the field after a defeat than in taking cities and provinces after a victory. For he who seeks to surmount the obstacles and remove the errors that beset us in our march to the knowledge of truth must indeed fight a battle, and he loses it who adopts a false opinion concerning a matter of some comprehensiveness and importance; and to regain his former position, requires greater ability than to make great progress when once in possession of certain principles. And as for myself, if I have succeeded in discovering any truths in the sciences, I am certain that they are only the results of five or six difficulties which I have overcome, and my struggles with which I regard as so many battles in which fortune was on my side; and I declare without hesitation, that I only need to gain two or three such victories to reach the goal of all my designs, and I am not yet so advanced in years but that I may hope to accomplish this before I die. But my obligation to husband the time that remains increases with the hope of being able to use it well; and the publication of the principles of my physics would undoubtedly occasion a great loss of time. For, however evidently and absolutely they might be proved, it would be impossible for them to accord with the opinions of all the world; and I foresee that they would be the occasion of various controversies and disturb-

ances." These are the reasons why every publication of his
works seemed as absurd to our philosopher, as for a con-
queror to write books, and engage in controversies concerning the art of war, while advancing from victory to victory.
It was represented to Descartes, that the publication of his
doctrine might be useful to him and also to his doctrine.
Some would call his attention to certain defects; others
would turn it to practical account by means of useful deductions from it: and thus, by the assistance of others, his
system would be improved and extended. But these considerations had no weight with him. For no one was in a
better position to criticise his doctrine than himself, since no
one else was so well acquainted with it; and, as to the application of his thoughts, they were not yet mature enough to have
practical results, and, if they were, no one could realize them
as well as he himself, since the discoverer is always the best
judge, the only master. And Descartes not only dreaded antagonists, but the school which might attach itself to him and
deform his work. He knew what the schools of every time
have made of their masters, and he was on his guard beforehand against the "Cartesians." He expressly requested posterity not to attribute any opinion to him which he had not
himself declared. Precisely those disciples are most injurious who not merely repeat the words of the master, but
seek to interpret and complete his doctrine, and pretend to
know more than he himself. "They are like the ivy, which
never strives to rise higher than the tree to which it clings,
and often even returns downward after it has reached the
top. For these also appear to me to sink, that is, to become
more ignorant than when they began to study, who, not
contented with the teachings of the master, credit him with
the solution of many problems of which he says nothing, and
of which, perhaps, he never thought. These people live in
obscure conceptions which are very convenient to such philosophers; for they can thus talk with the utmost boldness,
and engage in endless controversies. They are like a blind

man who wishes to fight with one who can see, without disadvantage, and therefore leads him into a very dark cellar; and they ought to be glad that I refrain from publishing my 'Principles of Philosophy,' for they are so simple and evident that they would throw open the window, and let the light into the cellar into which the combatants have descended." [1]

But this sincere reason was more than counterbalanced by other considerations. The first, which stood by the cradle of his works, and did not cease to influence him, was the feeling that he ought to maintain his credit and keep his word. The reputation which would come with the diffusion of his writings was an enemy of his repose, but the feeling of unfulfilled promises was also. Earnestly to seek a reputation, was as disturbing as anxiously to avoid it. Descartes did neither. He allowed himself to gain the reputation of being a great thinker; and did not wish to be considered a charlatan, who had a reputation to which he had no right, and excited hopes which he did not fulfil, because, as one was at last obliged to believe, he could not. "Although I am not immoderately fond of fame, — am, indeed, averse to it, if I may venture to say so, *in so far as I regard it as an enemy of repose, which I prefer to every thing else,* — I have never been careful to conceal my actions as if they were crimes, nor made any effort to remain unknown: for I should regard such a course as a wrong to myself; and, besides, it would have been unfavorable to the perfect tranquillity which I value so highly. And, since I have not been able to avoid acquiring some kind of reputation, while thus alike indifferent to becoming known and remaining unknown, I thought I ought to do my best to avoid one that was bad." But the most important reason that determined him to publish his writings was, as we have already said, his desire for self-instruction. Descartes leaves no doubt on that point. "I see more and more clearly every day," says Descartes, "how my plan of self-instruction suffers

<hr>

[1] Discours de la Méthode, Part VI., Œuvres, i. pp. 196–203.

by means of this delay; for I need a great number of experiments, which I cannot perform without the assistance of others; and, although I do not flatter myself with the hope that the public will be greatly interested in my endeavors, yet I will not do myself such an injury as to give ground to those who shall survive me, to make the reproach against me that they might, in many respects, have been much better instructed if I had not too much neglected to give the information by means of which they might have promoted my plans." [1] The philosopher expressly declares that this consideration was his second motive in writing the "Discourse." It is, therefore, one and the same reason, — his desire of self-instruction, — that determined Descartes first to avoid writing his thoughts, and then inclines him to it, then causes him to refuse to publish his works, and finally to undertake it.

2. *Writings on Method.* — He goes carefully to work. His first publication is not his system, but *tests* or essays (*essais*), relating only to method and its application. He does not yet publish his theory of method, but only a preliminary statement of his general position; no *traité*, but only a *discours, de la méthode*, intended only as a preface or announcement of the doctrine, and rather vindicating the practical importance than explaining the theory of method. "I do not here intend to unfold the nature of my method, but only to talk about it." [2] The practicableness of his method was to be proved by its actual application in mathematics and physics. Descartes therefore published three essays along with the more important one, which were so chosen that the first belongs to mathematical physics, the second to physics, the third to pure mathematics. The subject of the first is "Dioptrics," that of the second "Meteors," that of the last "Geometry." The "Dioptrics" treats of the refraction of light, of sight, and of optical glasses. In "Meteors," Descartes

---

[1] Discours de la Méthode.

[2] Œuvres, vi. p. 138 (letter to Mersenne, written in the summer of 1637). Cf. p. 305 (a letter to a friend of Mersenne, April, 1637).

seeks to unfold the nature of salt, the causes of winds and
thunder-storms, the configuration of snow, the colors of the
rainbow and the properties of single colors, the halos about
the sun and moon, and particularly parhelions, four of which
had been seen in Rome some years before (March 20, 1629),
and had been described to him in detail. The "Geometry"
proves the new method of analysis which he had discovered,
by the solution of entirely new problems. In "Dioptrics"
and "Meteors," he merely sought to illustrate the value and
usefulness of his method, while in "Geometry" his aim was
to give an incontestable proof of it. These essays were to
have appeared under the following title: "Sketch of a Universal Science, by means of which our Nature can be raised
to the Highest Degree of Perfection; in addition, Dioptrics,
Meteors, and Geometry, in which the Author has chosen the
Best Cases for testing that Science, and so explained them
that Every Reader can understand the Subject without any
Instruction in Learned Matters." [1] It was well that Descartes
preferred to this high-sounding title the simple name "*Essais*,"
and called the more important essay "A Discourse on the
Method of Rightly Conducting the Reason, and Seeking Truth
in the Sciences." He wrote for thoughtful, independent
readers, unperverted by book-learning, and, therefore, in
French; stating the following reason at the conclusion of
his "Discourse:" "And if I write in French, the language of
my country, rather than in Latin, the language of my instructors, it is because I hope that the natural and healthy reason
will estimate my opinions more correctly than the learning
which puts its faith only in the books of the ancients. People of sound understanding, who have been properly instructed, are the only judges I desire; and I am sure that
they will not be so partial to Latin that they will refuse to
listen to my reasonings because I expound them in their
native tongue." [2]

---

[1] Œuvres, vi. pp. 276, 277 (letter to Mersenne, March, 1636).
[2] Discours de la Méthode, Part VI., Œuvres, i. pp. 210, 211.

With the exception of the "Geometry," the work was
ready for the press in the spring of 1636. Since the firm
of Elzevir in Amsterdam was not so ready to make advances
as Descartes had expected, he had it published by Jean le
Maire in Leyden. The privilege of sale was granted by the
States of Holland, Dec. 22, 1636; and by France not till May
4, 1637. Mersenne had attended to the matter in France,
and delayed it. It was his fault, and likewise his service,
that the French license was a eulogy of Descartes, though
the latter had expressly wished to remain unmentioned, both
in his work and in the documents relating to it. The
" Essays " could not be sent until June, 1637.

3. *The Metaphysical Works.* — The path upon which he
entered led farther. It was impossible for him to stop with
these essays: he had said so much of his system, that it was
necessary to say more. In the fourth part of his "Discourse,"
the fundamental principles of the new doctrines had already
appeared. He had discussed the necessity of universal
doubt, the principle of certainty, the criterion of knowledge,
the existence of God and the soul, — in a word, the principles of his philosophy. But naturally, in view of the plan
of that work, these doctrines were rather stated than clearly
established, and thus guarded against every misconception.
And this danger was least avoided exactly where he was
most exposed to it, — in the passages discussing the existence of God, — and Descartes himself recognized this as the
weakest and obscurest part of his work, which, therefore,
required a thorough and immediate elucidation. But to
elucidate the concept of God, was to explain the fundamental
conceptions of his metaphysics. The work was already done.
It was his first work in the Netherlands, the sketch of the
" Meditations " written in Franeker. The book had been
written ten years when Descartes resolved upon its publication; and during his winter residence in Harderwijk
(1639–40), he gave it the final revision.

The investigation is described as it has arisen in his own

mind, advancing from problem to problem, from solution to solution. It makes upon the reader the impression of deeply experienced thoughts which have been subject to ever-repeated examinations, the constant companions of the philosopher for years, the friends of his solitude, which have attained to maturity with him. They have the character of the most lively soliloquy, a monological drama which the reader cannot help following with the most active sympathy. The question is concerning the existence or non-existence of truth. The problem of knowledge appears as the great question, upon the answer to which depends the destiny of the human spirit, and is by Descartes so experienced. There is no truth if doubt is not completely overcome, and there is no such victory if doubt has not defended itself and fought knowledge with every weapon which it possesses. We are not only made to understand the grounds of doubt, but also to feel the unrest of spirit which agitates the *doubter*, who strives after truth, and, in spite of the certainty of the victory which has already been won, describes the contests he has endured as if he were even now in the heat of the conflict. This union of contemplative repose with the most vivid representation of a mind aroused and stormed by an army of doubts, which the spirit of contemplation already marshals and masters, gives to the "Meditations" of Descartes an irresistible charm, and the character, in their kind, of an incomparable philosophical work of art.

For the first time Descartes appeared before the world undisguised, as the thinker which he was. He had finally spoken the fundamental thoughts, which he had been maturing for the last twenty years, for the instruction of the world. He did not disguise his opinions, but he attended to their publication with the greatest caution. The work was immediately intended only for scholars, and was, therefore, written in Latin. But this was not sufficient to protect it from suspicions and misconceptions. He was apprehensive of opposition to his physical principles from the Aristotelians;

to his theology, from the Church. The fundamental principles of his philosophy of nature were contained in the
"Meditations;" but the inferences from them were not
drawn, and if he did not expressly say to the scholastic philosophers that the question was concerning a purely mechanical physics, they would not observe it, and the victory
would be won before they knew that a battle had been
fought. Descartes therefore wished that nothing be said of
his physics at first. "*Il ne faut pas le dire*," was his instruction to his friend Mersenne on this particular.

But Descartes had made his theological principles so conspicuous that it was impossible to conceal them. He therefore sought to prevent every ecclesiastical suspicion by the
title and dedication. He says that the principal content.
of the "Meditations" is proofs of the existence of God and
the immortality of the soul; and he dedicated his work to
the doctors of Sorbonne, the theological authority of Paris,
whose university had been regarded as the highest theological authority of the Church since the time of the Middle
Ages. Convinced that rational proofs of the existence of
God and the immortality of the soul could convert unbelievers, and that they would not lead believers astray;
that they were, therefore, in harmony with the interests of
the Church, the claims of the Bible, and the decisions of the
last Lateran Council, — he submitted his work to the censorship and protection of the theologians of Paris. They
had no objections to make. Father Gibieuf, whom he particularly asked to examine it, gave him his entire approval.
Nevertheless, the Church opposed it eventually: twenty-
two years later, this work of Descartes, which laid the foundations of his philosophy, stood on the list of forbidden books
at Rome, with the remark, "*donec corrigatur*."

Descartes foresaw that the novelty of his thoughts would
make a stir among scholars, and provoke all sorts of objections. He therefore wished to learn the objections of the
most famous men beforehand, and to have them printed with

his replies as an appendix to the work. It was a shrewd measure: when the work first appeared, it was already attacked and defended. Criticism, which usually follows a work, and thus directs and often perverts public judgment, was here obtained beforehand, and published with the book itself, so that the author had the last word. Some copies were therefore made, and given to friends, who circulated them among capable men, and obtained their opinions, and in part reported them to Descartes, in part sent them committed to writing by their authors. Bloemaert and Bannius in Harlem, the only Catholic priests in Holland with whom Descartes was at all intimate, were his principal agents in this matter in the Netherlands; Mersenne, of course, attended to it in France. Bloemaert and Bannius gave the manuscript to a Catholic scholar of reputation, *Caterus* of Antwerp, a doctor of the theological faculty of Lyons, who was a missionary in Holland, and dwelt in Alkmaar. His opinion was the first which Descartes received and sent with his reply to Mersenne (November, 1640). Mersenne circulated the work among Parisian scholars, obtained the opinions of theologians and mathematicians, and sent two collections of them to Descartes. Three of them were made by men of ability and historical fame, two of whom were philosophers, one English and one French, contemporaries and antagonists of Descartes, both of whom read the "Meditations," and committed their opinions of it to writing at Mersenne's suggestion. The English philosopher was *Thomas Hobbes;* the Frenchman, *Pierre Gassendi.* At the end of the year 1640, Hobbes had come to Paris to reside again, to avoid the English civil war; and he spent there a number of years, the most important literary period in his life, since he wrote during that time his best-known important works. Mersenne requested him to read and criticise the "Meditations," soon after his arrival. Descartes received the first part of his objections Jan. 20, 1641, during his residence in Leyden, and replied to them the next day;

the second part was sent in the first week of February.
At this time, Gassendi, who was still engaged in his important work on Epicurus and his doctrine, went to Paris, and
became acquainted, through Mersenne, with Descartes' new
work, and was requested to state his opinion in writing.
Gassendi had an inordinate desire to be praised and quoted.
He was amiable in conversation, and extravagant in his
praises, except when the Aristotelians were concerned; but
he was too vain to be an impartial critic. He was out of
humor with Descartes because the latter had not cited his
explanation of parhelions in his essay on "Meteors," which
neglect he regarded as *præter decorum.* In an ill humor,
and without a thorough understanding of Descartes' doctrine, he wrote his objections ("Disquisitio Metaphysica seu
Dubitationes"), which Mersenne received at the end of
May, 1641. Of course the usual praises were not wanting
at the conclusion. He wrote a rejoinder (*instantiæ*) to Descartes' reply, which his scholar, Sorbière, published with
the announcement that a perfect triumph had been achieved
(1643). The third of the above-mentioned authors was
Antoine Arnauld, then a young theologian, and soon after
admitted among the doctors of Sorbonne, who was subse-
quently to earn the name of the "great Arnauld," and to
be one of the most famous of the Jansenists. Descartes
regarded his objections as the most important, on account
of their style, insight, and mathematical acuteness. Arnauld
may be regarded as the man through whose agency the
union was afterwards effected between the Cartesian philosophy and the Jansenists of Port Royal. Descartes had
wished Mersenne to give the manuscript also to Father
Gibieuf of the Oratory of Jesus, and to the mathematician
Desargues, whom he valued more highly than three theologians. Another opponent appeared, — Father *Bourdin* of
the Society of Jesus, professor of mathematics in the College
of Clermont, who in his lectures had already invidiously
attacked Descartes' "Dioptrics" and "Meteors," and now

was just as hostile to his "Meditations." His attacks were
very annoying to Descartes. He knew with what unanimity
the Jesuits acted. He saw himself involved in a controversy with an order with which he wished to maintain the
old friendly relations on grounds both of regard and policy.
That a member of the Society of Jesus should be so hostile
to him, must have been doubly painful to him at a time when
he was receiving the worst treatment from the Calvinists in
the Netherlands. The order, however, had nothing to do
with Bourdin's polemic. The provincial Dinet was favorable to Descartes, and composed the difference. Bourdin
himself ceased to be his enemy after he became acquainted
with him.

We have here to deal merely with the history of these
objectiones and *responsiones*, not with their contents. (They
constitute a second and larger part, as it were, of the
" Meditations.") . There were seven, arranged in chronological order. First came those of Doctor Caterus; the
reports of objections collected by Mersenne occupied the
second and sixth places; those of Hobbes were third,
Arnauld's fourth, Gassendi's fifth, and Bourdin's seventh,
though it was not possible to publish the latter in the first
edition.

The work first appeared in Paris under the title, " Meditationes de prima philosophia, ubi de Dei existentia et animæ
immortalitate " (1641). The philosopher now sought to
overcome his dislike of the name "Cartesius," since the
name Descartes was to him "*un peu trop rude en latin.*"
The second edition was published by Elzevir in Amsterdam,
under the changed title, " Meditationes de prima philosophia
in quibus Dei existentia et animæ humanæ a corpore distinctio demonstrantur." The reason for this change is
evident enough. The existence of God is a metaphysical
principle; but the immortality of the soul is not, while the
difference of essence between the soul and body is. This
difference forms the foundation of the entire Cartesian sys-

tem, and, strictly speaking, is the theme of the "*prima philosophia*." The second expression is, therefore, a correction of the first, which was chosen for theological and religious reasons, as the dedication declares. Descartes' theory of the immortality of the soul is based on the difference of essence between soul and body; and metaphysics deals with principles, not with deductions from them. The explanation given by Descartes' last biographer again sacrifices truth to emotion. While Descartes was engaged in publishing the "Meditations," his father died, and almost at the same time his daughter and eldest sister. Now, it was full of consolation to the philosopher, to read on the title-page of his work "*de animæ immortalitate*." It was not really the title of his work, but an epitaph! If such feelings demanded any expression in such a place, the words "*animæ humanæ a corpore distinctio*" would have been just as comforting.[1]

The "Meditations" developed the course of thought by which the fundamental principles of the new philosophy were discovered and established. His next work was the systematic exposition of his entire system. Descartes began it immediately after the publication of the "Meditations," and completed it within the course of the year. "The Principles of Philosophy," in four books, was published by Elzevir in Amsterdam in 1644, and was his second comprehensive and important work. The first book treats of the principles of human knowledge; the second, of the principles of bodies; the third, of the visible world; the fourth, of the earth. The first two form the doctrine of principles, strictly speaking, metaphysics and the philosophy of nature. In the progress of his works, the "Meditations" were, in time as in fact, the middle term between the methodological essays and the system of metaphysics. Descartes called them his "metaphysical essays," and thus aptly indicated that they combined the characteristics of "philosophical essays" and the "Principles of Philosophy." He wrote this work in the

---

[1] J. Millet: Descartes, son Histoire depuis 1637, pp. 23-25.

happiest period of his life.   The success of his previous publications had raised him above the fear of public literary
activity.   He was perfect master of the matter to which he
had to give form and order, and nothing could give greater
pleasure to his methodical mind than such activity as this.
He exercised the skill of the architect, which he gladly used
as an example, in order to show the imperfections of patch-
work in comparison with a systematic work produced by one
mind.   He erected this temple of his thoughts while he was
living in the free and idyllic leisure which the country
palace of Endegeest permitted him to enjoy; always in the
neighborhood of, and often in conversation with, the gifted
princess, who understood him perfectly, and knew how to
appreciate him.   The Countess-palatine Elizabeth was then
the world for whom he wrote; and he dedicated to her his
work, unconcerned about the doctors of Sorbonne.   But
already a storm was gathering about the new doctrine and
the philosopher.

CHAPTER VI.

BEGINNINGS OF A SCHOOL. DISCIPLES AND OPPONENTS.

I. CONTROVERSIES IN UTRECHT.

1. *Reneri and Regius.*

AS little as Descartes sought the diffusion of his doctrine, he could not prevent it from gaining friends and disciples, who soon formed the nucleus of a school; for whose public activity in teaching, his works offered a definite basis, and the universities of the Netherlands the first field of labor. With friends came antagonists. Even in its origin, the school was violently attacked. In attacking disciples, the master was attacked; every means of suppressing the new doctrine was tried; even the person of its author was threatened. The University of Utrecht was the place where the school began to form, and where it was first opposed. It was not so much a definite theory which provoked its antagonists, as Descartes' mental importance in general; it was the novelty and power of his thoughts, which excited the hostility of those who would gladly have made themselves the subject of the first command, "Thou shalt have no other gods before me."

In order to understand the course and character of the controversies of Utrecht, we must go back a little. In the first part of his stay in the Netherlands, Descartes had become acquainted with Henry Reneri (Renier) in Amsterdam, who studied in Liège and Lyons, was converted from Catholicism to the Reformed Church, and, therefore, disinherited by his father. An exile from his native country,

he had sought an asylum in Holland, and started in Amsterdam a private school. He had become acquainted with Descartes through Beeckman. Through his intercourse with
Descartes, Reneri became deeply interested in philosophy;
and by diligent study he made such attainments that he was
called to the University of Leyden after the death of the
Aristotelian there, from thence to Deventer, and in the year
1634 to Utrecht. Descartes' first disciple was the first professor called to the newly founded university, with whose
history that of the Cartesian system was interwoven during
its first years. Reneri's career as professor in Utrecht was
short but brilliant. For five years he was an ornament of
the university. After his early death (March, 1639), by
order of the city and university the highest honors were
paid to his memory. The funeral oration, delivered by Anton
Æmilius, professor of history and rhetoric, himself a disciple
of the new philosophy, was likewise a eulogy of Descartes.
The government wished that the philosopher and his system
should be mentioned with commendations, and that the
oration should be published. On its titlepage Reneri was
called the friend and disciple of Descartes, "the Atlas and
Archimedes of our century." Envy and hatred followed
close upon this public and somewhat extravagant praise:
they sought first to strike the philosopher through his
disciples.

Among Reneri's pupils in Utrecht was an exceedingly
talented young medical student by the name of Regius
(Henry le Roi), who had mastered the new doctrine with
enthusiastic zeal, and so expounded it in his private lectures
on physiology that he soon won a crowd of enthusiastic
students. There was only one chair of medicine in the
university, and this was filled by Straaten. He wished to
teach nothing but anatomy and practical medicine, and,
therefore, urged that another chair should be established for
botany and theoretical medicine. Regius was chosen for the
new position, and was appointed professor in ordinary in

1638. After Reneri's death he was the leader of the new philosophy in Utrecht, and, therefore, the first target of its enemies.

2. *Gisbertus Voëtius.* — The leader of his opponents was one of the most highly respected and influential men in Utrecht, — Gisbertus Voëtius, the first professor of theology in the University of Utrecht, and the first clergyman of the city. He had been one of the most violent Gomarists in the synod at Dort, and, since the victory of his party, one of the most overbearing. He strode along with a pompous air, his person carefully attended to, with an expression of perfect self-satisfaction. For a long time he had regarded his talents, merits, and worth as incomparable, and despised every thing in which he was deficient; and he was deficient in much. His scholarship was narrow and superficial; his reading limited, embracing little beyond the *loci communes*, some commentaries and abridgments. He made the grossest blunders in his writings, because he quoted authorities without having read and understood them. His judgment was without acuteness, his thoughts lacked connection and order; in philosophy, his ability and knowledge were limited by the ordinary scholasticism. It is difficult to believe that a person of such mediocrity could be so respected and feared, and become the dangerous antagonist of so great a thinker. His inclination, however, led him to a kind of activity for which he had most talent. He chose polemics, a field where much can be accomplished with a large audience, without learning and real culture. He was not a controversialist of ability, but a mere fighting-cock, fitted to please a mob. He lacked both the fairness and judgment necessary to a just and impartial estimate of an opponent. He hated Catholics and philosophers worst of all; and passion so blinded him that he was scarcely able to distinguish them, and in his malignity he regarded the same man as a Jesuit and an atheist. Yet he was shrewd enough to decry an opponent as an atheist when addressing Jesuits, and as a

Jesuit when addressing Protestants. He was disputatious, because he would not brook opposition, and because he wished to rule. His thirst for power made him eager for office, and affable. He wished to please the people, and excite their admiration, now by an air of devotion, now by his bold and impudent sermons and writings. With people in general, he took the *rôle* of the prelate, while with scholars it pleased him to appear as a pedant; but his strongest desire was to appear to all as a man whom every one had cause to fear. For this reason there was no other discourse he liked so well to deliver as castigatory sermons in the manner of a Capuchin, — which make a strong impression on people, — and, to avoid being considered a coward, he persecuted regardlessly persons of power and influence, for unimportant matters. He was a master of the arts of pleasing the people, and, therefore, won their esteem without seeming to make it an object. And so it came to pass, that he was really beloved and highly respected by the masses, an object of fear to many, and was called "the glory and ornament of the churches of the Netherlands (*ecclesiarum belgicarum decus et ornamentum*);" and this was the height of his ambition, as well as the expression of his own modest opinion.

By the side of this man, there arose in Utrecht an influential intellectual power in the doctrine and school of Descartes, which acknowledged no allegiance to him. Since it was praised on the titlepage of that funeral oration, Voëtius had been its enemy. He had exerted his influence a year before in behalf of Regius's appointment, after the latter had flattered him and allowed him to examine his creed. But now the zeal of Regius for Cartesianism, and still more his popularity as a lecturer, displeased Voëtius; and he plotted the ruin of Regius and Descartes. If he could only prove that the new doctrine was dangerous to Protestantism and, therefore, to the Netherlands! And, if he could show that the Cartesian philosophy was atheistic, it could be very easily done, since Regius was a Cartesian. To this end he read through the "Discourse," Descartes' first publication, and collected all the passages relating to theology; and, fortunately for his purpose, he found doubt so openly acknowledged, and vindicated with such disregard of consequences, that the atheistic tendencies of the work were to him self-evident.

3. *The Condemnation of the New Philosophy.* — At first the name of Descartes was not mentioned. Voëtius contented himself with selecting certain features of Descartes' doctrine, and attacking them as atheistic, in some academic theses in June, 1639. In this way he began his campaign, which, if he were successful, would end with the expulsion of Descartes from the Netherlands. For a long time the controversy was carried on in the form of academic theses and disputations. Voëtius made every exertion, and used his influence with the professors and magistrates, and his power as rector, to destroy Regius. On many an occasion, Regius, in his young and somewhat immature way, had shown the superiority of the new philosophy to the old, and had offended his colleagues by making the old ridiculous, and thus exposed himself to severe attacks. In June, 1640, when he defended the new doctrine of the circulation of the blood, discovered by Harvey and defended by Descartes, he was instructed not to depart so far from the traditional theories, and to defend the new doctrines only "*exercitii causa.*" The next year Voëtius was made rector. The controversy became more animated, though it was still carried on only by academic theses and disputations. Regius defended the thesis that the union of soul and body consists only in the composition of the two substances, and is not, therefore, an actual unity, — not a "*unum per se,*" but only "*per accidens.*" Now, it is exactly in this point that the most pronounced contradiction exists between the Cartesian system and the Aristotelian scholastic theory of the entelechy and substantiality of forms; and in his counter-theses Voëtius

declared the new doctrine heretical. The theory of the substantiality of the body, and the composition of man out of two substances (*"unum per accidens"*), is contrary to reason; the theory of the motion of the earth, which Kepler (!) introduced, contradicts the teachings of the Scriptures, as well as all the philosophy that has been hitherto accepted; and the denial of substantial forms leads to the same contradictions, promotes scepticism, endangers faith in immortality, the Trinity, incarnation, original sin, prophecy, miracle, grace, regeneration, etc. These theses denote the man, and the nature of his mind.

At this point the controversy, hitherto academic and carried on by means of disputations and theses, began to be conducted in writing. Contrary to the advice of Descartes and his friends in Utrecht, Regius published his defence against the theses of Voëtius. Indeed, Descartes was in general but little pleased with the polemical tone of Regius. The manner in which he inveighed against the scholastic philosophy could not but displease Descartes, from his whole mode of thought. He reminded Regius that the past ought not to be attacked for sport, and, indeed, he saw neither use nor plan in the controversy which the latter had in view. Should Regius publish his reply to Voëtius, — and Descartes counselled against it, — it ought to be moderate in its tone, and freed from all offensive expressions. Regius followed the last advice; but, however carefully he chose his words, however flattering they were to Voëtius, the latter could not pardon him for daring to reply to him at all. In addition to this, the reply was printed without license, the printer was a Catholic, and the publisher a Remonstrant. Voëtius discovered a whole nest of heresies that must be broken up. By command of the magistrates, the book was confiscated; but this only made it read the more, and its diffusion made the anger of Voëtius still hotter; and the result was, that at his urgent suggestion Regius was forbidden to lecture on *philosophical* subjects. He now turned

to attack the new philosophy as such, and defend the old.
His son wrote theses in reply to Regius; while one of
his creatures, a student by the name of Waterlact, wrote a
vindication of the already seriously threatened orthodox
philosophy. But Voëtius struck the home thrust through
the university of which he was master. The academic senate
decreed a formal disapprobation of the publication of Regius
and his doctrine, and likewise a formal condemnation of the
new philosophy. The decree was pronounced March 16,
1642, and contained the following declaration: "We, professors of the University of Utrecht, reject and condemn the
new philosophy, because, in the first place, it contradicts
the old, and subverts its principles; second, because it makes
students averse to the study of the old philosophy, and thus
hinders their cultivation, since they cannot understand the
terminology of the schools when they have once become
acquainted with the principles of this pretended philosophy;
and, finally, because not only do so many false and irrational views follow from it, but also immature youths can
easily draw inferences from it inconsistent with other sciences, particularly the true theology." Eight out of ten
professors subscribed to this division: the other two were
Cyprianus and Æmilius, the admirer of the philosopher.

4. *The Controversy between Descartes and Voëtius.* — The
condemnation was aimed at Descartes, although his name
was not mentioned; and he therefore now appeared on the
field of battle. Engaged in preparing the second edition
of the "Meditations," and in replying to Bourdin's objections, he found an excellent opportunity for describing the
intrigues of his enemy in Utrecht, in a letter written at the
same time to Dinet, in which he also examined the attacks
of his opponent among the Jesuits. He made no mention of
university, disciples, or opponents; but with a few strokes
he sketched a picture of the latter *ad vivum*: "There is
a man who is regarded by the world as a theologian, a
preacher, and a defender of the faith, who, through his con-

troversial sermons, in which he libellously attacks now the Catholic Church, now others of a different faith from his own, now the powers of the time, has won a high place in the respect and regard of the people. He makes a show of an ardent and ingenuous zeal for religion; interlarding his discourses, at the same time, with jests which please the ear of the common people. He is constantly publishing pamphlets which are not worth reading, citing therein various authors who testify against rather than for him, and whose works he probably knows only from their tables of contents. He speaks of every possible science in a bold and confident manner, as if he were entirely at home in them, and therefore passes for a scholar among the ignorant. But people of some judgment, who know how forward he is to begin quarrels with all the world, how often he substitutes insults for arguments, and, after he has been beaten, how insultingly he retires, openly ridicule and despise him if they are not of his faith. Indeed, he has been handled so roughly before all the world, that scarcely any thing for disputation now remains. Intelligent people of his own faith excuse and tolerate him as well as they can, but in their hearts they regard him with equal contempt." [1]

Voëtius recognized his portrait, and breathed vengeance. He ought now to have openly taken the field against Descartes, and led the fight directly against him; but he remained in ambush, and sought to find people to go into the fire for him. He wanted to find some one to attack the theories of the philosopher, another to write a libel against him, or to put his name to a pamphlet written by Voëtius himself. At the same time, before the public he took the *rôle* of the injured man. He was innocence itself, Descartes was a malicious slanderer. He failed in his first attempt to secure an ally to attack the theories of Descartes. nor could he have made it more unskilfully, or in a way that showed a greater lack of character. Voëtius, the sworn enemy of

[1] Œuvres, t. ix. pp. 34, 35.

Catholicism, wrote, to this end, to a *Catholic* theologian, who
was also Descartes' old and true friend, — Mersenne. And
how did he write? The letter was written in the beginning
of the controversies, before the university pronounced its
judgment of condemnation ; and in it we find these words:
" You have doubtless read the philosophical essays which
Descartes has published in French. He appears to wish to
be the founder of a new sect, unheard of till now; and there
are those who admire and pray to him as though he were
a god fallen down from heaven. These ευρηματα should be
subjected to your judgment and censorship. No physicist
or philosopher could overthrow him more successfully than
you, who are eminent in geometry and physics, — precisely
those departments in which Descartes imagines he is strong ;
and to do so would be a labor worthy of your learning and
your ability. You have defended truth, and, in the reconciliation of theology and physics, vindicated metaphysics
and mathematics. Truth, therefore, summons you to avenge
her." Disgusted by this letter, Mersenne treated Voëtius
as he deserved. He did not answer him for a long time ;
and when he did, he declined his proposal as emphatically
as he could, confounding its author so far as it lay in his
power. At the same time he sent the letter, with his answer,
to Descartes.

Voëtius succeeded in finding an ally to be responsible for
the libel. He found a man ready to give his name and pen
to a pamphlet sketched, and in part written, by himself, —
Martin Schoock, professor in Gröningen, formerly his pupil
and now his tool. The pamphlet was published a year after
that academic condemnation (March, 1643), under the title,
" Philosophia Cartesiana, sive admiranda methodus novæ philosophiæ Renati Descartes," in style and character a malicious
libel. The preface attacked the letter to Dinet, in which
Descartes had insulted Reformed religion, and the Evangeli-
cal Church of the Netherlands, particularly one of its most
eminent members. The rest of the pamphlet is an attack

on the new philosophy; charges it with having dangerous consequences, infidelity, atheism, and immorality. Descartes is a second Vanini, an atheist, and a hypocrite, like the latter who was justly condemned for his atheism and burned in Toulouse. This comparison, which smells of the stake, and is developed with great care and in great detail, is the unmistakable work of Voëtius.

The pamphlet was published in Utrecht. During the printing, Descartes received the sheets one by one; and as soon as he read the first, he began his reply, "Epistola ad celeberrimum virum D. Gisbertum Voëtium," the masterpiece of his polemics. He had a threefold purpose: first, to vindicate the picture of his antagonist, sketched in the letter to Dinet; second, to invalidate the pamphlet signed by Schoock; and, third, to criticise another of Voëtius' bungling works, which appeared while Descartes was writing. Thus the polemic grew under his hands, and the letter became a book of nine parts. Even before he received the last sheets of the " Philosophia Cartesiana," Voëtius published a libel entitled " On the Fraternity of Mary." The two publications, unlike as they are in their subjects, resemble each other so closely in their mode of thought, style, and polemical methods, that their kinship is easily recognized. Descartes now turns aside to take up this new subject, devotes to it the sixth part of his letter, and, after he has received the last sheets of the pamphlet, returns to his original subject. This interruption is unfavorable to the composition of his polemic. It makes a sudden leap into a new field, and absorbs foreign matter which increases its strength in appearance only, while in fact it scatters it and disturbs the impression of the whole. However, his procedure is explained both by his irritation, and particularly by the fact that it is an acknowledged production of Voëtius of which he is in possession, while he is compelled to write against a concealed author. If he can prove that the author of the Philosophia Cartesiana," and that of the " Confraternitas

Mariana," is one and the same man, he has scored an important point, and convicted Voëtius of the double meanness of reviling and lying.

The subject of the second publication has nothing in common with the first. There existed in Catholic times, in Bois-le-Duc, a Society of the Holy Virgin, in possession of certain rights and revenues, of which the most distinguished men in the city were members. After the downfall of the Spanish power, and the victory of the Reformation, this society had been acknowledged by the new government (1629). Its rights and revenues were preserved; though exactly for this reason it lost its ecclesiastical character, of which nothing remained but its name, and now existed merely as a civil society. But to prevent it from being a secret centre of Catholicism, and thus forming numerous intrigues dangerous to the state, the authorities required the admission of reformed members; and so the burgomaster of Bois-le-Duc, with thirteen of the most influential Protestants of the city, became members of the society. This event kindled the anger of Voëtius into a flame. He immediately hurled a thesis, always his first thunderbolt, against this "idolatry" in Bois-le-Duc. The authorities of the city, through one of their ecclesiastics, replied in a moderate and conciliatory tone to the charges of idolatry, religious indifference, and ungodly tolerance; but Voëtius or his companions made a counter-reply with an anonymous libel, and since this was forbidden in Bois-le-Duc he wrote the book, "De Confraternitate Mariana."

The two antagonists were now pressing hard upon each other. Four years had passed since Voëtius began the attack; and he had continued it in theses, disputations, lectures, sermons, and private letters. Through his influence the judgment of condemnation was pronounced by the University of Utrecht, and he boasted of it in a letter which fell into Descartes' hands; and finally he had concealed himself behind Schoock in order to insult the philosopher in a libel, and make him and his system an object of suspicion. After the lapse of years, Descartes himself entered the controversy, and wrote two articles, the letters to Dinet and Voëtius, both of which were handed in his name, by influential men, to the first burgomaster of the city of Utrecht.

A lawsuit now resulted from the controversy. Voëtius played the *rôle* of a martyr who had suffered for his faith. Descartes was a Jesuit, who had come into the Netherlands as the emissary and spy of the Jesuits, to excite dissensions and controversies; and this was why *Voëtius*, "the glory and ornament of the Church of the Netherlands," had been the first object of his attacks, the first victim of his slanders. He had never injured Descartes: the pamphlet against him was written by Schoock, not by himself. Thus he excited public sentiment in Utrecht, particularly that of the authorities, and arrayed it on his side, seeking from the magistrates protection, as a persecuted man, against the slanders of the foreign philosopher. The 13th of June, 1643, the authorities issued a summons to Descartes, to appear in person, and prove his accusations against Voëtius, especially to prove that Voëtius and not Schoock was the author of the pamphlet against him. If his accusations were true, they would result in the greatest injury to the university and the city. The summons was issued with all the forms of publicity; it was proclaimed before the people with the ringing of a bell; it was printed, posted, sent abroad. All this emanated from hostility to Descartes; for it was entirely unnecessary, as every one knew where to find him. He received the summons in Egmond, where he had lived for a short time, and answered it in writing in the language of the country. He thanked the authorities for the purpose of the investigation, and offered to prove his assertions; but, as a Frenchman, he disputed their right to institute judicial proceedings against him. Since a libel had been published against him in Utrecht, he had a right to expect that the investigation would first of all discover its author, and hold

him to account.   However, he felt that he was no longer
safe : he was apprehensive of a warrant, which could be
immediately executed in Egmond.   He went, therefore, to
The Hague, and committed himself to the protection of the
French ambassador, de la Thuillérie, who took up the matter; and through his influence the Prince of Orange put a
stop to further persecution.   That Descartes was unmolested,
was due to the stadtholder.   Sentence was certainly pronounced against him; his letters were condemned as libels,
and he was found guilty of slandering Voëtius (Sept. 23,
1643) : but the decision was published almost secretly, and
when it was proclaimed publicity was avoided with as much
care as it had been sought some months before when the summons was issued.   The authorities were in an embarrassing
position, and wished to get the matter out of the way by
pronouncing a sentence of condemnation in such a way as
to make it of no effect.   Voetius had thus attained the smallest part of his purpose.   If he had succeeded, Descartes
would have been driven from the Netherlands, and his condemned publications would have been burnt.   It was said
that he had already urged the executioner to make a huge
pile, in order that the flames might be seen at a great
distance.

5. *Conclusion of the Utrecht-Gröningen Controversy.* — But
the matter was not yet ended.   Descartes learned the decision without being officially informed of its purport and its
reasons.   What he heard necessarily increased his apprehensions for his safety, even for his reputation, since he seemed
to have been proved guilty of having falsely accused Voëtius
of having written the libel.   Schoock had spent the summer
in Utrecht, and had there declared most positively that he
alone was the author of the " Philosophia Cartesiana," that
he had written it without assistance or suggestion from Voëtius, and that he intended to state this in a new publication.
This made Descartes' position worse.   He received anonymous letters from those who were kindly disposed to him

in Utrecht and The Hague, warning him that he was in
imminent danger. He had reason to fear imprisonment, and
the seizure of his papers, in Egmond Van Hoef, where he
was then staying; and, therefore, intended to go back to
The Hague in November, 1643.[1] For the second time he
appealed for protection to the French ambassador, describing
to him in detail the situation in Utrecht. (The letter has
been in part preserved, and has been lately published by
Foucher de Careil.[2])

But, since Schoock had declared that he alone was the
author of the pamphlet, Descartes was compelled to bring
an action against him before the senate of the University of
Groningen. And there the matter terminated quite otherwise than in Utrecht. It happened that the accused was
just then rector of the university. To spare their rector,
and, at the same time, do justice to the philosopher, the
senate avoided pronouncing a formal decision, and made a
declaration satisfactory to Descartes, lamenting that Schoock
had engaged in the controversy against the latter, and
had brought utterly groundless charges against his system.
Schoock himself declared, under oath, that Voëtius had
urged him to write the pamphlet, the most of which was
written in Utrecht; that he had furnished the material for
it, and, during the printing, had added the strongest invec-
tives, and had put Schoock's name, against his will, on the
titlepage and to the preface. Schoock further swore that he
could not acknowledge the pamphlet in its present form as
his own, and that he must declare that it was unworthy
of a respectable man and a scholar. He said he repented of
nothing more bitterly, than that he had had any thing to do
with it; that he had broken with Voëtius, and had refused

<hr/>

[1] Œuvres inédites, vol. ii. pp. 22, 23. (Letter to the counsellor of state,
William, in The Hague, Nov. 7, 1643.)

[2] Ib., ii. pp. 43–63. (Letter to M. de la Thuillérie.) From the first words of
the letter, it is evident that Descartes had, for the first time, appealed to his
protection shortly before; which, it seems to me, his latest biographer over-
looks. J. Millet: Histoire de Descartes, ii. pp. 127–129.

his request to sign a false testimony. Now Descartes' accusation against Voëtius was completely proved, and the decision of the court in Utrecht was shown to be entirely
groundless. He sent the document stating the action of the
senate in Groningen, and the information laid before it, to
the authorities in Utrecht, with the reasonable expectation
that they would look into the matter, and make right the
wrong they had done him, by some public act. But nothing
was done, except to issue a prohibition to the printer and
publisher in Utrecht, forbidding them to sell or circulate any
publications for or against Descartes. Half of this prohibition was aimed at the philosopher; and the other half was
without effect, since both Voëtiuses, father and son, continued
to publish abuses of Descartes. The younger Voëtius wrote
a defence of his father, and a pamphlet against the University of Gröningen, in which Descartes and his system were
again slandered, and the contents of the first pamphlet were
re-affirmed, although the authorship of the elder Voëtius was
denied. The elder Voëtius brought an action against his
colleague Schoock, but let the prosecution drop. The two
worthies found it useful to compose their differences in good
time, since they had been partners in too many intrigues, and
each had reason to fear the revelations of the other.

Descartes finally concluded the controversy (the last week
of June, 1645), which, from its first occasion to the point of
time just stated, occupied a period of six years, with "An
Apologetic Letter to the Magistrates of Utrecht, against the
Two Voëtiuses, Father and Son." The entire course of the
controversy was narrated in detail; and from the letters of
Voëtius to Schoock, it was proved that Voëtius projected and
urged the defamatory pamphlet; that he made the comparison with Vanini; that he himself wrote the preface, the most
outrageous part of the pamphlet, and put it in Schoock's
hands. He said further, that the magistrates had for four
years treated him unfairly and unjustly, in favor of the two
Voëtiuses: first, in summoning him like a vagabond; second,

in condemning him as a slanderer, and in not retracting this decision even after the declaration of the senate of Gröningen ; third, in endeavoring to dispose of the matter without a word of restitution, by an apparently neutral but really partisan prohibition. He expected that the magistrates would at last give him the satisfaction which was his due.[1]

The magistrates of Utrecht remained deaf to all arguments. Their partiality appears the more odious when we consider the circumspect conduct, the peaceable character, and the retired life of Descartes. In a free country, where he sought nothing except leisure and solitude, he had, for no just reason, come pretty near being deprived of its hospitality, and his residence there had been made intensely disagreeable. His dislike of appearing before the world as an author had been justified : he must do penance for the attempt which he had made so hesitatingly and cautiously, with a long series of interruptions and disappointments.

II. ATTACKS IN LEYDEN.

When the affair at Utrecht was ended, the new philosophy had already struck roots in the University of Leyden, and had begun to be a subject of academic theses and disputations. Hooghland, a Catholic nobleman, the mathematicians Golius and Schooten, were friends and disciples of Descartes. Particular mention should be made of Adrian Heereboord, who circumspectly and successfully defended his theories in the university. As in Utrecht, disciples aroused opponents. Here, also, they came from the theologians, who emulated Voëtius, and were probably set on by him. Scarcely two years had passed since the conclusion of the Utrecht controversy, when the attacks of the theologians in Leyden became so violent that Descartes, at the suggestion of his friends, appealed from Egmond to the magistrates

---

[1] Lettre Apologétique de M. Descartes, aux magistrats de la ville d'Utrecht, contre MM. Voëtius père et fils (Œuvres, t. ix. pp. 250-322). Regius received this " fasciculum epistolarum," as he called it, June 22, 1645.

for protection.   And he had the same experience with these
magistrates as with those in Utrecht.

In the first months of the year 1647, Revius, a theological
tutor, had caused some theses to be defended against the
"Meditations," in which the philosopher was charged with
pure atheism and other heresies.   The man was so insignifi-
cant, and his attacks so coarse, that they had no effect.
Soon after, Triglandius defended theses, accusing Descartes,
not merely of atheism, but blasphemy and Pelagianism.
Descartes had called God a deceiver, and had explained the
faculty of the human will as greater than the idea of God.
As a matter of fact, Descartes had supposed the possibility
that the world is a mere phantom, the work of a deceptive
demon, in order to prove the contrary ; and he had declared
that the human will is more comprehensive than the understanding.   These attacks had so little the appearance of
mere misconceptions, that the friends of the philosopher perceived in them dangerous intentions, and advised him to take
measures against them.   On May 4, 1647, Descartes wrote to
the curators of the university and the magistrates of the city
of Leyden, requesting redress for the wrong inflicted upon
him by false accusations.   He was answered May 22, that the
rector of the university, as well as the professors of the theological and philosophical faculties, had been called together,
and strictly forbidden to make any mention of Descartes'
theories, whether to attack or defend them, and it was expected that he would engage in no further discussion of the
theories which had been attacked.[1]   The redress, therefore,
consisted in this, — that the theories which had been attacked
should be considered Cartesian, and that his entire system
was laid under a kind of interdict in the University of Leyden ; and, indeed, the philosopher himself required to submit
to this regulation.   Aroused by the injustice and unreason-
ableness of this procedure, Descartes replied to the magistrates, saying that he had probably not understood them ; it

[1] Œuvres, t. x. pp. 26, 27.

was to him perfectly indifferent whether his name was mentioned in the University of Leyden, or not; but for the sake of his reputation, he must demand the declaration that the theories which had been attacked were not his.[1] "Am I a Herostratus, that people are forbidden to mention me?" he wrote at that time to one of his friends in Holland. "I have never striven to have my name spread abroad, or desired that any pedant in the world should know any thing of me. But the matter has now gone so far, that they must either give me redress, or openly acknowledge that your theologians have a right to lie and slander, and that a man like me cannot expect the least justice against them in this land."[2] A little before this, he described his new grievances to the Princess Elizabeth. "I have written a long letter to the curators of the University of Leyden, to demand redress for the slanders of two theologians. I have not yet received their answer; but I do not expect much, since I know the disposition of the people in this country, and that they do not defend honesty and virtue, since they fear the frowns of theologians. The wrong will be plastered over, not healed." "If, as I foresee, I do not obtain justice, I intend to leave this country immediately." "I have just received letters from the Hague and Leyden, informing me that the meeting of the curators is postponed, and that the theologians propose to be the judges. In this case, I shall be subject to an inquisition worse than the Spanish ever was, and shall be branded as an enemy of their faith. I am, therefore, advised to appeal to the French ambassador, and the Prince of Orange, not to obtain justice, but to prevent, by their interference, the extremest measures of my antagonists. I do not think, however, that I shall follow this advice. I want justice; and if I cannot get it, I think it best to prepare to return as quietly as possible."[3]

Descartes was entirely correct, when, in his letter to the

---

[1] Œuvres, t. x. pp. 29–34.   [2] Ib., pp. 36–40.

[3] Ib., pp. 40–44. (The letter is dated May 12, 1647.)

Princess Elizabeth, he said that the Leyden attacks were a consequence of those of Utrecht, and spoke of a "theological league" that opposed him, determined to suppress his doctrine. The orthodox Calvinists of the Netherlands were agreed upon the condemnation of the new philosophy, and had no intention whatever to engage in discussions concerning its nature and grounds. They wished to make short work of it, and to forbid to theologians by *synodal* decrees any use of Descartes' doctrine in their discourses and writings. Ten years later they accomplished their purpose. It was the first conflict between modern philosophy and the Reformed Church.

With this, the idyllic life of the philosopher in the Netherlands was over. The Utrecht-Leyden difficulties had more and more embittered his feelings against the country and its inhabitants. He had every reason to feel insecure, and to think of a new and quiet residence.

CHAPTER VII.

LAST YEARS AND WORK IN HOLLAND.

I. NEW PLANS AND FRIENDS.

1. *Journeys to France.*

THERE were reasons enough to induce the philosopher, after so long an absence, and after he had so successfully finished the most important part of his work, to return to his own country. Although he had found many and able friends and disciples, particularly in the Hague, among the personal friends of the Prince of Orange and his counsellors, men like Constantine Huyghens van Zuytlichen (father of the famous Christian Huyghens), Wilhelm, Pollot, and others, he had been obliged to learn that the ruling party in the Church was hostile to him, had threatened to drive him from the country, and suspected him as a Catholic Frenchman. His opponents in the Netherlands wished to get rid of him, while his countrymen had long desired his return. It seemed unworthy of France, that a man who had increased the fame of the French name to such an extraordinary extent, should live in a foreign land. Even at the court, Descartes had found admirers. Sept. 6, 1646, a royal pension was bestowed upon him, unsought. With the prospect of a new one, the patent of which he received a year and a half later (March, 1648), he was invited to live in France, in a position suitable to his rank, and favorable to his leisure. Even before this, he had felt a desire to see old friends, and become acquainted with new ones; and, besides, after the death of his father, the duty of attending to the business affairs of his family occasioned him to break in upon his leisure in Egmond, and make a visit to France.

The two first journeys were made in the years 1644 and 1647, principally to attend to the business of his inheritance and his family. We learn from his letters that he left Egmond van Hoef, May 1, 1644; went by the Hague, Leyden, and Amsterdam to France; that he left Paris, July 10, for Brittany, to stay there two months.[1] At the commencement of October, he was again in Paris with his friend Picot; and in the middle of November, he returned to Egmond. The condemnation in Utrecht had already been pronounced, and action had been brought in Gröningen, against Schoock, when he set out upon the journey. Two years later we find him in the first week in June, in the Hague, about to start on another journey to France. He left Paris, July 15, to go again to Brittany and Poitou, to look after business matters. In the middle of autumn he was again in Egmond. Just before this, those unpleasant attacks in Leyden were made, and he quietly resolved to return. The thought of setting his feet on French soil was ever with him; and, therefore, he accepted that favorable invitation which was the only reason of his third and last visit to Paris.

He became acquainted with two of the critics of his "Meditations" in Paris, and, with them, forgot their disputes; viz., the Jesuit Bourdin on his first visit, and Gassendi on the last. In the summer of 1647 he made the acquaintance of the younger Pascal, whom he often met, and sought to convince that there is no "*vacuum*" in nature, and no "*horror vacuii.*" He insisted that we must not explain certain phenomena of the motion of fluid bodies — for example, the ascent of water in the tube of a pump — by such fictions, but by the pressure of the air.

2. *Clerselier and Chanut.* — Among the new friends and

---

[1] Œuvres inédites, ii. p. 31. (Letter to Wilhelm in the Hague, July 9, 1644. Descartes inquires in this letter concerning the Gröningen matter.)

enthusiastic admirers whom Descartes found in France, the
most important were two men with whom he became
acquainted in Paris, in the summer of 1644, and whose
names are interwoven with the destiny of the philosopher
and his works : they were the young advocate of parliament,
Claude Clerselier, and his brother-in-law, Pierre Chanut, then
president of the board of revenue, and next year French
ambassador to the court of the queen of Sweden. When he
went through Amsterdam on his way to Sweden (October,
1645), Descartes came from Egmond to see Chanut, for
whom he had formed a very warm friendship. Chanut was
particularly interested in questions relating to theoretical
ethics; and Descartes had so high an opinion of his judgment,
that he wished him to read and criticise his works. "Most
men have so little capacity for criticism, that I do not find it
useful to waste time with their opinions; but I shall regard
yours as the utterances of an oracle." In the same letter,
he wrote to his distant friend, " I often think regretfully,
that the world is much too large for the few excellent people
in it. I would that they all lived in a single city ; and I
would gladly quit my hermitage, to live there too, if they
would permit me. Although I shun the crowd, on account
of the multitude of intrusive boors one meets at every step,
I yet value intercourse with those whom one esteems, as the
greatest happiness of life. If *you* were in Paris, I should
have a strong motive to go there too." " I have been yours
from the first hour of our acquaintance, and I esteem you as
warmly as if I had spent my whole life with you." [1]

Chanut took the liveliest interest in the writings and
studies of Descartes, and spread his fame abroad whenever he
had the opportunity. He studied the " Principles" again,
and requested Clerselier to send him the French edition of
the " Meditations," that he might give it to the queen. He
rejoiced that Descartes had sketched a short essay on " The

[1] Œuvres, t. ix. pp. 409, 410. (March, 1646,) p. 417. (Letter dated Nov. 1, 1646.)

Nature of the Human Passions;" and he urged his friend to complete this work, which was connected with the questions relating to the theory of morals. This interest plainly animated the lonely philosopher, who was somewhat depressed by his recent experiences. "I would now gladly write of yet another undertaking," Descartes had said in the letter in which he mentioned that essay on the passions, "but I see how few men there are who think it worth while to read my writings; and this pleases me so little, that it makes me negligent." [1]

That the young queen of Sweden was to receive his "Meditations" from the hands of a friend, and read them at his suggestion, afforded to him a pleasant prospect, and plainly brightened his depressed mood, disgusted as he was with the conduct of a hostile or stupid multitude. Involuntarily his imagination placed the Northern queen by the side of the Princess Elizabeth, and found a resemblance between them. Vague wishes and hopes were excited, which reflected themselves in his next letter to Chanut. This letter deserves an important place among the self-revelations of the philosopher. Among the griefs and disappointments of the last years, he had often repented of his unfaithfulness to his motto, " *Bene qui latent, bene vixit.*" He wished now to see the world only in his friends. Perhaps Stockholm seemed to him that city of congenial minds to live in which he held the highest good. "Had I not an entirely exceptional opinion of your penetration, and the greatest wish to learn of you, I should not have begged you so importunately to examine my writings; for I am not in the habit of burdening people with such requests. I have let my works go into the world unadorned, destitute of the finery that attracts the eyes of those who judge merely by appearances, since I cared only for the attention of men of ability, who would take the pains to examine them for my instruction. This service you have not yet rendered me, though you have put me under great obligations in other

---

[1] Œuvres, t. ix. p. 413. (Letter dated June 15, 1646.)

respects, and I know that you speak well of me ; and Clerselier informs me that you wish to give my 'Meditations' to the queen. I have never been ambitious to be known by persons in such high station ; and if I had had the discretion which savages attribute to apes, no one would know that I write books. For it is said that savages believe that monkeys could talk if they would, but they refrain from doing so that they may not be forced to work. I have not been discreet enough to avoid writing, and therefore I am no longer in possession of the quiet and leisure that I might have enjoyed. However, the mischief is done. I am known by a multitude of the adherents of the schools, who look askance at my writings, and seek in all ways to injure me. I have, therefore, reason to wish to be known also by better people, who have both the power and the will to protect me. And I have heard such excellent things of this queen, that I am sincerely grateful to you for thinking of me in connection with her, though I have been in the habit of complaining when any one wished to make me acquainted with a person in eminent station. I would not have believed half that De la Thuillerie told me about the queen on his return from Sweden, if I had not myself experienced in the princess, to whom I dedicated my 'Principles,' that persons of great rank, of whichever sex, do not need to be old to excel others by far in scientific and moral culture. I only fear that the queen will not thank you for recommending my writings. Perhaps they would seem more worthy of being read if they treated of ethical subjects, but this is a theme upon which I dare not enter. The professors have fallen into a passion even on account of my harmless principles of physics, and they would give me no rest if I should write on ethics. A father (Bourdin) has accused me of scepticism, because I have refuted the sceptics ; and a clergyman (Voëtius) has decried me as an atheist, because I have attempted to prove the existence of God. What would they say if I should inquire into the true value of all things which we desire or shun, and into the state of the soul after death, and should seek to ascertain to what degree we have a right to love life, and what should be our state that we may not fear death? And however perfectly my views might accord with those of religion, and however useful they might be to the State, exactly opposite opinions would be attributed to me in both particulars. I hold it best, therefore, to write no more books at all, and to say with Seneca, 'Heavy is the burden of death on him who dies, known to all the world, but unknown to himself.' I will labor only for my own instruction, and impart my thoughts only in private conversations. How happy I should be could I have such intercourse with you! but I do not believe I can ever go where you now live, or that you can retire here. My only hope is, that, after some years, you will make me happy by spending some days in my hermitage on your return to France; and I can then talk with you with an open heart." [1]

His "beloved hermitage," however, lost its attraction for him soon after, through the attacks of the Leyden theologians; and the interruptions that followed, strengthened his wish to change his place of residence. His next plans were directed to France.

3. *Last Residence in Paris.* — But the affairs of that country, particularly those of the court, had grown more and more unfavorable to him; and the prospects which had been held out to him had vanished when he went to Paris for the last time, at the end of May, 1648. He had found the theatre of political events very much changed, even on his first journey (1644), after an absence of fifteen years. Louis XIII. had died a year before (May 14, 1643), a few months after Richelieu (Dec. 4, 1642), leaving the kingdom to a boy five years old, under the regency of his mother, Queen Anne of Austria, and the commanding influence of Mazarin, who had succeeded Richelieu. The new edicts of taxation, in the year 1644, had called forth remonstrances from the parlia-

---

[1] Œuvres, t. x. pp. 413–417. (The letter is dated Nov. 1, 1646.)

ment in Paris, and created disturbances among the people; and a keen observer could even then have seen the signs of a gathering storm. Now measures of violence on the part of the court, and opposition from the parliament, the division of parties, and the intrigues of party leaders, had gone so far that there was every indication of an outbreak of a civil war (May, 1648). The imprisonment of two members of parliament in August of this year had caused an insurrection; and when Descartes left Paris towards the end of the month, he saw the barricades erected with which the war of *Fronde* began. But the absolutism of the French monarchy was on the point of completion; and the last remaining shadow of a law-making power, independent of the crown, vanished after a series of battles.

Under such circumstances, no one could think of the position which had been promised Descartes, or even of the pension which had been assured him. The only advantage of his journey was a philosophical correspondence with Arnauld (June, 1648), and a last visit to his friend Mersenne, whom he left very sick, and of whose death he was informed soon after his return to Egmond. He had to abandon for a time his plan of living in France. "I should have done well," he wrote to the Princess Elizabeth soon after his arrival in Paris, " to remain in a country where there is peace already; and if these storms are not soon over, I shall return to Egmond in six or eight weeks, and wait there until the sky of France is clear. However, I find myself very happily situated, since I am perfectly free, with one foot in France, and the other in Holland."[1] But the storms increased, and Descartes felt still happier when he had both feet in Egmond. "Thank God," wrote he from this place, "the journey to France, to which I had formally pledged myself, is behind me: I am not sorry that I went, but I am yet gladder that I am back. I have found no one to envy, and those who live in the greatest splendor deserve the deepest sympathy.

[1] Œuvres, t. x. p. 136.

To learn how happy a quiet and retired life is, and how rich
is the man of moderate means, I could have chosen no better
time to make a visit to France." He has seen a queen under
barricades, and considers Elizabeth happy when he compares
her lot with that of the queens and princesses of Europe:
she is in a harbor, they are out on a stormy sea. "We ought
to be contented if we are in a *harbor*, even though we owe
our security to a shipwreck." [1]

Some months later he apologized to Chanut for not having
written of his return, declaring that he would rather say
nothing about it, since an account of his experience might
easily appear to be a criticism of those well-meaning people
who invited him to France. "I have considered them as
friends who invited me to dine; and when I accepted their
invitation, I found their kitchen in disorder, and their pots
upset. I have therefore returned without saying a word,
that I might not increase their chagrin. But I have learned
a lesson, and will never again undertake a journey on account
of promises, even when they are written on parchment." [2]

But Descartes did not always bear this deception with
such equanimity. In the very next letter to Chanut, he
gave a more detailed account of the matter, and he was
evidently somewhat annoyed. "I have never reckoned on
the favor of fortune, and have always sought to so order my
life that it might not be exposed to her influence: she therefore seems to be jealous, since she neglects no opportunity
to treat me badly. I have experienced this to my satisfaction in all three of the journeys I have made from this place
to France, particularly the last, which was enjoined upon me,
as it were, in the name of the king. To induce me to undertake it, letters had been sent to me written on parchment,
with the seals of the state, containing extravagant praises of
my merit, and the assurance of an excellent pension; and

---

[1] Œuvres, t. x. pp. 165, 166. (Letter to Elizabeth, Oct. 1, 1648, according to
Cousin's conjecture.)

[2] Ib., p. 310. (The letter was written Feb. 26, 1649.)

these royal documents were accompanied by private letters, promising still more after my arrival. But when I went, the matter resulted quite otherwise, in consequence of the sudden political disturbances. None of the promises were kept: the despatch of the patents had even been paid for by one of my relatives, to whom, of course, I had to return the money. It seemed that I had only travelled to Paris to buy the dearest and most useless parchment that ever came into my hands. So far I was entirely indifferent to the matter, and I should only have charged it to the account of the political disturbances, if the people who invited me had made any use of my presence whatever. And this annoyed me most, that no one desired any thing of me, except to see my face ; and I am really obliged to believe that I was invited to go to France, not for any serious purpose, but for the sake of the rarity, as though I were an elephant or panther. I know very well that I have no reason to expect the like in Stockholm ; but after the miserable results of all the journeys I have undertaken in the last twenty years, I cannot help fearing, that, if I should start upon a new one, I should have nothing else to expect than to be plundered by robbers on the way, or suffer a shipwreck that would cost me my life." [1]

The invitation to Sweden had been given, and unpleasant forebodings filled the mind of the philosopher. There was a third enemy more certainly to be foreseen than robbers or shipwreck, — the unfavorable climate, of which he himself had warned Chanut in earlier letters, and which was to prepare for him a premature death.

Paris and Descartes were not made for each other. Every time he lived there, the longing for solitude and quiet overcame him, and drove him repeatedly into suburbs, and finally out of France. In the same mood in which he left Paris twenty years before, he now returns to his village in Holland, and felt there as though he were in a harbor. It is one of the most noteworthy facts of Descartes' experience,

---

[1] Œuvres, t. x. pp. 325, 326. (The letter was dated March 31, 1649.)

without a knowledge of which we cannot understand his character and disposition, that this greatest thinker of France was perhaps the only Frenchman who could not live in Paris, and had an antipathy to the metropolis of the world. "If I venture in my vanity to hope for the approval of the queen," wrote he to Chanut soon after his last arrival in Paris, "you must attribute it, not so much to my disposition, as to the air of Paris. I think I have told you before, that it disposes me to chimerical fancies rather than to philosophical thoughts. I see so many here who deceive themselves in their opinions and calculations, that illusion seems to me an epidemic in Paris. The harmless solitude from which I have come pleased me far better; and I think I shall not resist my home-sickness, and shall soon return thither."

II. A NEW OPPONENT.—LAST LABORS.

1. *Regius' Apostasy.* — Descartes had reason, when he crossed the threshold of his literary career, to fear disciples who would not only follow him, but interpret his theories, and seek to improve them. He was to experience this to the fullest extent in the case of Regius, "The first martyr of the Cartesian philosophy." In the controversy which Regius had carried on with Voëtius by means of theses, Descartes was unable to entirely approve of the mode in which his disciple conceived of the relation between soul and body; and he particularly disapproved of his polemical methods when the controversy began soon after to be conducted in writing. When, four years later, Regius laid the manuscript of his text-book on physics (*fundamenta physicæ*) before Descartes, he found so many unproved assertions, so many false hypotheses, and in his theory of man such deviations from his own "Principles," that he strongly advised him not to publish it: he should limit himself to medicine, Descartes told him, since he had no talent for metaphysics, and the University of Utrecht had acted in his interest when it forbade him to lecture on philosophical subjects; not only was his mode of

exposition injurious to the theories of the philosopher, but he distorted them to such an extent, that Descartes would be obliged to publicly disclaim all responsibility for it if Regius published the work. Nevertheless, the book was published (September, 1646). Descartes wrote to the Princess Elizabeth that the book was not worth her reading : where it deviated from him, it was false; and where it seemed to accord with his doctrine, it was a wretched and ignorant plagiarism.[1]

Toward the end of the year 1647, two works appeared, attacking the Cartesian theories ; one bearing the title "Consideratio Reviana," and displaying its hostility, both in the name of its author and in the abuses which it contained. Descartes paid no attention to it. The second was an anonymous placard, discussing in twenty-one theses the theory of the human mind, and, without mentioning Descartes, so corresponding with the theories contained in Regius' work, that there could be no doubt of its authorship. In this placard, Descartes recognized an enemy in fact, if not in intention. It so distorted and caricatured his theories by pernicious and false conceptions, that, to obviate all misconceptions, he wrote a detailed criticism, of which, however, it seems that only a few copies were printed.[2] Who would have thought that the last antagonist with whom he would have to contend in the Netherlands, would be the same man whom he had once called his best and most trusted disciple?

We remark briefly, that the defection of Regius, which Descartes had noticed with such displeasure in the text-book on physics, consisted in an attempt to transform Descartes' fundamental doctrine, the dualism of soul and body, into materialism, and already indicated the direction which the French philosophy of the eighteenth century was to take in the hands of Condillac and La Mettrie. Thought and exten-

---

[1] Œuvres, t. ix. pp. 323–330. (Three letters to Regius in July, 1645, t. x. pp. 23–26.) (Letter to Elizabeth, March 15, 1647.)

[2] See following chapter.

sion are not to be conceived as opposite attributes of different substances, — according to Regius, — but as different attributes of one substance ; namely, body. The soul is a mode of body completely dependent upon its states and changes. The mind, therefore, neither has nor needs innate ideas, but gains all its ideas through the senses. The substantiality of the human mind, and its difference of essence from the body, are established by religion and revelation. So ran the text-book. The tendency is unmistakable : dualism prevails in religion, and materialism in philosophy. The theses of the placard aimed at the destruction of the Cartesian metaphysics. If any one wishes to know what Descartes would have said to Condillac and La Mettrie, let him read what he said to Regius. He saw before him a nest of fallacies.[1]

2. *The Last Works.* — After Descartes had laid the foundations of his system in the " Principles of Philosophy," and had developed it as far as the theory of organic nature, the most important subject that remained was man, the problem of anthropology, which comprehends three important subjects, — physiology, psychology, ethics. The first relates to the organs and functions of the human body ; the second, to the union of the soul with the body ; the third, to the problems and purposes of life. Physiology is closely connected with zoölogy. The human body in its developed form can only be understood through a knowledge of its origin, through the history of the development of the embryo, and this, in turn, through the history of the formation of animal bodies, the knowledge of which last the philosopher continually and industriously sought to acquire by studies in comparative anatomy. Here, nature was his immediate object of study. When any one visited him in Egmond, and inquired for his library, he pointed to a dissected animal. That Descartes sought to discover the secrets of life by studies in comparative anatomy and embryology, is a wonderful proof

---

[1] Œuvres, t. x. pp. 70-111. (Written in Egmond at the end of December)

of the methodical thinker, and must be valued more highly in the estimation of his biological labors than the worth or worthlessness of his results. Even in his " Cosmos " he was engaged in an inquiry concerning the origin of animals; and he had even then written an essay on the human body, intended to be included in that work. It was his " Traité de l'Homme " which treated of digestion, of the circulation of the blood, of respiration, of the motion of the muscles, of the organs of the senses and sensations, of the motions and functions of the brain. He now determined to remodel it; and the result was a new work, embracing animals and man, — " A Description of the Functions of the Human Body and an Explanation of the Formation of Animals; " or, as it is usually called, " Traité de la Formation du Fœtus." This work occupied him during 1647 and 1648. In a letter dated Dec. 23, 1647, the Princess Elizabeth expressed the wish that he would write an essay on education. Descartes answered that three reasons prevented him from undertaking it : " The third is, that I am just now engaged in another work, which I hope you will like better, — a description of animal and human functions ; since what I hastily sketched on that subject twelve or thirteen years ago, and showed you, has repeatedly fallen into unskilful hands, and I now feel the necessity of remodelling it, and have even ventured to develop the history of the animal from the commencement of its origin (I began it eight or ten days ago). I say of animals in general, since I would not undertake an investigation of what relates to man in particular, because I have not the necessary knowledge. The remaining months of the winter will be perhaps the most quiet period of the remainder of my life ; and I would rather use them, therefore, in this work, than in one which requires less concentration." [1]

His presentiment was true. It was the last quiet period of his life. The journey to France with its disappointments

<hr />

[1] Œuvres, x. pp. 121, 122. (The letter could not have been written before Feb. 1, 1648.)

was at hand.   Then came yet more distracting days, and then the end.

Descartes had already solved the chief problem of psychology, in his "Passions of the Soul."   It was the last work which he himself published — sketched in the winter of 1645–46, finished afterwards, and published the year he died. He would not write on morals and education, because he was unwilling to fan the flames of controversy which his other works had kindled; and he foresaw that such would be the result of engaging in discussions of questions of such practical importance.   He had expressed his thoughts on the worth and object of human life, in his letters to the Princess Elizabeth and the Queen of Sweden.

CHAPTER VIII.

THE CLOSE OF DESCARTES' LIFE IN STOCKHOLM.

I. THE INVITATION OF THE QUEEN.

1. *Christina of Sweden.*

WHEN Chanut went to Stockholm in the latter part of the autumn of 1645, the daughter of Gustavus Adolphus had sat for a year on the throne of Sweden. She was nineteen years old, in the zenith of her fortune and power, heiress of a powerful kingdom, and daughter of a man who united the fame of a hero with the glory of a martyr. The love and hopes of her people were fixed upon her, and the first measures of her reign seemed to realize the latter in a high degree. She was still young and unspoiled : her will was as yet master of those *bizarre* impulses, that capricious and fickle nature, that false and theatrical thirst for greatness, to which she lightly and blindly sacrificed her great destiny. The first princess of the North, both through her political and personal importance, and able to maintain this position, she became of her own accord a vagrant and adventurous woman, and did every thing in her power to make herself unworthy of her father. Her mental powers were in full bloom when Chanut sought to interest her in Descartes; and that which seemed peculiar and unbridled in her nature could be attributed to an excess of youthful vigor, and to that too masculine education which she had received according to the wish of her father. She was passionately fond of hunting, and gratified her taste for it with the best hunters. She was a bold and skilful rider, easily remaining in the saddle ten hours without dismounting from her horse. She preferred the dress of a man, and despised every adornment. She had hardened her body by fatigue, and strengthened it by a simple and hardy mode of life. She was not only queen in name, but knew how to command ; and she was so familiar with the business of the state, so independent in her decisions, so obstinate in their execution, that she made the members of her council feel her superiority. Her literary tastes and her intellectual interests were of a masculine character. She was fond of serious books and conversation, read daily some pages of Tacitus, spoke Latin, and studied Greek. Her exterior betrayed her restless and excitable spirit : the expression of her face and the tone of her voice changed quickly as she spoke. Hers was not a religious nature, although she was interested in religious questions, and ready to consider objections from any quarter. She was, therefore, particularly interested in the theoretical aspects of religion and morals, and often took or gave the opportunity for discussing such subjects in conversation. Thus it happened that one day, during a conversation with Chanut, who was full of admiration for the queen, she proposed the following questions : In what does the nature of love consist ? Can love to God result from our natural knowledge ? Which is worse, excess in love or in hate ? The content as well as the aphoristic style of the questions is very characteristic of the philosophical tastes of the queen. Chanut thought that no one could solve these problems better than Descartes, and wrote to him accordingly.

2. *Philosophical Letters.* — Descartes answered from Egmond, Feb. 1, 1647, in a cheerful mood. This " Letter on Love " was the first conversation, as it were, in which Descartes indirectly, and from a distance, engaged with the queen of Sweden ; for that she should read it was Chanut's intention in asking for the opinion of the philosopher. The letter is a little masterpiece, a real cabinet picture ; and any connoisseur of the philosopher, knowing nothing of its author-

ship, or the occasion of its writing, but familiar only with its ideas, the course of its investigations, and the choice of its expressions, would immediately exclaim, "A genuine Descartes!" He wrote no other work so limited in extent (it does not exceed the limits of an ordinary letter), in which he can be better understood, on the supposition that one knows how to read between the lines of a philosopher.

He distinguished intellectual love from that of passion, and then determined the nature of love in general, by an analytical inquiry: it consists in this, that we imagine an object whose presence or possession gives us pleasure, whose absence or loss gives us pain. We, therefore, desire this object with all the strength of our wills: we wish to be united, or form one whole with it, ourselves to be but a part of this whole. Love is necessarily united with *pleasure, pain,* and *desire.* These four directions of the will depend upon the nature of the soul proper, without union with the body. They are contained in the need for knowledge, which belongs to a thinking being. As thinking beings, we love the knowledge of things, feel pleasure when we have it, and pain when we are deprived of it, and, therefore, strive to possess it. Nothing is obscure here. Only the desire for knowledge moves our soul. We know what we love and desire, what rejoices us, and what afflicts us. The joys and sorrows of intellectual love, therefore, are not passions, but clear ideas. The love which is of the nature of passion or of sense, first arises when those clear ideas become obscured by the union of the soul with the body. There are bodily states or changes with which certain desires in our soul are coincident, although there is no resemblance or connection between them. In this way arise the obscure desires of sense and passion, which seek certain objects, and shun others; the possession of those gives pleasure, the presence of these, pain; those are loved, these are hated. Pleasure and pain, love and hate, are the four fundamental forms of the desires of sense, the elementary passions out of which, by composition and modification, all the rest arise. They are the only passions to which we are subject before birth, since they are active even in the nourishment of the embryonic life. Intellectual love coincides with the need for knowledge of our thinking nature; that of passion has its roots in the needs for nourishment of our organic nature. There is a conception of desirable objects (intellectual love) without bodily excitation, and without passion; and in like manner passion can exist without knowledge. There is love without passion, and passion without love. In the usual acceptation of the term, both are united in human love. Soul and body are united in such a manner that particular activities of thought and will accompany particular organic states, and mutually summon each other, like thoughts and words. Thus, the conception of desirable objects or love finds its involuntary bodily expression in the increased activity of the heart, and the more rapid circulation of the blood. This love which is both of soul and body, this union of intellection and passion, constitutes the feeling concerning whose nature the queen inquired.

From this it seems to follow that God, too exalted to be accessible, and too spiritual to be brought before our minds by means of the senses, can never be an object of love in the light of natural knowledge, since the representation of the Godhead to the senses is either the mystery of incarnation, as in Christianity, or the error of idolatry, as in the religions of paganism, where one, like Ixion, embraces a cloud instead of a goddess. Yet by deep reflection, the idea of God can become love, and, indeed, the most powerful of all passions, if we recognize in God the origin, and, therefore, the goal, of our mental life. But we must not regard this goal as a kind of becoming-divine, otherwise we fall into a dangerous error, which is not loving God, but desiring his divinity. Rather, we recognize in God the origin, not merely of our souls, but of the whole universe, which does not need to be a sphere in order to find its ground and stability in God alone.

This knowledge of the omnipotent will is so sublime that it fills us with joy, and with the effort to humbly follow the will of God. Therein consists the true love of God, illuminated by natural knowledge; and it is so powerful that it takes possession, even of the heart and nerves. The feeling of reverence does no harm to the feeling of love, but unites with it the wish to sacrifice one's self for the beloved object. Even friendship is capable of sacrifice; much more, patriotism. The more exalted the object of our love, the more joyous and willing is the subordination of ourselves; and there is, therefore, no obstacle to the union of the deepest love and reverence in the same feeling. Chanut himself, said Descartes, could best testify to the truth of this, since he experienced it. "If I asked you on your conscience, whether you love that noble queen near whom you now live, you might persist in saying that you feel for her only admiration, homage, reverence; but, in spite of it, I should maintain that your feeling is an ardent affection, since, as often as you speak of her, there flows from your mouth such a torrent of admiring words, that, as much as I believe you (I know your love of truth, and have heard of it from others), I am convinced you could not describe her with such animation if she had not excited your affections, and warmed your heart. Indeed, it is impossible to be so near such a luminary without being warmed by it."

Which is worse, an excess of love, or an excess of hate? The more our benevolence suffers through a passion, and our contentment decreases, and the more our pernicious excesses increase, the worse is the passion. There is no doubt that hate nourishes wickedness, while it poisons even kind natures; that it is a miserable and tormenting feeling, destitute of any real satisfaction, for the pleasure of hate is demoniacal, belonging to evil spirits in the place of torment. But as to pernicious excesses, the greater excess is also the worse. We must, therefore, inquire which of the two passions is in general more inclined to excess? And Descartes' answer is, love! It is more passionate, and therefore more powerful and more heroic than hate. Natures like Hercules, Roland, etc., have indulged in more excesses in love than in hate. Love unites, hate separates; and when love unites us to a worthless object, it injures us more than hate when it separates us from one that is worthy. And, finally, the more passionate the love, the more recklessly it seeks to remove every obstacle to its satisfaction. It thus excites hate in more than one direction, and with it an army of evils: love sowed the seed from which sprang the harvest that resulted in the burning of Troy.[1]

When the queen read the letter, she said to Chanut, "So far as I know Descartes, from this letter and your account of him, I count him the most fortunate of men; and his life seems to me enviable. Say to him that I have a high opinion of him." Descartes gave some more particular explanations, which the queen had requested, in a letter to Chanut, June 6, 1647. Soon she eagerly made another opportunity of asking for the opinion of the philosopher.

Among the scholars of Sweden, John Freinsheim of Elm, a German philologist, was then famous, because of his discovery of the supplements of Livy. A panegyric on Gustavus Adolphus had resulted in his call to Upsala as professor of politics and rhetoric, and five years afterwards he was called to Stockholm as historiographer and librarian of the queen. In his farewell address in Upsala, at which the queen with the French ambassador and some gentlemen of her court were present, he discussed the question of the highest good. The queen herself had suggested the subject. After she had heard the address, which was delivered in Latin, she remarked to Chanut, "These men can only treat such subjects superficially: we should hear Descartes discuss it." The question was accordingly proposed to him, and answered in a letter to the queen herself (November, 1647).

Descartes briefly sketched the foundations of his theory of

---

[1] Œuvres, t. x. pp. 2-22.

morals, and the principles by which his own life was guided. He proposed, not to determine the highest good in an absolute sense — this is God — but with reference to man, not humanity, whose highest good consists in the sum of all material and spiritual excellences, but with reference to individual man. So understood, the highest good must be attainable, something that we are able to possess or acquire, something, therefore, that lies in our power. Material goods are not in our power: the highest good must, therefore, be sought within the mind, in the territory of knowledge and will. But even knowledge in its different degrees is conditioned by one's capacities and circumstances, which are independent of us. There remains, therefore, the will as the only field in which the hidden treasure can be found. It is always in our power, it is our own highest faculty, our inner self, the core of our being. The will to seek knowledge lies in our power. We can firmly and continually carry out the resolve to act always according to our best judgment; and if we do so, we realize the ideal, both of the Stoics and Epicureans, for we are both virtuous and happy. This will alone is that which is truly worthy of reverence in this world. "I know that the gifts of fortune are usually valued more highly; but, as I am sure that your Majesty sets a higher value on your virtue than your crown, I declare openly that to me virtue appears as the only commendable thing." All other goods deserve to be valued, — not honored and praised, — provided they are considered as gifts of God, or as opportunities of which we are to make a good use by means of our free will. For honor and love are rewards, and only what the will does deserves to be rewarded or punished. The greatest good of man is the state of greatest contentment, and this, whatever its nature, exists within us; for the soul alone is contented, and only when it is in possession of some desired object. Its conception of good is frequently very confused: it conceives many goods as far greater than they really are, but its satisfaction always equals its estimate

of the good which it possesses. Now, no good is greater than
the excellent use of our free will. This will, therefore, and
it alone, is the highest good.[1]

It was very fortunate that these philosophical letters, the
occasion of which was a mere accident, treated of themes
lying, as it were, at the point of his pen. The question as to
the nature of love was closely connected with the sketch on
the "Passions," which he had written a year before. The
question as to the highest good related to the same subject,
which he had discussed shortly before that sketch, in the
letters on human happiness, which he had written to the
Princess Elizabeth. These letters had resulted in the sketch
on the passions. Descartes now sent both writings to Chanut, along with the letter to the queen, requesting Chanut
to permit no one to read them except the queen, and not
even the queen unless she expressly desired to.[2]

More than a year passed by before Christina answered
(December, 1648).[3] She had been occupied in the mean
time with quite other matters than the nature of love and
the highest good: the year 1648 was the date of the peace
of Westphalia. But she did not lose sight of Descartes; and
after she had communicated with him through letters, she
ardently wished to become personally acquainted with him.

3. *Invitation and Journey to Stockholm.* — Christina was
deeply interested in the work on the passions, and resolved
to study Descartes' philosophical works thoroughly. They
were her constant companions. She carried the sketch on
the passions with her when she went hunting, and the "Principles of Philosophy" when she went to her mines. She
made it the duty of Freinsheim to study this work, that he
might help her understand it; and Chanut was requested to
come to his assistance. "Since Friensheim has discovered

---

[1] Œuvres, t. x. pp. 59–64. (Written in Egmond, Nov. 20, 1647.)

[2] Ib., pp. 65–67.

[3] The answer of the queen is lost. Descartes spoke of its contents, and the
style of its French, in complimentary terms, in a letter to Chanut, Feb. 26, 1649.
Ib., pp. 307 and following.

that he needs a companion in this work," wrote Chanut good-humoredly to Descartes, " I am requested to read the 'Principles' with him. It is my duty to make myself agreeable to the queen, at whose court I serve the king of France ; and so it is now one of the duties of the French ambassador to Sweden, to study Descartes." While Descartes was in Paris, in the midst of the political commotions which destroyed his expectations relating to the immediate future, he learned with pleasure that his books were read at the court of Sweden, and that the queen studied philosophy, even on her hunts. He recommended the first book of the "Principles" instead of the "Meditations," because it was more concise, and likewise more easily understood. He further advised the queen not to delay with the theory of motion in the second book, and to give her attention merely to the important point of view, that, in the sensible properties of things, there is nothing objective, except size, form, and motion, and that, by these fundamental properties, even light and warmth are explained, which, like appetite and pain, exist only in our mind.[1]

But Christina soon found that the difficulties of his system could be better set aside by Descartes himself than by Freinsheim and Chanut, and that she could understand it better from Descartes' own mouth than from his books. She urgently requested Chanut to invite him to Stockholm — to repeat the invitation. The first letter which reached Paris, when Descartes had already left that city, did not reach him until the middle of February, 1649: he received the second about the end of the following month. He answered (probably March 31, 1649) in two letters to Chanut, one of which was to be shown to the queen, and the other confidential. In the former he accepted the invitation, and promised to

---

[1] Œuvres, x. pp. 308, 309. (Descartes replied to the queen at the same time, Feb. 26, 1649: he called his answer " un compliment fort sterile." In conclusion he assured her that his devotion to her could not be greater if he were a Swede or a Finlander.)

undertake the journey in the middle of the summer, in order
to spend the winter in Stockholm: in the latter he wrote
quite differently; many reasons for hesitation had obtruded
themselves upon him, many more than he had thought of at
first. He had had so many unfortunate experiences with
his philosophy and his travels, and had found so few who
were really able to appreciate his doctrine. At the first
glance, it seemed to many strange and peculiar; but after
they understood it, it seemed so simple and natural, that it
no longer excited their attention. For truth is, as it were,
the health of the soul; and, like that of the body, we prize
it only when we do not possess it. Besides, there is no place
less adapted to the study of such a philosophy than the court
of a queen, where there are so many things to distract the
mind. Still, if the queen had the necessary leisure and per-
severance, he would come. But if her interest was merely
a passing curiosity, he hoped Chanut would do all in his
power to save him from having to make the journey.[1]

All these considerations seemed to him more weighty in
his solitude at Egmond. He feared the long journey, the
strange country, the severe climate. "One does not wonder," he wrote some days after to Chanut, "that Ulysses left
the enchanted island of Calypso and Circe, where he could
enjoy every conceivable pleasure, to live in a stony and
barren country, because it was his native land. But a man
who was born in the gardens of Touraine, and who now lives
in a country, where, if not more honey, probably more milk,
flows than in the promised land, may very well be slow to
leave such a residence to go to a land of bears, in the midst
of rocks and ice."[2] But not only nature, but the court,
made him apprehensive. Envious antagonists, with their
slanders and intrigues of all kinds, would be no less abundant there than in his solitude in Holland. He feared that

---

[1] Œuvres, x. pp. 320–327. Cf. with the second letter, our account on p. 277.
[2] Ib., pp. 330, 331. (The letter was dated April 4, 1649, according to Cousin's
supposition.)

the queen would be an object of suspicion, even in her own country, because she had invited him. Already her preference for scholars and her studious habits were criticised; and it was deridingly said, that she was surrounding herself with the pedants of Europe, and that soon Sweden would be ruled by grammarians. He was very much afraid that hostile accounts of his system had been circulated in Sweden by assiduous opponents, who had heard of the purpose of his journey, and that thus his stay near the court of the queen might redound to her harm. He, therefore, wrote to Freinsheim with all frankness, and at the same time with the greatest delicacy, and asked for information and advice.[1] He received such an answer that he had reason to feel at ease.

Every step in the direction of limiting his independence and solitude, Descartes felt as a departure from his own proper element into one that was foreign to him. Whenever he was on the point of crossing this boundary, he stopped in hesitation. He thought of his journey to Sweden, as he had done of the publication of his works; then he would have preferred to be silent; now he preferred to remain where he was. Chanut had visited the philosopher in Holland in the spring, as he passed through on his way to Paris, where he was to remain until late in the fall, and had silenced many of Descartes' objections. Still, he would gladly have waited the return of his friend, in order to make the journey with him. But the impatience of the queen hastened him. She sent Flemming, one of her admirals, to Amsterdam, to offer to Descartes the services of his ship for the journey to Stockholm, where she hoped to see him before the end of April. But Descartes had already declared that he could not start before the middle of the summer. After he had prepared his work on the passions for the press, and given it to the

---

[1] Œuvres, t. x. pp. 335–337. (The letter was dated June 10, 1649, in Cousin's opinion. At the close of the letter, Descartes asked whether the queen would consent to the publication of his essay on the passions.)

publisher in Amsterdam, and carefully arranged all his affairs, he left Egmond, Sept. 1, 1649.

II. DESCARTES IN STOCKHOLM.

1. *Residence and Position.* — Descartes arrived in Stockholm early in October. Madame Chanut, the wife and sister of his two excellent friends, gave him a most hospitable reception in the absence of her husband, who was still in Paris. The queen received him with the highest marks of honor. Some days after his arrival, he wrote to his friend, the Princess Elizabeth, saying that he had only seen the queen twice, and had been quite as favorably impressed with her ability and attractiveness as he had dared to hope. Thanks to Freinsheim, he was free from the oppressive duties of court ceremony, and had to attend the court only when the queen wished to see him. Under the most favorable circumstances, he would not remain in Stockholm longer than the beginning of the next summer. Already he looked back with longing at his beloved hermitage in Holland. "It is easy for me there to make progress in the investigation of truth, and in this alone consists the chief purpose of my life." [1]

But the queen had plans with reference to Descartes, that contemplated a much longer stay. Through his residence in Stockholm, she not only wished to broaden her own culture, but to serve the cause of science in her country, and assist the philosopher in the prosecution of his own plans. She desired that he should be her instructor and friend; that he should found a scientific academy in Stockholm; and under her protection, and in the enjoyment of perfect leisure, complete the sketches he had brought with him, and finish the works he had begun. In this manner, Christina wished to promote the interests of the new philosophy, as well as be benefited by it. But to this end, it was necessary for Descartes to remain in Stockholm, not merely for a time,

[1] Œuvres, t. x. pp. 373–375.

and by way of a visit, but permanently. The queen, therefore, desired his formal settlement in Sweden, and intended
to have him take a place among the magnates of the land,
as the possessor of an hereditary estate. When Chanut
returned in November, the queen told him her plans, and
requested him to gain the consent of his friend. Descartes
was thoroughly averse to the proposal; pleaded that the climate was too severe for him. It was the only difficulty which
the queen would admit, and she easily set that aside. Descartes' estate should be in Southern Sweden; and Chanut
and a member of the council of the kingdom were commis-
sioned to find one for him among the possessions of the arch-
bishopric of Bremen and Pomerania, which Sweden had
just acquired by the peace of Westphalia, — an estate which
should yield him a splendid revenue, and be hereditary in his
family. The matter was already in progress, when it was
interrupted and postponed by Chanut's sickness, and it was
not finished when Descartes died. Thus, the peculiar
course of his destiny came very near making the greatest,
and, for German philosophy, most important, thinker of
France, the owner of an estate in German lands, through the
favor of the daughter of Gustavus Adolphus.

The philosophical instruction of the queen began in
November, after Descartes had come to feel somewhat at
home in his new surroundings. That she might study the
difficult subject when her mind was freshest, and be entirely
undisturbed by any business of state, Christina chose the
first hours of the morning. Descartes was obliged to go to
the palace every morning at five o'clock, in the cold of a
Northern winter, which, moreover, was unusually severe that
year, and await his royal pupil in the library. He had had
reason to fear the climate. After a walk with Chanut, Jan.
18, 1650, the latter was taken sick with an inflammation of
the lungs; and, for a time, his life was in danger. Descartes
nursed his friend with the greatest care; and, after nights of
wakefulness, he was every morning at five o'clock in the

library of the queen ; besides, he spent a portion of the after-
noons conferring with her concerning the proposed academy,
the statutes of which he sketched in the latter part of Jan-
uary, and submitted to the queen, Feb. 1.   It was the last
time he saw her.   These statutes show how little Descartes
was thinking of himself and his own advantage.   The very
first article excluded foreigners from the presidency, a position the queen had intended for him.

2. *Sickness and Death.* — Exhausted by his labors and the
care of his friend, he had less power to resist the attacks of
the terrible cold of the winter.   He was already sick when
he returned from his last conference with the queen, though
he forced himself to sit up.   The fever raged so much the
more violently the next day, and for a week he lay delirious.
Even on the fifth day his case seemed hopeless to the physicians.   Unfortunately, the first physician of the queen, du
Ryer, a countryman and friend of Descartes, was absent.
The second, van Weulles, was a Hollander, and a friend, it
is said, of Descartes' opponents in Utrecht.   The seventh
day his delirium ceased, his reason returned, but only to
enable him to perceive that death was near, and to bid him
direct his thoughts upon eternity.   He died Feb. 11, 1650,
at four o'clock in the morning, before the end of his fifty-
fourth year.

When the queen was informed of his death by the secre-
tary of the French embassy, she burst into tears.   She
wished to honor the memory of her "great teacher," and to
show to posterity that she knew how to appreciate him.
She proposed to bury him among the great dignitaries of the
crown, at the feet of the kings of Sweden, and to erect a
mausoleum of marble over his tomb.   Chanut persuaded
the queen to give up this plan.   He rightly felt that a
simple grave in the churchyard of foreigners would be more
fitting than a tomb of royal magnificence in the vault of the
kings of Sweden.   He was buried Feb. 12, 1650.   A simple
monument marked the place where he lay ; and an inscrip-

tion stated that here Descartes rested, whom the Queen of
Sweden had called to her court from his solitude in Egmond,
and to whom Chanut dedicated this memorial. In the year
of his death a medal was stamped in his honor in Holland,
with the symbol of the sun lighting the earth. It was painful to French patriotism, that the remains of the greatest
of French philosophers reposed in a distant land. Sixteen
years after his death, d'Alibert, one of his friends, assisted by
Terlon, who was then the minister of France to Sweden, had
his ashes conveyed to France at his own expense. They
were put on board of a ship in Stockholm, May 1, 1666, and
solemnly interred June 25, 1667, in the Church of Sainte-
Genevieve, the French Pantheon of to-day. It was a long
time before the authorities of the Church would consent to
show such high honors to the ashes of a man whose name
had stood for some years on the index. But his friends
overcame their opposition by attributing to Descartes "a
great service" to the Church. Queen Christina had resigned
her crown in June, 1654, and soon after had joined the Catholic Church. Now, Descartes had been her instructor for
some months; and these two facts, as disconnected as they
were, were joined together, and Descartes was represented
as a missionary who succeeded in converting the daughter
of Gustavus Adolphus. And since she herself was willing
to declare that her conversion was due to the influence of
Descartes, it was no longer the philosopher, but the proselyter,
whose ashes the priests received in the Church of Sainte-
Genevieve.

The testimony of the queen was false, given from a frivolous
readiness to oblige, as she herself declared frankly enough in
private. Nothing was more foreign to the character of Descartes than the disposition to make proselytes. He remained
true to the Church in which he was born, because he was
born in it; but with her proselyting, he had nothing to do.
His life, so far as he could direct it in harmony with his
genius, was given to philosophy and solitude.

CHAPTER IX.

A SURVEY OF HIS WORKS AND WRITINGS.

I. THE WORKS PUBLISHED BY DESCARTES HIMSELF.

THE writings which Descartes himself published, and whose origin we have become acquainted with in the history of his life, can be arranged in the two following groups, philosophical and polemical, the members of which follow each other in chronological order : —

1. *The Philosophical Works.*

1. " Essais philosophiques." Leyde, Jean le Maire, 1637. *Étienne de Courcelles* translated the essays into Latin, with the exception of the geometry; and the translation was revised by Descartes. Franz van Schooten, professor of mathematics in Leyden, translated the geometry into Latin, including in the translation de Beaune's observations and his own explanations. The title of the first was " R. Cartesii specimina philosophiæ, sive dissertatio de methodo recte regendæ rationis, Dioptrice et meteora ex gallico latine versa (par Étienne de Courcelles) et ab autore emendata." Amst., Lud., Elzevir, 1644. The title of the second was " Geometria a R. Descartes gallice edita, cum notis Florim. de Beaune, latine versa et commentariis illustrata a Fr. a Schooten." Lugd., Bat. J. Maire, 1649.

2. " Renati Descartes meditationes de prima philosophia, ubi de Dei existentia et animæ immortalitate. His adjunctæ sunt variæ objectiones doctorum virorum in istas de Deo et anima demonstrationes cum responsionibus auctoris." Paris,

1641. The second edition with the changed title (see pp. 247, 248), containing the objections of Bourdin and the letter to Dinet, was published in Amsterdam by Elzevir, 1642 : the third appeared the year Descartes died. Duke de Luynes translated the " Meditations " into French, and Clerselier the " Objections " and " Replies." Descartes revised these translations, and changed some passages in the Latin text. It was published in Paris, 1647.

3. " Renati Descartes principia philosophiæ." Amst., Elzev., 1644. The second edition appeared the year the philosopher died. The French translation was made under the direction of the Abbé Picot, and approved by Descartes, who accompanied it with a prefatory letter : " Principes de la philosophie, écrits en latin par René Descartes, et traduits en français par un de ses amis " (Paris, 1647). The letter to Picot, translated into Latin, was published in the following edition of the " Principles " as a preface.

4. " Les passions de l'âme." Amst., Elzevir, 1650. On the origin of the work, which was sketched in the winter of 1646, and finished in the summer of 1649, after the manuscript had been sent to the Princess Elizabeth, and afterwards to the Queen of Sweden, compare p. 272. A Latin translation appeared the year Descartes died.

2. *The Polemical Works.*

1. " Epistola Renati Descartes ad celeberrimum virum Gisbertum Voëtium, in qua examinantur duo libri nuper pro Voëtio Ultrajecti simul editi : unus de confraternitate Mariana, alter de philosophia Cartesiana." Amstelodami, Elzevir, 1643.

2. " R. Descartes notæ in programma quoddam sub finem anni 1647 in Belgio editum cum hoc titulo : explicatio mentis humanæ sive animæ rationalis, ubi explicatur, quid sit et quid esse possit." Amst., Lud., Elzevir, 1648. These " notes " are Descartes' reply to Regius (see p. 279). It is so rare, that even Pieters, the author of the annals of the

publishing-house of Elzevir, did not discover it until after the publication of his work. (Some years later it was attacked by Tobias Andreas, in a work called "Replicatio pro notis Cartesii." Amst., Elzev., 1653.)

II. THE REMAINS AND THE OPERA POSTUMA.

1. *Writings not in Descartes' Possession.*

Of the writings which Descartes left unpublished at his death, two are first to be mentioned which were written for friends, and were not, therefore, found with the rest of them; viz., (1) "Compendium musicæ," the first of his writings which have been preserved, which was written for Beeckman in 1618 (see pp. 179, 180), and published in Utrecht in 1650; (2) The fragment of an essay on mechanics, which was written for Constantine Huyghens in 1636, explaining certain machines, as the roller and pulley, inclined plane, wheel and axle, screw and lever. A second fragment, on lifting-machines ("Explicatio des engins"), which Daniel Mayor found, translated into Latin, and published in 1672, differs but little from the preceding. Poisson translated this fragment and the "Compendium musicæ" into French, publishing them under the following title: "Traité de la mécanique composé par M. Descartes, de plus l'abrégé de la musique du même auteur, mis en français avec les éclaircissements nécessaires par N. P. P. D. L." (Nic. Poisson, prêtre de l'oratoire.) Paris, Angot, 1668.

2. *Lost Writings.*

The rest of his unpublished works were in a box which Descartes took with him to Stockholm; and an inventory of its contents was there made, after his death, in the presence of Chanut. An essay on fencing was found, — probably his first essay, written even when he was in Rennes; a diary of the years 1619–21; three works on the theory of method; "Studium bonæ mentis," "Rules for the Direction of the Mind," a dialogue on the investigation of truth in the light of reason; a fragment called " Thaumantis regia" (palace of wonders); probably a study preliminary to his work in physics, in which, according to Baillet, the theory that animals are automata already appeared; fragments on mathematical, physical, and natural-history subjects; a part of the "Cosmos;" the essay on man and the formation of the fœtus; letters; the fragment of a French comedy, and verses in celebration of the peace of Westphalia.

Besides, Descartes had left a box in the care of his friend Hooghland, containing, in addition to valuable letters, an essay, " De deo Socratis," and, perhaps, the complete "Cosmos" in its original form. Millet thinks so;[1] though it is not possible to say with certainty, since the writings in Hooghland's care are lost, and likewise the catalogue of them.

Of those left at Stockholm, the essay on fencing, the original copy of the diary of the years 1619–21, the fragments on different scientific subjects, the "Thaumantis regia," the "Studium bonæ mentis," and the poems, cannot now be found.

It is no wonder that some of the unpublished writings left in Stockholm were irrecoverably lost. In view of the accident that befell the chest, we must say that it was by chance that so many, and certainly the most important, were preserved. Chanut sent the whole of them to his brother-in-law, Clerselier, in Paris, who intended to look after their publication. The ship reached the coasts of France without accident, and the boat in which they were put, reached Paris safely; but when they were being landed near the Louvre, they fell into the water, and lay there three days. They were finally fished out, and dried in sheets and leaves, and in this state reached Clerselier in the greatest confusion. The result was, that their publication was delayed, and involved insuperable difficulties, especially in the case of the letters. They had become so confused with each other, that it was

[1] J. Millet: Descartes avant 1637. Preface, pp. xxiii., xxiv.

impossible to restore them to perfect order. In some cases, heterogeneous parts could not be separated: in others, parts that belonged together could not be united.

3. *The Works edited by Clerselier.*

1. The fragment of the often mentioned "Cosmos," "Le monde, ou traité de la lumière." The first and incorrect edition was published in Paris in 1664, without Clerselier's knowledge, under the title, "Le monde de Descartes, ou le traité de la lumière." The edition corrected by Clerselier appeared in 1677.

2. "Traité de l'homme." This is closely connected with the "Cosmos," and was intended to form a part of it, "Chapitre XVIII." (see above, pp. 229, 230). Clerselier's edition, with remarks by Laforge, was published in Paris in 1664. Shortly before, Florentius Schuyl, professor of philosophy in Leyden, had published a Latin translation, "Renatus Descartes de homine." ("Lugduni, Batav.," 1662–64.) Clerselier found the translation bad, but the preface good; and he therefore incorporated the latter in French in his edition.

With this essay, likewise, and always united with it, appeared the "De la formation du fœtus," which Descartes himself had divided into paragraphs, as he had not done the "Traité de l'homme." Its whole title is, "La description du corps humain et de toutes ses functions, tant de celles qui ne dependent pas l'âme que de celles qui en dependent, et aussi la principale cause de la formation de ses membres."

3. "Les lettres de René Descartes," 3 vols., Paris, 1657–1667.

4. *Collection of Unpublished Works.*

It is strange that Clerselier did not publish two of the most important of his posthumous works, both of them relating to the theory of method. They were published a half-century after the death of the philosopher, in the first collection of his posthumous works, "Opera postuma Cartesii" (Amst., 1701), which contained in addition the fragment

"The World, or an Essay on Light," the tract on mechanics, the compendium of music, "Observations on the Procreations of Animals," and lastly, excerpts. The two important works which were then published for the first time are, —

1. "Regulæ ad directionem ingenii." It was intended to contain three parts, and each of these twelve rules. Only the first half is preserved, containing eighteen rules, with the statement of the three following without explanation. According to Baillet, the original text of this work was also in Latin. (Cf. above, pp. 203, 204.)

2. "Inquisitio veritatis per lumen naturale," a dialogue between three persons, likewise unfinished, and, according to Baillet, originally written in French. The title of the posthumous work runs, "La recherche de la vérité par les lumières naturelles qui à elles seules, et sans le secours de la religion et de la philosophie, déterminent les opinions que doit avoir un honnête homme sur toutes les choses qui doivent faire l'objet de ses pensées et qui pénètrent dans les secrets des sciences les plus abstraites."

III. EDITION OF COMPLETE WORKS.

1. *Collective Editions.*

Even before this first collection of posthumous works, collective editions, more or less complete, some of the philosophical works, others of his complete writings, as they were called, were published in Latin by Elzevir in Amsterdam. According to the annals of the publishing-house of Elzevir, "R. D. opera philosophica" appeared in the years 1644, 1670, 1672, and 1674. Besides, an edition of the philosophical works of the year 1656 is mentioned, and called "Editio tertia." The first edition of the "Opera omnia" was published in eight volumes, 1670–83; the second in nine, 1692–1701 and 1713. It was not really a complete edition, but a collection of separate editions, which contained in the last volume the "Opera postuma."

The first French edition in thirteen volumes appeared in

Paris in 1724–29. A century later (1824–26), Victor Cousin published his edition in eleven volumes. This is the edition which we cite, " Œuvres de Descartes, publiées par Victor Cousin."

2. *Arrangement of Letters.*

After the publication of the " Opera postuma," a complete edition of the works of Descartes involved not merely the labor of collecting, but also a critical work; since it was necessary to try to discover lost writings, and to collect those that were scattered, and, also, to determine the order of those extant. The collection and arrangement of the letters was necessarily a work of particular importance. By far the greatest and most important part of the letters were in Mersenne's hands, and fell, after his death, into the possession of the mathematician Roberval, who was an enemy to Descartes, and locked them up. They afterwards fell into the hands of La Hixe, who handed them over to the Academy. Baillet wished to write the life of Descartes; and the abbé, J. B. Le Grand, at the same time desired to publish the first complete edition of his works; after the death of Clerselier (1684), he inherited the remains of the philosopher, and had himself collected a number of scattered letters, and was, with Baillet, permitted by the Academy to use the letters which had been in Mersenne's possession. The edition was not published. The manuscripts which Le Grand possessed fell, after his death (1704), into other hands, and were entirely lost. The contents of a part were preserved by copies, and published in the " Opera postuma " in the year 1701. The copies of the letters of Descartes, made the year 1667, now in the library of the Academy, contain critical marginal comments on the dates, addresses, and connection of the letters, based on a comparison with the original manuscript; and they leave no doubt that a critical edition of them was at one time in preparation. It is not known who made these comments. Cousin, who arranged the letters (vols. vi.–x. of his edition), according to them, suspects that Montempuis, rector of the university of Paris, about the middle of the seventeenth century, was the author, since his seal was found in the copies. Millet, on the other hand, regards it as certain that Baillet and Le Grand made those comments, attempting together in the years 1690–92 to arrange the correspondence of Descartes.

3. Supplements.

In the remains of the philosopher was a diary of the years 1619–21, containing youthful writings, sketches, notes of different kinds, and referring to a time of which we have no literary evidence. Every thing, therefore, relating to this time, however unimportant in itself, should have been regarded as valuable and significant by those who were in-trusted with the edition of his works. According to Baillet, the diary was bound in parchment, and contained the follow-ing: some thoughts on the sciences in general, on algebra, " Democritica," " Experimenta," " Præambula," " Olympica," a sketch of twelve pages, in which that much-spoken-of mar-ginal note was written, denoting Nov. 10, 1619, as the day of a mental epoch. (See above, pp. 195, 196.)

Fortunately, there was one man in Clerselier's time who would gladly have preserved every line that Descartes wrote: it was no less a man than Leibnitz. During a stay in Paris, he became acquainted with Clerselier, who in the beginning of June, 1676, permitted him to examine Descartes' papers, and make copies of them, imperfectly arranged and inco-herent, as necessarily resulted from the condition of the manuscripts. He considered them the most valuable literary treasures which he possessed, and intended to publish them himself. " A man in Holland has for a long time intended," he wrote to Vernouilli, " to publish some posthumous works of Descartes. I, also, am in possession of some of Descartes' remains. I have the rules for the investigation of truth (which do not appear so extraordinary to me as they do to some), the fragment of a dialogue in French, his first thoughts on the origin of animals, etc. If the promised publication has not yet appeared, I should like myself to prepare such an one, with the addition of some unpublished writings by Galileo, Valarianus Magnus, and Pascal, along with my observations on the universal part of the 'Principles' of Descartes. I simply want a large number of free copies." Among the copies made by Leibnitz, there were besides notes on the "Principles," physical, physiological, and anatomical observations, mathematical writings, and especially passages from that notable diary which Leibnitz called, "Cartesii cogitationes privatæ."

They were not published. They passed from Leibnitz's library to that of Hannover. None of them were specifically catalogued except those on physiological and anatomical subjects, and those under the title " Excerpta ex Cartesii manuscriptis." The rest remained unknown and concealed, until lately Foucher de Careil discovered a part of them, and published them under the title, " Œuvres inédites de Descartes" (Paris, 1859–60).

A critically arranged, accurate, and comprehensive edition of Descartes' complete works is a work of the future. The translation of a work is not the work itself. The Latin writings should be published in their original text, either alone or along with the French translations.

BOOK II.

DESCARTES' DOCTRINE.

CHAPTER I.

I. SOURCES OF THE THEORY OF METHOD.

1. *Subject.*

WE must seek to enter the doctrine of Descartes by
the path of his method; and this, therefore, must
first be carefully studied. Descartes repeatedly and explicitly declared, that, in scientific investigation, method is the
important matter, and that he himself had found a new and
sure one, by the help of which he had made his discoveries.
And if he had not made this declaration, and if the proper
mode of searching for truth had not been the subject of some
of his works, the rest of them would have compelled us to
recognize a master of method, that is, of the art of bringing
light into thought, by the mode of their composition, and
the order and coherence of their ideas. No one can practise
this art as Descartes did unless he has studied it. As we
have been obliged to speak in the foregoing book of the
method of the philosopher, since it was the guide, not only of
his thinking, but also of his life, we cannot avoid some repetition here.[1]

Methodical thinking, and thoughts on method, are different
things: the former consists in the use and practice, the latter
in the theory, of method. All of Descartes' writings are methodical: strictly speaking, not one of them is methodologi-

---

[1] Foregoing book, chap. i. pp. 170-172; chap. ii. pp. 187-194; chap. iii. pp. 202-
204; chap. v. 224-vi. 240.

cal, not one of them is an accurate and complete exposition
or theory of the scientific mode of thought. Descartes promulgated no new organon, as Bacon did. Of the writings
which he himself published, there is but one which expressly
treats of method, the "Discours de la méthode." There is
another which so methodically discovers and expounds the
elements of knowledge, that, from the use of method, its real
nature is most distinctly evident, — the "Meditations." Of
the former, Descartes himself said, "No *traité*, but a *discours ;*
not an exposition of the theory of method, but only a conversation about it." If we judge it according to its title, we
might conclude that it does not perform what it promises;
but in truth it does more. We expect a theory of method,
and become acquainted with a man who has given his life
to science, and to this end has regulated and ordered it in
a completely methodical manner. The path to truth is not
merely pointed out with outstretched finger, but entered and
lived. Bacon sought to be only the Mercury along the road,
who remains standing on his pedestal, and points out to
others the road. Descartes lets us see how he himself
finds it, and advances along it. But it must be admitted
that our first expectation is not realized. There are four
brief rules for the investigation of truth in the second part
of the "Discours," stated in the most concise form, without
discussion or explanation.

2. *The Methodological Posthumous Works. Critical Questions.* — In addition to the "Discours," Descartes wrote two
fragments relating to the theory of method, "Regulæ ad
directionem ingenii," and "Recherche de la vérité par les
lumières naturelles," which were found among his unpublished writings after his death.[1] We are not informed when
they were written, and are therefore obliged to rely on
conclusions based chiefly on comparisons between them and
the "Discours" and "Meditations." The mere fact that
the first was written in Latin gives us reason to believe that

---

[1] See foregoing book, chap. ix. p. 303.

it belongs to the period in which Descartes wrote his scientific essays in that language, and was still entirely occupied with the question of method. It must have been written, therefore, before the philosophical essays. What the "Discours" compresses into four short rules, and only stipples, as it were, "The Rules for the Direction of the Mind" develop in detail, though not completely. This suggests that it was written before the "Discours," and that Descartes did not, therefore, wish to expound the regulative part of the latter. And there is finally another piece of internal evidence that decides the question. We know that Descartes regarded the method of mathematics as the type of the method of philosophy, and the "Rules" contain the following passage: "I have, therefore, *until to-day*, applied myself to this universal mathematical science, according to my ability, so that I can in future devote myself to higher investigations without fearing that my thoughts are not yet sufficiently mature."[1] When the philosopher wrote this sentence, he had *not* written the "Meditations." The "Rules" were therefore written before the "Meditations," and were probably composed in France after that conversation with Verulle, and before Descartes went to the Netherlands to write that work in Franeker.[2]

The date of the dialogue cannot be determined so certainly. Its contents and line of thought coincide so exactly, often in its very terms, with the "Meditations," that the connection of the two is perfectly manifest. Each leads up to the principle of certainty, "I think, therefore I am," in precisely the same manner; but the "Recherche" here breaks off in the middle of a sentence. What the "Meditations" express in the form of a monologue, is here developed in a dialogue between three. Eudoxe, the principal speaker, in his solitude in the country, represents the healthy and natural understanding, ignorant of the learning of the schools, and therefore not led astray by it; while Polyandre repre-

---

[1] Œuvres, t. xi., règ. iv. p. 224. [2] See foregoing book, chap. iii. p. 204.

sents the courtier and man of the world, who is interested in
philosophy, although he knows nothing about it ; Epistemon
is the polymathist, trained in the schools, who believes in
the books of the ancients, and despises the natural, untaught
understanding. Polyandre rapidly comprehends and with
increasing interest what Eudoxe, philosophizing in the spirit
of the " Meditations," draws out of him by means of questions in the Socratic manner; while Epistemon stands shaking
his head, and interjects his remarks here and there with the
air of a scholar. We see in Eudoxe, if not the philosopher
himself, the reader with philosophical tastes ; and in Polyandre the receptive pupil, such as Descartes wished for as
judges of his own writings at the conclusion of his " Discours." [1] There was a time when he did not think his
philosophy could become common property, and his doubt
an example for every simple and natural mind to follow.
When he composed the dialogue, he no longer held that
opinion. I hold it, therefore, highly probable, that it was
written after the " Meditations " and the " Discours," and
was related to the last, which hopes for a perfectly impartial
reader as the proof to a calculation. It was therefore written in French, and was designed to contain two books,
which were to develop Socratically the *whole* system of the
new philosophy. For this reason I think it was written
after the " Principles," since one must be completely master
of a subject to treat it in a dialogue. But that this dialogue,
as Millet assumes, is or was intended to be that "*traité de
l'érudition*" which the Princess Elizabeth asked the philosopher to write, appears to me doubtful, both because of the
subject and because of the reasons that led Descartes to
decline to undertake it.[2]

---

[1] See foregoing book, chap. v. p. 241.

[2] Cf. with foregoing book, chap. vii. p. 281, J. Millet: Histoire de Descartes, vol. ii. p. 326.

II. FALSE PATHS TO KNOWLEDGE.

1. *Defective Knowledge.* — The conviction at which Descartes early arrived, and which he energetically cherished, that science within and without the schools was in a wretched condition, had awakened in his mind ideas of the reformation of scientific thought. What displeased him was not the poverty or limited extent of knowledge, but the uncertain manner in which it was proved; it was not the lack of learning that left him discontented, since the Renaissance had increased the materials for culture to a very great degree; but the more thoroughly he examined the matter, the clearer it seemed to him that the lack of real knowledge was the cause of the wretched condition of the sciences. Science, as he saw it, lacked one thing that in his eyes was not merely the best, but every thing; viz., true *knowledge.* Descartes has been well compared with Luther. The objection that he neither was, nor wished to be, a Protestant is silly. We have here to do, not with the Catholic, but the reformer of philosophy, who did indeed sustain the same relation to science that Luther did to the Church. The Church lacked religion: that, in a word, was the conviction of Luther, based on his *need of personal salvation.* The sciences lacked true knowledge: that, with equal brevity, was the conviction of Descartes, based on his personal need of knowledge and truth. This incontestable parallelism throws light upon the problem and work of the philosopher. He occupies a position in philosophy which the Renaissance of philosophy never reached, and which it never could reach under the dominion of antiquity.

2. *Defective Method.* — We know that which we see follows from grounds, and these grounds must themselves be deduced from other grounds, and so on till we reach those that are rooted in absolute certainty. In other words, all knowledge consists in the correct arrangement and deduction of inferences. Each of these inferences is a link in a well-

articulated chain: each of them takes a step forward on the path of truth, and can be gained, therefore, only by progressing thought. But in order to walk, we must exert our own physical powers; and in order to make progress in thought, we must exert the powers of our mind. Method consists in this self-dependent and ordered thought. It is the only path to knowledge: all others lead to error and delusion. If, therefore, Descartes misses knowledge in science, he finds the reason for its absence in the lack of all methodical thought. Either one's own thought is lacking, as in the schools, where opinions are accepted on authority, or ordered thought, as is the case outside of the schools, where irregular desires of innovation and fantastic projects run wild.

What we accept on authority is not philosophical, but merely historical, knowledge. "And if we had read every word of Plato and Aristotle, without the certainty of our own judgment, we should not have advanced a step in philosophy: we should have increased our historical knowledge, but not our knowledge of truth."[1] The less of actual knowledge the learning of the schools and the ordinary philosophy — the vulgar philosophy, as Descartes calls it — possesses, the more restlessly and greedily it collects opinions which fill the memory, and swell up the mind, without giving it nourishment. "I believe that the body of a dropsical patient is scarcely more unhealthy than the mind of a greedy polymathist."[2] The hunting after, and catching at, all sorts of opinions are fatal to methodical thought, which exercises the utmost care in taking every step, and, therefore, advances slowly without any inclination to unhealthy and unprofitable speed. Polymathists are not thinkers, but collectors. The thinker seeks insight; and the clearer the insight, the higher he prizes it; and, indeed, unless it is perfectly clear, he regards it as valueless: the collector, on the other hand, seeks

[1] Œuvres, xi. Règles pour la direction de l'esprit, iii. p. 211.
[2] Rech. de la vérité, p. 338.

all sorts of so-called knowledge, and the rarest is to him the most interesting. The former prizes clearness, the latter rareness. The rarer his stock of knowledge, and the more difficult of acquisition, the more distinguished does the polymathist regard himself. He knows what others do not know: he is learned, they are ignorant. To pretended knowledge is thus added false imagination, the conceit of scholars, which even Montaigne regarded as a bane. In his deep aversion to the learning of the schools and polymathy, Descartes reminds us of that saying of Heraclites, πολυμαθὶτ νόου οὐ διδάσκει. And not less unprofitable than the blind search for knowledge, appeared to him the blind hunt for discoveries, such as uncalled innovators, the adventurers of science, seek to make. They are like those who seek for treasures, and who dig here and there in the hope that luck will enable them to light upon gold. They generally seek in vain; and if they find a treasure, they find it not "*par art*," but "*par un coup de fortune.*" [1] Bacon had a similar conviction when he saw the necessity of making thought a mode of discovery, and the process of discovery methodical, in order to transform it from a blind work of chance into an intentional work of art. Better not seek at all than seek in darkness. It is the worst method of making discoveries, but an infallible one for weakening the natural power of vision. The unlearned, healthy mind which has not developed its natural powers, but which, also, has not dulled them, is far more receptive to true knowledge than the mind which has been spoiled by polymathy, and an undiscriminating search for knowledge. Descartes wished to portray the character of the polymathist in his Epistemon. Of the many examples of charlatanry, he had seen one face to face in Chandoux.

III. THE PATH TO TRUTH.

1. *The Problem of Knowledge.* — How does knowledge result from thought? That is the question which the theory

---

[1] Règ. x. p. 253.

of method undertakes to answer, — a purely theoretical and absolutely universal one. The objects of knowledge are many and different, but knowledge itself is *one ;* and there can, therefore, be but one way in which we can certainly and undoubtedly, i.e., really, know. As the sun is related to the objects which it illuminates and reveals, so reason, the light within us, is related to the objects of thought. It is the same for all of them. How this light is produced, how it is made to attain perfect brilliancy, are questions, therefore, which are valid for all objects, for all sciences without exception. The theory of method which seeks to answer these questions has, therefore, the significance of a universal science ; and since it is valid for all the branches of knowledge, it makes them all fruitful. The faculty of knowledge is the capital which forms the basis of all our intellectual investments ; and to make it perfectly safe, is to increase the riches of knowledge immeasurably.

Every cognition is sure in the same proportion as the grounds from which it follows. Absolutely certain knowledge can be based only on absolutely certain grounds, and it is the mode of attaining such knowledge that the theory of method has to explain. The question is not how we may choose the less of two doubts, or the greater of two probabilities. Knowledge is the highest good, and we must not seek it by a method which can be recommended merely as enabling us to choose the less of two evils. Now, the more complex the cognition, the larger the number of its grounds, and the greater, therefore, its liability to error. In the field of complex knowledge we find at first mere probability, which involves doubt and uncertainty. If we wish to have absolutely certain knowledge, we must begin with the simplest conceptions, with the easiest problems, with objects that can be most easily known. The simpler the object, the sooner it can be perfectly examined in all its parts. Learning shows itself averse to clearness in its habit of preferring complicated and difficult questions to simple and easy ones, because one can thus maintain all sorts of theories and opinions, and engage in controversies on this side and on that. A single clear concept is more valuable and fruitful than many obscure and misty ones. The light in our minds is like real light: it diffuses itself. If it is perfectly clear in one place, clearness penetrates farther. If one conception is perfectly illuminated, others are illuminated along with it, and the day begins to dawn in our world of thought. And it is with fog in the mind as with real fog: when it begins to arise from the ground, soon the whole sky is obscured. We must take care, therefore, that the fog in our mind does not ascend, but that it falls to the ground; for if our conceptions are unclear in their foundations, the fog arises, and darkens our whole world of thought. Of what value is all learning if it is wrapped in darkness? It is not the subject of investigation that makes knowledge, but thought; and it is not true that difficult subjects, as they are usually treated, are more difficult than the knowledge of the simplest objects. On the contrary, "it is much easier," says Descartes, "to have a multitude of vague ideas on any question whatever than to penetrate to the truth in reference to the simplest of all questions." [1] Even so judged Socrates concerning the worth of true knowledge and the worthlessness of sophistical opinions, and of idle learning that boasted of them. In every great epoch of philosophy, the spirit of Socrates is present!

2. *The Method of True Deduction.* — We already see the starting-point of the road to truth, and the direction which it must take: it begins with the simplest perception, and advances to those which are composed of perfectly sure and clear elements, as a product of its factors. The method of knowledge is therefore *synthetic*, since it acquires and forms truths by progressive synthesis. Now, all derivative perceptions are only true when they are as sure and certain as those from which they are derived, and they have this cer-

---

[1] *Reg.* ii. p. 209.

tainty only when they evidently follow from them. That synthesis, therefore, consists in the logical derivation of every truth from the preceding, and of all from the first. This is the principle of the whole of knowledge: every derived perception is the basis of the following one. Proof by principles Aristotle called, in a narrower sense, syllogism: in Latin this syllogistic proof is called *deduction;* and with this name Descartes denotes his method, which he distinguished from the deduction of Aristotle as Bacon did his induction from the Aristotelian.

According to Descartes, there is no other criterion of truth than well-understood deduction. We must find the source of truth, and follow the course of the stream with the greatest care and accuracy step by step. "As to the object of scientific investigation, we dare not be guided by the thoughts of others, or even our own mere conjectures: we must follow what we ourselves clearly and evidently know, or can with certainty derive from what we know." The starting-point is the simplest truth; the goal, the complete knowledge of things. "We must give careful attention to these two points," says Descartes, "make no false assumption, and seek the way to the knowledge of all things." [1]

It appears that two paths lead to that goal, experience and deduction. The founders of modern philosophy stood at this parting-way, and left it in opposite directions. Bacon regarded experience as the only means of attaining to true knowledge; Descartes, deduction. Why Descartes rejected the Baconian method is evident. Experience begins with the facts of sense-perception, that is, with complex objects, the knowledge of which is exposed on all sides to deception. Among existing sciences, some are dialectical, others empirical: the only sciences which proceed deductively are *mathematical*, which, therefore, are alone free from error and uncertainty, since experience is subject to involuntary deceptions, but deduction is not. "From this it does not follow

[1] Règ. iii. p. 209, iv. p. 216.

that arithmetic and geometry are the only sciences that we ought to study, but that he who seeks the path to truth must occupy himself with objects that can be known as certainly as the deductions of arithmetic and geometry." [1]

Descartes distinguished this deductive method not only from the empirical, but also from the dialectical, mode of thought, which last prevails in the sciences of the schools. Experience is uncertain, dialectics useless, in reference to actual knowledge. This is the point in which Descartes opposed his deduction to that of Aristotle, which consists in the dialectic arts of the schools, the usual doctrine of the syllogism, which only enables us to arrange and state that which we already know in a logically correct form, but does not enable us to discover new truth. It does not produce knowledge, but presupposes it: it does not belong to philosophy, but to rhetoric. Touching the unfruitfulness of this kind of deduction or of the ordinary syllogism, Descartes entirely agreed with Bacon. "The dialecticians can form no syllogism whose conclusion expresses a truth that was not known before. The ordinary dialectics is, therefore, completely worthless for the discovery of truth, and is useful only in stating and explaining the results of our investigations: it has, therefore, no place in philosophy, but is strictly a part of rhetoric." [2]

Science, on the other hand, has to develop the known from the unknown, to find out new truths, to make discoveries, and, indeed, by means of the method which advances from discovery to discovery. Every new truth is a problem, which can be thoroughly and certainly solved, only when all the conditions are distinctly known from which the solution necessarily follows. They must, therefore, form a series, every member of which forms the evident ground of the one that immediately follows it. In such a continuity of progressing and new inferences consists that method of deduction which Descartes demands.

[1] Règ. ii. pp. 204–209.   [2] Règ. iv. p. 217, x. p. 256.

3. *Universal Mathematics. Analytical Geometry.* — We have
already mentioned in the history of his youth, how, exactly
in this particular, mathematics seemed to him a type, and
enabled him to ascertain his position with respect to the
other sciences.[1] He found in mathematics a kind of scientific thought corresponding to his needs, advancing in an
orderly manner from problem to problem, from solution to
solution, from discovery to discovery. There alone he found
a *method of solving problems*, and discovering the unknown by
means of the known. In this method, Descartes saw the
true spirit of mathematics, not in the usual school discipline,
which first states its proposition, and then proves it. He saw,
also, how, through the application, perfection, and generalization of this method, mathematics had made its greatest progress. Even the ancients understood the art of so solving
geometrical problems as to deduce unknown magnitudes from
those that are known. As by the analysis of a known fact,
the unknown conditions from which it follows can be discovered, so from a known problem, or the assumption of its
actual solution, the conditions are known which are essential
to this fact, that is, to the solution of the problem. The
ancients, therefore, called their method *analysis*, the practice
of which consisted only in the comparison of known magnitudes with those that are unknown. What the analysis of
the ancients was in reference to figures, the algebra of the
moderns is in reference to numbers. Arithmetic is more
comprehensive than geometry, and algebra is a generalization
of the analytical method. The next step in the improvement
of this method is to make it valid for the whole doctrine of
quantities, or, which is the same thing, to apply algebra to
geometry, to solve geometrical problems by algebraic calculations or by equations. This long stride consists in *analytical
geometry*, which Descartes discovered. The analysis of geometry is made by means of construction: analytical geometry
solves its problems by means of equations, by a logical opera-

---

[1] Foregoing book, chap. i. pp. 170-173; book ii. p. 184.

tion, therefore, which is independent of the intuition of space, the method of which both generalizes and simplifies mathematical thought. We cannot too carefully remember that Descartes discovered analytical geometry while he was studying method; for while he was trying to combine the analysis of the ancients and algebra, he perceived their identity. "The human soul has a divine aptitude for knowledge, which has borne its natural fruits in spite of the errors which have intrenched themselves in learning. We find the proof of this in arithmetic and geometry, the simplest of all sciences. Even the ancients used a certain analysis in geometry for the solution of problems: in arithmetic blossoms algebra, as we see, which aims to apply to numbers the method which the ancients applied to figures. These two kinds of analysis are involuntary fruits of our natural powers of thought: and I am not surprised, that, in application to such simple objects, they have yielded richer results than in other sciences, where greater obstacles stand in the way of their development; although there, also, if they are carefully cultivated, they can be brought to perfect maturity."[1]

Here Descartes alludes to his own particular problem, for the knowledge and solution of which, the mathematical method in the analysis of the ancients, the algebra of the moderns, and the analytical geometry, which he himself had discovered, formed preliminary stages. After he had made this method universal within the realm of mathematics or the theory of quantities, there only remained to make the knowledge of all things mathematical. He must take the last step in the extension and generalization of mathematical methods; he must apply analysis to the whole of human knowledge, analyzing its problem in order to determine from what conditions truth follows, and from what error; and, therefore, he must analyze all the voluntary and involuntary delusions of human nature into their elements. The quantity to which the method of analysis is to be applied, is the human

[1] Rëg. iv. pp. 217, 218.

mind; the philosopher himself in his own person.[1] The most complex of all objects is to be analyzed into its simplest factors. In this labor consisted the Titanic difficulty with which Descartes so long struggled. His path had led him through the territory of mathematics, to a point where he stood, as it were, before the last curtain. To raise this curtain, to completely unfold and universalize the method, as yet bound within and veiled by the theory of quantities, is the undertaking in which he engages. The problem is, to apply the methods of mathematics to the knowledge of the universe ; to treat mathematics, not as the theory of quantities, but as the *theory of science, as universal mathematics.* The method which in Descartes' own words was veiled and covered by the theory of quantities, was to be *uncovered* in the literal sense of the word. " That is the goal," continued Descartes in the passage above quoted, " which I have before my eyes in this essay. I should not lay so much emphasis on these rules, if they only served for the solution of certain problems with which arithmeticians and geometers pass away the time. I should then be devoting myself to trifles with perhaps a little more art than others. And if in this essay I often speak of figures and numbers, — because I can obtain such evident and certain examples from no other sciences, — the attentive reader will, nevertheless, easily see that I am in no way concerned with the ordinary mathematics, but that I am explaining a method which there appears in disguise rather than in its true nature. This method is intended to contain the elements of human reason, and to enable us to discover in every subject the truths that are concealed in it. And, to tell the truth, I am convinced that it excels every other means of attaining to human knowledge, since it is the origin and source of all truths." " I have therefore given up the special study of arithmetic and geometry, in order to devote myself to a *universal mathematical* science. I have first asked myself what one really means

---

[1] See foregoing book, chap. ii. pp. 189, 194, 195.

by 'mathematics,' and wherefore arithmetic and geometry are considered parts of it, and not astronomy, music, optics, mechanics and so many other sciences with just as good right. The word 'mathematics' means *science*, and the above-mentioned branches have therefore as much right to the name as geometry." " In a careful consideration of these matters, I have learned that all the sciences which have to do with the investigation of order and quantity, belong to mathematics, whether they inquire after this quantity in numbers, figures, stars, sounds, or in entirely different objects; and that there must, therefore, be a universal science, which, apart from every particular application, grounds every thing relating to order and quantity, and, therefore, deserves the peculiar and time-honored name of mathematics, since the other sciences are its parts." [1]

4. *Enumeration, or Induction. Intuition.* — In order to solve a problem methodically, we must know all its presuppositions, all the points upon which its solution depends. The complete enumeration of these points, the analysis of the principal question into the conditions necessary to its solution, Descartes calls enumeration, or induction. Through such a survey, we find our position with reference to the solution of the problem, and bring it under our power. Nothing prepares us more thoroughly and surely for the solution than the accurate and exhaustive knowledge of the problem. When the questionable points are known, and methodically arranged, from the condition upwards to the conditioned, we can advance with complete certainty from the first condition through all the intermediate terms to the solution of the problem. To take the simplest example, the progressive series of the numbers 3, 6, 12, 24, 48, etc., is based on the equality of the following relations, $3:6 = 6:12 = 12:24 = 24:48$; and the equality of these proportions is based on the fact that the following member is in every case twice as great as the one that immediately precedes it. The progress

of the series is apprehended by means of the relation of the
individual members to each other, and this by means of their
multiplication. The first proposition is $3 \times 2 = 6, 6 \times 2 =$
$12, 12 \times 2 = 24, 24 \times 2 = 48$. The second is, therefore, $3 : 6 =$
$6 : 12 = 12 : 24 = 24 : 48$; and from this follows the third, that
the numbers 3, 6, 12, 24, 48, etc., form a progressive series
with the geometrical ratio 2. In this way, continuity and
connection come into our world of conceptions, and our
ideas appear as members of series. The longer the series
of conceptions which deduction methodically arranges, the
wider the horizon, and the stronger the power of the mind
that grasps and masters it. But the longer the series, the
more distant its members are from the first condition upon
which they depend, and, therefore, from the source of their
light; and there is danger, that, with increasing distance, the
clearness of perception will decrease. We must, therefore,
frequently run through the whole series, each time more
rapidly, until we are completely master of it, and survey the
whole of it at a single glance. In this manner we disaccus-
tom ourselves to the natural dulness of the mind, and make
its horizon wider. Thought is quickened, and, at the same
time, a great relief is given to the memory. For to preserve a multitude of conceptions, there is no better means
than to unite them deductively in a thoroughly thought out
series. Methodical thought is the surest of all systems of
mnemonics.[1]

How does deduction begin? This question, which brings
us to the beginning of the system, and prepares the way for
a transition to it, we have purposely raised at the conclusion
of our discussion of the theory of method. Every member
of the series is based on the one that immediately precedes
it, and is, therefore, dependent upon all of the earlier members, and is the more dependent the farther it stands from
the first, which itself depends upon no other. The beginning of deduction is, therefore, not an inference, but an

[1] Règ. vi. pp. 226-233; vii. pp. 234, 235. Cf. xi. pp. 257, 258.

immediate certainty, a perception or *intuition*, as Descartes says, perfectly clear in the light of reason. Intuition is the starting-point of the path of knowledge, and it is made from that point on by means of deduction. These two kinds of knowledge are the only means of attaining to certainty, the single conditions which make science possible. "The starting-point can be apprehended only through intuition, the inferences from it only through deduction." "The entire method consists in the arrangement and succession of the objects in reference to which the mind is seeking to learn the truth. To follow the guidance of this method, we must follow obscure and complicated conceptions step by step backward into those that are ever simpler and simpler, until, from the intuition of the object of the simplest of all, we start step by step to the knowledge of each following and more complex conception. In this alone consists the perfection of method, and every one who wishes to wander through the labyrinth of science must hold it fast as carefully as Theseus did the thread. I know there are many who, through ignorance or lack of judgment, pay no attention to the theory of method, and often attempt to solve the most difficult problems in a way that suggests a man attempting to reach the top of a high building at a single spring, despising, or else not seeing, the stairs that lead up to it step by step. Thus proceed astrologists, who undertake to determine the effects of the stars without having made careful observations of their nature and motions. Thus proceed many people who, without a knowledge of the underlying principles of mechanics, undertake to make machines. Thus act the greater part of philosophers, who do not trouble themselves about experience, and suppose that truth will issue from their brains like Minerva from the head of Jupiter." [1]

The methodical solution of every problem requires the orderly *enumeration*, or *induction*, of its conditions, and the

[1] Règ. iii. pp. 211, 212, 214; v. p. 225.

analysis of those into the *intuition*, from which deduction
systematically advances. In this consists the sum of the
Cartesian theory of method. Deduction begins with intuition. But what is the object of that intuition? It can be
no other than the condition of all deduction, which, as such,
is not itself deducible. As all visible objects exist under the
condition that there is a power of vision, so all knowable
objects exist under the condition that there is a power of
knowledge or intelligence. The certainty of the last must,
therefore, precede the knowledge of things. This is the
foundation of deduction, and we are already in sight of the
beginning of the system — full of significance. On methodological grounds, Descartes requires the investigation of the
faculty of knowledge *as the first step ;* and the critical spirit
of his philosophy appears so clear and self-conscious in this
requirement, that we might here suppose that we are standing at the threshold of the Kantian philosophy. " The most
important of all the problems to be solved, is the determination of the *nature* and limits of human knowledge, — two
points which we embrace in one question, which must first
of all be methodically investigated. Every one who has the
least love for truth, must have examined this question; since
its investigation comprehends the whole of method, and, as
it were, the whole organon of knowledge. Nothing seems
to me more absurd than to contend, at random, about the
mysteries of nature, the influences of the stars, the unknown
events of the future, without having once inquired whether
the human mind is competent to such inquiries." [1]

The single object of intuitive knowledge is likewise the
first condition of all knowable things, hence, the guiding
principle of deduction ; viz., intelligence itself. Every thing
else I know through inferences, therefore through middle
terms : of one object I am directly and immediately certain,
— of myself, my own being, my own thought. " Every one
can intuitively know that he thinks, that he exists." [2] Des-

cartes states these propositions in his theory of method as examples of intuition or immediate certainty: they are the foundations of his system. We must now see how these fundamental truths are discovered, and how from this point the further problems are solved.

CHAPTER II.

THE BEGINNING OF PHILOSOPHY: METHODICAL DOUBT.

I. THE ORIGIN AND EXTENT OF DOUBT.

1. *The Teachings of the Schools.*

SINCE the diffusion of the Cartesian philosophy, its first propositions, "I doubt every thing," "I think, therefore I am," have become famous sayings, with which, as usually happens, the ignorant divert themselves. But he who does not clearly understand their origin in the mind of Descartes, knows nothing more of them than the mere words. How came such a cautious and circumspect thinker to entertain such a fundamental and far-reaching doubt? This concise and summary expression was not the suggestion of a moment, not a bold, quickly formed resolution, but the result of a long and uninterrupted self-examination. Between those first doubts in the scholar at La Flèche, and that doubt in the philosopher, with which he grounds his system, intervenes a long series of years. His first doubts were excited against the sciences of the schools and the learning of books. He found a multitude of conflicting theories heaped together out of different times and minds, propagated without examination, and taught by the authority and under the influence of the schools. His longing for truth would not tolerate the reception of such a disorderly mass of ungrounded theories. It demanded coherence in the theories assented to, and knowledge perceived, to rest on valid grounds, — a knowledge derived from one's own thought and experience, "from myself," as he said, "and the great book of the world," and not from books and the opinions of others.

But not even our own thought and experience of the world are a guaranty of truth. Both are liable to deception. To abandon our faith in teachers and books is of little avail, if we rest contented in the illusions of our own thought. Many boast of all sorts of doubts, and are at the same time the victims of the emptiest and most superficial self-deceptions. Apart from all artificial education, we have a natural propensity to accept things on authority; and we imagine ourselves independent where we are in the most utter dependence. To doubt the truth of *our own* opinions and our own intellectual excellence, goes deeper, and is, at the same time, more important, because it is so much the more difficult than a sceptical attitude towards external authorities. We have now to do with a doubt that shall follow our self-deceptions into their last hiding-place.

2. *Self-deception.* — We find in our minds a multitude of deeply rooted conceptions, based on prescriptive right, as it were, which through habit have become second nature, so that it is very difficult not to believe them. They are based on our first impressions, on the beliefs of childhood; and we are inclined to rely on them. Nevertheless, experience has taught us that many of these conceptions are false. Why may not the rest be? There is no guaranty of their truth; and if we would proceed surely, we must hold them all, if not false, at least uncertain and doubtful.[1]

Thus doubt forces its way into our inner world, attacking time-honored conceptions; and it will not pause until it meets with beliefs that are able to defy it. If the imaginations of childhood have been routed, or made to waver, nevertheless our sense-perceptions will stand their ground. But they also are deeply rooted; they are as old as the beliefs of childhood, and belong to the same general class; and it is improbable that they will prove the only exception to their uncertainty. The senses also have so often deceived us, that it is impossible for us to accept all their representa-

[1] Œuvres, t. i. Médit., i. pp. 235, 236, t. iii. Princ., sec. 1, pp. 63, 64.

tions as true.   If we are in earnest in our attempt to rid
ourselves of self-deception, we shall not give perfect trust to
their reports, and must, therefore, admit doubt even into
this supposed stronghold of certainty.   For the inconsiderate and, therefore, too hasty confidence in the reports of our
senses is also a self-deception.

But it nevertheless seems that *some* of the perceptions of
sense are of indubitable certainty.   Our own body and its
limbs, its present states and activities, are manifest phenomena, whose reality nobody questions.   But is this reality to
be accepted under all circumstances?   There are very many
and well-known cases, in which presentations of sense of
apparently the most certain character turn out to be empty
imaginations, which delude us with the appearance of reality.
As often as we *dream*, we experience this illusion.   We
experience what we dream, and dream what we have experienced.   The same phenomena are now objects of experience,
now the visions of a dream.   In the first case we regard
them as true ; in the second, false.   The nature of the presentation, therefore, is no guaranty of the reality of its object ;
and the objects of sense are not to be taken as real because
they are objects of *sense*, and also not because they are *these*
particular objects of sense, since, as such, they may just as
well be imaginary.   They exist in reality when they are not
dreams.   But to apprehend this reality, and guard it against
every doubt, there must be a criterion by means of which
we can accurately, infallibly, and invariably distinguish the
visions of a dream from the experiences of our waking states.
Now there is no such criterion.   " When I consider the
matter carefully, I do not find a single characteristic by
means of which I can certainly determine whether I am
awake, or whether I dream.   The visions of a dream and the
experiences of my waking states are so much alike, that I
am completely puzzled ; and I do not really know that I am
not dreaming at this moment ! " [1]

[1] Méd., i. p. 238.   Princ., i. sec. 4, pp. 64, 65.

In the progress of his self-examination, the fact of dreams forms an important moment, which repeatedly turns the scale in favor of doubt. In this case, it destroys our apparently strongest certainty, — that in the objects of sense. " How do you *know*," asks Eudoxe, " that your whole life is not a continual dream ? " [1] That reminds us of a sentence in Calderon's profound poem : —

> " In this wonder-world a dream is
> Our whole life and all its changes :
> All we seem to be and do
> Is a dream and fancy too.
> Briefly, on this earthen ball,
> Dreaming what we're living all."

So much is evident : the same phenomena which in dreams are completely imaginary, cannot be accepted as real in the state of waking, until we are able to distinguish the two states in the surest possible manner.

But there is yet something in the objects of sense that sets doubt at defiance. If all these objects are but the images of a dream, nevertheless all that is in them cannot be mere imagination : an image in a dream, like every other image, is a compound, which consists of certain elements without which its composition could not take place. However imaginary the image, its fundamental constituents *are given*, and have the surest claim on reality. Without certain elementary ideas, as space, time, extension, form, quantity, number, place, etc., there is no object of sense, no image, and, therefore, no image of a dream. As a painting presupposes, but does not make, colors, in like manner those elements are related to our world of confused and manifold conceptions. Before this last condition of sensible objects, it seems that doubt must call a halt.[2] But we must first inquire *by whom* those elements are given of which all our presentations and imaginations consist, and whether their reality is guaranteed

[1] Œuvres, t. xi. Rech. de la vérité, p. 350. [2] Méd., i. pp. 238-240.

by their author.   For that which is given and received from
without has not as such the stamp of truth, otherwise every
thing that we accept on authority might be accepted as true.
But in the beginning of our inquiry, we came in contact with
transmitted conceptions, and found them doubtful exactly
because they were transmitted.   To be sure, their uncertainty was based on the fact of their human origin ; while
those which we are now considering seem to be innate, and
not to belong to the things which men have transmitted.
Their origin, therefore, must be sought in a supra-human
source, — in *God* himself, as the ground of our being, and
the cause of the world.   Doubt thus stands in the immediate
presence of the highest object of faith ; and the question now
arises, whether, in the interest of the most searching self-
examination, we dare quiet ourselves with the assumption
that some of our ideas are of divine origin ; whether, with this
assumption, the possibility of deception is excluded.   The
more imperfectly we conceive of this God, whether as Fate,
Chance, or Necessity of Nature, the less has he the power to
preserve us from deception ; and the more perfectly he
appears as an all-powerful spirit, the more he has the power
to plunge us into deceptions.   And if he has the power, why
not the will also ?   Perhaps because he is good ; but if he
does not will that I err, why do I ?   Plainly his will does
not protect me from error, and he has the power to blind me.
It may be that I live in a world of phantoms, in a mere illu-
sionary world, perhaps that I may hereafter be delivered from
it, or that I may never attain to the light of truth.   It may
be that the divine omnipotence has so created me, that the
world which I represent to myself exists merely in my imagination, without truth and reality in itself.[1]   At all events,
this supposition is possible, and it is more than the fancy of
a self-tormenting hypercritic.   The idea that the sense-world
in which we live is a mere phantom world, which blinds and
deceives us, is the theme of the Mâyâ, one of the oldest reli-

[1] Méd., i. pp. 240–242.   Princ., sec. 5, pp. 65, 66.

gions in the world. In the course of the self-examination of
our philosopher, the plummet of doubt reaches so deep that
it penetrates to, and vindicates the possibility of, this conception, and thus demolishes the last bulwark, behind which
our ordinary beliefs, nourished by our confidence in the
senses, have protected themselves from scepticism. We
have, therefore, no beliefs that cannot and must not be
doubted, if we wish to completely rid ourselves of every self-
delusion. It may be that many of them are true ; but we do
not know it, since none of them are proved. We have no
reason to consider them certain, but reason enough to hold
them uncertain. Now, the declaration, " I doubt every thing,"
follows from the perception of this universal uncertainty.
" What can I allege against these reasons ? I have no arguments to weaken their force. I am at last compelled to the
open acknowledgment, that every thing which I have believed can be doubted, not thoughtlessly or lightly, but from
cogent and well-considered reasons ; and that, if the truth
is of any importance to me, I ought to guard as carefully
against assuming by chance that which is uncertain, as that
which is plainly false." [1]

II. DOUBT AS METHOD AND AS PRINCIPLE.

With our entire world of conceptions — which has not
stood the test of self-examination — we are prisoners to self-
delusion, and have grown accustomed to our fetters. Doubt
requires not only to break in upon and attack this habit
here and there, but all along the line, that it may utterly
destroy it : *it requires to wean us from the habit of self-delusion.* No habit is stronger than that of belief, and none is
more difficult to get rid of. And if doubt is really to have
the power to banish self-delusion, it is not enough for us to
conceive and understand it, and have a distinct idea of the
reasons for it : we must accustom ourselves to this mode of
thought, and live in this critical state of mind as heretofore

[1] Méd., p. 242. Princ., i. sec. 2. Rech., p. 351.

in the uncritical. That is as difficult as this was easy. The habit of self-delusion comes of itself; the weaning from it only through discipline of the mind and method. " But it is not enough by far to have observed this necessity: we must continually re-present it to our minds. For those familiar opinions are constantly returning and capturing the easily believing mind, which is subject to them, as it were, by prescription and domestic right. They return against my will, and I cannot wean myself from the habit of deferring to them, and confiding in them. Although I know very well how doubtful they are, nevertheless they seem so true that it seems more reasonable to believe them than deny them." [1]

Doubt becomes a principle: the critical direction of the mind becomes a conscious resolution of the will and a maxim. I wish to get rid of self-delusion, and not merely in this case or that, here or now, but in all cases and at all times. As self-deception is universal and habitual, so the doubt which is to banish it must be universal, and become at home in our mode of thought. We should note carefully the object of this doubt. It is not directed against this or that conception, the religious conception, for example, of which many first think when doubt is spoken of, but against a human state, the existence of which we can see with half an eye, against the state of self-delusion, imagination, blindness. He who rejects or opposes the doubt of Descartes, must approve of our self-delusion. He who holds it better not to give way to that doubt, must hold it better for us to continue in our self-blindness. It can, therefore, be only a deluded mind, not one that is earnestly religious, that fears such doubt. The opposite of self-delusion is truthfulness to one's self. This is the source of all truth and all the courage in seeking truth. He who is not true to himself has not the courage to look through his blindness; he has in general no courage in seeking truth; generally speaking, he is not true, and all the candor which he has in other matters

is at bottom false.   That, therefore, is the intention of the
Cartesian doubt and the task which it sets itself: be true to
yourself.   Do not persuade yourself, and do not allow yourself to be persuaded, that you are what you are not, that you
know what is not clear and evident to you, that you believe
that which at bottom you doubt, or ought to doubt.

Thus deeply inward is the inquiring and critical mind of
Descartes directed: he requires self-illumination in place
of self-delusion.   He has to do only with his own mind, and
not with the world; his doubt attacks merely the validity of
conceptions, and not states of the world; it is therefore not
practical, but only theoretical.   "I know that neither danger
nor error can arise from this: I have no reason to be afraid
of an excess of distrust, since I am here concerned, not with
practical, but merely with theoretical, problems.   I will suppose, then, not that the All-wise and perfectly good God is
the source of truth, but some malignant, and at the same
time powerful, demon, who has employed all his skill in
deceiving me.   I will suppose that the sky, the air, the
earth, colors, figures, sounds, and all the things I perceive
without me, are the illusions of dreams, with which that
spirit has laid snares for my credulity.   I will consider myself as without eyes, flesh, blood, or any of the senses, as
possessing all these things merely in imagination, and I will
resolutely continue and strengthen myself in this mode of
consideration.   If it is not then in my power to arrive at the
knowledge of truth, I shall at least be able to protect myself
from error.   I will face that lying spirit, and be he ever so
powerful and cunning, he shall not overcome me.   But the
undertaking is difficult, and a certain indolence is constantly
leading me back to my old habits of life: and like a prisoner
who rejoices in dreams over an imaginary freedom, and
dreads awakening, when he begins to suspect that it is only
a dream, and cherishes the pleasant fancy as long as possible,
so involuntarily I fall back into my old beliefs, and fear to
arouse myself from my slumber.   I fear the laborious exist-

ence that will follow this pleasant sleep, and which must
be spent, not in the light of day, but in the impenetrable
darkness of already excited doubts." [1]   To return is impossible.   The sun of truth must rise out of the ocean of doubt
itself.

[1] Méd., i. pp. 243–245. Pr., i. 3, p. 64.

CHAPTER III.

THE PRINCIPLE OF PHILOSOPHY AND THE PROBLEM OF KNOWLEDGE.

I. THE PRINCIPLE OF CERTAINTY.

1. *One's Own Thinking Being.*

I HAVE no conception the truth of which is evident to me. On the contrary, they are all of such a nature that I perceive their uncertainty. Experience, which has contradicted them in so many cases, testifies against the transmitted conceptions of childhood; the errors of the senses against the conceptions of sense; dreams, against the apparently most certain sense-perceptions; and, finally, against the reality of those elementary conceptions that lie at the foundation of all the rest, arises the possibility that the world of the senses universally is a mere unsubstantial, phantom world, that in the very roots of our being we are involved in deception and illusion. Thus, every thing is doubtful, and nothing certain except this very doubt. Every thing is doubtful; i.e., I doubt every thing. The second proposition is as certain as the first, and I am as certain of myself. If I subtract delusion from self-delusion, myself remains: if that is possible, this is necessary. Without a self, there can be no self-delusion and no doubt. Now I have found a point which doubt can never attack, because it depends upon it. "Archimedes demanded only a firm and immovable point in order to move the earth, and we also can entertain great hopes if we can discover the smallest certain and indubitable truth." Even suppose that

we have been banished by a wicked demon into a world of
illusion, nevertheless we are, no matter in what condition
of mortal blindness. If that demon deceives me, it is clear
that I also am : let him deceive me as much as he can, he can
never bring it to pass, that, so long as I think that something
is, I myself am not. And accordingly, after I have considered every thing again and again, I come at last to this
proposition, which stands firm : " I am, I exist," is necessarily true in the moment in which I express it or conceive
it.[1]

The next question is, What am I? We cannot answer,
" I am a man," or " I am this body," since it is possible that
all bodies are only phantoms. I cannot, therefore, explain
the essence of my being by activities which, like self-motion,
nourishment, sensation, can certainly be ascribed to the soul,
but not without the body. If I separate from myself every
thing that is doubtful, nothing remains but *the doubting itself*.
If nothing of that which I hold uncertain exists, my uncertainty yet remains. If I am nothing of that which I imagine
myself to be, my imagination yet remains. If every thing
is false which I affirm or deny, it is yet true that I affirm or
deny. Now, doubting, imagining, affirming, denying, etc., are
modes of thought. Thought remains after subtraction of
every thing that is doubtful ; in thought, therefore, consists
my unchangeable essence ; my thought is my true being ; I
think, therefore I am. " But why shall I imagine other
things? I am not that assemblage of members called the
human body ; also I am not a thin and penetrating substance
diffused through all these members, or wind, or fire, or
vapor, or breath, or any of the things which I imagine myself
to be. For I have supposed that all those things in reality
are not ; and though that supposition remains, I am nevertheless something." I am a thinking being. In this sentence,

[1] Méd., ii. pp. 246-248. Pr., i. sec. 7. In the Rech. de la vérité, Eudoxe
characterizes the doubt of every thing with the above expression of the
Meditations as " *un point fixe et immuable.*"

Descartes realizes, in relation to the knowledge of things, the requirement of Archimedes. If I should doubt the certainty of my thought, I should put in question the possibility of doubt itself, and should be obliged to return to the old delusions. The proposition, therefore, "I think, hence I am," excludes all uncertainty, and is the first and surest truth which every one finds who philosophizes methodically.[1]

If to the question, "What am I?" the answer is returned, "I am a man," we must inquire farther, and the unknown species be defined by the more unknown genus, according to the "tree of Porphyry." What is man? What is rational animal, living body, life, body, thing, etc.? A labyrinth of obscure conceptions. But the answer, "I am a doubting, and therefore thinking, being," cannot in like manner be resolved into an endless regress of questions, — what is doubting, thinking, etc.? To this objection of Epistemon, the philosopher of the schools, Eudoxe aptly replies, "We must doubt and think in order to know what it is." He who has experienced this activity does not inquire concerning its genus and species, since it is a matter of immediate knowledge.[2]

2. *The Principle of Certainty. The Mind as the Clearest Object.* — Every thing which is just as evident as the certainty of my own thinking being is just as true. Here the object of thought is directly present to the mind, and we know immediately both *that* it is and *what* it is. The presence of the object makes the perception of it *clear:* it is *distinct* because the object appears in its own nature unmixed with other things. "I call that clear which is present and manifest to the attentive mind, as we say we see an object clearly when it is present to the eye looking on, and when it makes on the sense of sight an impression sufficiently strong and definite; but I call that distinct which is clear, and at the same time so definitely distinguished from every

[1] Disc., iv. p. 158. Méd., ii. pp. 248-253. Pr., i. secs. 7-10.
[2] Rech. de la vérité, pp. 354-371.

thing else that its essence is evident to him who properly considers it." The truth of self-certainty has both characteristics: it is perfectly clear and distinct; and it would be less certain, that is, more uncertain, like every thing else, if it had these characteristics in a less degree. Clearness and distinctness are, therefore, the criteria of certainty or of truth. Our philosopher, accordingly, expresses the principle or "*regula generalis*" of truth by the formula, " *What I clearly and distinctly conceive is true.*" [1]

The principle of knowledge follows from the proposition of certainty. It is important to notice one of its consequences immediately. The less the clearness and distinctness of a conception, the less the certainty by which the truth and reality of its object is evident. Now, clearness is dependent upon the presence of the object, or the immediateness of the relation between perception and its object. The more mediate, therefore, the object, the greater the number of middle terms between perception and its object, and the more obscure the perception. Nothing is more immediately present to us than our own being: nowhere has any one a greater right to say that each is nearest to himself, than in knowledge. I am a thinking being or *mind*. Mind, therefore, is of all objects the clearest; its existence and nature are more evident than those of things without us, of material objects, the representations of which are mediate and dependent upon the senses; and obscure, because they are mediate; and confused, because the nature of my senses is mingled with the nature of the object. To make an object distinct, is to represent it to ourselves in its purity, and to separate from it every thing foreign to its nature; and that we can do only by examination and criticism, i.e., by judgment and thought. To clearly and distinctly represent a thing is, therefore, to *think*. From the principle of certainty, therefore, follows the principle in which the rationalism of Descartes' philosophy finds distinct expression: *True knowledge is possible only*

[1] Rech. de la vérité, pp. 354–371.

through thought. Thought alone makes our ideas of things clear and distinct.

Every conception which I have is my conception; and every conception, therefore, proves more certainly than it does any thing else, that I am. I say this body exists because I touch it: perhaps it does not exist, perhaps I only imagine or dream that I touch it. But one thing follows with incontestable certainty, — that I, who touch the body, or imagine I touch it, in reality am. That mind should be more clear and evident than body, appears absurd to the common consciousness: bodies are so distinct because we can see them with our eyes, and grasp them with our hands. That mind is more distinct than body, will seem less absurd, and the nature of the object perceived by means of the senses less distinct, if we earnestly try to conceive it. What do we distinctly conceive in a piece of wax, which we perceive as a hard object which we can grasp with our hands? It is not properties which we have just perceived; for the wax melts, and they are present no longer. What remains is something extended, ductile, changeable, which, by means of its extension, is capable of passing through an endless series of changes of size, and by means of its ductility and changeableness, and endless series of forms. This endless manifold can be conceived and comprehended by no presentation of sense, but only by thought.[1]

II. THE PROBLEM OF KNOWLEDGE.

1. *The Conception of a Being without us.* — If, now, true knowledge consists in the clearness and distinctness of conceptions, and if these are attainable only by thought, the question arises, How, by means of thought, do I come to a knowledge of *things?* My certainty reaches no farther than the activity of my thought: where this ceases, uncertainty begins. If we represent to ourselves the internal and external world as the hemispheres of the universe, the one lies

---

[1] Méd., ii. pp. 256-258. Pr., i. secs. 8-12.

in the circle of illumination, the other in shadow. If the
light within us does not illuminate the dark world without
us, we remain in uncertainty and doubt concerning its existence. This, therefore, is the question which the problem of
knowledge comprehends, — How does the certainty of the
existence of things without us follow from the certainty of
our own existence? To put the question in its most general
form, Is there any being at all without us, the existence of
which is as clearly and distinctly evident as our own thinking being? Have we a conception, from which the existence
of such a being manifestly follows?

Let us examine somewhat more closely the different kinds
of ideas we find in our internal world. Some of them seem
original or innate, others to have been voluntarily formed,
but most of them to have been received from without.
These last, the presentations of the senses, we consider effects
and copies of things without us, and, therefore, an indubitable evidence of their existence. We know indeed how
unfounded this opinion is, how the senses often, and dreams
always, deceive us. To be sure, the presentations of the
senses as such are never false. It is certain that I have this
perception, — that I present to myself the sun as a round disk
that moves of itself: only from this it does not follow that
the sun is a disk that moves in such a manner. The error
lies in this inference, it lies not in my presentation, but in
the fact that I hold my perception as the property and state
of a thing without me. In so doing, I am not merely having
a conception, but *judging* about it. It is a judgment when
we declare that a presentation in our minds is the effect and
copy of a thing outside of us. It is a *groundless* judgment
when we relate presentations of sense to external objects.
This is not the place to finally decide the question, whether,
by means of our sense-perceptions, the existence of bodies
can be proved. Here we only declare that the sensible properties which we find in our consciousness give no reason
to seek their cause or original without us. The reasons

which are adduced for that purpose prove nothing: it is in vain to appeal to the fact that they arise involuntarily, and that we refer them to an outward object by a natural instinct. These instincts are not infallible; and the fact that those sensations are independent of our will, does not exclude the possibility of their proceeding involuntarily from the conditions of our own nature. And even if they are effects of external objects, it does not follow that they are related to their causes as copies to their originals, since an effect may be very unlike its cause. We must declare, accordingly, that they in no way authorize the certain judgment, that there are things without us. If, therefore, any of our ideas is to make us certain of the existence of things outside of us, it cannot be a sensation.[1]

2. *The Principle of Causality.* — As çertain as is our own thinking nature by means of which we have ideas, so certain is the principle of causality: "From nothing, nothing becomes; every thing is the effect of a producing cause." If less should be contained in the cause than in the effect, this excess would have to be produced by nothing. From this it follows that the cause never can be less than the effect, but must contain more reality than, or just as much as, the effect. In the first case, it is related to the effect, as the artist to a work of art, since in him more is contained than in his work; in the second, as a form to its impression. That cause, Descartes calls " *causa eminens;*" this, " *causa formalis.*" If, now, we find an idea in our minds which contains more reality than our own nature, it is clear that we are neither its " *causa eminens* " nor its " *causa formalis,*" therefore not its cause at all; that, therefore, the cause of *this* idea must exist without us. The question is, whether we have such an idea.[2]

What we conceive are either substances or modes. Plainly those contain more reality than these; and we have now, therefore, to examine more closely the worth and value of

[1] Méd., iii. pp. 268-272.   [2] Ib., iii. pp. 272-275. Pr., i. sec. 17.

conceived substances. As such we take our own being and the things without us. These are in part like us, in part different from us; the latter are either higher or lower than we; the higher are God and angels; the lower are animals, or entities below animals. Angels are beings between God and men; and, if we have the ideas of these two, we can make that of angels, and do not need for this purpose any original without us. Men are beings like ourselves, whose bodies are different from ours. From the conception of our own being and bodily substances, we can form those of other men. The ideas of God and of body are accordingly the elements out of which the ideas of the remaining substances are formed by the activity of our own minds. What we represent to ourselves by way of the senses as belonging to objects, is obscure, and, therefore, either nothing or of less reality than our thinking nature: what we distinctly conceive in them is contained in our own thinking nature, or can be derived from it. In no case does the conception of a body contain more reality than that of our own being. There is, therefore, at first sight no reason why we could not be the producing cause of this conception. I am a thinking being: every other finite thing is less than I am. When, therefore, I conceive finite beings without me, the cause and the original of my conception does not need to exist without me. There remains, therefore, but one conception as the object of our question, — the idea of God.[1]

3. *The Idea of God.* — I am a finite being, God is infinite: I am imperfect and defective, God is perfect and without defects. It is, therefore, impossible for me to be the cause of this idea. Either I cannot have such a conception at all, or its cause must be a being of like reality; i.e., God himself. But I have the idea of God; and in this case, to have it is equivalent to having received it. Every conception, as every phenomenon, has its cause. If I clearly and distinctly perceive that I cannot be this cause, I know just as clearly

[1] Méd., iii. pp. 276–280. Pr., i. sec. 18.

and distinctly that it must be without me; that there is, therefore, a being without me. "If in one of my ideas, a so powerful reality is represented, that I am certain that it cannot be contained in me, either formally [1] or eminently, and that I cannot, therefore, be its cause, it follows *that I am not alone in the world,* but that yet another being exists as the cause of that idea. But if I have *no* such idea, I have no means of proving that a being exists different from me. I have considered the matter on all sides, and with all possible care, and up to this moment have been unable to reach any other result." [2]

Through the idea of God, the darkness without our lonely self-certainty is to be illuminated, and the problem of knowledge solved. The question now arises, How is the knowledge of things possible by means of the idea of God? This must be the subject of our next inquiry; and we may be sure, that, without it, the meaning and depth of the Cartesian philosophy are not understood.

[1] The following remark may serve to explain the expression, "formally contained:" producing is with Aristotle shaping, or forming. What is conceived, Descartes calls "*objective;*" what actually exists, "*formal.*" The conceived object is "*realitas objectiva;*" the actual object, "*realitas actualis sive formalis.*" That which contains the cause formally is nothing more or less than the contents of the effect.

[2] Disc., iv. p. 160. Méd., iii. p. 276.

CHAPTER IV.

THE EXISTENCE OF GOD. — HUMAN SELF-CERTAINTY, AND CERTAINTY OF GOD.

I. PROOFS OF THE EXISTENCE OF GOD.

1. *Cause of the Idea of God.*

AGAINST our self-delusion, Descartes had summoned self-examination, that fundamental doubt which left but one certainty; viz., that we doubt, that we think, that we are. From this followed the principle of all certainty, — that truth consists in clearness and distinctness of knowledge. The fact of causality is clear and distinct; it follows from the fact of certainty, since it is impossible for us to think and *not* to be; this would be activity without a subject, change without substance, effect without cause. From the principle of causality, it follows that we cannot be the cause of a conception which contains more reality than we ourselves do. Now, the idea of God contains more reality: therefore we cannot be the cause of it. There must, therefore, be a being without us, who has all the perfections that we conceive as belonging to him : the cause of the idea of God is God himself. To be a cause is to be active, and therefore real ; so that the existence of God is evident merely from the idea of God in us.

Since the solution of the problem of knowledge is to be reached through this point, it must first of all be fortified and protected against every doubt. Our certainty of the existence of God is based first of all on the certain fact that we exist, and have the idea of God. Is the inference valid ?

Does it follow that God really exists, because we are, and have the idea of God? Perhaps we ourselves are able, by means of our own powers, to produce this idea: perhaps neither God nor we ourselves, but another cause, has produced both us and the idea of God within us. If it can be proved, that, without the existence of the most perfect being, it is impossible for us and the idea of God within us to exist, these possibilities are excluded.

We must be perfect in order to produce the idea of the perfect, according to the requirement of the principle of causality. But in fact we are not perfect: and if we were in our capacities, this perfection would not be actual, but only potential; i.e., a becoming or growing perfection which is equivalent to existing imperfection. Becoming is endless: growing perfection is never completed. We are, therefore, always in a state which, when compared with the idea of God, is less perfect than this. A capacity for perfection is actual imperfection. Mere capacity is not yet activity, not producing cause; therefore, not the cause of the idea of God.

The principle of causality holds not merely of our ideas, but just as well of our existence. If we suppose that the cause of our existence is *not* the most perfect being, it must be one that is less perfect — either I myself, or my parents, or another being; perhaps one, perhaps several. If I had been my own creator, I should have had the power to give myself all those perfections which I am able to conceive : I should then have become God. But I do not possess these perfections : they do not, therefore, stand in my power, and I was not my own creator. Conserving is continued creating : he only who can create, can conserve. But I have not the power to conserve myself: therefore, I did not have it to create myself. The continuance of my existence is not in my power, nor in that of my parents : therefore, they also were not my creators. As a thinking being, I should have to be conscious of this sovereign power if I had it. But I

am conscious of the opposite : I am not, therefore, the cause
of my existence.   It is just as little thinkable that the
Divine perfections which I conceive have *more* than one
cause, since with unity those causes would lack true perfection, and would not, therefore, be what they would have to
be.   There remains, therefore, but one inference : *one* being
different from us, proceeding either from a higher being or
existing of itself, has produced that conception.   We must
deny the case of origin from a higher being, for this is to
suppose an endless regress of causes, which is impossible ; for
we would in that case never come to the producing cause,
and, therefore, never to the effect.   That producing being
which must be different from us, and *sui generis, can exist only
of itself :* it is God.   To deny the existence of God in this
sense, is to declare our own existence and the idea of God in
us impossible.   " From the fact alone that I am, and have
the idea of a most perfect being, or God, it follows with complete clearness that God also exists." [1]

2. *The Idea of God as Innate.* — We have received this
idea ; but since we have not received it through the senses
nor any other medium, we have received it immediately
from God himself ; it is originally given, or *innate;* God has
stamped it upon us as his work "as the mark of the artist."
This mark is not here different from the work, but is the
work itself : God is not merely the cause, but the archetype,
of our existence.   " From the fact alone that God created
me, I believe that God fashioned me after his image, and that
I am like him.   *In this exact likeness consists the idea of God.*
I am this exact likeness, and I therefore know the idea of God
by the same faculty through which I know myself.   When
I make my own nature an object of study, I see not merely
that I am a defective, dependent being, aspiring unceasingly
after higher perfection, after something greater and better,
but I see at the same time that that primordial Being upon
whom I depend contains in himself all perfections, and that

[1] Méd., iii. pp. 280-289.

not potentially as the goal of an endless striving, but in reality and infinitely. I apprehend the existence of God. The force of the proof lies in this, — that I am compelled to perceive that I myself, with the idea of God in me, could not possibly exist if God in reality were not, — I mean *the* God whom I conceive, — that is, the Being who has all the perfections which I do not comprehend, but can only touch, as it were, with my thoughts afar off, the Being who is destitute of every kind of imperfection." [1]

3. *Ontological and Anthropological Proofs.* — In order to prove the existence of God, Descartes used several different arguments; and it is a too superficial treatment of him to emphasize merely the ontological proof, as is usually done. We will inquire first what these proofs are, then their order, and finally their deepest motives.

The principle of certainty is, Every thing which we clearly and distinctly apprehend is true. Now, in the mere idea of God, I apprehend his existence clearly and distinctly, and it is accordingly indubitable. This is the inference from concept to existence, the so-called ontological argument which Anselm introduced into scholastic theology. The idea of God is given in us as a fact of our inner experience, as a fact in our world of conceptions, which cannot be produced by us, but only by God himself. Therefore, God exists. This proof concludes from the fact to the cause: it is *a posteriori*, and can, therefore, be regarded as a proof from experience.

The fact of our existence and of the idea of God in us can be stated in this manner: *we exist, and are endowed with the idea of a most perfect being.* Since we cannot ourselves be the cause of our existence, it must be such a being, different from us, as possesses all the perfections of which we have an idea: otherwise it would not be able to produce us with the ideas of them. This most perfect of all beings, or God, therefore exists. This proof concludes from the nature of

<hr>

1 Méd., iii. pp. 289-291.

man, so far as it is imperfect, and conceives perfection to
the nature and existence of God.   In it the two preceding
arguments, the ontological and empirical, are united.   We
call this proof *anthropological*, and add the remark, that,
without it the ontological or metaphysical argument cannot
be understood and estimated in the sense of our philosopher.
It is the real Cartesian proof of the existence of God.

The order in which Descartes develops his arguments is
worthy of remark.   Where he leads us along the methodical
course which his own thoughts took in their search for truth,
and therefore proceeds analytically in his exposition, he
states the anthropological argument before the ontological,
as in his essay on method and in his "Meditations," — there
in all brevity, here in detail.   But where he proceeds syn-
thetically in his exposition of the truths he has discovered,
he states first the ontological and then the anthropological
argument, as in the geometrical outline of the "Meditations," which was contained in his reply to the second objection and in the "Principles."   In the "Meditations" he
rests the whole force of his proof on the anthropological
argument, and does not develop the ontological argument
until afterwards, when he returns again to the idea of God.[1]

4. *The Anthropological Proof as Foundation of the Ontological.* — The ontological proof of Descartes is fundamentally
different from the scholastic one, in spite of its parallelism
with it.   This difference is so important, that the usual
failure to observe it is equivalent to a complete lack of
insight into the system of our philosopher.   Descartes must
have been convinced that the objections which overthrew
the scholastic argument did not touch his, since he was
acquainted with them, and considered them in detail in his
fifth "Meditation."   We will first notice the defects of the
usual ontological argument.

From the mere idea of God, his existence is claimed to

---

[1] Disc., iv. pp. 159-162.   Méd., iii. pp. 280-289.   Ib., v. pp. 312-317.   Obj. et
Rép., Propos., i.-iii.   (Œuvres, i. pp. 460-462.)   Princ., i. 18-22.

follow, just as evidently as, from the concept of a triangle, the fact that the sum of its angles is equal to two right ones, and, from the concept of a circle, the equality of its radii. As little as we can conceive a hill without a valley, so little can we think God without existence. As necessarily as hill and dale are united, so inseparable are the concept and existence of God. Either he is the most perfect Being, or he is nothing at all. For the most perfect being would not be what it is if any thing were wanting to it, and certainly not if it lacked reality. But here the following objection at once arises · Our idea of God is a conception, like every other, and we cannot see why that should be held of this conception which is held of no other, viz., that thought existence is actual existence. In every other case the conceived object is only possible, not actual. God alone, according to the ontological proof, constitutes an exception : he exists because I think him. But if I do not think him? Does not my thought stand in my own power? Are not my thoughts voluntary? It depends, therefore, upon me whether there is to be an argument for the existence of God, or not! We must, therefore, require as the first condition of an ontological proof, that the idea of God is not an arbitrary, but a necessary, thought, inseparably bound and united with our nature. If this necessity cannot be grounded in the nature of man, the ontological proof, even in its starting-point, is without foundation. From this it is evident that it requires to be *anthropologically* grounded and vindicated.

But even when that first condition is fulfilled, we are yet far from the goal. Suppose the idea of God in us is necessary : does his existence follow from it? If we are compelled to conceive the most perfect being, we must, of course, think it as actual ; but is, then, thought actuality already real? Is existence within my conception also existence without, and independent of it? It is impossible to see how my conception and thought should at any time go out beyond themselves, and testify to the reality of a being beyond all conceived and conceivable objects. So long, therefore, as the idea of God is only *my* conception, produced by my thought, however necessarily, so long is the existence of God also only my idea. The thought existence is and remains only possible: the reality, independent of me and my conception, is absolutely incapable of demonstration by the merely ontological argument. If the idea of God in me is to prove the existence of God, it must be more than merely my idea: it must not merely represent the existence of God, but in a certain sense be that *existence itself.* Suppose that this idea which I have were the expression of God's own nature, his immediate effect, and proclaimed itself as such to me, then, certainly, it would be a direct proof of the Divine causality, and, therefore, of the Divine existence. But how dare I consider as an effect of God an idea which I find as my conception, as one among others? And it is not enough that I *dare* so consider it: I ought rather to be utterly unable to regard it as any thing else. As certain as I am of myself, so certain ought I to be that this idea is not my product, but the effect of God in me. This is the point which is now to be proved, upon which every thing in Descartes' doctrine of God directly depends. If it can be proved that the idea of God in us (1) is necessary, and (2) cannot be our effect, the point in question is made out. It must be shown that an imperfect being such as we are cannot produce the conception of a perfect being. In any case, the knowledge of our own imperfection and weakness, therefore the investigation of our own nature, our self-examination, must be the first step on the way to the knowledge of God. But it is not merely the first step, but also the light on the way! This light, which Descartes' doctrine of God and its ontological argument alone imparts, is entirely wanting to the scholastic proof. In the latter the important matter is, that we conceive a perfect being: in Descartes' argument the important matter is, that we conceive a perfection *which we ourselves do not have, and because we do not have it.* With Descartes, therefore, the ontological argument goes hand in hand with the anthropological, which rests on human self-knowledge. If from the nature of man it is evident that he is compelled to conceive a perfect being, then, and only then, has the ontological argument a secure starting-point. And if, in like manner, it follows from human nature that the idea of God is not its product, but the activity and effect of God in it, then, and only then, can that proof reach its goal.

The conditions, accordingly, which our idea of God must fulfil, in order to be capable of proving his existence, are its necessary or original conception, and its divine origin. Descartes comprises both in his expression, " Innate Idea." Not from the mere idea of God is his existence inferred, but from the *innate idea,* which, as the activity or effect of God, is the expression in us of the divine existence. To infer his existence from this idea of God innate in us is equivalent to apprehending the existence of God from his existence in us. This is an immediate, not a mediate, inference : it is a simple certainty, not a syllogism. We advance from the concept of God to his existence, not as to something new, but rather existence is discovered in the concept, not as one characteristic among others, but this concept is the divine activity and existence itself. The knowledge of the existence of God is, therefore, dependent upon no middle terms, but is just as intuitive as the knowledge of our own existence. Both are alike evident, and alike certain. As from the " *cogito,*" " *sum* " immediately follows, so from " *Deus cogitatur,*" " *Deus est* " immediately follows. As certainly as I exist, so certainly exists a being without me : as certainly as I know that I am, so certainly know I now *that I am not alone,* that outside and independent of me exists yet another independent being. In the " *cogito, ergo sum,*" the mind was absorbed in itself, in a monologue as it were : it had turned from the consideration of outward things, and at first won no other certainty than that of its own existence. In the review of its ideas, *one* is discovered which excels all others; and the first glance, as it were, betrays its divine origin. While all other conceptions are ever repeating to the lonely thinker, "Thou art, thou art, I am only a mirror of your nature, an effect of your power," this alone proclaims to him, "*I am*, I reflect in thee another and far better nature than thine: I have not, therefore, sprung from thee, but from my archetype." In the case of all other objects, the fact of my conception proves the possibility of their existence; in this alone, its necessity. In all other cases, concept and thing, essence and existence, "*essentia*" and "*existentia*," are two different things: here alone they are one and the same.

II. THE CERTAINTY OF SELF AND THE CERTAINTY OF GOD.

1. *The Certainty of One's Own Imperfection.* — The sentence, "*Deus cogitatur, ergo Deus est*," is claimed to be as certain as the sentence, "*cogito, ergo sum*." The method of Descartes requires the deductive union of truths. Between these two propositions, therefore, there must be an immediate connection, and this must be evident; and since the "*cogito*" is indubitable, it must first of all be comprehended as the ground of the "*Deus cogitatur*." Our conception of God is necessary if it is immediately contained in that of our own thinking being and is given by it, if our self-consciousness and the consciousness of God form two sides of one and the same intuition, which belong together as thoroughly as right and left, above and below. This connection between "*cogito*" and "*Deus cogitatur*," between the certainty of self and the certainty of God, is the point to be proved and illustrated, without which the doctrine of Descartes remains misunderstood. This doctrine cannot, as usually happens, be conceived and expounded as if it first promises a method, and then does not keep its promise, but leaps from the fact of self-certainty to that of causality, and then to the ontological proof of the existence of God, derives from the essence of God some of his attributes, among them veracity,

and then courageously advances to the knowledge of things. If this were the fact with reference to the progress of Descartes' thoughts, there would be in them no methodical advance; and Epistemon's objection would be well taken, that we do not advance a step from the fact of self-certainty. "A beautiful knowledge indeed! You have a method to prove every thing, to avoid making a false step, and trip, therefore, around the same point, without taking a step in advance!"[1] Epistemon says what Descartes puts in his mouth! The philosopher was acquainted with this objection.

In order to discover the methodical progress from the certainty of self to the certainty of God, we must take the expression of the first, the "*cogito*" or the "*sum cogitans,*" exactly in the sense in which the philosopher conceives it and establishes it. His desire for truth requires self-examination, which consists in the perception that we deceive ourselves in many instances, and, therefore, possibly in all; that we have no reason to regard any of our opinions as true; rather, that we are in a state of universal uncertainty, and completely destitute of the truth. On this knowledge of self rests that all-embracing doubt which admits the possibility of delusion everywhere, and distinctly recognizes that we are destitute of the truth. The Cartesian doubt is nothing else than *the certainty of this defect, of this our universal intellectual imperfection.* In one and the same act, doubt reveals to us our thinking nature and our defective intelligence. Not for nothing follows the "*cogito ergo sum*" immediately from the *de omnibus dubito.*" *I am myself*, that being whose existence is immediately evident to me. *I am myself*, the being of whose possession of truth I doubt absolutely, as to whose intellectual excellence I am completely puzzled. He who does not find in the Cartesian "*cogito,*" that expression of one's own thought, certain of itself, the confession of one's own complete intellectual destitution so far as the state of thought referred to in the "*cogito*" is concerned, he does

---

[1] Rech. de la vérité. Œuvres, xi. pp. 372, 373.

not understand what that sentence means, and is ignorant, both of its theme and its origin. The certainty of one's own thinking being springs from doubt, and is penetrated with the conviction that one's own thought is destitute of knowledge and of truth, though sorely needing it.

But to be conscious of one's own imperfection is to strive for, and therefore to conceive, perfection. The idea of the perfect is, therefore, necessarily and immediately connected with the act — it is indeed contained in it — which makes us certain of our own imperfection. And exactly therein consists the profound and now evident connection between the Cartesian "*cogito*" and "*Deus cogitatur.*"[1]

2. *The Idea of the Perfect and its Primariness.* — As necessary as is the conception of myself, so necessary is the idea of God : as necessary as is the certainty of my own imperfect existence, so necessary is the conception of the perfect. This conception is necessary and inseparable from the thought most entirely our own, but from this we are as yet by no means entitled to infer the existence of God. There arises on the contrary, from the point we have won, a series of doubts of this inference. If the perfect is the goal of our endeavors, it can be nothing else than an idea in us, however necessarily such a goal may be conceived. When we become conscious of our powers, we are aware at the same time of our defects and limitations; and while in thought we increase our powers, and disregard their limitations, we come by the known "*via eminentia*" to the conception of a most perfect being, which is none other than our own imperfect self, with the omission of all that the first syllable indicates. Exactly, therefore, because the idea of the perfect proceeds from the consciousness of imperfect human nature, it is a mere work of the latter; it is only an idea, not God; and the anthropological argument which promised to support the ontological proof, seems at first to be very unfavorable to it.

---

[1] Cf. Disc. de la méth., iv. p. 159, concerning this progress in Descartes' thoughts.

It is true that from the idea of the imperfect, — if we omit the negations, — that of the perfect can be produced, and brought into consciousness. But the problem is not thus solved, but only referred to the question, *How does the idea of the imperfect arise?* How do we attain to the knowledge of our own imperfection? It is one thing *to be imperfect*, another to *know that we are*. In the one case, imperfection is a state in which I am involved: in the other, it is an object which I make clear to myself. This perception, at least, is not imperfect, but is as perfect as it is true. That I am involved in self-delusion is an undoubted proof of my defects: that I break through its barriers, and *perceive* my self-delusion, is an undoubted proof of a perception present in me, without which I should continue in the darkness of delusion, and the idea of my imperfection would never occur to me. If the question were as to the estimation of a work of art, every one knows that the art critic would see its defects more clearly than any one else, because he is familiar with the perfections of art, and knows what this particular work requires. There are no defects for idiots: either they find every thing good, or they condemn without discrimination. Only the critic sees imperfections: they can be apprehended only in the light of the perfect, the light which illuminates that "*via eminentia*" on which man supposes he first finds the idea of the perfect. It is no wonder that he finds it, since he had it already, and had to have it, when he perceived his own imperfection. Without truth, there is no desire for truth, no self-examination, no becoming perplexed with reference to ourselves and all our conceptions, no doubt, no certainty of self, no "*cogito ergo sum*."

3. *The Primariness, Reality, and Truthfulness of God.* — The relation is now reversed, and what seemed to be the inference, is in truth the ground. From the idea of the perfect, springs that of the imperfect: that is *more original* than this, therefore more original than the knowledge of our own imperfection, of our own thinking being. In our certainty

of God, our certainty of self has its roots. The idea of God
is not merely one among others, but is the only one of its
kind, because it is the source of all light. It is not merely
as clear and evident as the conception of our own being, but
far clearer, because it first illuminates this conception. "It
is of all our ideas the clearest and most distinct, and therefore the truest."[1] This sentence of Descartes is now first
intelligible.

But as the *primariness* of the idea of God, its independence
of our thought and existence, its causality in reference to
our knowledge of self, is evident, the reality of God is therewith clear of itself. It is proved that the idea of the perfect,
primary as it is, is not merely an idea, but God. Without
the reality of God, there is no idea of God, no idea of the
perfect in us, no perception of our own imperfection, no
" *de omnibus cogito*," no " *cogito ergo sum*." In this connection we see the progress of Descartes' thoughts in their
methodical conclusiveness.

And not only the fact that God is, now appears beyond
doubt (because the existence and idea of God first make
true doubt possible), but also *what* he is. The idea which
illuminates the state of our own intellectual imperfection in
the clearest manner, can be nothing else than intellectual
perfection itself, with which no kind of defect is compatible.
This God is, therefore, absolute truth and truthfulness itself,
which, with deception, excludes, also, from himself the purpose to deduce.[2] Thus is the last and most oppressive doubt
removed, that stood in the way of the possibility of true
knowledge, in our self-examination. Now I know that no
demon has banished me into a phantom world, and afflicted
me with incurable blindness. If I had remained a prisoner
in delusion, as in a dark, labyrinthine dungeon, with no way
out, I could not even doubt, since even doubt proves that I
am conscious of delusion, and that somewhat of the *infallible*
light has shone into my spirit. Now doubt is cleared up.

[1] Méd., iii. pp. 281, 282.   [2] Ib., iii. p. 291, iv. 294. Princ., i. sec. 29.

The knowledge of things is possible; my presentations are no phantoms; things are as I conceive them, when I consider them in that infallible light; i.e., when I clearly and distinctly apprehend them.

After we have thus become acquainted with the true nature of Descartes' proof of existence of God, and the true connection of its various parts, we cannot help perceiving that the statements concerning the idea, reality, and truthfulness of God, are not edifying assurances, but *principles*, which constitute the foundation of knowledge, and support the remainder of the system.

CHAPTER V.

THE ORIGIN OF ERROR.—UNDERSTANDING AND WILL.— HUMAN FREEDOM.

I. ERROR AS THE FAULT OF THE WILL.

1. *The Fact of Error.*

THE possibility of knowledge is established. With this certainty arises a new doubt, diametrically opposed to the first one, for the possibility of knowledge seems to be grounded in a way that excludes the possibility of error. At first nothing was clearer than our errors, now nothing is more unintelligible. If our thinking nature springs from the primary source of light and truth, if we are not prisoners to delusion, and if the world which we conceive is no phantom world, but truly real, whence comes the possibility of delusion, and that state of blindness in which we, in fact, find ourselves? The ground of it cannot be sought in God, therefore not in the nature of our conceptions, therefore only in ourselves. We are not deceived, but we deceive ourselves. All error is *self-deception*. The question is, In what does this self-deception consist, and from what source does it spring?[1]

It has already been pointed out, that, in the mere state of conception, no error takes place, and that the possibility of error first enters with *judgment*, which declares our conceptions, states, or properties of things without us.[2] In a judgment of such a kind, error is made or expressed, but this expression of error is not its source. What is asserted in a

---

[1] Med., iv. p. 3.   [2] See preceding chapter.

judgment is either true or false, but a true or false assertion is not yet my error. I have only erred when I hold a true judgment false, a false one true, a doubtful one certain, a certain one doubtful. To hold a true judgment false is to deny it, to hold a false one true is to affirm it. If I hold a doubtful judgment certain, and a certain judgment doubtful, I deny in the one case the uncertainty, and in the other the certainty. From this it appears, that not in judgment as such, but in our acceptance or rejection, in our *affirming* or *denying* of judgment, error properly consists; and its source can therefore only be contained in our faculty of affirming or denying, accepting or rejecting.

This faculty requires more precise determination. If we were *forced* to affirm every true judgment, and to deny every false one, we could not err. Error can therefore only arise from such a faculty of affirming or denying as excludes all force from itself, and depends entirely upon our inclination. This unconditioned or free faculty to affirm, just as well as to deny, the same proposition, is will, or the freedom of choice (free will). A judgment is the work of the understanding: the affirming or denying of it is the work of the will. Error consists in our preferring the false judgment to the true, in our preferring to assert the false: it is only possible because the choice between the two lies completely in our power. It is accordingly clear that the two faculties, understanding and will, co-operate to produce error, since by virtue of its freedom the will is guilty of error through the understanding, or what amounts to the same thing, since the will turns the understanding from the path of knowledge. [1]

2. *Will and Understanding.* — To make a thorough investigation of the source of error, the relation between these two faculties must be more closely examined. If the will were compelled to affirm the true judgment, to deny the false one, to leave the uncertain one undecided, it would be

[1] Méd., iv. p. 298.

bound to the understanding, by it mastered and guided, equally limited in its sphere of action. But as we have already seen, this is by no means the truth. Our understanding is limited. There is much that I cannot comprehend at all, or only obscurely and indistinctly: there is nothing which the will cannot affirm or deny, accept or reject, or towards which it cannot occupy an attitude of indifference; i.e., nothing which it cannot neither affirm or deny. It reaches farther, therefore, than the understanding: it extends to the unknown as well as to the known, and can affirm or deny the one as well as the other. "The will is therefore greater than the understanding." It is not merely greater, but since it extends to every thing, while the understanding is limited in its knowledge to a definite sphere, it is *unlimited*, while the understanding is limited. This unconditioned greatness of the will is our freedom, and likeness to God. "The will, or the freedom of the will," says Descartes, "is of all my faculties the only one which, according to my experience, is so great that I cannot conceive a greater. It is this faculty pre-eminently by reason of which I believe I am created in the image of God." But if will and understanding are so related to each other that the latter is subject to natural limits, while the former is completely independent of them, it is evident that neither of the two, taken by itself, can be the source of error, not the understanding alone, because as our natural faculty of knowledge, dependent upon God, it cannot be deceptive; not the will alone, since, as our unconditioned faculty of freedom, it is, in the proper sense of the word, divine.[1]

That concurrence of the two faculties through which error is caused must accordingly consist in this: The human will, by virtue of its freedom, perverts the understanding, and transforms its infallible light into a Will-o'-the-wisp. Error can be nothing else than a blameworthy ignorance.

3. *Blameworthy Ignorance.* — By means of its unlimited

[1] Méd., iv. pp. 298-300. Princ., i. 34-38.

character, the will extends both to the known and the unknown, to the clear and the obscure sphere of knowledge; and, by means of its freedom, it can both affirm and deny the one and the other. But if it affirms or denies independently of clear and distinct knowledge, it acts groundlessly; i.e., it judges without reasons, and errs therefore in any case, no matter what judgment it affirms or denies. Error, therefore, reaches farther than we at first determined. Even the affirmation of a true judgment is an error if it is made without grounds. I affirm the judgment without knowing that, and why, it is true: I judge in the darkness, and stumble through accident upon the truth, like a blind fowl upon a grain of corn. If I would be true to myself, I must confess that I do not know the truth with reference to the matter in question: I am in darkness, and avoid every assertion about it. But as soon as I judge, I imagine a certainty which I do not have; I deceive myself, therefore; i.e., I err. Or I pretend to others a certainty which I do not possess, and which I know that I do not possess; I, therefore, deceive others; i.e., I lie. If the affirmed judgment is false, the manifest error is a double one; it is an error, both in relation to the fact and personally: I am deceived in the fact, and deceived concerning myself. To repeat an earlier example, it is no error for me to conceive the sun as a moved disk. I err as soon as I judge that the sun is a moved disk; I err as to the fact and personally when I affirm the geocentric system; I err if I deny it without insight into the grounds of the system, and hold the opposite one true.

II. THE WISH FOR TRUTH.

1. *The Prevention of Error.* — Error consists in groundless assertion. It arises from the freedom of the will as the faculty of affirming or denying groundlessly. In this faculty lies likewise the power neither to affirm or deny; i.e., to withhold every groundless assertion, or, what amounts to the same thing, to avoid every error. As soon as I am true to myself,

I must be aware of my states of personal uncertainty, my lack of insight; and by means of this knowledge, I am able to abstain from every error and all mere apparent knowledge. But if in every case of error the possibility not to err stood open, every error into which we fall is our own deed and fault. We should not err if our knowledge were perfect: it is imperfect, and this imperfection is not our fault, but the defect or limit of our nature. Without this defect, there would be no possibility of erring; and in spite of it, we should avoid error if we carefully withheld our judgment, and never again wished to seem to know, except when in truth we clearly and distinctly perceive ; *if we in no case preferred groundless judgment to those that are grounded.* This choice constitutes error, and the freedom of the will makes this choice possible. Grounded judgments are few, while ungrounded ones are numerous. The appearance of knowing more than one really knows, is tempting, and occasions that misuse of freedom through which we prefer ungrounded judgments to those which are grounded. We can now say exactly what the understanding and will contribute to error. The contribution of the understanding lies in its limits, that of the will in its misuse. The limits of the understanding is a natural defect, the misuse of the will is a moral one ; namely, a lack of personal truthfulness, genuine knowledge of self, and self-examination.[1]

From the above explanation, it follows that error enters in a blameworthy manner as soon as we treat the unknown as known. To the unknown belongs also the unknowable. We are not able to know the purposes of God, and dare not, therefore, pretend to know any thing by means of these purposes: the teleological explanation of natural things is therefore erroneous. " Even from this reason I am convinced that that whole class of final causes can have no place in the explanation of nature, for it seems to me to be temerity to inquire after the purposes of God." Here Descartes and

[1] Méd., iv. pp. 304-308.

Spinoza meet; both deny the validity of the concept of purpose in the explanation of things; Descartes, because the purposes of God are unknowable; Spinoza, because they are impossible. The step from unknowableness to impossibility is not long, and is the logical advance of rationalism.[1]

That we err, is our fault, not the fault of God. In so far as our will causes error, it is at once evident that it does not belong among the works of God. But also the imperfection of our intellectual nature does not derogate from the divine perfection. The divine perfection requires the perfection of the divine works; but this consists in the *whole*, and suffers so little from the defects of individual things, that it rather results from it. The imperfection of our limited existence appears perfection when considered in reference to the whole, therefore also in reference to God. "What would perhaps have to be considered very imperfect if it existed alone, is perhaps very perfect considered as part of the whole." Here Descartes and Leibnitz meet. The vindication of the perfection of the whole from the imperfection of individuals forms the fundamental thought of the Leibnitzian Theodicee as the nullity of purpose and the concept of purpose of the philosophy of Spinoza.[2]

2. *The Lower and Higher Freedom of the Will.* — Our errors are the fault of our will: they are caused by it, and by it they can be avoided. We must, therefore, distinguish within the will certain states or stages according as it, by its action, is guilty of, or avoids, error. There are, therefore, different stages of freedom, lower and higher; and that which directly produces error must be considered the lowest. This consists in affirming or denying without reason; and results from the irrational action of the will, i.c., from mere arbitrariness, which is determined in its choice of judgments and actions by no kind of rational considerations. The indifference of the will is, therefore, the lowest stage of freedom. Freedom is so much the higher, and the will so much

[1] Méd., iv. p. 297.　　　　[2] Ib., iv. p. 297.

the freer, the clearer the reasons on account of which it affirms or denies; i.e., the more it acts in accordance with insight. "But that indifference which I experience when no sort of rational considerations incline me more to one side than the other, is the lowest stage of freedom, and proves, not its perfection, but the absence of knowledge. For if I always clearly knew what is true and good, I should never be in doubt what to judge and to choose, and I should thus be entirely free without ever being indifferent."[1] Thus the higher is distinguished from the lower, the rational from the indifferent and groundless, the enlightened by freedom from that which is blind, and destitute of knowledge. Through the latter alone, moral action is possible. Here we see the fundamental thought of Descartes' ethical doctrine.

3. *Freedom from Error.* — Here we again see in the clearest manner the beginning of the entire system. There was only one means of penetrating the blindings of our deeply rooted self-delusions: we had to become sceptical as to ourselves, to doubt of the validity and truth of all our conceptions, to accustom ourselves to this doubt, and to strengthen ourselves in this habit of self-examination, even as we had done in the habit of self-delusion. This intellectual transformation can take place only through the will, through the wish for truth. Now we see to the very bottom of our self-delusion, and of the doubt which is directed against it. Error lies not in our conceptions, not in judgments as such, but in affirming or denying them without reason; in an act of the will, therefore, which we have the power to withhold. It is thus the will in the last analysis which darkens the understanding, and plunges us into error: it is likewise the will which preserves us from error, and frees us from it.

We wish to affirm or deny without having thought or known: that is the untruth to ourselves, our self-delusion, our error. We wish to affirm or deny according as we have distinctly known: that is the truth to ourselves, the doubt of the

[1] Méd., iv. pp. 300, 301.

truth of our conceptions, the perception of our ignorance, the firm resolve to know, to think clearly and distinctly, and, so long as we are in the dark, *not* to judge. To act according to this resolution as an inviolable law is the business of the will and character. " Thus we acquire the freedom not to err as a kind of habit, and in this consists the greatest and chief perfection of man." [1]

Méd., iv. pp. 306, 307.

CHAPTER VI.

OPPOSITION BETWEEN SOUL AND BODY. — TRANSITION TO THE PHILOSOPHY OF NATURE.

I. THE SUBSTANTIALITY OF THINGS.

1. *The Existence of Bodies.*

AFTER we have proved the possibility of knowledge, and explained error, we must now consider the question as to the reality of the objects which we conceive as things without us. Faith in the senses affirms this reality: self-examination and doubt have shattered the faith in the truth of the presentations of the senses. The idea of God has made me aware that I am not alone in the world, and from the perfection of God it is self-evident that the imperfection of my existence belongs to the perfection of the whole. I am imperfect, because limited: I am limited, because I am not the whole, but only a part of it, not the only being except God, but only one among others. There are, therefore, besides me, yet other beings in the world.

My conceptions are true in so far as I do not deceive myself: things are as I conceive them if I think them clearly and distinctly. They appear to me as bodies. Is not this appearance my self-delusion? Are there in reality bodies? Certain it is that the presentation or picture of bodies is present to my mind, that I *imagine* their existence. If my thought alone can be the cause of this imagination, or, what amounts to the same thing, if thought and imagination are completely identical, there is no reason to refer the fact, that

I represent to myself bodies, to an external cause. But imagination, as it seems, is different from pure thought. I experience this difference as soon as I think or imagine the same object. It is difficult to imagine a figure with a thousand sides, though it is thought as easily as a triangle. Since, now, the essence of the mind consists in thought, the faculty of imagination appears not only to be dependent upon the mental nature, but to require the union of it with the body. It appears, that, without body, our imagination of it could not take place. The fact, therefore, of this imagination is claimed to be a valid reason for the existence of bodies. The entire argument rests on the unproved assumption, that thought and imagination are different, and that imagination is something else than a mere modification of thought. By such an argument in its most favorable interpretation, the existence of bodies can only be made probable, but never certain.[1]

But the attempted proof can apparently be supported with greater certainty on the fact of our sensations and similar experiences. How, without the existence of bodies, are such affections possible as pleasure and pain? impulses like hunger and thirst? moods like joy and sadness? sensations like hardness and softness, warmth and cold, color and tone? sensations of smell and taste? It is certain that we have such experiences; that, of all our experiences, they are the most vivid and importunate; that they come without our will, and, therefore, as it appears, from things without us; that we receive knowledge of the latter in no other way than through the impressions upon our senses, and we, therefore, regard them as the expression of things themselves, as their exact copies. Involuntarily we refer the presentations of our senses to bodily causes, as though we were guided by a natural instinct. We consider them as the elements of all our conceptions, since they are the first we have, and so come to think that all the ideas in our minds enter through the

---

[1] Méd., vi. pp. 322-325.

senses, and that all the impressions upon the senses are made by bodily causes. But we know how terribly we have deceived ourselves concerning the truth of the presentations of the senses, not merely in dreams where they have no reality at all, but also in states of waking, where perception represents the same object, now in one way, now in another, and at times even completely deceives us. The four-cornered tower appears round in the distance: after an amputation, pain is still experienced in the amputated member. Accordingly, we can prove the existence of bodies just as little by our sensations as by our imagination.[1]

So much is certain: we have sensitive presentations; they must be caused, and the power that produces them is either within or without us. If it is in us, it must be the understanding or will; and, in that case, they must either be thought or willed. But they are neither: they come without the action of thought or will, often indeed against the will. The cause, therefore, cannot be our mind, i.e., we ourselves; and it must, then, exist without us, either in God or in things of a nature different from God and our own spiritual being. Suppose that God is the cause: he must have produced them either immediately, or through intermediate causes of a higher nature than ours. They would in that case have originated in a way that is, and must remain, entirely hidden from us; while we are impelled by our very nature to seek their origin in an entirely different direction. Their true origin would remain not only veiled from us, we should not only be stricken with blindness concerning it, but we should be involved in a complete *delusion*, — a delusion not due to ourselves, not to any fault of ours, but to the very constitution of our nature. We should be led into error by God himself, and that is inconsistent with the divine truthfulness (intellectual perfection). It is, accordingly, certain that the cause of our sensitive presentations is not we, not God, but bodies themselves, for that is the name we apply to natures different

[1] Méd., vi. pp. 325–331.

from God and mind. *Bodies are*, but what are they? That is the next question.[1]

2. *Substances. God and Things.* — It is evident that bodies in reality exist as the cause of our presentations of bodies, that they exist independently of our thought, that our existence is not essential to theirs. Such an independent being, Descartes calls *substance*. " I say that two substances are in truth different, when each of them can exist without the other." " Exactly in this consists the nature of substances, that they mutually exclude each other. This determination is valid, both of bodies and minds: each exists independently of the other, and is in this respect substance, but only in *this*. For if a substance is a being that needs no other in order to exist, and is, therefore, completely independent, there can, strictly speaking, be but one which itself depends upon nothing, while every thing else depends upon it. If there were several of such substances, they would have to mutually exclude and condition, and therefore limit, each other. There can be, therefore, but *one* absolutely independent being, but one substance in the true sense of the word; and that substance is God. He is substance in an absolute sense; mind and body only relatively. God is infinite: mind and body, on the other hand, are finite because they mutually exclude and limit each other. There are, accordingly, two kinds of substances, — God and things. The former is infinite, the latter finite. We cannot call them species of substance, since they have no common genus. Descartes says explicitly, that the word substance cannot be used in the same sense (*univoce*) of things and God. God is the cause of all things. Minds and bodies are, therefore, dependent beings in relation to God, since they need for their existence the existence and activity of God. The concept of substance in relation to the world or the totality of finite things must, accordingly, be limited so as to indicate such beings as require for their existence *merely* the concourse of God. " By a substance

[1] Méd., vi. pp. 331-335. Cf. above, chap. iv. p. 358.

which in no way is in need of another being, but one being can be understood; namely, God. We cannot conceive how others can exist save by the concourse of God. The term substance does not, therefore, apply *univoce*, to adopt an expression of the schools, to God and other beings; i.e., no meaning of this word can be accepted which is common to God and to them." [1]

In this explanation, two conceptions have important results, — the *unity* of substance — in comparison with which things, minds and bodies, are not real substances — and the *concourse* of God. The first concept contains the motive of Spinozism; the second, of Occasionalism.

• 3. *Attribute and Modes.* — Substances are fundamentally different in nature. We can only know what they are from their manifestations or properties. That property which expresses the essence of substance, and necessarily belongs to, or dwells in it, is *attribute.* Attribute is the quality without which substance can neither be nor be thought. Within a substance, different and changing determinations are possible; its attribute remains, though it can assume a variety of forms, and express itself in a variety of ways; these forms are *modes,* or *modifications.* We can think substance and attribute without modes, but not modes without substance and attribute. Modes, therefore, are not necessary but accidental properties of substance, and in this respect we call them *accidents.* Thus, mind cannot exist without thought, though it may very well without imagining or desiring this or that object. Thought is the attribute of the mind: imagination and desire are modes of thought. In like manner, figure cannot be thought without space, though space can very well be thought without figure: figures are modes of space, while space itself constitutes a necessary attribute of body. A substance can only change its modes, not its essence. The change of its states, and therewith

_____

[2] Obj. et Rép. Def., v.-x. (Œuvres, i. pp. 453, 454, 464, 465. Pr., i. secs. 51, 52.)

change in general, falls under the concept of mode. In God, no change is possible: there is, therefore, in him only attributes, not modes.[1]

In these concepts all kinds of distinctions are contained. These exist either between different substances, or between substance and attribute as between different attributes, or between substance and mode as between different modes. The first kind of distinction Descartes calls *real*, the second *rational*, the third *modal*. Real, for example, is the distinction between mind and body; rational, that between mind and thought, body and extension, extension and divisibility; modal, that between body and figure, or figure and motion.[2]

II. THE ATTRIBUTES OF THINGS.

1. *False Attributes.* — We apprehend the essence of things by means of their necessary attributes or properties. The question in what these consist can now be accepted as the form into which the problem of knowledge resolves itself. What are things *in themselves?* What are they as objects of our clear and distinct conception? The question would be easy to answer if they were not at the same time objects of our obscure and indistinct conceptions. In the sifting of these two modes of thought lies the difficult and critical point, the problem without the solution of which there can be no knowledge of things. What we clearly and distinctly conceive in things is their true attribute : what we conceive in them obscurely and confusedly is their false attribute. We have, therefore, to undertake the critical separation of the two. When we subtract from the intuition of things their false attributes, only the true remain. What, therefore, are the false or imaginary attributes? Plainly all those which we ascribe to things as such, though they are only modes in which we conceive them. If we regard as a property of objects what is merely a property of our thought, we attribute to bodies what belongs to ourselves. The matter is then thor-

---

[1] **Princ.**, i. secs. 52-56.   [2] Ib., i. secs. 61, 62.

oughly confused, and a knowledge of the nature of things is impossible. The more habitual and involuntary is this mode of consideration, the more thorough is the confusion, and the more difficult the sifting. We consider the duration of a thing as a property contained in its nature, and say the duration of a thing consists of so many days, months, years, etc. These determinations are nothing but certain quantities or numbers of the motion of the earth or the moon. The thing that endures so many months has, as such, nothing to do with the moon. We compare its existence with the motion of the heavenly bodies: we number these motions, and measure thereby the duration of the thing, and thus make the determination of time, which the thing is claimed to have as a property. *We* make it; i.e., our thought. Time is not a property of things, but of our thought: it is a "*modus cogitandi.*" Number and measure are modes of thought. What is true of time is just as true of number and all those common predicates which thought forms in comparing things; therefore, of all those concepts of genera and species, the so-called universals, of which Porphyry distinguished the well-known five, — *quinque voces*, as they were called in the logic of the schools, — genus, species, difference, property, accident. "Triangle" is a genus; "right-angled triangle" is species and specific difference; the Pythagorean relation between the length of its sides is its property (*proprirem*), its rest or motion, its accident (*accidens*).[1]

The abstract characteristics of things are our modes of thought, their sensible qualities our *modes of sensation.* We suppose that the thing is hard or soft, cold or warm, sour or sweet, light or dark; that it has this or that color, this or that sound, etc. All these determinations are not properties of things, but states of sensations of our organs of sense. To apprehend the so-called sensible qualities clearly and distinctly, we must distinguish accurately our nature from the nature of things, and not ascribe to one what belongs to

---

[1] Princ., i. secs. 57–59.

the other. Sensations are in us, not in things. As soon as we mingle our nature with that of things, the conception of things is obscured, and knowledge confused. It seems as if light and color actually belonged to, or dwelt in, the things which we see; as if pain or titillation were in the member of our body in which we have that feeling. And we do not err so long as we merely assert that it so appears. The judgment that it *is* so first makes the error, this judgment that obeys the appearance! If we allow ourselves to be deluded by this appearance, we are involved in self-delusion. That we have these particular sensations, is true; that we conceive them as properties of things, is false. Sensations as states of feeling are clear; as properties of things, they are obscure. What in the nature of things corresponds to or causes this sensation is at first sight unknown. When, therefore, we attribute sensible qualities to things themselves, we conceive something of the nature of which we are ignorant; i.e., we have an obscure conception. We apprehend in bodies, extension, figure, motion, clearly and distinctly; not so colors and tones, warmth and cold, etc. Our sensation as a property of things is a thoroughly obscure conception. We judge that things are as we are sensible of them. It is now clear how much value belongs to this judgment. It is exactly equivalent to saying that things are as we conceive them, when we conceive them obscurely and confusedly. This judgment is fundamentally false. It is not the sensation which is false, but the judgment which is thoughtlessly and uncritically based upon it. Here self-examination is wanting. This defect in this place is "the first and most important cause of all our errors."[1]

2. *The Multitude of our Errors, and their Chief Source.* — To separate the true from the false attributes of things, a thoughtfulness is necessary, an attentive self-examination, and a maturity of mind, which we cannot possess in childhood. Under the first influence of things, we are not able to

---

[1] Princ., i. secs. 66–71.

distinguish between their real and apparent properties, and, therefore, suppose that they are like each other. Thus begins the confusion. We believe things are as we perceive them. We estimate the reality of bodies according to the kind and degree of our sensation: the stronger the impression, the greater appears to us their reality; the weaker the impression, the less their reality; and when we have no impression at all, nothing exists for us. Thus, we regard the stars as little points of light, the earth as immovable, its surface as level, the air as less real than stones and metals, etc. We live only in the objects which we conceive as external to us and sensible without being aware, and without thinking, of our perceiving activity. This self-forgetfulness, or this lack of recollection of self, conceals from us our own mental nature. Now, we believe that there are no other objects at all than those which we conceive as falling under the senses, no other substances than bodies, no other bodies than those we perceive by means of the senses. Most men live in this faith, and guide their thoughts and actions by it; and it is, therefore, no wonder that they think and act during their whole lives in darkness.

Our speech shapes itself in accordance with our habitual conceptions. Error insinuates itself into our use of language, and obtains through words a generally received and stereotyped expression, which offers the most obstinate resistance even to discovered truth. In spite of Copernicus and Galileo, in the habitual language of men, the sun never ceases to move around the earth. Communication takes place only by means of language. Errors are not merely fortified by words, but transmitted and propagated from generation to generation. Conceptions gradually cohere so closely with words, that it is very difficult to separate them; and most men hold on to the words merely without being conscious of the concepts. The word steps into the place of the thing. "Since we can remember words so much more easily than things, we hardly ever have the concept of a thing so distinct that we can separate it from the words that express it. And the thought of almost all men has more to do with words than things, so that they habitually assent to words which they do not understand, because they suppose that they once understood them, or received them on the most trustworthy authority." And this is the reason why the learning of books and the wisdom of the schools are so poor and barren in true knowledge : they repose on faith in words.

Words become stamped on the memory; and when they have been kept there a long time, it begins to appear as if the conceptions and things had been known for a long time along with them, and that, therefore, it is entirely unnecessary to examine them. Words become an easy and familiar object of memory, and familiar words pass for familiar things; i.e., *the strange passes for the familiar, and the familiar for the known*, and thus error is completed in its fundamental form. That which is merely familiar, is, as a rule, least known, since it is least examined, because it seems superfluous to examine it. The appearance of familiarity is the greatest foe to knowledge, and the strongest fortress of self-delusion. Thus, error is completed, and made chronic in the worst form, — worst because it is most averse to self-examination. "We err most frequently in supposing, in the case of many things, that we have known them for a very long time, and have left them in charge of memory, and now affirm them as objects with which we are entirely familiar, while in truth we have never known them."

It is not our conception of sensible things which is the error, but our *belief* in it. From this error the rest follow. Our language and our memory do every thing in their power to strengthen and diffuse our errors, and to bring self-delusion to such dominion that the desire for self-examination vanishes. "To philosophize in earnest, and to investigate the truths of all knowable objects," — so Descartes ends the first book of his "Principles," — "we must in the first place lay aside our prejudices, and be on our guard against giving our assent to communicated opinions until we have examined them carefully, and found them true. We must then methodically and carefully examine our opinions, and accept only those as true which we clearly and distinctly apprehend. In this investigation we shall first know that we are thinking beings, that there is a God upon whom we depend, and that from him follows the possibility of a true knowledge of all things since he is their cause. We shall find likewise that we bear in us eternal truths, like the law of causality; that we conceive likewise a bodily or extended divisible and movable nature as an actual object; that we have certain affections and sensations, the causes of which are yet unknown to us. In these few propositions are contained, as it seems to me, the most important principles of human knowledge." "The philosopher ought to accept nothing as true that he does not perceive to be such; and if he trusts the senses without examination, he reposes more confidence in the inconsiderate judgments of childhood than in the decisions of mature reason."

CHAPTER VII.

THE PHILOSOPHY OF NATURE. (ↀ) THE MATHEMATICAL PRINCIPLE OF THE EXPLANATION OF NATURE.

I. EXTENSION AS THE ATTRIBUTE OF BODY.

1. *Body as an Object of Thought.*

IN the progress of methodical inquiry, the reality of our mind, of God, and of bodies, has been put beyond doubt. We know clearly and distinctly that there are things without us which exist independently of our thought, and are, therefore, *substances;* that they are *finite* like ourselves in distinction from God, *bodily* in distinction from us who are spiritual. This perception of the opposition between mind and body forms the concluding point of the metaphysics and the starting point of the philosophy of nature: it is the transition from the doctrine of knowledge to the doctrine of body. The fundamental question of physics is, What are bodies in themselves? In what does their attribute consist?

From the opposition of the two substances, it follows that no property of spiritual beings can be mingled with the conception of body; that all mere subjective modes of conception, particularly our modes of sensation, must be subtracted from it. Bodies are what they are after the subtraction of all their sensible qualities. They are, even when we do not perceive them: their perceivable or sensible qualities do not, therefore, belong to their nature as such. A stone seems hard when we touch it: if it changes into dust, it does not cease to be stone, though it is indeed no longer hard. What is true of hardness, is true also of warmth and cold,

color, weight, etc. Color does not belong to the nature of
stone, since there are transparent stones: weight does not
belong to the nature of bodies, since there are some, as fire,
which are not heavy. In the sifting and criticism of the
concept of body, Descartes follows exactly the same course
as in the examination of mind. In the knowledge of self,
the point was to ascertain the *pure* concept of our nature;
in the knowledge of the world without us, the pure concept of body. In the former case, it was necessary to separate from our nature every thing that does not necessarily belong to it, every thing the reality of which can be
doubted; and nothing remained except the activity of thought
itself, and that constituted the attribute of mind. And in
like manner every thing must now be separated from the
nature of body that does not necessarily belong to it, every
thing which can be separated from it without annihilating
the independent existence or substance of bodies. Nothing
thus remains except pure materiality or extension, and this
is the attribute of body.

If the two attributes, opposed in their natures, are mingled with each other, as in considering our modes of thought
and sensation as properties of bodies, there arises a twofold
confusion, and we deceive ourselves, both concerning the
nature of bodies and ourselves. To conceive bodies as the
substance in which universal concepts and sensible properties inhere, is to transform them into thinking natures, or to
anthropomorphize them. The fundamental aim of the Cartesian philosophy of nature is just the opposite. It aims to
free physics from all anthropomorphism, and to apprehend
the nature of objects after the subtraction of the mental
nature of man. Involuntarily we attribute our properties
to body, and our mode of considering them is likewise the
veil which hides them from our eyes. To remove this veil is
therefore the first condition of knowing them. When the
veil, which is woven, as it were, out of our mental nature,
falls off, nothing else can be revealed than body in its naked-

ness, in its nature opposed to, and deprived of, mind; and this is merely extension. Mind is as the self-conscious, likewise the self-active, inner nature: all self-action is of a spiritual nature. Completely opposed to this is the inert state of the being which is acted upon merely from without; i.e., of extended being, or matter. Extension is, therefore, the attribute of body: the opposition between mind and body is equivalent to the opposition between thinking and extended substance.

Since all further inferences and problems of Descartes' philosophy depend upon this concept of extension, the grounding of it should be explained yet more searchingly. We must make clear to ourselves the fact, that, from the point of view of the Cartesian doctrine of mind, no other conception of body is possible, and that this, as an object of thought and the opposite of mind, contains no other attribute than extension. Body is to be considered purely physically, i.e., as a mere object of knowledge; and this can be done only when our consideration fulfils the conditions under which objects are first of all possible. The common opinion is, that they are given without any thing further, and we have only to open our senses to receive them, and await their impressions: they are the models; we, the table of wax. But the matter is not so simple. There is no object without a placing of myself over against it, without distinguishing myself from the thing, and the thing from myself; i.e., without separating my nature from the nature of the thing, and without stepping opposite to the external world as a self-conscious or thinking being. There is no object without subject, no "thou" without "I." There is no subject without the certainty of self, no self-conscious discrimination without thought. Thought only has objects, since it causes them to arise. They are as little given as thought itself, which is no existing, ready-made thing, but an activity which only reaches as far as we are certain of it, as it illuminates consciousness. Without the thinking certainty of self, the "*cogito ergo sum*," there are no objects, also no bodies as objects. In our sensations, things do not stand opposite to us : they touch us and grasp us. They are not our objects, but our states and affections : we are not free from them, but under their impression ; and, therefore, we do not know what they are, but only how we are sensible of them. To consider body as an object, according to the requirements of knowledge, is, therefore, exactly the same as taking an attitude, not of sensation, but of pure thought, towards body ; to place it over against the mind, and to separate it from every thing of a mental nature, i.e., to place it opposite to the mind, to consider it as the opposite of mind, as an inert, merely extended being, destitute of a self. If the mind is only a thinking being, body is only extended : if that according to its nature is bodiless, this is mindless. These two concepts mutually demand and support each other.[1]

2. *Body as Quantity of Space.* — Body is an extended substance : it is nothing more. As the mind is nothing without thought, so the body is nothing without extension. Between substance and attribute, there is no real difference. Body and extension are, therefore, identical. A body without extension is either a word without meaning, or a confused concept. Extension is distinguished in length, breadth, and thickness ; it has no other distinctions than those of spatial dimensions ; it is merely spatial. Extension and space are, therefore, identical. Body distinctly conceived is, therefore, nothing except quantity of space. The physical concept of it is, therefore, identical with the mathematical. Space is related to body as universal extension to a limited portion of it. Every body is a *limited* quantity of space : without it are others, some of which immediately surround it. The space which the body occupies is its *place*, and, in reference to its surroundings, its *position*. The external place is the space (*superficies*) in which the surrounding and surrounded bodies touch each other. The inner place is the space which

[1] Princ., ii. secs. 4, 9, 11. Œuvres, iii.

the body fills: the inner place and size of the body are therefore identical.[1]

Against the position that body and quantity of space (extension) are identical, two doubts arise, based on the *rarefaction* of bodies, and *empty* space. If body and extension were identical, the same body would have to occupy the same extension all the time, and could not be extended, now more, now less, which is the case in the rarefaction and condensation of bodies. But the supposition upon which the objection rests is not true. Rarefaction is not increased extension, since extension, or matter, consists in the multitude of parts; but rarefaction does not consist in increasing the parts of bodies, but in enlarging the spaces between them, or in other bodies entering into them. Thus, the sponge which is filled with water does not increase in size because its parts increase in number, but because there is more water than before in the spaces between them. The rarefaction and condensation of bodies does not, therefore, consist in their increased or decreased extension, but in the enlargement or diminution of their pores.[2]

But empty pores are *empty* space: this is extension without body, and is, therefore, an actual proof that body and extension are not identical. This objection also is invalid, and rests on confused concepts. Empty space is either understood relatively or absolutely: in the first case it is not empty, in the second it is without meaning. A water-pitcher, a cauf, and a trading-vessel are said to be empty when the first is empty of water, the second of fish, and the third of goods, although they are always filled with other bodies. We call the space empty which does not contain certain bodies which we expected to find there, or which in general are capable of being perceived by the senses. This customary (relative) concept of empty space has, however, led to the philosophical (absolute) concept. There is no necessary connection between a vessel and its contents; it can contain air, water, sand, and also nothing; and when every content is lacking, it is absolutely empty. Absolute emptiness is nothing, space is something; and there is just as little an empty space as a something which is nothing. A vessel can be empty of this or that thing, but not absolutely empty, since in that case it could not exist. In absolute emptiness, there would be literally nothing to separate the concave walls of a vase from each other; and these would have to fall together, and there would be no configuration and no vessel. In truth, there is no emptiness, but only the appearance of emptiness. Every body is extended, and is full in the same proportion as it is extended: it cannot be more or less extended, therefore not more or less full than it is whether it is filled with gold or lead or water or air, or whether it seems to be empty.[1]

II. THE MATERIAL WORLD.

Body and extension are identical: there is nothing empty. Where space is, there are bodies and only bodies; these stretch through the whole of space, however far it extends; it extends as far as extension. Within extension, there is nothing which is unextended or indivisible. There are *no* atoms: the smallest parts of bodies are always still divisible, therefore not atoms, but molecules or corpuscles. And just as little can extension anywhere cease or be bounded; for with this boundary, the unextended would have to begin, and the boundary itself could therefore no longer be extended. It is, therefore, absolutely impossible to enclose extension within bounds: it is absolutely boundless. Therefore the material world is infinite.

Since extension can nowhere be empty, or cease at any place, it is continuous, and forms a continuum. There are, therefore, not different kinds of extension or matter, therefore, also, not different material worlds. The material world is merely extended, boundless, and one. Beyond thought, there is no other world than the material.

[1] Princ., ii. secs. 16-19.

CHAPTER VIII.

THE PHILOSOPHY OF NATURE. (b) THE MECHANICAL PRINCIPLE OF THE EXPLANATION OF NATURE.

I. MOTION AS THE FUNDAMENTAL PHENOMENON OF THE MATERIAL WORLD.

1. *Motion as a Mode of Extension.*

ALL the phenomena or events of the inner world are modifications of thought: all the phenomena and modifications of the outer world are modifications of extension, which, we have seen, is the attribute of material substance. Now, if extension is infinitely divisible, its parts can be united and separated, and thus different formations or forms of matter result. This union and separation take place through the approach and removal of the parts ; i.e., through motion. Extension is therefore divisible, capable of form, and movable. Its possible changes consist in division, formation, and motion: there are no other modifications of extension. With the following declaration, Descartes concludes the second part of his " Principles : " " I frankly avow that I acknowledge in the nature of bodies no other matter than that which can be divided, formed, and moved in a great variety of ways, that which mathematicians call magnitude (quantity) ; that in this matter I consider merely its divisions, figures, and motions, and accept nothing as true that does not follow from these principles as evidently as the certainty of mathematical propositions. In this way all the phenomena of nature can be explained. I think, therefore, that no other principles in physics than those here expounded are necessary or admissible." [1]

[1] Princ., ii. sec. 64.

These principles can be simplified. All division and for-mation of matter takes place through motion. All the modifications of matter can, therefore, be analyzed into motion. The changes in the material world are all phe-nomena of motion: every change in matter and all the dif-ferences of its forms are dependent upon motion.[1] The stand-point of the Cartesian philosophy of nature is now per-fectly clear: the nature of bodies consists in quantity of space and their changes in motion; that is conceived math-ematically, this mechanically. Descartes' explanation of nature, therefore, rests completely on mathematical-mechan-ical principles.

2. *Motion as Change of Place.* — All motion consists in a spatial change. Now, the space which a body takes up in relation to other bodies is its place, or position. If a body moves, it changes its place: all motion is, therefore, change of place. "It is the action by means of which a body passes from one place into another."[2]

This concept must be more precisely determined that it may be guarded against the objection that the same body in the same time can be both moved and not moved. A body can change its place while it rests, as a man sitting in a ship which is moving with the current of the stream. He is changing his place with reference to the banks of the stream, but not with reference to the ship in which he is sitting; he remains in the same position with reference to the bodies that immediately surround him; i.e., he rests. Since motion can be considered only as a mode of a moving body, or as a change peculiar to it, it cannot be predicated of a body that changes its place without its own action. A body or (since all bodies are parts of one and the same matter) a part of matter moves only when it changes its place in relation to the immediately surrounding bodies; i.e., when it is trans-ported from the vicinity of the bodies that directly touch it to the vicinity of others. Now, that change of place which

[1] Princ., ii. sec. 23.   [2] Ib., ii. sec. 24.

has the character of such a transposition or translation (transport) from one place to another is motion in the strict sense of the word.

But this concept also requires a yet more precise determination, that it may meet the above objection from a new point of view. Change of place is always relative. If a body A changes its place in relation to the immediately neighboring parts of the matter B, B also changes its place in relation to A. It is possible that both bodies are active and in motion at the same time. But there are cases in the change of place of immediately neighboring parts of matter, in which only one of the bodies moves. Two bodies, A and B, move on the surface of the earth directly towards each other. This motion is reciprocal, and belongs to each of the two in like manner. Both bodies change their places at the same time in relation to the parts of the surface of the earth that immediately surround them: this change of place is also reciprocal, and the earth also must be considered to move in relation to A and B; i.e., it must at the same time move in two opposite directions, which is impossible. The bulk of the earth is, therefore, considered as resting in relation to the bodies of the earth and so many smaller bodies that move here and there on its surface. From this it is evident that a body is moved when it passes from the vicinity of those parts of matter that directly touch it, and which, in relation to it, are considered at rest. A ship that is urged forward by the stream, and backwards by the wind, with the same force, remains opposite to the same place on the bank: it does not change its place on the earth, but rests, while the particles of water and air which surround it are in constant motion. " If we would know," says Descartes, " what motion really is, in order to determine it precisely, we must explain it as the translation of place (transport) of one part of matter or of one body from the vicinity of those bodies which directly touch it, and are considered at rest, into the vicinity of others." "By a body, or a part of matter,

I understand the whole of the mass in motion, not taking
into consideration the parts of which it may be composed,
and which may have at the same time still other motions.
I say that it is the translation from one place to another, not
the force or activity which causes it, with a view of showing
that motion is always in the moving object, and not in the
thing that causes it, since I believe that these two things are
not usually distinguished with enough care. As figure is a
property of the figured, and rest of the resting, thing, so I
understand motion as a property of the moving thing, but
not a being for itself or substance." [1]

From this explanation certain inferences can be drawn,
both in relation to *simple* and *complex* and also *compound*
motions.

The first inference is, that every body has and can have but
one motion peculiar to it, since its active change of place
holds only in relation to the matter in its vicinity, and which
is at rest. But as part of a greater body, which itself has a
motion peculiar to it, it can, without damage to its own
motion, take part in an infinite multitude of other motions.
Thus, the wheels of a watch move in a way peculiar to
themselves, while they take part in the motion of the sailor
with the watch in his pocket, as he walks up and down in a
ship, with the sailor in the motion of the ship, with the ship
in that of the sea, with the sea in that of the revolution of
the earth on its axes, etc. The wheels of this watch have
their own motion, belonging only to them, while they, at the
same time, take part in a complication of a great multitude
of other motions. Without distinguishing precisely a body's
own motion from those in which it participates, we should
be unable to determine whether and how a body moves.
Now, this motion peculiar to a body, although in the same
time it is only this and no other, i.e., appears as simple, can
very well be compounded of, or result from, different motions ;
as, for example, a wagon-wheel in motion both revolves

1 Princ., ii. secs. 15, 24–30.

about its axle and advances in a straight line, or a point which is urged at the same time in different directions moves in the diagonal of the two.

It further follows from the concept of motion, that no body can be moved by itself alone while all others are at rest. There is no empty space, and, therefore, no empty place. If, therefore, a body leaves its place, another must enter into it at the same time, while it itself forces from its new place the bodies which it finds there, and forces them in turn to expel other bodies from the position they have occupied up to that time. There is, therefore, with every moving body the motion of several, which form a chain, the last link of which catches into the first, so that always a complex of bodies is moved which forms a ring or circle.[1]

II. THE CAUSES OF MOTION.

1. *The First Cause of Motion, and its Quantity.* — The law of causality requires that nothing should happen without a cause. The cause of motion is *force*, the opposite of motion is *rest*. Rest is arrested or hindered motion. No body can be moved, no motion can be stopped, without force. Rest, therefore, is not possible without force. The opposite opinion is a childish error, based on the experience of childhood, — that we need force and exertion to move a body, but none to cause it to rest. As soon as one tries to stop a moving body, or make it rest, he will at once learn whether it requires strength, or not.[2]

Motion and rest are the two opposite modes or conditions of body. Bodies are merely extended and movable: they neither move nor come to rest by means of their own force, since of themselves they are destitute of force. From whence, therefore, come motion and rest into the material world, since they do *not* come from the material world itself? Both must be caused; and as they can be caused neither by body nor by minds, their first cause can only be God. In

---

[1] Princ., ii. secs. 31-33.   [2] Ib., ii. sec. 26.

relation to minds, he is the principle of knowledge; in relation to bodies, the principle of motion and of rest.   He illuminates the mind, and moves bodies, or causes them to rest. Matter is created in a state in part of motion, in part of rest: both belong to it originally.   We must, therefore, conceive the material world as from the very beginning in part moving, in part at rest.

Now, if bodies of themselves have power neither to produce nor stop motion, they have, also, not the power either to increase or diminish it.   The quantity of motion and rest in the material world, therefore, always remains the same. If in one part of matter motion is increased, it must be diminished in another to exactly the same extent: if it vanishes in one form, it must appear in another.   *The quantity of motion in the world is constant.*   Descartes deduces this law from the unchangeableness of the Divine nature and activity.   The law is necessary because its opposite is impossible, both because of the nature of God and of bodies.[1]

2. *The Second Causes of Motion, or the Laws of Nature.* — From the unchangeableness of God, it follows that all the changes in the material world take place according to unchangeable rules.   These rules Descartes calls laws of nature. Since all the changes of matter are motions, all the laws of nature are laws of motion; and since God is the first cause of motion, these laws are characterized as its second causes (*causæ secundæ*).   Bodies are of themselves without force: none of them, therefore, can of themselves change from the state in which they happen to be.   They remain or continue in the given state of form and position, rest or motion, until an outward cause effects a change.

(1) In this consists the first law of nature.   All changes in the material world are due to *outward* causes.   We can call this the law of inertia or constancy, only we must not understand that this means *rest*, and imagine that a body of itself strives to rest, — to continue in a state of rest, and to

---

[1] Princ., ii. sec. 36.

return from a state of motion into that of rest. As if a body preferred rest to motion, and would rather be inactive than active! This conception is fundamentally false. If there were such an endeavor, every body would immediately place itself in a state of rest, as soon as the outward cause of its motion ceased to act. A body which we pushed with our hand would come to rest the moment our hand let it go. But it continues its motion until outward causes, i.e., others which it meets on its way, hinder it, and cause it to rest. Because we do not perceive these causes, we suppose that the body comes to a state of rest, not because of the action of outward causes, but of its own exertions. This judgment through our ignorance is our error.[1]

If we can venture to speak of any exertion of a body at all, it can only consist in an effort to continue in whatever state it is in, but not in one state at the expense of another, but in preserving the state in which it may happen to be, whether of motion or of rest; i.e., in opposing or offering resistance to every external cause which acts upon it. This effort to preserve its state coincides with the existence of body. Every thing seeks to preserve its existence, and defends itself against destruction : every body by means of its inertia or constancy defends itself against the destruction of its existing states; i.e., it opposes every external cause that seeks to change any of its states. Without such a resistance, the quantity of motion in the material world would not be constant. This resistance is, therefore, necessary. Now every act is an expression of force, and we can, therefore, speak of a force of resistance in bodies, and, in this sense, we can admit the validity of the concept of force in the material world. Bodies have indeed no original forces to exert, but only a force to oppose to external influences. "The power of every body to work upon another, or to make resistance to its influence, consists only in this : every thing strives to continue so far as it can in the state in which it finds itself,

according to the first of the laws of nature." Every part of
matter has this force ; the greater, therefore, the number of
parts of a body, the greater its force. The quantity of parts
is called *mass*, and the quantity of motion, *velocity*. The
greater, therefore, the mass in motion, the greater the action,
and therefore the force. The measure of force is, therefore,
equal to the product of the mass into the velocity.[1]

(2) From the law of constancy it follows that every body
in motion continues its motion, and of itself, — to be sure,
in a direction which remains unchangeably the same. If it
describes a curve, its direction is changed every moment;
and this can only happen under the constant influence of an
external cause. Unchanged uniform direction is a straight
line. Every body in motion must, therefore, strive of itself
to continue its motion in a straight line, and if, by reason of
an external cause, it is moved in a circle (as a stone in a
sling), to continue it in a tangent of the circle. Every body
must preserve its state of motion : it must, therefore, endeavor to continue to move in the direction of a straight
line, since every deviation from it can only be effected by
external causes. In this consists the second law of nature.[2]

(3) There is no empty space. Every moving body must,
therefore, meet another body with which it collides, as it
moves on its course, which it endeavors to prolong in a
straight line. A collision takes place between bodies moving either in opposite or the same directions, or between
bodies one of which is at rest. In the first case, three possibilities arise : either the masses and velocities of both bodies
are equal; or the masses are unequal, and the velocities
equal ; or the masses are equal, and the velocities unequal.
If one of the bodies is in a state of rest, there are likewise
three possibilities to be distinguished : either the body at
rest is greater or smaller than, or equal to, the body in
motion. In the second of the above cases, when the colliding bodies are in motion in the same direction, if the smaller

1 Princ., ii. sec. 43.   2 Ib., ii. sec. 39.

mass, moving more rapidly, overtakes the greater, three possibilities arise according to the relation of the differences of
size to the difference of velocities, which, however, are not
considered as separate cases.   All together, there are, accordingly, seven cases which Descartes distinguishes in the
collision of bodies, and consequently seven rules according to which the changes resulting from the collision take
place.[1]

These laws are determined under the following suppositions : (1) that in the states of different bodies, not their
motions, but only their *motion* and *rest*, are opposed to each
other, and, therefore, between bodies in motion no other
opposition is possible than that of their directions; (2) that
the colliding bodies are completely hard or solid ; (3) that
complete abstraction is made of every influence of other
bodies surrounding them which might increase or diminish
their motion, especially the influence of fluid bodies.   Under
these suppositions the law is to be determined in each of the
different cases according to which a body changes its motion
and direction in consequence of a collision.   The change
follows from the force of resistance exerted by a body, and
depends upon its size.   The greater force of resistance, so
Descartes thinks, overcomes the smaller, or hinders its
action.[2]

If, therefore, a body B is moving in a straight line, and
meets another body C having a greater force of resistance,
it cannot move the latter from the spot, or push it away,
since, according to the supposition, C is perfectly hard or
solid ; but B, in consequence of the resistance, cannot continue on its way, but must return in the opposite direction.
It therefore loses its direction, but not its motion, since
directions are opposed, not motions.   But if B has the
greater force of resistance, it will continue on its way with
the body C : it does not change its direction, but only the
quantity of its motion, of which it loses as much as it imparts

---

[1] Princ., ii. secs. 46-52.   [2] Ib., ii. secs. 44, 45, 53.

to the other body. Since the quantity of the motion (mass
in motion), i.e., the product of the mass into the (simple)
velocity, always remains the same, the velocity must decrease
in the same proportion as the moving mass is enlarged or
increased in size.   This can be increased only through
imparted motion; and, therefore, every body which puts
another in motion must lose as much of its own motion as
it communicates to that body.[1]

If we call the motion which one body communicates to
another, its action, and the loss of motion which it thereby
itself experiences, re-action, in every case of communicated
motion, *action and re-action are equal.*   And since within
nature no motion originates, but all is only imparted, since
it can only be produced by means of external, i.e., material, causes, that equation is the real, fundamental law of
the mechanically-moved material world.   That Descartes
treats this law, which he derives from the constancy or
conservation of the quantity of motion in the world,[2] as a
special case, and does not regard it as valid for all cases of
collision, is an error of his doctrine of motion, due to false
presuppositions.   If all changes of bodily states follow from
external causes, the loss of motion which a body suffers must
be considered as an effect, whose external cause is the force
of resistance exerted by the body to which it communicates
motion, however great or small that force of resistance may
be.   It is false that the smaller force is without effect in
relation to the greater, or that the greater can completely
prevent the action of the smaller;[3] it is false that in the
collision of bodies the one avails as the impelling, the other
merely as the impelled, body, and that every thing now
depends on this, whether that is greater or less than this;
finally, it is false that the opposition between rest and
motion is absolute, and that there are no oppositions between
motions.

From the principles of Descartes, it follows that bodies of

---

[1] Princ., ii. secs. 40–42.   [2] Ib., ii. sec. 42.   [3] Ib., ii. sec. 45.

themselves are destitute of force, that they only have a force
of resistance because they are obliged to continue in their
states, that all changes in the material world are due to
external causes, and all motion, therefore, to impulse and
pressure, and that, therefore, there are no inner concealed
causes, no secret forces, no so-called *qualitates occultæ* in general in the material world. *Gravity* is regarded as such a
force, an original property of a body belonging to it of itself.
Descartes denies it. Therein consists the opposition between
Galileo and Descartes: with gravity he was obliged to reject
gravitation and the power of attraction. Therein consists the
subsequent opposition of Newton to Descartes: he is, therefore, compelled to deny the so-called central forces, as well
as every *actio in distans*, and to explain the case of bodies,
as the courses which planets describe, by the impact, or the
external and immediate influence, of other bodies. Since
the laws thus far considered relate merely to the collision of
solid or hard bodies, all the motions which cannot be derived
from them must be explained by means of the distinction
between solid and fluid bodies, particularly from the constitution, motion, and influence of the latter.[1]

III. HYDRO-MECHANICS. — SOLID AND FLUID BODIES.

1. *Distinction between the Two.* — Since there are no other
opposite states in body than motion and rest, it is evident
that from these alone the opposite states of cohesion of solid
and liquid bodies must be derived. Perception plainly
teaches us that solid bodies resist every opposing motion,
every attempt to separate their parts, or move them out of
their places, — which is not the case with fluid bodies. Now,
as we have seen, according to Descartes, motion is not
opposed to motion, but rest. What, therefore, makes a body
solid, or its parts capable of resisting the intruding motion
which seeks to separate them, or move them out of their
places, can be nothing else than that these parts are every-

[1] Princ., ii. 53.

where in a state of rest; and the great mobility and separability of the parts of a fluid body consist in the fact that they are everywhere in motion, even in their smallest parts. Nothing can make the combination or connection of material things stronger than their rest; for, if this were not so, a particular kind of cement would have to hold or unite them together. Now, this medium could only be a substance or a mode; but the parts themselves are substances, and rest is a mode of those substances, — rest, which of all material states is the most hostile to motion. The fact that fluid bodies, as water and air, are able to dissolve many solid bodies by their influence, proves that their parts must be continually in motion, since they could not otherwise decompose those bodies.[1]

2. *Solid in Fluid Bodies.* — Parts of matter are either at rest or in motion, therefore bodies are solid or fluid. Since there is no empty space, there must be fluid bodies in every space where there are no solid ones. All pores are, therefore, filled by fluid bodies, and they surround solid bodies. Suppose, now, that fluid matter, the smallest parts of which are continually in motion, and at the same time in such a way that they are tending in every direction, completely surrounds a solid body: the latter will be in contact with fluid parts on all sides, and urged with like force in different directions, so that it is suspended, or at rest, in the fluid matter that surrounds it. There is no cause by virtue of which the body must move in one direction rather than another. As soon, therefore, as such a cause enters, giving to the body a definite impulse, though with but the smallest expenditure of force, it puts the body in motion. The smallest force suffices to move a solid body when it is completely surrounded by fluid matter.[2]

Now, suppose that the fluid matter in which the solid body is suspended, or at rest, is put in motion in a definite direction with its entire mass, like a stream towards the sea, or

[1] Princ., ii. secs. 54-56.　　[2] Ib., ii. secs. 56, 57.

air moved westward by an east wind: the solid body is
seized by the current, and borne onward with the fluid parts
which touch it and surround it. It will always, therefore,
have the same neighbors while it drifts with the stream, and
will not, therefore, change its surroundings or its place. It
is at *rest* in the fluid matter that surrounds it, the whole
mass of which is in motion in a definite direction.[1]

3. *The Heavens and the Earth. The Motion of the Planets.
The Hypotheses of Vortices.* — Descartes bases his theory of
the rest and motion of the *heavenly bodies* on his doctrine
of the rest and motion of solid and fluid bodies and the influence of the latter upon the former. The heavenly bodies do
not rest on pillars, and are not suspended by cords, nor are
they fastened in transparent spheres; but they are poised in
the spaces of the heavens, which cannot be empty, but must
consist of fluid matter, which surrounds the heavenly bodies
on all sides. They are distinguished in relation to size, light,
and motion. Some are self-luminous, as the fixed stars and
suns: others are opaque, as the planets, the moon, and the
earth. The sun is analogous to the fixed stars, the earth to
the planets. Some do not seem to change their position
with reference to each other, and appear to be immovable:
others change their places, and are regarded as wandering
stars. Those are called fixed stars, these planets. The system of the heavenly bodies, especially that of the planets,
appears, therefore, as a special case, and at the same time as
the greatest example in which fluid matter surrounds other
bodies on all sides.[2]

In order to explain the motion of the planets, the stand-
point must first of all be determined from which it is considered and judged. For every thing depends on whether
this stand-point itself is at rest or in motion in relation to the
planets. Three hypotheses have been advanced to explain
it, — that of Ptolemy in antiquity, and those of Copernicus
and Tycho Brahe in modern times. The Ptolemaic hypoth-

---

[1] Princ., ii. secs. 61, 62.　　　[2] Ib., iii. secs. 5-14.

esis is abandoned by science, because it is inconsistent with absolutely certain facts, which more recent observation and investigation have established, especially the phases of light of Venus, discovered by the telescope, and similar to those of the moon. Only, therefore, the hypotheses of Copernicus and Tycho Brahe can now come in question; and they agree in reference to the heliocentric motion of the planets, not in reference to the motion of the earth, which Copernicus affirmed, and Tycho Brahe denied. Is the earth at rest, or in motion? That is the point of controversy in deciding which Descartes asserts that he agrees with neither of the two astronomers. Although the Copernican hypothesis is somewhat simpler and clearer than that of Tycho Brahe, Descartes maintains that it has not distinguished with sufficient care between motion and rest, while Tycho has denied the motion of the earth in a sense which is inconsistent with the truth. Because Tycho did not sufficiently consider in what motion really consists, he maintained in words indeed that the earth is at rest; but at bottom his theory requires its motion, even more rigidly than that of Copernicus himself. One should, therefore, proceed more carefully than Copernicus, and more correctly than Tycho. "My position is different from that of those two philosophers only in this," says Descartes somewhat ambiguously, "that, with more carefulness than Copernicus, I deny the motion of the earth, and I seek to ground my theory with more truth than Tycho. I will here expound the hypothesis which seems to me the simplest of all and the fittest, both for the explanation of the phenomena, and for the investigation of their natural causes. I will, however, say explicitly, that I by no means desire that this theory of mine should be regarded as the complete truth, but only as an hypothesis or opinion which may possibly be erroneous."[1]

The two essential presuppositions of Descartes' hypothesis are the immeasurableness of the universe and the nullity of empty space. From the first, it follows that the universe

---

[1] Princ., iii. secs. 15-19. Cf. Introduction, chap. vi. pp. 125-130.

is not a spherical body, and does not consist in concentric spheres to which the stars are fastened; that there is, therefore, no celestial sphere beyond the farthest planet (Saturn), and that the sun does not lie in the same spherical superficies. From the second, it follows that the spaces of the heavens are filled with fluid matter, and that the heavenly bodies are surrounded by the latter, and subject to its influences. This is the point where Descartes applies his hydromechanic principles to the motion of the heavenly bodies; that is, to the planets and the earth. The earth is completely surrounded by fluid matter, and is acted upon uniformly in all directions, or borne onwards by its current, as a solid body in fluid matter. It rests in the heavens as a ship on the sea, which is moved by no wind, propelled by no oar, held fast by no anchor, but quietly floats with the current. And the same is true of the rest of the planets. "Each is at rest in that space in the heavens in which it is; and all the change of place which we observe in those bodies, follows only from the motion of the matter of the heavens which surrounds them on all sides." We cannot say, therefore, if we have the true idea of motion, that the planets and the earth are themselves moved. This would be the case if they changed their surroundings; i.e., if the space of the heavens which surrounds it rested while the planets wandered through it. But this space of the heavens is itself fluid in all its parts, is always matter in motion, which as such never ceases to surround the heavenly bodies, though the individual parts in contact with them are perpetually changing; i.e., now these, now those, parts of that matter are in contact with the superficies of that body. Thus, on the surface of the earth, water and air are in continual motion; while the earth itself, in reference to the parts of its waters and atmosphere, is not regarded as moved. It rests in its moved space in the heavens, in this flowing matter which surrounds it, and in reference to which it does *not* change its place. But although it rests, it does indeed change its position with reference to the other heavenly bodies. If any one, speaking in the usual way, persists in ascribing motion to the earth, it moves exactly as does a man who is asleep in a ship while it takes him from Dover to Calais.[1]

If, now, we suppose that that flow of the matter of the heavens which surrounds the planets and carries them onwards with it, describes a current *spinning round* like a vortex, in the centre of which is the sun, and that the earth is one of these planets, it is evident in what sense Descartes teaches the heliocentric motion of the earth, like Copernicus, without denying with him that it is at rest, and still less with Tycho affirming this rest in a cosmical centre. How he explains the motion of the earth and planets, not by virtue of their weight and attraction, but only by the impelling force of the matter that immediately surrounds and touches them, is also evident.[2]

The rotary-moving current, or the central motion of the matter, Descartes calls a *vortex*, or whirlpool-like motion (*tourbillon*),[3] and explains thereby the course of the wandering stars (planets, moons, comets). It is with this motion of the matter of the heavens as with the eddies of water which rotate about a centre in ever widening circles, and carry along with them the floating bodies that come within them. The nearer the centre, the quicker the rotary motion, the more rapid the rotation; and the more distant the centre, the slower the rotation. "As waters when they are forced to a reflux form an eddy, and draw violently within their rotary motion, and carry along with them, light floating bodies, as, for example, straws; as then these bodies, seized by the eddy, turn about their own centre, and those nearer the centre of the eddy always complete their rotation earlier than the more distant ones; as, finally, this eddy always, to be sure, describes a circular figure, but almost never a perfect circle, but extends itself, now more in length, and now in breadth, wherefore the parts at the periphery are not

equally distant from the centre, — so one can easily see that
the motion of the planets is of the same character, and
that no other conditions are necessary to explain all their
phenomena." [1]

Among these phenomena, the motion and time of rotation
of the planets, and spots of the sun, of the earth and moon,
the obliquity of the orbits of the earth and the planets
(ecliptic), the elliptic form of these orbits, the consequent
unequal distances of the planets from the sun, and the therefore unequal velocities, are particularly conspicuous. " I
need not farther show how, by this hypothesis, the changes
of night and day and of the seasons, the phases of the moon,
the eclipses of the sun and moon, the standing still and
retrogradation of the planets, the precession of the equinoxes,
the change in the obliquity of the ecliptic, and similar facts,
can be explained, since all these phenomena are easily
understood by any one who has a little knowledge of
astronomy." [2]

We now know upon what presuppositions the Cartesian
hypothesis depends, and in what it consists. It would lead
us too far from the system itself to show more particularly
how Descartes seeks to ground his hypothesis; how from
chaos this so-ordered world, fluid and solid matter, the rotary
currents of the fluid matter, the kinds of matter and heavenly bodies, arise according to the laws of motion. He
assumes that matter in its original condition was distributed
in a certain uniform manner; that in some places its parts
had a rotary motion, by means of which fluid masses were
formed which revolved around a common centre, while each
of their little particles moved about its own centre, from
which proceeded the distinction of central and peripheric
masses; that the rotating and differently shaped molecules,
by their mutual contact and friction, changed their configuration, blunted their corners, and gradually rounded
them off in such a way that they assumed the spherical form

[1] Princ., iii. sec. 30.   [2] Ib., iii. secs. 31–37.

of globules; that thus intervals arose which had to be filled
up, and were immediately filled up by yet smaller and more
rapidly moving particles, which decreased in size through
that mutual blunting and rounding off of the molecules;
that the excess of the thus resulting waste was driven into
the centres of the rotary currents, and constituted the
material out of which the *central masses* (*fixed stars*) were
formed, while the surrounding masses, moving in concentric
spheres, shaped in their smallest parts in the form of a
globule, constituted the space of the heavens. From the
laws of motion it follows that every body having a circular
motion, like a stone in a sling, constantly tends to fly off from
the centre, and proceed in a straight line. Every particle of
the central masses and the matter of the heavens has this
centrifugal tendency, and in this *light* consists. The kinds
of matter and the classes of the heavenly bodies are distinguished in reference to light. The heavenly bodies are
either luminous, transparent, or opaque. The central bodies
(fixed stars and suns) are luminous; the heavens are transparent; the wandering stars (the planets and comets, the
earth and the moon) are opaque. There are, accordingly,
three kinds of matter or elements: the first are those smallest
and most rapidly moving particles, of which luminous bodies
consist; the second the spherical molecules which form the
material of the heavens; the third the coarser matter, moved
with greater difficulty because of its size and form, which
constitutes the material of the wandering stars. Ether is
that subtile matter which fills every apparently empty space,
and is the lightest and most easily moved of all the kinds of
matter, and is always in rapid motion.[1]

When Descartes expressly says that his hypothesis for
explaining the system of the universe not only may be, but
in certain respects is, false, he plainly wished to protect himself from the fate of Galileo. For, according to the experience of Galileo, it was not enough to announce his theory of

[1] Princ., iii. secs. 54-64.

the universe as a mere hypothesis: it must be declared to be erroneous. Descartes made this declaration of his own accord beforehand, to avoid being compelled to make it afterwards. He acknowledged his error, because, as he said, his explanation conflicted with the biblical account of creation. The Bible asserts that the order of the heavenly bodies was created; while he explained it as gradually arising according to purely mechanical laws, in order to make it comprehensible by man.[1]

This equivocation is to be charged to the account of the time and his character, and, after the detailed discussions of that point in our history of his life, needs no further vindication or justification. In the attempt *to explain the origin of the system of the world by purely mechanical laws* lies the importance of Descartes' philosophy of nature. That was the object of his first work, which, for reasons with which the reader is already acquainted, remained unpublished, and was lost as far as the essay on light. Its essential contents are contained in the two last books of the " Principles ; " and we may fairly suppose, that, after the publication of this work, that of the " Monde " was superfluous.

But as to the relation of our philosopher to modern astronomy, particularly to Copernicus and Galileo, a definite judgment can now be pronounced. He did not mention Kepler's great discoveries, and probably was not acquainted with them. The geocentric hypothesis of Tycho he rejected. If one explains the heavens as rotating about the earth, and correctly understands motion in its relative and reciprocal sense, he must ascribe far more motion to the earth in relation to the heavens on the theory of Tycho than even Copernicus maintained.[2]

Descartes teaches that the motion of the planets is *heliocentric*, and that the earth is a *planet:* he teaches its daily revolution on its axes, and its yearly motion about the sun in an elliptic orbit. He, therefore, agrees essentially with

Copernicus and Galileo. But he bases his theory on mechanical laws of a different sort from those maintained by
Galileo. We have already become acquainted with his mode
of proof; it is a deduction from his principles; and whatever
may be its validity and truth, the difference between him
and Galileo is in no wise a pretence. That Descartes also
denied the motion of the earth, in a certain sense follows
from his concept of motion which he had to apply to the
heavenly bodies. In all these points, without ignorance of
the matter, there can be no talk of any kind of *accommodation*.
The Cartesian denial of the motion of the earth has nothing
whatever in common with the ecclesiastical: rather is it
completely opposed to it. Descartes affirmed that motion of
the earth which the Church, the Bible, Ptolemy, and common
opinion denied. For all that he said, " You see that in terms
I deny the motion of the earth, while in reality I maintain
the system of Copernicus." He affirms the heliocentric
motion of the earth, and that is the only question at issue.
It would have been more than sophistical if he had sought,
in opposition to Galileo, to *appear* to maintain the *rest* of the
earth, in agreement with the Church, or out of deference to it.
Perhaps it would not have been disagreeable to Descartes
if the world, and particularly the authorities of the Church,
had deceived themselves concerning this point of his doctrine. But that *he* sought to deceive any one concerning it, is
false, and can only be believed by those who are unac-
quainted with his works. Of the accommodation, therefore,
with which he is charged, only so much remains: Descartes,
after he had openly and honorably presented and established
his doctrine, declared that his hypothesis was false so far as
it conflicted with the faith of the Church. He acted as Galileo did, except that he anticipated the retraction with a view
of avoiding chicanes.[1]

4. *Emptiness and the Pressure of the Atmosphere.* — The
conviction that empty space is impossible, and that all

[1] Cf. book i. chap. v. pp. 230-235.

motions in nature can only be produced by external, material causes and their immediate influence, i.e., by pressure and impact, necessarily led Descartes to fundamentally deny with the vacuum, also the so-called "*horror vacui*" of nature, —a conception which still prevailed among the physicists of his generation, —and to declare it one of the greatest of errors. It is just as false to affirm the reality of empty space as to deny it with the Peripatetics on the ground that nature abhors a vacuum, and will not, therefore, permit it. It is to unite both errors to limit the "*horror vacui*" to a certain degree, as did the advanced physicists of Descartes' time, that in spite of it a certain void might exist in nature. By such hypotheses they sought to explain the ascent of fluids, as water in the bore of a pump, and quicksilver in a tube. Descartes opposed to the assumption of emptiness his subtile matter (ether), by reason of which there could be no vacuum anywhere. This was the point of controversy between him and Blaise Pascal, who denied the existence of his subtile matter, and maintained the reality of a void, on the ground of a moderate *horror vacui.*

When we perceive motions or rest, without at the same time being able to perceive their material causes, we are inclined to believe that no causes whatever are present. Thus, the motion of the atmosphere, the pressure which it exerts on all bodies which it surrounds and touches, is a constantly acting cause, however little the moving mass falls under the observation of senses. Descartes insisted that for the actual explanation of certain phenomena of the motion of fluid bodies, the *pressure of the atmosphere* (weight of the air) must be supposed instead of empty space and the horror of a vacuum. Even in the dialogue of Galileo, he met the assumption of the "*horror vacui*" where the cause of the phenomenon should have been sought in the weight of the air, and criticised it in the observations which he made on that work in a letter written in October, 1638. Nine years later, in a conversation with Pascal, he advised him to convince himself by an experiment of the nullity of emptiness and the reality of atmospheric pressure, by noting the height of quicksilver in a tube at the foot, and also at the top, of a very high mountain. He would find, that, as he went higher up the mountain, the column of quicksilver would fall, in consequence of the decreasing pressure of the atmosphere. He could easily have this experiment performed in Auvergne, where he resided. The experiment was made on the Puy-de-Dôme, and confirmed what Descartes predicted without having made the experiment. Pascal, however, did not mention this circumstance, and also gave the philosopher no account of the success of that experiment. Descartes attributed this unreasonable conduct to the hostile influence of Roberval, who was the friend of Pascal, and hence made a profession of enmity to Descartes.[1]

As to the matter itself, the priority of the discovery cannot be claimed for Descartes. The experiment which he recommended to Pascal in the summer of 1647, consists in the barometrical measurement of altitudes; and the barometer was invented by Toricelli some years before (1643). But Descartes was before acquainted with the law upon which the invention rests, as his letters in the years 1631 and 1638 show. And not even the testimony of his letters is required, since the law necessarily follows from his principles, as we have seen. Applied to the motion of floating bodies (solid bodies in water), the invention which goes by the name of the Cartesian diver could easily be made and explained by the activity and modifications of the pressure of the air.

[1] Concerning Descartes' doctrine of the pressure of the atmosphere, compare his letters, June 2, 1631, and October, 1638, to Mersenne (concerning Galileo), and those of June 11 and August 17, 1649, to Carcavi (concerning Pascal). (Œuvres, vi. p. 204; vii. p. 436; x. pp. 343, 351. Millet: Descartes, etc., ii. pp. 214-226. See above, book ii. chap. vii. pp. 270, 271.

CHAPTER IX.

UNION OF SOUL AND BODY.—PASSIONS OF THE SOUL.—NATURAL AND MORAL LIFE OF MAN.

I. ANTHROPOLOGICAL PROBLEM.

1. *Meaning and Extent of the Problem.*

THERE yet remains a problem after the fundamental questions of metaphysics are answered. These relate to the existence of God and the mind and body, and require their clear and distinct knowledge, i.e., the determination of their reality and essence; and this is only evident when it is conceived without any mingling with its opposite. The being of God required to be apprehended independently of all finite and imperfect things; that of the mind, independently of the body; that of the body, independently of the mind. Both, therefore, must be considered as completely opposite substances, the mind merely as a thinking, the body merely as an extended, being; the processes of the mind only as modes or kinds of thought; the processes of body only as modes or kinds of extension, i.e., as motions. God, as the real ground of all things, must, in reference to the mind, be regarded as the original source of knowledge, and, in reference to body, as the original source of motion.

If, now, there are processes of a mental nature which are united with certain motions in such a manner that the former cannot exist without the latter, we have a fact before us which involves a new problem. Such a fact cannot be explained by the dualism of mind and body, that fundamental concept of Descartes' philosophical principles. The new problem, therefore, is not metaphysical. A union of mind and body can only take place in a being which consists of them both. *We ourselves* are this being, and certainly among all finite substances *only* we, since we are thinking natures, and as such we immediately and, therefore, with absolute certainty, know our own being and existence. We are likewise united with a body which we conceive as ours. Our sense-perceptions prove that there are bodies without us; our affections and natural impulses, that one of them is ours. "Nature teaches me nothing more explicitly than that I have a body, with which it stands ill when I feel pain, and which needs food and drink when I suffer hunger and thirst. I cannot doubt that there is something real in these feelings. Those affections and impulses make it clear to me that I am not in my body like a pilot in a ship, but that I am united with it in the closest manner, and, as it were, mingled with it so that we constitute *one* being in a certain measure. Otherwise I should not feel pain by reason of my mental nature when my body is injured, but should perceive this injury merely in an intellectual way, as the captain perceives any damage to his ship. If the body needed food and drink, I should apprehend these states without having the unclear feelings of hunger and thirst. These feelings are, in fact, obscure conceptions, which proceed from the union and, as it were, mingling, of the mind with the body." Among all knowable minds, the mind of man is the only one which is united with body; and, therefore, the new problem is *anthropological*.[1]

The nature of the mind consists in thought; true knowledge in clear and distinct thought, which is both striven for and obtained by the absolute power of the will as well as hindered and prevented thereby. Genuine freedom of the will seeks true knowledge, and acts according to it. In this the human mind fulfils its nature and its destiny.[2] In the union with the body, its clearness is obscured, and its free-

---

[1] Méd., vi. pp. 335, 336.　　[2] Cf. book ii. chap. v. pp. 366, 367.

dom limited: it is, therefore, itself in a condition which is *not* conformable to its nature. Now, freedom of the will and clearness of thought appear as a goal to be reached, as a work to be done, as a problem to be solved, and only solved by a proper exercise of the power of the will. Thus, the anthropological problem comprehends that of *ethics*.

Nevertheless, this union of the mind with the body is, in its way, also according to nature, since it is grounded in the order of things. We cannot, therefore, regard our bodily life in Platonic fashion, as a decree or punishment due to a fall from the spirit world, and desire for the enjoyments of earth, but as the result of natural laws. But if the union of mind and body is in harmony with the laws of nature, it cannot even in reference to the mind be considered as contrary to nature, however little it conforms to the essence of the mind. We must, rather, with the naturalness acknowledge also the rightness of that union, and of every thing that necessarily follows from it, as impulses, inclinations, passions, etc. All these activities of human nature are, as such, good and necessary conditions or instruments of spiritual life. If they check and darken the latter, this is not the fault of nature, but of the will. Its original direction is not false, and the deviation from it is our error. Its natural character is not bad, but the degeneracy of it because of our will. What comes to pass in the dual nature of man requires to be naturally explained and morally vindicated; i.e., its worth in freeing the mind must be apprehended. It is particularly the passions which Descartes regards from a purely natural point of view, convinced that he thus considers them from an entirely new point of view. "How defective are the sciences which the ancients have handed down to us, is nowhere more evident than in their treatment of the passions. For as much attention as has been given to this subject, and as easy as it is to be understood, since every one can discover the nature of the passions in himself without any observation of outward things, the doctrines of the

ancients concerning it are so inadequate and uncertain that
I am obliged to entirely forsake the usual paths in order to
approach the truth with some confidence. I must write,
therefore, as if I had to do with a subject that no one has
considered before me." With these words, Descartes begins
his essay on the passions of the soul. "My intention is,"
says he in the prefatory letter, "to treat the passions of the
soul, not as a preacher, also not as a moral philosopher, but
only as a physicist." [1]

2. *The Cardinal Point of the Problem.* — Now, if Descartes
regards the passions as the principal object of consideration
in anthropology, he must find here the characteristic expression of human (mental-bodily) life, the ground of the knowledge of man's dual nature. The explanation of this fact is
for him the cardinal point of the problem of *psychology.* As
motion is related to body, so is passion to man : as there the
concept of motion had first of all to be more precisely
determined, so we must here ascertain in what the nature of
passion consists.

It is at once evident that all the passions are of a passive
nature. Nevertheless, every thing of a passive nature is not
passion. In opposition to the nature of body, the nature of
mind consists in self-activity, the source and power of which
is in the will. Every thing, therefore, which takes place in
us without being willed by us, is, in the widest sense, of a
passive nature. Of this nature are all involuntary functions,
even the apprehensions or perceptions which we form and
experience independently of every act of self-determination
and choice. Some of these perceptions are inner, and relate
merely to the mind, as the involuntary apprehension of our
thoughts and volitions. Our thinking nature is not passive,
but the apprehension of it is so far as this forces itself upon
us of itself, and we are compelled to be aware of it. There
are other perceptions which relate merely to body, either our

---

[1] Les passions de l'âme, part i. art. i. Rép. à la lettre, ii. Œuvres, t. iv.
pp. 34-38.

own or those that are external to it. To these belong the
feelings due to our senses or our sensations, as colors, sounds,
etc.; the bodily affections, as pleasure and pain; the bodily
impulses, as hunger and thirst. All these perceptions, inner
and outer, are of a passive nature, but are not passions in
the strict sense of the term. We are passive in them, but
not impassioned.[1]

There is a third class of passive states, which belongs
neither to the mind alone, nor to the body alone, but to both
at the same time, — states in which the soul *itself* suffers under
the influence and concurrence of the body. It can remain
indifferent in seeing and hearing, hunger and thirst, but not
in joy and anger. It alone is susceptible of joy and sorrow,
love and hate; but it could not be if it were destitute of a
body. Passion consists in *this* kind of passive experience.
It would be impossible for the passions to be able to arouse,
animate, and affect our souls as powerfully as they do if they
were not mental forces. It would be impossible for them to
have such capacity as they have to obscure and confuse the
mind, if they were not at the same time of a bodily nature.
They are states of the mind, not such as are produced by its
free energy, but which attack it and lay hold of it without
any exercise of the will. They are states of feeling, but not
such as exist in the body, but in the soul. They are, in a
word, emotions of the mind (*émotions de l'âme*), in which both
natures are mingled, the mental and bodily. "One can
define them as perceptions or feelings or emotions of the
soul, which appertain to it peculiarly, and are caused, sustained, and strengthened by the activity of the animal
spirits."[2]

3. *The Passions as Fundamental Phenomena of the Human
Soul.* — From this it is evident what importance Descartes
ascribes to the fact of the passions. He regards them as
fundamental phenomena, as the third and most important,

---

[1] Les passions, i. arts. xix., xxiii., xxiv.
[2] Ib., i. arts. xxv., xxvii.-xxix.

besides thought (will) and motion. Understanding and will are possible only in the mind; motion, only in the body; the passions only in man, who unites mind and body in himself. Thought requires nothing but mind, motion nothing but body: the passions, on the other hand, require the union of both. The dual nature of man is the *only real ground* of the passions: the passions are the *only ground of the knowledge* of the dual nature of man, which is not so evident from the fact of sensations and natural impulses. To understand why Descartes allows this importance only to the passions, and regards sense-perceptions and desires, on the other hand, merely as bodily processes, we must bring before our minds the foundation of his entire doctrine. From his stand-point, there is, so far as our knowledge extends, but *one* body which is united with a mind, or animated with a soul; and that is the human body. All other bodies, even animals, are mere machines, destitute of mind and soul. The soul is the mind; and the reality of the latter is evident only from its certainty of itself, and coincides with that. Without self-consciousness, there is no thought, no mind, no soul. Animals have no self-consciousness, and, therefore, no souls: they are, hence, nothing but moved bodies, or automata. But they have sensations and impulses; and, hence, these must be regarded as bodily motions, governed by purely mechanical laws, by which they must be explained. Animals feel, but they have no souls: the former is an undeniable fact, and the latter a necessary inference, in the system of Descartes. It is certain that animals see and hear, hunger and thirst: it is just as certain that they have no clear and distinct knowledge, no self-consciousness, and, therefore, according to Descartes' principles, neither mind nor soul. It only remains, accordingly, to regard sensations and impulses in general, and, therefore, even in man, as mechanical processes, having nothing in common with psychical activities. Thus, Descartes finds no fact which reveals to him the union of mind and body except the passions. One can ask whether the passions are not also of an animal nature, and whether sensations and impulses are not also of a psychical nature; one can dispute the Cartesian theses, which deny both, and even doubt whether the philosopher himself remained, and could remain entirely, true to them; but we have no right to question that he taught them, and was obliged to teach them, in consequence of his principles. The examination of this point is not now our purpose. We have as yet to do only with the exposition and proof of the system, and to follow the paths which Descartes trod. When we estimate his doctrine, we shall return to those questions, and then we shall examine them carefully.

II. THE UNION OF THE SOUL AND BODY.

1. *The Mechanism of Life.* — So far as the life of man is like that of animals, it must be explained by purely mechanical and physical causes, particularly motion and warmth. It has been falsely supposed that the soul moves and warms the body, and is, therefore, also the physical principle of life. For every flame proves that it is not the soul which imparts motion and warmth to the body. And if the human body becomes stiff and cold after death, it suffers this change, not because it ceases to be animated by a soul, or because the soul has left it. The living body is not, as such, animated with a soul; for if so, animals would have souls, and this conflicts with the principles of Descartes' doctrine. Life does not consist in the union of soul and body; death, not in their separation. Life is not the product which produces soul, but the presupposition under which the soul enters into a union with body, the condition without which such a union cannot take place. The truth of the matter is, therefore, the direct reverse of the usual opinion. Not because the body is animated with a soul is it, therefore, alive, but, because it lives, it can be animated with a soul. The body is not stiff and cold because the soul leaves it, but the soul leaves it because it is dead. Death is the destruc-

tion of life, and is a necessary result of physical causes. Life is mechanism : death is the destruction of that mechanism, and results when the living body suffers such an injury that the whole machine stops. To the error which makes the soul the principle of life, Descartes opposes the following explanation : "Death never enters because the soul is absent, but because one of the important organs of the body is destroyed. We can, therefore, decide that the body of a living man differs from that of one who is dead, exactly as does a watch (or an automaton of any kind ; i.e., a machine moved by itself) which has in itself the material principle of the motions which it is to perform, along with all the conditions necessary to its activity, and, when it is wound up, goes, — from one that is broken, in which the moving principle ceases to be active." [1]

The soul can be united only with a living body. Since it is of a mental nature, also, among finite beings so far as they are knowable by us, exclusively of a human nature, this union can only take place with the body of man.

The human body, like that of animals, is a machine. Its principle of life is the fireplace in it which prepares the warmth of life, and imparts it to the whole organism, — fire, whose material is the *blood*, and whose place is the · *heart*. Harvey's great discovery of the motion of the blood and heart of animals explained this fundamental principle in the mechanism of life, and made an epoch in the history of biology. Descartes became acquainted with it when he was finishing his "Cosmos," and absorbed in the investigation of the human body, and had come by his own path to a like conclusion. This doctrine appeared to him so important, and so great and evident a triumph of the mechanical physics and of the scientific method in general, that he expounded it as an example of the latter in the fifth part of his "Discours," and, referring to Harvey's fa-

[1] Les passions, i. arts. iv.–vi.

mous discovery, explained the motion of the heart and
the circulation of the blood through the arteries and
veins.[1]

According to these fundamental conditions, Descartes discusses the remaining parts and function of the machine of
the animal-human body. The organs of motion are the
muscles, those of feeling are the nerves. The heart is the
central organ of the blood and its motion, that of the nerves
is the brain. Descartes represents an organ as acting between the two, whose origin and activity he characterizes as
the most remarkable phenomenon of life. The finest, most
mobile, most fiery particles of the blood, which are produced
in the heart by a kind of distillation, ascend by mechanical
laws through the arteries into the brain, and are led from
thence to the nerves, and, through these, to the muscles.
They cause feeling and motion in those organs, and, therefore, administer the real functions of life ; and hence Descartes calls them animal spirits (*esprits animaux*). " The
most remarkable fact in these things is the origin of animal
spirits, which are like a very fine wind, or, better, a very
pure and active flame, which constantly ascends in the greatest abundance from the heart into the brain, and goes thence
through the nerves into the muscles, and imparts motion to
all the members. But why the most mobile and the finest
particles of blood, which, as such, make the best material for
the animal spirits, go rather to the brain than elsewhere, is
very simply explained by the fact that the arteries, which
carry them to the brain, ascend from the heart in the most
direct line ; and if several things are striving to move at the
same time in the same direction, while, as in the case of the
particles of the blood, which strive to go to the brain from
the left ventricle of the heart, there is not room enough for
all, it follows from the laws of mechanics, which are identical
with the laws of nature, that the weaker and less mobile must

---

[1] Disc. de la méth., part v. Œuvr., i. pp. 174–184. Les passions, i. art. vii.
See book i. chap. v. pp. 230.

give place to those that are stronger, and that these alone must make their way to the brain." [1]

In like manner, all our involuntary motions, as in general all the activities which we have in common with animals, depend only upon the arrangement of our organs and the motion of our animal spirits, which, excited by the warmth of the heart, take their natural course into the brain, and thence into the nerves and muscles, in the same manner as the motion of a watch is produced only by the force of its spring and the form of its wheels. [2]

2. *The Organ of the Soul.* — The human body is a very complicated machine, whose parts, as the heart, brain, stomach, arteries, veins, muscles, nerves, etc., are in universal interaction, mutually preserving each other, and constituting a community in which each serves, and suffers with, the other. This machine forms a whole, and each of its parts is an organ of the whole; its parts, therefore, are not merely aggregated, but articulated; the community or complex of organs constitutes an organism, or articulated machine. An organism is, therefore, a particular kind of machine. It is a machine whose parts form themselves, and combine of their own accord, and constitute, therefore, no mere aggregate, but a unity or a whole. Descartes is so in earnest with this definition, the characteristic of the organism, that he says of the living body directly, "It is *one*, and in a certain sense *indivisible.*" The soul, therefore, if it is to be united with the human body, cannot merely dwell in one of its parts, but must be present to the *whole* organism. For since every part of the living body is connected with every other, none can enter into an exclusive union with the soul; and since this, by reason of its nature, has nothing in common with extension and divisibility, it is impossible for it to enter into exclusive union with one part of the organism. [3]

But it can very well be especially united with one of the

---

[1] Disc. de la méth., part v. pp. 183, 184. Les passions, l. arts. x.-xiii.
[2] Les passions, i. art. xvi.   [3] Ib., i. art. xxx.

organs: indeed, there must be — in view of that fundamental difference of the two substances, which does not permit their immediate union — a particular organ through which the soul has intercourse with the whole organism. Since the principal question in relation to the two substances is how motions in the organs are transformed into sensation and perception, and sensation and perception into motion, it is easy to see that it is the animal spirits, those agents of sensation and motion, which are the medium of intercourse between soul and body. In the motion of the animal spirits, there are two centres, the heart and the brain; in the former, they are produced; to the latter they ascend, and from thence act upon the organs. If, therefore, the soul carries on its intercourse with the organism by means of the animal spirits, it must be especially connected with one of the two central organs. The more precise answer of the question is self-evident. Since the peculiar action of the animal spirits goes out from the brain, this only can be the special organ; and in this, to use Descartes' expression, must the "seat of the soul" be sought.

The place of the peculiar organ of the soul is in the central organ of the nerves, itself also central and lying in the middle of the brain, where the animal spirits from the two parts of the brain, the anterior and posterior cavities, commune with each other, and where motion can be most easily caused by them, and they themselves can move most easily. It is the pineal gland, or conarion, which Descartes explains as the real organ of the soul. He finds, besides, a particular reason in support of his hypothesis. The impressions upon the senses of sight and hearing are dual, like the organs by means of which they are received; while the object perceived, like our presentation of it, is single, which would not be possible unless a union of the double impressions was effected in the central organ. It appears necessary, therefore, that an organ should exist in the brain to receive the double impressions, and that this organ should be *single* in its nature.

Descartes finds this organ in the pineal gland, which he, therefore, regards as the principal seat (*principal siège*) of the soul, as that part of the human body with which it is united most closely (*étroitement*). The central position and singleness of that part of the brain were the reasons which persuaded the philosopher to localize there the psychical activity so far as it receives and causes bodily impressions.[1]

By the connection between soul and body, as that now is obvious, the natural origin of the passions is explained. The received impression is changed by the activity of the soul into presentation and motive. If such an impression is experienced as something hurtful to our life, as, for example, when we see a wild animal rushing upon us, there arises a conception of danger along with the presentation of the object. Without a conscious exercise of volition, the will bestirs itself to protect the body, whether by attack or flight. Involuntarily, accordingly, that organ of the soul is affected, and that impulse is given to the course of the animal spirits, which disposes the limbs either for a battle or flight. The disposition to resist is courage, that to flee is fear. Courage and fear are not sense-impressions, but impulses of the will : they are not mere conceptions, but emotions of the mind, or *passions*. The motion, which in such emotions is felt in the heart, as little proves that the passions have their seat in the heart, as a painful sensation in the foot proves that pain is in the foot, or the sight of the stars in the vault of the heavens points out their true place.[2]

3. *The Will and the Passions.* — This explanation of the passions by the mental-bodily nature of man is, by the assumption which it makes, and the principle of its explanation, very characteristic of the doctrine of Descartes. By the help of the animal spirits and the organ of the soul, which is, he maintains, the pineal gland, the philosopher seeks to prove the origin of the passions *in a purely mechanical way*. In this

---

[1] Les passions, i. arts. xxxi., xxxii., xxxiv., xli.
[2] Ib., i. art. xxxiii., xxxv., xxxvi., xl.

lies the central point and the *novelty* of his attempt; and it was this which Descartes had in mind, when, in the very beginning of his work, he declared, that, in his doctrine of the passions, he had been obliged to entirely leave the beaten paths, and that he intended to discuss them, not as a preacher or a philosopher, but merely as a physicist. The passions had been previously considered merely as psychical processes, and it had not been seen that they contain factors of a purely bodily character. Now, since they master the soul, and deprive it of its freedom for the time being, and, therefore, militate against its nature, the psychological explanation knew not how to help itself except by a division of the soul into higher and lower powers, into a higher and lower appetitive faculty, into a rational and irrational soul, to which latter it ascribed the passions. Thus, the soul was divided into different parts, and it was held to consist, as it were, of different persons or souls: its unity and indivisibility were abandoned, and thereby its nature completely denied. This is the point which Descartes attacked and characterized as the confusion in which all of the earlier theories of the soul were involved.

It is true that reason fights with the passions, that it can gain the victory or be overcome in this conflict, that in human nature two powers fall into a struggle, the stronger of which gains the victory. But it is a false explanation of this fact to say that that fight takes place in the mental nature of man, and that this rises against itself as it were. In truth, the conflict takes place between two motions of opposite direction, which are communicated to the organ of the soul, — the one from the side of the body by the animal spirits, the other from the side of the soul by the will. That is involuntary, and is determined by bodily impressions alone: this is voluntary, and is motived by the intention which the will decides. Those bodily impressions which stir up the moving animal spirits in the organ of the soul, and through this in the soul itself, are here transformed into presenta-

tions of sense, which either leave the will at rest, as is the
case in the usual perception of objects, or, by their immediate relation to our existence, disturb and move the will.
Presentations of the first kind are passionless, and there is
no reason for opposing them. Those of the second class, on
the other hand, necessarily excite passion, since they rush
violently upon the will, and provoke its counter-action. The
attack upon the will follows from bodily causes: it necessarily results from natural and mechanical laws, and in its
strength consists the power of the passions. The re-action
of the will is free: it acts with mental power, in itself destitute of passion, and is, therefore, able to oppose and master
the passions. In this strength consists the power over
the passions. Assaulted by the impressions of the animal
spirits, the soul can suffer fear, and, strengthened by its own
will, have courage, and master the fear with which passion
at first filled it. It can give the organ of the soul, and
thereby the animal spirits, the opposite direction, by reason
of which the limbs move to battle, though fear urges them
to flight. It is now clear what powers fight with each other
in the passions. What has been regarded as a conflict
between the higher and lower nature of the soul, between
reason and desire, between the thinking and sensitive soul,
is in truth a conflict between the body and the soul, between
passion and will, between natural necessity and the freedom
of the will, between nature (matter) and mind.[1] Even the
weakest minds can, by their influence upon the organ of the
soul, become master of and direct the motion of the animal
spirits, and through them the progress of the passions, in
such a way that they are able to control them completely.[2]

The mechanical origin of the passions does not prevent,
but is rather the basis of, their moral results. The freedom
of the mind requires to be won by a hard struggle, and this
can only happen through the subjection of the opposing
powers. These opposing powers are the passions, and are,

[1] Les passions, i. art. xlvii.   [2] Ib., i. art. 1.

therefore, necessary conditions of the freeing of the human mind. Therein consists their importance and worth. They would not be the *opposing* powers of the will if they did not have their origin in a nature opposed to the mind, and hence the necessity of their mechanical origin. They would not be opposing *powers* if they were not powerful, i.e., if they could not affect the will; and that is possible only when body and mind are united as in human nature. Hence, this is regarded as the necessary and only basis for explaining the passions. The foundation is now perfectly clear upon which, within the Cartesian system, the doctrine of the passions rests. The next question is, In what do they consist?

III. KINDS OF PASSION.

1. *Fundamental Forms.* — We have already distinguished those presentations of sense which are destitute of passion from those of an impassioned character. The ground of an impassioned feeling does not lie in the object as such, but in the interest which our will takes in its existence, or in the way in which the object is related to our existence, and in which we are sensible of this relation. The nature of the latter is infinitely variable, because of the difference of individuals and of the states of our souls at different times. What one regards with fear, another views with contempt, and yet another with indifference. And in the change of our states of life and of our temper of mind, the same object makes upon the same person an impression, now of joy, now of sadness, and now no impression whatever. There is, therefore, an endless variety of passions. Yet from the nature of passionate excitement in general, we can deduce certain simple and necessary forms, which are related to the rest as fundamental forms to their modifications, or as elements (given in the calculations of combinations) to their variations. The fundamental forms, Descartes calls primary or "*primitive;*" those derived from, or combined of, them, the special or "*particular*" passions. From this point of view,

our passions can be distinguished and arranged. What we are emotionally sensible of are not things, but their worth; i.e., the advantages or injuries which we receive from them, or imagine we receive. It appears that the third case, in which the object is experienced neither as useful nor hurtful, excludes all value, and therefore every excitation of passion. This is not so. There are objects which, merely by their power and novelty, take hold of the mind with irresistible force, without in the least exciting our desires. An impassioned excitation is also united with presentations of this kind on account of their involuntary and powerful effect, and this Descartes calls wonder. We see at a glance that this feeling is full of passion, and has neither the usual character of desire, nor, still less, that of indifference.

What we conceive as useful or beneficial to us appears as something worthy of desire, or as a *good ;* the opposite of it as an *evil*, the destruction of which is desired. We wish to possess the good, and to get rid of the evil. In the first case we wish to possess the object, in the second to be free from it, while we merely look at the admired object, wishing neither to possess nor be rid of it. There are, accordingly, in the first place, two fundamental forms of passion to be distinguished, — wonder and desire. Desire sustains either a positive or negative relation to its object: it wishes to have and preserve the good, and to be rid of and destroy the evil. In the former case it is love, in the latter hate. Now, desired objects are either future or present. The good which is near at hand allures, the imminent evil threatens. In both cases, desire is eager, and consists in the expectant hope or longing for the attainment of a good, and the avoidance of an evil. Since, now, in both cases the opposite can be realized, — since we may fail to attain the good and to avoid the evil, — desire is affected both by hope and fear; i.e., it is positive and negative at the same time. If the objects which excite our desire are present, we either find that we possess the desired good, or that an evil has befallen us. In the

first case we are filled with the feeling of *joy*, in the second
with that of *sadness*. Accordingly, there are the following
primitive passions, which lie at the foundation of all the rest,
— wonder, love and hate, desire, joy and sadness. Wonder is
the only passion which is neither positive nor negative; the
longing for an object is the only desire that is both at the
same time; all the remaining passions are desires either of
the one or the other character.[1]

2. *Derived or Combined Forms.* — We will first consider the
desires. We propose to call attention to the most important
forms of these particular passions, and to show that they are
either combined of some of the given elements, or that they
are species of them.

The fundamental values of the objects which we have
characterized as utilities and injuries are infinitely different
in degree. There is a measure for determining the strength
or greatness of our desires, and for distinguishing certain
principal gradations. We love or hate what seems useful
or hurtful to *us*. Our self-love is, accordingly, the measure
by means of which our desires for things are to be compared,
and the intensity of them estimated. We may love other
beings either less than, or as much as, or more than, we do
ourselves: our love for an object may be less than, or equal to,
or greater than, our self-love. In the first case, it is *inclination*
(*affection*); in the second, *friendship* (*amitié*); in the third,
devotion (*dévotion*). What we love in the highest degree, i.e.,
self-sacrificingly, are the powers upon whom our existence depends, and by whom it is conditioned, as God, our country,
humanity, etc. Among the objects which excite love and
hate in our soul are to be particularly emphasized the beautiful and ugly as objects of sensitive delight and repulsion:
the love of the beautiful is *delight* (*agrément*), the opposite
feeling is disgust (*horreur*). Both passions, because they
excite the senses, are the strongest kinds of love and hate,
but also the most deceptive.

---

[1] Les passions, ii. art. lxix.

Longing (*verlangen*) is desire (*begierde*), eager to possess the good which is near at hand, and to avoid the imminent evil; passionate and still uncertain hope. This expectation is either *hope* (*espérance*) or *fear* (*crainte*), according to the degree of its uncertainty. The highest degree of hope is *assurance* (*sécurité*), the highest degree of fear is *despair* (*désespoir*). Descartes incidentally calls jealousy a species of fear. When the hoped or feared result depends not on external circumstances, but merely on ourselves and our own activity; when we can gain the good, and avoid the evil, merely by our own power, and must choose the means for doing so, perform certain actions, and, therewith, contend with certain difficulties, — hope and fear are modified accordingly. The fear of making a mistake in the choice of means reaches no decision because of the multitude of doubts and questions, and becomes *irresolution*. The energetic hope of being able to oppose and overcome the difficulties that lie in the way of the realization of one's plans, is *courage* (*courage*) and *daring* (*hardiesse*); the opposite feeling, afraid of difficulties, and trembling before them, is *cowardice* (*lâcheté*) and *terror* (*épouvante*).[1]

The presentation of existing goods or evils excites in us the feeling of joy (*joie*) or sorrow (*tristesse*). If those goods or evils do not relate to us, but to others, it is the happiness or unhappiness of another that rejoices or saddens us. Joy and sorrow, love and hate, are modified accordingly. The rejoicing in the joy of others is good will, sympathy with their misfortunes is pity (*pitié*). When the prosperity of others disturbs us, we experience *envy* (*envie*); when we rejoice in their misfortunes, *malice*. Descartes made these feelings dependent on a moral condition, which ought not to be considered in a physical explanation of the passions. He considers the prosperity and misfortunes of others as deserved or undeserved, the persons in question as worthy or unworthy of them, so that what they experience of good or

---

[1] Les passions, ii. arts. lvii., lix.

evil happens to them justly. We have, then, before our eyes, not so much the happy and unhappy, as the deserved, states of others, and rejoice in the just, course of things. Only the deserved prosperity of others excites our good will, as the undeserved our envy: only the deserved misfortunes of others excite our malice, as the undeserved our pity. These emotions of the mind now appear as right, as so many kinds of our natural feeling of right, whose satisfaction is a source of joy, and whose wounding is painful. Envy and pity belong to the class of sorrowful feelings, good will and pleasure in the misfortunes of others to the feelings of joy. But the two latter are claimed to be different in this, that joy on account of deserved success is serious, while scorn and ridicule (*moquerie*) are mingled in the joy on account of deserved misfortune.[1] It is at once evident, that, in the explanation of these passions, Descartes has not kept physical and moral causes enough apart. Right feeling can strengthen our good will and pity, but it has nothing to do with malice and envy. The philosopher has here missed the physical explanation which he promised, and not spoken of the passions " as physicist."

The good and bad deeds of men are particular classes of useful and hurtful objects, and therefore give rise to particular feelings of joy and sorrow, which take different forms according as we ourselves or others are the authors of those deeds, and the actions of others affect us or not. Joy, on account of our own good, is *self-contentedness* (*satisfaction de soi-même*): the opposite feeling is *repentance* (*repentir*). The consideration that we gain in the opinion of others through our merits, is fame (*gloire*): the opposite thereof is *disgrace* (*honte*). The merits of others awake in us a *friendly feeling* (*faveur*), and, if our own well-being is promoted thereby, *gratitude* (*reconnaissance*); while an evil-doer excites our *indignation* (*indignation*), and, if he adds injury to ourselves, our *anger* (*colère*). The goods and evils which fall to our share are of longer or shorter duration. Long habit dulls

---

[1] Les passions, ii. arts. lxi., lxii.

feeling, and changes satisfied joy into *satiety* (*dégoût*), while
it gradually diminishes our sadness on account of our losses
and injuries. The good and bad times which we experience
pass by: we see those vanish with *regret* (*regret*), and perceive with *gladness* (*allégresse*) the termination of these.[1]

Among the primitive passions, Descartes characterized
wonder as the first, and as elevated above the contrariety of
the others. We must now enter somewhat more particularly
into the nature, and the particular kinds and characteristics,
of this passion. It is always called forth by a new and unusual, a rare and extraordinary, object, the impression of
which lays hold of our mind, and is experienced as a *surprise*.
Its power does not gradually increase, but is at once active
in all its strength, because it arrests all our habitual impressions. Wonder is, therefore, the strongest of all our passions,
and, like every surprise, has the character of a sudden effect.
In all the emotions of the mind, we are involuntarily seized
by an object; but nowhere is this seizure so pure and perfect
as in wonder, whose essence it constitutes. Therefore, in a
certain manner, somewhat of this mode of feeling is present
in all the passions. It may be so powerful as to exclude all
opposition, and not merely move the mind, but so chain it
that all the animal spirits in the brain rush to the place of
the impression, and concentre here, while all the rest of the
body is motionless, and we become petrified, as it were, as
we gaze at the object. Then wonder passes into *amazement*
(*étonnement*), and degenerates through excess.[2]

So long as we are affected only by the power of the new
and unusual impression, we have no consciousness of the
usefulness or hurtfulness of the object — which constitutes
the fundamental theme of the rest of the passions. Wonder
is, therefore, prior to these: it is the first of the passions, and
has not, like the others, an opposite. Its real opposite would
consist in a state of mind which permits itself to be affected

[1] Les passions, ii. arts. lxiii., lxvii.
[2] Ib., ii. arts. lxx., lxxii., lxxiii.

by nothing whatever, a state of mind completely passionless in its lack of receptivity to impressions. There is, therefore, no passion opposed to wonder; i.e., it has no opposite. But there are, indeed, differences in, or kinds of, wonder, dependent upon the object whose unusualness surprises us, varying according as its extraordinary character consists in its largeness or its smallness, or as we or other free beings are its object. Descartes calls the two fundamental forms of wonder, esteem (*estime*) and *contempt* (*mépris*); the corresponding estimate of one's self is either magnanimity (*magnanimité*) (self-respect) and *pride* (*orgueil*), or *humility* (*humilité*) and *abjectness of disposition* (*bassesse*) (false humility); while the surprising impression produced by the greatness or littleness of others excites our *reverence* (*vénération*) or *contempt* (*dédain*).[1]

Among these kinds of wonder, our estimates of ourselves are the most deserving of notice. Nothing stamps itself more distinctly in the demeanor of a man, in the expression of his countenance, in his gestures and gait, than an extraordinarily high or low estimate of himself. In our estimate of ourselves, there is a true and false exaltation of our worth, as there is a true and false disparagement of it. Descartes calls true self-esteem *magnanimity* (*magnanimité*), not haughtiness, but *generosity* (*générosité*): pride, on the other hand, is false self-esteem. Genuine humility he calls *humilité* (*humilité vertueuse*): false humility, on the other hand, is "*bassesse*." Now the criterion is to be determined for distinguishing the true from the false in the intensity and direction of our self-esteem. In general we may remark, that only *free beings* can be objects of esteem and contempt. Only *one* object is in truth worthy of esteem, as its opposite is contemptible, — our freedom of the will, by virtue of which reason rules in our nature, and the passions serve. In this free and rational mastery of self, all the moral worth of man consists. It is the only good that no favor of fortune can

---

[1] Les passions, ii. arts. liii.-lv.

give, but which can be earned only by labor and discipline
of the will which each one practises in himself. He who has
gained the mastery over himself, possesses that greatness of
soul from which that truly high and alone justifiable self-
esteem proceeds, that magnanimous disposition which Descartes calls *générosité*. Nothing is more valuable than this
good ; but nothing is more difficult to attain, since one must,
in comparison with it, regard the usual goods of life as of
no worth, and lift himself high above the weaknesses of
human nature. If one struggles earnestly to overcome his
own weaknesses, and to divest his freedom of them, he apprehends for the first time how numerous they are, and how
frail human nature is. Its littleness and covetousness are
therefore experienced in the same proportion as greatness of
soul is striven for and obtained. True self-esteem goes hand
in hand, therefore, with true humility. Only self-esteem that
does not proceed from the feeling of the greatness and freedom of one's own will, is false and perverted, as also is any
humility that is not based on the feeling of one's own weakness of will. Perverted self-esteem is haughtiness or pride,
as perverted humility is self-abasement and abjectness of disposition. As genuine humility is not merely compatible, but
necessarily connected, with generosity, so is pride with crin-
ging. "Pride is so unreasonable and absurd, that I should
scarcely be able to believe that men could stoop to it if so
much unmerited praise were not bestowed; but flattery is
so general, that every man, however faulty, finds himself
praised, not only without any merit, but even for his mean-
nesses, and that is why the most ignorant and stupid are
proud." "Men of the most abject disposition are frequently
the most arrogant and haughty, as great souls are the most
modest and humble. These preserve their equanimity in
prosperity and misfortune; while little and base souls depend
upon the caprices of fortune, and are puffed up by prosperity,
exactly as they are cast down by adversity. We often see,
indeed, that these people humble themselves in a disgraceful

manner before others who can serve or injure them, and, at
the same time, conduct themselves in the most insolent
manner towards those from whom they have nothing to
hope or to fear." Every energetic or free being can deserve
esteem. No man, therefore, is contemptible as such, and
least of all because he lacks certain external advantages
and gifts of fortune, as talent, beauty, honor, riches, etc.
If a man earns our esteem, we are sensible of respect or
reverence, which is composed of awe and admiration, while
another who deserves our contempt, seems so far below us,
that his baseness certainly excites our wonder, but not the
least fear.[1]

IV. THE MORAL AIM OF LIFE.

1. *Worth and Unworthiness of the Passions.* — At this point
the doctrine of the soul passes over into the *doctrine of morals*,
and completely illuminates the theme of the latter. To be
free is every thing. The freedom of the will, our highest
faculty, points out the direction and the goal. The exaltation of our spiritual nature above the senses, the freedom of
the will, which has in subjection our desires and passions, is
the purpose of human life, the highest good, the possession
of which alone constitutes our happiness, the only moral
worth, the single ground of our self-esteem. Descartes did
not expound his doctrine of morals in a special work, but
only discussed its principal points, in part in his work on the
passions, in part in the letters which he wrote to the Princess Elizabeth on the happy life (criticising and correcting
Seneca), and in those designed for the Queen of Sweden on
love and the highest good. We have seen the direct connection between those letters and the origin and completion of
the work on the passions of the soul.[2]

If the highest good consists in the freedom which masters

---

[1] Les passions, iii. arts. cxlix.–clxiii.

[2] See book ii. chap. iv. p. 218; chap. viii. pp. 284–291. The letters to Elizabeth on "*beate vivre*" are in Œuvres, t. ix. pp. 210–249.

the passions, it cannot be won without a conflict with the latter, and is, therefore, inconceivable without them. If the highest good is of all things the most worthy of desire, it must, in a certain sense, be an object of desire, and there must be a passion which of itself has a moral tendency. It is at these two points in the explanation of the emotions of the mind, that the doctrine of the soul and that of morals interpenetrate.

All our passions can be reduced to those six primitive ones whose simplest forms are wonder and desire. Even wonder, so far as it desires the conception or consideration of its object, is a desire. In the last analysis, therefore, all our passions are desires, and, as such, the natural motives of our actions. All human action is conditioned by the fact that something is wished or desired, and right action consists in right desiring. If we can determine the latter, we have found the fundamental rule which constitutes the theme of the whole of morals. This fundamental rule is very simple and evident. The possession of all desirable goods is either entirely, or in part, or not at all, dependent upon ourselves; i.e., upon our own powers. What we cannot acquire by our own activity, we cannot even really possess, and, therefore, also cannot reasonably desire. We, therefore, desire unreasonably what our power is not sufficient to enable us to acquire or appropriate, but which, on the contrary, depends upon conditions which lie wholly or in part beyond our power. Our wishes are unreasonable if it is impossible to realize them; and it is, strictly speaking, impossible when the necessary conditions do not lie within our power. So unreasonable are the general wishes of men: they desire most passionately what least depends upon their own energy, the external goods of life, beauty, honor, riches, etc. The rule of knowledge says, Think clearly and distinctly: only that which is clearly and distinctly apprehended is true. The maxim of the will says, Desire clearly and distinctly: only that which is so desired is good. Wish nothing that thou canst not obtain by thyself alone. Thy highest faculty is freedom. It cannot make thee beautiful, rich, respected, powerful, successful, in the eyes of the world, but only free: it makes thee, not a master of things, but only of thyself. Wish not to be more! Let the only good which thou desirest be this mastery over thyself: let it be the only goal of thy efforts, the single object of thy admiration! All other wishes are vain! [1]

2. *The Worth of Wonder.* — Right action, accordingly, is dependent upon a true knowledge of our strength and weakness. From the knowledge of the first springs the feeling of our true and attainable nobility; from that of the second, genuine humility. Nothing is more conducive to the latter than the consideration of the immeasurable universe, in which man is not the centre and purpose of things, but a vanishing point, too weak to alter the course of things according to his wishes. "Because the passions impel us to action only through the desires which they excite, our desires must be regulated; and therein consists the most important use of morality." "We have two resources against idle wishes: the first is a lofty and true estimate of one's self (*générosité*), of which I shall speak later; the other, the thought upon which we ought often to meditate. Divine providence has determined the course of things from eternity like a destiny or an unchangeable necessity, which latter is to be opposed to blind fate, in order to destroy this phantom of the imagination. For we can only wish what, in our opinion, somehow lies within the realm of possibility. What, on the other hand, is independent of our power, we can only regard as possible by conceiving it as depending upon that blind fate, and by believing that the like has already happened before. We believe in chance because we do not know the real causes of things. If an event, which in our opinion depends upon chance, does not happen, it is clear that one of its causes

---

[1] Les passions, ii. arts. cxliv.-cxlvi. Cf. letter to Elizabeth, Œuvres, ix. pp. 211-214.

is absent, and that, therefore, it could not happen, and that the
like never has happened ; namely, something without a cause.
If we had previously had this necessary course of things
clearly before our eyes, we should never have regarded the
matter as possible, and, therefore, never desired it." [1]   All
vain wishes are errors, while correct wishes are a necessary
consequence of a true self-respect and the greatness of mind
(*générosité*) that is based upon it.   Descartes, therefore, calls
this latter "the key, as it were, to all other virtues, and the
chief means for overcoming the passions." [2]

Self-esteem is a kind of wonder.   This is the emotion of
the mind which of itself takes the moral direction, and points
the way to all the others.   For wonder is a desire that sat-
isfies itself, not with the possession, but with the conception
or contemplation, of things, and, therefore, moves the mind
in a direction which precedes, and makes ready for, knowledge.   When we are affected by a surprising impression, by
a new, unusual, rare object, we are lost, as it were, in the
contemplation of it.   Nothing is now more natural than
the wish to complete this contemplation, or to make it plain
by a more thorough examination.   Knowledge consists in this
explanation.   From the desire to contemplation, the desire
for knowledge naturally follows.   Of all our passions, none
is of so theoretical a nature, and so favorably disposed to
knowledge, as wonder.   It is on the way to knowledge : it
stands at the beginning of the course.   That saying of Aristotle, that philosophy begins with wonder, is valid also with
Descartes, without conflicting with his characteristic declaration that philosophy begins with doubt.   The desire for
knowledge is one thing, the certainty of it another : the
former has its source in wonder, the latter in doubt.   We
know what importance Descartes ascribes to the will in his
theory of error.   Wonder involuntarily gives to the will a
theoretic direction, and makes it disposed to knowledge :
hence Descartes regards it not merely as the first among the

---

[1] Les passions, ii. arts. cxliv., cxlv.   [2] Ib., iii. art. clxi.

primitive passions, but as the most important of the passions in general.

We are speaking of natural and healthy wonder, which agitates the mind, but does not enchain it; which calls forth the desire for knowledge, but does not stifle it. Here Descartes distinguishes the two defective extremes, which Aristotle had done in reference to the natural impulses in general, the *too much* and the *too little*, defect and excess, dulness and the inability to resist the power of the impression, the incapacity to wonder and the inordinate desire of wonder. The first temper of mind consists in a determined equanimity, that allows itself to be affected by nothing; the second in a blind curiosity, that catches at new impressions, and yields itself to every one without an impulse towards investigation. This kind of wonder is not really an emotion of the mind, but a cessation of mental action; not really wonder, but, as Descartes had already said before, amazement. Exactly in this consists the value of wonder, that it is not most sensible of the useful or hurtful, but of the rare and extraordinary, character of impressions, and stamps it upon the mind in such a manner that it insures the continued activity of the mind, and excites our reflections. "The other passions can only serve to make useful or hurtful objects noticeable: wonder alone observes the exceptional. And we see that people without any natural inclination to this emotion are usually very ignorant."

"But much more frequently we find the opposite, that men abandon themselves too much to wonder, and are amazed at things that are either very little, or not at all, worthy of attention. And thus the theoretic value of this passion is either completely cancelled or perverted into its opposite. Intentional and special attention is of avail against a deficiency in wonder, and to this our will can always oblige the understanding as soon as we see that the observation of the object is worth the pains. But against excessive wonder, there is no other resource but to learn to know many things, and to distinguish the rarest and most unusual. Although only dumb and stupid men are by nature incapable of wonder, the capacity for it is not always proportioned to greatness of mental endowments. But it is especially a characteristic of such minds as have a good natural understanding, and who, without imagining themselves therefore great, are quick. Certainly the impulse to wonder diminishes in consequence of habit. The more rare objects any one has seen and wondered at, the more he forms the habit of not wondering at them any longer, and of regarding all succeeding ones as usual. But when the impulse to wonder exceeds all proper proportion, and fastens its attention ever only on the first impression of the object before it, without striving for a further knowledge of it, the habit thence arises of constantly catching at new impressions. And this is the reason which makes the disease of blind curiosity chronic : one then seeks out exceptional things merely to wonder at them, not in order to understand them ; and people gradually become so fond of wonder (*admiratifs*), that they are attracted as much by trifling as by the most important things."

3. *Freedom of Mind.* — Without passions, the soul would take no part in its bodily life ; without them, there would be for human nature neither goods nor evils in the world ; they alone are the source of our joyful and sorrowful existence. The more powerfully they move and affect us, the more receptive are we to the joys and sorrows of life, the sweeter its joys, and the bitterer its sorrows. And certainly its sorrows are so much the more painful, the less we are able to control our passions, and the more disagreeable our external circumstances. But there is a means of mastering our passions, and moderating them to such an extent, that their evils become very endurable, and all transform themselves into a source of joy. This single means is *wisdom*. With this declaration Descartes concludes his work on the passions of the soul.[1]

Wonder gives the natural impulse to enter the path that

---

[1] Les passions, iii. art. ccxii.

leads to wisdom. Wisdom releases the impulse to knowledge which cannot content itself without our self-knowledge,
without the perception of our self-delusion, without the fundamental *doubt* which leads to certainty, to a true self-knowledge, and, therefore, to a true estimation of ourselves, upon
which that enlightened self-respect, that genuine feeling of
freedom, is based, which coincides with true knowledge, and
determines moral worth. Thus, from the impulse to wonder
springs the impulse towards knowledge, and from this result
doubt and the certainty of self, and thence in the light of reason that wonder whose object is the greatest and most exalted of our faculties, the freedom of the will. Here arises
that affection of the mind which Descartes called magnanimous temper (*magnanimité* or *générosité*) (self-respect), and
which holds the reins of our moral life in its hands.

Before this knowledge vanish the imaginary worth of
things, the illusive goods of the world, the desires blinded
by such appearances, the power of all the passions whose object is this kind of desire or selfishness. So long as the soul
abandons itself to the control of these passions, it is driven
by them hither and thither: it can repress one while it follows its opposite, and thus exchange one master for another.
Such a triumph is merely apparent: it is not the soul, but one
of its passions, that triumphs, while it itself remains a slave.
But when by its own energy and freedom, acting upon its
clear and distinct knowledge, it lifts itself above the level of
the passions, then first does it conquer "*with its own weapons,*" and, therefore, in reality. This victory is the triumph
of the freedom of the mind. "What I call its own weapons
(*ses propres armes*) are the firm and certain judgments concerning good and evil according to which the soul is resolved
to act. Those are the weakest of all souls whose will, without the aid of knowledge, allows itself to be moved by the
passions of the moment, now in this direction, now in that:
these passions turn the will against itself, and bring the soul
into the most miserable condition into which it can fall.

Thus, on the one hand, fear represents death as the greatest of all evils, which is only to be escaped by flight; while on the other, honor represents this disgraceful flight as an evil which is still worse than death. The two passions drive the will in different directions; and this, mastered now by one, and now by the other, is continually at war with itself, and thus makes the condition of the soul slavish and miserable."[1]

Here the system of Descartes concludes, returning to its deepest foundations. What lay at the foundation of doubt was the will, which sought to break through self-delusion, and penetrate to certainty. Certainty consisted in the clear and distinct knowledge of self and of God: from thence followed the clear and distinct knowledge of things without us. In the light of reason, we saw the absolute opposition of soul and body. Our passions now prove the union of the two, for only in such a union could they have their source: they deny what clear knowledge affirms. Thus arises a contradiction between the perceptions of our free reason, and the involuntary affections of our mind. The problem contained in this contradiction is solved when we understand the passions, see through the imaginary worth of their objects, and destroy their power. That opposition of soul and body does not prevent their union in human nature, and this union does not prevent the opposition of the two. Rather in the exaltation of the soul over the bodily existence, in the freeing from the passions and desires, in a word, in the freedom of the soul, this opposition first finds its true and energetic expression. Our passions are related to our thinking nature as obscure conceptions to those which are clear, and in their obscurity lies their weakness. If the will, by virtue of doubt, could break through self-delusion, and, by the help of thought, could attain to clear and distinct knowledge, it can by clear and distinct knowledge also master the power of the passions; for desires also are self-delusions which blind us by

[1] Les passions, i. art. xlviii.

the illusory worth of things, and keep us imprisoned therein. Doubt meets and overcomes *each* of our self-delusions, even the power of the passions and the freedom of the soul ; i.e., the will, enlightened by knowledge, gains the victory over the passions also.

CHAPTER X.

THE FIRST CRITICAL TEST.—OBJECTIONS AND REPLIES.

I. OBJECTIONS.

1. *Stand-points and Tendencies of their Authors.*

WE have expounded the philosophy of Descartes in the connection of its essential parts, and now turn to examine it. And here we meet at once those objections to the " Meditations," objections which the philosopher himself invited, and to which he replied, and which he published along with his replies. It was the first test which the new system had to stand before its author and the world. Descartes wished to put his doctrine to such a test in its very first appearance before the world, and as the one who was best acquainted with it, to be also its first interpreter and defender. These critical discussions are therefore historically notable.[1]

If the objections are mingled with the exposition of the doctrine, and arbitrarily scattered in different places, as usually happens, their impression, as a whole, is completely lost, while that of the system is unnecessarily interrupted. There is no source from which we can better learn the first effect of the new doctrine on the philosophical minds of the time than these objections validly made from such different points of view by critics with and without reputation while the impression of the work, as yet in manuscript, was still fresh in their minds. We find here together the prevailing tendencies of the philosophical consciousness of the time,

[1] See book i. chap. v. pp. 245–247.

some of them in their most renowned representatives. It is, therefore, worth while to carefully consider this group of Descartes' first critics.

Not taking into account the reports of objections collected by Mersenne in the second and sixth places, Descartes received, and replied to, the objections of Caterus, Hobbes, Arnauld, Gassendi, and Bourdin, in the order in which we have just mentioned their authors. The later ones, which we may call the eighth and ninth, and which it was impossible to include in the edition of the "Meditations," were discussed by letters. To these belong the objections under the name of Hyperaspistes, and those of the English philosopher, Henry More. The former are scarcely worthy of notice, since they repeat what had already been said: the latter again attacked Descartes from the theosophical standpoint, disputing the mere materiality of extension, and maintaining an immaterial space, valid for spiritual being, and explaining the presence of God in the world as well as that of the soul in the body.[1]

The second and sixth objections, which express the doubts of different philosophers, and in which Mersenne indeed also found a place for his own, are in the manner of *dilettantes*. They are not, therefore, contemptible; for in an age as active in philosophy as Descartes', the desultory co-operation of *dilettantes* is no unimportant power. Caterus' objections relate only to the concept of God, particularly to the ontological proof, and, therefore, do not touch the fundamental principle and trend of the new doctrine.

To understand the chief objections, we must bring before our minds the fundamental thoughts on which the whole Cartesian system rests. The methodical knowledge of things in the natural light of reason or of thought was the problem and the universal theme of Descartes. So far as the light of knowledge is, and must be, *natural (les lumières naturelles)*,

---

[1] The letters between H. More and Descartes were written from December, 1648, to October, 1649. Œuvres, t. x. pp. 178-196.

his system is *naturalistic*.   So far as this natural light is, and
requires to be, *reason*, or pure (clear and distinct) thought,
this naturalism is *rationalistic*.   *Method* consists in the mode
in which that light is discovered, and so produced in thought
that it illuminates things.   These are the fundamental
thoughts.   He who attacks these, attacks the foundations
of the new doctrine.   This fundamental attack can be made
in three points.   We can defend the natural light of knowledge, but deny that it arises and shines in thought, holding
that it must be sought not in reason, but in the senses.   Such
a view denies not the naturalism, but the rationalism, of Descartes; not the philosophical (natural), but the metaphysical
(rational), knowledge of things: this view is empiricism or
sensualism.   This sensualism is as ancient as the atomic
mode of thought, and as modern as the Baconian philosophy.
The Renaissance had again animated the old doctrine of
Democritus, which Epicurus, and after him Lucretius, had
revived, even in antiquity.   Gassendi, whom we can regard
as a late product of the Renaissance, took this position against
Descartes, being a disciple of Epicurus.   From the revival
of philosophy by Bacon, who had founded empiricism, a
sensualistic school necessarily resulted, and this already involved materialism.   *Hobbes* opposed Descartes from this
point of view.   We have before us that antithesis which,
at the first glance at the course of the development of modern philosophy, we saw arising within it.[1]   It is the first of
the indicated oppositions.

But even the natural light of knowledge does not remain
undisputed.   The supernatural light of faith and of revelation, which illuminates the kingdom of grace and the Church,
is the adversary of naturalism : theology and, more particularly, Augustinianism, which the Reformation had revived
against the Romish Church, and which Jansenism sought to
support within Catholicism — Jansenism, which appeared at
the same time with the doctrine of Descartes, and can be re-

---

[1] See introduction, chap. vii. pp. 159-162.

garded as the most powerful expression of the religious consciousness of the time. Arnauld, who was imbued with Augustinianism, and was one of the most important theologians then living in France, and afterwards the leader of the Jansenists, opposed the new philosophy from this point of view.

There is an ecclesiastical rationalism which Scholasticism had developed, and whose problem was not to discover new truths, but to prove those dogmatically asserted. There can be no greater opposition than between the methods of Cartesianism and Scholasticism ; between thought, making no presuppositions and purified by doubt, and thought trained in and bound by dogmatism ; between synthetic deduction and the unfruitful doctrine of the syllogism, parading its " *barbara* " and " *celarent.*" The Jesuits, the neo-scholastics of the time, were adepts in the dialectic arts of the schools ; and through them, Descartes had become acquainted with this method at an early age, and thoroughly despised it. The Jesuit *Bourdin,* the author of the objections in the seventh place, concentrated his attack upon Descartes' method, seeking therewith to overthrow the new doctrine itself. That this method was attacked by a Jesuit, and the mode of his attack, were as characteristic as his polemic was unimportant.

2. *Points of Agreement and Disagreement.* — Among the tendencies of thought which found themselves in conflict with the doctrine of Descartes, there is no greater contrast than that between the Augustinian theology and the sensualistic (materialistic) philosophy, — Arnauld and Hobbes ! Both attacked the new system — namely, the rational knowledge of God and of things — at the same time. They attacked from opposite sides, the *metaphysical* foundations of the system, the principles, which claim to be discovered by methodical thought, and to be not merely more certain than any of those hitherto accepted, but absolutely certain and indubitable. Theology rejects these principles, because it acknowl-

edges none but the facts of religion and revelation ; sensualism, because it concedes to human knowledge no other
foundation than the facts of the sensible world and experience. These attacks upon the doctrine of Descartes were
unavoidable. They turn a blaze of light upon the fundamental features of the entire system in its naturalistic and
rationalistic character. And, therefore, we may regard the
objections of Hobbes, Gassendi, and Arnauld as the most
worthy of notice and instructive. Hobbes, although abler
and more modern than Gassendi, treated the matter somewhat
superficially, and was less accurate and searching in his criticisms than Gassendi. Descartes, therefore, broke off the controversy with the former, while he carried it to the end with
the latter. For this reason we may regard Arnauld and
Gassendi, both countrymen of the philosopher, as the most
important opponents against whom he attempted to defend
his doctrine.

Not less significant than the points of disagreement are
the points of agreement between the philosophy of Descartes
and the Augustinian theology, between Cartesianism and the
materialistic sensualism. As soon as we turn away from the
metaphysical (rational) basis of the system, the resemblances
on both sides are perfectly evident. The sensualistic philosophy is, from its entire foundation and nature, inclined to a
materialistic and mechanical explanation of nature. Descartes also gave this explanation : it could not be stricter.
Hobbes, who at first noted only this phase of the new doctrine, thought that it completely coincided with his own.
But the Cartesian explanation of nature is a necessary consequence of those dualistic principles with which we are now
acquainted : its purely materialistic and mechanical tendency
proceeds from an entirely different stand-point from that of
the sensualistic philosophers. They thought that because
nature is material, the mind is also. Because nature can be
explained only by mechanical laws, the activities of the mind
are also to be explained in the same manner. Descartes'

conception on the other hand is precisely the reverse of this. Because the mind is not at all material, the world of bodies is only material: because the phenomena of mind cannot at all be derived from material conditions, the phenomena of the body can only be explained by such conditions. Because the mind is the opposite of body, the body is also the opposite of mind. This was the point about which the contro- . versy arose between our philosopher on the one side, and Hobbes and Gassendi on the other.

In the opposition of the nature of mind to that of body, in this pronounced dualism, lay the central point of the new system. And just here where it was attacked by the sensualists, it exercised an involuntary attraction upon those Augustinian theologians. Descartes himself felt himself more closely related to these than to his philosophical opponents. He saw that *Arnauld* understood him far better than Hobbes and Gassendi, whose entire mode of thought repelled him; and he regarded the objections which the former made as the most important of all. We are acquainted with his profound investigation of the concept of God, and the decided importance of its results upon his entire system. When the philosopher declared, that, by this phase of his doctrine, he wished also to promote and strengthen the cause of religion, it was not an idle remark, or a merely cautious and conservative way of speaking. He was sincerely interested in the cause of religion, and Arnauld sympathized with him in this respect. Along with this, there was a verbal agreement with Augustine, which must have been welcome to the theologian, and must have seemed so much the more significant as it appeared in the very point which Descartes had called the fulcrum of Archimedes; viz., in the proposition of certainty. To prove the existence of God, Augustine took the certainty of self as his starting-point in his work on the freedom of the will. He puts these words in the mouth of Alypius as he addresses Euodius: " I will begin with the most certain truth. I ask you, therefore, whether you yourself are, and whether you are afraid of a delusion in your answer to this question, although no sort of error is possible here, for if you did not exist, you could not even be deceived." Exactly so had Descartes spoken in his " Meditations," without knowing that in his " *cogito, ergo sum*," he had had a predecessor in Augustine. When he learned this fact from Arnauld, he thanked him for the delightful surprise.

But similar starting-points as little prove a real and thorough agreement as similar conclusions. Trends of thought which set out from opposed principles may coincide in certain points, as, for example, the Cartesian and sensualistic doctrines in reference to the mechanical explanation of nature ; and even so, trends of thought may start from a common point, and diverge widely in their course. Thus it is in a certain respect with the Cartesian and Augustinian doctrines. If we follow them in their course, and compare their historical developments, we discover a contrast, a greater than which cannot be conceived. From the system of Augustine follows the ecclesiastical consciousness of the Middle Ages and the dominion of scholasticism ; from the system of Descartes, that of Spinoza. But such an opposition was still far from the consciousness of our philosopher. So far as the tendency of his philosophy was clear to his own mind, he could deceive himself concerning the fundamental opposition between his doctrine and the Augustinian theology, and regard the essential agreement of the two as certain. The existence of things, the knowledge of minds, the motion of bodies, as the creative work of God, were still valid for him. The human mind would be veiled in impenetrable darkness if the idea of God, and, therefore, God himself, did not illuminate it. The material world would be motionless and lifeless if God himself did not move it. Things could neither exist nor endure if God had not created them, and if he did not conserve them. Human knowledge is thus in its final ground *illumination ;* the existence of the world, *creation;* its duration, *continual creation.* All this Augustine also taught, but on supernatural grounds, resting on the fact of faith in the Christian revelation; while Descartes sought to prove it by the natural light of reason, whose original source he saw in God himself. The guiding principle of the Augustinian system is the Christian faith and the absolutely supernatural fact of redemption: the guiding principle of the Cartesian is only the natural light of reason — clear and distinct thought. Therein consists the absolute opposition of the two. Arnauld felt this opposition. His doubts were excited by the rationalistic mode of thought and its necessary consequences. The truth of the ecclesiastical doctrine of faith is not consistent with the method of clear and distinct thought. We know clearly and distinctly that modes cannot exist without substances, and properties not without the subject to which they belong. It is impossible for properties to exist, when the thing to which they belong no longer exists; for those to remain while this is transformed, for bread and wine to be transubstantiated into flesh and blood, and yet preserve their properties of form, color, taste, etc. It is impossible for substance and modes to be separated from each other: divine omnipotence itself cannot effect such a separation, for it would then act contrary to clear and distinct thought. Descartes denies this possibility, while faith in the transubstantiation of the elements affirms it. Arnauld and the authors of the objections in the sixth place urged these objections against the philosopher. We know clearly and distinctly that substances are independent of each other, and, therefore, can never constitute one being. Now, persons are substances; and the unity of three persons, as it is taught in the doctrine of the Holy Trinity, appears unthinkable. With the position that substance and modes are inseparably united, the doctrine of the Lord's Supper is at strife; with the position that substances are necessarily separate, the doctrine of the Trinity.[1] Arnauld remarked

---

[1] Obj., iv. (t. ii. p. 35). Ib., vi. (t. ii. pp. 327-329).

that the principle of certainty should be limited to philosophical knowledge, and not applied to morals and religion.
Descartes, in agreement with Augustine, should stop at the
boundary between faith and knowledge, as this rests on
reasons, while the basis of that is authority. Descartes had
no difficulty in agreeing with Arnauld, since that limitation
was in harmony with his feelings, and the guiding principle
of his life. But the problems of philosophy are more powerful than the inclinations and rules of life of philosophers.
The limitation which Descartes thought proper to impose
upon himself, the spirit of his doctrine could not continually
endure.

3. *The Points of Attack.* — We shall best find our attitude
with reference to the contents of the objections and their
points of attack by recalling the cardinal points of the system so far as they are contained in the "Meditations." The
salient points are methodical doubt, the principle of certainty,
the idea, existence and truthfulness, of God, the reality of
the sensible world, the cause of error, and the difference of
essence between mind and body. The objections concentre
about these important points, and can be arranged accordingly.

The new method and its sceptical vindication found its
principal opponent in the scholastic, who felt himself strong
and at home in the old doctrine of the syllogism and the
sorites. The principle of certainty by means of pure
thought, and the thereon based doctrine of the absolute independence of the mind, so far as the body is concerned, was
attacked by the sensualistic philosophers, assisted by their
sensualistic mode of thought, by which the consciousness of
most men is dominated. Against this point, therefore, there
are the greatest multitude of objections: here unite with
Hobbes and Gassendi those "different theologians and philosophers," from whom the objections in the second and sixth
places proceed. A multitude of objections are urged against
the proofs of the existence and veracity of God, particularly

against the inference that God cannot deceive us, in which the anonymous theologians vie with Caterus and Arnauld. Only that Arnauld, who had penetrated the spirit of the new doctrine more deeply, first saw that Descartes' ontological proof was different from the scholastic.

1. It is a universal characteristic of the philosophers of modern times, no matter what their point of view, that they thoroughly despise the old school, particularly the art of disputation, which had earned its triumphs in the lecturers' chairs of the Middle Ages. Their right to do so can best be judged from a concrete case, — when one sees before his eyes how a polemic of the old dialectic couches his lance against the founder of a new and synthetic method. In this respect, the objections of Bourdin are characteristic, and not without interest for the historian of culture. He seeks to prove, according to the rules of the syllogism, that Descartes' method is impossible; that it can neither begin nor advance, nor prove any thing whatever except pure nothing; that it is both absurd and nihilistic in the sense of complete nullity.

The proposition of certainty, with which methodical knowledge begins, rests on that absolute doubt which denies all certainty. The first proposition is, "Nothing is certain;" and then by means of it, it is proved that "something is certain." From a universal negative, a particular affirmative is affirmed, which, according to the rules of the syllogism, is impossible: so impossible is the proposition of certainty, the pretended beginning of all knowledge.

The same is true of the proposition of doubt. Because we have been deceived in some cases, the possibility of deception is asserted of all cases; because one thing is uncertain, therefore all things are uncertain, or nothing is certain. This inference is impossible, because we cannot deduce a universal from a particular judgment: so impossible is the proposition of doubt, the pretended beginning of philosophy. If the proposition of doubt is really valid, it must have a reactionary effect, and destroy itself; if nothing is certain, it is not even certain that any thing is uncertain : so impossible is not merely the inference, but also the beginning of doubt.[1]

The entire Cartesian philosophy, according to Bourdin, is wrecked on the impossibility of basing a universal judgment on a particular one — even the dualism between mind and matter, even the physics that rests on the doctrine that body is merely extended. If some bodies are extended, it does not follow that this is a property of all bodies, still less that it constitutes the essence of bodies, and that, therefore, the soul, because it is indivisible (unextended), can never be of a bodily nature. By such reasoning, one could prove to a peasant that the properties with which he is acquainted in his domestic animals are all essential to an animal ; that, therefore, the wolf is not an animal.[2]

As impossible as is every attempt to make a beginning of knowledge according to Descartes' method, so impossible is every attempt at progress. It sinks at every step into a bottomless abyss, into pure nothing. It is only necessary to judge the course of this method according to the rules of the syllogism, to state its attempts at progress in the regular forms of "*celarent*," "*cesare*," etc., in order to see whither it leads. Every being whose existence is doubtful is not actual ; the existence of body is doubtful, therefore body is not actual, and no actual being is body ; I am real, therefore I am no body. Now, according to Descartes, every thing is doubtful, consequently mind also. Mind, therefore, has as little reality as body ; and, therefore, we ourselves are neither mind nor body, hence nothing. Since, now, every thing must be either mind or body, and can be neither of the two, there is *nothing* at all. It is thus evident, that, according to the new method of knowledge, we can neither make a beginning, nor advance, nor reach any goal whatever of knowledge. We must, therefore, return to the old method of the schools, from the nihilistic to the syllogis-

---

[1] Obj., vii. (t. ii. pp. 393, 404, 412–415).   [2] Ib., vii. pp. 441–443.

tic, from the sceptical to the dogmatic, from Cartesianism to scholasticism.[1]

2. The objections of Hobbes, Gassendi, and Arnauld to the Cartesian doubt are, of course, of a different character. Hobbes discussed the matter with a somewhat lofty air: he impugns the novelty of the doubt and its validity in reference to sensible knowledge. Even among the ancient philosophers, both before and after Plato, there had been sceptics by profession; and Plato himself had said much of the uncertainty of the perceptions of sense. Descartes would have done better to leave this stuff alone: it is not modern, but belongs to the whims of antiquity. Gassendi is ready to agree to a *moderate* scepticism, after the fashion of the people of the world, but he finds the Cartesian excessive: it throws away the good along with the bad, and puts a new error in the place of the old. Whoever imagines or persuades himself that he has a doubt that deprives him of all certainty, deceives himself; and however much he protests that he regards nothing as certain, there are things enough which he cannot doubt, but which he regards as perfectly certain. The doubt of Descartes is, therefore, largely self-delusion. Arnauld, on the other hand, felt that this doubt shook the intellectual self-righteousness of man, and affirmed its validity so far as it was confined to natural knowledge, and avoided entering the territory of faith and morals on principle.[2]

3. The principle of certainty is contained in the "*cogito, ergo sum*," "I think, therefore I am: I am a thinking being (mind)." We must carefully separate the numerous objections which were urged against this particular point. As short as it is, it includes a series of important and definite assertions, which Descartes deduces from it. The "*cogito ergo sum*," therefore, offers more than one point of attack. From the "I think," taken strictly, follow two inferences: (1) *I*

<hr />

[1] Obj., vii. pp. 444–455, 461–463, 489–504.
[2] Ib., iii. (t. i. pp. 466, 467).   Ib., iv. (t. ii. p. 30).   Ib., v. (t. ii. pp. 91, 92).

am, or *I exist;* (2) *I am thinking,* or *I am mind.* The nature
of the inference is to be carefully considered in three points:
(1) the certainty of one's own existence follows only from
thought, from no other activity; (2) from thought follows
immediately *only* the certainty of one's own thinking nature,
nothing else; (3) this certainty follows from thought (not
mediately, but) *immediately.* It is not a conclusion, but an
immediate or intuitive certainty.

From thence result the following points of attack and
objections: (1) From the "I think" follows, to be sure, the
"I am, or exist," but not "I am mind." (2) The "I am"
by no means follows *only* from my thought, but just as validly
from all my other activities. (3) The "I think, therefore
I am," is an inference, and presupposes what it seeks to
prove so long as its major premise is not proved. It is a
petitio principii, and, as such, has no certainty. Hobbes,
under his own name, advances the first objection; Gassendi
the second; Descartes examines and refutes the third in
considering the objections in the second place.

From the "I think," it unquestionably follows that I am,
and that to my activities or properties those of thought
belong. We can, therefore, without doubt, conclude, I am
thinking, or, I am a thinking being, but not, I am mind, or,
my nature consists in thought: that is converting a property
of a thing into the thing itself. The first proposition is true;
the second absurd. Thought is as little a for-itself-existing
being as *taking a walk* is. One can just as well say, "I go
a-walking: there my nature consists in walking."[1] It is a
reasonable inference from the "I think," that I am a thinking being; i.e., a subject to whom, among other properties
or activities, those of thought belong. Plainly the activity
cannot also be the subject of the activity: thought cannot
also be the subject of thought. I can, indeed, say, I think
that I have thought; i.e., I remember what a particular
kind of thought is. But it is nonsense to say, "Thought

[1] Obj., iii. (t. i. pp. 468, 469).

thinks;" or, "I think that I think;" for this would lead to an endless regress, and make all thought impossible, since the subject of the thought would never attain to existence. Nothing is more evident than the distinction between subject and activity, thing and property. As the subject of thought, therefore, I am a being different from thought; i.e., *I am a body which thinks.* According to this conclusion, Cartesianism is overthrown, and sensualistic materialism enthroned in its stead.[1] Mind consists in the thinking activity of body; thought, in the union of words which denote conceptions or imaginations; and these are produced by the motion of, and impressions upon, the organs of the body. All ideas, therefore, have their origin in sense, and mind is nothing independent of body. Clear and obscure conceptions are nothing else than clear and obscure *impressions.* We see a near object distinctly; a distant one, indistinctly. Assisted by instruments, we see clearly what appears either indistinct or not at all to the unaided eye. The astronomical conception of the heavenly bodies sustains the same relation to the ordinary conception that telescopic vision does to unassisted vision, that distinct impressions do to indistinct. Both kinds of conception are sensible: all our conceptions are *only* sensible. So-called universal concepts are abstracted from our impressions, and have no real, but only a nominal, existence. What we perceive by the senses are not things themselves, but their properties. The concept of substance is, therefore, a conception without an object. We receive all our impressions from without: therefore, there are no innate ideas, no special dowry of the mind, which man has in comparison with the other beings of the world. Therefore he is different from animals only in degree, but not in kind.[2]

4. My thought is *not the only activity* from which the certainty follows that I am. To be sure, this certainty follows from the activity of my thought, but not because this ac-

---

[1] Obj., iii. (t. i. pp. 469, 470, 475). Cf. Obj., vi. (t. ii. pp. 318, 319).

[2] Ib., iii. (t. i. pp. 476, 477, 483, 485–487). Cf. Obj., vi. (t. ii. pp. 320, 321).

tivity is thought, but because this thought is my activity. The sentence, "I go a-walking, therefore I am," is just as certain as the "*cogito ergo sum.*"[1] If my being consisted in thought, I could not be without thought a moment: I should be thinking even in the embryonic state and in lethargic sleep. We cannot think without consciousness, but we can indeed exist without it: therefore our being and our thought are in no way identical.[2]

Moreover, according to Gassendi, the proposition of certainty does not give us what we had a right to expect in view of the promises of Descartes; viz., the most accurate and profound knowledge of our own nature. What new and particular thing do we learn when we ascertain that we are thinking beings? We learn what we have known for a long time. If we are promised fundamental instruction concerning the nature of wine, we expect an accurate chemical analysis of its constituents, but not the declaration that it is a fluid. We have the property of thought, as wine has that of fluidity. What further? Such a commonplace is the Cartesian proposition of certainty.[3]

5. But this proposition is not even certain; for, (1) according to the philosopher's own declaration, it depends upon our certainty of the existence of God, and is, therefore, exposed to all the doubts of the validity of the proofs of his existence (an objection which is repeated at different times); and (2) it is a *conclusion* which depends upon an unproved assumption. The complete syllogism is, "All thinking beings are, or exist: I think, therefore I am." Now, to prove the major premise, the truth of the conclusion must be assumed. This syllogism, therefore, is not merely a *petitio principii*, but also a *circulus vitiosus*, as the logicians say. These objections would be pertinent *if* the proposition of certainty were a syllogism. We await Descartes' reply.[4]

---

[1] Obj., v. (t. ii. p. 93. Cf. p. 248; t. i. pp. 451, 452).
[2] Ib., v. (t. ii. pp. 101, 102).		[3] Ib., v. (t. ii. pp. 122, 123).
[4] Ib., ii. (t. i. pp. 403, 404).

6. The final ground of all certainty and knowledge, according to Descartes, is the idea of God in us, whose cause can only be God himself. That, in brief, is the ontological argument whose profound basis, in the system of Descartes, we have become acquainted with in detail, and which none of his opponents knew how to appreciate. Here the objections are massed. To separate the points of attack, we must distinguish the points which the proof includes. It requires (1) that the principle of causality be applicable also to ideas; (2) that, in particular, the idea of God requires a real cause; (3) that this idea be innate; (4) that from this innate idea the reality of God be immediately evident; (5) that God be the cause of himself, and, therefore, infinite. Each of these propositions offers a point of attack.

Ideas are thought-things which have only a nominal existence. They require, therefore, no real or active causes, and, least of all, such as contain more "objective reality" than they themselves. Caterus laid special emphasis upon this objection to Cartesianism.[1]

The idea of God is not innate; for if it were, it would be always present, even in sleep. But many do not have it at all, none always. The cause of it, therefore, cannot be God. We are its cause: the idea of God is our creation; the work of the human understanding, which forms the conception of a perfect and infinite being by increasing the perfections with which it is acquainted, widening the limits, and abstracting from the imperfections. It is not true that the conception of an infinite being must be caused by this being. The infinite universe is not also the cause of our conception of it; but we attain to this idea by gradually enlarging our at first limited idea of the world, and at last extending it to the immeasurable.[2]

Our idea of God, therefore, contains nothing of the reality

---

[1] Obj., i. (t. i. pp. 355, 356).

[2] Ib., ii. (t. i. pp. 400-402). Ib., iii. (t. i. pp. 479, 480). Ib., v. (t. ii. pp. 139, 140).

of God. Nor can the existence of God be proved by the existence of things, since the assumption of a last or first cause is groundless; for the causal nexus is infinite, and we are not justified in setting limits to it. But even granting that there is a being which is cause of itself, its infinitude would in no way follow from this unconditionedness (aseity).[1]

The existence of God does not follow from the idea of God, still less, *clearly* and *distinctly*. For in that case the idea must, first of all, be clear and distinct. But it is the opposite, even according to Descartes' own doctrine; for we are finite and imperfect beings, while God is infinite and perfect. If the idea of God were the ground of all certainty, the fact that atheists regard their mathematical knowledge as indubitable would be incomprehensible.[2]

The idea of God is neither innate, nor is it clear and distinct. Hobbes went farther, and even disputed its possibility, maintaining that we have no faculty with which to form such an idea, and that it has no origin or object. Since it is not innate, it must have been abstracted from things. Now, it cannot be abstracted from bodies, also not from the presentation of the soul, since we have no definite presentation of the soul. The object of the idea of God must be an infinite substance, which excels all others in reality; but of substance in general we have no conception, and a thing that is more a thing than all others is unthinkable. All thought consists in inferring and deducing: the unconditioned is, therefore, inconceivable, and all investigations concerning it are useless. Now, the entire cogency of the Cartesian arguments rests upon the idea of God in us. If God did not in truth exist, the idea of God could not be in us. The existence of this idea, says Hobbes, is unproved, unprovable, and, in my opinion, impossible. Descartes, therefore, has not proved the existence of God, and, still less, the creation.[3]

[1] Obj., i. (t. i. pp. 359, 360). Ib., v. (t. ii. pp. 139–142).
[2] Ib., v. (t. ii. pp. 174, 175). Ib., vi. (t. ii. pp. 321, 322).
[3] Ib., iii. (t. i. pp. 484, 493).

7. If there is no rational knowledge whatever of God, we cannot base upon it the possibility of a knowledge of things. Descartes bases the knowledge of things upon the *veracity* of God, upon the impossibility of deception by God. Now, granting the knowledge of God, *this* inference is false, both in the light of revelation and in that of reason. Either the Bible contains that which is unworthy of belief, or there are deceptions which God has willed. He blinded Pharaoh, and caused the prophets to foretell things which did not come to pass: both the Old and New Testament teach that we wander in darkness. Further, on rational grounds it is impossible to see why deception is incompatible with the nature of God, or why it is unworthy of him. There are wholesome deceptions made with the best and wisest intention. Thus, parents deceive their children, and physicians the sick.[1]

That God *cannot* be the cause of our errors is accordingly to be rejected. Descartes explained error by the freedom of the will, and regarded it as the fault of the will. It was to be expected that theologians would raise objections against this fault, and sensualists against this freedom. If every act of belief on confused grounds is a fault, a perversion and misuse of the will, the *conversions* to Christianity have taken place on indefensible grounds, very few of which have resulted from the clearest and most certain conviction, and the mission of the Church is gone. Descartes regards the indifference of the will, i.e., completely indeterminate choice, as the lowest degree of freedom, while the highest is the will illuminated or determined by the perceptions of reason. Arbitrariness is incompatible with wisdom that is absolutely free: this is bound by the necessity of thought and the laws of reason, and there is in God no arbitrariness in opposition to it, — a doctrine very characteristic of the Cartesian standpoint, but very questionable from that of theology.[2]

[1] Obj., ii. (t. i. pp. 404-406). Ib., vi. (t. ii. pp. 322-324). Ib., iii. (t. i. pp. 501, 502).

[2] Ib., ii. (t. i. p. 406). Ib., vi. (t. ii. pp. 324, 325).

Sensualists cannot admit a faculty independent of all physical conditions, and, therefore, they dispute the freedom of
the will.   It has always been combated, never proved, and,
by the most strictly orthodox Calvinists, completely denied.
Even Hobbes appealed in this case to the Calvinists.   Freedom is not merely unproved, but unprovable, like every other
unconditioned.   It is, on physical grounds, impossible.   To
deduce error from the freedom of the will is to explain the
known by the unknown and the unknowable, the natural by
the impossible.   Error is rather the natural and easily to be
comprehended consequence of our limited faculty of knowledge.[1]

8. The Cartesian dualism follows from the certainty of
self illuminated by the idea of God; the perception that
mind and body are substances, and, indeed, completely
opposed to each other.   From thence is evident the independence of the mind of the body.   All his opponents, however they differ in their other opinions, *attack* this point.
The sensualists and theologians contest this doctrine in
common: their arguments are similar, though their motives
are different.   Sensualists wish to maintain the dependence
of the mind upon the body, because they wish to make the
body supreme.   Theologians are interested in opposing the
freedom and independence of the mind, because, with them,
the absolute dependence of human beings is of the utmost
importance.   The weakness of body is evident enough.   If
our mental nature is united with that of the body, and depends upon it, the frailty and weakness of man are made out
as the system of theology requires.   By their participation in
the nature of bodies, finite spirits are distinguished from God.
According to the opinion of the Church Fathers and the
Platonists, even spirits of a higher order have bodies; and accordingly the Lateran Council permitted angels to be represented by paintings.   So much the less has the human mind
a right to imagine that it is independent of body.   But even

---

[1] Obj., lii. (t. i. pp. 494, 495).   Ib , v. (t. ii. pp. 186-192).

if the difference of the two substances were sufficiently proved, the *immortality* of the soul is not yet proved. For, if the soul is immaterial, it can be destroyed by the divine omnipotence. Besides, such an argument would prove too much. For the souls of animals, since they are likewise different from body, would have to be immortal according to that reasoning, which it occurs to no one to maintain. To be sure, Descartes denies that animals have souls, declaring that they are nothing but machines; but this opinion is so utterly at variance with experience, that it is difficult to convince any one of it.[1]

Moreover, according to Arnauld, the proof that is said to be evident from the opposition between body and mind will not stand the test of a careful examination. What can be thought without the concept of another being, is held to be able to exist without the existence of that being, and, therefore, to be independent of it: thus it is with the concept of mind in relation to that of body, and conversely. This inference from idea to existence is incorrect, since it proves too much. I can conceive a right-angled triangle without knowledge of the Pythagorean proposition: I can conceive length without breadth, and this without depth. Nevertheless, there are no right-angled triangles without the properties which Pythagoras proved, and there is in reality no one dimension without the rest. That we can form the concept of mind clearly and distinctly without that of body, is therefore no proof of the immaterial existence of mind. Further, the opposition of substances cannot be inferred from that of their attributes (thought and extension), the concepts of which must necessarily be separated. What is true of thought is not for that reason just as true of mind; for, if it were, the nature of the latter would be identical with the conscious activity of thought, and all obscure and unconscious states of mind, as in embryonic life and sleep, would be impossible. Expe-

[1] Obj., vi. (t. ii. pp. 319, 320). Ib., ii. (t. i. pp. 408, 409). Ib., iv. (t. ii. pp. 15-16).

rience teaches us that the life of our souls is influenced by
our bodily states, that our mental development goes hand in
hand with that of the body, and that sound mental activity
is hindered by the obstruction of physical causes. The mind
slumbers in childhood: it is lost in madness. Facts like
these bear testimony against the purely spiritual nature of
man, and one does not need to be a materialist to find them
worthy of attention.[1]

No more detailed account is necessary to show how sensualists, on the ground of these and similar facts, affirm the
complete dependence of the mind upon the body, reject the
dualism of Descartes, and admit only a difference of degree
between man and the rest of the animal creation.

II. DESCARTES' REPLIES.

Since we have had in mind, and given due consideration
to, Descartes' replies to these objections, in our exposition of
his system, it is not to be expected that we shall now begin
to have a new perception of the purport and meaning of his
doctrine. If even the philosopher himself in most cases
could do nothing else in opposing the objections than return
to the " Meditations," and since the work was so mature and
thoroughly thought out that he found nothing to correct, his
explanations were fundamentally only circumlocutions and
repetitions of what he had already said. To avoid such
repetitions, we shall here proceed more briefly than in the
objections, noticing only those cardinal points of the system
which have always been subject to misunderstandings, though
they certainly have not justified them. They all relate to
the principle of certainty. This is completely misunderstood
when it is attempted to interpret it syllogistically, to construe
it materialistically, to prove it sensualistically, to nullify it
sceptically. As in all these cases, especially the three latter,
the misunderstandings, however gross, have a plausibility
that can easily deceive, we will hear how Descartes defends

[1] Obj. iv. (t. ii. pp. 11-15, 30).

the *immediate* certainty of his principle, whose first and immediate object is only our mental existence, whose ground is only the activity of our thought, and whose discovery proceeds from the *certainty of doubt* (not from its uncertainty).

1. *Reply to the Objection that the Proof is Syllogistic.* — The principle of the whole doctrine consists in our certainty of ourselves and of God, in our certainty of self illuminated by the idea of God, or, if one prefers this way of stating it, in the proof of our mental existence and that of God. We have shown in detail how closely and directly these two certainties are connected, and express the same thing in different relations.[1] What, therefore, is true of one, is true, also, of the other. Either they are both immediately, or both mediately, certain: in the latter case they are syllogistically proved; i.e., they remain unproved, and therefore invalid. When the Cartesian proof of God, especially the ontological form of it, is understood syllogistically, it is identical with the scholastic one, and is exposed to all the objections which the latter properly calls forth. Descartes corrects this misunderstanding in his reply to the objections of Caterus, showing in what his ontological argument differs from that of Thomas (he should have said Anselm); that his proof is not an inference, but an immediate certainty, since in the idea of God his existence is clearly and distinctly apprehended without middle terms. The same is true of the certainty of ourselves, which in like manner is not reached syllogistically or through middle terms, but is immediately or intuitively evident. Descartes makes that declaration in his reply to the second objections. "If any one says, 'I think, therefore I am or exist,' he does not infer existence from thought by means of a syllogism, but apprehends it as something immediately certain through the simple intuition of the mind."[1]

If one understands the doctrine of Descartes, the above-

[1] See book ii. chap. iv. pp. 354–359.

[2] Rép. aux Obj., i. (t. i. pp. 388–395). Ib., ii. (p. 427).

mentioned misconceptions seem so unintelligible as to be ridiculous. The Cartesian certainty of self rests not on this or that theorem, but on the consciousness of our intellectual imperfection, which must be evident by means of the *idea* of intellectual perfection. This idea, since it precedes and conditions our consciousness, is necessarily independent of the latter, and of an original character; i.e., it is not merely an idea, but *God.* If I am completely confused in myself and in all my thoughts, and declare my uncertainty with perfect conviction, one ought not to expect that any one will inquire upon what syllogism my conviction rests. He who does, knows not of what I speak. He knows neither the uncertainty in which I find myself, nor still less my incontestable certainty. The above objections to the doctrine of Descartes are based upon this kind of utter ignorance.

2. *Reply to the Materialistic and Sensualistic Objections.* — From the truth of self-certainty, the origin and depth of which Hobbes utterly failed to see, he deduced materialism. If I am a thinking being, I distinguish myself from thought as the subject from its property or activity: I am, therefore, a being different from thought; i.e., a body which thinks. Thought, therefore, is a bodily activity, or a kind of motion. The facts of experience prove that it is so. These everywhere show that the so-called mental life depends upon the states, impressions, and processes of the bodily nature; is, therefore, nothing except a phenomenon and effect of the body.

Descartes discusses these thoroughly superficial and grossly sophistical objections, which were unworthy of a Hobbes, as lightly and as slightingly as they deserved. Nothing is easier than to bring any two things into the relation of subject and predicate, and to declare that that must be different from this. We can then reverse the proposition, and prove the contrary. We can thus make the heavens the earth, and the earth the heavens; the mind the body, and, just as validly, the body the mind. Such a mode of proof has no validity at all, and is opposed to all sound logic and to the common use of language.[1]

Gassendi attempted to lessen the value of Descartes' certainty of self by maintaining that it can be proved sensualistically. That we are, is evident, not merely from our thought, but just as clearly from any other of our activities. "*Ambulo ergo sum*" must be accepted with the same right as "*cogito ergo sum.*" The proposition, "I go a-walking, therefore I am," is, according to Gassendi, just as certain as "I think, therefore I am." Descartes himself uses this example, in order to illustrate Gassendi's objection. Of all objections, *this*, to the common consciousness, is most plausible; and if it is well taken, the Cartesian principle of certainty is lost.

From every activity which I conceive, it follows, with indubitable certainty, that I am. The more particular determinations of the activity are completely incidental and indifferent. That *I conceive them* is the important matter, and the only ground upon which that certainty is evident. To conceive an activity, or be conscious of it, is *to think*. From every activity, so far as I conceive or think it, it follows that I am. If I do not conceive it, nothing at all follows for my consciousness. The taking a walk is a state of motion of the human body. It does not follow from thence that I am. Not till I conceive this body, and its state of motion as mine, can I say, "I take a walk." It is possible that this motion does not really exist; that it exists only in imagination or in dreams; that I do not take a walk; but it is impossible that I, who have this imagination, am not. The certainty, therefore, of my own existence does not follow from my motion, but *only* from my conception of it; i.e., from my thought. It makes no difference *what* I conceive, whether the object which I conceive is my own walking or that of another. It may be imaginary in both cases; but *that* I conceive them is certain, and from thence alone follows the certainty of my existence. "I think, therefore I am," is,

[1] Rép. aux Obj., iii. (t. i. pp. 472–474, 476–478).

therefore, indisputable. Gassendi, in opposing this proposition, was laboring under a twofold misconception, and involved in a double error. He did not see, that, abstracting
from my conception and my consciousness, there is no activity at all which I could denote as *mine*. Still less did he
see that it may be the activity of any other, or any object
whatever, *from the conception of which in me* the certainty of
my existence is immediately evident; that, therefore, in all
cases, my conception or thought is the only ground of certainty.[1]

3. *Reply to the Objection that Doubt is Nihilistic.* — The
proposition of self-certainty was exposed to a threefold attack.
Some regarded it as syllogistic, and therefore unproved.
Hobbes admitted its validity, but only of our bodily existence; Gassendi also, but on the ground of all our activities without distinction. All these objections to the
foundations of Descartes' doctrine are unsupported. We
have still to consider Bourdin's objection, who declared the
inference of certainty completely invalid and impossible,
since it depends on doubt.

We have already noticed those cheap dialectic arts by
means of which the author of the seventh objections attempted to disprove the doctrine of Descartes, by a *reductio
ad absurdum*, to prevent each of its steps, and, finally, as its
logical result, to deduce the proposition that nothing whatever is. Let us leave its scholastic buffoonery and caprioles
unnoticed, and attend merely to the principle with which the
controversial man sought to break down and overthrow
the new doctrine. The strength of the whole polemic lies in
this proposition: If the reality of all things is doubted, their
non-reality must be asserted; or, to speak more in Bourdin's
manner, If all things are doubtful, nothing exists in reality.
Two misconceptions, which, in opposition to the doctrine of
Descartes, we must characterize as a crude lack of understanding, lie at the foundation of this conception. The

---

[1] Rép. aux Obj., v. (t. ii. pp. 247, 248).

opponent regards "to be doubtful" and "to be unreal" (1)
as identical in meaning and (2) a state of things! In his
understanding, therefore, the Cartesian assertion, "I doubt
all things," is changed into, "There are no real things at
all."

To be doubtful, so far as it relates to an object, is *possibly*
not to be. When we doubt an object, or the reality of a
thing, we do not deny it, but leave it an open question
whether the thing is, or not, whether it is so, or otherwise.
"To be doubtful" is not a predicate which belongs to an
object in the same manner as extension, motion, rest, to
body. "Something is doubtful" means "It is doubtful to
me:" I doubt or am uncertain whether the thing is, or
not, whether it is so, or otherwise." "To be doubtful"
is, therefore, not a state of things, but merely of our
thought: it is the state of our uncertainty. The opposite of it is my certainty, and this exists only in my imagination or in truth. In the former case, it is self-delusion;
in the latter, knowledge. The path to truth leads not
through our self-delusion, but through our knowledge of it;
i.e., through the doubt of our own pretended or imaginary
certainty. This path Descartes trod, and therein consists his
doubt and its method. Either we must deny that we are
involved in self-delusion, which would be the height of self-
blindness, or we must be aware of this state, and fall into the
very same doubt which Descartes experienced and made typical. This doubt is the only protection against self-delusion,
and is unavoidable. It is as old as the experience that we
are involved in delusion, and it becomes new as often as this
experience is repeated; and this is the case in every man who
earnestly desires truth. Hobbes's objection, therefore, that
doubt is no modern discovery, did not make the least impression on our philosopher. New, or not, replied Descartes, it is
necessary, since I desire truth.[1] Least of all could Bourdin,
in his confident self-sufficiency, conceive the earnestness and

[1] Rép. aux Obj., iii. (t. i. p. 467).

depth of the Cartesian doubt. Nothing follows more clearly
and evidently from this doubt than self-certainty, because
it is already contained in it. It is not asserted that things
are unreal or non-existent, but their existence and properties are uncertain or doubtful. It is not asserted that things
are doubtful or uncertain, but that *I am* uncertain, and
indeed in all things. From "I am uncertain" follows immediately "I am," since it is contained in it.[1]

The necessity of doubt, the truth of self-certainty, the
grounding of the latter by our doubt or thought, — the only
and immediate validity of this ground, therefore the axiom-
atic certainty of our mental existence, — these foundations of
the doctrine of Descartes stand firm and sure, in opposition
to the objections. All of them attack it, but none of them
make the least impression upon it.

How is it with the system itself that rests on these foundations? This question leads us to the last inquiry, to the
examination of the system.

---

[1] Obj., vii. Remarque de Descartes (t. ii. pp. 385-387, 405-412).

CHAPTER XI.

A CRITICAL EXAMINATION OF THE SYSTEM.—UNSOLVED AND NEW PROBLEMS.

I. OBJECT AND METHOD OF THE INQUIRY.

THE criticisms which we have expounded in the foregoing chapter are not only worthy of note historically, but are also significant for the examination of the system to-day. They represent the doctrine of Descartes in the light in which it should be considered and estimated. That both theologians and naturalists opposed the principles of our philosopher, is, of itself, a proof that his system is neither theological nor naturalistic in the opinion of his antagonists. From opposite points of view they attacked the doctrine of rational principles or its metaphysical foundations. The natural light of clear and distinct thought appeared to the theological antagonists doubtful in relation to the ecclesiastical doctrines of faith; to the sensualistic, in relation to the empirical doctrine of nature. Those missed the supernatural light of revelation; these, the natural light of the senses. The light of reason (*la lumière naturelle*) which Descartes followed, falls not down from heaven, and does not proceed from the senses. Theologians regard it as merely natural, and, therefore, as something foreign to their modes of thinking; and sensualists, on the other hand, as not natural, and therefore as something equally foreign to their sensualistic modes of thought. To those, the new doctrine is too naturalistic: to these, it is not naturalistic enough. The one party fears that theology will become naturalized, and thus become disloyal to the Church; the other, that the doctrine of nature will become rationalized, and thus become alienated from experience.

Thus, in spite of their own opposition, the theological mode of thought which proceeds from Augustine and the scholastics, and the sensualistic, which in Gassendi started from Epicurus, and in Hobbes from Bacon, united against Descartes. At the same time, each of the two trends found a congenial side in the new doctrine; and it is a fact well worthy of remark, that, particularly between Descartes and Arnauld, there were points of agreement which both felt as a mental kinship. To none of the authors of the objections did Descartes feel so near: upon the agreement of none did he lay a greater emphasis. He hoped to have so united the theological and naturalistic systems in his doctrine, that they could enter into an alliance in which neither — least of all the theological — should be the loser. It is also true that both are contained in the new system, and not merely externally and artificially joined with each other, but *thought together*, in the mind of our philosopher. Now the question here arises, whether in Descartes' doctrine those tendencies are really united and are compatible which are in conflict with each other outside of the system, and meet in the polemic against it?

We cannot correctly, and from its own point of view, estimate a system by applying to it the measure of foreign opinions, and determining its value accordingly. Those objections with which we have become acquainted furnished an example of such a subjective estimation. Every thoroughly thought-out system, as it comes from the mind of a great philosopher, is in its kind a *whole* that requires to be apprehended and examined as such. It is, therefore, to be inquired whether it has really solved the problem which determines its fundamental thoughts. As necessary as is the problem, so necessary must be the conditions without which the solution cannot be given. These conditions are the principles of the system: the solution of the problem consists in their complete and logical development. To examine a system from its own point of view is, therefore, nothing else than to compare its solution with its problem, its results with its principles, its derivative propositions with those which are fundamental, and see whether it has performed what it intended. If the doctrine of a philosopher is completed and without defect, nothing remains but to recognize and diffuse it, — the task of disciples who regard the work of the master as perfect. To apprehend defects is the business of a searching and progressive examination, which at first assumes neither the correctness of the consequences, still less that of the principles, but only inquires whether *all* the inferences which could be deduced from those principles have actually been drawn. If not, the system is to be completed. Therein consists its *completion*, and this constitutes the proper and first business of a school. The second inquiry penetrates deeper: it relates to the correctness of the consequences; to the harmony of the derivative propositions with those from which they are deduced; to the application of the principles, whose validity is accepted without question: in a word, the question is as to the *logicalness* of the solution. If there are defects in this respect, the consequences must be so changed and corrected as to bring them in perfect harmony with the principles. In this consists the critical advance of the doctrine, — a work of the progressive school. When the system has been completed and corrected in the sense just explained, no more can be done while the principles remain undisputed. But if, in spite of it, the problem is not yet solved, the fault lies in the principles, — in the incongruity between the problem and the principles; in their lack of comprehensiveness. It is evident that the problems the system attempts to solve cannot be solved by means of its principles. To this the third inquiry leads, penetrating to the heart of the matter. It no longer concerns the completeness and correctness of the derivative principles, but that of those from which they are derived: it makes the really critical test which determines

whether the calculation is correct or not. Defects in inferences are secondary: those in fundamental principles, on
the other hand, are primary. If the calculation is not correct, defects of a fundamental character are discovered in the
system. The principles must now be changed, corrected, and
made conformable to the problem to be solved. In this consists the *transformation* of the system, and this transcends
the sphere of the school in the narrower sense.

Progressive stages can be distinguished, even in the transformation of a system; and we will now call attention to
the most important of them. In the first, which makes the
beginning, the fundamental principles are *partly* transformed,
in order to be brought into harmony with the system. The
extremest limits of the school are then reached, and it may
be questioned whether this advance belongs to the school.
If now, in spite of this change in the principles of the system,
the problem cannot be solved, we must advance to the second stage, to the *entire* transformation of the system; and
there is now no longer a question that the old school is completely abandoned. If the required goal is not reached on
the new road, it is evident that the fault, the error as it were,
in the calculation, must be sought not merely in the principles, but in the problem itself, in the mode in which it is put,
in the terms of the calculation as it were. The problem
must then be made soluble by a complete rectification, by a
change in the fundamental question. This transformation is
a *revolution* or *epoch*.

The rightly progressive examination of a great and epoch-
making system, from its own point of view, accordingly consists in the views which are immediately deduced from the
system, which take its direction, — first developing, then
correcting, and finally transforming it. While the problem
continues to be conceived in the form in which it has been
entertained up to this time, the principles are transformed,
at first partly, then completely. Finally, the problem itself
is transformed, the authority of the whole of the philosophy

of the past is overthrown, and a new epoch created. With this method of examining a system from its own point of view, progressing from question to question, coincides, as we see, the *course of the historical development* of philosophy itself.

The doctrine of Descartes is such a great and epoch-making system, to which all those stages of criticism and of progressing historical development can be referred. We touch upon them here by way of illustration, since they are expounded in detail hereafter. Thus, the first disciples of Descartes, men like Reneri and Regius (the latter in his earliest period), carefully unfold the principles. Geulincx and Malebranche make further developments. Spinoza affects their partial, and Leibnitz their total, transformation; while Kant completely demolishes them, and lays the foundations of a new epoch.

II. PRINCIPAL CRITICAL QUESTIONS.

In the light of reason, or of clear and distinct thought, Descartes had apprehended the reality of God as well as that of minds and bodies, their dependence upon God as well as their independence of each other. "Precisely in this consists the nature of substances, that they exclude each other." God is the infinite substance, minds and bodies are finite: those are thinking, these are extended, substances. There exists, accordingly, in our system a double and radical dualism: (1) the opposition between God and the world, and (2) within the world, between mind and bodies, from which that between men and animals necessarily follows.

This doctrine affirms the substantiality of God in distinction from the world, the substantiality of the world in distinction from God. In the first affirmation consists its *theological* character; in the second, its *naturalistic*. That God, according to Descartes, is the absolute, powerful Will, who illuminated minds, moved bodies, created and preserved all things, won the approval of the theologians, while the natural light of reason and the thereby evident substantiality of things was an object of their doubts. The nature of things was divided in the opposition between minds and bodies. If our system admitted nothing but the nature of things as real, it would be exclusively naturalistic. It would be materialistic if it affirmed only the substantiality of body. But its naturalism is limited by the validity which it concedes to the concept of God, since it regards things as depending upon the will of God, and limits materialism by the validity it concedes to the concept of mind, since it opposes mind to, and declares it independent of, matter. The materialists are, therefore, limited and repelled on two sides, and agree with Descartes only in this, that he affirms, also, the substantiality of matter, and, in consequence of it, explains the world by purely mechanical laws.

The same principle which forms the central point of the whole doctrine decides its twofold dualism. It advances through doubt to self-certainty, and thence to the knowledge of God and of body. From our self-certainty is immediately evident the independence or substantiality of mind, its difference of essence from God and bodies, therefore the opposition, both between finite and infinite, and between thinking and extended being. The dualistic character of the system is required by its principle, and is, therefore, fundamental. We must now inquire whether these dualistic principles are in harmony with the problem, whether all derivative propositions are consistent with those principles; i.e., whether the system itself does not teach that which opposes the dualism between God and the world, mind and body, man and animal? These questions relate to the principal critical points.

1. *The Dualistic System of Knowledge.* — Since, according to Descartes, substances mutually exclude, and are completely independent of, each other, there exists between them neither mutual nor one-sided dependence, neither reciprocal action nor causality, therefore no kind of community or connec-

tion. The problem of knowledge requires the universal connection of things, dualism their separation. Dualism, therefore, is in conflict with the problem which it claimed to solve, or that dualistic system of knowledge is involved in a contradiction with itself. The method of Descartes aimed to be (it is his own figure) the thread of Ariadne, the guiding principle, to lead knowledge step by step by a continuous and sure path through the labyrinth of the universe. Now, in more than one place the path of knowledge is severed by the yawing chasm of dualism. From this it is evident that the doctrine of Descartes cannot solve its problem by means of its principles, that the range of the problem of knowledge extends farther than that of the system.

2. *Dualism between God and the World.* — Were God in truth separate from things, and separated as the concept of substance and the dualistic doctrine demand, there could be no kind of connection between them, and there would be no possibility of the idea of God in minds, nor of motion and rest in bodies: those could not be illuminated, these could not be moved, by God. Our idea of God is according to the philosopher's own and necessary declaration, the effect, activity, existence of God in us. In like manner, the original state of motion and rest in the world of bodies is the act of the divine Will. Minds and bodies, accordingly, and, therefore, finite things in general, are dependent upon God, hence not substances in the strict sense of the word.

Descartes himself says it. The substantiality of God is one thing, that of things another: strictly speaking, only the first is to be accepted, not the second. Things are *not* substances in reference to God. Without God, minds are in darkness, so unilluminated that they are not even aware of their own imperfection, for only the idea of the perfect illuminates the imperfect: without the idea of God (without God), there is in minds no doubt, therefore no certainty of self, from which alone our substantiality is evident. With-

out God, there is in bodies neither motion nor rest. Without him, therefore, both minds and bodies, therefore finite
things in general, are as good as non-existent. They are
not merely dependent upon God, but even exist only through
him: they are his effects, he their cause. The more emphatically the substantiality of God is affirmed, so. much
the less can it be predicated of things, so much the more
does the independence of the world lose in importance,
until at last it has none at all. To the absolute independence of God correspond only the absolute dependence and
non-reality of things. They are creatures of God: the
concept of substance is transformed into that of *creature*.
To say both at the same time, Descartes calls things "*created
substances*," — which does not reconcile, or even conceal, the
contradiction, but openly declares it. The concept of a
created substance is a *contradictio* in *adjecto;* since by substance, according to the philosopher's own declaration, a
thing must be understood, that requires no other for its
existence, while the word creature denotes a being that can
neither exist nor be thought without the will of God.
And not merely for their existence, but also for their conservation, are things held to require the will and creative
power of God. Because they are not in and of themselves,
they also cannot be preserved by their own power. Descartes, therefore, with Augustine calls the conservation of
the world a continual creation (*creatio continua*). Finite
substances are, therefore, not merely in certain respects
dependent, and lacking in substantiality, they are in *every
respect*. Accurately speaking, there are no longer three
substances, but in truth but one: *God is the only substance.*
Descartes himself draws this inference, which is irreconcilable with his dualistic system of knowledge. "By substance
is only to be understood such a being as requires no other
for its existence. This independence can be conceived of
but *one* being; that is, of God. All other things we can
conceive to exist only under the concourse of God. There

is no meaning of this word which can be understood of God and his creatures in common."[1]

Here, now, is the point in which that principal critical question is decided: does the doctrine of Descartes so unite the theological and naturalistic systems, that each of the two has its rights? The question must at first sight be answered in the negative. The substantiality of things (the world) cannot maintain itself against the substantiality of God. The latter not merely preponderates, but has all of the weight, and finite substances finally lose all independence in comparison with the infinite. In the place of nature, the concepts of creation, of continual creation, step in; and these permit to things no independence of their own whatever. In the doctrine of Descartes, therefore, the theological element seems to gain such absolute supremacy, that Augustinianism in his system appears to gain the victory over naturalism.

But let us not be deceived by appearances. In truth, the God of Augustine is very unlike that of our philosopher. One thing is the ground of the knowledge of the God of Augustine; another, of that of Descartes'. That is evident from the fact of redemption, this from the fact of human self-certainty. The God of Augustine elects the one to happiness, the other to damnation; he enlightens the one, and strikes the other with blindness; he saves whom he will, and has mercy on whom he will; he is absolute sovereign power, and irrational arbitrary will.[2] But in the doctrine of Descartes, God is the cause (real ground) of our self-certainty, which constitutes the principle of knowledge according to the guiding principle of clear and distinct thought. This thought is the natural light within us which *never* deceives us, the source of which is God. To this God, therefore, deception is impossible. If there could be such a deception, human knowledge would be impossible, and the

---

[1] Princ. Phil., i. sec. 51.
[2] See Introduction, chap. iii. p. 51.

fundamental principle shattered on which knowledge rests
in absolute security.   Let us fix this point accurately in our
minds.   There is something which according to the doctrine of our philosopher is impossible, and therefore limits
the divine arbitrary will in the most significant manner.
That is impossible in God which would destroy knowledge
in us, and transform our natural light into a Will-o'-the-
wisp.   Descartes expressly says, "*The first attribute of God
consists in this, that he is absolutely truthful, and the giver of
all light.*   It is, therefore, unreasonable to suppose that he
can ever deceive us, or strictly and positively can be the cause
of the errors to which, as experience shows, we are subject.
To be able to deceive can perhaps by us human beings be
regarded as a mark of mind : *to will* to deceive is always
an indubitable consequence of wickedness, fear, or weakness, and can, therefore, never be asserted of God."[1]

Human knowledge is possible only if it is impossible for
God to deceive us.   But the less God wills and can will
our error, the less he is able to act according to arbitrary
will, but only according to the necessity which is in harmony
with law, and is one with his nature and will.   If he were
arbitrary will acting without grounds, as he is absolute
omnipotence, why should he not will to deceive us according
to his inscrutable determination, and how could we be sure
that he *never will?*   How are we able so to know the incomprehensible will of God as to perceive with absolute certainty that there is one thing he can never will, and that
is to deceive us?   In that case, we see likewise one thing
that he always desires, and that is our knowledge.   The
divine Will is, therefore, knowable, and it would not be if
it were arbitrary will acting without reasons.   It is not
that, since it cannot just as well will our error as our knowledge.   He desires only the latter: his will is, therefore, not
indifferent, but always illuminated by the most distinct
knowledge.   The divine Will is not different from the divine

[1] Princ. Phil., i. sec. 29.

light: the natural light, because it is infallible, is identical
with the divine. Now, in what is the being of God distinguished from that of nature? In one of his most noteworthy sentences, Descartes says, "It is certain that there
must be truth in every thing which nature teaches us.
*For by nature, in general, I understand nothing other than
God himself or the world-order established by God*, and by my
own nature in particular nothing more than the assemblage
of all the powers God has lent to me."[1]

We now see the bearing of the doctrine that God is the
only substance in the teachings of Descartes. The more
the naturalistic element steps into the background, and
vanishes in the presence of the theological, the more the
independence of things is absorbed by the independence of
God: by so much the more in the theological element itself
the naturalistic again appears, by so much the more does the
Cartesian God cease to be a supernatural being, by so much
the more is this concept of God *naturalized* and alienated
to the extremest opposition to the Augustinian. From the
dualistic declaration, "God *and* nature," already arises the
monistic "God *or* nature" (*Deus sive natura*). Decartes
hints at it: Spinoza elevates it to sovereign authority.
While Descartes seems to approach Augustine, he really
draws near Spinoza, and goes so far to meet him that he
actually pronounces the formula which contains Spinozism.
While in his personal inclinations, he feels drawn to the
Fathers of the Church, and to those theologians who were
imbued with Augustinianism, and rejoices in the agreement
which was remarked between his doctrine and Augustinianism, the spirit of his doctrine prepares a trend of thought
which will complete naturalism, and oppose the theological
system in the sharpest manner. The destiny of philosophy
is mightier than the persons through whom it speaks and
works. Descartes is on the road which leads to Spinoza,
while he supposes that he is laying the foundations of the

[1] Méd., vi. (t. I. p. 335).

doctrines of faith more deeply, and calls the doctors of Sorbonne to witness that he has completed a work beneficial to the Church. He is seized by the powers of whom it is said *nolentem trahunt!* The fundamental direction of his system which pierces through, and takes possession of, the theological, is the naturalistic.

Nevertheless, in the doctrine of Descartes, the concept of God as the *only* substance in no way attains to sovereign authority. Dualism protects itself against monism. In the nature of things, something remains behind which belongs peculiarly to them, and constitutes their unassailable fundamental essence. God moves bodies, which of themselves are only movable since they are only extended. Now, extension or matter, according to Descartes' own declaration, cannot be understood by means of that which is immaterial; and since God is not material, matter cannot come from God. It is, therefore, inconsistent with clear and distinct thought, hence also with the nature of God, to treat matter as Descartes does, as something created. We note here the characteristic contradiction which arises: body cannot be a substance in comparison with God; extension cannot be created. The fact that God is the only substance is again put in question, since along with God, extension, the essence of body, comes to be considered as independent of God. God illuminates minds: in this illumination, the natural light of reason, they cannot err. Nevertheless, they do err; and the ground of their error can be no other than they themselves, than their will. By virtue of this will they are beings with powers of their own, beings independent of God.

Two powers accordingly arise in the nature of things which lay claim to independent reality in opposition to the assertion that God is the only substance, — *extension* from the side of body, *will* from that of mind. But as soon as there is something that is independent of God or substantial, the proposition that God is the only substance can no longer be affirmed. Thus, we see in the doctrine of Descartes a series of unsolved problems which have necessarily arisen before us. The dualistic system of knowledge is in conflict with the problem of knowledge, with the solubility of this problem. The dualism between God and the world is in conflict with itself when the substantiality of one is denied. Substantiality is put in question on both sides: things are held to be creatures, and God the only substance; but the nature of things is in conflict with this concept through the independence both of extension and will.

3. *Dualism between Mind and Body.* — If the dualism between God and the world in the system of the philosopher falls into uncertainty, the cleft in the nature of things, on the other hand, the opposition between mind and body, appears in the most decided and certain form. From our self-certainty it followed that we are independent and conscious beings; i.e., thinking substances (minds). As soon as our doubt that there are things without us was removed, these had to be conceived as beings independent of us, in their way self-dependent, i.e., also as substances which can have nothing in common with mind, are, therefore, completely opposed to the latter, or, which is the same thing, as merely extended substances (bodies). Thus, the opposition between mind and body stepped into the full light of clear and distinct thought. Nothing that thinks is extended, nothing that is extended thinks. Thought and extension are different "*toto genere*," as Descartes says in replying to Hobbes. But if *only* the opposition or separation between mind and body can be thought clearly and distinctly, the union of the two must appear unthinkable or impossible in the natural light of reason; and if there is actually such a union, it is in conflict with the foundations of the system, and its explanation puts the doctrine of Descartes to the severest test. We have now to inquire whether the philosopher stands this test without denying his principles.

No objections to a system of knowledge are stronger than

the undeniable facts of nature itself. The negative instance
to the dualism of mind and body is *man*, since he is both
in one. In him mind and body are united, and indeed so
closely, that, according to Descartes' own declaration, they
constitute in a certain manner *one* being.[1] What becomes
of this fact when brought face to face with that clearly and
distinctly apprehended opposition of the two substances?
The philosopher declares, "In truth, mind and body are
completely separated: in the light of reason I see that
there is no community between the two." Human nature
proves the contrary, since it is such a community. According to dualism, natural things are either minds or bodies.
Man is a living proof of the contrary, a natural being who
is both at the same time. The voice of his self-certainty
calls to him, "Thou art mind:" the voice of his natural
impulses and desires calls just as distinctly, "Thou art
body."

After the Princess Elizabeth, Descartes' most receptive
disciple, had studied the "Meditations," the first question,
which she wished Descartes to answer by letter, was, How
is it with the union of soul and body? Descartes replied
that no question was more proper, but his answer to it
was not a sufficient explanation. He did not solve the
problem, but only changed it, and left it unanswered.
Clearly and distinctly one apprehends, he said, merely the
opposition of soul and body, not their union; that the
essence of the mind consists in thought and will, that of
body in extension and its modifications is an object of the
most distinct knowledge, while the union of the two and
their mutual influence is only perceived by means of the
senses. "The human mind is not capable of distinctly
conceiving the difference of essence between soul and body,
and, at the same time, their union, for it would then be
necessary to conceive both as a single being, and at the
same time as two different things, which is a contradic-

---

[1] Méd., vi. (t. i. p. 336).

tion.[1] " This confessed contradiction shows that the solution of the anthropological problem conflicts with the dualism of the principles.

There is no doubt that the complete nature of man consists in a union of mind and body; that, therefore, neither of the two substances, compared with human nature, has the character of completeness. The different relations in which mind and body require to be considered, must be carefully compared, that we may see whether the dualistic principles hold their own. Mind and body are finite substances, beings opposed to each other, constituents of human nature. They are finite in distinction from God, opposed in reference to each other, constituents which mutually complete each other in reference to man. In each of these three relations, the character of their substantiality is modified.

In the first relation, mind and body, as has already been shown, are not really substances, but *creatures (substantiæ creatæ)*. But if they are not substances at all, they cannot be opposed: their dualism is here wrecked on the concept of God, which cancels or invalidates the independence of things. In the second relation, they are *complete* substances (*substantiæ completæ*), since they are opposed to, and mutually exclude, each other. But their mutual exclusion is also reciprocity, therefore a kind of community. If two natures are so related to each other, that each must be conceived as the contrary of the other, neither can be conceived *without* the other. Both are bound together by the character of opposition, which constitutes their essence. The nature of body consists in nothing but extension, *because* it must consist in the complete opposite of thought. Thus, the dualism between mind and body is wrecked on the concept of substance itself, which excludes every relation of substances, therefore even opposition. In the third relation, i.e., in reference to human nature, mind and body are *incomplete* sub-

---

[1] Cf. the first two letters to Elizabeth in the spring of 1643 (t. ix. pp. 123–135). See book i. chap. iv. p. 220.

stances (*substantiæ incompletæ*) : each requires the other for its completion, and is, taken by itself, as little a whole as the hand is the whole human body. Descartes himself uses this comparison. If substance, according to the philosopher's own and often repeated declaration, must be a being requiring no other for its existence, an incomplete being, requiring completion, is *no* substance. Here the substantiality of mental and bodily nature, and therewith their dualism, are wrecked on the concept and fact of man. The contradiction is so apparent that the philosopher himself admits it.

With the doctrine of Descartes', that minds and bodies are independent of and completely separated from each other, the system itself is accordingly in conflict, since it maintains that both are creatures of God, that they are necessarily opposed in the world, and united in man. We must now examine more closely Descartes' solution of his anthropological problem, in the light of this contradiction of concepts.

Man is *one* being, consisting of *two* natures. How is this problem solved? This is the anthropological question from the point of view of Cartesianism. We cannot apprehend and affirm, both at the same time, wrote Descartes to his pupil. If, then, we affirm the one, we must deny the other. And there are passages in which this fundamental dualist, in involuntary acknowledgment of the individuality of our being, affirms the unity of human nature, in such a way that he denotes the union of soul and body in man as a substantial unity (*unio substantialis*), and denies the duality of their natures in such a way, that he transfers the fundamental property of the one to the other, at one time making the soul extended, at another the human body indivisible, and thus expunges the contradiction of attributes.[1]

Nevertheless, the fundamental doctrine of dualism remains the guiding point of view from which the union of the soul and body in man requires to be so explained, that the duality of natures may suffer no injury. They form not in truth,

---

[1] Les passions, i. art. 30.

but only "in a certain manner," *one* being. Out of relation
to man, they are in no way incomplete, since each is sufficient
for itself, and neither requires the other; but human nature
is first complete when they are both united in it, and, therefore, only in this relation has the connotation of incomplete
substances validity, as Descartes emphasizes in his reply to
the fourth objections. What nature has fundamentally separated, remains separated even in union. Fundamentally different substances cannot, therefore, be united, but only
placed together: their union is not unity of nature, but of
composition, not "*unitas naturæ*," but "*unitas compositionis.*"
Man is a compound of mind and body. In this conception,
both the opposition and union of substances are valid, and
only from this point of view can the anthropological question be put. The dualistic system has no other.

The question now arises whether these anthropological
principles are really consistent with the metaphysical,
whether soul and body, as constituents of a compounded
being, still remain those fundamentally different substances
which they are according to the dualistic principles of the
doctrine. Every compounded being is divisible, and, since
only extension can be divided, necessarily extended, therefore bodily or material; and the same holds of each of its
parts. The parts which, through external combination, constitute a whole, preserve their independence with reference
to each other, and remain substances; but only such substances can be brought into composition with each other as
are of the same kind, extended, material. Between the extended and the non-extended, the material and the immaterial, the bodily and the bodiless, substance, no kind of
composition is possible. If man is a compound of soul and
body, the fundamental difference of substances is gone. The
soul must touch the body with which it enters into the
closest union. The point where it touches it, or is connected with it, must be spatial, in a place, bodily: the soul
is now localized, and becomes, in this respect, itself spatial.

It is impossible to see in what respect it remains unspatial or immaterial. Extension is aggressive; if the soul, to speak figuratively, gives it the little finger, it takes the whole hand: if the thinking substance only has its seat anywhere, its independence of, and difference from, the body are lost, not merely in this, but in every, respect. If the soul is localized, even thereby is it also materialized, and made subject to mechanical laws. To these inferences Descartes is necessarily forced, and we have seen how he makes them in his work on the "Passions." He places the soul in the middle of the brain, in the conarion, where it both receives and causes the motion of the animal spirits. There it moves, and is moved by, body. Elsewhere he maintains that only bodies are movable, and, leaving out of consideration the first moving cause, that they are only moved by bodies. If this is true, the soul, since it is movable and moves bodies, must itself be bodily. It has become a material thing, however earnestly we have been assured that it is a thinking substance fundamentally different from body. That duality of natures which dualism asserts, and which is held to remain preserved in composition, is by this very position completely destroyed. That mechanical influence and connection which are said to exist only between bodies, are now asserted between soul and body. The composition of two substances, as the Princess Elizabeth aptly remarked, cannot be thought without the extension and materiality of the soul. The Cartesian anthropology is in conflict, not merely with the dualistic principles of metaphysics, but also with the mechanical laws of natural philosophy. That the quantity of motion in the world remains constant, that action and re-action are equal, — all these fundamental propositions of the doctrine of motion cease to be valid as soon as motions are produced in bodies by immaterial causes.

However the union of the two substances in human nature is thought, whether as unity or composition, in each conception it is in conflict with the fundamental dualism of the system, and necessarily results in the opposite.

4. *Dualism between Men and Animals.* — The union of the two substances is asserted only of human nature: only in *this* respect did Descartes regard them as incomplete beings, as only in relation to God created substances, therefore, in the strict sense of the term, not substances at all. Everywhere else dualism preserves its complete, unimpaired significance. Of all finite beings, man is the *only* one who consists of soul and body: among all living bodies, his is the only one that is animated with a soul. All other things (so far as our knowledge extends) are either minds or bodies: all other bodies, even animals, are soulless, mechanically arranged and moved masses, nothing but machines. This is the difference of essence between men and animals; and it necessarily results from the fundamental dualism of Descartes' doctrine, and is by no means a paradoxical fancy of the philosopher. Soul is mind: the mark by which mind is known is its self-certainty; this forms the single ground of the knowledge of our mental existence. Where self-consciousness is wanting, both mind and soul are wanting. Animals, therefore, are without souls, since they have no self-consciousness; while man, by reason of his self-consciousness, is of a mental nature. The opposition between man and animal is accordingly related to that between mind and body as a particular case to a universal proposition which includes it, or as an inference to its ground. And the proposition that animals are automata, follows from the difference of essence between man and animals.

We have now to inquire whether these inferences are in harmony with the principles, whether that particular case of dualism in the doctrine of Descartes can maintain itself as the system necessarily requires, and how the philosopher comes to terms with the facts which conflict with his doctrine from the side both of human and animal nature. We are now at the point which we have already spoken of,

where we must inquire more closely into this critical question.[1]   Its central point lies in the explanation of those phenomena of life which man has in common with animals, as
sensations and impulses. If Descartes denies passions to
animals because passions are emotions of the mind, still he
cannot deny that they have sensations. How are these to
be explained? Are they mental or bodily, psychical or
mechanical, modes of thought or of motion? In the answer
to this question, Descartes falls into a series of unavoidable
contradictions.

1. All true knowledge, according to the principle of certainty, consists in clear and distinct thought. If our thought
were only clear and distinct, there would be no error : the
will is guilty of error, because it affirms false judgments ;
these arise when we regard our presentations of sense (sensations) as properties of things. Sensations do not make the
error, but, without them, there would be no material out of
which the will could make them. If error consists in false
judgments, sensations consist in presentations of sense,
and these form the matter of judgment. Presentations are
only in mind : they are modes of thought. Sensations,
accordingly, are *psychical*. Among our different ideas are
also the presentations of body. Descartes at first leaves it
an open question, whether we ourselves, or things without
us, cause these ideas ; but he leaves *no* doubt that our sensations are presentations ; he accordingly relates sensations
merely to mind.[2]

2. Involuntarily we relate our sensations to bodies without
us as their cause. If there were no such bodies, our presentation of the world of the senses would be a natural delusion, one, therefore, in the last analysis willed by God
himself; and this, according to Descartes, is impossible.
Therefore, our presentations of the sensations are also caused
by bodies; i.e., they are at the same time bodily motions and

---

[1] See book ii. chap. ix. pp. 412, 413.
[2] Méd., iii. (t. i. pp. 277-279).

impressions, and can only exist in a mind which is united in the closest manner with a body. Now, Descartes relates sensations, not merely to mind, but to man as a being *composed* of soul and body.[1]

3. The share which the body demands in sensations becomes constantly greater and greater, and at last it is so great that the mind loses its part, and they become the complete property of the body. Since man has them in common with animals, they are also processes in the nature of animals, and, as such, merely mechanical, only impressions and motions, without conception or perception. Therewith sensation ceases to be what it is. From the position that animals are nothing but machines, followed the inference that they have *no* sensations, by means of which, in all seriousness, Cartesians attempted to justify vivisection. As soon as we consider sensations as phenomena of animal-human life, they can be referred only to *body*. We observe that the doctrine of Descartes is vacillating in reference to sensations, and is impelled in three different directions by means of its dualistic and anthropological principles. The first of the "Meditations" treats sensations and sense-perceptions as psychical facts, and relates them merely to the mind: the last regards them as anthropological, and relates them to the compound of mind and body. The work on the passions admits nothing but the passions as bodily-psychical events, and relates the sensations and impulses merely to body.[2] Thence results a twofold antinomy, — (1) thesis: sensations as unclear conceptions are modifications of thought, therefore psychical; antithesis: sensations as presentations of sense are not merely psychical, but at the same time bodily; (2) thesis: sensations as human processes are not merely bodily; antithesis: sensations as animal processes are merely bodily and mechanical.

4. If sensation is only mechanical, there can be no talk of

---

[1] Méd., vi. (t. i. pp. 336–340).
[2] Les passions, i. arts. xxiii., xxiv.

perception and feeling, since there are none whatever. What is asserted of animals must be asserted also of men, for the living body in both cases is nothing but a machine, incapable, therefore, of sensation, and that, too, in each of its parts, therefore in the brain. But if there are *no* sensations whatever in the true meaning of the word, then also no presentations of sense, no unclear thoughts, no errors are possible. Thus, the doctrine of Descartes inevitably comes into this characteristic position : it must both affirm and deny the fact of sensations and at the same time ; it is unable to do either. The attempt to explain them becomes involved, therefore, in an antinomy as well as a dilemma. If sensation is affirmed, it must also be affirmed in animals, and they can no longer be regarded as without souls : thus, the difference of essence between man and animal, mind and body, disappears. If sensation is denied, the conceptions of sense, obscure thought, human error, the state of our intellectual perfection, therefore our self-delusion, our doubt, our certainty of self, must also be denied. It is, therefore, as impossible to affirm them as to deny them. In a word, from the stand-point of Descartes' doctrine, the fact of sensation is unexplained and inexplicable.

III. NEW PROBLEMS AND THEIR SOLUTION.

1. *Occasionalism.* — These contradictions, which we have discovered and proved in the doctrine of Descartes, are problems which require to be solved, and which condition the historical development of the system. At first the correction of Cartesianism does not forsake its dualistic principles, but follows their guidance, and determines logical consequences accordingly. If mind and body are by nature opposed to each other, a natural union of the two as it takes place in men cannot be comprehended. It is, therefore, logical to declare it *incomprehensible*. As a matter of fact, it exists. Since it cannot result from natural causes, it is an effect of supernatural causes — can only be the product of divine

power.   Two facts proclaim that soul and body are united in
men, — the fact of our mental-bodily life and our perception
and knowledge of the material world.   In both cases, according to the dualistic principles, we must declare that the
union is possible neither through the mind, nor the body,
nor both together, but only through God.   The soul does
not move the body by means of its will, nor does the body
cause a presentation by means of its impression ; but God
brings it to pass, that the corresponding motion in our organs
follows upon our volition, and the corresponding presentation in our mind, upon the impressions of our senses.   Our
will and its volition are not the cause, but only the *occasion*,
in connection with which, and by reason of the divine activity, the motion that executes our designs takes place in our
bodily organs.   The same is true of our impressions of sense
in relation to ideas.   The *occasion* is not the producing, but
merely the *occasional*, cause (*causa occasionalis*) : the efficient
cause (*causa efficiens*) is, in both cases, God alone.   This
stand-point of Occasionalism, which Geulincx applied to the
anthropological problem, is the first and logical development
of Cartesianism.   If the dualistic principles are valid, the
union of the two substances which takes place in our perception and knowledge of the material world is likewise
incomprehensible.   If mind and body, thought and extension, are completely separated, how comes the idea of extension in our minds ?   This idea can be only in God : therefore
our knowledge of bodies, or our perception of things, is possible only in God.   To this explanation *Malebranche* comes,
in the logical development of the principles of Descartes
which he affirms and maintains.

The problem of man and of human knowledge is not
solved by Occasionalism : on the contrary, every appearance
of a natural explanation is avoided, and the impossibility of
a rational solution maintained.   So long as the opposition
of the two substances is regarded as fundamental, the questions of anthropology cannot be answered ; and the service,

as well as the advance, of Occasionalism consists in having illustrated this position of the anthropological problem.

2. *Spinozism.* — But a rational solution continues to be demanded by the doctrine of Descartes, since its problem is a universal knowledge of things. The union of soul and body requires, therefore, to be considered in the light of reason, and to be comprehended as a necessary effect of natural causes. Now, since the fundamental dualism of the Cartesian doctrine makes such an explanation impossible, all further advance depends upon a *transformation* which at first takes place only partially. The opposition of substances is denied, that of their attributes admitted. If thought and extension are the attributes of opposed substances, the union of soul and body is incomprehensible, and equivalent to a miracle. Those two fundamental attributes of things must be conceived as opposite attributes, not of different substances, but of *one.* This one is the *only* and divine substance: minds and bodies are not independent beings, but modes or effects of God, who, as the eternal and inner cause of all things, is equal to nature. The phrase "*Deus sive natura*" is now accepted as perfectly valid. Since the one divine Substance comprises in itself the opposite attributes of thought and extension, the two forces act as independently of each other as they are necessarily united: all things are effects both of thought and extension; i.e., they are both minds and bodies. These do not *become* united, they *have been* from eternity. They are not united only in men, but in every thing, since of every natural effect must be true what is true of the nature of the universe and its activity; viz., it is thinking and extended. As effects of the same universe, all things are bodies animated with souls, therefore alike in nature, and different only in the degree of their power. Therewith the dualism of substances, which Descartes had maintained, is annulled, — the difference of essence between God and the world, mind and body, man and animal. *Monism* has supplanted dualism;

and thus the naturalistic trend is completed, and raised to universal validity. *Spinoza* develops this trend, logically carrying out the fundamental thought of Descartes' doctrine, and transforming the principles accordingly. This fundamental thought was the logical requirement of a method of thought advancing along an unbroken path to the universal dominion of nature, and the logical outcome of the proposition that there is in truth but one substance. That there is but one substance, and that its attributes are of opposite natures, is the fundamental concept of Spinozism.

3. *Monadology.* — The opposition of attributes was still maintained, — the dualism between thought and extension. The transformation of the Cartesian doctrine by Spinoza was, therefore, only partial. In spite of its monistic character, the foundations of Spinozism still remain *partly* involved in the dualistic system of his master, and are, therefore, still dependent upon him. The next step in the historical development of philosophy must consist in the denial of that opposition of attributes also, and in the *entire* transformation of the principles of Descartes without changing the problem of knowledge.

If there is in truth but one substance, as Descartes had declared, and Spinoza had sought to establish, things are merely modifications of it, therefore absolutely dependent in their nature: no single and finite thing is independent — not even minds, not even the human mind. The self-certainty of the latter is, therefore, fallacious and impossible, since it is the expression and ground of its supposed substantiality. Without independence, there is also no self-certainty; without this, no certainty at all, and no possibility of knowledge. This is the point to which the doctrine of Descartes is immovably anchored. Upon it monism is wrecked; and in order to develop philosophy further, it is first necessary to return to the starting-point of the Cartesian doctrine, and to attempt so to advance from it as to avoid dualism, and fundamentally overcome it. Exactly therein

consists the entire transformation or reformation of philosophy. Substance must be so conceived that the self-certainty
of the human mind is compatible with it — that the independence of individuals is not thereby annulled, but rather
confirmed. Hence the conception of the substantiality of
individual beings : there is not one substance, but an infinite
number. If these substances are again to be opposed to each
other, and to be divided into the two classes of minds and
bodies, we have returned to Cartesianism, and must a second
time make our way through occasionalism to the monism of
Spinoza. The concept of substance is, therefore, so to be
transformed, that the opposition of thought and extension,
that remnant of dualism, may be obliterated. We cannot
get rid of this opposition so long as mind and self-certainty,
thought (conception) and self-conscious activity, are regarded
as identical, and the possibility of *unconscious* activity of
mind or unconscious conceptions is not evident. If there
are obscure conceptions, or if there is an unconscious life of
the soul, the territory and nature of mind are no longer limited
to self-consciousness, and bodies, because they are unconscious, are not, therefore, soulless, and the opposition between
mind and body (man and animal) grows less, and is resolved
into differences of degree, into gradations in the power of
conception, into degrees of development of beings animated
with souls, each of whom constitutes a self-active being or
individuality, determined by the degree of its power. The
concept of substance is transformed into that of individual
active beings or *monads*, the world appears as an ascending
series of such monads, as a system of development similar
to that which Aristotle had taught. The new system of
knowledge dissolved the dualism between thought and extension, mind and body, and thus removed also the opposition
between Descartes and Aristotle, between modern and
ancient philosophy. It so transformed the former that it
restored the latter. This is the stand-point of *Leibnitz* in
his doctrine of monads, a doctrine which dominates the

metaphysics of the eighteenth century, particularly German philosophy and the *Aufklärung*.

Descartes, Spinoza, and Leibnitz are the three greatest-philosophers of modern times before Kant. One can satisfy himself of their importance without any scholarly examination of their works. There are certain fundamental truths which are incontestably evident to every reflecting person from the consideration of his own mind and of the nature of things. There is no opposition in the world greater than that between self-conscious and unconscious beings. This opposition exists, and at first sight it makes no difference whether it is mediate or immediate. When we compare the dark world of body with the illuminated world of consciousness, a chasm yawns before us. Just as evident as is this opposition is the necessity of a universal, conformable to nature, and continuous *connection*, in which each thing proceeds from causes, and these themselves in turn are necessary consequences. The natural belonging-together of things demands such an inseparable connection or causal nexus. We must affirm and unite these fundamental truths: therein consists the third. The contrast in the nature of things is caused by their connection; i.e., the chain of things forms a *development* which rises from the lowest grades of unconscious beings step by step to conscious beings, from the natural world to the moral, from nature to culture, from the lower grades of human culture to the higher. The three fundamental truths are accordingly those of the opposition, the causal connection, and the development, in the nature of things. The first animates the dualism of Descartes; the second, the monism of Spinoza; the third, the harmonizing (evolutionistic) system of our Leibnitz.

4. *Sensualism.* — We have marked the path along which, in logical development of the principles of Descartes, philosophy advanced through the dependent stand-point of the school to a transformation of the metaphysical system. Let us now turn to the opposite tendency of Empiricism, that

we may compare it with Descartes, and see the paths which lead in a straight line from him to his opponents. Thus we shall ascertain the position of his system with reference to the different territories of modern philosophy.

The opposite stand-point of sensualism can be reached by a single step, as it were, from the doctrine of Descartes. If, for example, the nature of mind consists in self-certainty, whatever is in mind must appear in consciousness. Original or innate ideas must, therefore, *always* be present in *every* consciousness. But since, as a matter of fact, they are *not*, it follows that there are no innate ideas, that, therefore, nothing is innate to the mind, that it is on the contrary empty by nature, like a *tabula rosa*, and receives all its ideas merely through perception (outer and inner). In this way *Locke* attempted to refute Descartes in his "Essay on the Human Understanding," and to lay the foundations of sensualism. From sensualism arise two completely antagonistic trends, idealism and materialism. Let us compare both with our philosopher.

5. *Materialism and Idealism.* — According to Descartes, nothing can be accepted as true except that which is indubitably certain : our self-certainty was the ground and type of all knowledge. Now, we are immediately certain of nothing but our conceptions or ideas : these, therefore, are the only objects of our knowledge, our only certainties. Without us, or independent of the conceiving mind, there is nothing real ; no matter, as a thing independent of mind. All objects are only mental, not substances, therefore, not self-dependent beings existing for themselves, but phenomena. Only perceiving or conceiving beings are substantial. There are, therefore, only minds and ideas. This proposition is the fundamental theme which *Berkeley* develops in his *idealism*. We meet Berkeleyanism when we follow in a straight line the direction pointed out by the Cartesian proposition of self-certainty.

In order to maintain the dualism of thinking and extended substances, Descartes conceived the union of the two in man as a compound of mind and body, from which the position that the soul has a place and is material, inevitably followed. There a broad street for materialism was opened in his doctrine. If the soul has its seat in the brain, the materialists can easily conclude that the soul is the brain, thinking is feeling, feeling an activity of the brain — nothing more than a motion of the molecules of the brain. Not merely animals, but men also, are machines, and nothing but machines. We see a path before us which leads straight from Descartes to *La Mettrie*, from the "*cogito ergo sum*" to the "*l'homme machine*," from the French metaphysician of the seventeenth to the French materialism of the eighteenth century. This materialism was indeed a development of English sensualism, but in the Cartesian anthropology it found a point of support which even La Mettrie did not neglect. What is held of man is extended also to the universe. The universe is a machine. This sentence is the theme of the *système de la nature*.

6. *Critical Philosophy.* — But we have already seen how weak is the support which Cartesianism offers to materialism. There is no question, that from the principle of self-certainty, on which the system of our philosopher rests, the logical path leads not to materialism but to idealism. The real and truly objective world can be no other than that which is perceived. Now, we must carefully decide whether our conceptions are voluntary products or necessary results of the intelligence. Even in his first "Meditation," Descartes had declared that there are elementary conceptions which lie at the foundation of all the rest, without which no kind of conception of things is possible. He had laid special emphasis upon *space* and *time* as examples of such fundamental concepts. On further reflection, time appeared as a mere *modus cogitandi*, as a conception of a species which our thought makes and erroneously regards as a property of things themselves. Among the different ideas in our minds,

there is but one, not taking into account our idea of God, whose object Descartes proved, — the idea of things outside of us or of body whose attribute consists in extension or in *space*. Space constitutes the nature of bodies, which, independently of our intelligence, exist as things in themselves. Apart from our idea of God, space is the only one of our fundamental conceptions which expresses the nature of a substance independent of thought. If space were nothing but our conception, the same would be true of matter and the whole world of bodies, and we should then be as immediately certain of external things as of our own existence. Descartes affirms the reality of space because he regards bodies as things in themselves, as the external causes of our presentations of sense, as we are compelled to regard them by the natural instinct of reason. It would be a work of divine deception if it were otherwise. Descartes affirmed that the idea of space is original. His only reason for denying the idealistic character of space is the veracity of God. The same reason ought to have compelled him to accept the sensible qualities of body as properties of things in themselves; yet he declared this opinion the most wanton self-delusion, and insisted, that, in order to apprehend clearly and distinctly what bodies are in themselves, we must strip from the conception of them our modes of thought and sensation. If we withdraw from our conception of things certain conceptions, it is impossible to see why any thing should remain which is fundamentally different from thought. According to Descartes, nothing remains except space or extension. Space, then, must be that conception which we cannot renounce, or which we cannot strip off from our act of conceiving; i.e., the necessary act of our intelligence. If extension and thought are completely opposed to each other, as Descartes asserted, there cannot be in our thought any *idea* of extension, as Malebranche rightly inferred from that dualism. If there is in us the idea of extension, the fundamental conception of space, as Descartes emphatically maintains, thought and extension are not opposed to each other, but extension or space belongs to the nature of thought, to the constitution of our reason : space and the material world in it are, then, nothing but our conception. Now the question no longer is, " How are mind and body as opposite substances united?" but, " How does the mind attain to the conception of space, or how are thought and (external) intuition united?"   To precisely this question did *Kant* reduce the psychological problem of the doctrine of Descartes after he had proved that space is nothing in itself, but is merely our conception, the necessary intuition of our reason. Kant discovered this truth by his critical investigation which tests the natural light of the senses and of thought, but by no means presupposes its infallibility.   This is the turning-point in which not merely the principle of philosophy, but the *problem* itself, is transformed ; and the first inquiry is as to the possibility and conditions of knowledge, and this must be answered before one decides whether the nature of things is knowable and in what it consists.   When Descartes appealed to the veracity of God and of nature in order to make the infallibility of our intelligence dependent upon it, that light of reason in which bodies appeared as things in themselves, he laid the foundations of dogmatic philosophy.

Nevertheless, the problem of the critical philosophy is also contained in his system, and in his first methodological work is stated so clearly that Kant might have appropriated it word for word: "*What is the nature and what are the limits of the human knowledge? is the most important of questions.* Every one who has the least love for truth must once in his life have considered it, since its investigation includes the whole of method, and, as it were, the true organon of knowledge.   Nothing seems to me more absurd than to contend boldly and aimlessly concerning the secrets of nature,

the influences of the stars, and the hidden things of the
future, without having once inquired whether the human
mind is competent to such investigations."

With this view of Kant, for which the doctrine in the passage quoted offers a stand-point so favorable and to which it
is apparently so near, we conclude this book.

BOOK III.

DEVELOPMENT AND MODIFICATION OF THE DOCTRINE OF DESCARTES.

CHAPTER I.

I. CARTESIANISM IN THE NETHERLANDS.

1. *The New Rationalism and its Opponents.*

THE second half of the seventeenth century was the period
when the new doctrine was more and more widely diffused and accepted: it spread from the Netherlands to
Germany, and from France to England and Italy. It was
first and most widely diffused and most generally accepted
in France and the Netherlands, the two homes of the philosopher. The state of culture in these two countries presented
the conditions favorable to its development, and influences
hostile to it, though the character of both in France differed
from that of those in Holland.

The independence of Spain, which the United Netherlands
had achieved by war; their federation; the republican and
Protestant spirit of the people; the culture of powerful cities,
particularly a series of vigorous universities, some of them
recently invigorated, some of them recently founded, and
peculiar in their character, — offered to aspiring Cartesianism
free scope for the exertion of its powers. Some decades
after the first school began to be formed, the origin of which
Descartes himself had seen, there was no university in the
United Netherlands in which the new ideas had not gained
admission. Utrecht, Leyden, Gröningen, and Francker are
particularly to be mentioned. The new doctrine began to
be taught in the University of Utrecht by Reneri and Regius:

in Leyden it reached the zenith of its academic influence, both because of the number and the ability of its adherents; it not only controlled the departments of philosophy and mathematics in those universities, but it strongly influenced theology, physics, and medicine. The first labor of Descartes' disciples consisted in commenting upon and explaining his works, in paraphrasing the most important of them, the contents of which were by some even stated in verse. Then lacunæ were found in the system itself, which required to be filled up, and inferences which needed to be modified and more precisely determined. Therewith began the modification (*Fortbildung*) of the system, the work of its later disciples.

We have seen the attacks which the principles of the new system provoked. They proceeded in part from the ecclesiastico-theological, in part from the philosophical, side — from the old Aristotelian-scholastic and the new sensualistic-materialistic tendencies. The object of the first disciples of Descartes was to compose these differences, and particularly to adapt the new doctrine to the requirements of theology. They followed the example of Descartes in relation to matters of faith. In his system of metaphysics, with its proofs of the existence of God and the immortality of the soul, he had indeed intended to renew the alliance between theology and philosophy, faith and reason, and establish it more firmly than ever before. He hoped to have accomplished what scholasticism had labored for in vain, the rationalization of faith. But his demonstrations by no means disposed of the matter. In open conflict with biblical and ecclesiastical conceptions, he had taught the motion of the earth and the infinity of the universe. It was not enough to make theology rational, according to Descartes. The new theology had to prove its harmony with the *Bible;* and this could only be done by an artificial change in the interpretation of conflicting passages in the Bible, by an assumption that in such cases the biblical language was to be taken figuratively, in a word, by an *allegorical* explanation — the expedient which has always been resorted to whenever the attempt has been made to justify a speculative religious doctrine by the records of revelation. The natural, philological, historical interpretation had to give place to the so-called philosophical, that it might not stand in the way of the harmony which was to be proved. The Cartesian theologians of Leyden, Gröningen, and Francker developed and defended this theory of allegorical interpretation. *Wittich* (1625–1688), who was professor in Leyden, the most celebrated teacher in the university in his time, the leader of the new rationalism in the Netherlands, and later an antagonist of Spinoza, was the most distinguished expounder of this view. In the year 1659, his work, "On the Harmony between the Bible and Cartesianism," appeared. *Amerpool*, in Gröningen, in his "Cartesius Mozaizans" (1669), even sought to prove that the Mosaic account of creation and the Cartesian cosmogony were in harmony by reading the hypothesis of vortices into the first chapter of Genesis. The spirit of Philo seemed to have taken possession of the Cartesians. Their uncritical, extravagant mode of interpretation went so far that *Schotanus*, who put the Cartesian metaphysics in rhyme, compared the six Meditations with the six days of creation! *Coccejus*, a theologian who taught in Leyden at the same time that Wittich was there, independently of the rationalists of the philosophical school, used the allegorical mode of interpretation to show that the New Testament is contained typologically in the Old. The Cartesians, and followers of Coccejus, were, therefore, regarded as allies by their opponents in the Netherlands, as the Cartesians and Jansenists were in France.

With the greatest impetuosity the orthodox representatives of the Church in the Netherlands attacked the new school with its anti-biblical doctrines and its allegorical mode of interpretation, which it charged with treating the foundations of faith in an arbitrary manner, and seeking to subject theology to the claims of reason. They demanded the separation of the two, the formal exclusion of Cartesianism from pulpits and lecturers' chairs. Their leaders were the *Voëtians*, who so influenced the civil authorities, the academic curators, and theological faculties, and excited them against the new doctrine, that enemies appeared against it in Utrecht and Leyden, even in the lifetime of the philosopher.[1] Soon after the death of Descartes the synod of Dort pronounced a prohibition (1656) which was confirmed by the decrees of Delft in the following year.

But these measures accomplished nothing of importance. Their chief result was that those who diffused the doctrine did not acknowledge that they were disciples of Descartes. When *Heerebord*, professor of theology in Leyden, published his "Philosophical Investigations" in the year the decrees of Delft were enacted, he announced himself as an independent thinker, who availed himself of the freedom of faith and of thought in the Netherlands, to speak alike impartially of Aristotle and Thomas, of Patricius, Ramus and Descartes. He declared in the preface that he was the slave of no philosopher, that he proposed to be neither the scourge nor the martyr, neither the "Momus" nor the "Mimus" of the authorities of the schools. *Lambert Velthuysen*, a private individual in Utrecht, and an advocate of the Cartesian rationalism even in its application to the Bible, later an opponent of Spinoza, defended the motion of the earth, and said in the preface of his work that he was not a theologian, but a free man in a free country.[2]

2. *Attempts to Compose Philosophical Differences.* — Some of the physiologists and doctors of the Cartesian school sought to give a sensualistic interpretation to the system, and to give a materialistic character to its explanation of the relation between the soul and body. *Regius* in Utrecht,

---

[1] Cf. book i. chap. vi. p. 250-267.

[2] Francisque Bouillier : Histoire de la philosophie Cartésienne, 3d éd. (Paris, 1868) t. i. chap. xii. pp. 269-271 ; chap. xiii. pp. 283-291.

and *Hooghland* in Leyden, who in his "*Cogitationes*" (1646) so developed the fundamental doctrines of Descartes that the only Cartesianism of his work was the dedication, made this attempt at the same time. Regius had been once praised as a disciple, and Hooghland was the friend, of the philosopher. Descartes regarded Regius as an apostate, and publicly rejected him;[1] Hooghland, as a well-disposed man without a calling to philosophy, and without understanding of his doctrine: he thought his work as immature, and he expressed his disapprobation of it in a letter to the Princess Elizabeth. Descartes would not enter into any kind of compromise with these deserters to those enemies whom he had so forcibly opposed in his replies to the objections of Hobbes and Gassendi. He repudiated every attempt to accommodate his doctrine to sensualism and materialism, though he approved of the efforts to harmonize it with the theology of the Church, and even with the physics of Aristotle. Every agreement between the opposing tendencies of modern philosophy seemed to him the grossest caricature of his own doctrine, though he regarded it as advantageous to it to enter into an alliance with the old authorities long familiar both in Church and the schools. There was no Cartesian sensualism and materialism, but there was a Cartesian theology, and an Aristotelian-Cartesian philosophy of nature ought to be possible. In this way his doctrine increased in influence without losing any thing of its own significance, since its disciples insisted on its principles, and sought to reconcile opposing views to it by a change in their interpretation. Thus, a Cartesian interpretation was put upon the Bible, that Descartes' doctrine might appear biblical; and in like manner, a Cartesian interpretation was given to Aristotle, that his stamp, as it were, might be put upon the doctrine of Descartes, and the old school of physics no longer take umbrage at his doctrine. The most important representative of this trend was *J. Raey*, professor of

---

[1] See book i. chap. vii. pp. 278-280.

medicine in Leyden.   He published in 1654 his "Clavis
philosophiæ naturalis seu introductio ad naturæ contempla-
tionem Aristotelico-Cartesiana:" he sustained the same relation to Aristotle in the interests of theology, that Wittich
did to the Bible in the interests of physics.   Descartes
himself declared that no one was better able to teach the
new doctrine than Raey.   We shall hereafter have occasion
to mention Clauberg among the prominent men of the later
school: Raey was his teacher, Wittich his pupil.

The oppositions were too open and pronounced to be
tempered or denied.   Descartes' theory of knowledge was
necessarily contested by the orthodox, and his doctrine of
mind by the materialists.   According to the former, reason
is independent of authority: according to the latter, mind
is independent of matter.   The Gröningen professor, *Tobias
Andrea* (1604–1674), endeavored to maintain and defend
the system against its common enemies.

3. *Opponents in Lyons.* — Of course those artificial and
transparent attempts to change the interpretation of the old
doctrines were unable to deceive the disciples of the old school
— physicists as little as theologians.   The more the new
doctrine disguised itself, the more dangerous it necessarily
appeared.   Its opponents combined to attack their common
enemy.   In Lyons, the university of Catholic Netherlands,
the physicist *Plempius*, with the approval of the theologians,
led the movement against advancing Cartesianism.   The
papal nuncio in Brussels supported these zealots by admoni-
tions and prohibitions sent to the rector of the university.
The Jesuits took hold of the matter; and the result was,
that on Nov. 20, 1663, the philosophical works of Descartes,
particularly the "Meditations," the declaration against
Regius, the letters to Dinet and Voëtius, and the work
upon the passions, were placed upon the index of forbidden
books.   That even the declaration against Regius' *materialistic interpretation* of Cartesianism was mentioned in this prohibition, is as remarkable as that *Gassendi's* works were not

prohibited. But in view of the objections of Bourdin and the mode of thought of the Jesuits, it is not surprising that they regarded sensualism as rather to be commended than condemned, precisely because of its doctrine of the sensibility. But little resulted from the Romish prohibition in Lyons and Catholic Netherlands, but it was the more effective in France.[1]

II. FRENCH CARTESIANISM.

1. *Ecclesiastico-Political Persecutions.* — The condition of public affairs in France, the natural home of Cartesianism, was unfavorable to its diffusion. Both political and ecclesiastical power were centralized — the French king was the most absolute of monarchs, to whose command the institutions of learning were subject, while he himself was under the influence of the Jesuits. These facts, along with the popularity of Epicureanism which Gassendi and his disciples had revived, and which was promoted by the French spirit of the time, were great obstacles to the progress of Descartes' ideas. Three years after the Romish prohibition, the interment of Descartes' ashes in a church in Paris was forbidden; and after permission had been granted, the funeral ceremony and the erection of a monument were forbidden (1667). The king forbade the doctrine of Descartes to be taught in the *Collége Royal* (1669), in the University of Paris (1671), and that of Angers (1675). The new opinions were forbidden to be diffused, "*car tel est notre bon plaisir.*" The theological faculty in Caen would not confer degrees upon Cartesians (1667), and in the University of Paris the prohibition was renewed twenty years after that royal command which had come through the hands of the archbishop. That such a repetition seemed necessary shows how little the official persecution, to which Descartes' doctrine was exposed in France from 1670 to 1690, succeeded in accomplishing its intended

---

[1] Fr. Bouillier: Hist. de la phil. Cart., i. chap. xii. pp. 270-278 ; chap. xxii. pp. 466, 467.

purpose.   Descartes' doctrine was too strong to be overthrown by those persecutions.

The desire to suppress Cartesianism and to persecute it so
violently came from the Church, and was intensified by the
ecclesiastico-political spirit which then ruled in France.   The
war against Jansenism had been going on for years, and had
already entered the stage which terminated in the complete
overthrow of the Port-Royalists when the persecution of
Cartesianism assumed its intolerant character.   The new
philosophy was regarded as an ally of Jansenism; and
Arnauld, the spokesman of the latter, was a Cartesian.   If
the Jansenists were to be thoroughly overthrown, it would
not do to overlook the Cartesians, and the campaign against
Jansenism must be extended against Cartesianism also.   No
centrifugal tendencies would be tolerated in the French
Church.   From this ecclesiastico-political position, which
Louis XIV. occupied in union with the Jesuits, the disciples
of Descartes appeared in the ranks of the Jansenists, and
behind them the threatening Calvinists and Lutherans.
This was the real motive of all the Jesuitical polemics
against Cartesianism.   Its positions were contested that its
connection with Jansenism might be deduced from its inferences, and from its connection with Jansenism its hostility
to the Church.   The sceptical foundation of the system, the
Cartesian doubt, seemed proof enough that in this point
the unconditional validity of the authority of the Church
was fundamentally denied.   But the manifest contradiction
between the Cartesian metaphysics and the doctrine of
transubstantiation passed for the real ground of accusation.
If accidental validity only is conceded to forms, — not substantial, as with the scholastics, — if they are nothing but
modifications of substances, and are inseparably united with
them, it is absolutely impossible for the form and properties
of a thing to continue while the thing itself is changed, for
the body and blood of Christ to appear in the form and
among the properties of bread and wine — to illustrate the

principle by the case of pre-eminent interest to the Church. Descartes taught, that, under all conditions, substance continues and forms change : the Church teaches, that, in the sacrament of the eucharist, forms continue while the substance itself is changed.   According to Descartes' principles, there is indeed transformation, but no transubstantiation : according to the Church, there is, in the sacrament of the eucharist, transubstantiation, but no transformation.   According to Descartes, the essence of body consists in extension, and this in space : it is, therefore, absolutely impossible for the same body to exist in different spaces or places.   The real or bodily presence of Christ can, therefore, in no way exist in the sacrament.   Those fundamental positions concerning substance and its modifications, substance and its attributes, body and its extension, are accordingly absolutely *anti-eucharistic.*   Denying the substantiality of forms, and maintaining that of extension, they are in fundamental conflict with exactly that tenet of the Roman-Catholic Church in which *cultus* and *dogma* are inseparably interwoven.   All these considerations were laid before the philosopher himself ; and in his reply to the objections of Arnauld, and in his letters to the Jesuit Mesland, he vainly attempted to set them aside, and to give to his system an orthodox interpretation.   The points in dispute related to metaphysical necessities ; i.e., to such truths as are incapable of being changed, even by the will of God.   Had the question as to the position of a philosophical system on the doctrine of transubstantiation been of a merely academic character, it would be almost impossible to comprehend how such discussions in the golden age of French literature should have played such an important part in modern philosophy.   But it was an *ecclesiastico-political* question of pre-eminent importance.   We must realize, that, in the conception and doctrine of the sacrament of the eucharist, the ecclesiastical parties of the sixteenth century were divided ; that at this point the great chasm arose which tore Protestantism from Catholicism, and even separated the

Lutherans from the Reformed Church; that the Jesuitical stress on cultus, and particularly their administration of the Lord's Supper, the frequent and unspiritual confessing and communing, insisted upon by the Jesuit fathers, was one of the first objects which the French Jansenists, especially Arnauld, violently attacked; that in the age of Louis XIV., the question was not merely as to a splendid modern literature, but as to the complete restoration of the unity of the French Church, as to the repression of Jansenism and the revocation of the Edict of Nantes, — we must realize these things before we can understand the significance of the charge that Descartes' doctrine was anti-eucharistic. That charge involved the charge of having Jansenistic, and at bottom Calvinistic, tendencies; of being one of the most dangerous opponents of the Romish Church, and the unity of the Church in France. The question was not as to the inclination and wishes of the philosopher, but as to the *principles* of his doctrine. The Jesuit *Valois* epitomized the objections which they urged against it in the following title: "The Antagonism of the Doctrines of Descartes to the Church, and their Harmony with Calvin " (1680).[1]

2. *The Classic Period of French Literature and the Supremacy of Descartes' Philosophy.* — But these antagonists were completely mistaken — however correct their inferences may have been — when they regarded the Cartesian philosophy as a matter of an ecclesiastical party, and supposed that its destiny was bound up with that of the Jansenists and Protestants in France. They had very much under-estimated its importance when they looked upon it as a mere theological revival. It was a new theory of the world, a new system of knowledge and of nature, shaped and illumined by the strictest and most consistent method of thought, based on the most certain principles, and presented so clearly and beautifully that it must have made a very powerful impression upon the sensitive mind of the French,

---

[1] Fr. Bouillier, i. chaps. xxi., xxii. See Introduction, pp. 153–157.

and upon the Augustan age of their literature and poetry. Against such a coalition of forces, the persecution of ecclesiastical enemies, and even the powerful disfavor of the court, could accomplish nothing permanent. Public institutions of learning were closed to the Cartesian philosophy: it was diffused in a surer and less public manner through literature, by private scientific circles, by the intellectual society of the metropolis — which set the fashion for the rest of France. In the year 1635 Richelieu had founded the French Academy for the guidance and development of the language and literature. The next year appeared "The Cid" of the great *Corneille*, in which the character of high tragedy and the genius of the poet were perfectly expressed: a year later Descartes published his first works, the "Discours" and the "Essais." The epoch of classic French literature had begun. When the ashes of the philosopher were brought, a generation later, from Stockholm to Paris, the scientific circles and societies in the latter city were permeated by his thoughts. The same year (1666) Colbert founded the Academy of Sciences, and supplemented the work of Richelieu, by establishing an institute which was to sustain the same relation to mathematics and physics that the Academy did to the French language and literature. The latter reached its zenith in that time. The three stars of classic poetry shone at the same time, — Corneille, already setting; Molière, in his zenith; Racine, the pupil of Port Royal, just climbing towards the zenith: his "Andromache" appeared in 1667, a poem not less characteristic of his genius than "The Cid" of the genius of Corneille.

There are a peculiar affinity and harmony of spirit between the great philosopher and the great tragic poets of this period. The former set forth in his scientific works what the latter embody in their dramas; viz., the *passions of the soul*. The theme of their poems is not the characteristics of persons, but the portraiture of passions. To be able to express these as powerfully as possible, they seek the most plastic materials, the event most in harmony with their purpose, the most eloquent examples. The actions and characters which they bring before us in their correct works are only the organs through which powerful emotions express themselves forcibly and grandly. There was one passion which Descartes distinguished from the rest, one which he considered as *sui generis*, as the noblest and purest of all. He called it "*magnanimité*" and "*générosité;*" the nobility of the soul — self-esteem based on an heroic self-denial.[1] This passion in manifold forms lives in the poems of Corneille, who has been called the "great" because of this exalted characteristic, which, with the rhetorical power that is characteristic of the French, produces agreeable emotions. Of remaining passions, none is more powerful than love, none more tormenting than jealousy. These passions were most powerfully and eloquently expressed by the authors of "Andromache" and "Phädra." If one wishes a personal illustration of that emotion which Descartes extolled as "*magnanimité*," he need only recall Corneille's Chimène in his "Cid," who, to avenge the death of her father, did every thing in her power to sacrifice her lover, the idol of her heart; and she saw in such a denial of self, the perfection of strength of soul, and the culmination of fame : "*Je veux que la voix de la plus noire envie élève au ciel ma gloire et plaigne mes enmis, sachant, que je t'adore et que je te poursuis.*"

In the life of our philosopher himself, and in his principles, which brought on a conflict with the great authorities of the world, — venerable because of the power which they have inherited from the past, — and which demanded personal submission to them, we find a characteristic in harmony with that exalted emotion portrayed in the poems of Corneille.

The intellectual tendencies of the time, whether consciously or not, were determined by the influence of Des-

---

[1] See book ii. chap. ix. p. 431 and following.

cartes. A new species of poetry, which felt itself superior
to the Renaissance, and was filled with the consciousness of
its greatness and originality, associated itself with the new
philosophy. It would no longer imitate the ancients, but
would improve upon them, give itself rules, and methodically apply them, that it might produce works worthy of
acceptance as examples. The thoughts of philosophers and
the inventions of poets were controlled by a regular, carefully considered art. Descartes was the first to discipline the
reason, to subject it to an art of thought, to realize the requirement upon which he insisted, and to leave to his age a
luminous example in his works. His doctrine furnished the
foundation for a new work on logic, "L'art de penser," written
in Port Royal by Arnauld and Nicole (1662): *Boileau* wrote
a book on the art of poetry, "L'art poétique," which has
been aptly called the "Discours de la méthode" of poetry.[1]
Even in poetry nothing must please but reason and truth:
"*Aimez donc la raison ; que toujours nos écrits empruntent d'elle
seule et leur lustre et leur prix.*" "*Rien n'est beau que le vrai ;
le vrai seul est aimable !*" Even in poetry, brevity and clearness, the avoidance of every thing superfluous and bombastic,
are required. The most evident coherence, and therefore
unity of place, time, and action, were made rigid laws for
dramatic works. All these rules are just such as Descartes
would have laid down if he had treated of the art of
poetry. They correspond to his doctrine which demands in
the works produced by men — no matter upon what material
they work, whether stones, ideas, or actions — absolute unity
and the closest coherence. Irregular and confused accumula-
tions from various ages were as repulsive to the author of
the "Discours de la méthode" in the sciences as in houses
and cities. He would certainly have objected to similar ac-
cumulations in dramatic works. The tendency, which, in
the second half of the seventh century, controlled French
mind and taste in its greatness as well as in its limitations,

---

[1] Bouillier, i. chap. xxiii. p. 491.

manifesting itself in science and art, even in the gardens of Versailles, was based on a certain mode of thought, the principles of which are nowhere more distinctly and consciously expressed than in the doctrine of Descartes. We can, therefore, easily understand that Cartesianism in France and Paris was a power far greater than the decrees of the king whom it even made dependent upon itself, as it were, *incognito*. It was a *fashion* of the time to which men involuntarily paid homage. The tendency of the time was Cartesian.

3. *Fashionable Philosophy and Satire.* — It is, therefore, no wonder that the world of fashion and distinction and the ladies of the time cultivated Cartesianism or made a profession of it. The Duchess du Maine was compared with Queen Christina on account of her reverence for Descartes: the scholarly Dupré was called, "*la Cartésienne.*" Out of love to her daughter, Madame de Erignon, whose life was devoted to the study of the philosopher, Madame de Sévigné was drawn to share her interests. Jestingly she called Descartes, in her letters to her daughter, "*votre père,*" and the latter, "*ma chère petite Cartésienne.*" She visited in Brittany a relative of the philosopher who bore his name, and wrote to her daughter, "*Je tiens un petit morceau de ma fille.*" She used the proverb of Cartesianism in order, with inimitable grace, to express her maternal tenderness: "*Je pense, donc je suis; je pense à vous avec tendresse, donc je vous aime.*" She gave her daughter an account of a philosophical discussion after a dinner in which one of the guests had maintained that thought depends upon the senses, and her son had defended the contrary opinion according to Descartes. In one of her letters she aptly and wittily reveals the hold of the new philosophy upon the society of the time, and the nature of her own interest in the matter which was the subject of general interest, though it was frowned upon by the court; she regarded it as a modern and fashionable fancy, of which one could not afford to be ignorant: "Corbinelli and

Lamousse have undertaken to instruct me in Cartesianism. I wish to learn it like ombre, not in order to play, but to see others play."[1]

As soon as a philosophical system becomes a fashion, it is easy to make it ridiculous, especially if it collides with the opinions of the world by apparently paradoxical positions, and, nevertheless, is cultived by women, and affected by many. It was inevitable, therefore, that in witty Paris and in the time of Molière, Cartesianism, as the fashionable philosophy, should be made an object of satire. There was a harmony unsought between Descartes and the tragic poets in their conception of human nature and the passions, and the opposition between Descartes and Molière was just as natural. The disciple of Gassendi ridiculed the female disciples of Descartes in his "Femmes savantes" (1672). In the tragedies and comedies of the France of that time, in Cornielle and Molière, we can see the reflection of the two opposing currents of French philosophy, — the Cartesian and Gassendish. But we must not conceive the matter pedantically, and think of philosophical discipleship. If Gassendi had not instructed Molière, and if the latter had not been acquainted with Lucretius, whose poem he translated, he would have been in sympathy with the sensualism of the natural understanding, and opposed to the dualistic and spiritualistic doctrine of Descartes. He needed no personal malice nor that of a school to induce him to make the extravagances and affectations of Descartes' female disciples ridiculous. The comic poet chose such subjects as though he were called to do so. I shall not venture to decide whether, in the character of Marphurius, in "Mariage force," he was ridiculing the Cartesian doubt, and not rather that universal scepticism found in every time. In "Femmes savantes," he satirized, not exclusively, I admit, but in some of the most effective passages, the follies to which the fashion of Cartesianism had given rise in women. His char-

[1] Bouillier, i. chap. xx. pp. 438-440.

acters are not pronounced Cartesians, but women who
enthuse in an unintelligent manner over every thing that
smacks of learning. One praises Plato, another Epicurus, a
third finds "corpuscles" perfectly lovely, and "a void" too
hateful for any thing, and thinks herself subtile in preferring
"subtile matter:" "*Je goûte bien mieux la matière subtile.*"
Now, these are Cartesianisms which are treated by women as
matters of taste exactly as though they were fashionable
articles. "*J'aime ses tourbillons,*" said Armande; and his
mother continued, "*Moi, ses mondes tourbants.*"   Molière
portrays as most ridiculous the intense desire to regard the
body with its needs and impulses, the sensitive nature of
man, as contemptible stuff (*guenille*), the association with
which the soul must regard as beneath its dignity. The master of the house, Chrysole, is of a different opinion, and replies
to his wife entirely in the style of Gassendi: "*Mon corps
est moi-même, et j'en veux prendre soin, guenille, si l'on veut;
ma guenille m'est chère.*"   Also the lover Clitandre wishes to
know nothing of the spiritualistic doctrine which separates
the mind from the senses: "*De ces détachements je ne connais
point l'art; le ciel m'a dénié cette philosophie.*"   And Bélise,
the most ridiculous, and therefore the most successful, character of the comedy, bases on the Cartesian dualism her
theory of refined love, which belongs only to thinking substance, and has nothing in common with matter: "*Mais nous
établissons une espèce d'amour, qui doit être épure comme l'astre
du jour: la substance, qui pense y peut être reçue, mais nous
en bouissons la substance étendue.*" [1]

That a satire of the fashion of Cartesianism appeared as
late as the year 1690, written by the Jesuit *Daniel*, and
entitled, "Voyage du monde de Descartes," proves how long-
lived the "Femmes savantes" were. The author takes com-
fort by considering past fashions. In his jests we recognize
the associate of Bourdin. The whole satire sprang from
that sensualistic temper in which the Jesuits were in har-

---

[1] *Femmes savantes,* act ii. sc. 7; iii. 2; iv. 2; v. 3.

mony with Gassendi, particularly as opposed to Descartes.
What they attacked in Cartesianism by objections, accusations, satires, was its spiritualistic character. To make that
ridiculous, Daniel represented the philosopher as the magician of his doctrine, as it were, who had power to really
separate the soul from the body, to lay the latter aside like
a garment for a time, and to make journeys simply as a soul.
During such an absence of soul, the body of the philosopher
had been buried in Stockholm, and now the latter dwells in
the third heavens, engaged in constructing the universe out
of the subtile matter which he found there in store. He who
wishes to solve the riddle of the universe in the easiest way
must visit this architect of the world up there in his workshop ; it is only necessary for such an one to throw off his
body, and set out upon his journey as pure soul ; and this
can very easily be done by a well-trained Cartesian, since the
master had bestowed upon his disciples his own miraculous
powers.   In this way, a disciple, eager for knowledge, made
his " Voyage du monde de Descartes." [1]

The spiritualism of Descartes' doctrine was a result of
its dualistic conception of the relation between the mind
and the body, and that contains the questions which gave
rise to the first attempt to critically develop the system.

[1] Bouillier, i. chap. xx. p. 443; chap. xxvii. p. 576.

CHAPTER II.

THE FIRST ATTEMPTS TO CRITICALLY DEVELOP CARTESIANISM.

I. THE FRENCH SCHOOL.

1. *Rohault and Régis.*

AMONG the French Cartesians who were prominent in the diffusion and development of Cartesianism, both by their oral discussions and their writings, especial mention should be made of *Rohault* of Amiens (1620–1672), the son-in-law of Clerselier, and *Sylvain Régis* of Angers (1632–1707). The former was a man with a talent for mechanical invention; and by his lectures on physics, — delivered in Paris on Wednesdays, — and the explanations and disputations connected with them, he won a very large audience, in which all classes of society were represented, for the new doctrine, and by his work on physics (" Traité de physique ") he extended the influence of his instruction far beyond France. A year before his death, his " Entretiens de philosophie " appeared, in which he sought to reconcile the Cartesian doctrine with the Aristotelian physics, and the theology of the Church, in the manner with which we have already become acquainted in the Netherlands. He was the man who brought that testimonial from the Queen of Sweden which opened the door of St. Genevieve for the ashes of Descartes. Régis was his pupil, and was sent by the Cartesian society in Paris to the southern part of France to teach the new doctrine there: in the years 1665–71 he was thus engaged, first in Toulouse, then in Montpellier, with the most extraordinary success. When he returned to Paris to continue the lectures of his teacher, the persecution of Cartesianism with which we are acquainted had begun. At the advice of the archbishop, Régis felt obliged to discontinue his lectures, and was unable until 1690 to publish his "System de philosophie," which contained in four parts logic, metaphysics, physics, and morals.

What particularly attracts our attention in his works is not so much the deviations from Descartes in his ethics and politics in the direction of Hobbes, and in his doctrine of ideas towards Gassendi, as his modification of Cartesianism in reference to the relation between God and the world, soul and body. In these points we find ideas in harmony with Occasionalism, and particularly with Malebranche. If God is, strictly speaking, the only substance, he is the only real cause. We must, therefore, distinguish between the primary causality of God and the secondary causality of things. But if the divine activity is truly original, it alone also truly produces, and natural things must be regarded as intermediate causes or instruments through which God works. They are not forces, but only "instruments." From this point of view, the natural interaction between soul and body necessarily appears as the result of the divine will: through the body God causes the processes in the soul to arise, through the soul the motions in the body. Now, the instrumental cause has indeed no producing causality of its own, but only acts in connection with the divine will, which it influences, and whose action it modifies, as the nature of the instrument does the activity of the artist. Régis thus leaves something to the soul that depends upon the soul itself; it cannot produce motion, though it can indeed determine its direction; it is a *director*, not a producer, of motion. Thus the divine and human will concur in the production of the bodily motions which correspond to the processes of the soul. The relation of the two substances remains, therefore, undetermined and indefinite. If one determines and changes the direction of a motion, he thereby causes motion. We may regard Régis' position as an attempt to harmonize Cartesianism, not merely with its sensualistic opposite, but also with the innovations which had already appeared within the Cartesian school itself. By the latter, we mean the theories of the French Occasionalists, and of Malebranche, whose principal works were published before those of Régis were written. Scarcely had the latter entered upon that brilliant career of instruction in Toulouse, when French Occasionalism appeared in the writings of two older Cartesians.[1]

2. *De la Forge and Cordemoy.* — In the year 1666, the physician and physiologist, *Louis de la Forge*, a friend of Descartes, and, with Clerselier, the editor of "Traité de l'homme," published his work "On the Human Soul, its Powers and Activities, also its Union with the Body according to the Principles of Descartes," and the advocate *Géraud de Cordemoy*, his six "Philosophical Essays on the Difference between Soul and Body."[2] The relation of the two substances in respect to both their union and separation is the most important of the subjects discussed in these works.

De la Forge explains the connection between soul and body as the work of the divine will, and, in like manner, the interaction between the two, with the exception of those motions which depend upon our will which he regards as *voluntary*. The human soul, accordingly, appears as the producing and immediate cause of all conscious and voluntary actions (motions); God, on the other hand, as the producing and immediate cause of all unconscious and involuntary processes. As to the latter, the bodily impression cannot cause the conception, but only occasion God to cause it, and conversely. He thus maintained one-half of Occasionalism. He accepted Occasionalism except in the

---

[1] Concerning Rohault and Régis, cf. Bouillier, I. chap. xxiv. pp. 508–510, 517–524.

[2] *Louis de la Forge:* Traité de l'âme humaine, de ses facultés et fonctions et de son union avec le corps d'après les principes de Descartes. *Cordemoy:* Dissertations philosophiques sur le discernement de l'âme et du corps.

case of the so-called voluntary motions. If these are not in fact voluntary, and if they are as independent of our will as they are of our knowledge, we must declare that the human will causes no bodily actions whatever, and, on the basis of Dualism, carry out the theory of Occasionalism.

Cordemoy took this step. He was the first Occasionalist among the French Cartesians, and his Occasionalism was due to the logical development of his dualistic principles. There is but *one* active cause, as there is but one kind of self-active being; viz., mind, or will. Bodies have no wills, therefore they are not causes. No body, as such, can change another body, none can affect the mind. Thinking substances are fundamentally different from extended ones. The human mind (will), therefore, cannot move a body, and it has just as little power to direct motion. There is but one cause that moves body, and there is but one that causes the interaction between mind and body; and that is in both cases the divine, because infinite and all-powerful, Will. When two bodies meet, neither of itself moves the other, but their collision is only the occasion upon which the cause that moved the first body moved the second also. If mind and body exist together in man, and the will puts forth a volition to make a definite movement in an organ of the body, the volition is only the occasion upon which God so causes, and so directs, the motion that it corresponds to the purpose. Our will, therefore, is not the efficient, but only the occasional, cause of motion: motion takes place independently of us, voluntary as well as involuntary. Our will causes neither motion nor its direction.[1]

The principles of Occasionalism were stated in the clearest manner by Cordemoy, and we see how far Régis remained behind. But the Occasionalistic system had been developed still more comprehensively and profoundly in the Netherlands, and had taken a course similar to that from De la

---

[1] Bouillier, i. chap. xxiv. pp. 511-516.

Forge to Cordemoy; viz., from Clauberg to Geulincx. The logical development and application of the dualistic principles of Descartes was the animating thought that found expression in different tendencies.

II. THE SCHOOL IN THE NETHERLANDS.

1. *Clauberg.* — *John Clauberg* of Solingen in Westphalia (1622–1665) had heard Tobias Andrea in Gröningen, had become acquainted with Clerselier and De la Forge during a visit to France, and then continued his philosophical studies in Leyden under Raey, where he gave special attention to physics, before he began to teach philosophy in Herborn. He was professor of philosophy in the University of Duisburg during the last thirteen years of his life (1652–1665). A German by birth, and convinced of the philosophical destiny of his mother-tongue, Clauberg was one of the first to teach philosophy in the German universities. He was full of enthusiasm for Cartesianism, and, except the Holy Scriptures, he valued no works more highly than those of Descartes, and he labored with untiring zeal to defend and explain them. In reply to the theological opponents of Cartesianism, — Revius in Leyden, with whom we are already acquainted, and his own associate Lentulus in Herborn, — he wrote his "Defensio Cartesiana" (1652): he explained the "Meditations," defended the Cartesian doubt as the path to truth ("Initiatio philosophi"), and wrote a logic which served to develop the system, sought to unite the old and new philosophy, and may be regarded as a forerunner of the French manual, "L'art de penser."

None of his works has a greater claim on our interest than the essay "On the Union of Soul and Body in Man" ("De animæ et corporis in homine conjunctione"). The fact of the mutual influence of soul and body cannot be explained by natural laws in view of their substantial difference, but must be regarded as a miracle, due to the exercise of divine power. But the soul, because of its essence, is far more powerful than the body; it has more power over the body than the body has over it; it cannot produce the motion of the body, but it can indeed direct it; it is not its physical but its "*moral* cause." To use Descartes' figure, it is related to the body like a driver to a wagon: the wagon is moved by the horses, but the driver determines their course. But the body can exert *no influence whatever* upon the soul: it is completely incapable of any psychical effect. Its impressions and motions merely precede, prepare for, i.e., *occasion*, the corresponding psychical changes, but do not cause them. The soul exercises a directive power upon the body: upon occasion of the bodily impressions, it produces the corresponding impressions by virtue of its own thinking nature. Accordingly, in comparison with either God or body, it is not so important as it ought to be on the principles of dualism. Clauberg reminds us of La Forge in limiting Occasionalism to the influences of the body, and of Régis in ascribing a directive influence to the human will on the bodily motions; though Régis, later than Cordemoy, retraced his steps, and resumed the stand-point of old Cartesianism, while Clauberg only departed farther from it, and in the vacillations and half-heartedness of his Occasionalism he may be regarded as having entered upon the path that terminated in the critical development of it.[1]

2. *Balthasar Bekker.* — From the Cartesian dualism, it follows that God is the only real substance and the primitive source of power, the only producing cause in the true sense of the word, in comparison with whom natural things have only a secondary, instrumental, occasional efficiency, and the mutual influence of soul and body exists only by virtue of the divine will. Motion in bodies, and knowledge in minds are caused, and the first cause of both is God. No being except God, therefore, can exert a causative force upon minds and bodies, and, therefore, upon man, who consists of the two. This fact overthrows a whole class of generally

---

[1] Bouillier, i. chap. xiii. pp. 293-298.

accepted opinions. If there are intermediate beings between God and us, spirits below God and of a supernatural character, they cannot exert any influence whatever upon man, nor can they alter the nature of things at all. By the light of reason, we see, as Descartes proved, only the reality of God, minds and bodies: we see in bodies no property except extension, no activity except mechanical motion, and, in minds, nothing but understanding and will. We must, therefore, deny that these intermediate beings (demons) exert any power in the world of things, and indeed we dare dispute even their existence. There are undoubtedly many worlds unknown to us, and many unknown beings; but there are no demonic actions, and, therefore, no demonic causes, at least none capable of appearing to us, and exerting an influence upon us. In this point, the new rationalism opposes all demonology, and attacks a multitude of opinions which have been entertained in the most different forms from the earliest times, and were entertained, as it were, in the very presence of Descartes' doctrine. There are, as objects of knowledge and reasonable belief, neither demons nor angels, — either good or bad, — no souls of men separate from the body, returning to the world of apparitions, — either happy or damned, — neither Devil nor ghosts, — hence no leagues with the Devil, and no magic based upon it, — neither enchanters nor witches, no power capable of enchanting men and things in opposition to the laws of nature; in a word, no "enchanted world." What throws light upon the world is reason, and faith in God, which is based upon it: what bewitches and enchants it is *superstition*, the objects of which are demons, and which is itself produced by ignorance and deceit. We can judge what strength and courage of conviction were necessary to maintain such a position in a century in which the existence of the Devil was firmly believed by orthodox Christians and people in general, and with such strength that witches were burnt in the name of justice. It was a preacher in the Netherlands, and a doctor of theology, who developed this bold position with such energy and thoroughness that his work became famous, was hotly attacked by some, and imitated by many. He paid the penalty for it by losing his position and by being excluded from the communion of the churches, a sacrifice to, and a proof of, his fidelity to his convictions. He was the boldest and most interesting of the Cartesian theologians.

Balthasar Bekker of West Friesland (1634–1698) began to preach soon after the completion of his studies (which he had begun in Franeker, and continued in Gröningen) in the village of Öosterlittens; afterwards he went to France, where he labored until 1674, when he accepted a call to Lönen, and three years later to Weesop; shortly after he was invited to Amsterdam (1679), but he lost his position in consequence of his principal work (1694). He had already excited the suspicion and hatred of the orthodox by an earlier work: now he was suspended from his position by the authorities of the city, and, since he remained loyal to his convictions, he was dismissed from it by order of the synod.

His first work, published in 1668, contained his philosophical creed, — a defence of Cartesianism ("De philosophia Cartesiana admonitio candida et sincera"): the second, an "Investigation of Comets," written in the language of the Netherlands, opened the campaign against superstition, which he attacked in the form of fear of comets. In 1680 the dreaded heavenly body had appeared, and the minds of men were thrown into terror. On this occasion, and with a similar purpose, *Pierre Bayle* published in Rotterdam at the same time (1683) his work on comets. Bekker's comprehensive and great work, written in the tongue of the Netherlands, was published in the years 1691–94 under the title, "The Enchanted World" ("De Betoverde Weereld"), and gave in four books a complete and methodical discussion of his subject. The first book gives an account of faith in demons as it is found in different peoples and religions, in the heathens of ancient as well as

modern times, in Jews and Mohammedans, in Catholic and
Protestant Christians, and thus fixes the subject to be
investigated in its entirety. In the following books, the
matter itself is examined: in the second, from the point of
view of reason and the Bible; in the third and fourth, from
that of the facts which are urged as proofs of demons; viz.,
the *magical* arts, — particularly enchantment and prophesy-
ing, — the appearances of spirits, and the demonic states of
being possessed. The author then distinguished traditional
doctrines and testimonies from experiences — subjective
in their origin — to which people appeal, and which they
allege as present actual facts in proof of demonology. Bekker took this occasion to recount a number of facts that had
come under his own experience and observation, and which
had convinced him of the nullity of the pretended demonological facts. (The above biographical account is based on
these statements of the fourth book.) *The faith of Christians in demons*, particularly that of the *Reformed Church*,
was the real object against which Bekker's entire work was
directed. It was the faith in the Devil and in leagues with
the Devil, in enchanters and witches, which he sought to
completely destroy. He wished to prove to the Church that
its faith in demons was rooted in superstition. His arguments were drawn in the main from three sources; viz.,
from the historical origin of the Christian faith in demonology, from pure reason, and from the Bible.

Faith in demons, like the faith in a plurality of gods to
which it belongs, is of pagan origin, and was inherited by
primitive Christianity from paganism. It penetrated primitive Christianity, and it became powerful in the Romish
Church, in the faith and cultus of which it formed, along
with magic, an essential element. This element was partly
destroyed, partly preserved, by the Reformation, and accepted by it as an inheritance from Catholicism: this is
particularly true of the belief in the existence of the Devil.
Thus, the belief in demons and magic in the Romish Church

is nothing but paganism in Christianity, and the belief of
the Reformed Church in the existence of the Devil is nothing but Papacy in Protestantism.   It is one of the most
serious errors of the time to detest the Romish Church on
account of things which we admire in pagan religions, and
not to see that these things have remained in their essence,
having merely changed their forms.   And it is just as
absurd to regard the Romish Church as the work of the
Devil, and the Pope as Antichrist, and still continue under
the yoke of papal authority by believing in the power of the
Devil.   Until we have entirely broken with the authority
of the Church and its traditions, we have no right to detest
the Papacy, since that is inseparable from the authority of the
Church.   To Papists we should say, " Your faith in demons,
and your magic, is pagan: why, therefore, do you hate paganism?"   To Protestants, "Your belief in demons and the Devil
is Catholic: why, therefore, do you hate Papacy, and admire
paganism?"   The Reformed Church sustains the same relation to the Papacy that the Papacy does to pagan religions:
they have inherited and accepted their superstitions, and
condemned the faith from which they received them.[1]

The philosophical stand-point from which Bekker proved
that demonic effects are unknowable, that belief in demons
is absurd, and that superstition comes from paganism, was,
as we have already seen, the *Cartesian*, which is based on
the dualism of God and the world, mind and body.   He
rejected the Spinozistic conception of God, and conceived
the relation between the soul and body, not strictly according to Occasionalism, but according to the old Cartesianism,
which according to its principles denied the natural interaction of the two, yet admitted it as a fact.   God alone can
exert power upon nature: man is the only finite being whose
mind has any power over his own body.   Hence all faith in
demons is without foundation.[2]

---

[1] The Enchanted World, book i., chiefly xxiv., secs. 16–22.
[2] Ib., book ii., chiefly i., 3–15, ii. 4, iii. 1, iv. 8, vi. 11, vii.

But all arguments against demons and their activity are
destitute of cogency, so long as they are opposed by the
Bible, which, in so many places, speaks of the appearance of
angels and the Devil, of good and bad spirits, of archangels,
and of Satan. The author of " The Enchanted World " was
a firm believer in the Bible: he dared not, and would not,
doubt what he found there. Hence, in order to be certain
that there are no demonological actions in the world, that
there is no influence exerted by supernatural agents, he had
to convince himself that these things are not asserted by
the Bible. To gain this conviction, and state the grounds
of it in detail, was plainly the most difficult problem of his
works; and it is evident from some of its statements, that it
required many years to bring the perceptions of his reason
into harmony with his faith in the Bible. Thus, for example,
he had for a long time literally understood and accepted
the history of the fall, and the temptation of the Devil who
is spoken of as a serpent. After he had repeatedly and
carefully examined all the passages pertaining to this subject along with the necessary philological considerations, he
had reached this conclusion: (1) that none of the passages
in question teach 'any thing concerning the origin and
nature, property and order, of good and evil spirits, and
that, therefore, the Scriptures contain no *doctrine* of *demons ;*
(2) that none of them assert an *immediate* activity of angels
(good spirits) upon men, or (3) the real activity of the
Devil. When angels appear, it is never as independent
beings, but either as intermediate causes or instruments of
the divine power, or as images and signs (rhetorical figures)
of the presence of God; or finally, when they appear in
bodily form, and eat and drink, as did those messengers
who were sent to Abraham and Lot, they are not supernatural beings, but men. When God is spoken of as coming
on the wings of cherubim and of the wind, the cherubim
are evidently to be understood in the same figurative sense
as the wind; and when the heavenly hosts of worshipping

spirits are mentioned as surrounding the throne of God, angels mean nothing but the throne; and both are images of human forms trying to glorify God. The idea of the Devil, on the other hand, as an independent spirit arrayed against God, having and exerting a power of his own in the world, and possessing a kingdom on earth, is perfectly absurd. Where the Bible speaks of the appearing and actions of the Devil, we must interpret it either *allegorically* as in the history of the temptation in Paradise, and in the controversy, mentioned in the Epistle of Jude, between the archangel and Satan over the corpse of Moses, or the narrative relates to a *vision* as in the history of the temptation of Jesus. In all other cases, the occurrence is referred to the Devil by the interpreters of the Scriptures through a misunderstanding, while in reality the narration refers only to *divine* or merely human actions. Thus, it was not Satan who caused the sufferings of Job, but God who tried him; and it was not the persecutions of the Devil which Paul had to endure, but those of evil men, whether the officer with his scourge, or the enemies of the apostle with their slanders.[1]

This was the attitude of our theologian towards the Holy Scriptures. To harmonize his faith in the Bible with his disbelief in the Devil, he interpreted the Bible in harmony with the laws of nature, only he confined this method to the explanation of demonic miracles while he acknowledged the divine as worthy of belief. Later rationalism extended the natural mode of explanation to *all* miracles. As to the question of biblical miracles, there are three points of view. The orthodox say, "Miracles are worthy of belief *because* they are narrated in the Bible." Rationalists say, "They are not worthy of belief, *therefore* they are not narrated in the Bible." Those who occupy the third point of view, which is later than the two preceding, affirm their

[1] Ib., book ii., chiefly viii.; ix., sec. 11; x. 18-23; xi. 12, 13; xiv.; xv. 9; xviii. 3-12; xx. 23-26; xxi.; xxiii.

minor premise though their conclusion is negative. They say, "Miracles are not worthy of belief *although* they are narrated in the Bible." The second of these points of view was Bekker's, supported by the rationalism of the Cartesian doctrine; though he by no means occupied that attitude towards all the miracles of the Bible, but only towards the accounts of demons. That is the remarkable position of this man in the history of philosophy and theology.

CHAPTER III.

THE SYSTEM OF OCCASIONALISM. — ARNOLD GEULINCX.

I. GEULINCX' LIFE AND WRITINGS.

THE special representative of Occasionalism in its complete and systematic form came from Catholic Netherlands, — *Arnold Geulincx*[1] of Antwerp (1625–1669), a pupil, and afterwards a teacher, in the University of Lyons. He here studied philosophy and medicine, took his doctor's degree, and for twelve years delivered lectures on philosophy, — the last six as the first representative of the department. His lectures were attended by a large and enthusiastic crowd of students until he was forced to stop, and flee in a state of the greatest destitution to Leyden, where he was hospitably and benevolently received by the Cartesian Heidanus. Through his influence, Geulincx, after he went over to the Reformed Church, was permitted to deliver private lectures in the University of Leyden, which were indeed as well attended, though they were not so lucrative, as those in Lyons. The assistance of Heidanus was to him a deliverance. He himself, in the preface of his logic, called the misfortune that had overtaken him a "*naufragium rerum;*" and Bontekoe, who, under the name Philaretus, published his most important work after his death, placed on the titlepage the words "*post tristia auctoris fata.*" His position must have been desperate at that time, since Philaretus says in the preface that he must have starved or begged if Heidanus had

---

[1] The name is spelled in different ways in the titles of his works, — Geulincx, Geulinxs, Geulinx, Geulincs, Geulinck.

not come to his assistance. What drove him from Lyons is not clearly known. We may surmise, that, on account of the persecution of the Cartesians there by the party of Plempius and the Jesuits, Geulincx lost his position, and, being poor, suffered on account of economic difficulties, and was oppressed by the orthodox. The Abbé Paquot, a licentiate of theology from Lyons, in his literary memorabilia (1768), states that debts and official dissensions compelled the unhappy man to have recourse to flight. But his great influence upon the students of the university, and the theses in which he attacked and derided scholasticism, were reasons enough to make him an object of hatred to his antagonists.

He had not leisure enough to publish all his works. The first work which he published in Leyden was a collection of the theses which he had defended in Lyons, — "Saturnalia, seu quæstiones quodlibeticæ in utramque partem disputatæ" (1660). Two years later his restoration of logic appeared, — " Logica fundamentis suis, a quibus hoctenus collapsa fuerat, restituta." This was followed by the first part of his most important work, — "Γνῶθι σεαυτὸν sive ethica" (Amsterdam, 1665), the whole of which was published after his death by Philaretus (Bontekoe).

His Physics and Metaphysics are next in importance, two posthumous works, in which he opposed the Cartesian standpoint to the Peripatetic; viz., "Physica vera" (Lugdunum, 1680), and "Metaphysica vera et ad mentam peripateticam" (Amsterdam, 1691). Contemporaneously with these, his observations on the Principles of Descartes were published in Dort, — "Annotata præcurrentia" and "Annotata majora in principia Renati Descartes."

Geulincx' Logic and " L'art de penser," the logic of Port Royal, appeared the same year; his Ethics a year before the writings of Louis de la Forge and Cordemoy upon the relation between soul and body. He was independent of both of them, and, therefore, the first and real founder of Occasionalism.

II. GEULINCX' DOCTRINE.

He was the first who was in all respects in earnest with the Cartesian dualistic principles, and who set himself the task of making the strictest and most logical application of them. He found likewise that in one of its essential parts the structure of the master still needed to be supplemented and completed. Descartes' system required a theory of ethics: he had indeed stated its elements and outline in his work on the passions, but he had left this part of his system undeveloped.

Geulincx undertook to supply this defect. Only a true knowledge of self can furnish the guiding principle of our conduct, and solve the problem of ethics. Hence the title of his most important work, " Γνῶθι σεαυτὸν sive ethica." Know thyself, know from what thou art, thy true relation to the world, and, hence, thy destiny in the world! Now, human nature consists in the union of soul and body. In what does this consist? The problem of ethics leads us to that of anthropology, and this to the fundamental questions of metaphysics: what is the nature of the soul and of the body? How are finite substances distinguished from the infinite substance? The doctrine of morals rests therefore on metaphysics, and has three questions to answer, — What am I? What is body? What is God? Geulincx, accordingly, divided his metaphysics into Autology, Somatology, and Theology. Spinoza also called his most important work "Ethica." It may be that the title of Geulincx, whose work probably appeared before Spinoza's, was not without influence upon the latter.

1. *The Doctrine of Principles.* — All knowledge rests on the certainty of self, the Cartesian " *cogito, ergo sum.*" The only object of immediate, and, therefore, absolute, knowledge, is our own being. Only thinking beings can be objects to themselves, and be evident to themselves. Only thinking activity is immediately certain of itself, and every activity

which is certain of itself must be of a thinking nature.
The spheres of my thinking activity and that of my self-certainty are exactly equal : so far as one extends, so far
extends the other, so far extend *I myself.*

It is, therefore, clear that *I myself* am active only as far as
my consciousness reveals my activity. If there is in me an
activity of which I am not immediately certain, which does
not fall within the illuminated circle of my consciousness, I
am not in truth *myself* active : I am not the being who produces this activity, and thus it is evident that something
takes place in me of which I am not the producing cause.

My activity coincides with my consciousness. But the
activity which lies in the light of consciousness is perfectly
clear and transparent : I see not merely that it happens, but
I see through its entire course ; I know *how* it happens. If,
therefore, an activity takes place in me of which I do not
know *how* it happens, I am not really conscious of this activity : it does not lie in the circle of my certainty of self. It
is, therefore, not in truth *my* activity : I am not its cause.

The inference, therefore, which Geulincx immediately
draws from the Cartesian " *cogito, ergo sum,*" and declares the
self-evident principle of his doctrine, is this : It is impossible
for self-activity to be unconscious, and it is equally impossible for unconscious activity to be self-activity. He who
does not know *how* an event takes place in him cannot be
the cause of this event. If you do not know, or if you are
not conscious, *how* you do any thing, you yourself do not do
it, and it is not your action. Every activity presupposes
that it is thought and willed. What, therefore, happens in
you without your thought and will does not happen through
you : you are not its cause. In other words, *Every unconscious and involuntary activity is not yours.*[1]

Activity without previous thought and will is impossible.

---

[1] " *Impossibile est, ut is faciat, qui nescit, quomodo fiat. Quod nescis, quomodo
fiat, id non facis* " (Metaph., pars i.; Scientia, v.). " *Qua fronte dicam, id me
facere, quod quomodo fiat nescio ?* " (Tract., i. sec. ii. § 2, par. 4).

This "impossible" contains the whole of Occasionalism. My thought is modified in a variety of ways. I have experiences which I do not consciously produce, which, like my sensations, come involuntarily, the origin of which I do not know. They are independent of my thought and will: I myself am my thought and will. They do not, therefore, depend upon me: they, therefore, presuppose a will foreign to mine, which produces them in me. This foreign will produces in us the multitude of sensations either immediately through itself, or through us, or through bodies. Our own nature as thinking is one, simple, indivisible. That foreign will, therefore, cannot produce in us sensations through ourselves, and for the same reason not through itself, since as a thinking being it is likewise simple. The only means of its activity, therefore, is body, but mere extension, as uniform as it is, cannot produce that variety of experiences: it must, therefore, be body in its variety, i.e., in its changes, which is the means employed by that foreign will in producing in us the experiences that do not depend upon ourselves. Now, all changes in body are motions, and our involuntary experiences must, therefore, be produced by a will not our own by means of the motion of bodies.[1]

Now, mind, by reason of its nature, is inaccessible to any motion. Motion is the approach or withdrawal of parts; but the mind has no parts, and therefore it cannot be moved. Only the divisible is movable, and the mind is indivisible. Between mind and body, therefore, there is no natural community. There is no influence, no *incursus*, of body into mind. If, therefore, by means of the body something takes place in mind, the body cannot be the producing, but only the instrumental, cause of it; not the cause, but only the instrument; not "*causa efficiens*," but "*causa occasionalis*" (occasional cause).[2]

There are a great number of bodies different because of

---

[1] Metaph., i.; Scient., ii., iv., vi., vii.
[2] Metaph., pars. i.; Scient., viii.

their motions; among these bodies or parts of the material world *one* is the instrument, by means of which a multitude of sensations are produced in me: with this body, my soul is united. The union of a soul and a body is *man:* I am man so far as I am united with a body in which a will not my own causes my motions, and through these motions causes experiences in my soul. To enter into those conditions of human nature, i.e., into this union with a body, is to be born: to leave those conditions is to die. The constitution of human nature is not my work: I do not produce it, and I do not know how it is produced. I only know that it is not caused by me, that it must, therefore, be caused by a will other than mine. In the world in which I live, I am accordingly myself the work of a will not my own.

My power extends only as far as my will, and my will should not be directed to objects beyond my power. Where I can do nothing, I ought not to will any thing. ' *Ubi nihil vales, ibi nihil velis!* '" In this point, the doctrine of morals empties into metaphysics, the " *ostium fluminis moralis,*" as it were, as Geulincx says.[1]

We see plainly how closely the occasionalistic mode of thought is connected with the ethical, and conditions the latter. What does not take place through my will and with my consciousness is not my deed· this sentence contains *in nuce* the whole of Occasionalism.

The immediate inference is obvious. My connection with the body, and with the world in which I am born, live, and die, is not my work, since it lies beyond the sphere of my will and my consciousness. This world is not the scene of my activity, and it ought not, therefore, to be the object of my will: this sentence contains the whole sum of ethics.

If, with Descartes, we admit the validity of the opposition of thinking and extended substances, in view of the actual union of soul and body, no other conclusion is possible than the Occasionalism of Geulincx. It does not explain the fact

---

[1] Metaph., i.; Scient., xi.; cf. ix., x.

of that union, but rather the impossibility of comprehending it on natural principles. If the absolute opposition of soul and body is once accepted, nothing else can indeed be inferred than the impossibility of their natural community.

Experience shows that there is an apparent interaction between soul and body. Certain motions in our bodies are followed by certain states of consciousness in our souls, and, in like manner, certain volitions are followed by certain motions which correspond to those volitions. It is easy to say that the will moves the body, and the impressions upon the senses produce the sensations. But how is it possible, we must ask, for the soul to act upon the body, or the body upon the soul, since both are substances fundamentally different in nature, and excluding each other? In such a relation any mutual influence is impossible. Bodily processes can never be caused by the soul, and the body has just as little power to cause changes in the soul. Thus, philosophy overthrows what experience seems to teach ; viz., the mutual causal relation between soul and body.

But if, in spite of all this, a causal relation does exist, it must be so conceived that every reciprocal influence of one upon the other, every natural interaction (*influxus physicus*), is excluded. It is not the will that causes motion, nor the impression which causes sensation; but this is their relation : when an impression or a motion takes place in an organ of my body, on occasion of this, the corresponding sensation is produced in my soul, and in like manner, on occasion of a volition, the corresponding motion in my bodily organ. The causal relation is only *occasional.* Both sides are entirely independent of each other: no kind of natural causal nexus, therefore, exists between them. They are in complete harmony, but such a one as excludes every natural accommodation of one to the other : they are in a *miraculous* harmony which admits no natural explanation. I feel, in harmony with the impressions upon my senses; but the cause of this sensation is neither body, since it cannot act upon the soul, nor I myself, since the sensation is involuntary, and I do not know how it arises. My body moves in harmony with my volitions; but the cause of this motion is neither the body, since this is a merely extended substance incapable of itself of any kind of activity, nor am I myself the cause, since my own activity is not of the nature of motion, but only of thought and will.

This union of soul and body is the greatest wonder of the world. It is absolutely impossible to comprehend *how* will and motion, sensation and impression, correspond to each other. This correspondence appears perfectly magical, considered from the natural point of view. That I, through my will, set my body in motion, is not less wonderful than if I thereby set the whole material world in motion. It is no less wonderful, said Geulincx, that the tongue in my mouth trembles when I pronounce the word "earth," than if the earth had thereby trembled.[1] This shows how perfectly Geulincx understood his point of view. The wonder is not diminished because the body is *mine* upon which I act, since it consists precisely in the fact that a part of the material world is *my* body, or, what is the same thing, that there is one body which is connected with me who am a soul.

What is the source of this union of soul and body? Since they are not united of themselves, but, on the contrary, exist independently of each other, they must be united by a particular activity, — one that proceeds from neither of the two sides, one whose cause can neither be soul nor body. The cause of this activity, therefore, can only be *God*. There is no action, no activity whatever without will. The activity which unites the soul with the body is not ours: it is not our will. Its cause must, therefore, be a will that is independent of us, and there is no being of this nature but God. Thus, the problem of Occasionalism is solved theologically.

From this point of view, Geulincx develops his concept

---

[1] Ethica Tract., i. sec. ii. § 2, par. 14.

of God. He it is who unites the soul with the body. Man consists of both, pre-supposes, therefore, the existence of minds and bodies. The union of the two requires the motion of bodies, and this is possible neither through minds nor through bodies, but only through God. God, therefore, must be conceived as moving will which is more powerful than the infinite material world; i.e., he must be conceived as *omnipotent will.* He causes in us the states of conscious-ness which do not depend upon our thought and will. Therefore, he must be conceived as a thinking being; i.e., as *mind.* He works in minds and bodies: he is related to things, therefore, as an active being to those that are passive. *He* acts, *they* are acted upon, are passive. All things depend upon him: he depends upon nothing. God is the absolute being: he is of himself (*a se*), cause of himself, unlimited, perfect, necessary, eternal. That he should not exist is impossible: it is impossible for minds and bodies to be united except through him. What contradicts the nature of things, contradicts also the divine nature; or rather, the eternal truths are a necessary consequence of the divine intelligence in which they dwell. These truths cannot be changed, even by the divine will: he can only affirm them, and act according to them. Thus, the Occasional mode of thought elevates more and more distinctly the eternal necessity of things into a divine necessity, upon which the will depends, and which forms, as it were, nature in God.[1]

In this point, Geulincx is borne along by a current of thought which struggles towards Spinoza.

Natural minds are related to the divine Mind as dependent and conditioned beings to one that is independent and unconditioned, as particular to universal, as limited to unlimited. Geulincx still wavered between the theological and naturalistic conception. He regarded finite minds as creatures, and at the same time as modes of God: the former conception is theological, the latter naturalistic.

---

[1] Metaph., pars. iii.; Scient., vii.

He denotes minds as "*mentes creatæ, particulares, limitatæ :*"
he calls them "*aliquid mentis.*" Thus, the creatural relation
becomes a partitive one ; the theological conception, naturalistic ; the creatures of God, modifications of God. The
more Geulincx feels compelled to concentre all activity in
God, the more must he limit the field of self-activity in
things, so that at last they have no existence for themselves,
but are only effects or modes of God.[1]

2. *Ethics.* — Theology and autology unite in the point
which determines the outlines of ethics. We know ourselves
as creatures of the power of God, as dependent upon him,
and permeated by his activity. This perception of our entire
dependence upon God is at the same time the perception
of our entire lack of power. Our knowledge of self harmonizes with our knowledge of God in the sentence, "*Ubi
nihil vales, ibi nihil velis.*" This thought determines ethics.
Of this principle which it receives from metaphysics it
makes a virtue, in which lies the spirit of renunciation of
the world.

There remains to man nothing higher than to bring his
will and actions in harmony with his knowledge, than to
affirm what his reason teaches him, than to obey it willingly
and perfectly. This love of reason is the fundamental form
of all virtue, of all moral action : its different kinds are
the cardinal virtues, which, from this point, can easily be
determined. We must first perceive the voice of reason by
making a careful study of ourselves, then obey it, doing
what it commands, and, finally, make this obedience the
guiding principle of our conduct, the constant rule of our
lives. Thence the fourth and highest duty naturally follows : we must pretend to be nothing except what we in
truth are, — instruments in the hand of God. In view of
the knowledge of our entire dependence, and utter weakness, we must renounce every idle wish, every false self-
exaltation, and become truly humble in the inmost recesses

[1] Metaph., pars. iii.; Scient., ii.

of our nature. Thus Geulincx determines the four cardinal virtues which proceed from the love of reason or the will conformable to it; viz., diligence, obedience, justice, and humility. The last is the daughter of virtue, and the sum of them all.[1]

This humility is the moral expression of a true estimate of self, and this is itself a necessary consequence of true self-knowledge. Thus, the highest of the virtues appears as the fulfilment of the injunction, γνῶθι σεαυτόν. When we know what we in truth are, every kind of self-exaltation is impossible: those apparent worths which blind our self-love vanish; we see the vanity and nothingness of all our idle wishes and desires; and the host of worldly cares, which are nourished by our self-love, cease to give us pain.

Our self-examination reveals the fact that we conceive a world of which we ourselves form a part, that in this world we are united with a body which we call ours: we see that we have produced, and can produce, nothing of this world; that we do not know how we act upon our body, and cause motions in it; that these motions, therefore, are as little our work as the changes in the rest of the universe; that, therefore, the world which we conceive can neither be the scene nor the object of our activity. Where we can do nothing, we ought to will nothing. Hence we should desire nothing for our body, but should merely contemplate it: we should relate ourselves to this machine which we call our body as to the world in which we live, not practically, but merely theoretically, because, in truth, we can do nothing more. Thus we obey the injunction, " *Ubi nihil vales, ibi nihil velis.*"[2]

---

[1] " *Virtus est amor rationis. Ratio est in nobis imago divinitatis*" (Eth. Tract., i. cap. i. § i. par. 6). " *Diligentia est auscultatio rationis. Obedientia est executio rationis. Justitia est adæquatio rationis*" (Eth. Tract., i. cap. i. § i. par. 6). " *Humilitas est virtutum cardinalium summa. Humilitas circulum absolvit: ultra eam virtuti nihil addi potest. Igitur filia virtutis humilitas* (Ib., § i. par. 2).

[2] " *Sum igitur nudus spectator hujus machinæ. Esse me in hoc mundo-me spectare hunc mundum*" (Eth. Tract., l. sec. ii. § 2, par. 8, par. 14).

The power of our will reaches no farther than our thought: it does not reach beyond our inner world. In this alone should we live and act. A complete renunciation of the world, directed to God, necessarily springs, therefore, from true knowledge of self. We renounce our own self as far as this is of a worldly nature. Our worldly existence, our well-being, and our value in the world, cease therewith to be objects of our interests, cares, and wishes. This renunciation is not an act of vanity, but of piety and modesty. From the false relation to the world, which our self-deception deludes us with, we turn to the true, revealed by our self-knowledge; and this destroys our self-love, and demands the abandonment of all idle wishes.

This kind of renunciation and genuine self-abasement in opposition to self-exaltation, Geulincx calls "*despectio sui.*" It is the consequence and the negative expression, as it were, of the "*inspectio sui.*" Self-knowledge and resignation are, accordingly, the constituents of humility, which is nothing else than submission to the divine order of things, and that state of the mind which is destitute of all the cares of self-love, the "*incuria sui*," as our philosopher well explains the "*despectio sui.*" [1]

Here we see most plainly how the ethical doctrine of the Occasionalists irresistibly tends towards Spinozism. Geulincx himself calls love of reason — the principle of his Ethics — love also of God. He says that the highest of the virtues depends upon love of God and reason. In the "*amor Dei intellectualis*" of Spinoza's Ethics, we find the culmination of what Geulincx had meant by the "*amor Dei ac rationis.*"

But we must first consider the system of Occasionalism in

---

[1] "*Humilitos est contemptio sui præ amore Dei ac rationis. Requiritur ad humilitatem contemptus negativus sui ipsius, quo quis de se non laboret, de non curet, nullam sui præ amore rationis rationem ducat. Amor enim Dei ac rationsi (qui est ipsa virtus) hoc agis in amonte, ut se ipse deserat, a se penitus recedat. — Humilitas est incuria sui. Partes humilitatis sunt duæ; inspectio sui et* **despectio** *sui*" (Eth. Tract., i. sec. ii. § 1).

its application to the *theory of knowledge;* i.e., in the completed form which Malebranche developed in France. He stands between Geulincx and Spinoza. His most important work appeared nine years after the Ethics of the one, and three before that of the other.

CHAPTER IV.

MALEBRANCHE'S STAND-POINT, LIFE, AND WORKS.

I. THE INTUITION OF THE WORLD IN GOD.

IN criticising the doctrine of Descartes, we have already seen that it contains two opposing elements; viz., the theological and naturalistic, the affirmation of the substantiality of God and the world as the totality of natural things. The concept of God requires the complete dependence of things, while that of nature requires their own peculiar independence. This contradiction Descartes could not tolerate. God is, in his system, the only real substance; while minds and bodies are not really substances, though they are called by that name. God in truth is the only substantial and efficient being. Is the action of this being free, or necessary? Does it proceed creatively from arbitrary will, or is it determined by unchangeable laws? Is it will, or nature? Must we conceive it according to Augustine, or Spinoza? Descartes was personally inclined to the former: the tendency of his doctrine was towards the latter. While he seemed to approach Augustine, he actually approached Spinoza.[1]

This characteristic required to be developed in a peculiar system. Starting from Descartes, it struggles towards Augustine, but turns directly towards Spinoza; and, though it violently resists him, against its will it goes so far to mete him that it even crosses the boundary of his system. The stand-point of this trend of thought is remarkable and signi-

---

[1] Cf. book iii. chap. xi. pp. 471–478.

ficant in that in it, on Cartesian principles, Augustinianism and Spinozism almost touch each other, and, at the same time, violently repulse each other.

We find the problem already adumbrated in Descartes. How is a knowledge of things, particularly of bodies, possible, if minds and bodies are substances, opposite in nature, which completely exclude each other? Plainly such a knowledge from those two sides is *not* possible: it *cannot* be by means of the nature of minds and bodies. Descartes himself had shown profoundly how the idea of the perfect reveals in us the idea of the imperfect, how in the light of this idea we become conscious of our own imperfection, i.e., of ourselves, perceive our self-delusion, fall into doubt, and thereby first attain to the certainty of our thinking being. He had shown how in this certainty of self, the existence of things outside of us, the reality of bodies, becomes evident to us through the idea of God, and *only* through this. Our knowledge of things thus appears, even according to Descartes, in its last analysis as an *illumination* through God, as a seeing of things in God or in the light of the divine reason.

This claim is very plainly hinted at by Occasionalism: it is suggested by that assertion of Geulincx, "If you do not know how you do any thing, you do not do it at all: it is not your own activity."[1] Now, we have the perception of the external world without knowing how this perception arises. Our conscious reflection finds it, and pre-supposes it. This intuition, the world as presentation, is not our work; and it is just as little an effect of the external world upon our minds, for such an effect is impossible. Our intuition of the world is, therefore, only possible through God: only in him can we present to ourselves the world without us. We see things in God. That is the central point of the doctrine which *Nicholas Malebranche* made his own. Therewith are indicated the fundamental features which constitute the philosophical character of this man, his importance and position in the course of the development of the Cartesian doctrine. He was a religious and theological thinker of the Augustinian type, and an enthusiastic disciple and profound student of the new philosophy. The type of an *Augustinian Cartesian* was embodied in him. His mode of thought was that of Occasionalism, like Geulincx's: he was the most outspoken opponent of Spinoza, whom he abhorred as an atheist, whose doctrine he rejected — with all sincerity, and in perfect conviction — as atheistic and chimerical. But in spite of it, of all the opponents of Spinoza, there was no other who approached him more closely: of all the Cartesians, there was no other who had so manifestly cleared the way for the fundamental thoughts of Spinoza as Malebranche. While he fled from him, he fell into his hands. It was his historical work to apprehend with religious zeal, and logically develop, the Augustinian element in the doctrine of Descartes. To devote himself to this problem in perfect freedom from disturbance, he found the favoring conditions in the society of priests of the Oratory of Jesus, which, in the midst of the noisy metropolis, occupied a quiet dwelling in Rue St. Honore.

II. THE ORATORY OF JESUS.

Even after the Council of Trent, the desire was active in Catholicism for a deeper theological culture to purify men without alienating them from the Church. To this end, the Oratory of Jesus was founded in Paris, a society of priests without vows. A scientific centre had grown up in that retired society which was regarded as one of the first of the theological circles of France. Their rivals were the Jansenists and Jesuits, — the former with similar aims and tendencies, the latter with opposed. It is no wonder that the Jesuits were hostile to the Oratory; that, with their purpose of restoring the Church, they attacked a society of priests which seemed to them a lot of secret reformers. Wherever Augustinianism was active, the Jesuits were suspicious.

And it was very powerful in the Oratory.   Plato and Augustine were there rated more highly than Aristotle and
Thomas.   The characteristic difference of the two was
manifest in their attitude towards the philosophical movements of the time.   The fathers of the Oratory embraced
Idealism; the Society of Jesus Sensualism.   We have seen
already that the latter were the outspoken opponents of
Descartes, whose doctrine of mind they attacked with the
weapons of Gassendi, while the former sympathized with
Descartes, whose doctrine of God had affinities with Augustinianism.   In this revival of Augustinianism within the
Catholic Church, in this anti-Jesuitical attitude, in this
friendliness towards Cartesianism, the priests of the Oratory
may be compared with the recluses of Port Royal.   But
this mental kinship could not prevent a very bitter and
obstinate controversy from breaking out between the greatest
thinker of the Oratory and the greatest theologian of Port
Royal, between Malebranche and Arnauld.

The founder of the Oratory himself in a certain way
assisted in founding the new philosophy.   Fourteen years
after the founding of the Oratory of Jesus, Cardinal Bérulle
had that memorable conversation with Descartes, in which
he pledged him to put his doctrine on paper, and publish
it (1628).[1]   At his advice, the philosopher went into retirement, and wrote the " Meditations : " Bérulle died too early
(1629) to see the publication of Descartes' works.   His
successor, De Condren, remained faithful to the purposes of
the founder, and recommended the study of these works to
the members of the Oratory.   The Fathers Gibieuf and De la
Barde were personal friends and admirers of the philosopher:
Poisson explained the Essay on Method and the "Geometry,"
and translated the fragment of Mechanics and the Compendium of Music.   The spirit of Descartes was at home in the
Oratory.   His doctrine appeared to the fathers in complete
harmony with Augustine, as the longed-for alliance between

[1] See book iii. chap. iii. pp. 203-205.

religion and reason, Christianity and science. In this feeling, *André Martin*, the first of the members of the Oratory
who publicly taught Cartesianism at a university (Angers),
wrote under the name of Ambrosius Victor, his " Philosophia
Christiana," a work that prepared the way for our philosopher. In his " Athei detecti," the Jesuit Hardouin called
André Martin the teacher of atheism, whom Malebranche
followed. Those persecutions with which we are already
acquainted, which, through the influence of the Jesuits, were
aimed at the doctrine of Descartes, soon threatened the Oratory also. To preserve it from destruction, the superiors of
the society warned the members in 1678 against further cultivating the pernicious doctrine. Then it appeared how deeply
Cartesianism had struck roots. They made answer, " If Cartesianism is a pestilence, more than two hundred of us have
caught it." Four years before, Malebranche's most important
work had appeared. The Cartesian doctrine in alliance with
the spirit of religious contemplation and the Augustinian
mode of thought was already accepted in the Oratory when
Malebranche became a member of it.

III. MALEBRANCHE'S LIFE AND WRITINGS.

1. *Incidents.* — Fontenelle's memorial oration and the biographical remarks of the Jesuits André and Adry, which
have recently been discovered by the Abbé Blampignon, are
our sources of information concerning the life of Nicholas
Malebranche, which externally was very monotonous.[1] He
was born in Paris, Aug. 6, 1638, the son of a royal officer,
and the last and weakest of many children. Even in early
life he was obliged to endure an operation, in consequence
of which his fate prescribed a celibate life. Nature herself,
in harmony with his inclination, directed him to the clerical
office. When he arrived at the age of manhood, — usually
the period of greatest vigor, — he had to suffer for twenty
years with a nausea at the stomach, that made every attempt

---

[1] Bouillier, ii. chap. ii. p. 16.

to take nourishment painful.   In body he lacked every thing that belongs to strength and beauty.   He was unusually tall and slender, extremely thin, and besides he was deformed by a very large curve of the spine.   His head alone was well developed, his eyes fiery, and the expression of his countenance was mild and amiable.   He bore his bodily afflictions with the greatest patience, lived temperately, and in great quietness, and thereby attained a quiet of mind which strengthened his intellectual powers, and preserved his life. No one had believed that with such a body he could live to be seventy-seven years old.   That he might have the care of his mother as long as possible, he remained with his parents until his sixteenth year.   Destined for the clerical calling, he took his philosophical course in the College de la Marche, and then pursued his theological studies in Sorbonne.   These studies left him with feelings similar to those with which Descartes left the school of La Flèche.   Thus dissatisfied, he became at the age of one and twenty a priest of the Oratory of Jesus.   Even then he was not at once seized by the prevailing intellectual current.   His was one of those profound natures who must themselves experience what they are to believe.   His philosophical needs and talents remained concealed until his twenty-sixth year.   They manifested themselves only in the fact that none of the learned, philosophical, and historical studies with which he had been occupied in his first five years in the Oratory, satisfied him. At the end of that time he had the painful experience that his thirst for knowledge remained without satisfaction.   That Cartesian desire for knowledge, out of sympathy with the Renaissance, with its study of history and antiquity, would not let him rest, though he was unable to discover in himself the source of truth, and had no idea where it was to be found.   Then one of those significant accidents that never fail to appear in the lives of such men, revealed to him his true vocation.   His path one day lay through Rue St. Jacques; and he entered a book-store, where his attention

was called to the latest literary novelty, the "Traité de
l'homme" of Descartes, which had just been published. Attracted by the title, Malebranche took the book with him.
As he read it, his curiosity changed into the greatest admiration. For the first time he saw a strict, evident, well-
arranged method of explanation and exposition : for the first
time he felt the charm of philosophy. There was what he
had so long sought for, as it were, instinctively and in vain.
He had to put the book down more than once because his
throbbing heart would not let him read further. Now his
work becomes clear to him. He will study the works of
Descartes, at first nothing but these. At a single stroke,
as it were, he felt alienated from all other objects, and
entirely absorbed in the doctrine of Descartes. After he
had devoted ten years to the study of it, and had thoroughly
mastered it (1664–74), he published his most important
work, "On the Investigation of Truth." The book soon
made him famous. After it appeared, he was called
"*Auteur de la recherche de la vérité.*" The Oratory shared
in this fame, and in a general assembly the fathers voted
him thanks, and congratulated him.

A series of writings followed this principal work, extending even to the last year of his life. Their essential theme
was the unity of religion and theology, of Christianity and
metaphysics, of Augustinianism and Cartesianism (when
logically developed). It was *this* unity which Malebranche
represented.

2. *Controversies.* — As much as he loved peace, he could
not prevent his writings from provoking opponents, who did
not cease to attack him ; and he never tired of defending
himself. That he, a priest of the Oratory, presented to his
generation the doctrine of Augustine in alliance with that of
Descartes, and by the depth of his thoughts as well as by
the beauty of their exposition gained influence over men,
necessarily embittered the Jesuits, who felt his triumph over
Pelagianism and Scholasticism as a double defeat. Some of

them inclined towards him when Arnauld, their more obstinate and most dreaded enemy, took the field against him.
Malebranche's doctrine of divine grace, which he developed
in a particular work (1680), separated the two who were
friendly to each other before. Arnauld opened the contest
with his book "On True and False Ideas" (1683), which
was aimed at Malebranche's theory of knowledge. In the
following years (1683–86), polemic after polemic appeared.
The opponents rivalled each other in the violence and bitter-
ness of their criticisms, until finally the matter seemed to
rest. Then arose the controversy between Régis and Malebranche concerning the pleasures of sense and their moral
worth. Arnauld seized this opportunity to renew the controversy, after a long pause, with undiminished violence.
Malebranche had finished the first part of his reply when
his irreconcilable enemy died, Aug. 8, 1694, in his exile in
the Netherlands. Malebranche also remained unreconciled;
and even after the death of his opponent, in the feeling of
the injustice which he had suffered, he could not restrain
himself from replying. His essay on grace had found decided opponents among the ablest and most influential theologians of the French church, particularly in *Bossuet* and
Fénelon, both of whom were favorable to Cartesianism.
Bossuet vainly endeavored to bring Malebranche to other
thoughts; he feared that the philosopher of the Oratory
would sow the seed of heresies; and, at his suggestion, his
disciple and friend, Fénelon, wrote a violent reply to the
essay on grace, which, however, remained unpublished, and
did not appear until a century after the death of its author.
The relation between Malebranche and Bossuet changed
when, some years later, a bitter conflict broke out between
the latter and Fénelon (the bishops of Meaux and Cambray)
concerning the question whether, in the love of God, the
passive state of entire self-denial — as the mystics and quiet-
ists insist upon it — is necessary or to be condemned? Bossuet rejected the quietistic view to which Fénelon inclined.

Malebranche then wrote his essay "On the Love of God" (1697), which maintained Bossuet's position, and so won him that he took the first step towards a closer friendship with Malebranche, which was never again disturbed.

The most important subject of controversy between Malebranche and Arnauld related to the doctrine of divine providence and grace, of unconditional predestination, determining every single event, of groundless arbitrary divine will, capable of being limited by no kind of necessity and freedom on the part of others (the independence of the human will). The divine will is not to be bound by the divine wisdom and the unchangeableness of his being, by the necessity of a best constitution of the world and the unchangeableness of its laws. He causes not merely the facts which happen, but the occasions of their happening; and certainly, this divine activity concerns not merely the universal order, but each particular case. As soon as an unchangeable law prevails, — whether a physical or moral necessity, — God is subject to it; and the creed of the Church that declares an omnipotent Creator, is false. These are, in brief, the considerations which, in the polemical form of unrelenting censure and bitter reproach, the strictly Jansenistic Arnauld urges against his opponent. Every acknowledgment of a necessity in God, every attempt to construct a *théodicée*, every optimistic theory which regards the divine will as bound to create the perfect and best, appeared to him as a characteristic of naturalism — in opposition to Christian faith — which he had reason enough to find in Malebranche's doctrine: he might have found it, even in the doctrine of Descartes. It was the point in which Malebranche, against his will as it were, affirmed the eternal necessity of things in God. He affirmed it without injury to his piety and his orthodoxy, which could not have been more sincere. And, therefore, Arnauld's judgments seemed to him so unjust: he was frightened from the mirror which the latter held before him as he was terrified by the doctrine of Spinoza.

Divine predestination concerns also the motions of external bodies; through these, those of our bodies, the occasional causes of our volitions and actions, which, therefore, can by no means be independent of God. This kind of psychical predestination by the motion of bodies was called "*prémotion physique.*" Upon this subject the Jansenist *Boursier* wrote an elaborate work in which he rejected every limitation of divine predestination, and taught it in the sense of "*prémotion*" (*præmotion*).[1] (He agreed with Malebranche in four points, and was friendly to him.) But human freedom was not thereby to be denied. Malebranche defended it in his "Thoughts on Prémotion Physique," and aptly characterized the contradiction of Boursier, who put human actions entirely within the power of God, and still attempted to maintain their freedom. We might just as well say, "God changes a globe into a cube without injuring its spherical form, or a cube into a globe without removing its corners." It was Malebranche's last work in the last year of his life.

He lived in his cell in the Oratory in the deepest retirement for more than a half-century. Sometimes he enjoyed the quiet of the country at the house of a hospitable friend. He was so accustomed to the solitude of his retired life, and was so absorbed in his thoughts, that he seldom spoke, and was called in the Oratory the "silent and meditative man." His fame as a philosopher and an author brought him many visitors. Scholars who came to Paris wished to see the man who wrote the work on the investigation of truth. Even during his last sickness he became acquainted with the English philosopher, Berkeley, and had an eager conversation with him concerning the existence of matter. It is said that the exertion hastened his death.[2] He died after four months of suffering, Oct. 13, 1715.

---

[1] De l'action de Dieu sur les créatures, traité dans lequel on prouve la prémotion physique. (Paris, 1713.)

[2] Cf. my work, Francis Bacon and His Followers, 2d ed. (Brockhaus, 1875), book iii. chap. xi. p. 669.

The century of the French illumination (*Aufklärung*) forgot the doctrines of this man, but not his fame.   Voltaire
called him "the great dreamer of the Oratory;" Buffon,
"the divine Malebranche."   His style was admired: even
Voltaire called him a master of philosophical style.   Some
have been pleased to call him the French Plato, a comparison which Malebranche deserves neither as a thinker nor
an author, and which neither his doctrine of ideas nor his
dialogues justify.   Perhaps we can more correctly say, that,
after Descartes, he was the greatest metaphysician of France,
if we do not forget that the distance between them is great.
In truth, Descartes stands in France alone and incomparable.

3. *Writings.* — Malebranche's   public   literary   activity
covers a period of more than forty years.   It began with his
most important work, " De la recherche de la vérité," the
first three books of which appeared in 1674, the three following in the next year.   Six editions of it were published during the lifetime of the author, the last of which (Paris, 1712)
is the completest.   Seventeen explanations (*éclaircissements*)
were added to this.   The Reformed preacher Lenfant, to the
great delight of its author, translated the work into Latin,
" De inquirenda veritate libri sex " (Genevæ, 1685).

" Conversations chrétiennes, dans lesquelles on justifie la
vérité de la religion et de la morale de Jésus Christ " (Paris,
1677), followed the above-mentioned work.   It was written at
the request of Duke Chevreuse, and published without the
name of its author.   Next came "Traité de la nature et de la
grâce, en trois discours " (Amsterdam, 1680).   This essay was
the occasion of the controversies above spoken of.   Then followed " Méditations chrétiennes et métaphysiques" (Cologne,
1683), which is regarded as his masterpiece in point of
style.   Although the first edition consisted of four thousand
copies, a second was soon necessary.   The same year "Traité
de morale " appeared (Cologne, 1683).   (According to Bouillier, Malebranche was said to have written this work at the
request of the Princess Elizabeth, — which is difficult to be-

lieve, as the latter had died three years before.[1]) After the first work, which laid the foundation of his philosophy, the most important for his philosophical point of view is "Entretiens sur la métaphysique et sur la religion" (Rotterdam, 1688). It is the most concise statement of his doctrine.

His last works were "Traité de l'amour de Dieu" (Lyons, 1677), "Entretiens d'un philosophe chrétien avec un philosophe chinois sur l'existence et la nature de Dieu" (Paris, 1708), "Réflexion sur la prémotion physique, contre le P. Boursier" (Paris, 1715). His controversial writings against Arnauld were published in four volumes, — "Recueil de toutes ses réponses à Arnauld" (Paris, 1709).

The result of Arnauld's attacks was that the essay on nature and grace was put on the Romish Index, May 29, 1689, and, indeed, without the remark "*donec corrigatur.*" The Latin translation of his most important work, the "Traité de morale," and the "Entretiens sur la métaphysique et sur la religion," met the same fate twenty years later. As painful as this was to the pious Malebranche, his convictions remained unshaken. We must follow the truth, wrote he to a friend, "*per infamiam et bonam famam.*"[2]

---

[1] Bouillier, ii. chap. ii. p. 37.

[2] Ib., chap. ii. p. 25. Even in his lifetime a collection of his works was published in eleven volumes (Paris, 1712). Genoude and Lourdoueix published complete collective editions in two quartos (Paris, 1838). The three principal works (Recherche de la vérité, Méditations chrétiennes, Entretiens sur la métaphysique) were published with a revised text and an introduction in four volumes by Jules Simon (Paris, 1877).

CHAPTER V.

MALEBRANCHE'S DOCTRINE. (a) THE PROBLEM OF KNOWLEDGE OF OCCASIONALISM.

I. DUALISM AND OCCASIONALISM.

1. *The Substantiality of Things.*

THE principle which determines the doctrine of our philosopher consists in the application of the principles of dualism to the possibility of our knowledge of things. How can the nature of body be evident to mind, when there is no sort of natural community between the two, but rather a complete opposition ? In his maintenance of the latter, Malebranche is through and through Cartesian. With Descartes, he explains the difference of essence between thinking and extended substances as the foundation of philosophy, and, also, defines substance as that being which can exist, and be thought, without another, while the opposite is true of its states or modifications, the manner of its existence (*manière d'être*). Now, thought is independent of extension, and conversely ; thinking and extended substances (minds and bodies) are, therefore, independent of each other, and hence, in this respect, substances.[1]

Extension is divisible ; its parts can be united or separated : in this way spatial relations arise, which form different and changing orders. The order in which the parts unite is figure : its change in space is motion. The only modifications of extension are form and motion : the corresponding modifications of thought are intellect and desire. Intellect

---

[1] Entret. sur la métaphys., chap. l.

expresses itself in the threefold form of sense-perception, imagination, and pure reason; the faculty of desire in the twofold form of inclination and passion.

How is a true knowledge of things possible by means of human knowledge subject to such modifications? We are exposed to errors, and must inquire into their sources in order to find the path to truth. For aught we can yet say, it is possible, that, on account of its nature, our thought is in danger at every step of falling into errors, that the Will-o'-the-wisps of error are seen in each of its modifications, and mistaken by us for the light of truth. These illusions are to be laid bare. True knowledge sees things as they are in themselves without any foreign addition. But through our sensation and imagination, we do not consider things as they are in themselves, but as they affect us, and as they are to our sensibility, through the impressions they make upon it. And while we are under the power of our inclinations and passions, we have just as little power to perceive the true nature of things. We do not see what they are in themselves, but how we are sensible of them, how we regard them, and what they are worth to us in the state of life in which we exist. What, therefore, we are conscious of through sense and imagination, through inclination and passion (by which we are blinded), is not the true nature of things, but always only their relation to us. What we are conscious of is, in the last analysis, only our states of consciousness dependent upon the impressions made upon our senses. And pure understanding (*esprit pur*) taken by itself, opposed, as it is, in its isolation to things without us, independent, as it is, to the rest of the modifications of thought, can, at first view, reveal to us clearly and distinctly neither the nature of things nor their relations.

Our modes of presentation and desire are, accordingly, so many sources of error, so many paths upon which the truth is not to be found. To investigate the truth, these erroneous paths must be avoided, and, therefore, must first of all be known.   The problem of our philosopher is, therefore, divided into the investigation of those five sources of error and the universal method of truth.   There are, accordingly, six books in the whole work: (1) "On the Senses;" (2) "On the Imagination;" (3) "On the Understanding, or Pure Mind;" (4) "On the Inclinations, or Natural Affections;" (5) "On the Passions;" (6) "On the Universal Method of Truth."   The fundamental question was the problem of knowledge; and the conception of it was, as we see, absolutely determined by the dualistic principles of the Cartesian doctrine.[1]

2. *The Inactivity of Things.* — The nature of the material world consists only in extension that is divisible, movable, capable of form.   Bodies can be moved, but they are incapable of self-motion.   Extension is destitute of energy, bodies are not moving forces.   Every change that takes place in the material world is a motion, but no body has power to produce motion: none is its producing, efficient cause.   Now, motion is the *only* kind of effect that can be attributed to bodies.   If they are unable to cause motion, they are unable to cause *any thing whatever:* they are of themselves completely inactive, entirely destitute of power to act upon mind and change its states.   Matter cannot modify mind.   It cannot affect it either agreeably or disagreeably: it cannot make it happy or unhappy.   Now, since the universe consists of minds and bodies, and bodies exert power neither upon matter nor mind, it follows that they do not exert power at all, but that power is exerted through them.   If we call the acting force cause, we must declare that bodies are incapable of being causes, that bodies are no real or actual causes.

It might seem that the motion whose cause body cannot be, is produced by minds.   But how can minds move body, since the nature of both is such as to exclude any kind of connection?   Now, composition or union is a kind of connection, and is inconceivable without motion.   Man is a

<hr/>

[1] Recherche de la vérité, liv. i. chaps. i., iv.; liv. iii. conclusion.

union of soul and body; but neither can the soul of itself attract the body, nor the body the soul. A human being, therefore, is a union of two substances, neither of which could have produced the union. The cause of human existence is not to be found, therefore, in nature, not in things, neither in minds nor bodies. The will of man moves nothing, not even the smallest body. I will to move my arm in a particular direction, and the motion takes place. If the will were the producing cause of the motion, a necessary connection must exist and be knowable between it and the motion: the motion must have, in that case, depended upon the will mediately or immediately, therefore upon consciousness, and we must be the more capable of producing motions in our bodies, the more plainly we see the connection between will and motion in all its connecting links, and the anatomist must be also the strongest athlete. The motion of the arm follows the volition without our perceiving the connection, without our knowing the series of connecting links that communicate motion from the will to the body. Motion, therefore, takes place in entire independence of our thought and knowledge. Now, since will is a modification of thought, motion takes place independently of our volition: it follows after it, but not out of it. Even if we were able to follow motion from one organ of the body to another, its connection with the *will* would not thereby be known. Suppose it is the animal spirits which, by means of the nerves, set the muscles in motion, and through these the arm: we only see how one moving body moves another, but not how the will produces motion in the animal spirits, not how the soul moves the body. This connection is unknown and unknowable. It is a natural impossibility, since there is between will and motion, thought and extension, no community resulting from their natural activity.

Body moves neither mind nor body, nor is it moved by mind. If now, nevertheless, bodies are united with each other and with minds in harmony with law, if there is an

order of things, the cause of it is not the efficient nature of
things themselves.   Things are not active beings ; they are
not real and true causes ; they do not act.   Yet natural
events appear everywhere dependent upon natural causes.
When bodies collide, their motion is changed according to a
constant law.   If we will to move the arm, the arm in fact
moves.   In the former case, the collision of the bodies
appears the material cause of the change in motion that follows it: in the latter, the will seems the cause of the motion
of the arm.   This natural causality must be affirmed, and at
the same time the activity of natural things must be denied.
What remains, therefore, but to maintain that natural causes
are not the efficient causes of things?   A ball strikes a ball ;
it imparts to the latter its motion ; it is the natural cause of
this motion.   But since the ball can never be the producing
cause of motion, it cannot be the producing cause of imparted motion.   In brief, the natural cause is not the producing.   What is it, then ?   What is a cause without
activity ?   It is not active but passive cause, not the force
but the medium and mere vehicle of efficiency, not the efficient but the occasional cause, not real cause but mere occasion.   The so-called natural causes are all of them merely
occasional.   In this point, Malebranche completely agrees
with Geulincx, although he does not directly appeal to him.
He is a Dualist, like Descartes, and an Occasionalist, like
Geulincx.   His Occasionalism was the necessary consequence
of the Dualism which he maintained as a fundamental
principle.[1]

3. *The Causality of God.* — Now, if all natural causes are
merely occasional, what is the producing cause?   The negative answer is evident from the simple conversion of the following sentence : if no natural thing is a real or true cause,
a real or true cause is also no natural thing, no finite, imperfect thing whatever, but the infinite and perfect being
alone ; i.e., *God* himself, who can be but *one*, since his per-

---

[1] Rech. de la vérité, liv. vi. part ii. chap. iii.   Entret., vii.

fection is not relative, but absolute. There is but *one* true cause, and it includes all true energy in itself; and, without it, there is no kind of active power. This one true cause is God. That is the conclusion of the true philosophy, which, in this point, is in entire harmony with true religion. Only by means of the principles of the new philosophy, i.e., the doctrine of Descartes, is this great and decisive truth clearly and distinctly conceived. Only from this point, therefore, is the harmony between reason and faith, philosophy and religion, possible. Malebranche fixes upon this point of coincidence as his goal, and keeps it constantly in mind.

From this fundamental view, the opposition of this philosophy to the old is at once evident. There is but *one* true cause: all the rest are occasional, therefore not in truth causal at all. God is the only cause. In comparison with him, natural things are not less causal, but *not causes at all*, not causes in the relative sense, but, in the strict understanding of the term, not causes at all. The question is as to the difference between God and the world, God and things; and it is precisely in this point that Malebranche found the difference between the new philosophy and the old. We cannot explain the difference between God and the world by the different kind of causality or activity of the two. In that case, God would be regarded as the absolute, highest, and first cause, and things as relative, lower, and secondary causes; God and the world would then differ only in degree; things would be causes, only with less power. Malebranche states with the utmost emphasis that the contrast between false and true, pagan and Christian, philosophy, consists in the affirmation and denial of secondary causes. He insists upon their absolute denial. Under whatever name they are affirmed, whether as forms, faculties, qualities, energies, plastic forces, as soon as things are regarded as causes or agencies, "philosophy falls into the most dangerous of all errors." For what is the necessary result? To be a cause is to effect, to produce, to create. There is no efficiency that is not of a productive, creative nature. No finite and natural thing can create: none can change of itself or by means of another finite thing. To exert a power of causality is to create: to be a cause is to be God. These assertions Malebranche regards as identical. If things are causes, they are, therefore, of a divine nature: as secondary causes, they are divinities of the second and a lower degree, "little deities;" and nature herself a world everywhere filled with divine or demonic powers. Is not this paganism? To admit secondary causes is to affirm paganism. With this mode of thought, says Malebranche, the heart may be a Christian, but the head is a pagan. The error is contrary to reason because it is based on an absurd proposition: a secondary cause is a little deity; i.e., a deity which is none, a pure chimera. It is also pernicious because of its inevitable moral consequences. What one regards as divine, he must affirm. Natural things appear to partake of the divine nature, and the human will is blinded by such an imagination, and insnared in desires for the world; the love for God becomes stifled by the love for his creatures; the mind must certainly be a pagan, and the heart, filled with such desires, can hardly remain a Christian. Hence Malebranche called this error the most dangerous in the philosophy of the ancients.[1]

II. CHRISTIANITY AND PHILOSOPHY.

1. *The Divine Will as the Law of Nature.* — Things, accordingly, exist, persist, and act, only by means of the divine causality. They exist through God; i.e., they are creatures, minds as well as bodies. Body of itself is neither at rest nor in motion. God, therefore, is the author, both of rest and motion in the material world. He alone is the author of the union of soul and body; therefore, of human existence. He causes in our mind, both sensation and knowledge. Without the divine assistance we could not

---

[1] Rech. de la vérité, liv. vi. part ii. chap. iii. "*De l'erreur la plus dangereuse de la philosophie des anciens.*"

move a finger nor pronounce a syllable. "Without God," said Malebranche, "man in the world would be as immovable as a rock, and as dumb as a block. Without him, the union of body and soul is impossible. He must unite his ever active will with our ever powerless desires that our will may show itself by the corresponding action.[1] A creature is from its very nature destitute of power as the divine will is omnipotent by reason of its nature. To effect is to create. To suppose that a finite will acts creatively, is a cause, has effects, is as great a contradiction as to suppose that the all-powerful will of God is not creative.[2] The existence of the world and its conformity with law is, therefore, only the effect of God. All the activity in the world is his creating activity. The world exists, i.e., it is created: ·the world endures, i.e., creation does not pause, does not cease, does not pass away, works continually. The continuance of the world is preservation by God: the preservation of the world is continual creation.

The causal nexus of things is the divine will, only this. It is the indissoluble bond that connects all creatures; by it alone things are connected; by it alone soul and body are united, by it alone the world endures and lives. "The universe is in God, but God is not in the universe." Malebranche uses the first sentence to state his own theory; the second, that of Spinoza; and he does it expressly to denote the doctrine of the latter, and to reject it (as atheistic). If God is in the universe, producing activity is in things themselves, and the door is thrown wide open for that most dangerous of all errors which deifies things. But if the universe is in God, he alone is the cause of every thing.[3]

The world exists because God wills it: it obeys law because the divine will is steadfast and constant. "God is wise; he loves order, and will not violate it; he acts in accordance with it, does not at any time disturb it." The

---

[1] Entret., vii.   [2] Rech. de la vérité, liv. vi. p. ii. chap. 3.   [3] Entret., viii.

motions of the material world, and the union of soul and
body in man, take place according to this eternal order.

The divine purpose in this union can be none other than
to test the human soul. Its duty is to stand this test, to
keep its independent and higher nature free and pure in
immediate union with God, in spite of its union with the
body. "God can unite minds with bodies, but he cannot
subject minds to bodies." Reason enables us to see clearly
that the soul is independent of its body. Experience
daily convinces us of the contrary. We are dependent
upon our bodily states, and miserable because of this dependence.

2. *Error as the Consequence of Sin.* — Whence this dependence? God never willed it, nor caused it: he could do
neither. It was not our original state (immediately dependent upon God), but the wretched condition which we have
brought upon ourselves: we have fallen, and thereby come
under the power of the body. Human nature is oppressed
by the yoke of the body because of the guilt of sin: it is
original sin that has deprived us of the independence of the
soul. Sin pre-supposes freedom. In the state preceding the
fall, the soul was independent of the body, and dependent
directly on God. How was freedom possible in such a state
of dependence? This possibility is inconceivable. "Freedom," said Malebranche, "is a mystery."

The divine will is unchangeable. God wills the independence of the mind, and he does not cease to will it even
after we have lost it through the guilt of sin. He willed
it originally according to his wisdom, and wills now to
restore that which has been lost, according to his mercy: he
desires to save us from sin through Christ. God's will
being the only cause, we live in a double union: our mind is
united with God, upon whom it directly depends, and likewise with a body, upon which it does *not* depend. The fall
of man reversed this relation: it estranged us from the
divine light, and made us subject to the body. Now, God

can still only will our restoration ; i.e, salvation.[1] If philosophy, by its own resources, can point out that the path of holiness alone can lead us to truth, Malebranche's object is accomplished ; viz., the unity of philosophy and religion, of metaphysics and Christianity, of Cartesianism and Augustinianism. To understand Malebranche, we must realize with all clearness *how* in his mind the two parts meet, and with what important results the Christian religion and Augustinianism co-operate in his solution of the problem of knowledge.

Truth consists, as Descartes taught, in the clear and distinct conception of things. Obscure and confused conceptions are not true: our sensations are caused by our external impressions; our imaginations by our inner. Neither teach what things are in themselves, but only what they are for us. Neither the senses nor the imagination, therefore, give us knowledge ; and, as Malebranche repeatedly urged, we must carefully distinguish between feeling (*sentir*) and knowing (*connaitre*) if we wish to avoid error. Our sensations are not, as such, false, since only through them do we learn how other bodies are related to ours: they show what is useful or hurtful to our body, what tends to preserve or endanger our life ; and as long as sensations are regarded only in *this* sense, they do not lead us into error. They do not lead us into error until we use them to attain a knowledge of things. " We should consider the senses as false witnesses in relation to the truth," said Malebranche, " but as true counsellors in relation to the preservation and needs of life ! "

To seek to know through the senses is nothing else than to make our judgment and thought dependent upon them. And that is the root of error. We err as soon as our thought falls under the control of the senses. But how is it possible to *avoid* this after the mind has once become dependent upon the body? Dependence is the penalty of

---

[1] Entret., iv.

sin, in consequence of which thought comes under the dominion of the senses, takes them as guides to knowledge, and thereby falls completely under the power of error, and no longer distinguishes between feeling and knowing.

3. *Knowledge as Illumination.* — But if error is the penalty of sin, we can get rid of it only by a thorough eradication of sin; i.e., by salvation or the immediate union of the soul with God. We err necessarily and inevitably while the soul depends upon the body with which it was united by God, but to which it was by no means subjected by God: we know the truth just as necessarily and inevitably when the soul depends upon God, when our mind is immediately united with the divine. Error is the guilt of sin, the darkening of the soul by the body which controls it: knowledge is the illumination of the soul by the divine light. It is possible only through God, as error is possible only by turning from God, by subjection to the yoke of the body; i.e., by sin.

From this point we can get the clearest perception of the inmost motive and problem of Malebranche. He took the Cartesian Dualism for his foundation, and logically developed it into Occasionalism. This logically denies the activity of things, and admits only the causality of the divine will. Malebranche opposes this conception to the philosophy of the ancients, i.e., to Naturalism, and in this point agrees with Augustine. But even the divine causality cannot destroy the dualism of mind and body, since the foundation and principle of the doctrine would thereby be destroyed: the divine causality, therefore, cannot make the mind dependent upon body. This dependence is not possible in, and by means of, God, but it exists, nevertheless, in fact. It is, therefore, only possible through ourselves, through our estrangement from God, through sin which darkens our mind and causes error. But if error is the result of sin or our estrangement from God, knowledge, or the destruction of error, is only possible through our union with God and his illumination.

Now, if it can be proved by purely philosophical arguments that our knowledge of things is only possible in and through God, that we see things in God, a very important regressive inference results. If knowledge is only possible through union with God, error can only arise by our fall from God: error is, therefore, a proof of sin; and since, as experience shows, we are inevitably involved in it, the same is true of the sin which causes it. The error in which we live, and which clings to us, is a proof of *original sin*. That is the central point of Augustinianism, which is, dogmatically, the acutest and completest expression of the Christian doctrine. The core of the doctrine of Malebranche now lies plainly before our eyes. The proposition that knowledge is only possible as illumination, that we see things in God, forms the connecting link between philosophy and religion, metaphysics and Christianity. Every thing, therefore, depends upon the philosophical proof of this proposition, and the vindication of it as the theory of knowledge. This is the problem which is still to be solved.

CHAPTER VI.

(b) SOLUTION OF THE PROBLEM: THE INTUITION OF THINGS IN GOD.

I. OBJECTS AND KINDS OF KNOWLEDGE.

AS different as are the objects of human knowledge, so different are its kinds. The objects of our knowledge are God, our own minds, other finite minds, and body. The perfect can never be evident from the imperfect, nor the infinite from the finite. Our knowledge of God is not, therefore, deduced, but original, and is of all our knowledge the clearest and most distinct. The consciousness of God is the light by which we know. *Bodies*, on the other hand, are not knowable of and through themselves: they are not of an intelligible, but of a material, nature, extended substances, independent of us, and opposite to us in nature. It is as impossible for mind to go beyond the limits of its thinking nature as for body to go beyond extension. How can they affect each other? How can mind be acted upon by matter? How can matter make its way into mind? The objects of the mind are only *conceived* things (ideas). If there are ideas which present the nature of body clearly and distinctly, then, and only then, is a knowledge of things possible.

If we were not ourselves of a mental nature, we should never learn that there are other minds: if we did not know by our own experience what sensations, conceptions, and desires are, we would have no suspicion that similar facts exist in other beings. We know other minds only by means of analogy, not, therefore, immediately, but by a comparison guided by our own inner experience. We suspect that they are similar to us: we know it, as Malebranche says, "*par conjecture.*" *We ourselves* are the original with which we compare them: the criterion for the knowledge of men is the *knowledge of self.* In what does this consist? We need no medium for it as we do for the knowledge of the nature of body; only a conception or idea could be such a medium: but in the knowledge of self, the being which we conceive coincides with the conceiving being; the knowledge of self, therefore, does not take place through ·*ideas.* It has the character of *immediate* certainty. Malebranche denotes it by the term "*conscience.*" But this immediate consciousness does not extend beyond our inner experience: we know of ourselves nothing more or less than what we inwardly and directly perceive. Before we experience joy and pain, we do not know what emotions (*affecte*) are: we know ourselves only so far as we have experience of ourselves, only through inner perception, or, as Malebranche says, "*par sentiment intérieur.*" [1]

We are not in a position to comprehend, to make clear to ourselves, to realize, all the possible modifications of our thought, all possible inner experiences in our consciousness. There is, therefore, no clear and distinct knowledge of self; but there is indeed an idea which presents to us the nature of body clearly and distinctly. Malebranche, therefore, does *not* admit the Cartesian assertion that the nature of mind is more clearly evident to us than that of body. Descartes saw that sensible qualities are our states of sensation, conceptions modifications of thought, but only because they could *not* be modifications of extension. He was by no means able to so evidently deduce the different sensations from the nature of thought as the different figures from that of extension. Mathematics is clearer than psychology, and that is a distinct proof that the nature of body is more

---

[1] Rech. de la vérité, liv. iii. part ii. chap. 7.

evident than that of the soul : the evidence for the latter is
plainly less. If both were knowable only in the same degree, we could as easily and clearly deduce colors and tones
from mind as the figures of a triangle, square, etc., from
extension (body). If two ideas are equally clear, and at
the same time completely different, they could never be
mistaken for each other, and their difference would always
be evident to us. Soul and body are fundamentally different. If the ideas of soul and body are alike clear, how
is it that so many men cannot distinguish them, but conceive the body far more distinctly than the difference of
one from the other? The explanation is, that the nature
of the soul is by no means so evident to our consciousness,
that our knowledge of self is by no means absolutely clear,
that it is rather, as Malebranche expresses it, a " *connaissance
confuse.*" [1]

We can illustrate the difference of knowledge in respect
to its objects and kinds by sight. What makes things visible
is light : we see things in light. We cannot see our own act
of seeing, but we are certain of it through our experience ;
and from this certainty of our own power of seeing, we infer
that of others. As our power of seeing is related to the
light, so is our power of knowing to God. As our power of
seeing is related to things in the light (images of things), so
is our power of knowing to the ideas of body. As our inner
experience of color is related to our seeing, so is our knowing to our own soul ; and as our own power of seeing is related to that of others, so is our·knowledge to other minds.

Of the four objects of knowledge, only one, accordingly, is
completely evident and clear ; viz., *body.* Bodies can be
known only through *ideas*, and through ideas only bodies are
knowable. The question concerning the knowledge of
things is, accordingly, resolved into the question concerning
ideas.

---

[1] Rech. de la vérité, liv. iii. part ii. chap. vii. par. iv.; Eclairc., xi.; Entret.,
iii.

II. MALEBRANCHE'S DOCTRINE OF IDEAS.

1. *The Origin of Ideas.* — How is a clear knowledge of things possible? Reduced to its simplest and ultimate form, this question runs, How are ideas possible, and what is their origin? The ideas of things are immediate objects of our consciousness, and as such they are in our mind. The question is, *How* came they in our mind, whence have we received them? There are, at first view, three possibilities for the solution of this problem: ideas are given to us either by the body, or by the soul, or by God. There are two cases of each of the two last possibilities: either the soul, creating ideas, produces them out of itself, or they belong to the soul as its properties: they are modifications of thought which we know through inner experience. God produces ideas in the soul, either by stamping them all at once upon it, and making them innate, or creating single ideas anew in the soul every time, as occasion demands.[1]

Let us suppose the first case: there are bodies, which, according to the Peripatetic view, produce ideas in us. Now, bodies themselves cannot enter into the soul: there must, therefore, be copies, or resembling forms, that peel off from body, touch our senses, and impress themselves upon it (*espèces impresses*), then are made intelligible, are transformed into sensation, and become consciousness (*espèces expresses*). If the images of a body go out from the body itself, they must be parts of it. But, if so, the material substance must become less and less, until it is finally completely resolved into images. If those forms are parts of bodies, they are themselves material, and therefore impenetrable. Now, since they fill all space, from the stars to human eyes, it is impossible to see how they penetrate these spaces which are filled, and, in the thousand-fold crossings and disturbances to which they are necessarily subject, can produce definite and distinct impressions.[2] And, even granting that these

---

[1] Rech. de la vérité, liv. iii. part ii. chap. i.
[2] Ib., liv. iii. p. ii. chap. ii.

copies as effects of bodies are communicated to the organs of our senses, this communication would still consist in motion. Now, how is it possible for motion to be transformed into sensation? "I am indeed able," said Malebranche, "to follow the activity of the sun, for example, through all the space between it and me; but since this space is filled, I see, of course, that the sun cannot make an impression upon me where it is, that its activity must be transmitted even to the place where I am, even through my eyes, and through these to my brain. But advancing thus from motion to motion, I do not comprehend how the sensation comes into existence. This transformation of motion into sensation has always appeared to me perfectly incomprehensible. What a wonderful transformation! An impression upon my eyes metamorphosed into a flash of light! I see this flash, not in my soul, of which it is a sensation, not in my brain, where the motion terminates, not in my eye, where the impression is made, but in the air, — in the air, I say, which is completely incapable of such a modification. What a miracle!"[1] Sensation can never result from motion. If so, body would be able to modify the soul, and body and soul could not be opposite in nature. From whatever point of view we consider the matter, it is evident from every reason that it is impossible for bodies to produce ideas in us.

There remain, therefore, but two alternatives: either the cause of ideas in the soul is the soul itself, or God.

It may be that the soul produces ideas out of itself, or possesses them among its properties (as modifications of thought). Let us examine these alternatives. The first case has three possibilities; viz., the soul produces ideas either out of nothing, or out of material impressions, or according to the object to which the idea relates, like a copy according to its original. To produce something from *nothing* is to create. But the soul has no creative power, and does not, therefore, create ideas. But if it cannot produce ideas at

---

[1] Entret., iv. par. vi.

all, it cannot produce them out of material impressions; for ideas are spiritual beings (*êtres spirituels*), and material impressions are of a bodily nature. How can spiritual things be made out of bodily? If man cannot create an angel, said Malebranche, he also cannot produce him out of stone. At least, the latter is as difficult as the former. It must, therefore, on the above supposition, be the objects themselves according to which the soul forms ideas. But to copy objects, we must have them before our minds, therefore have ideas of them. Why, then, does the soul need to produce ideas since it already has them? Such an hypothesis is not an explanation of the origin of ideas, since it presupposes it, and subjects it to a condition which represents the producing of ideas as entirely unnecessary. Thus, in whatever way we consider the matter, we come to the same conclusion: it is impossible for the soul to produce ideas.[1]

Let us take the second case. Ideas are contained in the soul; it possesses them by virtue of its very nature; they belong to its natural qualities, as the sensations of cold and heat, colors and tones, as the affections of joy and pain, as the passions of love and hate, etc. The soul is, if not the cause, the *natural subject*, of ideas. Since its nature is higher and nobler than that of body, it must contain more reality than body: in the nature of the soul, that of body is also expressed and contained therein in an eminent manner (*éminement*). The intelligible world will, accordingly, comprehend in itself the sensible and material: conceptions or ideas of body are, accordingly, ideas of body, and as such, like all other modes of thought, natural manifestations of the soul. In that case, it is our thought in which ideas exist: it is our knowledge of self, or our inner experience through which we become conscious of ideas. But this entire theory contradicts the fundamental principles of our philosopher. Whatever may be the relative rank of soul and body, their relative grade of being, they are decidedly and certainly

[1] Rech. de la vérité, liv. iii. p. ii. chap. iii.

opposed to each other. Now, how can thought conceive
extension, how can extension be an object of our conception,
how can ideas of body be modifications of thought, or natural
qualities of the soul? From Malebranche's point of view,
it is manifestly impossible for the soul to possess ideas of
body by virtue of its very nature. Now, since it can neither
produce nor possess them, it is in every sense impossible for
ideas to proceed from the soul.[1]   God alone, therefore,
remains as the cause of ideas.

2. *The World of Ideas in God.* — We have received ideas
neither from bodies nor from ourselves: God, therefore, as
it seems, is the only source from which we could have
received them.   In this case, there are two possibilities:
either God has stamped all ideas upon the soul once for all,
and they are innate, or he produces every idea in us anew
whenever we require them.

Let us take the first case: all our ideas are innate.   Now,
it is evident that they are infinite in number: take a single
class, as that of geometrical figures; it is without limit.
There are countless figures, and even single figures, as a
triangle, an ellipse, etc., has countless forms: there are an
infinite multitude of triangles, an infinite multitude of
ellipses, according to the distance of their foci.   All our
ideas are, accordingly, an infinite multitude of countless numbers.   Our soul is finite, the world of ideas is infinite.   How
can the finite soul conceive this infinite world, and not
merely conceive, but even receive it into itself?   As little
as God can impart his infinity to the soul, so little can
he make the world of ideas innate.   The theory of an
innate world of ideas is in conflict with the nature of the
human mind, which never ceases to be a creature or limited
substance.

Let us take the second case, — the only one, as it appears,
that still remains: we have received ideas from God, not
all of them at once, but single ones, one after another, as we

---

[1] Rech., liv. iii. p. ii. chap. v.; Entret., i.

require them. As often as we will to present to ourselves a definite object, God produces the idea of it in our minds. We have not had the idea before: on the contrary, we have been entirely without it. But without any idea of an object, how can we think of it? How can we will to bring it before our minds? Is not thinking of an object equivalent to seeking the idea of it? How can we seek that of which we have no idea at all? It is, accordingly, impossible for God to produce the idea of an object in our minds according as we need it, if we do not in any manner whatever, however obscurely, already possess the idea. But if we already possess it, it is unnecessary for God first to produce it.[1]

By this path, therefore, we reach no result, or rather the negative one that we can neither receive ideas from bodies, nor from ourselves, nor from God. There is, therefore, no source from which ideas can flow into our minds; it is, accordingly, altogether impossible for us to have them; *we* are not the being that has them, *we* are not the subject of ideas. From this negative conclusion follows the positive: the only possible source of ideas is God. It is impossible for God to convey ideas from his being into ours, either by making them innate, or by creating them each time anew. It is, therefore, clear that ideas arise in God, and also that they can be, and remain, nowhere but in him. Ideas are in and through God alone: he alone is the infinite and all-embracing being (*être universel*), the only cause of ideas, and, through them, of things.[2]

Now we have reached the solution of the problem. Ideas are, and remain, only in God: knowledge of things is possible only through ideas, therefore only in God; i.e., *we know or we see things only in God.*

3. *Intelligible Extension and Universal Reason.* — If we know things through ideas, they are the ideas which are evident to us, and which cause our knowledge. They could

---

[1] Rech., liv. iii. p. ii. chap. iv.

[2] Ib., liv. iii. p. ii. chap. v.; Entret., ii.

not have such a power upon our minds if they were not of
a higher nature than the latter. The only truly efficient
being is God. If, therefore, ideas are of an efficient nature
(*efficaces*), they are divine. Thus, the proof of the assertion
that ideas are in God, is found in the fact that we know by
means of ideas. This proof, said Malebranche, will have
the force of a demonstration to those who are accustomed
to abstract thought.[1]

The things which we know clearly and distinctly through
ideas are only *bodies :* these, in all their forms and changes,
are modifications of extension, and nothing else. It is,
therefore, the idea of extension by means of which all
bodies are known, and nothing else. All ideas, accordingly,
can be reduced to this one, *intelligible extension,* — *l'étendue
intelligible,* — as Malebranche, in his dialogues, most simply
denotes the fundamental form of all ideas.[2]

Intelligible extension is neither a modification of extension nor of thought. No modification of extension is
intelligible, no modification of thought can be a conception
of extension. Intelligible extension can, therefore, neither
belong to extension, since it is intelligible, nor to thought,
since it is extension. It cannot, therefore, belong to finite
beings at all, to beings contrasted with others, but only to a
being which is without opposition, which is unlimited and
infinite. The idea of extension is only possible in God; and
since only this idea makes the external world knowable, it
is clear that we see all things in God. The idea of extension is related to the ideas of bodies, as extension as such to
actual bodies. As extension is modified in bodies, so is the
idea of extension in the ideas of body. As extension constitutes the condition and principle of the material world,
so the idea of extension is the fundamental form and principle of the world of ideas. It is the *primordial idea (idée
primordiale).* As ideas are related to things, so intelligible

---

1 Rech., liv. iii. p. ii. chap. vi.
2 Entret., i. pars. 9, 10.

extension is related to actual. Ideas are in God, things are outside of him. Those are of a creative nature; these are creatures; or, to express this relation in Platonic terms, ideas are the archetypes, things, copies. Thus, Malebranche called intelligible extension *the archetype* of the material world.[1]

After we have shown how the idea of extension is related to the ideas of bodies, and to body itself, there remains the question, How is this idea related to minds? It forms in minds the clear and distinct object of their intuition: this object is in all minds the same. In the intuition of this object, therefore, *all* minds agree; and however different we may be in other respects, this conception is the same in all of us. As the idea of extension expresses the essence of all bodies, so the intuition of it expresses the essence of all minds, — *the universal reason (la raison universelle).* There is but *one* reason, and this remains unchangeably like itself. The multiplicity and variety of individual minds are cancelled in it: it does not belong as a modification to the nature of finite minds, for in that case reason would be as different as individuals; but by reason of its universality and unchangeableness, it belongs to the nature of God.[2]

Universal reason and intelligible extension mutually correspond to each other. They are related to each other as subject and object: universal reason is the subject for which intelligible extension is the object, and conversely. God comprehends the universal reason in himself; this, intelligible extension; this, the ideas of all bodies, therefore the objects of clear and distinct knowledge. To make this knowledge ours, we must take the point of view from which alone the objects of knowledge, the ideas of body, i.e., the intelligible extension, appears. This point of view is the universal or divine reason. In it, said Malebranche, minds exist. This expression is identical in meaning with the proposition, we see things in God. "God sees in himself

---

[1] Entret., iii. par. i.; Ib., ii. par. i.; Ib., iii. par. ii.
[2] Ib., i. par. x.; Ib., iii. par. iv.

intelligible extension, the archetype of matter, of which the world consists, and where our bodies dwell : *we* see only in God, since our minds dwell only in the universal reason, that intelligible substance which comprehends in itself the ideas of all the truths which we discover." [1]

[1] Entret., i. par. x.; Ib., xii.

CHAPTER VII.

(c) THE RELATION OF THINGS TO GOD. — PANTHEISM IN MALEBRANCHE'S DOCTRINE.

I. THE UNIVERSE IN GOD.

1. *God as the Place of Minds.*

WE are now in the very centre of the system. Malebranche combines two important proofs in order to establish his doctrine of ideas and the intelligible world in God, the real theme of his philosophy. He deduces the one from the fact of our knowledge, the other from the creation of the world.

The fact that we perceive and know a world without us is undeniable, but it is explicable neither by means of the powers of our senses nor by body. What we perceive through our senses is always only our own impressions and states, not the properties of external things as such. The external world is not sensible, but material. Matter cannot of itself act upon our mind: it cannot impart itself and represent itself to mind. The capacity to be intuited and known does not belong to its properties: the material world as such is not knowable. It is conceivable that the mind could have sensations of body while bodies themselves were destroyed, while all its real properties ceased to exist. And that is an evident proof that the capacity to be presented to the mind does not belong to matter. The material world is not conceivable: the world, therefore, which we conceive is not material. Hence the world as conception or object can only be of an *intelligible* character; and since it is produced neither by nor in our thought, its cause can only be God, and it can continue to exist nowhere else than in him. Malebranche's proof can be most concisely expressed as follows: Without an intelligible world, there can be no knowledge; without God, no intelligible world: hence our knowledge of things is only possible through and in God.[1] The other proof, deduced from the doctrine of creation, leads to the same conclusion. God must conceive what he creates. Creation pre-supposes the creator and the idea of the world, God and the idea of things. Without the eternal presence of things in God, there is no creation, no world, therefore, also, none knowable to us. If things are to be evident to us, their ideas must be present to us; and since these are only in God, our presence in God is necessary in order to conceive them. There is no other stand-point for true knowledge. Truth consists in our clear and distinct conception of an object; and this must be strictly distinguished from all other conceptions, and is, therefore, possible only in the intuition of the intelligible world, i.e., in God. We must be in God in order to have clear thoughts. Our conceptions are confused when we are out of him. Hence the expression Malebranche used to state this fact: "God is through his presence so closely united with our souls, that we can say that he is the place of minds, exactly as space is the place of bodies. *God is the intelligible world or the place of minds, as the material world is the place of bodies.*"[2]

2. *Things as Modes of God.* — Our objects of knowledge are particular and finite things. The particular cannot be conceived without the universal, since it is its more precise determination; the finite not without the infinite, since it is its limitation. Now, God is the absolutely universal and infinite being. Hence the ideas of things are related to the idea of God, as the particular to the universal, as the limited to the unlimited. What is true of ideas must, indeed, be

---

[1] Entret., i.   [2] Rech., liv. iii. part ii. chap. vi.

true of things themselves. Things are related to God as
particular beings to the universal one, as finite to the infinite
one. They are, in a limited and imperfect way, what God
is infinitely and perfectly: they take part in the divine
being, are "participations" of it. Thus Malebranche arrives
at the significant assertion, "All particular ideas are only
participations of the universal idea of the infinite in so far
as God's being does not depend upon his creatures, but *all
creatures are nothing but imperfect participations of the divine
being.* All ideas which we have of creatures in particular
are only limitations of the idea of the Creator." [1]

God himself, according to Malebranche, is the single purpose of all divine activity. This certainty is evident from
the simplest thought, as well as from the revelations of the
Scriptures. What God creates, he creates for himself: he
alone is the cause and the end of all his creatures. Minds
exist only to consider the works of God, and therein to perceive God himself: they exist by means of this intuition, in
which they see the image of God, — which is, as it were, the
mirror of God. As he alone is the end of creation, so he is
the only object of our knowledge, and the only goal of our
efforts. The consideration and love of God is the fundamental cause of our conceptions and desires, of our entire
spiritual life. "If we did not see God," said Malebranche,
"we should not see *any thing:* if we did not love him, we
should not love *any thing.*" Every volition is a striving for
God, love for him. Without this love, we could neither
love nor desire any thing. Without God, our being is inactive and dead, our thought without light, our volitions without an end. Without him, there is neither power to think nor
to desire. To think is to know God, to will is to love him.
In this point, a manifest contradiction appears between philosophy and experience. The former sees in God the constant goal of our efforts: the latter shows that we constantly
desire the particular and perishable goods of the world. If

[1] Rech., liv. iii. part ii. chap vi.

the first is necessary, the second appears impossible: if we
admit the testimony of experience, we must declare the
theory of philosophy to be the greatest of all errors. Malebranche *denied* that there was any contradiction, and maintained that his theory was in harmony with experience.
Our worldly desires are, in his eyes, no exception to his
theory that love to God is the sole, animating cause of our
volitions.   It is with our desires precisely as with our conceptions: our ideas of things are participations of the universal idea of God, our desires for things are participations
of the love for God.   Our love for the particular and transi-
tory goods of the world, and our love for God as the most
universal and eternal good, stand in the same relation as the
particular and the universal, the finite and the infinite, the
limited and the unlimited, the conditioned and the unconditioned.   What the latter is perfectly and infinitely, the former is imperfectly and finitely.   *Our desires for things are
modifications of our love for God.   What, indeed, can things
themselves be except modifications of God?*   It is not we who
draw such inferences from the position of our philosopher:
he himself declares them openly and freely.   "We can only
love particular goods," said Malebranche, "by turning the
love for God, which he infuses into us, into the direction of
those goods."   Those particular goods are worldly things:
our love for worldly things is accordingly a determination
of our love for God.   All our desires are modifications of
the will whose fundamental direction is towards God.   If
we desire worldly things, the will is directed towards creatures, but in truth its object is the Creator.   The movement, therefore, which impels it towards creatures is only a
determination of that movement which struggles towards
God.   But if our love for creatures is only a determination
of our love for God, creatures themselves must be regarded
as determinations of God.   Hear Malebranche's own declaration: "*All the particular ideas which we have of creatures
are only limitations of the idea of the Creator, as all desires in*

reference to creatures are only determinations of the movement of the will which is directed towards the Creator." [1] God's power produces things and their modifications; his wisdom includes the ideas of all things in itself; his love is the inmost motive of all natural effort. The *being* of God consists in this power, wisdom, and love: they are God himself. Hence the divine being, in which all things have their existence and their ideas, is the only cause and purpose of their activity. "Let us," said Malebranche, concluding this most important section of his most important work, "let us abide in this conviction, viz., that God is the intelligible world or place of minds, as the material world is of bodies; that all things receive their modifications through his power, find their ideas in his wisdom, are moved necessarily and in harmony with law! And since his power and love are he himself, we believe with the apostle Paul that he is not far from every one of us, for in him we live and move and have our being." [2]

II. MALEBRANCHE'S PANTHEISTIC TENDENCY

That sentence of Paul's is found in the Bible, and pantheists eagerly quote it. The farther Malebranche advanced in the development of his fundamental thoughts, the more prominent became the features of his pantheistic mode of thought, not as the object of the philosopher, but the inevitable destiny of his doctrine which accepted two diametrically opposite views of the world, the Augustinian and the naturalistic, and sought to combine them. And exactly in this is it a true and necessary reflection of the period

---

[1] "*Nous ne pouvons aimer des biens particuliers qu'en déterminant vers ces biens le mouvement d'amour que Dieu nous donne pour lui. Ainsi comme nous n'aimons aucune chose que par l'amour nécessaire, que nous avons pour Dieu: nous ne voyons aucune chose que par la connaissance naturelle, que nous avons de Dieu: et toutes les idées particulières, que nous avons des créatures, ne sont que des limitations de l'idée du Créateur, comme tous les mouvements de la volonté pour les créatures ne sont que des déterminations du mouvement pour le Créateur*" (Rech., liv. iii. p. ii. chap. vi.).

[2] Rech., liv. iii. p. ii. chap. vi.: "*Que nous voyons toutes choses en Dieu.*"

which revived Augustinianism with intense fervor, and, at
the same time, was irresistibly filled with that naturalism
which mastered the new era of philosophy. Between the
two tendencies, as between two diverging lines, there are
very different distances at different stages of development.
At one point they are very wide apart; at another they approach each other: the point in which they *meet* is Malebranche. Descartes, Geulincx, Plato, are the connecting
links — the stages, as it were, of the course along which his
doctrine passes; Descartes and Plato being the two extremes.
Malebranche's method of combining them was not eclectic.
There was *one* fundamental thought that urged him through
these different stages: from Descartes, as a starting-point,
through the Occasionalists to Augustine; from Augustine,
through Plato, to a naturalistic conception of God, which
was on the very point of becoming Spinozism.

The dualistic principles of Descartes formed the starting-
point of Malebranche, and he accepted Occasionalism without
qualification. He maintained the absolute inactivity and in-
substantiality of things, the activity and substantiality of God
alone. From this point, there is but *one* step to Augustinianism. Even our knowledge of things depends upon God: it
is only possible as illumination. "We see things in God."
This assertion is Augustinian in reference to the ground of
our knowledge, and Platonic in reference to its objects; for
what we see in God are the *ideas* of things, the intelligible
world. If, according to Descartes' doctrine, — consistently
developed, — an absolute opposition exists between us and
things without us, between minds and bodies, an opposition
excluding every kind of community, we can know only in
the light of God, and things are knowable only through
ideas.

It is only *bodies* which are knowable through ideas. Now,
bodies are modifications of extension: hence the idea of the
latter, *intelligible* extension, is our proper object of knowledge, the fundamental form into which Malebranche analyzed

ideas. Here we see most clearly the Cartesian origin of his system. Only when the nature of body consists simply in extension, as the Cartesian dualism requires, does the essence of knowable things, or the idea of the whole material world, consist in intelligible extension.

The intelligible world is in God: God is the intelligible world. It is the object of the universal reason: God is the universal reason. The intelligible world is *our* object of knowledge, in so far as we are in the universal reason, or God. These are not mere inferences from Malebranche's doctrine, but *literal* statements of it. There remains between God and the world no other difference than that between intelligible and actual extension. The latter is what the former is not; viz., creature. But by what characteristics is the creatural character of extension distinguished from its divine and eternal nature? We cannot say that intelligible extension is infinite while matter is finite, for the latter is, indeed, infinite. According to Malebranche's explicit statement, that the intelligible world is the archetype of the actual world, such an absolute difference between ideal and real extension can no longer exist. We find no characteristic to distinguish the two; and, even if there were such, it would not be knowable. The difference between these two kinds of extension is, therefore, in no case an object of knowledge. But since the whole difference between God and the world is analyzed into *this* distinction, we are obliged to decide that between God and the world, according to Malebranche, an *evident* difference no longer exists.

But we must go still farther. In the range of the doctrine of our philosopher, deductions appear, which not only obliterate the *knowable* difference between God and real extension, but their essential difference. Even Malebranche declared that the ideas of things are "limitations" of the idea of God, our desires for things are "determinations" of our love for God, and creatures themselves imperfect "participations" of the divine being. What is true of all things, must be true of *bodies*. Even ideas of bodies are limitations of the ideas of God; even bodies themselves participate in the divine nature, and are related to God as our desires are to the love of God; *they are determinations or modifications of God*. Now, bodies are modifications only of extension. If they are, likewise, modifications of God, God must be *the* extension, the modes of which are bodies; i.e., he is *real* extension.

The Occasionalistic principles, which Malebranche applied without qualification or reserve, irresistibly lead to just this conclusion. Completely powerless as natural things here appear, without all substantiality, without any power to act independently, they can be nothing more than mere modifications of God: they take part in the being of God, and, therefore, coincide with him. They are in a determinate, finite, imperfect manner, what God is perfectly, infinitely, indeterminately. Here from the nature of things a highly important regressive inference can be drawn of God. Things are either minds or bodies. If minds must relate themselves to thought as body does to extension, things are either the modifications of thought or extension. Now, if both are modifications of God, God must unite both these attributes in himself. He is the *one* and only substance — whose activity consists both in thought and extension. This proposition takes us into the heart of Spinozism, a purely naturalistic system, to which the doctrine of Descartes has led us through Geulincx and Malebranche, to which Malebranche himself was driven by the Cartesian-Occasionalistic, Augustinian, Platonic mode of thought, however strongly he opposed the doctrine of Spinoza, and wished to maintain that of Augustine. I remark in passing, that the pantheistic feature of his doctrine is by no means to be considered as a form of its later development — as some have contended — on which Spinoza's works exerted a certain influence, but that it is found even in his ·most important work, and nowhere more distinctly appears than in that most important section which treats of

the fundamental theme "that we see all things in God."
Spinoza's most important work appeared three years later.
It is not true, therefore, that Malebranche, in his dialogues
on metaphysics and religion, gave more scope to the pantheistic mode of thought than in his work on the investigation
of truth. The later work is different from the earlier, only
in relation to the doctrine of the universal reason and intelligible extension; but this difference is not connected with
the pantheistic development of the doctrine, but with its
simplification and concise conception.

God is universal reason; he is the intelligible world;
therefore, also, intelligible extension. So said Malebranche.
God is an infinite, thinking, and extended being. So said
Spinoza. The whole difference between them consists only
in intelligible extension, which Malebranche identifies with
God, while he distinguishes the actual from him. But even
this remnant of Platonism vanishes in presence of the explicit
assertion that things, therefore bodies also, participate in
the being of God — in presence of the inference which Malebranche cannot guard against, that things, therefore even
bodies, are modifications of God. This naturalistic feature
inevitably moulded the doctrine of our philosopher, and gave
to its conception of the divine will that deterministic character, which the Jansenists rightly regarded as a limitation
of the unconditional will of God, and was, therefore, so
violently opposed by Arnauld. We can easily understand
that Malebranche, who was not conscious of this tendency
of his doctrine, and of the logical result of his ideas, though
he was indeed aware of the religious spirit and purpose of his
entire system, — we can easily understand that he regarded
these attacks as the wretchedest and the most hostile mis-
interpretations. It had been his aim to put the honor of God
beyond every thing, by ascribing to him *alone* all power and
activity; and he could not see how he had thereby infringed
upon the divine will. It is true that Malebranche affirmed
these two propositions: God is absolutely and infinitely

powerful, and acts according to eternal and necessary laws; and God is absolutely free, acting independently of any laws. He did not see the contradiction in which he was involved, and appealed to the second proposition when he was reproached with the first, and when his opponents objected that it was impossible for the activity of God to be controlled by law, and, at the same time, for the will of God to be absolutely free.

If any one wishes so to present to himself this contradiction in Malebranche's own conceptions that he may see the two contradictions close to each other, there is scarcely a more striking example than that letter (first discovered and published by Cousin) which the philosopher wrote, March 21, 1693, to a certain Torssac on the immortality of the soul. Some attempt to prove the immortality of the soul, he said, from the substantiality of the mind and the impossibility of destroying it: but if God created the soul from nothing, he can also annihilate it; and immortality must, therefore, be based on the power and will of God. But such a method of proof affords no mathematical certainty. "Since every thing depends upon God, and the world *by no means* necessarily proceeds from his nature," "there is between voluntary effects and their cause no such connection as between truths and their principles." The immortality of the soul cannot, therefore, be rigorously demonstrated. Nevertheless, Malebranche will give good proofs (*de bonnes preuves*). The most important is, "God's mode of action *must* correspond to his attributes; he *must* act as he is: the guiding principle of his volitions is found in his essence; it consists in the *unchangeable order* of his perfections. Now, if God is wise and omniscient, he is unchangeable and constant in his purposes, — and he would not be if we were not immortal. *God's nature forms the rule and the inviolable law of his activity*, and I discover in him nothing that could induce him to will our annihilation. We cannot judge the divine will according to ours, and in general we must resist our inclination to anthropomorphize the causes of things if we would know them rightly." Malebranche found the decision of the question of immortality in divine revelation and the incarnation, since the end of divine creation can be none other than the salvation of the world.

In this letter, the fundamental features of the philosopher lie before us. He affirms the freedom of the divine will, making every thing dependent on his unconditional decrees: he denies it, making the will of God dependent on the eternal necessity of the divine nature, which is revealed in Christ's work of salvation. Cousin aptly said, "Malebranche was, with Spinoza, the greatest disciple of Descartes: he was in a literal sense the Christian Spinoza."

Only a little while before he died, Malebranche was compelled, in a confidential correspondence with the well-trained mathematician and physicist *De Mairan*, to defend himself against Spinozism, and to meet the charge that the latter is a necessary consequence of his own doctrine. These eight letters, written in the last year but one of his life (Sept. 27, 1713–Sept. 6, 1714), the publication of which we likewise owe to Cousin,[1] are a highly interesting and instructive proof of Malebranche's relation to Spinoza: they show in what Malebranche saw the chief distinction of their doctrines, and how, finally, without having weakened the conviction of his friend, he grew weary of defending himself, and laid down his pen without having accomplished his object, and discontinued the painful discussion. De Mairan, forty years younger than Malebranche, with a reverential devotion to him, acquainted with his works as well as with those of Descartes, — himself inclined to Descartes, — had just read and re-read Spinoza's works, attracted by the mathematical arrangement of its propositions, and the clearness and cogency of its proofs: he had reflected upon them in perfect quiet ("*dans le silence des passions*," as he

---

[1] V. Cousin: Fragments de philosophie Cartésienne (Paris, 1852). Correspondence de Malebranche et de Mairan, pp. 262-348.

said, quoting a beautiful expression of Malebranche's), and
he was unable to break the chain of its demonstrations.
He was by no means blinded by admiration, since the
religious and practical inferences from the doctrine seemed
to him questionable enough. He turned to Malebranche
with the urgent request, "Overthrow this system for me,
whose proofs are so cogent, and whose consequences are so
depressing." He had already read and examined a number
of refutations; but they did not convince him, since he saw
that none of them understood the system they attempted to
demolish. Now he hoped that the deepest thinker of the
time would point out the fundamental error of that terrible
system. For Malebranche himself, he urged, had spoken in
his "Meditations" of such a fundamental error, of such a
"false principle" which had compelled Spinoza to deny
creation, and heap error on error. Was it contempt or
sympathy that caused him to say in that passage, "*le misé-
rable Spinoza*"?[1] De Mairan took him at his word: "Point
out this error, and prove it!" Malebranche had studied the
works of Spinoza neither dispassionately nor thoroughly, but,
as he himself confessed, had read them formerly (*autrefois*),
and never completely (*en totalité*). Besides, philosophizing
by letter was troublesome to him. But, if he had had the
most thorough knowledge, he could have taken no other
position in opposition to it than the one here formulated,
which he repeated *ad nauseam*.

His answer to Mairan literally confirms the judgment
that we have pronounced concerning the difference of the
two systems. Spinoza's fundamental error was, he said,
that he did not distinguish *intelligible* and *material extension*,
the world in God and the created world, the ideas of things
and creatures, and, therefore, denied creation. This confusion was the false principle of his doctrine and the ground
of all his errors. And just as literally does Mairan's third
reply agree with our view. There are two kinds of con-

---

[1] Méditationes chrétiennes. Méd., ix. § 13.

fusion : we can identify things which are different, and we may seek to distinguish those that are not different. Malebranche is involved in a confusion of this second character concerning the relation of the intelligible and real (created) extension. De Mairan aptly wrote, "Reverend Father, your distinction between intelligible and created extension only serves to confuse the true ideas of things. What you call intelligible extension, is, according to all the properties you ascribe to it, *extension itself* (*l'étendue proprement dite*). What you call created extension, is related to intelligible, as modifications to a substance." In brief, Malebranche's doctrine, rightly understood, is Spinoza's.